*Software
Specification
Techniques*

INTERNATIONAL COMPUTER SCIENCE SERIES

Consulting editors   **A D McGettrick**
University of Strathclyde

J van Leeuwen
University of Utrecht

Software Specification Techniques

Narain Gehani
AT & T Bell Laboratories

Andrew McGettrick
University of Strathclyde

ADDISON-WESLEY PUBLISHING COMPANY

Wokingham, England · Reading, Massachusetts · Menlo Park, California
Don Mills, Ontario · Amsterdam · Sydney · Singapore · Tokyo
Mexico City · Bogota · Santiago · San Juan

© 1986 AT & T Bell Telephone Laboratories, Incorporated

All rights reserved. No part of this publication may be reproduced, stored in a retrieval system, or transmitted in any form or by any means, electronic, mechanical, photocopying, recording or otherwise, without prior written permission of the publisher.

Photoset at AT & T Bell Laboratories, N.J.
Printed in the U.S.A.

British Library Cataloguing in Publication Data
Software specification techniques.
   1. Elecronic digital computers—Programming
   I. Gehani, Narain   II. McGettrick, Andrew D.
   001.64′25   QA76.6

ISBN 0-201-14230-9

Library of Congress Cataloging in Publication Data
Software specification techniques.
   Bibliography: p.
   1. Computer programs—Specifications—Addresses, essays, lectures.   I. Gehani, Narain, 1947-
II. McGettrick, Andrew D., 1944-
QA76.6.S6437   1985   001.64′25   85-1437
ISBN 0-201-14230-9

BCDEF89876

To
INDU
and
SHEILA

Preface

Computer software, rapidly overshadowing hardware in cost and complexity, is becoming the dominant and critical component in computer systems. A problem that frequently occurs in software design is that specifications are not met—causing irritation between the software designers and the users. Software that does not meet its specification may even lead to lawsuits between the person or organization paying for the software and the software designer. Eventually, such software must be modified, incurring both additional costs and delays in software delivery dates.

Why might software not meet its specifications? Often the specification of a system is not completely known when system design and implementation are started. Although one can be idealistic and say that system design and implementations should not be initiated until a complete specification of the system is available, in practice it may be possible to completely specify a system only after experience with a partial implementation of the system (especially in case of systems that are novel).

Although informal specifications are easy to read and understand, they are often incomplete, vague and ambiguous, and cannot be used to mechanically verify that the software constructed actually conforms to the specifications. In an effort to correct the deficiencies of informal specifications, formal specifications have been proposed as an alternative. From these specifications, prototype systems (generally inefficient) can be automatically generated. Such systems can be very useful in establishing the appropriateness of the specifications, determining the viability of the proposed system and in making changes to the specification of the system prior to its actual design and implementation.

Formal specifications do not render informal specifications obsolete or irrelevant; although they can be checked to some degree for completeness, redundancy and ambiguity, and can be used in program verification, they are often hard to read and understand. Consequently, informal specifications are still necessary as an aid to the understanding of the system being designed; informal and formal specifications complement each other.

This book will be of special interest to software designers and computer scientists interested in specifying systems accurately and correctly. It will also be very appropriate as one of two or three text books used in a course on software engineering, software design and program verification.

In this book, we will focus on formal specification techniques. Several of these have been proposed in recent years. We will examine various aspects of formal specification techniques, e.g., general principles, specific techniques, actual experience in using these specification techniques and the automatic generation of prototype systems from the specifications.

The book is a collection of recent papers on specifications. It is organized into four sections:

(1) Specifications—Requirements and Techniques

(2) Particular Approaches

(3) Case Studies

(4) Specification Systems

Each section begins with an introduction to tie papers in the section together and provide continuity between the sections.

To reduce the size of the book, we have deleted several appendices and some text referencing these appendices. We have explicitly indicated the places where we have deleted some material.

Narain Gehani
Murray Hill, N.J.

Andrew McGettrick
Glasgow, Scotland

Acknowledgments

We are grateful to Elsie Edelman for her invaluable assistance in the preparation of the manuscript.

We are indebted to the authors and publishers for giving us their permission to reprint their papers. The individual credits are listed below:

- Liskov, B. H. and V. Berzins 1979. An Appraisal of Program Specifications. In *Research Directions in Software Technology*, edited by P. Wegner, pp. 276-301, MIT Press.
- Balzer, R. and N. Goldman 1979. Principles of Good Software Specification and Their Implications for Specification Languages. *Proceedings of IEEE Conference on Specifications of Reliable Software*, 58-67.
- Swartout, W. and R. Balzer 1982. On the Inevitable Intertwining of Specification and Implementation. *CACM*, **25** (7) (July), 438-440.
- Goguen, J. A. 1981. More Thoughts on Specification and Verification. *ACM SIGSOFT*, **6** (3), 38-41.
- Guttag, J. V. 1979. Notes on Type Abstraction. *Proceedings of Conference on Specifications of Reliable Software*, 36-46.
- Parnas, D. L. 1972. A Technique for Software Specification with Modules. *CACM*, **15** (5) (May).
- Jones, C. B. Systematic Program Development. To appear in *Proceedings of the Symposium on Mathematics and Computer Science*, North Holland.
- Bartussek, W. and D. L. Parnas 1978. Using Assertions about Traces to Write Abstract Specifications for Software Modules. *Proceedings of Second Conference of European Cooperation in Informatics, Lecture Notes in Computer Science*, **65**, 211-236, Springer-Verlag.
- Zave, P. 1982. An Operational Approach to Requirements Specification for Embedded Systems. *IEEE Transactions on Software Engineering*, **SE-8** (3), 250-269.
- Gehani, N. H. 1982. Specifications: Formal and Informal—A Case Study. *Software—Practice and Experience*, **12**, 433-444.
- Guttag, J. V. and J. J. Horning 1980. Formal Specification as a Design Tool. *Seventh Annual ACM Symposium on Principles of Programming Languages*, 251-261.

- Jacob, R. J. K. 1983. Using Formal Specifications in the Design of a Human–Computer Interface. *CACM,* **26** (4), 259-264.

- Sufrin, B. 1982. Formal Specification of a Display-Oriented Text Editor. *Science of Computer Programming,* **1**, 157-202.

- Mateti, P. 1983. A Specification Schema for Indenting Programs. *Software – Practice and Experience,* **13**, 163-179.

- Feather, M. S. 1982. Program Specification Applied to a Text Formatter. *IEEE Transactions on Software Engineering,* **SE-8** (5) (September), 490-498.

- Sunshine, C. A., D. H. Thompson, R. W. Erickson, S. L. Gerhart and D. Schwabe 1982. Specification and Verification of Communication Protocols in AFFIRM Using State Transition Models. *IEEE Transactions Software Engineering,* **SE-8** (5) (September), 460-489.

- Zave, P. and R. T. Yeh 1981. Executable Requirements for Embedded Systems. *Fifth Annual Conference on Software Engineering,* San Diego, 295-304.

- Burstall, R.M. and J.A. Goguen 1981. An Informal Introduction to Specifications Using CLEAR. In *The Correctness Problem in Computer Science,* edited by R. S. Boyer and J. Stothers Moore, Academic Press, 185-213.

- Goguen, J. A. and J. J. Tardo 1979. An Introduction to OBJ: a Language for Writing and Testing Formal Algebraic Program Specifications. *Proceedings of the Conference on Specifications of Reliable Software,* 170-189.

- Ambler, L., D. I. Good, J. C. Browne, W. F. Burger, R. M. Cohen, C. G. Hoch and R. E. Wells 1977. GYPSY: A Language for Specification and Implementation of Verifiable Programs. *Proceedings of the ACM Conference on Language Design for Reliable Software, SIGPLAN Notices,* **12** (3), 1-10.

- Klausner A. and T.E. Konchan 1982. Rapid Prototyping and Requirements Specification Using PDS. *ACM SIGSOFT Software Engineering Notes,* **7** (5), 96-105.

Contents

Preface   vii

Acknowledgments   ix

REQUIREMENTS AND TECHNIQUES   1

An Appraisal of Program Specifications   3
(B. H. Liskov and V. Berzins)

Principles of Good Software Specification and their Implications for Specification Languages   25
(R. Balzer and N. Goldman)

On the Inevitable Intertwining of Specification and Implementation   41
(W. Swartout and R. Balzer)

More Thoughts on Specification and Verification   47
(J. A. Goguen)

PARTICULAR APPROACHES   53

Notes on Type Abstraction   55
(J. V. Guttag)

A Technique for Software Module Specification with Examples   75
(D. L. Parnas)

Systematic Program Development   89
(C. B. Jones)

Using Assertions about Traces to Write Abstract Specifications for Software Modules   111
(W. Bartussek and D. L. Parnas)

An Operational Approach to Requirements Specification for Embedded 131
Systems
(P. Zave)

CASE STUDIES 171

Specifications: Formal and Informal — A Case Study 173
(N. H. Gehani)

Formal Specification as a Design Tool 187
(J. V. Guttag and J. J. Horning)

Using Formal Specifications in the Design of a Human–Computer Interface 209
(R. J. K. Jacob)

Formal Specification of a Display-Oriented Text Editor 223
(B. Sufrin)

A Specification Schema for Indenting Programs 269
(P. Mateti)

Program Specification Applied to a Text Formatter 289
(M. S. Feather)

Specification and Verification of Communication Protocols in AFFIRM 303
Using State Transition Models
(C. A. Sunshine, D. H. Thompson, R. W. Erickson, S. L. Gerhart and
  D. Schwabe)

Executable Requirements for Embedded Systems 341
(P. Zave and R. T. Yeh)

SPECIFICATION SYSTEMS 361

An Informal Introduction to Specifications using CLEAR 363
(R. M. Burstall and J. A. Goguen)

An Introduction to OBJ: A Language for Writing and Testing Formal 391
Algebraic Program Specifications
(J. A. Goguen and J. J. Tardo)

GYPSY: A Language for Specification and Implementation of Verifiable 421
Programs
(A. L. Ambler, D. I. Good, J. C. Browne, W. F. Burger, R. M. Cohen,
  C. G. Hoch and R. E. Wells)

Rapid Prototyping and Requirements Specification using PDS 441
(A. Klausner and T. E. Konchan)

References 455

REQUIREMENTS AND TECHNIQUES

In recent years software specification has emerged as an independent area of study in computer science. There are important benefits which stem from writing specifications, i.e., stating in precise terms the intended effect of a piece of software. For then it is possible to talk about such issues as the correctness of an implementation, a measure of the consistency between that specification and the effect of the program. The range of benefits are actually wider than this; they relate to methods of programming, to possible approaches to validation and verification of programs, and even to the management and control of large software projects.

Yet the topic is clouded in controversy. There are debates about whether specifications should be formal or informal, about the nature of the languages used for specifying programs, about the relationship between languages for specification and languages for programming, about whether a program can itself be viewed as a kind of specification. Is it always possible to realize a specification in the form of a corresponding piece of software? How much freedom should an implementer be given?

The whole subject matter of software specification has been given considerable impetus recently by the U. S. Department of Defense. In January 1983 this body issued a document entitled "Trusted Computer Systems Evaluation Criteria" which set criteria for assessing and classifying the degree of security associated with computer systems. A spectrum of possibilities involving control of access, security domains and verification is provided. The highest security classification, A1, would be awarded to systems that could be shown to have been formally specified, formally developed and proved correct.

The papers in this first section address and debate the problems discussed above and many others. The paper by Barbara Liskov and Valdis Berzins is an authoritative account of more recent developments. In their paper Robert Balzer and Neil Goldman itemize what they consider to be the important properties that should be associated with good specifications and specification languages; these observations provide useful measures against which to judge later papers. In the next paper, William Swartout and Robert Balzer suggest that specification and implementation cannot and should not be separated. In the final paper, Joseph Goguen discusses the important relationship between formal program specification to program verification. Without such a specification, program verification is meaningless.

BARBARA H. LISKOV *and* VALDIS BERZINS
Massachusetts Institute of Technology

An Appraisal of Program Specifications

1. INTRODUCTION

Every program performs some task correctly. What is of interest to computer scientists is whether a program performs its intended task. To determine this, a precise and independent description of the desired program behavior is needed. Such a description is called a *program specification*.

Several kinds of program specifications may be usefully distinguished. In constructing software, the first phase consists of an analysis of the requirements for the software. The result of this phase is a *requirements specification*. A requirements specification is an informal description of intended system behavior; it is often very large, running into hundreds of pages. The requirements specification details both the tasks that the system should perform, and some constraints on the speed and resource utilization with which these tasks should be accomplished.

After the requirements analysis phase, there are one or more design phases, which define a system structure meeting the requirements specification. Large programs are not constructed as single monolithic entities, but as a number of interconnected subprograms or modules. Most often these modules are organized in a hierarchical fashion, with modules higher in the hierarchy implemented in terms of (by means of calls on) modules lower in the hierarchy. The result of a design phase is the identification of modules, and a graph structure showing which modules are to be used in implementing which other modules. Later design phases are often used to elaborate the structure of modules that were considered only as indivisible "black boxes" in earlier design phases.

A common problem in system construction is that the kind of behavior expected by a user of a module may not be the same as what the module provides. This problem can be avoided, or at least greatly reduced, if the design phase provides specifications of the module. The module specification serves to document the intended module behavior and to communicate this behavior to the implementor of the module and to programmers who will use that module in implementing other modules. Two kinds of module specifications are of interest: *functional specifications*, which describe the effect of the module on its external environment, and *performance*

3

specifications, which describe constraints on the speed and resource utilization of the module.

In this paper, we survey existing techniques for providing formal functional specifications for program modules. We believe these techniques can form a basis for the functional part of requirements specification; this is discussed further in Section 4. The techniques we discuss are not applicable to performance specifications. Some work has been done in this area (see Wegbreit [1976] for some recent work), but much remains to be done.

In the remainder of this section we discuss the advantages of formal specifications. Section 2 contains a discussion of module specification techniques for sequential programs. In Section 3, we review recent work on specifying parallel programs. Section 4 evaluates formal specification techniques and discusses expected future developments.

1.1 Advantages of Formal Specifications

Program specifications can have various degrees of formality. At the informal end of the spectrum, the specifications can be expressed in some convenient combination of English, diagrams and a variety of standard mathematical notations. Sometimes specifications are required in a prescribed format, where the order of the sections and the information to be found in each section are given, but the contents of the sections can be in any language. These kinds of specifications are in common use today.

The ISDOS system [Teichroew and Bastarche 1975] is a step up from this. The interface specifications for the modules of the proposed software system are expressed in a precisely defined formalism, which is parsed by machine, and checked for various completeness and consistency properties. The specifications for the functional behavior of the modules, however, are informal, unconstrained and unchecked.

A specification is formal if it is written entirely in a language with an explicitly and precisely defined syntax and semantics. Examples of suitable formal languages are first order predicate calculus and a programming language for which the semantics has been defined by one of the known techniques (for example, the part of PASCAL that has been axiomatized [Hoare and Wirth 1973]). However, a program should not be its own specification, because this eliminates the redundancy needed to make verification meaningful. An independent description of desired behavior is always required.

There are advantages in using formal, rather than informal specifications. Formal specifications can be studied mathematically while informal specifications cannot. For example, a correct program can be proved to meet its specifications, or two alternative sets of specifications can be proved equivalent. Formal specifications can also be meaningfully processed by a computer. Certain forms of inconsistency or incompleteness in the specification can be detected automatically [Guttag 1975]. Since this processing can be done in advance of implementation, it should prove to be a valuable aid to program design. In addition formal specifications can sometimes be realized automatically (for a recent survey see Bierman [1976]), although the resulting implementation may not be as efficient as one designed by a programmer.

Even in cases where these mathematical tools will not be used, formal specifications are advantageous. When specifications are used as a communications medium among programmers during system design and implementation, it is essential that the programmers reading a specification all agree on what that specification means. This is more likely when the specification is formal, for two reasons. First, there is only one way to interpret a formal specification, because of the well-defined and unambiguous semantics of the specification language. Second, the formality of the language encourages greater rigor in the definitions. It is easy to hide incompletely designed program behavior under vague informal descriptions. Rigorous informal specifications are probably just as difficult to construct as formal ones; informal specifications appear easier to construct because they are usually incomplete.

Specifications are a useful component or program documentation. A well written specification will be easier to understand than a program because it is written in a language chosen for ease of expression, rather than for efficiency of implementation. In addition, specifications are helpful during program maintenance and modification: if the implementation of a module is changed, but the specification is still valid, then the modules using that module need not be changed. Again, formal specifications should be provided, so that the meaning of the specification is well defined.

Formal and informal specifications can complement one another nicely. Informal specifications have the virtue that the main points of the behavior can be communicated in an understandable and effective manner; unfortunately, often details of the behavior are not specified. Formal specifications contain all the details, but there may be insufficient emphasis on the main points. Therefore, we recommend that formal specifications always be accompanied by informal specifications as comments. In this way, the reader can get the idea of the specification quickly and easily, but also has sufficient information to understand fully what is meant.

2. SPECIFICATIONS FOR SEQUENTIAL PROGRAMS

Specifications are closely related to modularization. If a module implements a clean abstraction, then it will have a simple specification. Conversely, if a module performs an arbitrarily chosen set of actions, sharing logical interdependencies with other modules, then the specification is likely to be at least as complicated as the implementation, and hence virtually useless.

There are two kinds of abstractions that have proved to be particularly useful in program construction: procedural abstractions and data abstractions. A procedural abstraction performs a mapping from a set of input values to a set of output values. The domain and range of a procedural abstraction consist of data abstractions, and the behavior of the procedural abstraction is defined in terms of the behavior of these data abstractions. A data abstraction provides a set of data values and a set of operations to manipulate the values. Although each operation can be thought of as a procedural abstraction, it is more convenient for implementation and specification to treat the data abstraction as a unit.

In the following sections we present an overview of some existing formal techniques for specifying procedural abstractions and data abstractions, assuming that we are dealing with sequential programs only. Then we consider some of the problems with existing techniques.

2.1 Procedural Abstractions

A procedural abstraction can be viewed as a mapping from its inputs to its outputs. Procedural abstractions are implemented as procedures or subroutines; common examples are a square root routine, a sort package and a compiler.

Some procedures exhibit nonfunctional behavior (compute different results for the same inputs on different occasions). This is because they have implicit inputs (for example, global variables they read) or outputs (global variables they change). If all of the logical inputs and outputs are considered, then any procedure can be described as a mapping from inputs to outputs.[1] For example, a random number generator may have a state variable called the seed, which is uses to compute the output value, and which it updates in preparation for producing the next value, so that the seed is both an implicit input and an implicit output. Such a random number generator can be described as a function of type (seed → seed × value).

The specification of a procedural abstraction has two parts: the interface specification and the behavioral specification. The interface specification consists of the name of the module, and the types and sources or destinations of the inputs and outputs. (Typical sources for input and output are formal parameters of the procedure or global variables.) The interface information is syntactic in nature and must be given in the declarations of most high level languages, at least for the explicit inputs and outputs.

There are two main techniques for specifying the behavior of procedural abstractions that meet the criterion of formality: input/output specifications and operational specifications. In either case, the module is treated as a black box and the specification describes the relationship between the inputs and outputs of the module.

2.1.1 Input/Output Specifications

The input/output approach describes the relationship between the inputs and the outputs by giving a pair of constraints. Provided that the actual input satisfies the input constraints, the output is guaranteed to satisfy the output constraints.

---

1. This approach works provided the procedure does not depend on some parallel activity (e.g., input from a terminal, the real time clock). Parallelism is discussed in Section 3.

Early work on formal I/O specifications was done by Naur [1966], Floyd [1967], and Hoare [1969]. Their work was motivated largely by a desire to *prove* that programs have certain properties (e.g., "correctness"). They attached assertions to various points in a program and sought to prove that the assertions were true whenever control reached the associated points in the program. The assertions were expressed in the ordinary notation of mathematical logic, since this is a natural language in which to do proofs. Each pair of assertions acts as a specification for the program fragment between them. Hoare introduced the notation P{program text}Q, for expressing I/O specifications, where the assertions P and Q are sentences of mathematical logic. Assertions are written in terms of program variables, logical variables and the names of procedures. A program variable in an assertion stands for the value of the variable at the instant when control reaches the point in the program associated with the assertion. The logical variables have static values and are implicitly universally quantified. A procedure name in an assertion denotes the function computed by the associated procedure: the arguments of the function are the parameters of the procedure and the result is the return value of the procedure. Assertions should refer only to procedures that are functional and have no side effects. In the case of nonfunctional procedures with side effects, the specification technique should establish standard notational methods for referring to the functions that compute the outputs and the side effects of a procedure (e.g., see Hoare [1971b]).

A small but nontrivial example of an I/O specification for a well known functional abstraction, the greatest common divisor, is given in Figure 1. The interface specification tells us that *gcd* has no side effects, since the return value is the only output. The input assertion states that both inputs must be positive. The output assertion states that both inputs must be evenly divisible by the output and that the output must be the greatest such number, in the sense that if must be divisible by any common divisor of the inputs. Note that use of the abbreviation, *divides(x, y)*, to enhance the readability of the specification. An important part of constructing specifications is the

---

Interface: gcd (integer, integer) **returns** integer

Behavior: x > 0 & y > 0 {gcd(x, y)}
                    divides (gcd (x, y), x) & divides (gcd (x, y), y)
                    & $\forall$ i: integer [divides (i, x) & divides (i, y)
                    $\Rightarrow$ divides (i, gcd (x, y))]

Abbreviations: divides (x, y) $\equiv$ $\exists$ i: integer [y = x * i]

Figure 1.   I/O specifications for gcd.

identification of appropriate abbreviations; such abbreviations play a role in specification construction analogous to the role played by procedural and data abstractions in program construction.

Hoare's notation P{program text}Q specifies only partial correctness: it states how the program behaves, provided that it terminates. Note that such a specification is satisfied by an infinite loop. The definition was formulated in this way because it is often convenient to use different techniques for showing partial correctness and termination. Proof techniques based on I/O constraints that specify total correctness have also been developed [Dijkstra 1975, 1976; Manna 1969]. In these formalisms, whenever the input constraints are met the program is guaranteed to terminate in a state satisfying the output constraints. The specification of an abstraction necessarily includes the termination requirements,[2] regardless of whether the proofs are done separately or together.

One of the main benefits obtainable from specifications of modules is that proofs of program properties can be decomposed using such specifications: to prove something about the result of a procedure call, one need only refer to the specification and not to the code implementing the function. Hoare [1971b] has studied some of the issues involved in proofs of programs containing procedure calls. His discussion is complicated by the possibility that data may be shared between different parameters of a procedure. If a function designed under the assumption that two input objects are independent is passed actual input objects that are identical or share subcomponents, then quite startling and unexpected behavior may result, especially if the function changes the input objects. These complications do not apply to parameters that are passed by value (copied).

2.1.2 Operational Specifications

The assertions of an input/output specification describe properties of program states; the computation that transforms a legal input state into a legal output state is not described explicitly. In an operational specification, the transformation is described explicitly by giving a program that computes the intended function. An operational specification differs from an implementation because, for the purposes of specification, simplicity is important and efficiency is not. The specification language should be chosen to make the specification as simple as possible. Note that it is not necessary to have an implementation for the specification language (it may be convenient for testing purposes), although the specification language must have a precisely defined meaning. McCarthy [1963] gives some early examples of operational definitions of functional abstractions. McCarthy's formal language is very simple, using only recursion and conditional expressions.

---

2. If the program is not intended to terminate, then this must be explicitly stated.

Interface: gcd (integer, integer) **returns** integer

Behavior: gcd (x, y) = **if** x ⩽ 0 ∨ y ⩽ 0 **then** error ("unexpected input")
 else search-from (x, y, min (x, y))

Abbreviations: search-from (x, y, z) = **if** mod (x, z) = 0 & mod (y, z) = 0
 then z
 else search-from (x, y, z − 1)

Figure 2. Operational specifications for gcd.

An operational specification for the greatest common divisor function is given in Figure 2. The specification uses the integer operation *min*, which returns the less of its two arguments and the integer operation *mod*, which returns the result of reducing its first argument modulo the second argument. The function *search-from* starts with the largest number that has a chance of being a common factor of x and y, *min(x, y)*, and tries all possibilities, biggest first, until it finds a common divisor. The algorithm will always terminate, since the inputs are positive and since 1 is a divisor of any number. This function does indeed satisfy the I/O specifications given above, although it is not easy to prove that it does because the notions of "greatest" used by the two specifications are different.

A proof that a procedure correctly implements the abstraction defined by an operational specification is really a proof of the equivalence of two programs. Methods have been developed for doing such proofs when the two programs are recursive [McCarthy 1963; Greif 1972].

There is a hazard of inadvertently giving incomplete specifications for both the I/O constraint and the operational specification techniques. For the I/O constraint method, it is possible to make the output constraints too strong, so that for some inputs there is no output value satisfying them. For the operational technique, it is possible to write incomplete conditionals or nonterminating recursions. Such specifications are misleading and should not be written on purpose even if they specify the desired behavior. If incomplete specifications are desired, then the conditions under which the output is not defined, or in which an error occurs, should be explicitly identified.

2.2 Data Abstractions

A data abstraction consists of an abstract data type, or a family of related abstract data types. An abstract data type is a set of objects capable only of particular kinds of behavior, which correspond to a finite set of allowable operations on objects of the type [Liskov and Zilles 1974]. All other operations on the data type must be realized using the ones in the finite set.

The meaning of an abstract data type is completely characterized by the behavior of the operations; this is guaranteed by limiting access to the representation of an object to just the operations of the type. Note that the data representation may be changed freely, provided only that the behavior of the operations is preserved. All data types can be cast into this framework. For a discussion and a multitude of examples, see Hoare [1972b].

Common examples of data abstractions are fixed-point numbers, arrays and databases. Data types may be provided by the programming language, or they may be defined by the programmer. Some programming languages (such as Alphard [Wulf, London and Shaw 1976a], CLU [Liskov, Snyder, Atkinson and Schaffert 1977] and Simula67 [Dahl, Myhrhaug and Nygaard 1970]) provide support for user-defined data types, and user-defined types can be simulated in any programming language by appropriate coding conventions.

A data abstraction also has an interface specification and a behavioral specification. The interface specification consists of the name of the type and the names and types of the associated operations. In the following, we discuss two methods of specifying the behavior of an abstract data type: axiomatically and via an abstract model.

2.2.1 Axiomatic Specifications

Axiomatic specifications define the behavior of an abstract data type by giving axioms relating the operations. There are variety of axiomatic approaches. One of the best developed methods is based on data algebras; using the recently developed theory of heterogeneous algebras [Birkhoff and Lipson 1970], this approach was developed by Zilles [Liskov and Zilles 1975; Zilles 1974], Goguen, et al. [Goguen, Thatcher, Wagner and Wright 1975], and Guttag [Guttag 1975].

All objects of an abstract data type must have been produced by some sequence of the constructor operations of that type. Other operations of the type, called inquiry operations, yield results of different types and provide the only way to extract information from an object of the type. A complete set of axioms has to define the values of the inquiry operations for any object of the abstract data type.

Let us consider the array data abstraction as an example. This abstraction corresponds to a family of data types, parameterized by the type t of the array elements. Arrays are considered to be objects that can be created, changed and interrogated. There are five array operators. The *alloc* operation creates a new array; parameters to *alloc* specify the lower and upper bounds of this array. The *store* operation changes an array by replacing one of its elements, while the **fetch** operation retrieves an element. The *top* and *bottom* operations yield the upper and lower bounds of the array. Note that we consider an assignment to an array element to be equivalent to an operation on the array, which changes the state of the array as a whole. For uniformity, we use functional notation, introducing the operations *store* and *fetch*. In more conventional notation, $store(x, i, a)$ would be written as $a[i] := x$, and $fetch(i, a)$ as $a[i]$.

AN APPRAISAL OF PROGRAM SPECIFICATIONS

Interface:

alloc (integer, integer)	**returns** array[t]
store (x: t, v: integer, a: array[t])	**changes** a
fetch (integer, array[t])	**returns** t
bottom (array[t])	**returns** integer
top (array[t])	**returns** integer

See P/2 for the meaning of As

Axioms: *behaviors relating operations*

1. alloc (i1, i2) = **if** i1 > i2 **then** error ("bad array size") *operation { bottom, top*

2. store.a (x, i, a) = **if** i < bottom (a) ∨ i > top (a)   *check i with the bounds*
   then error ("index out of bounds")

3. fetch (i1, alloc (i2, i3)) = **if** i1 < i2 ∨ i1 > i3 **then** error ("index out of bounds") *check i1 with the bounds i2, i3.*
   transformation on third argument of store **else UNDEFINED** *leave to implementor*

4. fetch (i1, store.a (x, i2, a)) = **if** i1 = i2 **then** x **else** fetch (i1, a)

5. bottom (alloc (i1, i2)) = i1   *specify a new array*

6. bottom (store.a (x, i, a)) = bottom (a)   *store op doesn't change the bounds*

7. top (alloc (i1, i2)) = i2

8. top (store.a (x, i, a)) = top (a)

arrays have fixed size ∴ no other ops that change arrays.

Figure 3. Axiomatic specification for the type array[t].

Figure 3 shows a specification for arrays. The specification has two parts, specifying the interface and the behavior of the data abstraction. In addition to the types of the inputs and outputs of the operations, the interface specification tells us that the operations *alloc, fetch, top* and *bottom* return values, but have no side effects, while the operation *store* returns no value, but changes the state of its third argument, labeled "a". The axioms in Figure 3 should be interpreted as describing the relationship between the operations and the state of an array. The transformation on the third argument of *store* is denoted by *store.a*. The axioms apply only if the arguments of the operations satisfy the type constraints given in the interface specification. The axioms are numbered for ease of reference.

According to the last four (5-8) axioms, the arguments to *alloc* specify the bounds of a new array, and the *store* operation does not change the bounds. Thus arrays have fixed sizes, since there are no other operations that change arrays.

According to the first axiom, arrays must have at least one element, and an attempt to create an empty array will cause a runtime error. According to the second and third axioms, any attempt to examine or modify an element outside the bounds will also cause an error.

Axiom 4 says that the *store* operation updates the indicated element of the array and has no effect on the rest of the elements. Axiom 3 says that all of the elements of a new array are undefined; this means that the axioms do not constrain the behavior of the implementation in this case.

The interested reader may want to compare this axiomatization to the one given by Hoare [1972b], which presents a cleaner and more abstract view of arrays in which all array elements have defined values. We believe that the arrays described by Hoare are better than the ones we define. We chose to define the behavior as above because it corresponds more closely to that provided by common programming languages.

2.2.2 Abstract Model Approach

In the abstract model approach, the objects of the data type are represented in terms of other data abstractions with known properties established by formal (probably axiomatic) specifications given in advance. Then the operations of the type being defined can be specified in terms of the operations of the known abstractions selected as the representation. The operations are specified using the methods for specifying procedural abstractions. Often it is most convenient to give I/O specifications for some of the operations, and operational specifications for the rest.

This approach is analogous to the operational method for procedural abstractions, where a function is specified by giving a particular algorithm for computing it. It must be emphasized here again that clarity and simplicity are important for specifications, while efficiency is not. It is often convenient to choose representations that use objects of standard mathematical domains, such as sets and sequences, which are not supported by most programming languages. Careful choice of representation can greatly simplify the specifications of the operations.

As an example, we will give an abstract model representation for the array data abstraction described above. The representation will use tuples and sequences.

A tuple is a set of named elements, which may be of different types. Tuples are like mathematical Cartesian products, except that the components are referenced by named selectors rather than by numerical indices. Tuples are similar to records in the programming language PASCAL [Wirth 1971b], except that they are static (cannot be updated). For example,

tuple[a: integer, b: real]

denotes a tuple type, with two components whose selectors are "a" and "b", and whose types are integer and real.

AN APPRAISAL OF PROGRAM SPECIFICATIONS

{a: 3, b: 4.1}

is an element of this type. If x denotes this element, then

x.a = 3   and   x.b = 4.1.

Sequences contain zero or more elements, all of which must have the same type; the elements are numbered from 1 to n. Sequences cannot be updated. Sequence operations include:

<> Denotes the empty sequence.

length(s) Returns the number of elements in s.

s_i If $1 \leq i \leq$ length(s), then the ith element of s.

addfirst(x, s) Creates a new sequence with x as the first element, followed by the elements of s in order.

butfirst(s) If length(s) > 0, returns a new sequence containing all but the first element of s in their original order.

An abstract model specification for arrays is shown in Figure 4. The "low" and "high" components of the representation are the bounds of the array, while the "elements" component contains information about the array elements with defined values; each such element is represented as a pair consisting of a value and its index in the array. If the bounds are legal, the *alloc* operation returns an array without any defined elements. The *top* and *bottom* operations return the appropriate components of the representation. The *store* operation simply adds the new index-value pair to the front of the elements sequence, without bothering to remove any old elements. The *fetch* operation searches the elements sequence from the front, finding the most recently stored value, if there is one. Note that the definition of *fetch* does not state what happens when an attempt is made to fetch an undefined element.

Interface:

alloc (integer, integer)	**returns** array[t]
store (x: t, v: integer, a: array[t])	**changes** a
fetch (integer, array[t])	**returns** t
bottom (array[t])	**returns** integer
top (array[t])	**returns** integer

Representation:

array[t] = **tuple** [low: integer,
                     high: integer,
                     elements: sequence [**tuple** [index: integer, value: t]]]

Operations:

alloc (i1, i2) = **if** i1 ⩽ i2 **then** {low: i1, high: i2, elements: < >}
                         else error ("bad array size")

bottom (a) = a.low

top (a) = a.high

store.a (x, i, a) = **if** a.low ⩽ i ⩽ a.high
                    then { low: a.low,
                              high: a.high
                              elements: addfirst ({index: i, value: x}, a.elements) }
                    else error ("index out of bounds")

fetch (i, a) = **if** a.low ⩽ i ⩽ a.high **then** getval (a.elements, i)
                          else error ("index out of bounds")

getval (elements, i) = **if** length (elements) = 0 **then** UNDEFINED
                       else if elements$_1$.index = i **then** elements$_1$.value
                       else getval (butfirst (elements), i)

Figure 4. Abstract model specification for the type array[t]

It is important not to read too much into abstract model specifications for data abstractions, or into operational specifications for procedural abstractions. The implementation must have the same behavior as the specifications, but it is not constrained to using the same representations and algorithms for realizing that behavior. For example, an implementation of arrays is not constrained to retain the old array values. Indeed, the strategies used for the specification and the implementation often *should* be different, because speed and simplicity do not always go together.

2.2.3 Comparison of Axiomatic and Abstract Model Techniques

It is not clear which of the abstract model and axiomatic approaches is better. Abstract model specifications are probably easier for programmers to construct and understand, since they are more like programs; however, they tend to supply detailed information that is not really part of the abstraction.

AN APPRAISAL OF PROGRAM SPECIFICATIONS

Proofs of program properties can be given using either specification techniques. Proofs of implementations are probably equally difficult in the two approaches, although this is still a matter of research. A proof in the axiomatic approach must show that the axioms are satisfied by the operations of the implementation [Guttag, Horowitz and Musser 1976]; in the abstract model approach, a homomorphism is constructed from (an algebra derived from) the implementation to (the algebra described by) the abstract model [Hoare 1972a].

The axiomatic technique is well suited to proofs of programs using the data abstraction: the axioms, and theorems derived from them, can be used directly in the proof. For abstract model specifications, however, it is probably better to prove a set of theorems from the specifications and then use the theorems in proofs rather than use the specifications directly.

The complexity of a specification in either approach depends on the complexity of the abstraction. In general, the more potential error conditions an abstraction has, the more complicated is its behavior. For example, the array definitions in Figures 3 and 4 are complicated by the fact that array elements can have undefined values. As was mentioned earlier, we believe that this is a deficiency of the array abstraction. In our experience of writing specifications we have found that slight changes in an abstraction often result in both a simpler specification and a better abstraction; this is another reason why specifications can be a useful aid in design.

The specification technique proposed by Parnas [1972a], in which a module is viewed as a state machine, can be formalized using either the axiomatic or the abstract model approach. Formalization using axioms is being investigated by Parnas and Handzel [1975]. Formalization via the abstract model approach is appropriate for the specification technique in use at SRI [Robinson and Levitt 1977], in which "hidden" functions are added to the state machine when needed to define the behavior completely; this formalization is being studied at SRI and at MIT [Principato 1978].

2.2.4 Problems for Further Research

There are a number of issues concerning procedural and data abstractions that are not sufficiently well understood. One such issue is how to specify the behavior of a program when an error is detected during execution. Models for error handling are needed both for programming languages (see Goodenough [1975]) and for specification techniques. In the absence of such a model, the behavior of a program in the presence of errors is often left unspecified, and winds up being determined by what is easiest to implement at each installation. At best, as in the examples above, the errors are named, and the conditions under which they occur are specified. Parnas has described one model for program behavior in the presence of errors [Parnas 1972a; Parnas and Wuerges 1976], but his model is informal and incomplete. Another model that appears to be promising is described in Schaffert.

Side effects are also not well understood. A side effect is said to have occurred when the value of some variable, x, changes, but no explicit assignment to x has been made. Since all changes to values must occur through variables, there must be some other variable, y, which refers to the value of x. Two common ways in which variables come to share the same values are through a call by reference, or through pointers.

Hoare [1971b] discusses some of the issues introduced by sharing via the call by reference mechanism. It is not hard to describe the effects of procedures that change their arguments. The difficulty lies in describing the effects of sharing that may occur at some times and not at others. For instance, it is possible to cause two parameters passed by reference to share the same variable by invoking a procedure with that variable for both arguments. The behavior in such a case may be different than if the inputs were distinct. Specifications and proofs must treat such cases separately. As the number of variables that may be sharing a value increases, the number of ways the sharing may happen increases drastically, making the enumeration impossibly tedious. Furthermore, these special cases are often uninteresting. We believe that linguistic methods for limiting sharing are desirable (e.g., Lampson, Horning, London, Mitchell and Popek [1978]) but also that more convenient notations for describing shared data are needed.

An additional construct that is useful in sequential programs is the control abstraction, a program unit that produces a sequence of values, one at a time, for use in a generalized **for** statement (see Liskov, Snyder, Atkinson and Schaffert [1977]; Shaw, Wulf and London [1977] for discussions of control abstractions). Some work has been done on specification and verification of control abstractions [Shaw, Wulf and London 1977], but more is needed. Control abstractions introduce a kind of quasi-parallelism between the program producing the values and the body of the **for** loop; it may be that specification techniques for parallel programs, discussed below, are appropriate here.

3. SPECIFICATIONS OF PARALLEL PROGRAMS

A sequential computation has a single site of execution activity, where the instructions of a program are executed one after another by a *process*. Sequential programs are executed by only one process at a time. In a parallel computation there may be many sites of activity, with a separate process executing instructions at each site. A parallel program is executed by an arbitrary (and possibly variable) number of processes, where more than one process may be actively executing instructions at the same time.

If a process can run without communicating with other processes, then the program executed by that process can be viewed as a sequential program, and the techniques used in the preceding section can be used to specify its behavior. This is often the case in a time-sharing system, where the jobs belonging to different users do not interact. However, for many useful and interesting applications, processes must cooperate to perform some joint task.

In this section, we discuss specification techniques for describing the behavior of parallel programs in which concurrent processes interact.

Concurrent processes can interact either by explicitly passing each other messages via a queue or I/O stream, or by changing the state of a shared data object. We will assume that processes interact by changing shared data. However, our discussion applies also to situations where processes interact by passing messages, since the I/O stream can be treated as a shared data object.

Interacting processes generally have to be *synchronized* to keep them from interfering with each other. For example, a process performing a computation sequence that changes the state of a shared object can interfere with another process in the middle of a computation sequence that depends on the state of the same object. Computation sequences that change or depend on the state of a shared object are known as *critical sections* with respect to that object. Whenever a process is in a critical section, all other processes have to be prevented from performing some subset of the possible operations on the associated shared object in order to prevent destructive interference.

New techniques are necessary for specifying the behavior of cooperating parallel programs because it is necessary to express new kinds of information. In a sequential program, the values passed in as parameters (or free variables) are the same as the values that get operated on, so that the behavior of a procedure can be viewed as a function from the inputs to the outputs. When there is concurrent activity, some other process may change the states of some of the input objects between the time of the call and the time the procedure actually gets executed, as well as several times during the execution. Sometimes this kind of behavior is desired, and sometimes it is not.

For example, consider the specification of an operation, *dequeue*, that dequeues an element from a FIFO queue. If the input queue is not empty, *dequeue* should remove and return the oldest element on the queue. This behavior is desired for both sequential and parallel programs. The desired behaviors for empty queues are different, however. In a sequential program, some sort of error condition is desired, because there is no oldest element, and never will be. In a parallel program, the desired behavior is that *dequeue* should wait until the queue is no longer empty (presumably some other process will eventually place an element in the queue).

Note that the value returned by a *dequeue* operation is not determined solely by the input values it receives. The value depends also on the inputs to subsequent *enqueue* operations, and on the history of previous *enqueue* and *dequeue* operations (including the number of previous *dequeue* operations also waiting for values).

Thus we see that a procedure cannot always be viewed as an indivisible operation in a parallel programming environment. In the queue example, we have to consider two suboperations, the request to retrieve an object from the queue, and the actual retrieval. Another example is the readers/writers problem [Courtois, Heymans and Parnas 1971], where three suboperations are considered for readers: attempting to read, actually reading and end of read.

Just as for sequential programs, careful modularization is needed to make the specifications manageable. The hard problem in parallel programming is to synchronize the processes correctly, which must be done whenever processes share data. If data abstractions are used properly, the operations of the abstract data type can be made to coincide with the critical sections associated with objects of that type, and hence processes need to be synchronized only when they perform these operations. Thus the specification of a data abstraction can include a local and complete specification of the synchronization requirements for all processes using the data abstraction. Much current research is concerned with defining linguistic mechanisms to support the use of data abstractions in parallel programming (e.g., monitors [Brinch Hansen 1973; Hoare 1974; Howard 1976], serializers [Hewitt and Atkinson 1976]). Languages where interprocess interactions are limited solely to messages passed via shared message buffers are also being investigated (e.g., Gypsy [Ambler, Good, Browne, Burger, Cohen, Hoch and Wells 1977]).

Specification techniques for parallel programs are not as well understood as are techniques for sequential programs. However, some techniques are emerging that appear to be promising. These techniques differ in the way information about the activities of concurrent processes is represented. Two approaches are discussed below.

3.1 The State Variable Approach

One way to specify the behavior of a parallel program is to describe the states of the machine before and after the program is executed. Owicki has followed this approach. In Owicki [1975] she extended Hoare's I/O constraint technique to parallel programs, by adopting his notation and giving proof rules for a language with primitives for parallel execution and synchronization. Owicki's work, like Hoare's, is geared toward proofs of program properties. The work reported in Owicki [1975] deals with arbitrary program fragments and hence can also be used to specify the operations of a data abstraction. Owicki is currently working on applying her techniques to the problem of specifying and verifying the behavior of data abstractions shared by concurrent processes.

Owicki found that her axiomatization is incomplete without a rule of inference which says that a program has a property if it can be shown that the program, when augmented by adding auxiliary variables, has that property. The auxiliary variables are used to encode information about the interactions between processes in the state of the program. For example, an auxiliary variable may be used to record the number of processes that are currently performing a given operation on a given shared data object. Auxiliary variables may be introduced into a program only as the targets of assignment statements. Their values may not be used by the program, although they may be used in assertions about the program. Consequently, the auxiliary variables can be removed from a program without affecting the

```
Incs := 0;

cobegin   S₁: ···
          // ··· //
          Sᵢ: while true do
              <non critical section>
              InCS(i) := 1;
              <critical section>
              InCS(i) := 0;
              <non critical section>
              end;
          // ··· //
          Sₙ: ···

coend;
```

Invariant: $\forall i,j\ [(1 \leq i \leq n\ \&\ 1 \leq j \leq n\ \&\ \neg(i=j)) \Rightarrow \neg(InCS(i)=1\ \&\ InCS(j)=1)]$

Figure 5. State variable specification of mutual exclusion

outcome of the computation, and any property of a program that can be proved by introducing auxiliary variables must also hold for the original program.

An example of a specification using Owicki's technique is shown in Figure 5. The program fragments labeled $S_1, \ldots, S_n$ (separated by the delimiters "**cobegin**", "**//**" and "**coend**") are all identical except for the auxiliary variables. Each program fragment is executed by a separate process, and each contains a critical section. We wish to specify that the critical sections are mutually exclusive: no two distinct processes may be executing a critical section at the same time. In order to express this property formally, we introduce an array of auxiliary variables called *InCS*, which is indexed by the subscripts of the process labels S_i. All of the components of *InCS* are initially zero. Just before process S_i enters its critical section, *InCS(i)* is set to one, and just after process S_i leaves its critical section, *InCS (i)* is set to zero. These are the only places in the program where *InCS* is mentioned. Therefore we know that *InCS(i)* = 1 whenever process S_i is in its critical section. The invariant assertion says that no two distinct components of *InCS* have the value one, which implies that no two processes are in their critical sections at the same time, as we require. The invariant is asserted to hold at all points in the program between the **cobegin** and the **coend** statements. This example is adapted from Owicki [1975], where the author proves that the appropriate invariant holds for a program with a similar structure and a particular synchronization scheme, thus establishing that the mutual exclusion requirement is met.

Robinson and Holt have considered the problem of specifying the synchronization constraints associated with shared data as a part of the specification of the data abstraction. For each operation, they introduce an abstract program consisting of a sequence of suboperations. Some of the suboperations update "state functions", which are generally used to count the number of processes currently active in a given section of code (cf. Owicki's auxiliary variables). The synchronization constraints are expressed by invariant assertions involving the state functions before and after certain suboperations of the abstract program. Just those program states that do not violate the invariant are legal. Suboperations that would result in an illegal program state have to be suspended until it is safe for them to proceed.

Robinson and Holt point out that a proof of correctness of an implementation must include a proof that the implementation preserves the invariants. They also discuss a way of verifying the correctness of the specification. This involves constructing the state machine that has those state transitions allowed by the invariant. This state machine can be checked automatically for various properties, such as freedom from deadlock; it may also be presented to the user for review. Methods for determining properties of specifications are even more important for parallel than for sequential programs, because it is especially difficult to determine that the specified behavior does indeed correspond to the user's expectations when there are interacting concurrent processes involved.

3.2 The Event Approach

The earliest event-oriented specifications for concurrent programs are path expressions [Campbell and Habermann 1974; Habermann 1975; Flon and Habermann 1976]. Path expressions are tied to data abstractions; the execution of a suboperation of an operation of the data type is taken to be an event. Path expressions are constraints on the order in which events can happen. Habermann gave informal descriptions of several versions of path expressions, which he intended as synchronization primitives for a high-level programming language; for one version [Campbell and Habermann 1974] an algorithm for implementing path expressions using Dijkstra's P and V operations [Dijkstra 1968b] was presented. Lauer and Campbell [1975] gave a formal definition of a slightly different version, using the Petri net formalism [Hack 1972; Petri 1962]; this kind of path expression is a regular expression (as in automata theory), which generates a set of strings corresponding to all of the legal sequences of events. Finally, Flon and Habermann [Flon and Habermann 1976] discussed proofs of correctness of parallel programs specified by path expressions, connecting a new kind of path expression with invariant assertions.

A more formal and abstract view is taken by Greif [1975]. This work is based on the assumption that it is not possible to define a global notion of time, or a total ordering on events, that all observers can agree upon. Rather,

AN APPRAISAL OF PROGRAM SPECIFICATIONS

a local view is taken; two events are ordered only if some communication has taken place that allows the ordering between the events to be deduced, much as in the relativity theory of physics. Time is described as a partial ordering, so that there may be pairs of events that are not ordered with respect to one another, and hence can be "simultaneous" or "concurrent". An event is supposed to be instantaneous and indivisible. Events are usually defined as the beginning or the end of some step in the computation.

Greif describes a computation as a partially ordered set of events: some events are known to come before certain other events. The partial order can be viewed as a history of the computation. Each event is associated with exactly one process, so that the set of events in a computation can be partitioned into disjoint subsets (one for each process).

Synchronization constraints are expressed as axioms constraining the legal partial orders, admitting some computations but not others. For example, Figure 6 shows the axiom for mutual exclusion. S_1 and S_2 denote the sets of events corresponding to two distinct invocations of the critical section (possibly by different processes).[3] The axiom says that the computations S_1 and S_2 may not overlap in time: either every event of S_1 must happen before any event of S_2 does, or vice versa. The notation "x < y" means that the event x occurs strictly before the event y. Note that the axiom is independent of the number of processes involved, so that it can be used even in situations where the number of processes is variable.

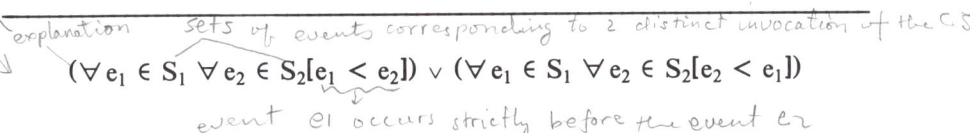

$$(\forall e_1 \in S_1 \; \forall e_2 \in S_2[e_1 < e_2]) \lor (\forall e_1 \in S_1 \; \forall e_2 \in S_2[e_2 < e_1])$$

Figure 6. Event axiom for mutual exclusion

Greif's formalism is powerful enough to handle real concurrency, with multiple processors that may be in widely scattered locations. The formalism can be used to state requirements concerning priorities and various other fine points of scheduling, such as the absence of deadlock and starvation. It cannot describe performance properties, such as throughput, because only the order of events is discussed, and not the actual elapsed time between two ordered events.

4. FUTURE RESEARCH DIRECTIONS

We believe that the use of formal specifications can enhance the reliability and decrease the cost of software, and that research in this area should be

---

3. Although we have not done so here, the sets S_1 and S_2 can be defined formally using Greif's techniques.

supported and encouraged. In the remainder of this section, we discuss future research directions that we believe have promise.

In Sections 2 and 3, we discussed current work in specification techniques. Considerable gains have been made in understanding and defining specifications, but much remains to be done. In the area of sequential programs, useful specification methods have been invented for both functional and data abstractions. The main work that needs to be done is to establish proof techniques associated with the various methods, to extend the methods to those aspects of program behavior not yet covered (e.g., errors, side effects and control abstractions), and to develop specifications languages that make the techniques easy to use.

In the area of parallel programs, specification methods need considerable development. It is not even clear what the important aspects of the behavior of a parallel program are. The concepts need to be developed before they can be precisely defined. For example, the input/output behavior of a module is usually treated separately from other aspects, such as the priority and the degree of concurrency. However, these aspects are not completely independent, and it is not yet known how to describe the relationship between them in a useful way. Once standard concepts dealing with orderings and synchronization are developed, standard notations for these concepts should be introduced, with the result that specifications can be given at a higher level.

As specification languages come into existence, they should be used to specify programs so that the techniques can be evaluated. We have only limited experience with specification of programs of reasonable size [Price 1973; Ragland 1973]. The study of specifications should focus on well-modularized programs consisting of modules supporting data and functional abstractions. The utility of specifications in program construction should also be evaluated.

The specification methods discussed in this paper are suitable for describing a program design, or at least those parts resulting in modules supporting data or functional abstractions. To the extent that an entire system can be considered to be an abstraction, or a group of abstractions, the technique ought to be useful for describing system behavior, although the difficulty of describing very high-level abstractions is formidable (consider the complexity of a specification of a programming-language processor). Attempts to specify real applications will be valuable in determining the applicability of the techniques to describing entire system behavior.

The use of specifications during program design will be enhanced if tools exist for increasing the level of confidence that a set of specifications does indeed capture the intended concepts and behavior. For instance, properties and implications of a specification can be derived, and reviewed by the user [Guttag 1975]. A catalog of properties that are useful gauges of behavior and a set of methods for extracting these properties from a specification are needed as a preliminary step towards building an automated facility to assist the user in evaluating a proposed specification or system design.

For specifications to contribute most effectively to the programming process, computer support of specifications is desirable. We expect that ultimately there will be systems that support program development in an integrated fashion. Such systems will be organized around a database containing information about abstractions (see Liskov, Snyder, Atkinson and Schaffert [1977] for a description of such a system). For each abstraction, the database will include specifications, source code and object code of implementations, and the known properties of the abstraction (e.g., that a particular implementation has been verified). Many programs will run on the data base, including specification and programming language processors and verifiers.

Very little work has been done in the area of formal requirements specifications. In one study that has been done [Bell and LaPadula 1973], properties of the desired system behavior were specified using a model. The specifications resulting from the system design must be checked to see if they satisfy these properties, which we envision as a set of interdependent constraints the user expects the system to satisfy. We speculate that the techniques used in formally specifying a system design can be carried over to this phase, with the benefit that conflicts and inconsistencies among the requirements can be caught early.

ROBERT BALZER and NEIL GOLDMAN
USC/Information Sciences Institute

Principles of Good Software Specification and their Implications for Specification Languages

1. INTRODUCTION

Many computer languages have been designed without goals being explicitly stated beforehand. We attempt to reverse this process by carefully developing the goal structure before designing a language to satisfy it.

A few other languages have been constructed using a similar paradigm, most notably PASCAL [Wirth 1971b] and EUCLID [London, Guttag, Horning, Lampson, Mitchell and Popek 1978]. Each was strongly influenced by the unique goal structures chosen (simplicity for PASCAL and provability for EUCLID). Similarly, we expect our language, not yet designed, to be strongly influenced by the goal structure chosen.

Our contribution lies in the extent to which we have developed an explicit set of goals and their implications on the structure and features of any language that would satisfy these goals.

2. CRITERIA FOR JUDGING SPECIFICATIONS

In order to establish the criteria to be used in judging software specifications, we begin by considering their primary uses. First, and most important, a software specification is a contract between the specifier and the implementor defining the system to be constructed. It therefore must be clearly and unambiguously understandable by both parties. Thus, understandability is the first criterion for judging specifications.

Second, it must be possible to ascertain whether an implementor has fulfilled such a contract; that is, to test, in the broadest sense, whether a specification and an implementation are equivalent (i.e., consistent). In addition, before entering into an implementation contract, a specifier must be able to ascertain that the specified system meets the needs for which it was designed. Thus, the specification itself must be testable. Hence testability is the second criterion for judging specifications.

Finally, because this contract will change over time, it must be easy to modify the specification. Hence, maintainability is the third and final criterion. Optimization (the process of reducing the computing resources required to execute a program) is conspicuous by its absence from the list of criteria. This is intentional. Not only is optimization the proper concern of the implementor, but it conflicts with each of the identified criteria.

Optimization represents the spread of information which, by increasing the interdependence of the components, increases the complexity of the whole. This reduces the understandability, maintainability, and testability of the specification. Thus, not only is optimization *not* a proper criterion for judging specifications, but specification languages should actively attempt to preclude the optimizations of specifications (as opposed to their implementations).

3. PRINCIPLES OF GOOD SPECIFICATION

Principle #1: Separate functionality from implementation.

First, by definition, a specification is a description of *what* is desired, rather than *how* it is to be realized (implemented). Specifications can adopt two quite different forms. The first form is that of mathematical functions: Given some set of input, produce a particular set of outputs. The general form of such specifications is find [*a/the/all*] result such that P(input), where P represents an arbitrary predicate. In such specifications, the result to be obtained has been entirely expressed in a *what* (rather than *how*) form. In part this is because the result is a mathematical function of the input (the operation has well-defined starting and stopping points) and is unaffected by any surrounding environment.

Principle #2: A process-oriented systems specification language is required.

Consider instead a situation in which the environment is dynamic and its changes affect the behavior of some entity interacting with that environment (as in an "embedded computer system"). Its behavior cannot be expressed as a mathematical function of its input. Rather, a process-oriented description must be employed, in which the *what* specification is achieved by specifying a model of the desired behavior in terms of functional responses to various stimuli from the environment.

Such process-oriented specifications, presenting a model of system behavior, have normally been excluded from formal specification languages, but they are essential if more complex dynamic situations are to be specified. In fact, it must be recognized that in such situations both the process to be automated and the environment in which it exists must be described formally. That is, the entire system of interacting parts must be specified, rather than just one component.

Principle #3: A specification must encompass the system of which the software is a component.

A system is composed of interacting components. Only within the context of the entire system and the interaction among its parts can the behavior of a specific component be defined. In general, a system can be modeled as a collection of passive and active objects. These objects are interrelated and over time the relationships among the objects change. These dynamic relationships provide the stimulus to which the active objects, called agents, respond. The responses may cause further changes and, hence, additional stimuli to which the agents might respond.

PRINCIPLES OF GOOD SOFTWARE SPECIFICATION

Principle #4: A specification must encompass the environment in which system operates.

Similarly, the environment in which the system operates and with which it interacts must be specified.

Fortunately, this merely necessitates recognizing that the environment is itself a system composed of interacting objects, both passive and active, of which the specified system is one agent. The other agents, which are by definition unalterable because they are part of the environment, limit the scope of the subsequent design and implementation. In fact, the only difference between the system and its environment is that the subsequent design and implementation effort will operate exclusively on the specification of the system. The environment specification enables the system "interface" to be specified in the same way as the system itself rather than introducing another formalism.

It should be noted that the picture of system specification presented here is that of a highly intertwined collection of agents reacting to stimuli in the environment (changes to objects) produced those agents. Only through the coordinated actions of the agents are the goals of the system achieved. Such mutual dependence violates the principle of separability (isolation from other parts of the system and environment). But this is a *design* principle, not one of specification. Design follows specification and is concerned with decomposing a specification into nearly separable pieces in preparation for implementation. The specification, however, must accurately portray the system and its environment as perceived by its user community in as much detail as required by the design and implementation phases. Since this level of required detail is difficult, if not impossible, to foresee in advance, specification, design, and implementation must be recognized as an iterative activity. It is therefore critical that technology exist for recovering as much of this activity as possible as the specification is elaborated and modified (during both initial development and later maintenance) [Balzer, Goldman and Wile 1976].

Principle #5: A system specification must be a cognitive model.

The system specification must be a cognitive model rather than a design or implementation model. It must describe a system as perceived by its user community. The objects it manipulates must correspond to the real objects of that domain; the agents must model the individuals, organizations, and equipment in that domain; and the actions they perform must model those actually occurring in the domain. Furthermore, it must be possible to incorporate into the specification the rules or laws which govern the objects of the domain. Some of these laws proscribe certain states of the system (such as "two objects cannot be at the same place at the same time"), and hence limit the behavior of the agents or indicate the need for further elaboration to prevent these states from arising. Other laws describe how objects respond when acted upon (e.g., Newton's laws of motion). These laws, which represent a "physics" of the domain, are an inherent part of the system specification.

Principle #6: A specification must be operational.

The specification must be complete and formal enough that it can be used to determine if a proposed implementation satisfies the specification for arbitrarily chosen test cases. That is, given the results of an implementation on some arbitrarily chosen set of data, it must be possible to use the specification to validate those results. This implies that the specification, though not a complete specification of *how*, can act as a generator of possible behaviors among which must be the proposed implementation. Hence, in an extended sense, the specification must be operational.

The operationality may exist only in a theoretical sense, since it involves replacing existentially and universally quantified objects in the specification by brute force generation and testing (the British Museum algorithm) of all possibilities (which may be infinite). One way in which the specification can be used to partially test an implementation without relying on the British Museum algorithm is to use the possibilities generated by the implementation on a specific run in place of the search required by the British Museum algorithm. The specification then becomes a validation filter for the generated possibilities (it does not, however, guarantee that all valid possibilities were generated by the implementation, only that those generated are valid).

Principle #7: The system specification must be tolerant of incompleteness, and augmentable.

No specification can ever by totally complete. The environment in which it exists is too complex for that. A specification is always a model—an abstraction—of some real (or envisioned) situation. Hence, it will be incomplete. Furthermore, as it is being formulated it will exist at many levels of detail. The operationality required above must not necessitate completeness. The analysis tools employed to aid specifiers and to test specifications must be capable of dealing with incompleteness. Naturally this weakens the analysis which can be performed by widening the range of acceptable behaviors which satisfy the specification, but such degradation must mirror the remaining levels of uncertainty.

Principle #8: A specification must be localized and loosely coupled.

The previous principles deal with the specification as a static entity. This one arises from the dynamics of the specification. It must be recognized that although the main purpose of a specification is to serve as the basis for design and implementation of some system, it is not a precomposed static object, but a dynamic object which undergoes considerable modification. Such modification occurs in three main activities: formulation, when an initial specification is being created; development, when the specification is elaborated during the iterative process of design and implementation; and maintenance, when the specification is changed to reflect a modified environment and/or additional functional requirements.

With so much change occurring to the specification, it is critical that its content and structure be chosen to accommodate this activity. The main requirements for such accommodations are that information within the

PRINCIPLES OF GOOD SOFTWARE SPECIFICATION 29

specification must be localized so that only a single piece (ideally) need be modified when information changes, and that the specification is loosely structured (coupled) so that pieces can be added or removed easily, and the structure automatically readjusted.

4. IMPLICATIONS FOR SPECIFICATION LANGUAGES

Having set forth the principles of good specification in the previous section, we now derive some important implications of these principles for specification languages. References to the principles, and to earlier implications, are parenthesized and are referenced by principle (P) or implication (I) number (e.g., P1 or I3).

Implication #1: Logical data specification and access.
  Since a specification must deal with functional behavior rather than an implementation (P1), the data manipulated in the specification must be representation independent. The specification must thus be described at the logical level by defining the methods of getting from one data item to another (access paths) and the operations that can be performed upon a data item.

Implication #2: Uniform data specification.
  Since the logical data specification should make no implications about data representation (P1), the principle of parsimony requires that a single uniform data specification be used for all data and that this specification not preclude any possible representations.

Implication #3: Relational data model.
  This requirement of uniformity (I2) has strong implications. It forces a quite unconventional specification of data to be adopted. The conventional view of data as having a "value" and being composed of a collection of parts is fraught with difficulty. What is the "value" of a data item, what is its range, when is the "value" used rather than the item, and how far does the "boundary" of the data item extend? There are no easy answers to these questions, which arise from choosing a representation-oriented view. Instead, a functional view leads to a very simple, yet general, data specification which avoids these difficulties.
  Objects are associated with one another, and their relationships can be used to access them. An object has no "value" or "boundary". Rather it is defined by the set of associations it forms with other objects. This definition is necessarily circular, but such circularity causes no problems because after some point further chains of associations become irrelevant for the processing being performed.
  Thus data is defined simply by specifying the relations existing among the objects. There are only five basic operations that can be performed on such data. Objects can be created or destroyed. Similarly, relations among two or more objects can be created or destroyed. Finally, objects can be accessed from other objects via one of these relations. The symmetry of the relational

specification is particularly nice since it is just as easy to access one object from another via a particular relation as it is to use the second object to access the first via that same relation. Using database terminology, this means that the database is fully associative, or equivalently, fully inverted (that is, inversion is a physical technique for implementing logical associativity).

It should be noted here that although this type of data specification is quite unconventional in software and system specifications, it is becoming prevalent within the database community. Unfortunately, because this community is concerned with efficiency, it has adopted a particular canonical form of relational specification (third normal form [Codd 1971]) rather than allowing the full generality of the formalism. Clearly, for the purposes of functional specification such a restriction should not be included. Instead the recent database work on semantic models [Hammer and McLeod 1978; Chen 1976; Smith and Smith 1977a, 1977b; Pirotte 1977] more closely matches the general relational model required.

It should also be noted that the semantic net representation [Quillian 1968] widely used in the artificial intelligence community is entirely equivalent to the general relational specification (actually, to a relational specification using only binary relations). The reasons for adoption of semantic nets by the artificial intelligence community are quite instructive. Artificial intelligence systems are designed to deal with uncertainty which arises in the data to be processed and/or the processing to be applied to it, which prevents optimization of the data structures and necessitates a very general expression of its functionality. These reasons are very similar to our own, although the motivation is distinct. We need to express the functional characteristics of the data while delaying consideration of representation and optimization to the implementation phase of development.

Implication #4: Global model.

A model of the objects, both passive and active, manipulated by the agents and serving as stimuli for them must be maintained (P3). Since new agents can be added to the specification or their stimuli changed (P8), any object may serve as part of an agent's stimulus, and hence must be globally maintained.

This global database represents a dynamic model of the environment in which the system operates. The model's dynamics are governed by the sequence of actions performed, and these actions, together with the changes made to the objects in the model, constitute the observable behavior of the agents. The agents also gather information from the global model to make decisions of whether or not to perform an action, and if so, which one. These information-gathering and decision-making processes constitute a model of the agent; it is just such a model that can be embodied in computer software.

System specifications contain one or more such agents. The objects and actions of the global model must also be defined, and models of each agent provided. However, much variability is allowed in the completeness of specifying an agent model (P7). The model must define which actions the agent is allowed to perform, but it need not specify the information-gathering processes used by the agent in deciding which actions to perform or their order. It may contain partial descriptions of these processes or merely constraints on the behavior of the agent.

If each agent is completely specified, the system can be simulated (P1); that is, the global model, operating with particular or symbolic data, can be advanced through successive stages. If the agents are incomplete, such simulated behavior can be accomplished only by having the user interactively inject agent actions into the sequence of actions being performed. As the completeness of agent description decreases, the amount of automatic analysis and checking which can be performed decreases correspondingly. However, partial descriptions should be retained as consistency checks when supplanted by more complete descriptions or when agent behavior is provided by the user.

Implication #5: Global database with inference.

The global model must be maintained in a data base which supports inference (derived relationships). The global model is a simulation of the environment in which the system operates. Normally such environments are quite rich and many of the relations between objects can be deduced (inferred) from other relations within the model. Since the specification can, and will, undergo such modification, the principle of locality and loose coupling (P8) requires that neither the use of information nor its method of derivation be explicitly determined in the specification. That is, any information requested from the global model should be available independent of whether it was directly produced by some action or can be inferred from such directly produced data.

For each data item a choice must be made between explicitly representing that item in a database and maintaining it as actions are performed, or deriving (inferring) it when needed. Such choices are quite critical to the efficient operation of a system, but they are implementation choices and have no place within the system specification (P1). Inference mechanisms provide a way of delaying these choices until implementation without sacrificing the operationality of the specification (P6). The need to hide the distinction between explicit and implicit data through the use of inference implies that the global model is maintained in a database accessible only through an interface which supports inference.

It should be noted that the "computation rules" of data-flow languages [Prywes 1977; Hammer, Howe and Wladawsky; Langefors] are a special case of inference rules. The advantage of specifying computation via such rules is that the control structure has been suppressed from the specification and these rules are invoked whenever necessary. This suppression of the control structure enables the user to specify the functional relations between objects (*what*) without specifying when (*how*) to compute them (P1).

When appropriate, this method of specification should be heavily utilized. However, its applicability is limited to static situations in which the global model isn't changing (no actions are being applied). Rather, only the state of explicit knowledge about the global model is being altered as information is derived from other information.

A common specification mistake is the failure to differentiate the actual actions occurring in the global model, from "information actions". The actual actions are performed by agents to alter the relationship between objects producing stimuli to which other agents may respond. "Information actions", on the other hand, don't alter any relationships between objects, but rather draw conclusions from the existing relationships. They are merely an implementation mechanism for hiding the distinction between explicit and implicit data, and hence should not be explicitly invoked in the specification. Instead, only the functional basis (the inference rules) for such "information actions" should be specified (to be used as needed).

Implication #6: Descriptive reference.

Since the global model is being maintained in a database which obscures the distinction between explicit and implicit data (I5), references to data from the model must operate indirectly through some language processed by the database rather than by direct access to the data itself. The use of a data-request language with the support of an inference mechanism is one step in the direction of separating the specification of what data is required (functionality) from its method of access (implementation) (P1). A second step is the use of a fully associative relational database (I3). The final step is the capability to access data by describing its attributes—descriptive reference. Thus, a pattern is used to specify which relations the desired object(s) must have to other objects, which are proscribed, and which alternatives are acceptable. These conditions must be simultaneously satisfied for an object to match the pattern—the descriptive reference. The objects used to describe the desired object may themselves be descriptively described, and so on, so that very general descriptions can be composed. These descriptive references require a quite complex pattern match mechanism, but the specification is only concerned with functionality. A major portion of a systems implementation will, however, be concerned with simplifying these data-access mechanisms by proper choice of data structures and use of facilitating computations.

For compactness of expression, it is desirable that the appearance of a descriptive reference create a lexically scoped association between a model time, the description, and a name called a placeholder. The placeholder can then be used elsewhere in that lexical scope as a shorthand for the description itself or for the object which satisfied the descriptive reference at the time contained in the association (see Implication #7). It should be noted that this association between a reusable name (normally an object type) and a pattern to specify either the object currently or originally satisfying the pattern closely parallels the use of descriptive reference in natural language.

Implication #7: Historical references.

The explanation of descriptive references above introduced the notion that the description might be used to reference either the object currently satisfying the pattern or the object which satisfied it at some previous time—

PRINCIPLES OF GOOD SOFTWARE SPECIFICATION

the time at which the placeholder association was formed. This is a particularization of the general capability to obtain the object satisfying the pattern at an arbitrary earlier time.

The need for such a capability becomes clear when the alternative is investigated. Without such a capability, historical references such as "the location of the plane when first spotted" must be implemented by recognizing at the appropriate point (the time at which the plane was first spotted) that the object satisfying the descriptive reference (location of plane) must be saved so that it can later be used where required. This is a clear violation of both the principles of functional specification (P1) and loose coupling (P8).

The capability of satisfying descriptive references as of some arbitrary earlier point in time remedies these problems by merely specifying what data is desired (not how to obtain it) and by localizing the specification at the point of consumption (rather than creating an explicit coupling between the production and consumption points through a shared variable). Naturally, this capability implies some ability to specify earlier times. It should be clear that the only meaningful method of time specification is the specification's own history; that is in terms of the sequence of actions performed on the global model. By reasoning similar to that motivating the need for descriptive references for objects (I6), so too are descriptive references required for the actions which mark the passage of time.

The coupling of descriptive references for both objects and actions provide the capability to examine (but not change) the entire history of a system. This includes the ability to examine any previous state of the system, to determine whether one state preceded another, or to use the historical time order to access data within a state (e.g., "the last plane launched before the storm").

Implication #8:   Elimination of variables.

The use of historical references (I7) means that a required object, the only type of "value" allowed (I3), can *always* be recomputed even if the system state has been altered. In most languages, which have no historical reference, modification of the state forces the saving of the required value in some variable because it cannot be recomputed later. Here, since recomputation is always possible, there is a choice between saving the value (storage) and recomputation. By the principle of locality and loose coupling (P8), the choice must be universally in favor of recomputation. Otherwise, an explicit coupling is established between the consumption and the production through the shared (non local) use of a variable.

Thus, values are always recomputed, as needed; they are never stored. This eliminates the need for variables. They serve no purpose other than holding saved values.

It should be noted that the use of placeholders (I6) represents a compromise with the complete elimination of variables. Placeholders are a type of variable, but they "hold" descriptive references rather than values and must be satisfied as of some time to yield a value (object). Thus they are like procedures in which the name is used as a shorthand for the definition, the definition must be applied to yield a value, and the association between name and definition is static for the lifetime of the name rather than being reassigned as with conventional variables. This "structured" use of placeholders is, we feel, warranted, even though it causes a named-based sharing (P8), because of the notational inconvenience which would otherwise result from recopying the reference. Furthermore, such recopying would itself violate the localization principle (P8). So it is quite clear that some compromise must be accommodated.

Implication #9: Constraint capability including strong data typing.

By the same reasoning which eliminated variables (I8) because their use would introduce explicit coupling between the producer and the consumer, the need for constraints is also established. Without a constraint statement, which is a global prohibition of some class of states of the data model, the constraints would have to be integrated ("compiled") into the specification at all the appropriate places. Such integration ("compilation") violates both the principles of locality (P8) and separation of function from implementation (P1), and prevents the specification from paralleling the user's cognitive model (P5) in which such constraints naturally exist.

One major category of constraints are type restrictions on objects. Normally, only certain types of objects can participate in the various roles of an association or action. These restrictions must be locally specified (P8). Furthermore, since a real world object may belong to many different types simultaneously (e.g., a particular individual may be an adult, a farmer, and a employee, as well as being a person), so too must the modeled objects (P5). In general, a lattice of types must be supported, and, for all the obvious reasons, the association between types and objects must itself be part of the relational database so that, like other associations, it can be supported by inference, associativity, constraints, etc.

Implication #10: Nondeterministic constructs.

For the constraints (I9) to be more than mere documentation of properties already guaranteed by the specification, they must actually constrain the set of allowable interpretations of the specification. Since the specification is operational (P6), the constraints proscribe those behaviors which would violate the constraints. Thus, the specification may contain nondeterministic constructs for which the choice rule is free except that no constraint may result. A key aspect of the *implementation* of the specification is determining choice rules which guarantee that the constraints wouldn't be violated.

For obvious reasons, this nondeterminism must exist in both the data and control spaces. The data-nondeterministic construct has already been introduced—descriptive references (I6). When more than one object can satisfy the reference, and one is desired, then a nondeterministic choice must be made. The control construct merely indicates that a nondeterministic choice must be made among the specified actions (e.g., "either launch another plane or allow a returning one to land").

Implication #11: Result specification.

The nondeterministic constructs (I10), in conjunction with constraint (I9) described above, provide a mechanism for describing desired behavior without specifying precisely the mechanism by which it should be achieved (P1): merely that some appropriate combination of choices for the nondeterministic constructs will result in the specified behavior without violating any constraints.

In a similar way, it should be possible to specify choices among alternative operations by the results desired or to be avoided (e.g., Achieve S by doing X or Y or Z). These required and/or proscribed results act like local constraints which must be satisfied nondeterministically by at least one specified method for achieving the desired state (to maintain the operationality of the specification (P6)).

It should also be possible to use such result specifications to control the conditionality of some action (e.g., "launch another plane unless it would leave the ship vulnerable to attack").

Such result specifications in which properties of the state resulting from performing some operation are used to determine whether to perform that operation are novel. Normally, such decisions are made by determining what conditions existing in the current state would, after performance of the specified action, yield the specified state. Here, through result specifications, the specified conditions are simply evaluated in the state existing after (hypothetically) performing the operation. This is analogous to a historical reference (I7) in which the specified time has not yet occurred and, like historical references, its need is justified by considering the alternative. Without such a capability, the desired (or proscribed) resulting state must be described in terms of the current state of the model before the operation is applied. This translation of conditions across the application of an operation is highly dependent upon the exact nature of the operation, and is a type of "compilation" which violates the principles of functionality (P1)—by specifying how to calculate the criteria (in the current state) rather than merely specifying the criteria (in the future state) to be used; the principle of locality and loose coupling (P8)—by explicitly using the definition of the operation to determine the current state criteria; and the principle of cognitive modeling (P5)—by preventing the natural expression of the future states and their use within constraints.

Implication #12: Future reference.

This capability enables references to be made to objects that will satisfy a description as of some future time (e.g., "refuel all planes which will be launched today"). This capability can be thought of as the extension either of historical references into the future, or of result specifications to objects. Its justification is similarly motivated. Its absence would require determining the criteria, expressed in terms of the current state, for those objects which will satisfy the description as of the specified time, and would hence violate both the functionality (P1) and locality and loose coupling (P8) principles.

Again, it is an implementation, rather than specification, issue to determine effective mechanisms to efficiently calculate such references in the current state.

Implication #13: Demons.

There are two separate reasons for including demons in a system specification language. The first is based on the relationship between the system being specified and its environment (P4). This environment is conceptualized as a set of agents which affect a global model (I4) by performing actions on the objects in that model. One or more of these agents constitute the system being specified. They, and the environment agents, must react to changes which occur in the global model. This can only be done by either integrating the agents into a single control structure which activates each one at the appropriate time, by having each constantly poll the model for interesting changes, or by providing a demon capability which activates an agent whenever specified changes occur in the model. Since both integration and polling represent implementation techniques (P1) for achieving demon capability, and integration further violates the principle of locality (P8), the specification should be expressed directly in terms of demons.

The second reason for including demons in the specification language concerns the interactions between various parts of the system being specified. Like constraints, demons provide a method of localizing the response to some change in the global model, rather than distributing the response to all the places the change could have been initiated from (P8). Also, by localizing the response, protection is provided for future additions which might also initiate the change (P7). Thus demons provide a method of specifying a response *whenever* some change occurs, not just for those which are explicitly known.

Implication #14: Logical aggregation.

Descriptive references (I6), inference mechanism (I5), and a fully associative database (I3) are required to separate the functional description of data items from the implementation mechanisms needed to access them (P1). These capabilities provide functional access to individual data objects. But process-oriented specifications (P2) also deal with collections or aggregations of objects which satisfy some common criteria. These aggregations are formed so that an operation, or sequence of operations, can be applied to each object in the aggregation or to the entire aggregation as a whole. Such aggregations are the basis for concise specification by expanding into a much larger set of individual actions to be applied to the individual objects of the aggregations, and correspond to the loop-control structures of programming languages.

These aggregation constructs must satisfy all the requirements for separating functional description from access mechanisms (P1) described above. Hence, they should be compatible with the descriptive reference capability so that they can be used in conjunction with historical and/or

PRINCIPLES OF GOOD SOFTWARE SPECIFICATION

future references. In addition, they must hide the implementation distinction (P1) between explicit aggregations (where each object belonging to the aggregation is explicitly represented), implicit ones (in which only the rule of membership is represented), and combinations thereof without sacrificing the operationality of the specification (P6). This implies that all operations utilizing the members of an aggregation operate indirectly through some language processor so that implicit aggregations can be made explicit as objects belonging to the aggregation are needed. Since these same requirements exist for descriptive references themselves, the aggregation capability should exist not merely in a form compatible with descriptive references, but as an extension of that capability.

There are two detailed issues which arise in the functional specification of aggregations. First, the operations performed on the elements of an aggregation may affect the membership of other objects in that aggregation. If so, then the specification must be completed by specifying whether the aggregation membership is static as of some specified time, or dynamic with additions and deletions allowed during its use. The second detailed issue occurs when the order of selecting objects belonging to the aggregation affects the resulting state of the global model. The order of selecting objects will be non-deterministic unless an explicit ordering has been specified.

Implication #15: Alternative constructs (contexts).

The aggregation capability (I14) provides a mechanism for functionally specifying a collection of objects and treating them similarly. But a capability is also required to treat the objects of an aggregation as mutually exclusive alternatives. Each of the alternatives must be separately investigated before a decision can be made as to which to select. During these investigations the exploration of the individual alternatives must not interfere with one another. Each exploration must be carried forth as if it were the only one being investigated so that actions performed in one exploration are not apparent in any other and constraints are applied only within an exploration (so that each exploration remains self-consistent but the explorations are not necessarily consistent with each other). Upon completion of the explorations it must be possible to compare the resulting states and determine which subset to retain (either the resulting state or the alternative which started the exploration may be retained).

This alternative construct capability is merely a generalization of the result specification capability (I11) described earlier and is similarly motivated.

Implication #16: Analogous specification.

Often two or more processes are very similar to each other. In such cases, it is more convenient to specify one in terms of another by specifying the similarities and differences rather than repeating the common portions (which would violate P8). More importantly, if, during maintenance, the definition of the base process should change, this change would automatically be reflected in all the analogously specified processes (in cases where this effect was not desired, a new exception clause could be added to analogously specified processes for which the maintainer, guided by a simple maintenance tool, indicated that the effect should not be promulgated). This capability directly supports the ability to make specifications more complete (P7) by localizing the base description (P8) and by explicitly maintaining the dependencies between process descriptions.

Implication #17: Normal-case specification.

In support of the ability to deal with incomplete specifications (P7), it must be possible to specify the behavior of the process for the normal case and then augment that description with the additional and/or alternative behavior required in the various special cases which can arise. This capability is itself a special case of the general analogous specification capability (I16) described above.

The important aspects of this capability are that each exception should be independently specified (P8) and that these alternatives are automatically organized (P1) so that the most specific applicable alternative is chosen in each case, and the normal case processing is performed only when none of the other alternatives are applicable.

These two capabilities (I16 and I17) are intended to provide the basis for gradually developing a specification by augmentation and modification. This implies the ability for the specification to refer to parts of itself as the basis for the incremental specification.

Implication #18: Process models (scenarios).

Often only an incomplete model of an environmental agent (P4) exists so that only certain aspects of its behavior are known. It must be possible to specify the known aspects (P7), leaving the others open, while preserving the operationality of the specification (P6).

One common form of incompleteness is knowledge of the possible actions which an agent can perform, but lack of information of the decision mechanism employed by the agent. This form of incompleteness can be easily modeled by "scenarios" which utilize nondeterminism mechanisms (I10) to embed processing options into an expression (such as path-expressions) describing the range of the possible behaviors to be performed by the agent and possible conditions under which these scenarios will be performed.

Though it is beyond the scope of this paper, we note that an analysis aid could be provided to determine whether the system being specified adequately responds to the range of possible behaviors specified for the environment agents.

5. CONCLUSION

Strong constraints have been placed on future specification languages by carefully considering design principles of "good" specifications which were themselves derived from the primary uses of specifications. These constraints imply the need for an ultra-high-level language which combines the database concept of a global model containing alternative viewpoints (hiding the distinction between explicit and implicit data) with the control structures (both asynchronous demon structures and conventional branching and looping structures) of programming languages.

This combination obviates the need for conventional variables which are replaced by placeholders which retain access to specific portions of the global model. In addition, the need for several novel features such as the ability to access the global model as of any historical or future state and the ability to choose a course of action based upon the desirability (or lack thereof) of its results have been identified.

As mentioned in the Introduction, a language satisfying these constraints has neither been designed nor implemented; but work in this direction has begun. The SAFE [Balzer, Goldman and Wile 1977] project has an implemented language called AP2 [Goldman 1978] which provided the experience base from which the conclusions in this paper were derived. This existing language already satisfies half the constraints (Implications 1-6, 8, 9, and 13) and work is under way on including the rest, cleaning up and simplifying the existing features and providing a habitable syntax. We have also begun implementation of a "smart" compiler for this (planned) language which would remove the need for much of the run-time support otherwise required. The purpose of this compiler is to make it feasible to run a specification for selected test cases, rather than to optimize it for production usage. This modest goal makes the implementation of the compiler not only feasible but rather straightforward.

WILLIAM SWARTOUT and **ROBERT BALZER**
University of Southern California

On the Inevitable Intertwining of Specification and Implementation

For several years we [Balzer 1967; Balzer, Goldman and Wile 1976; Balzer and Goldman 1979; Balzer 1981] and others [Bauer 1976; Burstall and Darlington 1975; Dijkstra 1972; Hommel 1980; Knuth 1974; Parnas 1972b; Wirth 1971a] have been carefully pointing out how important it is to separate specification from implementation. In this view, one first completely specifies a system in a formal language at a high level of abstraction in an implementation-free manner. Then, as a separate phase, the implementation issues are considered and a program realizing the specification is produced. Depending on the development methodology being employed, this realization is produced either manually (software engineering), semiautomatically (program transformation), or automatically (high-level languages and automatic programming). The key issue here is not how one arrives at the realization, but rather that all current software methodologies have adopted a common model that separates specification from implementation.

Unfortunately, this model is too naive, and does not match reality. Specification and implementation are, in fact, intimately intertwined because they are, respectively, the already-fixed and the yet-to-be-done portions of a multi-step system development. It is only because we have allowed this development process to occur, unobserved and unrecorded, in people's heads that the multi-step nature of this process was not more apparent earlier. Only with the appearance of development methodologies such as stepwise refinement and program transformation did this essential multi-step aspect become clear.

It was then natural, though naive, to partition this multi-step development process into two disjoint partitions: specification and implementation. But this partitioning is entirely arbitrary. Every specification is an implementation of some other higher-level specification. Thus simply by shifting our focus to an earlier portion of the development, part of the specification becomes part of the implementation. This explains why it is so hard to create a good specification—one which is high level enough to be understandable, yet precise enough to define completely a particular class of behavior.

The standard software development model holds that each step of the development process should be a "valid" realization of the specification. By "valid" we mean that the behaviors specified by the implementation are a subset of those defined by the specification. However, in actual practice, we find that many development steps violate this validity relationship between specification and implementation. Rather than providing an implementation of the specification, they knowingly redefine the specification itself. Our central argument is that these steps are a crucial mechanism for elaborating the specification and are necessarily intertwined with the implementation. By their very nature, they cannot precede the implementation.

To distinguish such steps from valid implementation steps, we will call them *specification modifications*. They arise from two sources: physical limitations and imperfect foresight. We will consider these in turn.

The systems we implement employ physical devices (including computers). These devices have limitations (such as speed, size and reliability) which are specific to the device. Often, one finds cost-effective partial solutions rather than total solutions. This introduces either a restriction that limits the domain of input (e.g., names can only be eight characters) or introduces the possibility of error. In the latter case, one must then define what to do when such errors arise. In either case, the semantics of the specification has been changed, and the alteration is only meaningful in terms of an already fixed implementation decision.

Clearly, such specification modifications cannot precede the implementation decisions they are predicated upon. These "imperfect implementations" are in fact quite common and include modifications due to finite resources or economic considerations and modifications that limit the domain of a specification to a subset of "expected" situations. One reason the specification modifications are not well recognized is that they are usually folded into the "initial" specification, which necessarily therefore also includes (implicitly) the associated implementation decisions, rather than existing explicitly as separate development steps.

The second source of specification modifications is our lack of foresight. The systems we specify and build are complex. We are unable to foresee all the implications and interactions in such systems. During implementation we examine these implications and interactions in more detail in terms of the more concrete implementation being created. Often we find undesirable effects or an incomplete description. This insight provides the basis for refining the specification appropriately. Which version of the specification is modified (i.e., where in the development the modification is inserted) depends upon which implementation decisions need to be reconsidered because of the new insight, and which implementation decisions it is dependent upon.

Such improved insight may (and usually does) also arise from actual usage of the implemented system. These changes reflect not only unanticipated implications and interactions in the implemented system, but also changing needs generated by the existence of the implemented system. Incorporation of these specification modifications is precisely the same as above, i.e., they must be integrated at some appropriate spot in the development.

Thus a much more intertwined relationship exists between specification and implementation than the standard rhetoric would have us believe. Implementation is a multi-step process. Each stage of this process is a

SPECIFICATION AND IMPLEMENTATION

specification for what follows. However, many of the steps in this development are not mathematically "valid". They do not implement the specification, they alter it. Many of these specification modifications arise from physical limitations of one form or another. Such "partial" or "imperfect" implementations provide the structure for elaborating the specification to handle the imperfections. The rest of the specification modifications arise from our lack of insight concerning the systems we are implementing. Inadequacies or incompletenesses are discovered during implementation and/or use, and result in the need to revise some appropriate version of the specification and reconsider some of the implementation decisions.

If we were to try to retain the old model of separation of specification from implementation, then we would have to define specification as that portion of the development process beyond which only valid implementation steps occurred (i.e., no specification modifications), and implementation was the rest. Unfortunately, such a distinction can only be made after the fact, and hence is not useful for system builders.

These observations should not be misinterpreted. We still believe that it is important to keep unnecessary implementation decisions out of specifications and we believe that maintenance should be performed by modifying the specification and reoptimizing the altered definition. These observations should indicate that the specification process is more complex and evolutionary than previously believed and they raise the question of the viability of the pervasive view of a specification as a fixed contract between a client and an implementer.

1. AN EXAMPLE

Consider the following specification of the controller for a package router:[1]

The package router is a system for distributing *packages* into destination *bins*. The packages arrive at a *source* station, which is connected to the bins via a series of *pipes*. A single pipe leaves the source station. The pipes are linked together by two-position *switches*. A switch enables a package sliding down its input pipe to be directed to either of its two output pipes. There is a unique path through the pipes from the source station to any particular bin.[2]

Packages arriving at the source station are scanned by a reading device which determines a destination bin for the package. The package is then allowed to slide down the pipe leaving the source station. The package router must set its switches ahead of each package sliding through the pipes so that each package is routed to the bin determined for it by the source station.

After a package's destination has been determined, it is delayed for a fixed time before being released into the first pipe. This is done to prevent packages from following one another so closely that a switch cannot be reset between successive

---

1. This specification was obtained from Hommel [1980].
2. This is equivalent to viewing the router as a binary tree having switches as nodes, pipes as branches and bins as leaves.

packages when necessary. However, if a package's destination is the same as that of the package which preceded it through the source station, it is not delayed, since there will be no need to reset switches between the two packages.

There will generally be many packages sliding down the pipes at once. The packages slide at different and unpredictable speeds, so it is impossible to calculate when a given package will reach a particular switch. However, the switches contain sensors strategically placed at their entries and exits to detect the packages.

The sensors are placed in such a way that it is safe to change a switch setting if and only if no packages are present between the entry sensor of a switch and either of its exit sensors. The pipes are bent at the sensor locations in such a way that the sensors are guaranteed to detect a separation between two packages, no matter how closely they follow one another.

Due to the unpredictable sliding characteristics of the packages, it is possible, in spite of the source station delay, that packages will get so close together that it is not possible to reset a switch in time to properly route a package. *Misrouted* packages may be routed to any bin, but must not cause the misrouting of other packages. The bins too have sensors located at their entry, and upon each arrival of a misrouted package at a wrong bin, the routing machine is to signal that package's intended destination and the bin it actually reached.

When we received this specification, we considered it to be an excellent example of an abstract specification which had successfully separated the description of intended behavior from the implementation of that behavior. It was only during our attempt to formalize this example into our specification language that we came to the disturbing realization that the "excellent specification" was contaminated with many implementation decisions. For example, someone has made the decision to use gravity to move the boxes from one switch to the next. Alternatively, this "package mover" could have been implemented by, say, a set of conveyor belts. If conveyor belts had been chosen, it might have been possible to make them more dependable than the gravity/chute implementation, and if so, the specification for the controller might not have to deal with "misrouted boxes" at all. Moving up a level, the choices of organizing the switches into a tree and making it binary are both implementation decisions. In fact, the package router could have been implemented using a gantry crane that would pick up boxes at the source and drop them in their appropriate bins. If that were the case, it would not have made much sense to talk about trees, switches, and package movers. Thus we can see that in this example (and we take it to be fairly typical) implementation decisions are made before specification is complete and these decisions can have a major effect on the further specification of the system. Turning things around, if we wanted a specification that contained no implementation commitments it would have to represent information about all the possible implementation technologies, a potentially enormous task.

The package router specification given above also illustrates how an implementation choice can force a modification to the specification. The goal of any package router is to distribute packages into their correct bins. However, particular implementation decisions already present in the specification presented (chiefly, the decision to slide boxes down chutes) introduce the possibility of boxes bunching up, preventing the system from routing all boxes to their correct destinations (because the switches do not and cannot have infinitely fast switching time). The notion of "misrouted boxes" must be introduced to specify what should happen when the goal cannot be achieved. If a different implementation decision had been made which assured that boxes would arrive correctly, the notion of misrouted boxes would be irrelevant.

2. CONCLUSION

From the standpoint of constructing aids for capturing the specification and evolution of programs, interleaving specification and implementation into a single development structure will result in a more coherent and realistic structure for making modifications. By contrast, if we attempted to construct such an aid keeping complete specifications and implementation separate, we necessarily would have trouble capturing specification changes like those described above which are forced by implementation decisions.

While the interleaving of specification and implementation seems to occur quite frequently in practice, work directed toward formal specification and aids for creating such specifications seems to have paid little attention to this phenomenon. We have attempted here to illustrate several situations where this interleaving plays an important part in the software development process. Therefore, our software development aids must begin to address these issues.

Complete means: if it's true, you can prove it
consistent " : if you can prove it, it's true.
standard paradigms   Hoare rules.

$P\{Q\}R$ ← post-condition
↑   ↑
precondition pgm or fragment of pgm.

$$\frac{P\{Q\}R \quad R \rightarrow S}{P\{Q\}S} \qquad \frac{P\{Q\}R \quad S \rightarrow P}{S\{Q\}R} \qquad \frac{P\{Q_1\}R_1 \quad R_1\{Q_2\}R}{P\{Q_1; Q_2\}R} \qquad \frac{P \wedge B\{S\}P}{P\{\text{while } B \text{ do } S\} \neg B \wedge P}$$

↑
sequence operation (composition)

if the pgm halt, it's correct (can be proved)
but if its not halt, its not sure whether correct or not.

Hoare-style rule only can prove partial correctness.

logic lang. (complete & consistent set of rules of inference)
                                                    ↑
                                            formal description
                                            of the spec. lang.
         ↑
   formal description of
   the system description lang.
                                            ↑
                                    properties to be verified
         ↑   — correctness
   system description   — totality (finishes)
   (written in system description   — security or trust/ ?
   lang)

JOSEPH A. GOGUEN
SRI International

More Thoughts on Specification and Verification

1. INTRODUCTION

This note discusses program specification, emphasizing the relationship to verification. It begins with a discussion of what formal verification is, and then discusses what is today the most common paradigm for formal program verification, the use of a verification condition generator. A number of difficulties are pointed out with this paradigm, and these are used to motivate the use of a formal specification language. A brief discussion of the state of the art in specification languages is given. The next section considers some problems with a naive approach to program transformations, and then suggests how these might be solved by using a formal specification language. Finally, some additional uses of specifications are briefly discussed.

2. THE FORMAL VERIFICATION PROBLEM

It is meaningless to talk about formal verification unless each of the following has been provided:

(1) Some properties which are to be verified, expressed in a formal language, hereafter called the specification language of the verification problem.

(2) A formal description of the system about which these properties are to be verified, expressed in a formal language, hereafter called the system description language of the verification problem.

(3) A formal definition of the specification language which relates it to some underlying logical language having a precise mathematical semantics and a set of inference rules which is consistent and complete.

(4) A formal definition of the system description language which relates it to the same underlying language.

One simple class of well-posed specification problems in the above sense is given as follows: the properties to be verified are expressed by a set of sentences in first-order logic; and the system for which they are to be verified is described by another set of first-order sentences. Thus, both the

47

specification language and the system description language are the same as the underlying logical language, which is first-order logic.

A number of problems arise if an attempt is made to apply the simple framework of the previous paragraph to program verification. Among these problems we particularly mention (a) the extreme awkwardness of the sentence sets which result, and (b) the insuperable difficulties involved in carrying out the proofs, both (b1) because of their inherent complexity for most cases of genuine practical interest, and (b2) because of the need to go beyond simple first-order logic in order to prove many properties of interest (for example induction is often useful in proofs about particular structures such as the integers). Indeed, almost the entire history of formal verification can be seen as trying to find ways around these difficulties, by using languages which are richer in one sense or another than first-order logic.

I do not intend to suggest that the only worthwhile approaches to programming are based on formal verification, but I do believe that the product will be better if it is possible to do this in a sufficiently inexpensive way.

3. THE STANDARD PARADIGM

At this time there is a more or less standard paradigm for formal program verification, in which the system description language is some standard programming language, defined by a set of Hoare-style rules of inference for its various constructs, in which the underlying logical language and the specification language are both variants of first-order logic. A verification condition generator (vcg) is then used to provide the assertions which, if actually proved, will suffice to verify the desired specification properties. There are a number of problems with this standard paradigm:

(1) Expressing complex specifications in first-order logic, or any of the usual simple logical languages, yields very complex sentences, which are consequently often wrong.

(2) It is impossible to give a complete set of Hoare-style rules for programming languages as rich as the ones usually used in computer science.

(3) We do not know how to give simple Hoare-style rules for some common features or today's programming languages.

(4) It is necessary for the user to supply so-called invariants, in order to prove the correctness of programs with iteration or recursion.

(5) It is often very difficult to prove the hypotheses which are generated by the verification condition generator, and consequently it is very difficult to believe any proofs which may be offered.

(6) In order for this standard paradigm to rigorously correct for a given programming language, one should have a formal definition and a correctness proof for the verification condition generator used for that language.

(7) One should also have some independent check of the correctness of the Hoare-style rules, such as proof that they are valid in some model, and are therefore also consistent.

A rather general such proof has recently been given by [Moriconi and Schwartz 1981]; it applies to any set of Hoare-style rules which satisfy certain restrictions. Unfortunately, it excludes many important rules in general use; possibly this method can be extended. On the other hand, the completeness result is only relative to the completeness of an underlying first-order set of axioms for the data structures involved, so that the entire system will always be incomplete. (By Gödel's theorem, not even the integers can be axiomatized in this way.)

Despite these difficulties, the vcg approach remains the most practical way to verify given programs against given specifications.

4. SPECIFICATION LANGUAGES

In an effort to overcome particularly the first two of the difficulties listed in the previous section, a different approach, using specification languages which are much more powerful than any standard logical language, is being developed. To overcome the first difficulty, these specification languages support structured presentations of the properties to be verified. This has the same kinds of advantages for specifications as for programs: it is easier to read, to write, and to modify them. To overcome the second difficulty, these languages often incorporate some kind of higher-order properties, such as induction, into their underlying logic.

Unfortunately, many advocates of the specification language approach have thrown out the baby with the bath water, so to speak, by not giving any formal definition of the specification language they are using. Without this, it seems to me, one cannot say that anything is really being verified at all. Most specification language descriptions do not even mention the underlying logical system which is being used.

At this time, I know of only one specification language which has been given a complete formal definition; this is the CLEAR language of Burstall and Goguen [1977, 1980]. Related systems, subsets of which could be given semantics in a similar way, are OBJ [Goguen and Tardo 1979], HOPE [Burstall, MacQueen and Sannella 1980], and AFFIRM [Gerhart et al. 1980]. However, only CLEAR gives a really satisfactory account of parameterized abstract specifications.

Another very promising direction is to use an entire first-order axiom system for set theory as an underlying logic; this is being explored at Oxford by [Abrial, Schuman and Meyer 1979]. I would like to also mention work at SRI on a specification language based on the semantics of CLEAR, which is very flexible in terms of its domains of application, and is syntactically much more readable and writable than CLEAR; this language is called ORDINARY [Goguen and Burstall 1980a], and is in part inspired by the previous generation SRI specification effort, SPECIAL [Levitt, Robinson and Silverberg 1979]. For a set of requirements for specifications languages, and a more detailed discussion of their nature, see Goguen [1980].

5. MECHANICAL VERIFICATION

An important variant of the standard paradigm supports mechanical verification of the properties desired of a given system by using, instead of first-order logic, some closely related language which happens to be processed by a suitable mechanical theorem prover. This goes a long way towards increasing confidence in the alleged proofs of the desired properties, and may go some ways towards making them easier to find. The underlying logical language of the some theorem provers, for example that of [Boyer and Moore 1979], involves some built-in data types, and supports the use of induction over those types. However, this cannot be done within a purely first-order framework; see point 5 of Section 3.

This brings up the perhaps embarrassing subject of "lemmas." Many workers in verification, perhaps because their theorem provers cannot handle induction, apparently make use of a file of assertions, typically properties of data types of the kind which require inductive proofs; during verification, this file is consulted if the theorem prover gets stuck. The trouble is that the "lemmas" in this file have actually not been verified mechanically.

6. SPECIFICATIONS VERSUS TRANSFORMATIONS?

There are apparently some individuals who claim that the use of specifications is unnecessary and/or actually harmful in program development. Following the pioneering work of Burstall and Darlington [1977], they argue for starting with a very simple (and possibly very inefficient) program which obviously does the job, and then transforming it into an efficient program which does the same job, using a sequence of simple program transformations known to preserve semantics. This approach is alleged to be better than starting with a precise specification, and then producing a program which satisfies it. However, the argument fails to take account of some important facts:

(1) There are many tasks for which even the simplest possible inefficient program is very complex, and yet there is a very simple specification of what we want it to do. For example, we can specify that margins should be right justified in the output of a text-formatting program much more easily than we can give an algorithm for doing it. In general, one can express constraints on algorithms which do not determine exactly how it will be implemented more easily than one can give some particular implementation; this is the basic idea of abstraction.

(2) There are many transformations the correctness of which depends upon verifying that certain properties hold for the part of the

SPECIFICATION AND VERIFICATION

program to which they are applied. For example, transformations which optimize the evaluation of expressions in general require that certain laws of arithmetic are valid for values of the type being evaluated. This implies that we need specifications of how programs are supposed to work, and not just the programs themselves, in order to be sure that transformations really produce correct programs. It also means that we will need deduction in order to do the verification of correctness of application.

(3) Transformations do not actually apply to large complex programs, but only to parts of programs, for example, to an arithmetic expression which is to be evaluated. But how are we to know that this part of the program to which we want to apply a transformation will not be side-effected by some other part of the program? This also requires that we have some theory about how the program operates; that is, it requires specifications of program parts, and it requires knowledge of how the program parts are related to one another.

(4) So far, transformations have not been applied to very complex problems, such as operating systems, and it is not clear that the methodology can be extended without substantial further research.

(5) The idea of building up libraries of specialized transformations for optimizing particular classes of problems, while initially attractive, has worked badly in practice, in that such transformations are in fact so rarely applicable to other problems that a reasonably comprehensive library would be so large as to be very difficult to make effective use of.

It was just such considerations which led Burstall and Goguen [1977] to work on structured specifications, as in their language CLEAR. In order to make further progress in program transformations, we felt it would be helpful to have structured specifications of how programs are supposed to work. After working in this direction for some time, we came to believe that in fact program transformations as often naively conceived without semantics are inadequate, but that fortunately it is possible to explicitly correlate program structure with theory structure, and thus address the validity of transformations. (These ideas are sketched in Goguen and Burstall [1980b], a report on a proposed system called CAT.) We do not feel that there is a conflict between transformations and specifications, but rather that there are some tough problems about transformations to solve which specifications are needed. It may well be that the study of transformations is more difficult than the study of specifications. Transformations cannot be relied upon to yield correct programs, unless they are somehow connected with knowledge about what the programs do, that is, with specifications. Not only programmers ought to understand the effects of what they are doing, but also program transformers! This point has been recognized by many workers in the field, for example, the members of IFIP Working Group 2.3.

Incidentally, the theories required for validating transformations are often closely tied in with theories of the data structures involved, and it was this which suggested the value of an algebraic approach to specification. However, subsequent work on CLEAR convinced us that this was by no means necessary, and the latest version can accommodate any desired underlying logic which satisfies certain simple conditions [Burstall and Goguen 1980].

7. OTHER USES OF SPECIFICATIONS

Experience has shown that the approach of writing a specification and a program separately, and then attempting to verify that the program satisfies the specification, can lead to considerable difficulties, especially for complex programs. However, this does not mean that specification and verification are dead issues, only that they should perhaps not play such naive roles. One approach is to develop programs systematically in connection with a methodology which incorporates verification, as in Levitt, Robinson and Silverberg [1979]. A semantically based transformation system, as described above, could verify satisfaction of the conditions under which the application of a transformation is actually meaningful. In general, an approach which takes some account of the structure of the program development process (and not only of the program) will be simpler than one which attempts to verify the correctness of a single program.

There also seems to be a role for using specifications to guide implementation, possibly with a certain amount of verification performed as the implementation proceeds. The specifications and the verification need not be entirely rigorous for this to be of some genuine value. One might interpret the suggestions of Guttag [1975] and Guttag, Horowitz and Musser [1978] in this light, for example. Design verification is another area in which verification is useful. Here, one does not attempt to deal with the code itself, but rather one proves useful properties about relatively high-level specifications. This approach has been taken, for example, in the PSOS project at SRI Neumann, Boyer, Feiertag, Levitt and Robinson [1977].

to describe the effect of programs. The resulting approach to specification is usually referred to as a denotational or mathematical approach. The paper by Cliff Jones highlights the main features of the VDM approach and compares VDM with other techniques.

In their paper Wolfram Bartussek and David Parnas start by expressing surprise at the unsatisfactory nature of the specification of certain abstract data types which seemed intuitively acceptable. (It can be imagined that these are implemented as a module or package.) The detailed investigation by the authors leads them to the idea that the concept of a trace should be used as a formal mechanism with which to argue about properties of specification such as completeness, consistency and the correctness of a particular implementation. In this context a trace is regarded as a sequence of calls to routines supplied by a module. As might be expected, only a certain subset of the set of all possible traces may be acceptable. These legal traces, as they are called, describe all possible forms of acceptable behavior and are therefore interesting.

The final paper by Pamela Zave indicates an approach that is radically different from the others. Behind it is a belief that the more traditional specification methods have proved unsatisfactory in certain application areas. In looking at the requirements specification for embedded systems, for example, there is often a need for the specification method to permit the expression of parallelism, timing constraints and more generally performance requirements. To overcome these problems an "operational" kind of specification language is introduced, enabling the ready construction of prototypes.

The principle of data type induction can be used to prove that all data belong to a data type T satisfy some property P. To be specific,

Data type induction: Let T be a data type, & p a predicate (i.e. $P: T \to \{0,1\}$). Let $f_1, f_2, \ldots f_k$ be the set of all operations that have ranges which are subsets of T. If, for all i,

$P(t_{i_1}) \land P(t_{i_2}) \land \cdots \land P(t_{i_n}) \Rightarrow P(f_i(s_{i_1}, s_{i_2}, \ldots s_{i_m}, t_{i_1}, t_{i_2}, \ldots, t_{i_n}))$

where the t_i's $\in T$, then $P(t)$ $\forall t \in T$.

Use strong induction on the # of steps needed to compute t_i, where $t_i \in T$. Each invocation of a f† f_i above counts as one step.

To show $P(t)$ $\forall t$ computed in 0 steps consider those f_i which have no arguments of type T. Let $T_0 = \{t_i | t_i = f_i(s_{i_1}, \ldots s_{i_m}) \text{ for } m \geq 0\}$. If P holds for each element of T_0, then the conclusion follows vacuously.

To show that if $P(t)$ holds for all t, computed in k steps or less, then $P(t)$ holds for all t computed in $k+1$ steps. Consider such a t, which must be the result of some f_i, i.e. $t = f_i(s_{i_1}, \ldots s_{i_m}, t_{i_1}, \ldots t_{i_n})$, where the t_i's are computed in k steps or less, & hence $P(t_i)$ holds for all the t_i's. Since the truth of $P(t_i)$ $\forall i$ implies $P(t)$, the conclusion follows.

PARTICULAR APPROACHES

An (almost) inevitable conclusion of the previous section is that formal methods and formal approaches to specification are desirable and an important area of study. What should the basis of the formal approach be? Should it be some branch of mathematics, formal logic, some other familiar and mature area of study or even some unfamiliar and immature area? A variety of possibilities exist and some of these will be explained in the following papers.

The first paper by John Guttag is tutorial in nature and deals with two approaches to the specification of abstract data types; both of these come into the category of axiomatic methods. The first approach, advocated by C. A. R. Hoare, involves essentially modeling the behavior of programming constructs, e.g., in terms of mathematical entities. Here the behavior of the programming entities are described in terms of familiar mathematical concepts and notation. Since its introduction the notion of Hoare's has been encapsulated in modified form into various programming languages as the module or package. The second approach, proposed by John Guttag, characterizes a specification by means of syntax and semantics. The latter are described by (a) a set of axioms in the form of equations detailing the relationships between various entities, and (b) a number of circumstances under which error or exceptional conditions will arise. This latter approach is usually referred to as the algebraic approach to specification. Throughout the paper, it is important to be aware of important issues which address questions relating to the relative merits of these approaches.

In the next paper, which is one of the early papers dealing with the importance of software specifications, David Parnas proposes a semi-formal specification technique for specifying software modules. Specifications should be precise enough to specify what a software module does and they should not contain information not relevant to the module user, e.g., the details of the module implementation.

The next paper discusses the specification techniques embodied in the Vienna Development Method (VDM). Its origins lie in the Vienna Definition Language (VDL) developed in the sixties at the IBM Laboratories in Vienna. VDL was used in a certain kind of specification exercise, namely that of providing a formal definition of the programming language PL/I. The development of VDM itself is rather different. It is based on the view that mathematical ideas such as sets, tuples and functions provide a suitable framework in which

JOHN GUTTAG
University of Southern California

Notes on Type Abstraction

1. INTRODUCTION

A key problem in the development of programs is reducing the amount of complexity or detail that must be considered at any one time. Two common and effective approaches to accomplishing this are decomposition and abstraction.

One decomposes a task by factoring it into sub-tasks each of which can be treated independently. Unfortunately, for many problems the smallest separable sub-tasks are still too complex to be mastered in toto. The complexity of such problems must be reduced via abstraction. By providing a mechanism for separating those attributes that are relevant in a given context from those that are not, abstraction serves to reduce the amount of details that one needs to come to grips with at any one time.

One of the most significant aids to abstraction used in programming is the self-contained, arbitrarily abstract, function by means of an unprescribed algorithm. Thus, at the level where it is invoked, it separates the relevant detail of "what" from the irrelevant detail of "how." Similarly, at the level of the implementation, it is usually unnecessary to complicate the "how" by considering the "why," i.e., the exact reasons for invoking a subroutine are rarely of concern to its implementor. By nesting subroutines, one may develop a hierarchy of abstractions.

Unfortunately, the nature of the abstractions that may be conveniently achieved through the use of subroutines is limited. Subroutines allow us to abstract single events. Their applicability is thus limited to problems that are conveniently decomposable into independent functional units. Type, or data, abstraction is not amenable to such an attack.

The large knot of complexly interrelated attributes associated with a data object may be separated according to the nature of the information that the attributes convey about the data objects that they qualify. Two kinds of attributes, each of which may be studied in isolation, are:

(1) those that describe the representation of objects and the implementations of the operations associated with them in terms of other objects and operations, e.g., in terms of a programming language's primitive data structures and operations;

55

(2) those that specify the names and define the abstract meanings of the operations associated with an object.

Though these two kinds of attributes are in practice highly interdependent, they represent logically independent concepts. At most points in a program one should be concerned solely with the latter. The user of a data object should have no more interest in the details of its implementation than does the user of a high-level language in the details of the object code produced by the compiler.

If at a given level of refinement one is interested only in the effect of the operations associated with certain data objects, then any attempt to abstract data must be based upon those characteristics, and only those characteristics. The introduction of other attributes, e.g., a representation, can only serve to cloud the relevant issues. Here, we will use the term "abstract type" to refer to a class of objects defined by a representation-independent specification.

On the other side of the fence, those responsible for providing an implementation of an abstract type need to be isolated from consideration of exactly how objects of the type are to be used. This isolation takes place at two levels: On a conceptual level this isolation involves a reduction in the number of concerns that must be dealt with at any one time. On a more concrete level, it involves the assurance of the validity of data-type induction (called generator induction elsewhere, e.g., Spitzen and Wegbreit [1975]). Consider a type, T. Let $f_1,...,f_n$ be the set of all operations that have as their range values of type T. Let $P(t)$ be any predicate on values of type T. If the truth of P for all arguments of type T of each f_i implies the truth of P for the results of applications of the f_i, then it follows that P holds for all values of type T. Assuming strong type checking, the validity of this principle follows by induction on the number of computation steps used to generate any value of type T. The data type induction principle is analogous to that of complete induction over the integers. The basis step of the induction occurs when one shows that P holds for the results of those f_i with no arguments of type T.

Most of the recent work on incorporating abstract data types into programming languages has emphasized the use of strong typing and class-like constructs to provide isolation for the implementors of abstract types. In Euclid, for example, the author of a module may assure the validity of data type induction through careful use of the import and export lists. If no "var" globals are imported, the value of any instance of the module is a function of the values of the data structures that are local to the module and global to the module routines. If furthermore no portion of the data structure is exported as "var," the principle of data type induction is established.

It is certainly possible to use abstract types as a programming tool without actually making provision for them in the programming language. There are, however, several advantages to be gained from having a facility for the definition of abstract types within a programming language. Perhaps the most significant of these is that it increases the likelihood that the program text will accurately reflect the thought processes that led to its construction.

TYPE ABSTRACTION

Thus the program should be easier to read and comprehend, particularly for those who were not involved in its construction.

A second reason for the inclusion of facilities for the definition of abstract types within a programming language is to permit type checking. Much has been written about the benefits to be gained from extensive type checking. Gannon [1975] and Morris [1973] contain particularly good discussions. Morris suggests the type checking serves two distinct purposes: authentication and secrecy. By authentication, he means that type checking can be used to prevent programs from attempting to perform operations on values of other than the appropriate type: trying to divide one queue by another, for example. What Morris calls secrecy has often been called protection or security. Its purpose is to prevent users from writing programs that depend upon the particular representation chosen for a type. If one can actually define a type *Queue*, rather than merely a data structure to be used as a queue, the compiler can prevent the user from modifying or accessing values of type *Queue* except through the operations provided as part of that type. This inhibits him from destroying the integrity of the data structure (thus allowing data type induction), and from writing programs that rely upon the representation of the type (thus allowing the substitution of a different representation).

2. THE SPECIFICATION OF ABSTRACT TYPES

The class construct of SIMULA 67 [Dahl, Nygaard and Myhrhaug 1968] has been used as the starting point for much of the more recent work on embedding abstract types in programming languages, e.g., Clu, Alphard and Euclid. While each of these offers a mechanism for binding together the operations and storage structures representing a type, they offer (within the base language) no representation-independent means for specifying the effect of the operations. The only representation-independent information that one can supply in the language proper are the domains and ranges of the various operations. One can, for example, define a type *Queue* (of *Integers*) with the operations:

```
new:       → Queue
add:       Queue × Integer → Queue
front:     Queue → Integer
remove:    Queue → Queue
empty?:    Queue → Boolean.
```

Except for intuitions about the meaning of such words as *Queue* and front, the operations might just as easily be defining type *Stack* as type *Queue*. The domain and range specifications for these two types are isomorphic. To rely on one's intuition about the meaning of names can be dangerous even when dealing with familiar types; when dealing with unfamiliar types, it is almost impossible. What is needed, therefore, is a language for specifying the semantics of the operations of the type.

This language must be a formal one. An informal language, such as a natural language, is often not efficient—either for the communication of abstractions or for their creation. (This is not to say that informality has no role to play in the abstraction process. At times the high connotational content of an informal language makes it a valuable tool for both creative thinking and the communication of the fruits of that thought.)

Unlike formal languages, informal languages do not force precision. In fact, it is only by dint of great care and expertise that it is possible to write precise specifications in a notation as informal as a natural language. Thus, at times, an informal language may prove more a hindrance than a help in organizing one's thoughts. The problem is compounded when one attempts to use an informal notation for communicating an abstraction to others. Not only might the specification be underdefined, hence ambiguous, but the language in which the specification is stated will almost certainly be ambiguous. If all goes well, someone will perceive the ambiguity, and it will be resolved. More often, the people involved will merely form their own, different, conceptions of the abstraction. Of course, the use of a formal language is no guarantee that specifications will be unambiguous or even consistent. It is, for example, quite possible to specify ambiguous grammars or empty languages in BNF. What a formal language does provide are objective criteria for recognizing ambiguity and inconsistency, thus increasing the likelihood that such failings in a specification will be recognized.

A good formal specification technique is a technique that facilitates the production of good formal specifications. Good specifications may take many forms, but all of them have certain attributes in common. A good specification must be restrictive enough to ensure that nothing unacceptable to the specifier will meet the requirements imposed by the specification. Yet it must also be sufficiently general to ensure that few, if any, acceptable entries are precluded. And finally, a good specification must be well tailored to its intended application. In most cases this implies that it must be perspicuous enough to facilitate communication among people, and at the same time suitable for purely formal reasoning.

That a good specification must be sufficiently restrictive (or specific) is a statement that should need no justification. It is the assumption that lies at the base of most arguments in favor of formal specifications. The importance of the generality criterion is less obvious. It is not essential to ensure that no acceptable model is precluded, but whenever one introduces unnecessary constraints one runs the risk of eliminating some of the more desirable (e.g., efficient or elegant) solutions to the problem at hand. That a certain tension exists between the goals of generality and restrictiveness is clear. The use of weakest pre-conditions [Dijkstra 1976] to specify a programming language represents one attempt to strike an optimal balance between the two. Often, however, it is counterproductive to strive for this optimal balance—for to do so may lead to less elegant and less useful specifications. In these cases, one must be willing to accept some loss of generality.

There are many possible approaches to the formal specification of abstract types. Most, however, can be placed in one of two categories: operational or

TYPE ABSTRACTION

definitional. In an operational specification, instead of trying to describe the properties of the abstract type, one gives a recipe for constructing it. One begins with some well-understood language or discipline and builds a model for the type in terms of that discipline.

The operational approach to formal specification has many advantages. Most significantly, operational specifications seem to be relatively (compared to definitional specifications) easily constructed by those trained as programmers—chiefly because the construction of operational specifications so closely resembles programming. For abstract types containing a small number of moderately simple operations (i.e., operations readily expressible in the modeling domain), operational specifications seem to offer a sufficient degree of perspicuity. As the operations to be specified grow more complex, however, operational specifications tend to get too long to serve as an adequate tool for communication among people. As the number of operations grows, problems arise because the relations among the operations are not explicitly stated, and inferring them becomes combinatorially harder. This can be reflected in the difficulty in reasoning about programs that use the type. A final serious problem associated with operational specifications is that they often force one to over-specify the abstraction. By introducing extraneous detail they are likely to associate non-essential attributes with the type.

The extent to which an operational specification is unnecessarily restrictive depends upon the level of abstraction achieved by the specification. With an operational specification, one must infer the properties of the abstract type from the properties of the operational model. In general, one can infer properties other than the necessary ones. Loosely speaking, the greater the number of inessential properties that may be inferred, the lower the level of abstraction. The level achieved depends largely upon the level of abstraction of the language in which the specification is given. A Pascal implementation of an abstract type, for example, scarcely qualifies as an abstract specification. The Vienna Definition Language allows more abstract specifications. Parnas's state machine model [Parnas 1972a] seems to allow still higher levels of abstraction.

In a definitional specification, one explicitly lists properties required for the values and operations forming the abstract type. The primary advantage of this mode of specification is that it tends to define the type quite generally, in that only essential characteristics need be specified. The specification is thus an abstraction encompassing a relatively large (compared to an operational specification) class of implementations. In addition to increasing the generality of the specification, the absence of superfluous detail tends to increase the clarity of the specification. If the type has many operations, the ability to state explicitly the relationships among the operations makes the specification a better tool for formal reasoning.

There are very many number of formalisms that can be used to construct definitional specifications. The two most prominent approaches (in programming) are the axiomatic specifications of Hoare [1969] and Scott's lattice theoretic approach to mathematical semantics [Scott 1970]. The axiomatic approach is the more widely used of the two; nevertheless mathematical semantics offers several advantages. Donahue [1976] cites two advantages as particularly notable. Firstly, mathematical semantics is a more powerful specification technique because the domain of discourse is far less limited. Secondly, by virtue of the fact that the notion of a computation appears explicitly, a mathematical semantics definition seems to provide considerably more guidance for implementors.

These apparent advantages, however, are in reality two-edged swords. Just as a well-designed programming language should encourage its users to write better programs by constraining the programs they may write, a well-designed specification language should place severe constraints on the specifications its users may write. Thus, the freedom of expression offered us by mathematical semantics may be more a bane than a boon. The explicit appearance of the notion of a computation saddles mathematical semantics definitions with some of the same over-specification problems associated with operational specifications. This will almost certainly lead to problems if one is interested primarily in proof-theoretic (rather than model-theoretic) properties of the type being specified. For these reasons, we shall be concentrating on axiomatics in the remainder of these lectures.

We shall look at two axiomatic approaches to the specification of abstract types: first the approach suggested by Hoare [1972a] and then algebraic axioms [Guttag 1975]. Today, variants of Hoare's method predominate, e.g., Wulf, London and Shaw [1976a] and London, Guttag, Horning, Lampson, Mitchell and Popek [1978]. The algebraic approach does, however, seem to be gaining some currency, e.g. Dahl [1978].

3. THE HOARE APPROACH (as embodied in Euclid)

As stated above, Hoare's approach has enjoyed widespread use. Most of its users have departed in some ways from the notation originally used by Hoare. Here, we shall use the notation of Euclid's [Lampson 1978] modules. We begin by looking at an example from "Proof Rules for the Programming Language Euclid," London [1978]. The module *smallintSet* provides the abstraction of a set of integers in the range 1-100. The abstract operations are insertion and removal of individual elements and a membership test. When a variable of type *smallintSet* is declared, it is initialized to the empty set. The set will be represented by a *Boolean* array, S, of 100 elements,

    S: **array** 1..100 **of** Boolean

where $S(i)$ if and only if i belongs to the set.

    type smallintSet =
        pre true
        module smallSet
        abstract invariant true
        concrete invariant true
        exports (insert, remove, has, :=)

TYPE ABSTRACTION

```
var S: array 1..100 of Boolean

procedure insert (i: integer) =
    pre 1 ≤ i ≤ 100 and smallSet = smallSet'
    post smallSet = smallSet' union {i}
    begin S(i) := true end insert

procedure remove (i: integer) =
    pre 1 ≤ i ≤ 100 and smallSet = smallSet'
    post smallSet = smallSet' - {i}
    begin S(i) := false end remove

function has (i: integer)
    returns hasResult: Boolean =
    pre 1 ≤ i ≤ 100
    post hasResult = (i ∈ smallSet)
    begin hasResult := S(i) end has

initially
    post smallSet = { }
    begin for j in S.indexType
          loop S(j) := false
          end loop end initially

abstraction function setValue
    returns resultSet = imports (S)
    begin resultSet = {j | S(j) and 1 ≤ j ≤ 100} end setValue
end smallintSet
```

The module is a mechanism for providing encapsulation and the support of type abstractions, and as such provides distinct pictures to its users and its implementors. To the user the module presents a picture intended to deal only with those properties pertinent to the ways in which the abstraction can be used. These "abstract" properties are captured in the pre- and post-conditions associated with **initially**, **finally**, and the exported routines. The implementor of the module must deal not only with the user's view, which defines the object he must implement, but also with the module's data structures and the bodies of the module's routines. The abstraction function is the bridge between the two perspectives with which the implementor must deal.

In general, the abstraction function maps a sequence of concrete identifiers to an abstract identifier. In the above example, *setValue* maps the array S to the *smallintSet resultSet*. If, for example, S were to have the value false in all positions except the 31st and 40th, we could deduce from the definition of the abstraction function, *setValue*, that *resultSet* =

$$\{j \mid S(j) \text{ and } 1 \leq j \leq 100\} = \{31, 40\}.$$

To see exactly how Euclid modules work, let us examine the structure (but not the details) of the proof rule given for modules in London [1978]. The rule contains a conclusion and eight premises. We now explain the structure of the rule and describe the purpose and workings of each premise.

The conclusion of the rule involves the instantiation of a module identifier in a scope. Premises 1-5 are properties required of the module definition. These properties, which must be verified only once for each module definition, deal with the internal consistency, or well-formedness, of the definition. Premise 6 states that the instantiation pre-condition is met; this must be proved each time a variable of the module type is declared. Premise 7 tells us that we may use the information contained in the module definition (which we verified in connection with premises 1-5) to prove what we need to show about uses of variables of the module type. Thus the module rule has the structure:

$$\frac{1, 2, 3, 4, 5, \quad 6, \quad [7.1, 7.2, 7.3, 7.4] \vdash P\{x.\text{initially}; S; x.\text{finally}\}R}{P\{\text{var } x:T(a); S\}R \text{ and Post-of-finally}}$$

We now describe each premise in a bit more detail. In premises 1-5, the substitution of a call of the abstraction function for the name of the module converts a predicate on the abstract identifier to one involving concrete identifiers.

Premise 1: Show that the concrete invariant implies the abstract invariant. In our example, since each invariant is the constant true, this is trivial. Had we chosen the slightly more interesting abstract invariant *cardinality(smallSet)* $\leqslant$ 100, we would have arrived at the verification condition:

true $\Rightarrow$ cardinality($\{j \mid S(j)$ **and** $1 \leqslant j \leqslant 100\}$) $\leqslant$ 100.

Premise 2: Show that the module pre-condition across the declaration of the module's local variables and the body of **initially** establishes the post-condition of **initially** and the concrete invariant. Again, to show that the invariant will hold is trivial. To show that the post-condition of **initially** is established we must prove:

true {**var** S:**array** 1..100 **of** Boolean
    begin for j **in** S.indexType
        loop S(j) := false
        end loop end}
setValue(S) = { }.

We replace *setValue* by its definition, and this proof becomes straightforward.

Premise 3: Verify that the body of each exported procedure is correct, i.e., that the conjunction of the procedure's pre-condition and the concrete invariant is a sufficient pre-condition to ensure that the body of the procedure will establish its post-condition and preserve the concrete invariant. Not

TYPE ABSTRACTION

surprisingly, this premise bears a strong resemblance to that of the procedure call rule. It differs only in the presence of the module invariant and the need to use the abstraction function. This need arises from the fact that the pre- and post-conditions deal with abstract objects, while the body of the procedures deal with concrete ones. Looking at *insert*, the verification condition generated is:

$1 \leq i \leq 100$ **and** $\text{setValue}(S) = \text{setValue}(S')$ **and** true
$\{S(i) := \text{true}\}$
$\text{setValue}(S) = (\text{setValue}(S') \textbf{ union } \{i\})$ **and** true

Again, using the definition of *setValue*, the verification of this premise is trivial.

At this point let us pause in our analysis of the individual premises, and look a bit more closely at the way we have been using the abstraction function *setValue*. Notice that we have been using the substitution of *setValue*(S) for *smallSet* as a device to convert predicates in the abstract domain of *smallintSets* to predicates in the concrete domain of arrays. We thus seem to be using *setValue* as a mechanism for moving from the abstract to the concrete — despite the fact that the functionality of *setValue* goes the other way, from the concrete to the abstract. That we use a mapping that goes in this direction is crucial, since the mapping in the other direction may not be a function. Consider, for example, a type *BoundedQueue* (with a maximum length of three). An implementation of this type might be based on a ring-buffer and top pointer. Given this implementation we might well discover that a queue containing the elements *A*, *B* and *C* in that order has the attainable concrete representations:

$\rightarrow A \rightarrow B \rightarrow C \_\_\_\_$ $\rightarrow B \rightarrow C \rightarrow A \_\_\_\_$

In this example, the concrete representation of a particular abstract value is not a function of that value, but is rather a function of the history of insertions and deletions from the queue. The realization that the mapping from abstract to concrete may be one too many, and the circumvention of this apparent problem through the use of an abstraction function (called a "representation" function by Hoare) represents the essence of the substantial insight and contribution of Hoare [1972a].

Premise 4: Verify that the body of each exported function is correct. Premise 4 is analogous to premise 3 except that the concrete invariant is assumed to be preserved, since Euclid functions are guaranteed to be side-effect free. (In London, Guttag, Horning, Lampson, Mitchell and Popek [1978], this was split into two premises, numbered 4 and 5.)

Premise 5: Show that the body of finally establishes the post-condition of the module. (There is no finally in our example.)

Premise 6: Show that at the point where a variable of the type is declared, the state implies the module pre-condition with the actual parameters substituted for the formals.

Premise 7: This premise deals with reasoning about uses of the module variable, x, in the scope S. In showing that the state at the point where x is declared implies a pre-condition that is sufficient to ensure the truth of R after executing the body of **initially** followed by S and the body of **finally**, we may use the four formulas 7.1-7.4. These formulas give the properties of the module procedures, functions, **initially** and **finally** respectively. Formulas 7.1 and 7.2 correspond to the conclusions of the procedure and function call rule; the only difference is that the abstract invariant may be used in proving the pre-conditions and is assumed following the calls. (This is the source of much of the utility of the module construct. It allows us to prove theorems using data type induction.) Formula 7.3 treats $x.initially$ as a parameterless procedure call that establishes the invariant. Formula 7.4 treats $x.finally$ as a parameterless procedure call for which the abstract invariant may be used in establishing its pre-condition. (If x is declared to be an array of modules or a record containing modules, then $x.initially$ and $x.finally$ must be replaced in 7.3 and 7.4 by a sequence of calls to initialization and finalization routines respectively.)

Conclusion: The conclusion of this proof rule simply states that if all of the premises have been shown to hold, one may conclude that if P holds before executing the statements: **var** $x: T(a)$; S, then R and the post-condition of finally will hold upon exciting the scope in which x is declared. An example of the application of this proof rule to prove some properties of a program containing our example module definition is contained in London, Guttag, Horning, Lampson, Mitchell and Popek [1978].

The above may strike the reader as excessively complicated. That would be an accurate appraisal of the situation. Part of the complexity of the above discussion (and more importantly the proof rule behind it) stems from the linguistic eccentricities of Euclid and the fact that we are dealing with partial rather than total correctness. (The latter issue is most relevant to the part of the rule dealing with the module's functions, and is manifested in the complexity, not dealt with here, of clauses 4 and 7.2.) Much of it, however, reflects more fundamental problems with the basic approach. Despite the fact that the various operations of type *smallintSet* are intricately related to one another, these relationships are not directly expressed in the (abstract) specification of the type. Rather, we supply stand-alone pre- and post-conditions for each operation. This leads us to introduce a third domain of discourse in which to express the meanings of the operations. In our example, we want to supply the programmer with the abstraction *smallintSet*. We implement this abstraction using the Euclid primitives *array*, *Boolean* and *integer*. We specify it using the (presumed well-defined) third domain of discourse supplied by the operations on mathematical sets. To prove the correctness of our implementation of *smallintSet*, we must map a Euclid data structure onto mathematical sets. To reason about programs that use type *smallintSet*, we must reason in terms of mathematical sets. This can be a serious problem. Presumably, one introduces an abstraction primarily because one feels that some advantage is to be gained by thinking in terms of it. Perhaps little is lost when one is forced to reason in terms of mathematical sets rather than *smallintSet*s. They are, after all, rather similar abstractions. For the sake of argument, however, let us assume that our domain of already well-understood types doesn't include mathematical sets. It may well prove to be the case that the programmer is forced to reason in terms of some abstraction quite different from that he wished to introduce into his program. If this is the case, then much of the rationale for introducing the type abstraction is lost.

4. ALGEBRAIC SPECIFICATIONS

An algebraic specification of an abstract type consists of three parts: a syntactic specification, a semantic specification, and a restriction specification. The syntactic specification provides the syntactic and type checking information: the names, domains, and ranges of the operations associated with the type. The semantic specification is a set of axioms which defines the meaning of the operations by stating their relationships to one another. The restriction specification deals with pre-conditions and exception conditions. The word "algebraic" is appropriate because the values and operations can be regarded as together forming an abstract algebra. Goguen, Thatcher and Wagner [1975] and Zilles [1975b] have strongly emphasized the algebraic approach, developing a theory of abstract types as an application of many-sorted algebras. Implementations are treated under this approach as other algebras, and the problem of showing that an implementation is correct is treated through showing the existence of a homomorphic mapping from one algebra to the other. We shall in these lectures, as we have in our own research, de-emphasize the use of algebraic terminology and methods, preferring instead the terminology and methods of programming and logic.

At the heart of any specification technique lies the specification language. We begin by assuming a base language with five primitives: functional composition, an equality relation (=), two distinct constants (true and false), and an unbounded supply of free variables. From these primitives one can construct a richer specification language. Once a type abstraction has been defined, it may be added to the specification language. One might, for example, want to include a type *Boolean* with an *if-then-else* operation defined by the axioms:

if-then-else(true, q, r) = q
if-then-else(false, q, r) = r

Throughout we shall assume that the expression *if-then-else*(b, q, r), which we will write as **if** b **then** q **else** r, is part of the specification language. We shall also assume the availability of infix *Boolean* operators as needed. The axiomatization of these operators in terms of the *if-then-else* function is trivial. Finally, we shall assume the availability of type *Integer* with the standard operations.

Let us now look at a simple example (with no restriction specification). Consider a type *Bag* (of *Integers*) with the operations:

empty-bag:	→ Bag
insert: Bag × Integer	→ Bag
delete: Bag × Integer	→ Bag
member-of?: Bag × Integer	→ Boolean.

There are, of course, many ways to implement type *Bag*. Some (e.g., a linked list representation) imply an ordering of the elements, some don't (e.g., a hash table implementation). These details are not relevant to the basic notion of what a bag is. A bag is nothing more than a counted set, and a good axiomatic definition must assert that and only that characteristic. The axioms below comprise just such a definition.

declare b:Bag, i, i':Integer

1) member-of?(empty-bag, i) = false
2) member-of?(insert(b, i), i') = **if** ?=?(i, i')
           then true
           else member-of?(b, i')
3) delete(empty-bag, i) = empty-bag
4) delete(insert(b, i), i') = **if** ?=?(i, i')
         then b
         else insert(delete(b, i'),i)

As an interesting comparison, consider the following specification of type *Set*:

empty-set:	→ Set
insert: Set × Integer	→ Set
delete: Set × Integer	→ Set
member-of? Set × Integer	→ Boolean

declare s:Set, i, i' :Integer

1) member-of?(empty-set, i) = false
2) member-of?(insert(s, i), i') = **if** ?=?(i, i')
           then true
           else member-of?(s, i')
3) delete(empty-set, i) = empty-set
4) delete(insert(s, i), i') = **if** ?=?(i, i')
         then delete(s, i')
         else insert(delete(s, i'), i).

Except for the change in the **then** clause of axiom 4, this specification is, for all intents and purposes, the same as that for type *Bag*. The two specifications thus serve to point out the similarities and isolate the one crucial difference between type *Set* and type *Bag*.

Once one has constructed a specification, one must address the question of whether or not one has supplied a sufficient number of consistent axioms. The partial semantics of the type is supplied by a set of individual statements of fact. If we can use the statements to derive an equation that contradicts the axioms of one of the underlying types used in the specification, the axioms of the specification are inconsistent. Ultimately, any inconsistent axiomatization is characterized by the fact that it can be used to derive the equation *true* = *false*. If, for example, one were to add the axiom:

$$\text{member-of?}(\text{delete}(b, i), i') = \textbf{if } ?=?(i, i')$$
$$\textbf{then } \textit{false}$$
$$\textbf{else } \text{member-of?}(b, i)$$

to the specification of type *Bag*, one would have created an inconsistent specification. There would exist values of type *Bag* for which it would be possible to prove both *member-of?*(b, i) = *true* and *member-of?*(b, i) = *false*, depending upon which of the axioms one chose to use. *Member-of?*(*delete*(*insert*(*insert*(*empty-bag*, 3), 3), 3), 3) is an example of an expression for which such a contradiction could be derived.

Determining the consistency of an arbitrary set of equations is in theory an unsolvable problem. In practice, however, it is often relatively simple to demonstrate consistency. The construction of a model is perhaps the most widely used technique. To show that an axiomatization of an abstract type is consistent, it suffices to construct an implementation of the abstraction that can be proved correct using a consistent proof theory. From a practical point of view, this is often the best way to demonstrate consistency. The chief drawback to this approach is that if the specification is inconsistent, it is possible to expend considerable effort trying to construct a model that does not exist. This problem can be avoided by proving the consistency of a specification prior to attempting to implement it. This can be done by treating the equations of the specification as left-to-right rewrite rules, and demonstrating that they exhibit the Church-Rosser property. Informally, a set of rewrite rules is Church-Rosser if whenever one applies a rewrite rule to reduce a term, and then a rule to reduce the resulting term, etc. until there is no longer an applicable rule, the final result is independent of the order in which one chooses to apply the rules. A useful method for proving that a set of rewrite rules exhibits this property is presented in Knuth and Bendix [1970].

Having established the consistency of a set of axioms, one should next address the question of its completeness. The notion of a complete axiom set is a familiar one to logicians. The exact definition used depends upon the environment in which one is working. The statements that a complete axiom set is "one to which an independent axiom cannot be added", or "one with which every well-formed formula or its negation can be proved as a theorem", or "one for which all models are isomorphic (i.e., the axiom set is categorical)", are all common. Our notion of completeness is equivalent to none of these statements, thus we introduce the qualifier "sufficiently" to differentiate it from these other, more common, concepts. Guttag and Horning [1978a] discuss sufficient-completeness at length and with some formality. Here we treat it only briefly and relatively informally.

The syntactic specification of a type, T, defines a free word algebra. The set of words, $L(T)$, contained in this algebra is a set of expressions that may occur in a program that uses the abstract type. For an axiomatization of a type to be sufficiently-complete, it must assign meaning to certain ground (i.e., without variables) terms in this language. We begin by partitioning the operations of the type into the sets S and O, where S contains exactly those operations whose range is the type being specified, the type of interest. Looking at type Bag, for example $S = \{empty\text{-}bag, insert, delete\}$ and $O = \{member\text{-}of?\}$. Intuitively, S contains the operations that can be used to generate values of the type being defined, and O the operations that map values of the type into other types. The need for operations to generate values of the type of interest is clear, thus S will always be non-empty.

In principle, one could define a type for which O were empty. Such a type, however, would be singularly uninteresting. With no way to partition the values of the type of interest (O empty implies no predicates) or to relate these values to values of other types, no value of the type could be distinguished from any other value. For all one could observe, every value of the type of interest would be equivalent to every other value of the type. For all intents and purposes, there would be only one value of that type. The ability to distinguish among the values of the type of interest thus rests solely upon the effects that these values have when they appear in the argument lists of the operations contained in O. It is this observation that lies at the root of our definition of sufficiently-complete.

For any abstract type T, and any axiom set A, A a sufficiently-complete axiomatization of T if and only if for every ground word of the form $o(x_1,...,x_n)$ contained in $L(T)$ where o is a member of O, there exists a theorem derivable from A of the form $o(x_1,...,x_n) = u$, where u contains no operations of type T. The above axiomatization of type Bag, for example, is sufficiently-complete because it can be used to reduce to either true or false any word in the set:

{$member\text{-}of?(b, i)$ | b is either $empty\text{-}bag$ or any sequence of inserts and deletes applied to $empty\text{-}bag$ and i is any integer}.

It can be shown that the problem of establishing whether or not a set of axioms is sufficiently-complete is undecidable. If, however, one is willing to accept certain limitations, it is possible to state reasonable conditions that will be sufficient to ensure sufficient-completeness. Such conditions are discussed in Guttag and Horning [1978a].

Before leaving the issue of sufficient-completeness, we should make it clear that while sufficient-completeness is a weaker completeness criterion than is generally used, there are circumstances in which it is still too strong.

TYPE ABSTRACTION

Consider, for example, adding an operation

    choose: Set ⟶ Integer

defined by the single equation

    member-of?(s, choose(s)) = true

to type *Set*. Our axiomatization of type *Set* would no longer be sufficiently-complete, since it would be impossible to prove that a word such as choose(insert(insert(empty-set, 3), 2)) is equal to any particular integer. Nevertheless, this may well be exactly the specification needed. If we have no reason to care which value the choose operation selects, any sufficiently-complete axiomatization would be unnecessarily restrictive. Given this not sufficiently-complete specification, we interpret *choose* as a not fully specified function. That is to say, given an arbitrary value of type *Set*, *s*, the value of *choose*(*s*) is not predictable. However, we require that *choose* be a function, i.e., that for all values, *s* and *s*1, of type *Set*

    s = s1 => choose(s) = choose(s1).

In some circumstances, even this may be too restrictive. Insisting that *choose* be a function of sets may preclude the most efficient implementation of the operation. If, for example, we implement sets as linked lists, it may prove convenient to return the last element added to the list. If one wishes to allow this flexibility, one must specify *choose* as a relation rather than as a function. At this point, it should be noted that we believe that in practice the need for specifications that are not sufficiently-complete is relatively limited, and that routinely checking the sufficient-completeness of a specification is a useful activity.

We turn now to a somewhat more comprehensive example:

    type Stack[elem-type: Type, n:Integer]
    where ( )

    syntax

newstack:		⟶ Stack
push:	Stack × elem-type	⟶ Stack
pop:	Stack	⟶ Stack
top:	Stack	⟶ elem-type
isnew:	Stack	⟶ Boolean
replace:	Stack × elem-type	⟶ Stack
*depth:	Stack	⟶ Integer

    semantics

declare stk:Stack, elm:elem-type

axioms (handwritten annotation)

    1) pop(push(stk, elm)) = stk
    2) top(push(stk, elm)) = elm
    3) isnew(newstack) = true
    4) isnew(push(stk, elm)) = false
    5) replace(stk, elm) = push(pop(stk), elm)
    6) depth(newstack) = 0
    7) depth(push(stk, elm)) = 1 + depth(stk) *recursive* (handwritten)

restrictions

    pre(pop, stk) = ~isnew(stk) *not a new stack.* (handwritten)
    pre(replace, stk, elm) = ~isnew(stk)
    isnew(stk) => **failure**(top, stk)
    failure(push, stk, elm) => depth(stk) $\geq$ n

In this example, the lower-case symbols in the first line are free variables ranging over the domains indicated, i.e., *n* ranges over the set of integers and *elem-type* over the set of types. This tells us that we can have a type *Stack* of any type of elements (but all elements in a stack must be of the same type). What we have defined is thus not a single abstract type, but rather a type schema. The binding of *elem-type* to a particular type and *n* to a particular integer, e.g., *Stack*[*Real*, 18], reduces the schema to the specification of a single abstract type. The empty **where** clause indicates that the choice of which type to bind *elem-type* to and which integer to bind *elem-type* to and which integer to bind *n* to is completely unrestricted. In general, however, we provide for **where** clauses such as:

    where n > 0 **and** elem-type **has**

        op: elem-type × elem-type ⟶ elem-type
        const: ⟶ elem-type

    declare e1, e2:elem-type

    op(e1, e2) = op(e2, e1)
    op(e1, const) = e1.

The second portion of this **where** clause restricts the types to which elem-type may be bound. That is, it may be bound only to types that contain some nullary operation and some binary predicate exhibiting those properties specified in the two equations. It would thus be possible to bind elem-type to type *Integer*, with *op* bound to + and *const* to 0, or to type *Set*, with *op* bound to *union* and *const* to the *empty-set*, e.g.,

    Stack[Set **with** (union, empty-set) **as** (op, const), 18].

The * preceding depth in the syntactic specification of type *Stack* indicates

TYPE ABSTRACTION

that depth is an auxiliary function. Auxiliary functions, which have also been called hidden functions, may not appear as part of programs using the abstraction. They are part of the specification of the abstraction, but not of the abstraction itself. As Thatcher, Wagner and Wright [1978] proves, the introduction of auxiliary functions is necessary if one relies on equations as the basis of a specification technique. Even when not strictly necessary, however, the introduction of an auxiliary function may greatly simplify and clarify a specification in much the same way as the introduction of a non-essential procedure can simplify and clarify a program.

The restriction specification serves two purposes. A pre-condition specification limits the applicability of the axioms. In the absence of a restriction specification, the weakest pre-condition (wp) associated with each function, f, of the abstract type is (roughly speaking) defined by

$$wp(x := f(Y), Q) = (\text{axioms} \Rightarrow Q(f(Y) \text{ for } x)).$$

If a pre-condition, **pre**(*f*, *Y*), is added to the specification of the abstraction, it becomes:

$$\textbf{pre}(f, Y) \text{ and } (\text{axioms} \Rightarrow Q(f(Y) \text{ for } x)).$$

The formula **pre**(*replace*, *stk*, *elm*) = ~*isnew*(*stk*), for example, indicates that axiom 5 holds only if ~*isnew*(*stk*). This is equivalent to replacing axiom 5 by the conditional equation

$$\sim isnew(stk) \Rightarrow (replace(stk, elm) = push(pop(stk), elm)).$$

(For a careful discussion of conditional equations see Thatcher, Wagner and Wright [1978].) Notice that the burden of checking (or proving) the pre-condition lies with the user of type *Stack*. The implementor of the type need not insert a check in the implementation of replace.

Failure specifications, on the other hand, place a burden on the implementor of the type. A formula of the form $P(X) \Rightarrow \textbf{failure}(g, X)$ states that if the operation *g* is invoked with arguments *X* such that $P(X)$, then *g* must fail, i.e., failure is required. By this we mean that *g* must not terminate normally. Formally,

$$\textbf{failure}(f, Y) \Rightarrow wp(f(Y), Q) = \text{false}.$$

It may abort, loop or even (if the programming language permits it) execute a jump to some external routine. A failure specification thus serves to restrict the domain of an operation. $Isnew(stk) \Rightarrow \textbf{failure}(top, stk)$, for example, combines with the syntactic specification of *top* to tell us that *top* is a partial function that accepts a stack as its argument and is defined if and only if that stack is not empty. Note that this is not equivalent to using the syntactic specification

$$top: Stack - \{newstack\} \rightarrow elem\text{-}type.$$

This would imply that *top* would never be called with *newstack* as the actual parameter, thus absolving the implementor of *top* from having to insert in his code a check on the suitability of the argument passed to it.

A formula of the form **failure**(*g*, *X*) => *P*(*X*) states that if the operation *g* is invoked with arguments *X* and fails to terminate normally, then *P*(*X*) must have been true at the point where *g* was invoked. That is to say failure is optional if *P*(*X*) is true, but must not occur if *P*(*X*) is not. The formula **failure**(*push*, *stk*, *elm*) => *depth*(*stk*) $\geq$ n, for example, gives the implementation of *push* the option of failing whenever the depth of the resulting stack would exceed *n*.

Initially, we had hoped to limit ourselves to one form of **failure** specification. In particular, we had hoped to limit ourselves to the specification of optional failures and pre-conditions. It seemed that if a condition, *P*(*X*), were sufficient to guarantee failure, then $\sim P(X)$ should be used as a pre-condition, obviating the need for the failure specification. However, just as one can take comfort in knowing that the definition of a programming language guarantees that subscript errors will be reported, the programmer who uses type *Stack* may take comfort in knowing that should he try to compute the top of newstack, his computation will not proceed. This security is particularly important if the program using type Stack has not been formally verified, for then there is no guarantee that the specified pre-conditions hold at the point of invocation. The need for optional **failure** specifications is more pervasive. It stems from our desire to make our specifications as unrestrictive as possible. When dealing with capacity constraints, in particular, it is often the case that the specifier of the type needs only to establish a bound, and the exact choice of where to fail is best left to the implementor of the type. The implementor of type *Stack*, for example, might find it convenient to allow the depth of the stack to reach the first power of two not less than *n*. A related example involves the specification of a type *Number* with restriction specifications dealing with overflow and underflow. In some applications, it is crucial that calculations be carried out in exactly the precision asked for. In other applications, one need only require that the precision used be at least as great as that requested. The use of an optional **failure** specification in the latter case may allow a significantly more efficient implementation of type *Number*.

5. A FEW CLOSING COMMENTS

For verifications of programs that use abstract types, both algebraic and Hoare-like specifications of the types used provide rules of inference that can be used to demonstrate consistency between a program and its specification. That is to say, the presence of axiomatic definitions of abstract types provides a mechanism for proving a program to be consistent with its specification, provided that the implementations of the abstract operations that it uses are consistent with their specifications. Thus a technique for factoring the proof is provided, for the axiomatic definitions serve as the specification of intent at a lower level of abstraction. For proofs of the correctness of representations of abstract types, the axiomatic specifications provide the minimal set of assertions that must be verified. A lengthy discussion of the use of algebraic axioms in program verification appears in Guttag [1978b]. Discussions of the use of Hoare-like specifications in program verification appear in Hoare [1972a] and Wulf [1976].

Any discussion of the relative merits of these two specification techniques in program verification must be highly subjective. One can invert arbitrarily many examples for which one or the other approach is clearly more convenient. Those examples favoring the Hoare-like approach are characterized by the choice of a type abstraction closely related to a type available in the underlying specification language. Those examples favoring the algebraic technique are characterized by the choice of a type abstraction not readily represented by a type available in the underlying specification language. These two classes of examples illustrate two facts:

Fact 1: If there exists some domain of discourse about which a great deal is known, and the abstraction we wish to provide is readily mapped into that domain, then a great deal is to be gained by performing that mapping and reasoning in terms of the better understood domain.

Fact 2: If we are forced to map the desired abstraction into a dissimilar domain and then reason in terms of that domain, we will have lost any advantage we had hoped to gain by introducing the abstraction.

Given these two facts, any evaluation of the relative utility of these two approaches to type abstraction must be based upon a subjective evaluation of the way in which type abstraction will be used. In particular, one must address the question of what kinds of abstractions will prove most useful. Will they be primarily close variants of a small set of currently well-understood abstractions? Or, given suitably imaginative programmers, will they often be quite distinct from any already well-understood abstraction? These are questions to which only experience can provide answers.

ACKNOWLEDGMENTS

The discussion of Euclid modules is derived in part from London, Guttag, Horning, Lampson, Mitchell and Popek [1978]. Both the exposition of the module rule and my understanding of it can, to a great extent, be attributed to many hours spent discussing the subject with Ralph London. The discussion of algebraic axioms is in part a condensation of material appearing in earlier papers and in part a preliminary discussion of work currently in progress. I thus owe a significant debt to my past and present collaborators: Jim Horning, Ellis Horowitz and Dave Musser. I would also like to thank the participants of the Summer School on Program Construction, whose response to my lectures led to substantial revisions in these notes. Finally, I thank Lisa Moses for gently guiding me and this paper through various computer-based document preparation systems.

This work was supported in part by the National Science Foundation under grant MCS78-01798 and the Joint Services Electronics Program monitored by the Air Force Office of Scientific Research under contract F44620-76-C-0061.

[Handwritten notes:]

in chi's paper:

The strength of the algebraic approach is that it provides a simple notation which is easy to comprehend & w/ which it is easy to construct a spec. that is complete & usually consistent.

The algebraic appr. results in a specification which is reasonably clear & concise.

The spec. tech. proves to be easily extensible in the sense defined in

---

The meaning of "WP(S,R)ie
"the weakest P-C for 1

D. L. PARNAS
Carnegie-Mellon University

A Technique for Software Module Specification with Examples

Because of the growing recognition that a major contributing factor in the so-called "software engineering" problem is our lack of techniques for precisely specifying program segments without revealing too much information [Buxton and Randell 1970; Parnas 1971a], I would like to report on a technique for module specification which has proved moderately successful in a number of test situations.

Without taking the space to justify them [Parnas 1971a] I would like to list the goals of the specification scheme to be described:

1. The specification must provide to the intended user *all* the information that he will need to use the program correctly, *and nothing more*.

2. The specification must provide to the implementer, *all* the information about the intended use that he needs to complete the program, and *no additional information*; in particular, no information about the structure of the calling program should be conveyed.

3. The specification must be sufficiently formal that it can conceivably be machine tested for consistency, completeness (in the sense of defining the outcome of all possible uses) and other desirable properties of a specification. Note that we do not insist that machine testing be done, only that it could conceivably be done. By this requirement we intend to rule out all natural language specifications.[1]

---

1. It should be clear that while we cannot afford to use natural language specifications we cannot manage to do without natural language explanations. Any formal structure is a hollow shell to most of us without a description of its intended interpretation. The formal specifications given in this paper would be meaningless without a natural language description of the intended usage of the various functions and parameters. On the other hand, we insist that once the reader is familiar with the intended interpretation the specifications should answer all of his questions about the behavior of the programs without reference to the natural language text.

The experience of the author has shown if one makes use of names with a high mnemonic value, both reader and writer tend to become sloppy and use the intended interpretation implied by the mnemonic name to answer questions which should be answered from the formal statements. For that reason the function names have not been designed to be highly mnemonic but are instead rather obscure. The functions will only be completely understood after the reader studies the text which follows. The use of obscure mnemonics is clearly a matter of personal taste, and should not be considered essential to the technique being described.

4. The specification should discuss the program in the terms normally used by user and implementer alike rather than some other area of discourse. By this we intend to exclude the specification of programs in terms of the mappings they provide between large input domains and large output domains or their specification in terms of mappings onto small automata, etc.

The basis of the technique is a view of a program module as a device with a set of switch inputs and readout indicators. The technique specifies the possible positions of the input switches and the effect of moving the switches on the values of the readout indicators. We insist that the values of the readout indicators be completely determined by the previous values of those indicators and the positions of the input switches.

[*Aside:* The notation allows for some of the push-buttons to be combined with indicator lights or readouts (with the result that we must push a button in order to read), but we have not yet found occasion to use that facility. A simple extension of the notation allows the specification of mechanisms in which the values of the readout indicators are not determined by the above factors, but can be predicted only by knowing the values of certain "hidden" readout indicators which cannot actually be read by the user of the device. We have considerable doubts about the advisability of building devices which must be specified using this feature, but the ability to specify such devices is inexpensively gained.]

In software terms we consider each module as providing a number of subroutines or functions which can cause changes in state, and other functions or procedures which can give to a user program the values of the variables making up that state. We refer to these all as *functions*.

We distinguish two classes of readout functions: the most important class provides information which cannot be determined without calling that function unless the user maintains duplicate information in his own program's data structures. A second class, termed *mapping functions*, provides redundant information, in that the value of these functions is completely predictable from the *current values* of other readout functions. The mapping functions are provided as a notational convenience to keep the specifications and the user programs smaller.

For each function we specify:

1. The set of possible values: (integers, reals, truth values, etc.)

2. Initial values: (either "undefined" or a member of the set specified in item 1). "Undefined" is considered a special value, rather than an unpredictable value.

3. Parameters: each parameter is specified as belonging to one of the sets named in item 1.

4. Effect: with the exception of mapping functions, almost all the

SOFTWARE MODULAR SPECIFICATION

information in the specification is contained in section 4. Under "effect": we place two distinct types of items which require a more detailed discussion.

First, we state that if the "effect" section is empty, then there is absolutely no way to detect that the function has been called. One may call it arbitrarily often and observe no effect other than the passage of time.

The modules that we have specified have "traps" built in. There is a sequence of statements in the "effect" section which specifies the conditions under which certain "error" handling routines will be called. These conditions are treated as incorrect usage of the module and response is considered to be the responsibility of the calling program. For that reason it is assumed that the "error" handling routine's body will not be considered part of the module specified, but will be written by the users of the module. If such a condition occurs, there is to be no observable result of the call of the routine except the transfer of control. Where there is a sequence of error statements, the first one in the list which applies is the only one which is invoked. In some cases, the calling program will correct its error and return to have the function try again; in others, it will not. If it does return, the function is to behave as if this were the first call. There is no memory of the erroneous call.

This approach to error handling is motivated by two considerations which are peripheral to this paper. First, we wish to make it possible to write the code for the "normal" cases without checking for the occurrence of unusual or erroneous situations. The "trap" approach facilitates this. Second, we wish to encourage the proper handling of errors in many-leveled software. In our opinion this implies that each routine receives all messages from the routines that it uses and either (1) hides the trap from its user or (2) passes to its user an error indication which is meaningful to a program which knows only the specification of the routine that it called and does not know of the existence of routines called by that routine. The reader will find that our insistence that (1) response to errors is the responsibility of any routine which called another routine in an "incorrect" way and (2) that when such an error call is made, there is no record of the previous call, places quite a demand on the implementers of each module. They must not make irreversible changes unless they are certain that they can complete the changes to be made without calling any "error" routines. The reader will note that we generally specify a separate routine for each case which might be handled separately. The user may make several routines have identical bodies, if the distinction between those cases is not important to him.

The remaining statements are sequence independent. They can be "shuffled" without changing their meaning. These statements are equations describing the values (after the function call) of the other functions in the module. It is specified that no changes in any functions (other than mapping functions) occur unless they are implied by the effect section. The effect section can refer only to values of the function parameters and values of readout functions. The value changes of the mapping functions are not mentioned; those changes can be derived from the changes in the functions used in the definitions of the mapping functions. All of this will become much clearer as we discuss the following examples.

In some cases we may specify the effect of a sequence to be null. By this we imply that the sequence may be inserted in any other sequence without changing the effect of the other sequence.

1. NOTATION

The notation[2] is mainly ALGOL-like and requires little explanation. To distinguish references to the value of a function before calling the specified function from references to its value after the call, we enclose the old or previous value in single quotes (e.g. 'VAL'). If the value does not change, the quotes are optional. Brackets (" [" and "] ") are used to indicate the scope of quantifiers. "=" is the relation "equals" and *not* the assignment operator as in FORTRAN.

We propose that the definition of a stack shown in Example 1 should replace the usual pictures of implementations (e.g., the array with pointer or the linked list implementations). All that you need to know about a stack in order to use it is specified there. There are countless possible implementations (including a large number of sensible ones). The implementation should be free to vary without changing the using programs. If the using programs assume no more about a stack than is stated above, that will be true.

Example 2 shows a "binary tree." This example is of interest because we have provided the user with sufficient information that he may search the tree, yet we have *not* defined the values of the main functions, only properties of those values. Thus, those values might well be links in a linked list

Example 1

Function PUSH(a)
possible values: none
integer: a
effect: call ERR1 *if* a > p2 $\vee$ a < 0 $\vee$ 'DEPTH' = p1
 else [VAL = a; DEPTH = 'DEPTH' + 1;]

Function POP
possible values: none
parameters: none
effect: call ERR2 *if* 'DEPTH' = 0

---

2. Although this paper introduces a new notation it must be emphasized that the notation is not intended to be a contribution of this paper. In making a specification we include some information about a module and omit some. We are concerned primarily with the choice of the information to be supplied. We introduce notation only as needed to make that choice clear. Although we have made some attempt to adhere to a consistent notation, this paper is not a proposal that this notation be considered a language to be adopted for specification writing. We are not yet at a point where that is an important issue.

SOFTWARE MODULAR SPECIFICATION

the sequence "PUSH(a); POP" has no net effect if no error calls occur.

Function VAL
possible values: integer initial; value undefined
parameters: none
effect: error call *if* 'DEPTH' = 0

Function DEPTH
possible values: integer; initial value 0
parameters: none
effect: none

p1 and p2 are parameters. p1 is intended to represent the maximum depth of the stack and p2 the maximum width or maximum size for each item. implementation, array indices in a TREESORT [Floyd 1964] style implementation or a number of other possibilities. The important fact is that if we implement the functions *as defined* by any method, any usage which assumes only what is specified will work.

Example 2

In the following module all function values and parameters are integers except where stated otherwise. In the interest of brevity we shall not state this repeatedly. For some values the values are *not* predicted by the definition. They are chosen arbitrarily by the system. This is done because the user should not make use of any regularity which might exist in the values assigned. The necessary relations between the values of those functions and the values of other functions are stated explicitly. Such incompletely defined functions are noted with an *. The user may store the values of those functions and use them to avoid repeated nested function calls.

Intended Interpretation:

> FA = *fa*ther, LS = *l*eft*s*on, RS = *r*ight*s*on,
> SLS = *set ls*, SRS = *set rs*, SVA = *set val*,
> VAL = *val*ue, DEL = *del*ete, ELS = *exists ls*,
> ERS = *exists rs*.

Function FA(i)*
possible values: integers
initial value: FA(0) = 0; otherwise undefined
effect: error call *if* 'FA' (i) undefined

Function LS(i)*
possible values: integers
initial value: undefined
effect: error call *if* 'ELS'(i) = *false*

Function RS(i)*
possible values: integers
initial value: undefined
effect: error call *if* 'ERS' (i) = *false*

Function SLS(i)
possible values: none
initial value: not applicable
effect: error call *if* 'FA' (i) is undefined
　　　　error call *if* 'ELS' (i) = *true*

　　LS(i) and FA(LS(i)) are given values such that
　　[FA(LS(i)) = i and 'FA' (LS(i)) was undefined]
　　ELS(i) = *true*;

Function SRS(i)
possible values: none
initial value: not applicable
effect: error call *if* 'FA' (i) is undefined
　　　　error call *if* 'ERS' (i) = *true*

　　RS(i) and FA(RS(i)) are assigned values such that
　　[FA(RS(i)) = i and 'FA' (RS(i)) was not defined]
　　ERS(i) = *true*;

Function SVA(i, v)
possible values: none
initial value: not applicable
effect: error call *if* 'FA' (i) is undefined
VAL(i) = v

Function VAL(i)
possible values: integers
initial value: undefined
effect: error call *if* 'VAL' (i) is undefined

Function DEL(i)
possible values: none
initial value: not applicable
effect: error call *if* 'FA' (i) is undefined
　　　　error call *if* 'ELS' (i) or 'ERS' (i) = *true*
　　FA(i), VAL(i) are undefined
　　if i = 'LS'('FA'(i)) *then* [LS('FA'(i) is undefined and ELS('FA' (i)) = *false*]
　　if i = 'RS'('FA'(i)) *then* [RS('FA' (i)) is undefined and ERS('FA'(i)) = *false*]

Function ELS(i)
possible values: *true, false*
initial value: *false*
effect: error call *if* 'FA'(i) undefined

Function ERS(i)

possible values: *true, false*
initial value: *false*
effect: error call *if* 'FA' (i) undefined

To make this specification complete the names of the error routines must be supplied.

Example 3 shows a more specialized piece of software. It is a storage module intended for use in such applications as producing KWIC indexes. It is designed to hold "lines" which are ordered sets of "words," which are ordered sets of characters, to be dealt with by an integer representation. For this example there are some restrictions on the way that material may be inserted (only at the end of the last line) which reflect the intended use. That might well be a design error, but for our purposes the important thing to note is that the restrictions are completely and precisely specified without revealing any of the internal reasons for making such restrictions.

Some readers may feel that the specification reveals an obvious implementation in terms of arrays. In fact, the module was implemented several times in tutorial projects and this obvious implementation was never used. Such an implementation would be impractical in most cases and a much more complex implementation was needed. The details of that implementation are hidden by this description of the module.

The limitations of the module ($p1$, $p2$, $p3$) were expressed in terms of the array model for several reasons, among them ease of use and the fact that it permits the array implementation. The decision to use those three parameters rather than one "space" parameter is a questionable one because in some cases we may exceed the apparent capacity without exceeding the real capacity. In our experience this has not been a problem.

In making the line holder of Example 3 it may prove advantageous to (1) separate out the problem of storing the individual characters that make up a word from the problem of storing the makeup of lines out of words, and (2) avoid duplicate storing of identical words. Both can be accomplished by use of the mechanism defined in Example 4 as a submodule for that described in Example 3. The implementer of the "line holder" would pass the individual characters of the "words" to the symbol table whose definition guarantees him that he will receive a unique encoding of every symbol. Note that the specification in Example 4 does not rule out an implementation which stores duplicate copies of words, but it does require that all receive the same encoding.

It is important to note that the user of the "line holder" will never know or need to know of the existence of the symbol table inner mechanism.

Example 3

Definition of a "Line Holder" Mechanism. This definition specifies a mechanism which may be used to hold up to $p1$ lines, each line consisting of up to $p2$ words, and each word may be up to $p3$ characters.

Function WORD
possible values: integers
initial values: undefined
parameters: *l*, w, c all integer
effect:
    call ERLWEL *if* $l < 1$ or $l > p1$
    call ERLWNL *if* $l >$ LINES
    call ERLWEW *if* $w < 1$ or $w > p2$
    call ERLWNW *if* $w >$ WORDS(l)
    call ERLWEC *if* $c < 1$ or $c > p3$
    call ERLWNC *if* $c >$ CHARS(l, w)

Function SETWRD
possible values: none
initial values: not applicable
parameters: *l*, w, c, d all integers
effect:
    call ERLSLE *if* $l < 1$ or $l > p1$
    call ERLSBL *if* $l >$ 'LINES' $+ 1$
    call ERLSBL *if* $l <$ 'LINES'
    call ERLSWE *if* $w < 1$ or $w > p2$
    call ERLSBW *if* $w >$ 'WORDS' $(l) + 1$
    call ERLSBW *if* $w <$ 'WORDS' (l)
    call ERLSCE *if* $c < 1$ or $c > p3$
    call ERLSBC *if* c .noteq. 'CHARS' $(l, w) + 1$ call ERLSWD if $l < 0$ or $l > p4$ LINES = 'LINES' $+ 1$
    then WORDS(l) =
    CHARS(l, w) = c
    WORD(l, w, c) = d

Function WORDS
possible values: integers
initial values: 0
parameters: *l* an integer
effect:
    call ERLWSL *if* $l < 1$ or $1 > p1$
    call ERLWSL *if* $l >$ LINES
    call ERLWSL *if* $1 >$ LINES

Function LINES
possible values: integers
initial value: 0
parameters: none
effect: none

Function DELWRD
possible values: none
initial values: not applicable
parameters: *l*, w both integers

SOFTWARE MODULAR SPECIFICATION

effect:
 call ERLDLE *if* $l < 1$ or $l >$ LINES
 call ERLDWE *if* $w < 1$ or $w >$ 'WORDS' (l)
 call ERLDLD *if* 'WORDS'$(l) = 1$
 WORDS$(l) =$ 'WORDS' $(l) - 1$
 for all c WORD$(l, v, c) =$ 'WORD' $(l, v+1, c$ *if* $v \geqslant w$
 for all $v > w$ or $v = w$ CHARS$(l, v) =$ 'CHARS' $(l, v+1)$

[margin note: not error handling ?]

Function DELINE
possible values: none
initial values: not applicable
parameters: *l* an integer
effect:
 call ERLDLL *if* $l < 0$ or $l >$ 'LINES'
 LINES = 'LINES' $- 1$
 if $r = 1$ or $r > 1$ *then* for all w, for all c
  (WORDS(r) = 'WORDS' (r+1)
  CHARS(r, w) = 'CHARS' (r+1, w)
  WORD(r, w, c) = 'WORD' (r+1, w, c))

Function CHARS
possible values: integer
initial value: 0
parameters: *l*, w both integers
effect:
 call ERLCNL *if* $l < 1$ or $l >$ LINES
 call ERLCNW *if* $w < 1$ or $w >$ WORDS(l)

Example 4

Symbol Table Definition.

[margin note: there is no where indicate that Example 4 (module) has been called (used)]

p1 = maximum number of symbols
p2 = maximum number of characters per symbol
p3 = maximum value of character

(The above interpretation is the intended one)

Function STRTSM
possible values: none
initial values: not applicable
parameters: none
effects: call ERFAST *if* 'MAYIN' = *true*
   MAYIN = *true*

Function MAYIN
possible values: *true, false*
initial values: *false*

parameters: none
effects: none

Function CHARIN
possible values: none
initial values: not applicable
parameters: call ERCHIL *if* c < 0 or c > p3
    call ERMNIN *if* 'MAYIN' = *false*
    call ERBUFX *if* 'BUFFERCNT' = p2
    BUFFER('BUFFERCNT' + 1) = c
    BUFFERCNT = 'BUFFERCNT' + 1

Function BUFFER
possible values: integers
initial values: not applicable
parameters: c, an integer
effects: call ERBUFE *if* c < 1 or c > 'BUFFERCNT'

Function BUFFERCNT
possible values: integers 0 < BUFFERCNT ⩽ p2
initial values: 0
parameters: none
effects: none

SYMEND
possible values: integers 0 < SYMEND ⩽ 'SMCNT' + 1
initial values: not applicable
parameters: none
effects: call ERNOIN *if* 'MAYIN' = false
    call ERNUTN if 'BUFFERCNT' = 0
    MAYIN = false
    if there is an s (0 < s ⩽ 'SMCNT') such that
    'BUFFERCNT' = 'CHCNT' (s) and
    [*if* for all c (0 < c < 'BUFFERCNT')
     BUFFER(c) = 'CHAR' (s, c)] then
     SYMEND = s
    else [call ERSYL *if* 'SMCNT' = p1
     for all c (0 < c < 'BUFFERCNT')
     [CHAR('SMCNT' + 1, c) = 'BUFFER'(c)
     CHCNT('SMCNT' + 1) = 'BUFFERCNT']
     SMCNT = 'SMCNT' + 1]
    BUFFERCNT = 0

Function CHAR
possible values: integers 0 < CHAR ⩽ p3
initial values: not applicable
parameters: s and c, both integers
effects: call ERNOSY *if* a < *l* or s > H'MSCN
    call ERNOCH *if* c < 1 or c > (s)'TC'TN'C

SOFTWARE MODULAR SPECIFICATION

Function SMCNT
possible values: integers 0 ⩽ SMCNT ⩽ p1
initial values: 0
parameters: none
effects: none

Function CHCNT
possible values: integers 0 < CHCNT < p2
initial values: not applicable
parameters: s, an integer
effects: call ERNOSY if s < 1 or s > 'SMCNT'

Example 5 is intended to exhibit the situations in which mapping functions are useful in specifications. This module is an alphabetizer, intended to work with the "line holder" shown earlier. It determines values for ITH in such a way that (1) every integer between 1 and the number of lines is a value of ITH and if $i < j$ then the line numbered ITH(i) does not come before the line numbered ITH(j) in the alphabetic ordering.

Note that ITH as defined might be an array in which the values specified as stored by the routine ALPH, or it might be a routine which searches for the appropriate line each time called. An interesting alternative would be to make use of FIND [Hoare 1971a] within ITH so that the computation is distributed over the calls of ITH and so that in some situations unnecessary work may be avoided. We repeat that the important feature of this specification is that it provides sufficient information to use a module which is correctly implemented according to any of these methods, *without the user having any knowledge of the method*.

Example 5

Alphabetizer for line holder. This module accomplishes the alphabetization of the contents of the modules referred to above by producing a pointer function, ITH, which gives the index of the ith line in the alphabetized sequence.

Function ITH
possible values: integers
initial values: undefined
parameters: i an integer
effect:
    call ERAIND *if* value of function undefined for parameter given

Function ALPHC
possible values: integers
initial value: ALPHC(l) = index of l in alphabet used
    ALPHC(l) infinite if character not in alphabet
parameter: l an integer
effect:
    call ERAABL if l not in alphabet being used, i.e. *if* ALPHC(l) = ∞

Mapping Function EQW
possible values: *true, false*
parameters: $l1, l2, w1, w2$ all integers
values:
    EQW($l1$, w1, $l2$, w2) = for all c ('WORD'($l1$, w1, c) = 'WORD'($l2$, w2, c))
effect:
    call ERAEBL *if* $l1$ < 1 or $l1$ > 'LINES'
    call ERAEBL *if* $l2$ < 1 or $l2$ > 'LINES'
    call ERAEBW *if* w1 < 1 or w1 > 'WORDS'($l1$)
    call ERAEBW *if* w2 < 1 or w2 > 'WORDS'($l2$)

Mapping Function ALPHW
possible values: true, false
parameters: $l1, l2, w1, w2$ all integers
values:
    ALPHW($l1$, w1, $l2$, w2) = *if* $\neg$ 'EQW'($l1$, w1, $l2$, w2) and
    k = min c such that ('WORD'($l1$, w1, c) $\neg$ eq. 'WORD'($l2$, w2, c))
    then 'ALPHC'('WORD'($l1$, w1, k)) < 'ALPHC' ('WORD'($l2$, w2, k))
    else *false*
effect:
    call ERAWBL *if* $l1$ < 1 or $l2$ > 'LINES'
    call ERAWBL *if* $l2$ < 1 or $l1$ > 'LINES'
    call ERAWBW *if* w1 < 1 or w1 > 'WORDS'($l1$)
    call ERAWBW *if* w2 < 1 or w2 > 'WORDS'($l2$)

Mapping Function EQL
possible values: *true, false*
parameters: $l1, l2$ both integers
values:
    EQL ($l1, l2$) = for all k ('EQW' (li, k, $l2$, k))
effect:
    call ERALEL *if* $l1$ < 1 or 1 > 'LINES'
    call ERALEL *if* $l2$ < 1 or $l2$ > 'LINES'

Mapping Function ALPHL
possible values: *true, false*
parameters: $l1, l2$ both integers
value:
    ALPHL($l1, l2$) = *if* $\neg$ 'EQL' ($l1, l2$) then
    (let k = min c such that 'EQW'($l1$, k, $l2$, k))
    'ALPHW'($l1$, k, $l2$, k) else true
effect:
    call ERAALB *if* $l1$ < 1 or $l1$ > 'LINES'
    call ERAALB *if* $l2$ < 1 or $l2$ > 'LINES'

Function ALPH
possible values: none
initial values: not applicable
effect:
    for all i $\neg$ < l and i $\neg$ > 'LINES' (
    ITH (i) is given values such that (

for all j ¬ < 1 and j ¬ > LINES
there exists a k such that ITH(k) = j
for i ≥ −1 and i < 'LINES'[that'ALPHL'(ITH(i), ITH(i+1))]

2. USING THE SPECIFICATIONS

The specifications will be of maximum usefulness only if we adopt methods that make full use of them. Our aim has been to produce specifications which are in a real sense just as testable as programs. We will gain the most in our system building abilities if we have a technique for usage of the specifications which involves testing the specifications *long before* the programs specified are produced. The statements being made at this level are precise enough that we should not have to wait for a lower level representation in order to find the errors.

Such specifications are at least as demanding of precision as are programs; they may well be as complex as some programs. Thus they are as likely to be in error. Because specifications cannot be "run," we may be tempted to postpone their testing until we have programs and can run them. For many reasons such an approach is wrong.

We are able to test such specifications because they provide us with a set of axioms for a formal deductive scheme. As a result, we may be able to prove certain "theorems" about our specifications. Example "theorems" might be:

1. The specification never refers to $F1(p)$ unless it is certain that p is less than 9.

2. Whenever $F3(x)$ is true $F4(x)$ is defined and conversely.

3. It is not possible for $F5(x)$ to take on values greater than $p3$.

4. Error routine ERRX will never be called.

5. There exists a sequence of function calls which will set $F2(x) = F5(x) = 0$.

6. There will never exist distinct integers i and j such that $F1(i) = F2(j)$.

By asking the proper set of such questions, the "correctness" of a set of specifications may be verified. The choice of the questions, therefore the meaning of "correctness," is dependent on the nature of the object being specified.

Using the same approach of taking the specifications as axioms and attempting to prove theorems one may ask questions about possible changes in systems structure. For example, one may ask which modules will have to be changed, if certain restrictions assumed before were removed.

It would be obviously useful if there were a support system which would input the specifications and provide question answering or theorem proving ability above the specifications. That, however, is not essential. What is essential is that system builders develop the habit of verifying the specifications whether by machine or by hand before building and debugging the programs.

Incidentally, the theorem proving approach might also be considered as a basis for a program which searches automatically for implementations of a specified module. We see this as more difficult and perhaps less urgently needed than the above.

3. HESITATIONS

To date the technique has received only limited evaluation. It has been used with reasonable success in the construction of small systems with simple modules in an undergraduate class. The largest completed specification is a description of a simplified man-machine interface for a graphics based editor system [Parnas 1971b]. However, any attempt to use this on a larger project (where the probability of failure without the technique is high) is in a very early stage. Clearly the idea needs further practical use before its usefulness can be evaluated. I hope that some of my readers will be in a position to do this.

There appears to be a weak limitation on the technique in that it makes it easy to describe objects which receive data in small units, and where the calling program must be aware of the period between receipt of such small units. So far we have not found a way to follow the technique for such objects as a compiler where the user sends one very large unit and does not want to know of internal steps in the processing of individual characters, phrases, etc. For such situations we have been forced to make use of techniques similar to that of Wirth and Weber [1966]. We did, however, combine the two techniques with some success.

In usage of these techniques it has become clear that there is a great initial resistance to their use. This approach to the description of programs as somewhat static objects, rather than sequential decision makers, is unfamiliar to men with lots of programming experience. The first few attempts always fail and require the patient guidance of an instructor. The idea is, however, simple and is eventually mastered by almost everyone.

C. B. JONES
University of Manchester

Systematic Program Development

1. INTRODUCTION

This paper provides an overview of one method which can be used to systematically develop computer programs. The so-called "Vienna Development Method" (VDM), on which the paper is based, is described in a number of publications (e.g. [Bjorner 1981; C. B. Jones 1980; Bjorner and Jones 1982]). VDM uses mathematical notation in order to be unambiguous but, at least in its applications, does not use particularly deep mathematical results.

Some of the techniques used in VDM deviate from those in wide use (the "accepted" approach). Such heresies are, in the opinion of the originators of VDM, the result of relying strongly on intuition gained from the application of the method to non-trivial problems.

The overall concern is how to create programs which are (known to be) correct with respect to their specifications. The idea of proving programs correct is now widely discussed. To support a formal proof, a specification must be recorded in a formal notation. Post-facto proofs of the correctness of large programs are likely to be unattainable. It is now widely accepted that correctness criteria are needed for individual design steps: thus it is the program design which is justified rather than (just) the finished code. Using formal concepts in this way makes it possible to relax proofs to the level of "rigor" used in most mathematical arguments. The knowledge of what and how to formalize ensures that sloppiness will not arise. The aim is to record program development in a formalizable notation.

One reason for concentrating on justification during design is the large impact which errors made early in the development cycle have on the productivity of programmers. Much more emphasis is put here on data structures and their refinement than on programming language control constructs. This is precisely because experience suggests that data structure decisions occur in the early stages of design.

This paper focuses on the formal aspects of program development: there are clearly many considerations which are not going to be helped by such formal methods. In order to avoid misunderstanding, it will be best to consider the development method as providing a structure in which a design can be documented. How the original specification is agreed, how the design ideas are generated, or how the designers are managed, is not intended to be constrained.

2. DATA TYPES

There are a lot of publications concerned with the specification of data types and these often confuse, rather than answer, the question "what is a data type?" An answer is given below in terms of behaviors but, before making this precise, it is necessary to clarify the scope of the intuitive idea as seen from VDM experience.

When considering data types, the natural mathematical comparison is with something like natural numbers: a set of values and a collection of total functions. With care, the functions (operators) can be defined without mentioning the values. Data types such as lists (sequences) fit this mold fairly well—although it becomes much harder to ignore the partial functions such as those yielding head and tail. Just as with integers, it is natural to build up complex list expressions which denote list values; list values can be compared; and, in a procedural language, list values can be assigned to variables. A data type like stack is different. The operators might be called "operations" in order to recognize that they change the state of the stack by "side effect." This state can be an important aid in writing a specification. Since the result of some stack operations depends on the history of other operations which have been applied, the state defines equivalence classes of such histories. Furthermore, comparison and assignment of stack values might not be considered desirable. Finally, with many such data types, the problem of partial and even non-deterministic operations cannot be avoided.

It is, of course, possible to present data types, even within the many complications, in the mold of more mathematical objects. One must, however, be careful when forcing things into artificial molds. With stacks it is natural to think of the POP operation both returning a value and having a side-effect on the state; it is doubtful whether the separation into two functions each yielding one result contributes to understanding. Where non-determinism is involved, this separation is even more questionable.

The behaviors (cf. Ganzinger [1983]; Sannella and Wirsing [1983]; Schoett [1982]) with which it is intended to explain data types, must recognize the side-effects as well as partial and non-deterministic operations. The appropriate model would appear to be on the one hand a set of terms, built up from operations which do not yield error; and on the other hand, a definition of the meaning of any such term given as a relation on its inputs and outputs.

The *specifications* of data types is an area where VDM deviates from the most widely accepted approach—that is the property oriented (algebraic, axiomatic) style. "Algebraic presentations" appear well-suited for basic data types like lists. Their attraction would appear to have more to do with mathematical tractability than with their ability to handle the full range of data types needed in computing science.

There is an interesting question concerning the interpretation of equations. [Kamin 1983; Bothe 1981] discuss the "final" interpretation. In some sense, the set of generating operators of a data type can be seen to create a model on which the other operators are defined. The question can then be asked whether this is the most convenient model.

VDM takes a model oriented approach to describing data types. Thus, if a relational database system is to be specified, the state might be modeled using (among other things) a mapping from relation names to sets of tuples.

The problem of representing mappings from keys to data occurs over and over again in computer systems. Unlike the database example, this could easily be specified via its properties—it will however serve as an example which is small enough to be carried through to its implementation. In the model oriented specification given below, pre-conditions are used to indicate the partial operations and, in general, non-determinism is handled by (relational) post-conditions.

3. SPECIFICATION

The examples given in this paper use the VDM notation. In most cases, this should have obvious meaning, a full description can be found in the references.

The top-level specification of the mapping from Keys to Data is made trivial by the availability of a suitable class of objects in VDM. Thus:

$$Mkd = \textbf{map Key to Data}$$

The initial object in Mkd is:

$$m_0 = [\ ]$$

The operations can be defined:

INSERT(K: Key, D: Data)

ext wr M: Mkd

pre k $\notin$ **dom** m

post m = $\overleftarrow{m}$ $\cup$ [k $\mapsto$ d]

FIND(K: Key) D: Data

ext rd M: Mkd

pre k $\in$ **dom** m

post d = $\overleftarrow{m}$(k)

DELETE(K: Key)

ext wr M: Mkd

pre k ∈ **dom** m

post m = $\overleftarrow{m}$ \ {k}

(The "hooked" variables in post-conditions denote the value of the corresponding variable at the beginning of the operation; undecorated lower case names refer to the value of corresponding (upper case) variables at the point where the assertion is relevant.)

Each of these operations has been specified to be partial in order to illustrate the proof rules below. Although the operations are deterministic, relational post-conditions have been written. The experience with VDM suggests that non-determinism often arises during design: even with this small example, this point is illustrated below. Notice that selective access to the state is given by means of **rd/wr** externals.

The most serious objection raised against model oriented specifications is that they might overspecify a system. This notion of "bias" has been made precise in earlier papers and a test has been devised to check that overspecification is avoided:

> A model specification is based on some set of objects. The model is biased (with respect to some given set of operations) if there exist different elements of the set of objects which cannot be distinguished by any of the operations.

Thus bias can be seen as preserving a part of the history (of an object) which cannot be detected by the operations: the equivalence class induced by the state is not coarse enough. (A representation which passes the bias test might contain redundant information such as duplication. The test only rules out non-unique representations.)

In practice, this test has uncovered few examples of bias in existing specifications. It is important to recall that the notion is defined with respect to a set of operations. In C. B. Jones [1980] it is shown how deleting the operations available for stacks dictates simplifications to the model based solely on this bias test. (One tantalizing example where the removal of bias might be interesting is the use of locations in the environments of denotational semantics.)

In some cases, bias can be eliminated by the use of data type invariants. But invariants play a larger part in discussing representations (cf. Binnode below).

4. REPRESENTATION

This section is concerned with showing that the behavior of one data type models the behavior of another. Normally, a representation (of an abstraction) is chosen because it is closer (than the abstraction) to the final implementation or because it can be manipulated efficiently. But the new representation is just a data type (cf. Bintree below) and is specified in the way described above. The problem of proofs about partial functions leads to a digression in this section.

The mappings (Mkd) can be represented by binary trees:

Bintree = [Binnode]

Binnode :: Bintree Key Data Bintree

where

invBinnode(mk-Binnode(lt, mk, md, rt)) $\triangleq$
 ($\forall$ lk $\in$ collkeys(lt) lk < mk) $\wedge$ ($\forall$ rk $\in$ collkeys(rt) . mk < rk)

Initial (Bintree) object: t_0 = **nil**

The set of objects satisfying the definition written with "::" is defined as:

Binnode = {mk−Binnode(lt, mk, md, rt)|
 lt, rt $\in$ Bintree $\wedge$ mk $\in$ Key $\wedge$ md $\in$ Data}

The use of the constructor function (mk-Binnode) as the parameter of the data type invariant (or below in cases) provides a way of naming the values of the sub-fields of a constructed object.

The definition of the function which collects the keys is:

collkeys: Bintree $\rightarrow$ **set of** Key

collkeys(t) $\triangleq$

cases t:

nil $\rightarrow$ { }

mk-Binnode(lt, mk, md, rt) $\rightarrow$ collkeys(lt) $\cup$ {mk} $\cup$ collkeys(rt)

From here on "Binnode" (and thus "Bintree") is taken to be the set of objects which satisfy the invariant: these are called the "valid" objects.

Notice that Bintree is biased with respect to the operations of Mkd: there are different ways of arranging the tree which, viewed as a mapping, are indistinguishable. Thus Bintree would not be used in the (abstract) specification; as a step of refinement, however, it is quite acceptable.

Following C. B. Jones [1979] it is now possible to build a "theory" of the Bintree data type. Firstly, two lemmas are stated without proof:

Lemma (collkeys1)

$\forall$ t $\in$ Bintree . collkeys(t) $\in$ **set of** Key

Lemma (collkeys2)

$\forall$ nd $\in$ Binnode .

(**let** mk-Binnode(lt, mk, md, rt) **in**

is-disj(collkeys(lt), {mk}) $\wedge$

is-disj(collkeys(lt), collkeys(rt)) $\wedge$

is-disj({mk}, collkeys(rt)) $\wedge$

($\forall$ k $\in$ collkeys(nd) .

(k<mk $\Rightarrow$ k $\in$ collkeys(lt)) $\wedge$ (mk<k $\Rightarrow$ k $\in$ collkeys(rt))))

The "collkeys1" lemma claims that the function is total; "collkeys2" defines some obvious results which are used in proofs below.

The next step in developing the Bintree theory is to define some functions; to locate a key in a tree:

findb(K: Key, T: Bintree) D: Data

pre k $\in$ collkeys(t)

findb(k, mk-Binnode(lt, mk, md, rt)) $\triangleq$

if k=mk **then** md

else if k<mk **then** findb(lt, k)

else findb(rt, k)

Notice that the pre-condition shows that the set of keys is non-empty and therefore the (recursive) definition of findb can be written assuming that the tree is not equal to **nil**.

* * *

This function is not total, the pre-condition shows an inter-relation between the arguments which cannot be expressed by limiting either set. (It would, of course, be possible to shift the problem by defining a subset of the cross product of the two sets via set comprehension.) Thus the lemma on the findb function is:

Lemma (findbl)

The function findb is total (w.r.t. its pre-condition) on valid Bintrees.

$$\forall k \in Key, t \in Bintree . k \in collkeys(t) \Rightarrow findb(k, t) \in Data$$

This logical expression manifests a problem which has to be faced by specification languages. Since findb is partial, the consequent of the implication can be undefined when the antecedent is false. Conventional ("two-valued") logic does not cope with this problem. Objections to this approach and an alternative solution are presented in Barringer, Cheng and Jones [1983]. The proof theory for that system is given in Appendix I. The system has a number of properties worth mentioning here:

(a) the and/or operators are commutative

(b) the "law of the excluded middle" does *not* hold

(c) the deduction theorem does not hold (without additional assumptions).

Perhaps the most important property of the system is what it *cannot* prove. It is not possible to show that:

$$x/0 = 1 \lor x/0 \neq 1$$

But it is possible to derive:

$$x = 0 \lor x/x = 1$$

which is equivalent to:

$$x/x = 1 \lor x = 0$$

Given that the proof system is deliberately weaker, it is not surprising that some proofs are more difficult than in normal logic. Thus in Gries [1981] a short proof is given of:

$$\frac{(E1 \lor E2) \land (E1 \lor E3)}{E1 \lor (E2 \land E3)}$$

by using the "law of the excluded middle." In the logic of partial functions the following natural deduction style proof is required:[1]

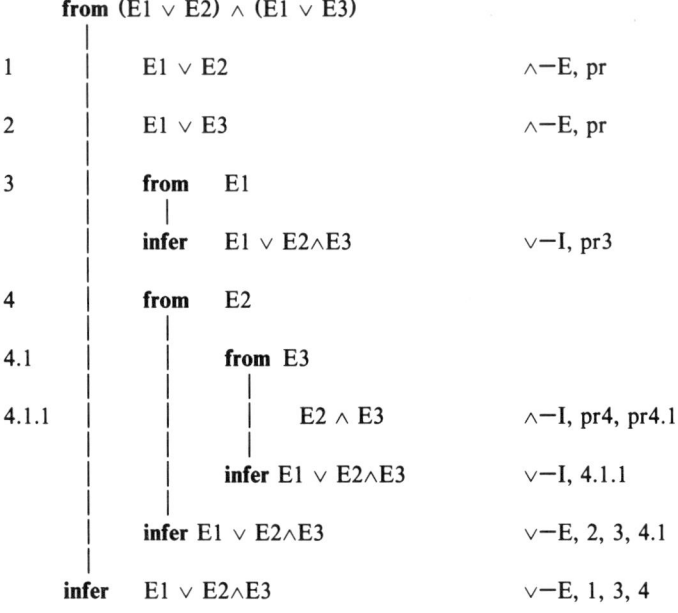

* * *

This same proof style can be used to prove lemma "findbl." The proof uses structural induction. The induction rule for Bintree can be stated:

$p(\text{nil})$,

$t = \text{mk-Binnode}(lt, mk, md, rt), \text{invBinnode}(t), p(lt), p(rt) \vdash p(t)$

$t \in \text{Bintree} \vdash p(t)$

The proof uses the abbreviation:

$p(k, t)$:

$k \notin \text{collkeys}(t) \vee \text{findb}(k, t) \in \text{Data}$

---

1. Definitions of the basic operators $\vee{-}I, \vee{-}E, \wedge{-}I$ and $\wedge{-}E$ are given below:

$\vee{-}I$ is defined as $\dfrac{Ei}{E1 \vee E2}$ $(1 \leqslant i \leqslant 2)$ $\wedge{-}I$ is defined as $\dfrac{E1, E2}{E1 \wedge E2}$

$\vee{-}E$ is defined as $\dfrac{E1 \vee E2, E1 \vdash E, E2 \vdash E}{E}$ $\wedge{-}E$ is defined as $\dfrac{E1 \wedge E2}{Ei}$ $(1 \leqslant i \leqslant 2)$

E, E1, E2 denote logical expressions.

SYSTEMATIC PROGRAM DEVELOPMENT

A formal proof is:

```
              from  t ∈ Bintree, k ∈ Key

1             |  k ∉ collkeys(nil)                              collkeys, set

2             |  p(k, nil)                                      ∨−I, 1, p

3             |  from  t = mk-Binnode(lt, mk, md, rt) ∧
              |        invBinnode(t) ∧ p(k, lt) ∧ p(k, rt)

3.1           |  |  k ∈ collkeys(t) ∨ k ∉ collkeys(t)           collkeysl, set

3.2           |  |  from  k ∉ collkeys(t)
              |  |  infer p(k, t)                               ∨−I, pr3.2, p

3.3           |  |  from  k ∈ collkeys(t)

3.3.1         |  |  |  k<mk ∨ k = mk ∨ mk<k                     collkeysl, pr3.3, Key

3.3.2         |  |  |  from  k = mk
3.3.2.1       |  |  |  |  findb(k, t) = md                      findb, pr3.3.2
              |  |  |  infer findb(k, t) ∈ Data

3.3.3         |  |  |  from  k<mk
3.3.3.1       |  |  |  |  k ∈ collkeys(lt)                      collkeys2, pr3.3, pr3.3.3
3.3.3.2       |  |  |  |  findb(k, lt) ∈ Data                   pr3, p, −1
3.3.3.3       |  |  |  |  findb(k, t) = findb(k, lt)            findb, pr3.3.3
              |  |  |  infer findb(k, t) ∈ Data                 −2, −1

3.3.4         |  |  |  from  mk<k
              |  |  |       − similar −
              |  |  |  infer findb(k, t) ∈ Data

3.3.5         |  |  |  findb(k, t) ∈ Data                       ∨−E, 3.3.1,
              |  |  |                                           3.3.2, 3.3.3, 3.3.4
              |  |  infer p(k, t)                               ∨−I, −1, p
              |  infer p(k, t)                                  ∨−E, 3.1, 3.2, 3.3
              infer k ∉ collkeys(t) ∨ findb(k, t) ∈ Data        indn, 2, 3, p
```

One of the nice features of such natural deduction proofs is that they can be used in a less-than-formal way by considering the outer levels of the proof.

Similar considerations arise with the function for inserting values into trees—the proof is more interesting because of the need to strengthen the statement of the lemma in order to obtain an induction hypothesis which carries through.

>insb(K: Key, D: Data, T: Bintree) R: Bintree
>
>**pre** $k \notin \text{collkeys}(t)$
>
>insb(k, d, t) $\triangleq$
>
>> **cases** t:
>>
>> **nil** $\longrightarrow$ mk-Binnode(**nil**, k, d, **nil**)
>>
>> mk-Binnode(lt, mk, md, rt) $\longrightarrow$
>>   **if** $k < mk$ **then** mk-Binnode(insb(k, d, lt), mk, md, rt)
>>
>>   **else** mk-Binnode(lt, mk, md, insb(k, d, rt))

Lemma (insbl)

The function insb is total (w.r.t. its pre-condition) on (valid) Bintrees; it preserves the invariant:

>$\forall\, t \in \text{Bintree}, k \in \text{Key}, d \in \text{Data}\;.$
>
>>$k \in \text{collkeys}(t) \lor \text{insb}(k, d, t) \in \text{Bintree}$

Proof by structural induction

>abbreviation p(k, t):
>
>>$k \in \text{collkeys}(t) \lor$
>>
>>>insb(k, d, t) $\in$ Bintree $\land$
>>>
>>>collkeys(insb(k, d, t)) = collkeys(t) $\cup$ \{k\}

SYSTEMATIC PROGRAM DEVELOPMENT

```
       from t ∈ Bintree, k ∈ Key, d ∈ Data

1          insb(k, d, nil) = mk-Binnode(nil, k, d, nil)            insb

2          invBinnode(insb(k, d, nil))                             1, inv

3          collkeys(insb(k, d, nil))    = {k}                      1, collkeys
4                                       = collkeys(nil) ∪ {k}      3, collkeys

5          p(k, nil)                                               ∧-I, 2, 4, ∨-I, p

6          from  t = mk-Binnode(lt, mk, md, rt) ∧
                 invBinnode(t) ∧ p(k, lt) ∧ p(k, rt)

6.1           k ∈ collkeys(t) ∨ k ∉ collkeys(t)                    collkeysl, set

6.2           from  k ∈ collkeys(t)

                 infer  p(k, t)                                    ∨-I, pr6.2, p

6.3           from  k ∉ collkeys(t)

6.3.1                collkeys(t) = collkeys(lt) ∪                  pr6, collkeys
                                   {mk} ∪ collkeys(rt)

6.3.2                k < mk ∨ mk < k                               -1, pr6.3, Key

6.3.3                from  k < mk

6.3.3.1                    k ∉ collkeys(lt)                        pr6.3, 6.3.1

6.3.3.2                    invBinnode(insb(k, d, lt))              -1, p, pr6

6.3.3.3                    collkeys(insb(k, d, lt))
                                = collkeys(lt) ∪ {k}               -2, p, pr6

6.3.3.4                    insb(k, d, t) = mk-Binnode(insb
                              (k, d, lt), mk, md, rt)              insb, pr6.3.3

                        infer  p(k, t)                             ∧-I, -1, -2, ∨-I, p

6.3.4                from  mk < k

                           — similar —

                        infer  p(k, t)

                  infer  p(k, t)                                   ∨-E, 6.3.2, 6.3.3, 6.3.4

              infer  p(k, t)                                       ∨-E, 6.1, 6.2, 6.3

       infer p(k, t)                                               indn, 5, 6
```

The function delb is harder to write but it and its proof could be tackled by enthusiastic readers.

* * *

With this theory of Bintrees, the actual proofs relating to refinement are all trivial. The task is to show that a series of operations on Bintree "model" those on the abstract mapping (Mkd) data type. The key to these proofs is to relate the underlying objects by a function which retrieves the abstraction from the representation. In this case:

    retrm: Bintree $\rightarrow$ Mkd

    retrm(t) $\triangleq$ **cases** t:

        nil $\rightarrow$ [ ]

        mk-Binnode(lt, mk, md, rt) $\rightarrow$

            merge([k $\mapsto$ d], retrm(lt), retrm(rt))

The reason for the choice of direction of this function is precisely because the increase in bias results in many representatives corresponding to one abstraction.

One requirement on retrieve functions is that they be total (on valid representations). This follows here since the invariant guarantees that the domains of the mappings to be merged are disjoint. Another property required of the representation and its retrieve function is that the representation be "adequate":

    $\forall$ m $\in$ Mkd . $\exists$ t $\in$ Bintree . retrm(t) = m

Intuitively, this requires that there must be at least one representation for each abstract state. A proof can be performed by induction on the domain of the mapping—since only existence is required, a completely imbalanced tree can be generated.

Also note:

    $\forall$ t $\in$ Bintree . **dom**(retrm(t)) = collkeys(t)

This ensures that the domains of the following functions are "large enough."

The relation can now be seen to preserve:

    retrm(t_0) = m_0

        $\forall$ t $\in$ Bintree, k $\in$ Key, d $\in$ Data.
           k $\notin$ collkeys(t) $\Rightarrow$

$$\text{retrm}(\text{insb}(k, d, t)) = \text{retrm}(t) \cup [k \mapsto d]$$

$\forall\, t \in \text{Bintree},\, k \in \text{Key}.$
$\quad k \in \text{collkeys}(t) \Rightarrow \text{findb}(k, t) = (\text{retrm}(t))(k)$

The INSERT operation on Bintrees can be defined:

INSERTB(K: Key, D: Data)

ext wr T: Bintree

pre $k \notin \text{collkeys}(t)$

post $t = \text{insb}(k, d, \overleftarrow{t})$

The general form of the rule to show that operations "preserve invariants" (valid results exist) is:

$$\forall\, \overleftarrow{\sigma} \in \Sigma\,.\, \text{preOP}(\overleftarrow{\sigma}) \Rightarrow \exists\, \sigma \in \Sigma\,.\, \text{postOP}(\overleftarrow{\sigma}, \sigma)$$

In this case, the result follows from lemma "insbl."

There are two rules which show that an operation on a representation models one on an abstraction. The domain rule ensures that the pre-condition is not too restrictive:

$$\forall\, t \in \text{Bintree}\,.\, \text{preOP}(\text{retrm}(t)) \Rightarrow \text{preOPB}(t)$$

The range rule ensures that no contradictory results can arise:

$$\forall\, \overleftarrow{t},\, t \in \text{Bintree}\,.\, \text{preOP}(\text{retrm}(t)) \wedge \text{postOPB}(\overleftarrow{t}, t) \Rightarrow$$

$$\text{postOP}(\text{retrm}(\overleftarrow{t}\,), \text{retrm}(t))$$

Here, both results are immediate consequences of the theory above. Indeed, the form of the rules might appear unnecessarily general. It is worth remembering that both operations can be non-deterministic and that the operation on the representation should be allowed to have a larger-than-required pre-condition. To illustrate the former point, notice that the post-condition of INSERTB could be:

post $\text{retrm}(t) = \text{retrm}(\overleftarrow{t}\,) \cup [k \mapsto d]$

This is highly non-deterministic and could, for example, cover tree balancing.

For the model of the FIND operation, one might use:

FINDB(K: Key) D: Data

ext rd T: Bintree

pre k ∈ collkeys(t)

post d = findb(k, $\overleftarrow{t}$)

Here the invariant is preserved since there is no state change and, for the same reason, the modeling proofs are simpler.

* * *

In order to illustrate the way in which design steps can be isolated by the proofs, a sketch is given of a second step of data refinement. The trees used above cannot be constructed directly in a language like Pascal. Instead each node must be created as a record on the heap and nested trees must be represented by pointers. Thus:

Heap = **map** Ptr **to** Binnoderep

Root = [Ptr]

Binnoderep:: LP: [Ptr]

             MK: Key

             MD: Data

             RP: [Ptr]

Without formalizing the statement, it is clear that the mapping should be well-founded and that all used keys should be in the domain of the map.

The remainder of the refinement step can be seen from:

collkeysh: Root × Heap ⟶ **set of** Key

collkeysh(p, m) ≜

    if p = **nil then** { }

    else(**let** mk-Binnoderep(lp, mk, md, rp) = m(p) **in**

        collkeysh(lp, m) ∪ {mk} ∪ collkeysh(rp, m))

findbhn: Key × Ptr × Heap ⟶ Binnoderep

pre k ∈ collkeysh(p, m)

findbhn(k, p, m) ≜

    let mk-Binnoderep(lp, mk, md, rp) = m(p) **in**

    if k = mk **then** m(p)

    else if k < mk **then** findbhn(k, lp, m)

    else findbhn(k, rp, m)

FINDBH(K: Key) D: Data

ext rd RT: Root
    rd HP: Heap

pre k ∈ collkeysh(rt, hp)

post d = MD(findbhn(k, $\overleftarrow{rt}$, $\overleftarrow{hp}$))

The point about isolation of development steps can now be made in two directions. The argument that the Heap representation is valid with respect to the Bintree does not rely on the earlier argument that Bintree is a valid representation for the map Mkd. Furthermore, the development, in the next section, of code to match the specifications on Heap is insulated from understanding Bintree.

5. DECOMPOSITION

A specification of a system should be abstract both in the data types it uses and in the fact that post-conditions make it possible to define (non-constructively) what result is required. The preceding section shows how the data can be refined to the point where it can be represented in the programming language. However, the post-conditions must eventually be realized by (i.e. decomposed into) sequences of statements. This section shows how such decomposition can be supported by correctness arguments.

This area is, of course, widely discussed in the literature and textbooks like Gries [1981] tend to focus on this topic. (Even C. B. Jones [1980] makes the mistake of covering it before data refinement.) But here again, VDM falls into heresy: the well-known Hoare-logic (cf. [Apt 1981]) cannot be used because of VDM's reliance on relational post-conditions. Aczel [1982] writes:

"For example, the program

    while $(y + 1)^2 \leq x$ **do** $y := y + 1$

meets the specification having precondition y = 0 & x ⩾ 0 and postcondition $y^2 \leq x < (y + 1)^2$.

It is a familiar fact that this specification does not explicitly express all that we have in mind. For example if the above program is prefixed by x := 0; the resulting program will still formally meet the specification, although the implicit understanding that x is supposed to remain fixed has been violated. One natural convention is to make this understanding explicit by using special symbols for variables that are to remain fixed throughout a computation. But a more flexible and powerful approach ... is to allow the postcondition of a specification to depend on the starting state of a computation. So, in our example the postcondition should be

$$(y^2 \leq x < (y + 1)^2) \ \& \ (x = \overleftarrow{x})$$

where we use $\overleftarrow{x}$ to denote the value of x at the start of the computation. In his book, Cliff Jones presents some rules for proving the total correctness of programs for his notion of specification. His rules appear elaborate and immemorable compared with the original rules for partial correctness of Hoare. Moreover, they are not complete."

In short, C. B. Jones [1980] had the right idea but used awful notation! Fortunately Peter Aczel suggested a far better way to present the proof rules.

The most important of the proof rules is that for the repetitive construct. Peter Aczel's presentation of this rule is:

$$\frac{\{P \wedge B\} \ S \ \{P \wedge R\}}{\{P\} \ \textbf{while} \ B \ \textbf{do} \ S\{P \wedge R^r \wedge \sim B\}}$$

If all mention of R is suppressed, this is identical to the Hoare rule. However, R is very important—it is a relational (i.e. two state) predicate which captures input/output behavior. If R is transitive and well-founded, and R^r is its reflexive closure, then this rule captures total correctness for relational post-conditions. It is interesting to contrast the use of R with the "variant" in Dijkstra [1976]: it can be seen that here, as well as providing a termination proof, R is used in the correctness argument.

These proof rules are used on a number of examples in C. B. Jones [1983a]; again, an important property is that a proof at one stage provides specifications which completely isolate the justification of the next stage. (It is, in fact, the imbedding of specified operations within a program construct which requires that the rules are capable of handling non-determinism. In C. B. Jones [1981] proof rules are justified with respect to a relational denotational semantics; two semantic functions are given—one for the relational meaning and one for the termination set; a satisfaction (*sat*) ordering is defined between such semantic objects; the principal programming language constructs are shown to be monotone in the *sat* ordering.)

Here, the rules are used to justify annotated programs. This goes back to the style in King [1971] but shows how to incorporate relational post-conditions. Furthermore, a style has been adopted which emphasizes the link

SYSTEMATIC PROGRAM DEVELOPMENT   105

to the natural deduction proofs shown above.

For the task of multiplying two numbers (using successive addition), the top-level development might be:

```
ext I, J, M, : Z
pre true
 |  pre true
 |   |  if I < 0 then
 |   |
 |   |
 |   |       post i ⩾ 0 ∧ i ∗ j = ⃖i ∗ ⃖j
 |  post i ⩾ 0 ∧ i ∗ j = ⃖i ∗ ⃖j
 |  ;
 |  pre i ⩾ 0
 |      — see below —
 |  post m = ⃖i ∗ ⃖j
post m = ⃖i ∗ ⃖j
```

This could be formally justified using the conditional and composition rules.

The actual multiplication step can be achieved by:

```
ext wr I, J, M: Z
pre i ⩾ 0
 |  M := 0
 |  ;
 |  pre i ⩾ 0
 |   |  while I ≠ 0 do
 |   |  inv i ⩾ 0
 |   |  rel m + i ∗ j = ⃖m + ⃖i ∗ ⃖j ∧ i < ⃖i
 |   |   |  ext wr I, J: Z
 |   |   |  pre i ≠ 0
 |   |   |   |  while is-even(I) do
 |   |   |   |  inv i ⩾ 1
 |   |   |   |  rel i ∗ j = ⃖i ∗ ⃖j ∧ i < ⃖i
 |   |   |   |   |  I, J := I / 2, J ∗ 2
 |   |   |  post i ∗ j = ⃖i ∗ ⃖j ∧ i ⩽ ⃖i
 |   |   |  ;
 |   |   |  M, I := M + J, I − 1
 |  post m = ⃖m + ⃖i ∗ ⃖j
post m = ⃖i ∗ ⃖j
```

This could be formally justified by (two applications of) the while rule. Notice how the inner specification (preserving m + i ∗ j) naturally introduces non-determinism in a deterministic program: this inner specification can be realized by the final multiple assignment yielding a linear algorithm; the same specification is satisfied by the $\log_2 i$ algorithm.

Clearly this presentation says little about discovering invariants (cf. Gries [1981])—indeed, it would appear that there is more work to be done since both **inv** and **rel** must be found. Experience so far suggests that there are natural ways of seeking the required predicates but this is not the place to pursue this topic.

As an illustration of a more interesting problem, consider the task (suggested by Tony Hoare) of describing how a hand calculator performs division of I by J—result in Q leaving remainder I. In a first stage (SL) J is shifted left until it is larger than I—the number of shifts is counted in N. The second stage (SR) shifts J back and at each step keeps the expression J•Q+I constant. There are two places this must be done: shifting at SRS and re-establishing i < j by stepping down I at SRC. The following presentation is made simpler by assuming that all variables are natural numbers.

```
pre j ≠ 0
 | pre   j ≠ 0                           {SL}
 | ext   I: rd, J, Q, N: wr
 | |     Q := 0; N := 0;
 | |     while J ≤ I do
 | |     inv
 | |     rel j • 10ⁿ = ⃖j • 10ⁿ
 | |       | J, N := J • 10, N + 1
 | post  j = ⃖j • 10ⁿ ∧ i < j ∧ q = 0
 | ;
 | pre   10ⁿ div j ∧ i < j               {SR}
 | |     while N ≠ 0 do
 | |     inv 10ⁿ div j ∧ i < j
 | |     rel j / 10ⁿ = ⃖j / 10ⁿ ∧ j • q + i = ⃖j • ⃖q + ⃖i ∧ n < ⃖n
 | |       | N, J, Q := N − 1, J / 10, Q • 10;   {SRS}
 | |       while J ≤ I do                        {SRC}
 | |         ext J: rd I, Q: wr
 | |         inv                                 (0 ≤ i)
 | |         rel j • q + i = ⃖j • ⃖q + ⃖i ∧ i < ⃖i
 | |           | I, Q := I − J, Q + 1
 | post  j = ⃖j / 10ⁿ ∧ j • q + i = ⃖j • ⃖q + ⃖i ∧ i < j
post ⃖j • q + i = ⃖i ∧ i < ⃖j
```

As a final example of a decomposition proof, the binary tree problem is picked up from the preceding section. The Pascal equivalents of the data objects are:

```
type Ptr = ↑ Binnoderep
Binnoderep = record
                LP: Ptr
                MK: Key
                MD: Data
                RP: Ptr
             end
ROOT: Ptr
```

The FINDB function can now be coded as follows:

```
function FINDBH(K: Key) Data
{ext rd RT: Ptr
     rd HP: Heap}
{pre k ∈ collkeysh(rt)}
var P: Ptr;
begin
    P := RT
    ;
    {pre k ∈ collkeysh(p)}
        while K ≠ P ↑ MK do
            {inv k ∈ collkeysh(p)}
            {rel findhn(k, p) = findbhn(k, p⃖) ∧
                 depth(p) < depth(p⃖)      }
            with P ↑ do
                if MK < K then P := LP
                else P := RP;
    {post p = findbhn(k, p⃖)}
    ;
    FINDBH := P ↑ MD
    {post d = MD{findbhn(k, rt⃖))}
end
```

6. CONCLUSIONS

The material in C. B. Jones [1980] and Bjorner and Jones [1982] focuses on different parts of VDM; this paper brings in ideas like the logic of partial functions which are not mentioned in either book; perhaps the time has come to answer the question "What is VDM?" The only reasonable answer would appear to be that it is a specification technique which is formal enough to support implementation justification. This is very broad. One important characteristic of VDM is that the choice of techniques is motivated by computing science and not (just) mathematical elegance. In some cases (the proof rules in the appendix) the story has a happy ending in that elegance is married to utility.

* * *

There are a number of topics which need further research. New proof rules (e.g. for recursive procedures) must be developed in the relational post-condition style. The proofs here have all assumed that parameters are passed by value; the obvious (recursive) procedure for INSERTBH needs to share a variable parameter with part of the tree. Proof rules for more powerful parameter passing will require care (cf. Reynolds [1973]). The specification of exception conditions is a topic which has received some attention (e.g. Bron, Fokkinga and Haas [1976]; Cristian [1984]; Cottam [1984]) — one of the difficulties is to remain relatively language independent. The **exit** mechanism of the VDM metalanguage might be a suitable procedural construct.

The need, in a development method, for the isolation property in a development method is referred to above. To achieve this for parallel, interfering, processes is difficult — some first steps are described in C. B. Jones [1983a, 1983b]; similar ideas are being pursued in a temporal logic setting by Howard Barringer and Ruurd Kuiper.

In the area of data types, model oriented specifications need a proper basis for parameterized data types and their refinement.

ACKNOWLEDGMENTS

My debt to Peter Aczel should be clear from the preceding discussion. The binary tree example was first developed by Elizabeth Fielding. The work here is supported by SERC research grants and has benefited from discussions at meetings of IFIP WG 2.3. My thanks are due to Julie Hibbs for coping with another of my bizarre manuscripts.

APPENDIX I
Logic Proof Rules

[*Appendix deleted*]

APPENDIX II
Rules for Data Types

[*Appendix deleted*]

APPENDIX III
Rules for Sequential Programs

[*Appendix deleted*]

WOLFRAM BARTUSSEK and **DAVID L. PARNAS**
University of North Carolina at Chapel Hill

Using Assertions About Traces to Write Abstract Specifications for Software Modules

1. INTRODUCTION

The Role of Specifications in Software Design

We are concerned with the building of software products that are so large that we cannot manage the task unless we reduce it to a series of small tasks. We further assume that each of the subtasks (which we call modules) will focus on one portion of the design and hide the details of that aspect of the design from the rest of the system. This has become known as the "information hiding principle", encapsulation, data abstraction, etc. [Parnas 1971a; Parnas 1972b; Parnas, Shore and Weiss 1976]. The design process will only go smoothly if the intermodule interfaces are precisely defined. Ideally, the interface description states only the requirements that the component must satisfy and does not suggest any other restrictions on the implementation. We term such a description of the requirements a *specification* [Parnas 1977]. We also note that any software product is but a module in a still larger system; its requirements should be specified as precisely as each of its components.

For a trouble-free development process it is also necessary that one be able to verify the reasonableness of decisions before proceeding to make further decisions. If we reverse one of our decisions later (or find that it was inadequately described), we may have to discard all work done subsequent to that decision. If we have written a formal specification for a module, we should be able to verify that the specification has such basic properties as consistency and completeness. These aspects will be discussed later in this paper.

What Are Specifications?

A fair amount of confusion has been caused by the fact that the word "specification" is used with two distinct meanings in the computer literature. The dictionary definitions of the word "specification" cover any communication which provides additional information about the object being described—any communication that makes the description of the object more specific. In engineering usage, the word has a narrower meaning. A specification is a precise statement of the requirements that a product must satisfy. A description of the number of ones in the binary representation of a

111

computer program is a specification in the general sense but it is rarely a specification in the engineering "specification".

Brief History of Work on Specifications

We distinguish two classes of specifications for software, which we shall denote as P/P (Precondition-Postcondition) and DA (Data Abstract). P/P specification techniques are based on the pioneering work of Floyd [1967] and subsequent work by Hoare [1969], Dijkstra [1975], and others. P/P techniques describe the effect of a program in terms of predicates that describe acceptable states of data structures. The *Precondition* is a predicate that describes the states in which the program may be started. The *Postcondition* describes the states after program termination. Dijkstra's predicate transformers replace both of these predicates by a rule for transforming a postcondition into a precondition [Dijkstra 1975, 1976]. P/P specifications describe the change of state that the program must effect, but not how to effect it. Usually, the effect of each individual program is described separately and in terms of the data structure accessed by the program.

In DA specifications the specification of a module does *not* refer to the data structure used within a module. That data structure is not part of the requirement; it is part of the solution. It does not belong in a statement of requirements because it depends on implementation decisions. Early work on specifications that "hide" implementation data structures was done by Parnas [1972a]; more recent work by Guttag [1975, 1977] put a sounder mathematical basis behind the work and suggested some notational improvements.

The DA specification work is motivated by a desire to give a "black-box" description of a software module. The user is told only of a set of programs that access the data structure within the module. Some of these (here termed *V-functions*) return values that give information about parts of the data structure. Others (here termed *O-functions*) change the internal data. In most cases, the execution of an O-function will *eventually* cause a change in the value of a V-function. The effects of the calls of the O-function may not be visible in terms of V-function values until some other O-functions have been executed.

Parnas's early work was done on an *ad hoc* basis. The notation was developed to meet the needs of specific examples [Parnas 1972a]. The early examples had the property that the effects of O-functions were immediately visible and could be described in terms of the new values of the V-functions. Only in later examples did [Parnas and Handzel 1975] seek to extend these techniques to cases where there were delayed effects.

The problem of delayed effects led Price and Parnas [Price 1973; Parnas and Price 1973, 1974] to include "hidden" functions in their specifications. "" functions are not available outside the black box. They need emented; their purpose is purely descriptive. The effects of O-functions are described in terms of the values of the hidden functions. These hidden functions are still in use at SRI [Roubine and Robinson 1977] and elsewhere.

In spite of all disclaimers, the hidden functions do suggest data structures and possible implementations of the program. Liskov and Berzins [1979] and others have suggested writing specifications simply by giving possible implementations—i.e., by giving a program whose behavior would be acceptable and asking that the programs produced be "equivalent."

The equivalent program approach and the hidden functions disturb us. They violate the basic motivation for DA specifications by providing information that is not a requirement. Some of the properties of a hypothetical implementation may not be required of the actual program. "One must be very careful not to read too much into such specifications" [Liskov and Berzins 1979].

Guttag's method does not rely on hidden functions to describe delayed effects. His papers [Guttag 1975, 1977] describe a systematic way of writing the specification. However, there were cases that he could not handle without the introduction of hidden functions. One of those examples, the stack with overflow, will be used later in this paper [Guttag 1977].

In this paper, we propose yet another approach. It allows the specification of modules with delayed or hidden effects without any reference to internal data structures. The only statements made are about the effects of calls on user accessible O-functions or user accessible V-functions.

When Is a D/A Specification Complete?

For simplicity, we assume that our modules are always created in the same initial state and could be returned to that state (reinitialized). We further assume that for each access program (O-function or V-function) there is an *applicability condition*. If this condition holds, the program may be called. In states where the condition does not hold, the module will "trap" or refuse to return through the normal exit [Parnas and Wuerges 1976]. Values of V-functions after a trap occurs will not be discussed in this paper.

A *trace* of a module is a description of a sequence of calls on the functions starting with the module in the initial state. A trace is termed a *legal trace* if calling the functions in the sequence specified in the trace with the arguments given in the trace when the module is in its initial state will not result in a trap. A specification *completely determines the externally visible behavior of a module* if for every legal trace ending with a call of a V-function, the value returned by that V-function can be derived from the specification. We term such a specification *complete*. A specification is *consistent* if only one value can be derived.

There are situations in which one may want a specification that is *not* complete in the above sense. In this paper, however, we will concern ourselves with the problem of recognizing complete and consistent specifications.

2. A FORMAL NOTATION FOR SPECIFICATION BASED ON TRACES

A specification will consist of two main parts. The first part, which we call *syntax*, gives the names of all of the access programs, and the type of each of the parameters. For O-functions we will indicate that it changes an object of the type being specified. For V-functions we will give the type of value that it delivers. This information is necessary for recognizing whether a program using the functions could be compiled by a typical compiler. The notation used is that used by Guttag [1975, 1977].

The second part of the specification will be called the *semantics*. It consists of three types of assertions.

1. **Assertions about trace legality.** These assertions identify a subset of the set of legal traces, that is a set of traces such that calling the functions as described in the trace (starting with a module in its initial state) will not result in traps. Additional legal traces may be implied by the equivalence assertions (see below). Any traces that cannot be shown to be legal using these assertions will be considered illegal traces.

2. **Assertions about the equivalence of traces.** These assertions specify an equivalence relation on traces, such that (1) equivalent traces have the same legality (either both are legal or both are not legal) and (2) that they have the same externally visible effect on the module or data item. These assertions of equivalence often enable us to extend the class of traces known to be legal. Equivalence is usually weaker than equality. Two traces are *equal* if they are identical in every respect (the same sequence of function calls with the same parameters).

3. **Assertions about the values returned by V-functions at the end of traces.** These statements describe the values delivered by V-functions for a subset of the set of legal traces. The traces discussed directly in this section of a specification are called *normal form* traces. Using the equivalence statements, one can derive the values of V-functions at the end of other traces by finding an equivalent normal form trace.

Remarks: In our examples, we have assumed that equality is defined for values of the types returned by the V-functions. In the unlikely event that we have no equality operator, V-function values would have to be described in terms of the operators that are available.

Since assertions about values of V-functions are made only using normal form traces, assertions about equivalence of traces will also

USING TRACES TO WRITE ABSTRACT SPECIFICATIONS

be used to show that any legal trace can be transformed to a normal form trace.

The three classes of assertions together with the syntax definition form a specification or statement of requirements. An implementation will be considered correct if and only if the assertions are true of it. Any property that one can deduce from the assertions must be a property of any correct implementation.

A program that uses the module in such a way that the program's correctness depends *only* on properties of the module that can be deduced from the specification's assertions will be able to use any correct implementation of the module.

Notation

(1) *Notation for describing the syntax* (taken from Guttag)

<Function Name>: <type of parameter> × ... × <type of parameter> ⟶ <type of result>

(2) *Notation for describing traces*

A trace will be represented as a string from the language described by the following syntax. The parsing of a trace into component subtraces is deliberately ambiguous. The trace denotes execution of the functions named in a left-to-right sequence.

<subtrace> ::= ∅ | <syntactically correct function call> | <subtrace>.<syntactically correct function call>

<trace> ::= ∅ | <subtrace>[.<subtrace>]*

[<T>]* denotes any number of occurrences of <T>.

"∅" denotes an empty trace. *Note that the symbol "∅" never occurs in a trace.*

We will sometimes use the following shorthand notation.

Let p_i, $m \leqslant i \leqslant n$, be a list of actual parameters and $X(p_i)$ a syntactically correct function call. Then $X_M^N(p_i)$ denotes the same as

$$X(p_M).X(p_{M+1}) \cdot \ldots \cdot X(p_{N-1}).X(p_N)$$

If the list of parameters is empty, then X_M^N is simply X.X. ... .X with n−m+1 repetitions of X. If M>N, then X_M^N denotes the empty trace. For N ⩾ 1 we write $X_1^N(p_i)$ as $X^N(p_i)$.

It is always assumed that a function call correctly adheres to the rules of the syntax section.

(3) *Describing legality of sequences*

We introduce the predicate $\lambda(T)$ where T is a trace. $\lambda(T)$ is true if T is a legal trace. The appearance of the assertion $\lambda(T)$ in a specification is a requirement that calling the functions as described in T will not result in a trap.

Assuming that the module will not "trap" if it is not used, we *always* assume $\lambda(\emptyset) = true$. (The empty trace is always legal.) It follows from our discussion of traces that if T is a trace and S is a subtrace, then

$$\lambda(T.S) \Rightarrow \lambda(T) .$$

In other words, the prefix of any legal trace is a legal trace.

(4) *Describing the values of V-functions at the end of traces*

If T is a legal trace, X is a syntactically correct call on a V-function, and $\lambda(T.X)$ is TRUE, then $V(T.X)$ describes the value delivered by X when called after an execution of T.

(5) *Describing equivalence of two traces*

If T_1 and T_2 are traces then $T_1 \equiv T_2$ is an assertion that:

for any subtrace S (including the empty subtrace), $\lambda(T_1.S) = \lambda(T_2.S)$,

and

for any subtrace S (including the empty subtrace) and V-function X,

$$\lambda(T_1.S.X) \Rightarrow V(T_1.S.X) = V(T_2.S.X)$$

Then "$\equiv$" is an equivalence relation. Note that the equivalence of two traces does not imply that they are the same in every respect, only in those respects specified above. For example, one may *not* conclude that two equivalent traces have the same length or that the prefixes of equivalent traces are equivalent. Note too that the above does not define a particular equivalence relation; that is done in each specification.

In the following specifications we have omitted universal quantifiers for variables representing traces (T) and values of specific types.

3. SOME SIMPLE EXAMPLES (to be explained and discussed in the next section)

Example 1. **A Stack for Integer Values**

Syntax:

PUSH: <integer> × <stack> ⟶ <stack>

POP: <stack> ⟶ <stack>

TOP: <stack> ⟶ <integer>

DEPTH: <stack> ⟶ <integer>

Legality:

(1) $\lambda(T) \Rightarrow \lambda(T.PUSH(a))$

(2) $\lambda(T.TOP) = \lambda(T.POP)$

Equivalences:

(3) $T.DEPTH \equiv T$

(4) $T.PUSH(a).POP \equiv T$

(5) $\lambda(T.TOP) \Rightarrow T.TOP \equiv T$

Values:

(6) $\lambda(T) \Rightarrow V(T.PUSH(a).TOP) = a$

(7) $\lambda(T) \Rightarrow V(T.PUSH(a).DEPTH) = 1 + V(T.DEPTH)$

(8) $V(DEPTH) = 0$

Example 2. **An Integer Queue**

Syntax:

ADD: <integer> × <queue> ⟶ <queue>

REMOVE: <queue> ⟶ <queue>

FRONT: <queue> ⟶ <integer>

Legality:

(1) $\lambda(T) \Rightarrow \lambda(T.ADD(a))$

(2) $\lambda(T) \Rightarrow \lambda(T.ADD(a).REMOVE)$

(3) $\lambda(T.REMOVE)) = \lambda (T.FRONT)$

Equivalences: *allow other traces; the seq. ADD.REMOVE may either be replaced by REMOVE.ADD or (at the start of a trace) deleted, resulting in a trace equivalent to the original one.*

(4) $\lambda(T.FRONT) \Rightarrow T.FRONT \equiv T$

(5) $\lambda(T.REMOVE) \Rightarrow T.ADD(a).REMOVE \equiv T.REMOVE.ADD(a)$

(6) $ADD(a).REMOVE \equiv \emptyset$

Values:

(7) $V(ADD(a).FRONT) = a$

(8) $\lambda(T.FRONT) \Rightarrow V(T.ADD(a).FRONT) = V(T.FRONT)$

The above specification assumes that only one queue exists and omits the queue parameter in the calls on the access programs.

Example 3. **Sorting Queue = (SQUEUE)**

Syntax:

INSERT: <integer> × <squeue> ⟶ <squeue>

REMOVE: <squeue> ⟶ <squeue>

FRONT: <squeue> ⟶ <integer>

Legality:

(1) $\lambda(T) \Rightarrow \lambda(T.INSERT(a))$

(2) $\lambda(T) \Rightarrow \lambda(T.INSERT(a).REMOVE)$

(3) $\lambda(T.FRONT)) = \lambda (T.REMOVE)$

Equivalences:

(4) $\lambda(T.FRONT) \Rightarrow T.FRONT \equiv T$

(5) $T.INSERT(a).INSERT(b) \equiv T.INSERT(b).INSERT(a)$

(6) $INSERT(a).REMOVE \equiv \emptyset$

(7) $\lambda(T.FRONT)$ **cand** $(V(T.FRONT) \leq b) \Rightarrow$
$T.INSERT(b).REMOVE \equiv T$

Values:

(8) V(INSERT(a).FRONT) = a

(9) λ(T.FRONT) **cand** V(T.FRONT) $\leqslant$ b $\Rightarrow$
V(T.INSERT(b).FRONT) = b

Note the value of X **cand** Y is *false* if X is *false*, and the value of X **cand** Y is the value of Y if X is *true*. Y need not have a defined value if X is *false*.

Example 4. Stack that Overflows (Stac)

Syntax:

PUSH: <stac> × <integer> ⟶ <stac>

POP: <stac> ⟶ <stac>

VAL: <stac> ⟶ <integer>

Legality:

For all T, λ (T)

Equivalences:

$0 < N \leqslant 124 \Rightarrow \text{PUSH}^N(a_i).\text{POP} \equiv \text{PUSH}^{N-1}(a_i)$

$\text{PUSH}(a_0).\text{PUSH}_1^{124}(a_i) \equiv \text{PUSH}_1^{124}(a_i)$

T.VAL $\equiv$ T

$N \geqslant 0 \Rightarrow \text{POP}^N.\text{PUSH}(a) \equiv \text{PUSH}(a)$

Values:

V(T.PUSH(a).VAL) = a **mod** 255

Example 5. Alternative Formal Specifications (Guttag Type) for STAC

This alternative includes two "hidden functions," which are marked in the syntactic specifications with asterisk.

Type:

stac

Syntactic Specification:

NEWSTAC: ⟶ <stac>

PUSH(s, I): <stac> × <integer> → <stac>

POP(s): <stac> → <stac>

VAL(s): <stac> → <integer>

SPSLFT(s): <stac> → <integer>

*ADD(s, I): <stac> × <integer> → <stac>

*DEQ(s): <stac> → <stac>

Semantic Specification:

SPSLFT(NEWSTAC) = 124

SPSLFT(ADD(s, I)) = SPSLFT(s) − 1

POP(NEWSTAC) = NEWSTAC

POP(ADD(s, I)) = s

DEQ(NEWSTAC) = NEWSTAC

DEQ(ADD(s, I)) = **if** SPSLFT(s) = 124
         then s
         else ADD(DEQ(s), I)

PUSH(s, I) = **if** SPSLFT(s) > 0
         then ADD(s, I)
         else ADD(DEQ(s), I)

VAL(NEWSTAC) = undefined

VAL(ADD(s, I)) = I **mod** 255

where * denotes a hidden function

4. DISCUSSION OF THE SIMPLE EXAMPLES

Example 1 is the classic example for abstract specifications. It is a stack with unlimited capacity. The legality section shows that any sequence of PUSH operations is a legal trace. The first statement in the value section shows the value of TOP after any trace that ends with a PUSH. (7) shows that PUSH always increments the value of DEPTH. (8) specifies the initial value of DEPTH to be zero. The equivalence section allows us to reduce any legal trace with PUSH, TOP, and POP to one that is equivalent but contains only PUSH operations. We will be able to determine the value of the V-functions for any legal trace by making such reductions.

In Example 2 (an integer queue) the "legality" section allows traces that consist of any number of ADDs but each occurrence of REMOVE or FRONT must be preceded directly by an ADD. However, the equivalence statements allow other traces because the sequence ADD.REMOVE may either be replaced by REMOVE.ADD or (at the start of a trace) deleted, resulting in a trace equivalent to the original one. The value section shows

USING TRACES TO WRITE ABSTRACT SPECIFICATIONS

the value of FRONT after (a) an item is added to an empty queue and (b) an item is added to the queue that already has a value of FRONT (same as before). To find the value of FRONT after a trace that has REMOVEs in it, one must apply (5) and (6) repeatedly until one has an equivalent trace that does not contain a REMOVE. Each application of (5) can move a REMOVE to the left one place. When REMOVE follows the first ADD directly, both can be deleted using (6).

In Example 3 we have a queue that always shows the largest item at the front. The largest object is also the one removed by REMOVE. The legal traces are the same as those in Example 2 (except for an obvious change of function names). The most important difference is (5) in which it is asserted that the order of two consecutive inserts is irrelevant. Assertion (7) shows the effect of a REMOVE after an INSERT that had a parameter larger than the value at the front of the SQUEUE. In that case it simply cancels the effect of the INSERT. However, because of (5), we can always rearrange the order of INSERTs so that the last one is the one that inserts the largest value. This allows us to use (7) for any REMOVE at the end of a trace with at least two inserts in it. (6) describes the effect of REMOVE in the case that it is preceded by only one INSERT. The value section shows us the value of FRONT after an INSERT in an empty queue and after inserting a value that is greater than the value of FRONT.

The discussion of the first three examples is intended to show that the formal specifications do correspond to our intuitive notions of the way that these modules perform. The correspondence with intuition must, of necessity, remain informal. The demonstration of completeness can be performed systematically. This will be discussed later on.

The fourth example is the problem that John Guttag could not specify without the use of hidden functions [Guttag 1976] (which follows from restrictions of the mathematical model underlying his technique). His specification is included as Example 5. We believe that the brevity of our specification shows the advantages of the trace method. This is a situation in which the values of V-functions for some legal traces are deliberately not defined. Any syntactically correct trace is legal. The module will never "trap." However the value of VAL initially (or after a POP on an "empty stack") is not defined. The implementation can deliver any value in these situations without violating the specifications. If a value, I, greater than 255, is inserted only I mod 255 will be stored.

The above examples show a number of advantages over previous methods of DA specifications. There appears to be no need for hidden functions; the specifications are quite compact and the individual statements are simple. The derivations needed to demonstrate completeness are sometimes quite involved but they need not be performed during the implementation or during the verification that an implementation is correct.

The ideas are rather new and we are aware of a number of important unanswered questions. Nonetheless, we believe that this report demonstrates that the method is as good as any of the previously published ones and can help to discover design errors early in the design process.

5. A COMPRESSED HISTORY OF THE DEVELOPMENT OF AN ABSTRACT SPECIFICATION

In this section we present the history of the development of an abstract specification for a "table/list"-(T/L) module. The programs offered by this module support the processing of linearly ordered data structures, regardless of whether they are implemented as tables or lists. This module is currently implemented to help in generating address translation tables as we need them for a virtual memory mechanism within a family of operating systems [Parnas, Handzel and Wuerges 1976]. It is also expected that this specification can be used for various other table or list handling purposes.

An Informal Picture of the T/L Module

Because it is the purpose of this report to introduce a method of describing such modules, we must begin with an intuitive description of our example. One physical implementation of this module would be by means of a set of children's blocks where it is possible to write one "entry" on the upper surface. The blocks are arranged in a single row and covered with an opaque lid with a single window. Through this window one may read the entry on a single block, insert and remove blocks, or change the entry written on the block that shows through the window. The entry on the block that shows through the window is referred to as the *current entry*. Because the cover is opaque it is not possible to tell how many blocks are currently under it, but the cover is fitted with signals that tell whether or not there is a block to the right of the current entry, whether or not there is a block to the left of the current entry, and whether there are any blocks under the cover at all.

The operations that we want to perform include reading the value of the current entry, moving the lid one place to the right, moving the lid one place to the left, moving the lid and all blocks at the right hand side of the current block to the right so that a new current block may be inserted through the window, and removing the current block (moving the lid and all blocks to the right of the deleted block one place to the left).

It was our goal that all operations that could be easily performed with the physical model described above be allowed by our specification.

In our specification we will have five operations (O-functions): INSERT, DELETE, ALTER, GOLEFT and GORIGHT. ALTER will just be a shorthand for a sequence of DELETE and INSERT. The first two indicators mentioned above will be named EXLEFT (EXist entries to the LEFT), EXRIGHT, and the third is represented by EMPTY. The current entry will be available through the V-function CURRENT. The precise relationship among the V-functions and the way that their values are changed by the module's operations will be described in the specifications.

USING TRACES TO WRITE ABSTRACT SPECIFICATIONS 123

Example 6.   (Incorrect) Version of a Specification for a Table/List Module

Syntax of Functions

O-Functions:	INSERT(e):	<entry> × <TL>	→	<TL>
	DELETE:	<TL>	→	<TL>
	ALTER(e):	<entry> × <TL>	→	<TL>
	GOLEFT:	<TL>	→	<TL>
	GORIGHT:	<TL>	→	<TL>

V-Functions:	CURRENT:	<TL> → <entry>
	EMPTY:	<TL> → <boolean>
	EXLEFT:	<TL> → <boolean>
	EXRIGHT:	<TL> → <boolean>

Legal Traces

(1) $\lambda\,(T) \Rightarrow \lambda\,(T.INSERT(e))$

(2) $\lambda\,(T) \Rightarrow \lambda\,(T.INSERT(e).CURRENT)$

(3) $\lambda\,(T.CURRENT) \Rightarrow \lambda\,(T.EXLEFT)$

(4) $\lambda\,(T.CURRENT) \Rightarrow \lambda\,(T.EXRIGHT)$

(5) $\lambda\,(T.CURRENT) \Rightarrow \lambda\,(T.ALTER(e))$

(6) $\lambda\,(T.CURRENT) \Rightarrow \lambda\,(T.INSERT(e).GOLEFT)$

(7) $\lambda\,(T.GOLEFT) \Rightarrow \lambda\,(T.GOLEFT.GORIGHT)$

Equivalences

(8) $T.EMPTY \equiv T$

(9) $T.INSERT(e).DELETE \equiv T$

(10) $T.GOLEFT.GORIGHT \equiv T$

(11) $T.ALTER(e) \equiv T.DELETE.INSERT(e)$

(12) $\lambda\,(T.CURRENT) \Rightarrow (T.CURRENT \equiv T)$

(13) $\lambda\,(T.EXLEFT) \Rightarrow (T.EXLEFT \equiv T)$

(14) $\lambda\,(T.EXRIGHT) \Rightarrow (T.EXRIGHT \equiv T)$

Values

(15) $V\,(EMPTY) = true$

(16) $\lambda\,(T) \Rightarrow V\,(T.INSERT(e).CURRENT) = e$

(17) $\lambda\,(T) \Rightarrow V\,(T.INSERT(e).EMPTY) = false$

(18) $\lambda\,(T)$ **cand** $(V(T.EMPTY) = true) \Rightarrow V(T.INSERT(e).EXLEFT) = false$

(19) λ (T) **cand** (V(T.EMPTY) = false) $\wedge$ (V(T.EXLEFT) = false) $\Rightarrow$
    V(T.INSERT(e).EXLEFT) = true
(20) λ (T) $\Rightarrow$ V(T.INSERT(e).EXRIGHT) = V(T.EXRIGHT)
(21) λ (T.GOLEFT) $\Rightarrow$ V(T.GOLEFT.EXRIGHT) = true
(22) λ (T.GORIGHT) $\Rightarrow$ V(T.GORIGHT.EXLEFT) = true
(23) λ (T.ALTER(e)) $\Rightarrow$ V(T.ALTER(e).CURRENT) = e
(24) λ (T.ALTER(e)) $\Rightarrow$ V(T.ALTER(e).EMPTY) = V(T.EMPTY)
(25) λ (T.ALTER(e)) $\Rightarrow$ V(T.ALTER(e).EXLEFT) = V(T.EXLEFT)
(26) λ (T.ALTER(e)) $\Rightarrow$ V(T.ALTER(e).EXRIGHT) = V(T.EXRIGHT)
(27) V(T.INSERT(e).GOLEFT.CURRENT) = V(T.CURRENT)
(28) V(T.INSERT(e).GOLEFT.EXLEFT) = V(T.EXLEFT)

A. The First Version (Example 6)

We do not display the original specification but instead present a translation using traces. We were not using traces for specification purposes at the time that the original was written. The use of traces makes many deficiencies in the first version obvious. They were originally discovered after much hard labor. We show an abbreviated history of the development to provide evidence controverting the claim that abstract specifications state "only the obvious".

The "syntax" section is as in the earlier examples. We use elements of a type "entry" only to store them into the data structure of the T/L module, or to fetch them. We assume that the relation of equality over entries is defined elsewhere.

Statements (3) through (5) tell us that V-functions EXLEFT and EXRIGHT and O-function ALTER(e) have the same applicability condition as CURRENT.

The "equivalences" section should allow the reader to transform any legal trace to one shown to be legal by (1) through (7). The alert reader will notice that this section does not satisfy this requirement. This will be investigated in some detail later.

Statement (8) is unconditional because a call on EMPTY can always be added to or removed from any trace without making the module trap.

Statements (9) and (10) say that subtraces INSERT(e).DELETE and GOLEFT.GORIGHT have no effect. Statement (11) is supposed to tell us that a call on ALTER has the same effect as two consecutive calls on DELETE and INSERT, provided that INSERT has the same actual parameter as ALTER. Statements (12) through (14) tell us that V-functions CURRENT, EXLEFT and EXRIGHT can be removed from a legal trace to get an equivalent trace.

Statement (15) gives the initialization of the module. Statement (16) through (20) describe the effects of INSERT at the end of a legal trace on the values of EMPTY, CURRENT, EXLEFT and EXRIGHT.

Statements (23) through (26) define the effects of ALTER at the end of a trace on the four V-functions. Note that only CURRENT is changed.

Statements (27) and (28) say that two consecutive calls on INSERT and GOLEFT have no effect on the values of CURRENT and EXLEFT.

B. Discussion of Flaws in the First Version of the T/L Module Specification

The use of traces and the way in which the present specifications are divided into sections allows us to discuss flaws in version 1 of the T/L module in a straightforward way and to omit two or three intermediate stages of the original development. However, all errors below were actually included in the original design of the T/L module (where a different method of specification was used) and allowed to remain in the design after formal discussion among the members of our group.

Incompleteness

In examining the first specification we first attempt to make certain that the specification is complete. We will (by definition) consider the specification to be incomplete if there are some traces ending in calls on V-functions which can be shown to be legal but for which no value can be derived.

One example of incompleteness concerns the value of the function EXRIGHT. Only (20) and (26) make any statement about the value of EXRIGHT and these make no statement about the initial value of EXRIGHT or V(INSERT(e).EXRIGHT) which can be shown to be legal.

The specification is similarly incomplete with respect to EXLEFT.

Another form of incompleteness can be found by attempting to derive the value of V(INSERT(a).INSERT(b).GOLEFT.EMPTY). There is no statement about the value of EMPTY when immediately preceded by GOLEFT and no equivalence assertion that would allow us to remove GOLEFT.

Specification Versus Intuitive Understanding

In addition to the instances of incompleteness that have been demonstrated, we can show that a number of statements in the "legal trace" section and "equivalences" section do not meet our intuitive expectations. There is a problem with the legality of traces beginning with a call on GOLEFT. For example, we would expect that a call on GOLEFT before the first entry has been inserted into the data structure should not be permitted. However, the value of $\lambda(\text{GOLEFT.GORIGHT})$ can by statement (10) always be calculated to be $\lambda(\emptyset)$, which is (by definition) "true." Since by definition $\lambda(T.X) \Rightarrow \lambda(T)$ we can conclude that (for $T \equiv \text{GOLEFT}$ and $X = \text{GORIGHT}$) we have $\lambda(\text{GOLEFT}) = \text{true}$. A similar problem exists concerning the legality of traces ending with a call on GOLEFT.

Statements (2) and (6) eliminate the possibility of insertion to the left of the leftmost entry. We can move the window in our cover over the leftmost entry but not further. An insert would then make EXLEFT true again (statement (19)) but we would have inserted to the *right* of the leftmost entry.

The mnemonic "EMPTY" was an obstacle to a straightforward solution. Imagine that one moves left from the left end. By statement (18), EMPTY would become true although there are entries in the data structure.

We will eliminate these problems by renaming "EMPTY" to "OUT" and allowing one move to the left beyond the left end. The value of CURRENT is then undefined, while OUT is true, EXLEFT is false, and EXRIGHT is true. This is in contrast to the new initial state (no entries in the data structure) where EXRIGHT is false.

A problem that initiated the development of the specification technique presented in this paper is best formulated by posing the following question.

How can the designer be sure that he specified the effects of all traces that he wants to be executable programs?

Or, put in another way and applied to our example, how do we determine the subset of

$$(\text{INSERT}(e), \text{DELETE}, \text{ALTER}(e), \text{GOLEFT}, \text{GORIGHT},$$
$$\text{CURRENT}, \text{OUT}, \text{EXLEFT}, \text{EXRIGHT})*,$$

(where "*" is the Kleene star) that comprises the set of executable, i.e. legal traces? (Rules for including V-functions are easy to find and are therefore not considered now.)

We now note some quantitative properties of such traces: Let $|X|$ denote the number of calls on X in a given trace. Then for all legal traces:

$$|\text{GOLEFT}| > |\text{GORIGHT}|$$
$$|\text{INSERT}| > |\text{GOLEFT}| - |\text{GORIGHT}|$$
$$|\text{INSERT}| > |\text{DELETE}| + |\text{GOLEFT}| - |\text{GORIGHT}|$$

These relations alone, however, help little. The obviously unreasonable trace

GORIGHT.GOLEFT.GOLEFT.INSERT(a).INSERT(b)

satisfies the above inequalities.

We therefore have to make some additional assertions to characterize the set of legal traces.

The specification of Example 6 did not capture the language of the module, as we intuitively understand it. For example:

λ (INSERT(a).INSERT(b).GOLEFT.GOLEFT) = **false**

Other examples can easily be found.

USING TRACES TO WRITE ABSTRACT SPECIFICATIONS

Example 7. Table/List Module with Unlimited Capacity

Syntax

O-Functions:	INSERT:	<entry> × <TL>	⟶ <TL>
	ALTER:	<entry> × <TL>	⟶ <TL>
	DELETE:	<TL>	⟶ <TL>
	GOLEFT:	<TL>	⟶ <TL>
	GORIGHT:	<TL>	⟶ <TL>
V-Functions:	CURRENT:	<TL>	⟶ <entry>
	OUT:	<TL>	⟶ <boolean>
	EXLEFT:	<TL>	⟶ <boolean>
	EXRIGHT:	<TL>	⟶ <boolean>

Legal Traces

(1) $\lambda(T) \Rightarrow \lambda(T.INSERT(a))$
(2) $\lambda(T) \Rightarrow \lambda(T.INSERT(a).GOLEFT)$
(3) $\lambda(T.GOLEFT) \Rightarrow \lambda(T.CURRENT)$

Equivalences

(4) $T.OUT \equiv T$
(5) $T.EXLEFT \equiv T$
(6) $T.EXRIGHT \equiv T$
(7) $\lambda(T.CURRENT) \Rightarrow T.CURRENT \equiv T$
(8) $\lambda(T.GOLEFT) \Rightarrow T.GOLEFT.GORIGHT \equiv T$
(9) $T.INSERT(a).DELETE \equiv T$
(10) $T.INSERT(a).GOLEFT.DELETE \equiv T.DELETE.INSERT(a).GOLEFT$
(11) $\lambda(T) \Rightarrow T.INSERT(a).INSERT(b).GOLEFT \equiv$
     $\qquad\qquad\qquad\qquad T.INSERT(b).GOLEFT.INSERT(a)$
(12) $T.ALTER(a) \equiv T.DELETE.INSERT(a)$

Values

(13) $V(OUT) = true$
(14) $V(EXLEFT) = V(EXRIGHT) = false$
(15) $\lambda(T) \Rightarrow V(T.INSERT(a).CURRENT) = a$
(16) $\lambda(T) \Rightarrow V(T.INSERT(a).OUT) = false$
(17) $\lambda(T) \Rightarrow V(T.INSERT(a).EXLEFT) = $ **not** $V(T.OUT)$
(18) $\lambda(T) \Rightarrow V(T.INSERT(a).EXRIGHT) = V(T.EXRIGHT)$
(19) $\lambda(T.CURRENT) \Rightarrow V(T.INSERT(a).GOLEFT.CURRENT)$
     $\qquad\qquad\qquad\qquad = V(T.CURRENT)$
(20) $\lambda(T) \Rightarrow V(T.INSERT(a).GOLEFT.OUT) = V(T.OUT)$

(21) $\lambda(T) \Rightarrow V(T.INSERT(a).GOLEFT.EXLEFT) = V(T.EXLEFT)$
(22) $\lambda(T.GOLEFT) \Rightarrow V(T.GOLEFT.EXRIGHT) = true$

C. The Current Specification for the T/L Module

After discovering the above errors (over a period of several months) we made an observation that allowed us to write the specification given in Example 7.

Any legal trace for the T/L module must be equivalent to a trace in which there is a (possibly empty) sequence of INSERTs followed by any number of repetitions of the sequence INSERT.GOLEFT. This observation is based on our intuitive model of the object that we are trying to specify. (We have no other possible basis.) We could create the table contents $a_0, a_1, ..., a_i, ..., a_N$, where a_i is the current entry, by successively inserting $a_0, a_1, ..., a_i$ and then executing INSERT(a_j).GOLEFT for $j = n, n-1, ..., i+1$. Each INSERT(a_j).GOLEFT sequence leaves CURRENT unchanged but inserts a block to the right of current.

Traces in this form are the *normal form* traces of this module. We will therefore have to provide a set of assertions that allow to transform any legal trace to such a normal form trace.

The assertions labeled "legal traces" in Example 7 ((1)−(3)) state that all traces in normal form (and some additional traces) are legal. We also indicate that CURRENT may be called whenever a GOLEFT would be allowed.

The assertions (4)−(7) state that the V-functions do not effect any changes on the module. (8) and (9) give the obvious facts that GOLEFT can be canceled by a GORIGHT that follows it and that an INSERT can be canceled by a DELETE that follows it. Note that (8) only applies when GOLEFT is legal.

If our specification is a good one, we should be able to show that every legal trace is equivalent to a trace in normal form. The V-functions can be trivially deleted. We are able to delete a DELETE if it immediately follows an INSERT and a GORIGHT if it immediately follows a GOLEFT. Using statement (11) we can move a GOLEFT right or left through a sequence of INSERTs to get an equivalent trace. That will allow us to remove instances of DELETE by bringing an INSERT up to them if only GOLEFTs intervene. Using assertion (10) one may transform sequences containing GOLEFT.DELETE and DELETE.GOLEFT into equivalent sequences where either the DELETE has been moved to the left (bringing it closer to the INSERT that it cancels) or the GOLEFT has been moved to the right (bringing it close to any GORIGHT that would cancel it). Assertion (12) allows the removal of all occurrences of ALTER. Repeated application of these rules allows the removal of all functions except INSERT and GOLEFT.

Completeness of the Current Specification

To demonstrate completeness we examine primarily the value section (13)−(22). (13) and (14) specify the initial values of all V-functions except CURRENT. The failure to specify an initial value for CURRENT is not an instance of incompleteness because CURRENT is not a legal trace. Using (15)–(18) we have specified the values of all four V-functions for traces containing only INSERT.

Using (19)–(22) we can determine the values of the V-functions for any trace of the form T.INSERT(a).GOLEFT provided that we know the values of those functions after T. It follows that we know the values for any trace in the normal form. Since the equivalence statements allow any legal trace to be reduced to an equivalent trace in that form, the specification is complete.

Consistency

Demonstration of consistency is more complex. It is quite clear that the value section ((13)–(22)) is in itself consistent, but it is necessary to show that the transformations allowed by the equivalence section that produce a trace ending in a given V-function result in traces with the same value. Such a proof is beyond the scope of this paper.

6. CONCLUSION

It is clear that when we entered into the design of the T/L module interface we did not expect the difficulties that we encountered. Each proposal seemed intuitively obvious and the formal specifications that we wrote appeared to correspond to our intuition. Several people examined the specifications (which were written using weakest preconditions); all thought that they were acceptable. The types of difficulties described in connection with the first version of the T/L module specification came as a complete surprise. We had expected that writing the formal specifications was "only a formality" for so simple a module.

Our first conclusion then is simply that writing the formal specifications is useful *even* for simple modules. Had we been forced to make the change from the first version to the second version *after* coding was under way, it would have been expensive in terms of the amount of code (both in the module and in programs that use the module) needing revision.

Once we became aware of the difficulties, we found attempts to convince ourselves of the correctness of new versions to be extremely frustrating. The specifications that were written (using predicate transformers for programs consisting of calls on the functions) did not lend themselves well to examination for completeness and consistency. The mathematical model underlying those specifications is complex and there were difficulties intrinsic in the decision to talk about programs rather than traces. Although we have not yet produced a complete formal proof that this specification is complete and consistent, the intuitive justifications are far more convincing than our more formal arguments about the old specifications. Our second conclusion therefore is that the concept seems to be superior to other forms of data abstract specification known to us.

It is becoming popular among software specialists to speak of "front end" investment. The proposal is that by investing time and intellectual energy in the early design phase one can reduce the overall systems costs because of time saved at the later stages. A weakness of the majority of such proposals is that they provide little in the way of specific suggestions about what to do at those early stages. There is little evidence that the effort invested in the early stages will actually pay off. There is lots of evidence that just writing vague statements of good intentions ("The system will have a user-oriented interface") will *not* pay off. In this paper we have made a specific proposal for the use of that "front end" energy. We have shown how to write such specifications, and indicated how one may evaluate them for completeness and consistency.

Further work on verifying properties of these specifications is clearly necessary. As Price has shown [Price 1973], there are clear advantages to doing as much verification as possible before implementation begins. Similar views are found in [Neumann, Boyer, Feiertag, Levitt and Robinson 1977] but Price includes some (machine assisted) proofs.

ACKNOWLEDGMENTS

The authors are grateful to Professor D. Stanat for his advice while the research was being performed and on the writing of this paper. Dave Weiss, Lou Chmura, John Shore and Janusz Zamorski also made helpful comments. This research was supported by the U.S. Army under contract #DAAG 29-76-G-0240. W. Bartussek was also supported by the German Academic Exchange Service (DAAD) under stipend #4-USA-CDN-AUS-NZ-3-EB.

PAMELA ZAVE
AT&T Bell Laboratories, Murray Hill, NJ 07974

An Operational Approach to Requirements Specification for Embedded Systems *

1. INTRODUCTION

Recently the study of system requirements has emerged as a major area of research in software engineering. It has become clear that the stated requirements for a system have tremendous impact on the quality and usefulness of the ultimate product, and on the efficiency and manageability of its development. Yet, despite their leverage, relatively little is known about deriving and specifying good sets of requirements.

At the same time, the prominence of "embedded" (roughly equivalent to "real-time") systems has been increasing, due largely to hardware advances which have made them feasible for a broader category of applications than ever before. We will argue that embedded systems are characterized by the urgency of their performance requirements; to the extent that all computer systems would benefit from the ability to state and satisfy precise performance requirements, knowledge of embedded systems can be useful to developers of all types of system.

This paper presents a new approach to the problem of specifying the requirements for embedded systems. It offers a substantial increase in formality, expressive power, and potential for automation over the current widely known requirements technologies.

2. THE REQUIREMENTS PROBLEM

2.1 The Role of Requirements in the System Life Cycle

The development of a computer system begins with the perception of a need for it. During the requirements phase, analysts should arrive at a deep understanding of that need and propose a system to fill it. The product of the requirements phase is the requirements specification, which plays a unique and crucial role in the rest of development. It states what system is to be developed, at what costs, and under what constraints.

---

* Copyright © 1982 IEEE. Reprinted, with permission, from *IEEE TRANSACTIONS ON SOFTWARE ENGINEERING*, Vol. SE-8, No. 3, pp. 250-269, May 1982.

The project cannot be a complete success unless the requirements have the informed consent of everyone who will be involved, including members of the development organization (designers, programmers, and managers), the originating organization (managers or sales people who determine the cost and value of the system), and the ultimate users of the system. This consensus can only be achieved through feedback and negotiation, with preliminary versions of the requirements specification being the major vehicle of communication.

During design and implementation, the requirements specification defines the "top" for top-down design, and the product toward which management effort is aimed. At the end of development, it is the standard against which the system is compared for success or failure, acceptance or rejection.

Requirements are often neglected, for reasons that are all too familiar: lack of awareness of their importance (which is disappearing), lack of useful requirements analysis and specification techniques, and natural reluctance to incur costs and delays at the beginning of a project. Yet the consequences of this shortsightedness, which include canceled projects or unprofitable products, unhappy users, chaotically structured systems, budget and schedule overruns as endless changes are made, and even lawsuits, are so serious that no one involved in software engineering can afford to ignore them. Other introductions to the role of requirements in system development can be found in [Boehm [1976]; Bell and Thayer [1976]; Ross and Schoman [1977]; Yeh [1980]; Heninger [1979]; Balzer and Goldman [1979]; Davis and Rauscher [1979].

It should be noted that even with the most optimistic view of current progress on requirements analysis and specification, in which problems of communication and complexity can be solved, certain other problems will remain very difficult to deal with. One is that vital decisions must be based on forecasts of costs and even feasibility, while such forecasting is perhaps the weakest point of our software technology. Another is that the requirements are constantly changing, even as we try to write them down. And systems that are used evolve continually throughout their lifetimes Belady and Lehman [1979]; Lehman [1980], creating "maintenance" costs which may eventually dwarf those of initial development.

As consciousness of the economic and technical importance of evolution in the system life cycle grows, we may develop a new concept of the life cycle based on iterated (re)developments, large and small, as in Conn [1980]. In such a model, the requirements specification will evolve with the system, serving throughout its life as definition, documentation, and contract. Needless to say, this expanded role will place even greater demands on the quality and modifiability of our requirements specifications.

2.2 Goals for Requirements Specifications

Progress in software engineering has almost always been made from the bottom up: from machine language to axiomatic specifications, for example, we have proceeded first by learning to do something and then by understanding it well enough to find suitable abstractions of it. This paper takes the same approach to requirements. It seems unlikely that we will find really effective techniques for requirements analysis before we know how to write a good requirements specification recording the results of that analysis. Therefore we will concentrate on specification techniques (although useful results on specification cannot help but suggest analytic methods and principles).

Goals for requirements specifications have been examined by many of the cited authors, and are discussed at more length in Zave [1980a]. In short, the things we do with requirements specifications are (1) use them as vehicles for communication, (2) change them, (3) use them to constrain target systems, and (4) use them to accept or reject final products.

For (1) and (2) they must be understandable and modifiable. For (3) they must be precise, unambiguous, internally consistent, and complete. They should also be minimal, i.e., define the smallest set of properties that will satisfy the users and originators. Otherwise the specification may overconstrain the target system, so that some of the best solutions to design problems are unnecessarily excluded. For (4) they should be formally manipulable (if verification is to be used) or testable (if acceptance testing is to be used).

The remainder of this paper is concerned with a requirements specification approach (and language) that promises to help us achieve many of these goals. It is also somewhat specialized for a particular class of systems, namely....

3. EMBEDDED SYSTEMS

Common examples of embedded systems are industrial process-control systems, flight-guidance systems, switching systems, patient-monitoring systems, radar tracking systems, ballistic-missile-defense systems, and data-acquisition systems for experimental equipment. The class of embedded systems is an important one, partly because it already includes some of our oldest and most complex computer applications, and partly because it is expanding rapidly in volume and variety as a result of the microprocessor revolution.

3.1 What Makes a System *Embedded?*

The term "embedded" was popularized by the U.S. Department of Defense in conjunction with its common languages (Ada) development project. "Embedded" refers to the fact that these systems are embedded in larger systems whose primary purposes are not computation, but this is actually true of any useful computer system. A payroll program, for instance, is an essential part of a business organization, which is a system whose primary purpose is selling products at a profit.

The common concept that unites the systems we choose to call "embedded" is *process control*: providing continual feedback to an unintelligent environment. This "theme" is easily recognized in flight-guidance systems and switching systems; even in a patient-monitoring system, sick patients are not exercising their intelligence in interacting with the system, and nurses can be viewed as providing a mechanical extension to the system's feedback loop.

The continual demands of an unintelligent environment cause these systems to have relatively rigid and urgent performance requirements, such as real-time response requirements and "fail-safe" reliability requirements. It seems that this emphasis on performance requirements is what really characterizes embedded systems, and causes us to be more aware of their roles in their environments than we are for other types of system.[1]

Fig. 1 shows an informal classification of systems, based on properties that show up at the requirements level. Requirements for "support systems" are generally much less definite than requirements for applications systems. And while the performance requirements for embedded systems may be couched in absolutes, the performance requirements for support systems will be relative to resources and resource utilization, and the performance requirements for data-processing systems will be relative to load, resources, and psychological factors. The most complex systems, such as nationwide airline-reservation systems, should probably be viewed as having subsystems of all three types.

TYPE	CHARACTERISTICS	EXAMPLES
EMBEDDED SYSTEM	SPECIAL-PURPOSE (APPLICATION)	INDUSTRIAL PROCESS-CONTROL SYSTEM
	ABSOLUTE PERFORMANCE REQUIREMENTS	FLIGHT-GUIDANCE SYSTEM
DATA-PROCESSING SYSTEM	SPECIAL-PURPOSE (APPLICATION)	BATCH BUSINESS PROGRAM
	RELATIVE PERFORMANCE REQUIREMENTS	ON-LINE DATABASE SYSTEM
SUPPORT SYSTEM	GENERAL-PURPOSE	OPERATING SYSTEM
	RELATIVE PERFORMANCE REQUIREMENTS	SOFTWARE DEVELOPMENT TOOL

Figure 1. A requirements-level system classification

---

1. Thus, "embedded" is almost synonymous with "real-time," but we prefer the newer term because it does not exclude performance requirements dealing with reliability.

3.2 The Special Problems of Embedded Systems

The special nature of embedded systems exacerbates many software engineering problems, and thus demands particular attention even during the requirements phase.

Few organizations have logged as much experience with embedded systems as the Department of Defense, which spends 56 percent of its approximately $3 billion annual software budget on them [Fisher 1978]. Here is a pointed summary of that experience:

> Embedded computer software often exhibits characteristics that are strikingly different from those of other computer applications. The programs are frequently large (50,000 to 100,000 lines of code) and long-lived (10 to 15 years). Personnel turnover is rapid, typically two years. Outputs are not just data, but also control signals. Change is continuous because of evolving system requirements—annual revisions are often of the same magnitude as the original development [Fisher 1978].

Clearly coping with complexity and change will not be easier in the domain of embedded systems.

In addition to the performance requirements, which have already been established as a major distinguishing factor, embedded systems are especially likely to have stringent resource requirements. These are requirements on the resources, mainly physical in this case, from which the system is constructed. This is because embedded systems are often installed in places (such as satellites) where their weight, volume, or power consumption must be limited, or where temperature, humidity, pressure, and other factors cannot be as carefully controlled as in the traditional machine room.

The interface between an embedded system and its environment tends to be complex, asynchronous, highly parallel, and distributed. This is another direct result of the "process control" concept, because the environment is likely to consist of a number of objects which interact with the system and each other in asynchronous parallel. Furthermore, it is probably the complexity of the environment that necessitates computer support in the first place (consider an air-traffic-control system)! This characteristic makes the requirements difficult to specify in a way that is both precise and comprehensible.

Finally, embedded systems can be extraordinarily hard to test. The complexity of the system/environment interface is one obstacle, and the fact that these programs often *cannot* be tested in their operational environments is another. It is not feasible to test flight-guidance software by flying with it, nor to test ballistic-missile-defense software under battle conditions.

4. AN "OPERATIONAL" APPROACH

The approach taken in this paper is to specify the requirements for an embedded system with an explicit model of the proposed system interacting with an explicit model of the system's environment. Both submodels consist of sets of asynchronously interacting digital processes, although some of the processes in the environment model may represent discrete simulations of nondigital objects such as people or machines. The entire model is executable, and the internal computations of the processes are specified in an applicative language.

We call this an "operational" approach because the emphasis on constructing an operating model of the system functioning in its environment provides its primary flavor. It has been embodied in a *S*pecification *L*anguage which, since, it is based on the ideas above and is therefore *P*rocess—oriented, *A*pplicative, and *I*nterpretable (executable), named PAISLey.

In the remainder of this section, the basic ideas behind PAISLey will be explained, illustrated, and justified in detail. Section 5 addresses apparent disadvantages of an operational approach, and Section 6 defines PAISLey.

4.1 Explicit Modeling of the Environment

Fig. 2 shows a partial requirements model for a simple patient-monitoring system. The *patient, nurse,* and *doctor* processes are all digital simulations of these natural objects. They represent, of course, only the roles played by these people with respect to patient monitoring. The *patient* process also models a sensor attached to the patient (this model is only partial because the complete one would have multiple patients, sensors, terminals, etc.).

The *reader* process reads sensor data at specified intervals of real time, sending a warning to the terminal if the reading is so implausible as to suggest sensor malfunction. The *monitor* process checks the reading against medical safety criteria, sending a warning if it falls outside a safe range. Sensor data also go to the *database* process, which responds to queries from the terminal and also purges old data to maintain themselves at a reasonable

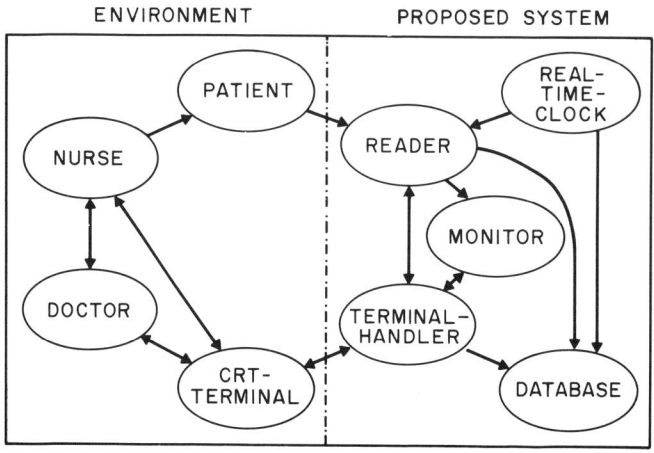

Figure 2. Partial model of a patient-monitoring system

size. Many parameters, such as sensor-reading frequencies and safe ranges, can be set by doctors and nurses.

The boundary between the environment and the proposed system is determined simply by which parts are "givens" for the contractor and which parts must be supplied by the contractor. The boundary is arbitrary (from a technical viewpoint), and is not even part of the formal PAISLey specification.

Including an explicit model of the environment has several advantages for requirements specification. The reason that the interface between an embedded system and its environment is complex, asynchronous, highly parallel, and distributed is that is consists of interactions among a number of objects which exist in parallel, at different places, and are not synchronized with one another. Organizing these interactions around the objects (processes) which take part in them is an effective way to decompose this sort of complexity. Furthermore, assumptions and expectations on both sides of the boundary can be documented. The result is a specification which is far more precise and yet comprehensible than could be obtained by treating either side of the interface as a "black box," which is what happens when the environment is not modeled.

Another reason for having an environment model is that the environment (when construed broadly enough) is the source of all changes to the system. Modeling it is therefore a promising way to anticipate changes and enhance the modifiability of both specification and target system.

The final advantage of specifying the environment is that many performance constraints are most naturally attached there. The patient-monitoring system has a real-time response requirement on database queries, which is neatly expressed as a time limit on the component of the terminal specification which waits for the response after sending a query. The system must also be able to handle a certain load. Since this load is completely determined by the numbers of sensors and terminals and the rates at which they create work for the system, it is most directly specified by a model of those peripherals.

The other significant aspect of constructing an environment model is that it is a valuable tool for requirements *analysis*, as well as specification. In fact, the best way to analyze requirements may be to start with the environment model, and work "outside-in" to a proposed system which supports a desirable model of operation in the environment. The extreme case is automation of an existing manual system—in the absence of changes to existing procedures, the requirements can be derived simply by modeling the current operation, and drawing a boundary to distinguish the automatable part! Yeh *et al.* [1979]; Yeh, Roussopoulos and Chang [1979] discuss "conceptual models," which are models of system environments constructed for the purpose of requirements analysis.

In the patient-monitoring system, since only the *patient* and *crt-terminal* processes interact directly with the proposed computer system, only these are necessary for precise specification of the system interface. The *nurse* and *doctor* processes appear strictly as vehicles for requirements analysis.

Wondering how doctors and nurses interact leads the analyst to ask which kinds of information a doctor expects to get from a nurse on duty, and which kinds he would like to find in the database. Wondering how nurses interact with patients and the display leads the analyst to ask how the display screen should be allocated to medical histories versus emergency messages, how often warnings concerning an ongoing crisis need be displayed, and whether information from the monitoring system is needed at the patient's bedside. These questions are never asked (or answered) in the numerous treatments of patient-monitoring systems appearing in the requirements literature.

Even if the analysts can achieve understanding of the requirements in some other way, early concentration on the environment may lead to better communication with users (who are much more interested in their environment than your system), and more open-minded problem-solving, unbiased by preconceived notions or similar systems the analysts have worked on.

4.2 Processes

Another key feature of the operational approach is that the primary units of specification are processes. A process is a simple, abstract representation of autonomous (distributed) digital computation. It is specified by supplying a "state space," or set of all possible states, and a "successor function" [2] on that state space which defines the successor state for each state. It goes through an infinite sequence of states (although a "halting" process can be specified by having it go into a distinguished "halted" state which it will never leave), asynchronously with respect to all other processes (Fig. 3).

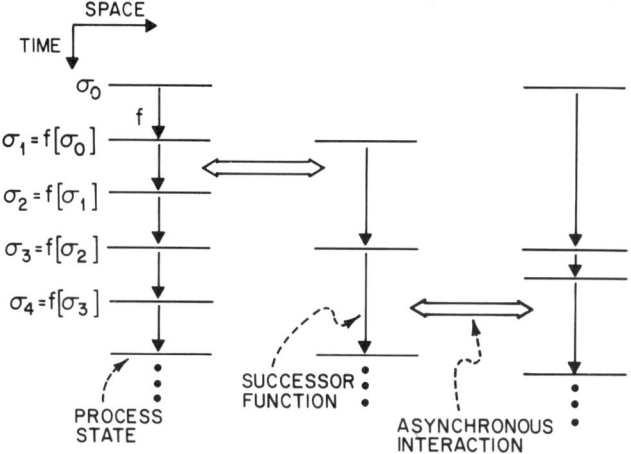

Figure 3. Process in action

---

2. Throughout this paper mappings will be called "functions," despite the fact that mappings named in specifications are often relations. The reason is that "function" gives a more accurate impression: the intention is always to produce a unique value when the mapping is invoked in the eventual target system, even though that value cannot always be determined by a known functional expression.

A process is cyclic, with its successor function describing its natural cycle. The natural cycle of a process simulating a sick patient, for instance, would be a single step of the discrete simulation algorithm. The successor function of such a process might be declared as

$$\text{patient-cycle: PATIENT-STATE} \rightarrow \text{PATIENT-STATE,}$$

where the set "PATIENT-STATE," which is its domain and range and also the state space of the process, contains values encoding possible states of the patient between simulation steps. The natural cycle of the *doctor* process might be to take one action, either asking one question of a nurse, giving one order to a nurse, or taking part in one transaction with the patient-monitoring system.

There can be no question about the *generality* of processes. They were originally used as abstractions of concurrent activities within multiprogramming systems [Horning and Randell 1973], and many recent articles have shown that they can be used to represent I/O devices, data modules, tasks, monitors, buffers, or any other identifiable structure within a computer system (e.g., Hoare [1978]; Brinch Hansen [1978]; Mao and Yeh 1980]). Process-based models of computation have been the focus of extensive theoretical work and the language Smalltalk [Ingalls 1978]. Our varied examples are persuasive evidence that the notion of digital simulation of nondigital objects is similarly powerful in describing the environments of computer systems.

The *appropriateness* of using processes to specify requirements for embedded systems is based on our observation that in these systems asynchronous parallelism—among environment objects, between environment objects and the system, and within the system (if only for reasons of performance)—occurs occurs naturally *at the requirements level*. One happy result of recognizing that parallelism is environment specifications which should be highly intuitive, even to naive users. This is because the specifications are populated by identifiable models of the same autonomous, interacting objects from which the real world is made.

Perhaps the best way to appreciate processes is to consider the alternatives: representations of processing used in other requirements languages. The one most commonly found in requirements documents is data access or "dataflow". Data-access graphs show major system functions, and identify the data structures which are their inputs and outputs (e.g., Fig. 4). Data access is the basis of PSL/PSA [Teichroew and Hershey, III 1977] and SADT [Ross 1977; Ross and Schoman 1977], and has probably been rediscovered thousands of times by isolated requirements writers.

Data access may be adequate for many data-processing systems, such as the one depicted in Fig. 4. This is because major subfunctions ("check-inventory", "send-invoice") are implemented as major subprograms, and subprograms are invoked in some implicitly understood sequence, whenever their input files are ready. Data access is seriously inadequate for embedded systems, however, because control is all-important in embedded systems and

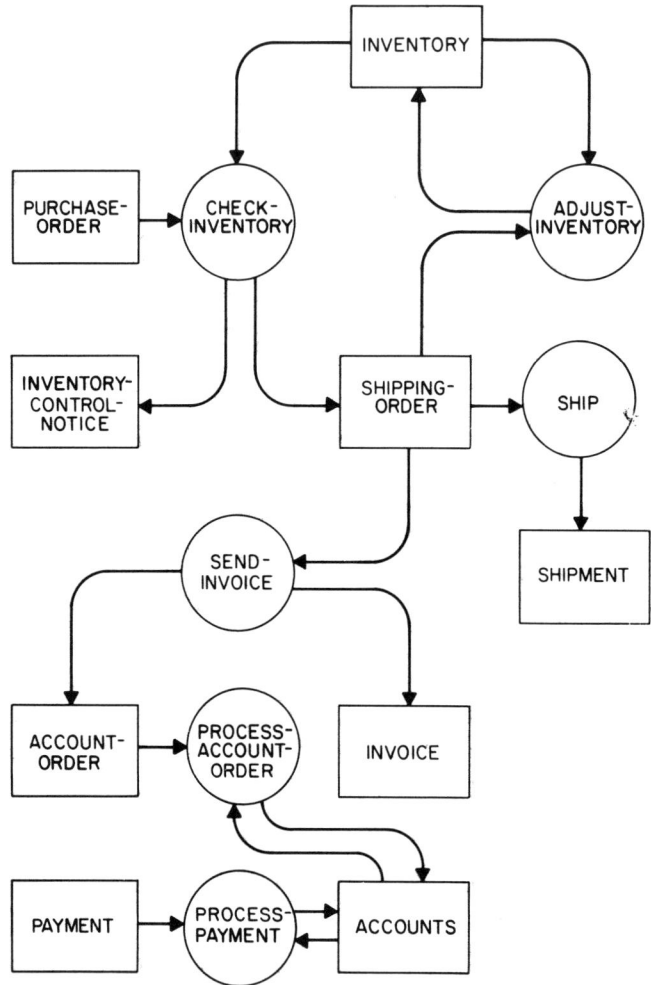

Figure 4. A data-access graph for filling orders from an inventory

must be represented in any intelligible model. If a data-access graph is mistakenly interpreted as representing control as well, the concepts of control expressed will be simplistic and misleading.

In Fig. 4, for instance, the following problems would arise if control were implied. (1) A distinction must be made between inputs which are always present (such as the "INVENTORY" database) and inputs which invoke a function whenever a new instance appears (such as "PURCHASE-ORDER"). The situation is even more complex when there is an input value (such as the current output of a sensor attached to a hospital patient) which is always available, but only read at certain real-time intervals (and the interval itself is a variable stored in some system database). (2) Functions (such as "process-account-order" and "process-payment") may have to be executed concurrently to meet performance requirements, in which case they must synchronize their uses of shared resources or databases (such as "ACCOUNTS"). (3) Functions may no longer execute in a predefined sequence (because of simultaneous access from multiple terminals, the need for internal housekeeping, etc.), and so a complex interplay of events and states must be anticipated.

The control arrow in SADT adds an explicit representation of control to data-access graphs (an illuminating discussion of its significance can be found in Ross [1977]), but its informality prevents it from being precise or expressive enough for embedded systems. Processes and their interactions, on the other hand, are well-suited to the task of specifying complex control, as would be expected from their historical origins in the specification of operating systems.

Other representations of processing appearing in requirements languages are stimulus-response paths in RSL [Bell, Bixler and Dyer 1977; Alford 1977; Davis and Vick 1977] and finite-state machines [Heninger 1979; Davis and Rauscher 1979]. A finite-state machine is very much like a single process—permitting no explicit parallelism, decomposition of complexity, nor modeling of the environment.

Stimulus-response paths (e.g., Fig. 5) represent sequencing, control, and parallelism explicitly, and do make it possible to decompose the requirements. The "R-net" in Fig. 5 shows parallelism between "STORE_FACTOR_DATA" and "EXAMINE_FACTORS," and is only one of several R-nets specifying the entire system. The fundamental differences between PAISLey and RSL appear to be as follows. (1) PAISLey representation emphasizes the *cyclic* nature of system components, while the RSL representation emphasizes *sequences*. Both are obviously useful ways of characterizing embedded systems, and only time will tell if one is superior to the other in a majority of instances. (2) The PAISLey notation integrates data, processing, and control in a unified whole, while in RSL the various concepts are separated—R-nets for control, PSL/PSA-like notation for data-access properties, etc. We believe that the unified approach will ultimately prove stronger in terms of comprehensibility, modifiability, and ability to determine internal consistency.

4.3 Executability

In the operational approach, requirements specifications are executable. This means that, under interpretation, the specification becomes a simulation model generating behaviors of the specified system.

It is of vital importance to be able to interpret specifications regardless of their level of abstraction. Not only are requirements by their nature abstract in many respects, but they must also be developed by successive refinements of understanding, each version of which should benefit from this facility. We will defer until Section 4.4 a discussion of *how* this can be done, and deal here only with the advantages of doing so.

Executability is a powerful tool for understanding a specification in all its ramifications. An executable specification can be tested and debugged by the analysts who wrote it. Its behavior can be validated by users in the course of

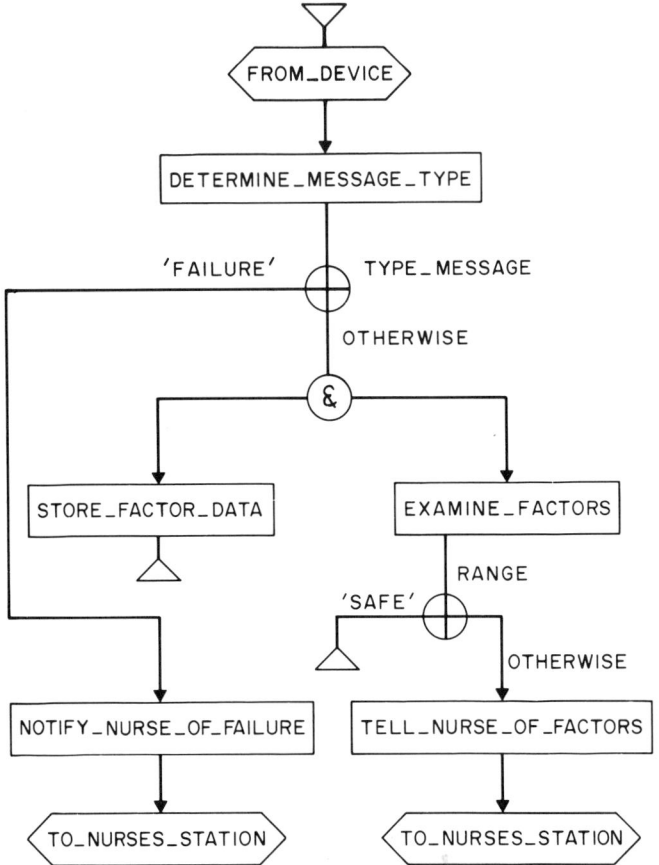

Figure 5. A stimulus-response path (part of a patient-monitoring system) specified in RSL (from Alford [1977])

demonstrations. If developed in enough detail, it can even be released on a small scale as a prototype of the proposed system.[3]

The ability to test is no panacea, as must be obvious from the literature on program testing—and with embedded system specifications there is the additional complication that any test must choose one of many relative-rate-dependent process execution sequences. Nevertheless, the problems inherent in testing programs have never caused us to give up on it, and requirements testing, once established in common practice, might seem likewise indispensable.

---

3. In most cases a practical requirements specification, even if executable, will be far more abstract (less detailed) than the system it specifies. Other differences between executable specifications and implementations lie in their performance, resource, and accessibility properties. A prototype falls somewhere between an executable specification and an implementation, because it must get some exposure in the field, and this requires performance, resource, and accessibility properties which are adequate at some minimal level.

Furthermore, an executable requirements model can continue to be useful after the requirements phase. The environment part of the model can be used as a test bed during system development, which will be particularly valuable for embedded systems because of the aforementioned difficulties of testing them "in the field" (in fact, it is almost always necessary to write an environment simulator for exactly this purpose). The model of the proposed system can be used to generate sample behaviors for acceptance testing.

It is also possible to attach performance constraints in such a way that they can be simulated along with the functional requirements, and this is done in PAISLey. Simulation can then be used to predict performance where it is too complex to determine analytically. This type of simulation is an important feature of SREM, the integrated set of tools by which RSL is supported.

There is a final, critically important, advantage of executability that has nothing to do with testing or simulation. It is that the demands of executability impose a coherence and discipline—because the parts of a specification must "fit together" in a very strong sense—that could scarcely be obtained in any other way. If an executable requirements specification is shown to be internally consistent, that means it will continue to generate behaviors without ever halting, deadlocking, or going into an undefined state. In other words, it is guaranteed to be a valid specification of *some* system interacting with *some* environment. Clearly this is the utmost that any formally defined notion of internal consistency could do for us, since deciding whether they are the *right* system and environment is a matter of validation by the originator/user, or verification of consistency with externally defined axioms of correctness.

4.4 Specification in an Applicative Language

Within a process, computation (i.e., the successor function of the process) is specified using a purely applicative language. "Applicative" (or "functional") languages are those based on side-effect-free evaluation of expressions formed from constants, formal parameters, functions, and functional operators ("combining forms" for functions, such as composition). Well-known examples of applicative languages are the lambda calculus, pure LISP, and the functional programming systems of Backus [1978].

1) *Advantages of Applicative Languages:* Applicative languages are currently receiving a great deal of favorable attention because of their numerous theoretical and practical advantages ([Backus 1978; Iverson 1980; Smoliar; Friedman and Wise 1977, 1978a, 1978b, 1979, 1980], among others), most of which can be exploited in requirements specifications. To begin with, because applicative languages are interpretable, they support the executability property: processes are executed by repeatedly replacing their current states by successor states, and successor states are discovered by interpreting the applicative expressions which define them.

For purposes of high-level specification, the most important property of applicative languages is their tremendous powers of abstraction, i.e., of decision deferment. Consider, for instance, the functional expression "f[(g[y], h[z])]," which says that the function "g" is to be applied to the argument "y" and "h" is to be applied to "z" (the "[ ]" symbols denote function application or composition). Then "f" is to be applied to the values produced (the "( )" symbols are used to construct tuples of data). The expression says exactly what is needed to compute the desired value, but does not otherwise constrain the data, control, processor or other resource structures used to do so. Are "g[y]" and "h[z]" evaluated sequentially or in parallel? In what data structures are their values stored? Perhaps the arguments "y" and "z" are even shipped off to special "g"- and "h" -processors, respectively, at different nodes of a network!

Furthermore, a primitive function has several interesting interpretations, all of which enable additional decompositions of complexity. A primitive function can represent a set of deferred decisions, to be made later by defining the function in terms of simpler primitives. It can also represent a mapping which will always remain nondeterministic from the perspective of the requirements model, because it depends on factors outside the scope of the model. For instance, in specifying a terminal we might declare a primitive function

think: DISPLAY $\longrightarrow$ INPUT,

where DISPLAY is the set of all CRT screen images and INPUT is the set of all input lines, to represent the human user's thought processes. Finally, in PAISLey a primitive function can be an abstraction for an interprocess interaction (see below). Because of these many options, applicative languages have been used successfully to describe phenomena ranging in level of abstraction from digital hardware to distributed system requirements [Fitzwater and Zave 1977; Smoliar 1979].

An interpreter for an abstract specification language makes expedient and non-functionally significant decisions about such matters as control and space allocation. The only other thing needed for interpretation is some sort of implementation of functions and sets left primitive in the abstract specification. This can be done in many ways, perhaps the simplest of which is to choose values of primitive functions randomly or by default. Another way to interpret primitive functions is to display their arguments at a terminal and ask the analyst to supply a value, thereby creating an interactive testing system. In either case, the effect is to simulate the decisions which have been made without interference from the decisions that have not been made.

Other advantages of applicative languages are that they are well-suited to formal manipulations such as verification, and may have great potential for efficient implementation (see [Backus 1978]). In procedural languages, on the other hand, assignment statements thwart top-down thinking, complicate the formal semantics, and force memory to be referred to and accessed one word at a time.

2) PAISLey as an Applicative Language: PAISLey is not a purely applicative language because states in general, and process states in particular, are not applicative concepts. In [Zave] it is explained that, while many aspects of even embedded systems can be specified applicatively, the specification of most performance requirements, real-time interfaces with the environment, and certain resource requirements all necessitate the introduction of some nonapplicative structure such as processes.

In fact, the process structure makes PAISLey specifications easier to write than typical large applicative programs. The system is decomposed into processes, and process computations are decomposed into cycles or steps, before applicative programming comes into use. The current state of a process "remembers" all its relevant history. Thus the applicative expressions which must be written are quite simple relative to the complexity of the system as a whole.

Since PAISLey is a blend of the applicative world and the nonapplicative world of processes and states, the "seam" must be a smooth one. The two worlds meet at the mechanism for interprocess interaction, which is necessitated by the existence of processes but designed to fit smoothly into the applicative framework. Interactions take place through a set of three primitives called "exchange functions" which carry out the side effect of asynchronous interaction, but look and behave *locally* (intraprocess) exactly like primitive functions. Exchange functions are defined and explained in Section 6.3. They are a unique mechanism which seems to fulfill our purposes very well, and also offers an interesting new perspective on asynchronous interaction mechanisms for distributed processes.

Applicative languages have, in some circles, a reputation for unreadability and general unsuitability for large-scale software engineering. We believe that this reputation is due to typelessness and recursion, neither of which is present in PAISLey.

Recursion is what purely applicative languages use to specify repetitive computation, and is analogous to looping (iteration) in procedural languages. Both are analogous to the repetitive application of a successor function to produce successive process state, which is how unbounded repetition is specified in PAISLey.

In most applicative languages, the only type of data object is the list or sequence, and all functions are applied to one list and produce one list. Since every function should be prepared to accept argument lists of any internal structure, there must be a distinguished "undefined" value produced whenever the internal structure of the argument is unsuited to the semantics of the function (as in [Backus 1978])—and this mismatch must first be detected! Multiple arguments to or values from functions must be packaged in single lists, yet the existence of this substructure (or any other substructure, for that matter) cannot be explicitly acknowledged.

Of course, deliberate substructure in data items is ubiquitous, and it is common practice to document it with the use of data types. Furthermore, typing in a language provides a useful form of redundancy which is susceptible to automated checks of internal consistency.

In PAISLey nonprimitive sets can be defined using set union (A ∪ B), cross-product (A × B), enumeration ({'true,' 'false'}), and parenthesization. The domain and range sets of every function, primitive or not, must be declared (although a function need not have arguments). The domain and range declarations can use arbitrary set expressions. Here are three example declarations:

    f: ⟶ A;
    g: B × C ⟶ D ∪ E;
    h: S ⟶ T.

When a function is applied to arguments, their types must be consistent with the domain declaration of the function. Consistency can be defined with the assistance of coercion, however, so that the composition "h[g[f]]" is perfectly legal if the definitions

    A = B × C;
    S = INTEGERS;
    D = {0, 2, 4, 6, 8};
    E = {1, 3, 5, 7, 9}

have been made. This notion of typing provides all the documentation and redundancy desirable for engineering goals, without sacrificing any of the flexibility attributable to typelessness. All that it requires is the ability to compare any two set expressions for containment, which is easily done *given this particular language of set expressions.*

5. QUALMS ABOUT OPERATIONAL REQUIREMENTS

Despite the obvious advantages of operational requirements, one cannot help but have certain reservations about the idea. In this section we examine its apparent disadvantages.

5.1 Encroaching on Design

Are not operational specifications actually *design* specifications rather than *requirements* specifications? This question is often prompted by the precision, potential for detail, and executability of PAISLey specifications.

From a certain technical viewpoint, requirements should specify only the functional and performance properties of the proposed system. Design begins when resources are introduced. The physical resources from which the system is to be built must be managed so that performance goals are met. The human resources who will implement and maintain the system must be managed so that they are used effectively; this depends on skillful modularization of the code to be written. Adopting this as a definition of the boundary between requirements and design, a requirements specification does not stray into design if it avoids unnecessary management of resources and unnecessary structuring of code.

PAISLey enables the requirements analyst to do this. This point is illustrated copiously in Zave [1980a], using as an example the specification of a process-control system from Zave and Yeh [1981]. We will confine ourselves here to explaining why one aspect of a PAISLey specification, its process structure, does not overconstrain resource management or code structure.

Processes are virtual structures, and a specification is partitioned into processes on the basis of factors such as functionality, synchronization, and performance—all of which belong to the requirements level. Thus a requirements analyst should use as many processes as "make sense" to him. Only in design should there be concern about how a large number of virtual processes are to be realized on a smaller number of physical processors, perhaps through time-multiplexing with priority scheduling. And the processes, representing dynamic structure of the target system, say nothing about its static code structure at all.

This technical view of requirements is elegant and satisfying, but it is not the whole story. Pragmatically, a requirement is any property of the proposed system that is necessary to satisfy the originating organization of the acceptability of the system, and these properties may very well include decisions about resources. Use of a particular computer or software subsystem may be required because the originating organization already owns it, and management insists that it be used. The new system may have to interface with an existing computer system, and thus be compatible with its resource management policies. The capabilities of the proposed system may even have to be trimmed to fit the resources available. This is common with really large systems such as ballistic-missile-defense systems and massive database systems. Another example would be a system to monitor experimental equipment on a satellite. Since facilities must be shared with other experiments, the amount of memory in the on-board computer allocated to each experiment is an administrative decision which must be made (at least tentatively) before work on the individual projects can begin.

The reality is that a system develops through a hierarchy of decisions, each decision constraining those below it in the hierarchy. No system is developed in a political or economic vacuum, and almost no system performs its function without interfacing with any preexisting computer system. Thus, even though resource decisions may be premature at the requirements level, any requirements language which is unable to record them will be terribly fragile, performing adequately only in the most idealized of situations.

PAISLey can record resource decisions because resource structures are like any other structures occurring in digital systems. They can definitely be specified if there is a general model of digital computation, which PAISLey offers. Hardware and software modules, for instance, can be specified as processes, and then included as part of the environment of the proposed system. This is a great strength of the operational approach—the promise of no unpleasant surprises when new applications, constraints, or economic contexts are encountered.

The ultimate test of whether or not a decision belongs in the requirements is whether or not the system could be constructed in any other way. This is illustrated in [Zave 1980a], using the requirements from an early real-time simulation system [U. S. Air Force 1965]. It is shown that decisions about the communication network, time-stamps, and the simulation time frame, while seemingly design decisions, are actually derivable during requirements analysis from feasibility considerations. The specification in PAISLey of each such decision is also described.

5.2 Too Much Precision

There can be little question that specifications written in PAISLey are too precise and based on too many technical principles, for customers, end users, managers, and other untrained personnel to understand. At the same time, their rigor can be invaluable to the trained analysts who will write them (this is based on numerous experiences of being confronted by surprise with the vagueness of my own ideas about a system). Informal analysis must always come first, but we have not yet fully exploited the potential of formal languages for expressing approximate or incomplete knowledge and real-world concepts.

There is not really a conflict here, simply because nontechnical people do not have to use the same representations that the analysts do. Analysts can communicate with them using simplified diagrams and narrow views derived from the current PAISLey specification. A process diagram such as Fig. 2, for instance, can have its interaction arrows labeled with the types of data being transferred. If this is done, the diagram does not differ substantially in form or content from the ever-popular data-access graph!

The single most successful feature of SREM (RSL) and PSL/PSA is that specifications are stored in a database from which a variety of up-to-date reports can be generated automatically. We envision PAISLey's being installed in such a database, and hope that user-oriented reports and diagrams could likewise be produced by tools running on the current specification.

5.3 Interface with Data-Oriented Specification Techniques

Other researchers have investigated the problem of requirements for data-processing systems, using as a starting point for their formalisms data definition languages, i.e., languages originally developed to describe the "conceptual schemas" (abstract, virtual, semantic structures) of databases. The notion that a requirements model should be an explicit representation of the proposed system interacting with its environment has also been derived in this context. A philosophy of data-oriented modeling is presented in Balzer and Goldman [1979], while Yeh, Roussopoulos and Chang [1979]; Roussopoulos [1979]; Mittermeir [1980]; Smith and Smith [1979]; Goldman and Wile [1980] exemplify it.

It is clear that a data-oriented technique is a more natural way than using PAISLey to develop requirements for data-processing systems. Yet data-processing systems cannot ignore performance and concurrency, and embedded systems cannot ignore data. Thus our goal is to view both process-oriented PAISLey specifications and data-oriented specifications as projections of the same underlying, all-encompassing model (Fig. 6). In this view the two types of specification are compatible and complementary, so that analysts are free to use either or both (in parallel) as the application domain and phase of development suggest. It is argued in Zave [1980a], by describing the data definition facilities of PAISLey in traditional database terms, that the structure of PAISLey is not inconsistent with this goal.

6. THE PAISLEY LANGUAGE

In this section full details of PAISLey are presented, including a new mechanism for process interactions and specification of performance

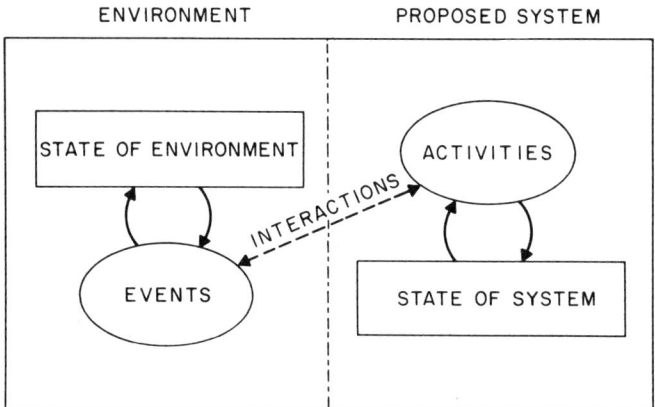

Figure 6. The conceptual model underlying both process-oriented and data-oriented system specifications

requirements. An LALR grammar for PAISLey in BNF form can be found in the Appendix.

6.1 Language Philosophy

PAISLey is intended to be simple. In particular, only features which are directly associated with run-time semantics are included.

For production purposes the language must be supported by a system which, in addition to storing specification fragments and collecting them into executable configurations (not to mention providing tools for static analysis and report generation), offers such conveniences as scopes, versions, macros, parameters, libraries, meta-notations, etc. The current frenzy of research on "programming environments" makes it plain that the design of such an environment is not a trivial task, and should probably not be undertaken simultaneously with development of the specification semantics. Specifications prepared using any of the above features would be translated into PAISLey (as currently defined) before interpretation.

Stylistically, PAISLey follows APL in using distinct symbols for distinct operators (but has far fewer of them!). This leads to a concise notation in which essentially all words are user-chosen mnemonics. In this decision and the one above, we apply exactly the same philosophy as Hoare [1978].

One other important principle is that every operational structure must be realizable with a bounded amount of resources (time and space). There is a bounded number of processes, no process state can require an unbounded amount of storage, and no process step can require an unbounded amount of evaluation time. The purpose of this is performance, i.e., making it possible to design systems which are guaranteed to meet their performance requirements. Clearly, if a computational path contains an unbounded loop, or may have to construct a data structure of unbounded size, no guarantee that it meets an absolute time constraint is possible. In PAISLey the only unbounded "structure" is the infinite succession of process steps of each process, and this one exception cannot be avoided.

Boundedness is enforced by requiring the sizes of system structures to be fixed. This gives the specification a static character which will greatly facilitate proofs of internal consistency, correctness, and other formal properties.

6.2 Sets, Functions, Processes, and Systems

Statements in PAISLey are delimited by semicolons, and comments are enclosed in double quotation marks.

Names are typed for greater readability. The names of functions are always in lowercase letters, and the names of sets are always in small capital letters (hyphens and integers may be used in either, but they must begin with alphabetic strings). Constants are either numbers, or strings enclosed in single quotation marks.

There are four kinds of statement: system declarations, function declarations, set definitions, and function definitions. Since a system is a fixed tuple of processes, we use the tuple-construction notation for a system declaration. A process is declared using a function application which applies its successor function to an expression evaluating to its initial process state. Thus a system consisting of four processes, three being terminals and the fourth being a shared database, would be declared as

>   (terminal-1-cycle[blank-display],
>   terminal-2-cycle[blank-display],
>   terminal-3-cycle[blank-display],
>   database-cycle[initial-database]
>   ),

where the following domain-range declarations would be appropriate:

>   terminal-1-cycle: DISPLAY → DISPLAY;
>   blank-display: →DISPLAY;
>   . . .
>   database-cycle: DATABASE → DATABASE;
>   initial-database: →DATABASE.

Terminal processes have the contents of the current displays as their process states. Note that there is no explicit naming of processes or systems, as it is not needed for the run-time semantics.

Function declarations give *properties* of functions, i.e., specify their domains and ranges or their performance (see Section 6.4). All function declaration statements begin with the function name and a colon. Domain-range declarations (of which we have seen many) are mandatory for all functions except intrinsic ones. (This is because intrinsic functions are either intrinsically typed or may have to handle several different types in the same specification.) Domain-range declarations are optional for intrinsic functions, and performance declarations are optional for all functions.

When a function is nonprimitive (defined), its declarations may be redundant, because its properties may be deducible from its definition. Declarations of nonprimitive functions can and should be checked for consistency with their definitions.

Set definitions define set names in terms of set expressions, which use set union, cross-product (which has precedence over union), enumeration, and parenthesization (all but parenthesization shown in Section 4.4(2)). Note that the size of all data structures is bounded, because all tuplets (members of sets defined by cross-product) are of fixed size.

Function definitions define function names in terms of function expressions, and may use formal parameters to do so. The structure of the argument may be imitated in a formal parameter list, thus giving names to argument substructures. Here, for instance, are some possible beginnings for function definition statements:

> new-func-1= ...;
> new-func-2[p]= ...;
> new-func-3[(p, q)]= ...;
> new-func-4[(p, (q, (r, s)))]= ....

Now in a defining function expression (for all but "new-func-1") the argument's first component can be referred to as "p", as an alternative to selectors such as "car" and "cdr" in LISP. Formal parameters have the same syntax as function names; the argument structure must, of course, agree with the function's domain declaration.

Function expressions may use function names, formal parameters, constants, applications of functions to arguments, tuple construction, and conditional selection. Conditional selection (the "McCarthy conditional") has the syntax "/p1: f1, p2: f2, ...'true': fn/" and evaluates to the value of the first functional expression "fi" such that the predicate (Boolean-valued functional expression) "pi" evaluates to 'true'. Note that there is no unbounded iteration, such as would be provided by *while ...do ...*, nor is recursion allowed. Fixed iteration can be specified using composition. The result is that the number of primitive operations to evaluate any function, including a successor function, can be bounded *a priori*.

As a simple example, consider the following specification of the successor function of a process representing a CRT terminal:

> terminal-cycle: DISPLAY ⟶ DISPLAY;
>
> terminal-cycle[d] = display [display-and-transact [(d, think-of-request[d])]];
>
> think-of-request: DISPLAY ⟶ REQUEST;
>
> display-and-transact: DISPLAY × REQUEST
> ⟶ DISPLAY × (RESPONSE ∪ ERROR-MESSAGE);
>
> display-and-transact[(d, r)] = (display[(d, r)], transact [r]);
>
> transact: REQUEST ⟶RESPONSE ∪ ERROR-MESSAGE;
>
> display: DISPLAY × (REQUEST ∪ RESPONSE ∪ ERROR-MESSAGE)
> ⟶ DISPLAY.

The process handles one transaction per process step, reflecting both the request and the response in the display. The primitive function "display" can carry out scrolling or whatever other formatting is desired.

Even aiming for a minimum of conveniences, it is impossible to do without some feature for defining groups of nearly identical items. In PAISLey this is done at all levels using the same index notation, as seen in

VECTOR = #1..10<× INTEGER>,

which defines members of the set "VECTOR" to be 10-tuples of integers. Index notation always denotes a sequence of the expression in angle-brackets, with the first symbol in the brackets used as the sequence delimiter. The integers after the "#" give the lower and upper bounds of the sequencing count. The only index notation without a delimiter symbol is the one for bounded functional composition (application), which makes "#1...3<func>[arg]" equivalent to "func[func[func[arg]]]."

In most cases what we want is a group of statements or expressions which differ slightly. This is done by operating on names, which are defined so that "syllables" (alphabetic substrings delimited by hyphens) are semantically meaningful. If the header for an index notation begins with a "syllable" before the "#", any syllable matching it in a name in the repeated expression will be replaced by successive integers from the lower bound to the upper bound.[4] Thus,

BIG-SET = J#1...3< ∪ LITTLE-SET-J>

is equivalent to

BIG-SET = LITTLE-SET-1 ∪ LITTLE-SET-2 ∪ LITTLE-SET-3,

and the system declaration

(k#0..9999<, terminal-k-cycle[blank-display]>,
database-cycle[initial-database]
)

creates a system with 10,000 terminal processes (an airline reservation system!), where the successor function of the thirteenth one is "terminal-12-cycle."

Index notation can even extend over groups of statements. Suppose we want our 10,000 terminals to be identical except that some identification must be built into "transact," the primitive function whose elaboration will send to and receive from the central system. This can be done by making slight modifications to the terminal specification already given, as follows:

---

4. The matching of index syllables does not discriminate between upper- and lower-case letters, so that an index syllable has scope over set and function names alike.

k#0..9999

<; terminal-k-cycle: DISPLAY ⟶ DISPLAY;

  terminal-k-cycle[d] = display[display-and-k-transact[(d, think-of-request[d])]];

  display-and-k-transact: DISPLAY × REQUEST
                         ⟶ DISPLAY × (RESPONSE ∪ ERROR-MESSAGE);

  display-and-k-transact[(d, r)] = (display[(d, r)], k-transact[r]);

  k-transact: REQUEST ⟶ RESPONSE ∪ ERROR-MESSAGE:

>;

think-of-request: DISPLAY ⟶ REQUEST;

display: DISPLAY × (REQUEST ∪ RESPONSE ∪ ERROR-MESSAGE)
                                          ⟶ DISPLAY

6.3 Asynchronous Interactions

1) *Definition of Exchange Functions:* Asynchronous interactions between processes are specified using three types of primitive functions known collectively as "exchange functions." An exchange function carries out two-way point-to-point mutually synchronized communication. It has one argument, which provides a value to be output, and always returns a value which was obtained as input. Thus within the process an exchange function looks like any other primitive function; it has, however, the side effect of carrying out a process interaction. By making interaction primitives masquerade as functions, we achieve compatibility with applicative notation.

An exchange function whose evaluation has been initiated interacts by "matching" (to be explained) with another pending exchange function. The two *exchange* arguments and terminate, so that each returns as its value the argument of the other.

Each exchange function has two attributes to be specified, namely a type ("x," "xm," or "xr") and a channel (a user-chosen identifier which has the syntax of a function name). The exchange function with type "x" and channel "chan" is named "x-chan," the exchange function with type "xr" and channel "real-time" is named "xr-real-time," etc. Only exchange functions with the same channel can match with each other.

The "x" is the basic type of exchange function. It can match with any other pending exchange function on its channel, including another of type "x". If no other exchange is pending, it will wait until one is. If there are several pending match possibilities, a match will be chosen nondeterministically, with the proviso that there must be no lockout (a situation where a pending exchange waits indefinitely while its match opportunities are given to other, more recently evaluated, exchange functions).

Competitive situations occur in most systems. To enable succinct specification of them we have exchanges of type "xm," which behave exactly like "x's" except that two "xm's" on the same channel cannot match with each other. They can then compete to match with an exchange of some other type as the examples will show.

Embedded systems typically have real-time interfaces, especially with the processes in their environments. To specify these we need a third type of exchange function, the "xr," which behaves like the others except that it *will not wait* to find a match. If evaluation of an "xr" is initiated and there is no other pending exchange on its channel, the "xr" terminates immediately without matching, returning its own argument as its value. It is always possible to determine whether or not an "xr" matched by giving it an argument distinct from any that it could obtain by exchanging.

Fig. 7(a) shows the possible matches of exchange types within a channel. Fig. 7(b) (contributed to the understanding of exchange functions by Friedman [Filman and Friedman]) shows the derivation of the three types. There must be both fully synchronized primitives ("synchronizing"), and also those which do not synchronize themselves ("free-running"). There must be exchanges which can match with their own kind and those that compete with their own kind. This makes four possibilities, except that a free-running type which exchanges with its own kind would be impossible, because it would require "matching" two simultaneous, instantaneous events.

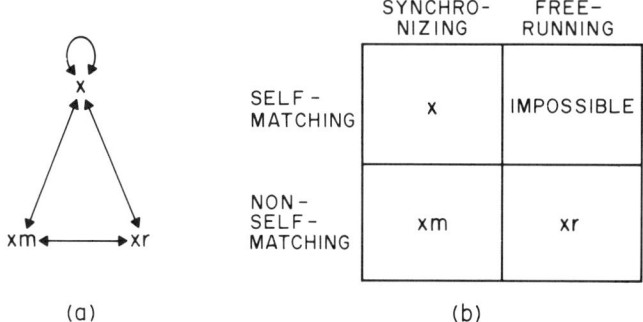

Figure 7. The three types of exchange function.
(a) Possible matches on a channel. (b) Derivation of the types

2) *Examples of Fully Synchronized Interactions:* In this section we will use exchange functions to specify the interactions between multiple transaction-processing terminals and a central database. "transact" in the terminal specification of Section 6.2 can be elaborated as follows:

transact[r] = receive-response[send-request[r]];

send-request: REQUEST ⟶ FILLER;

send-request[r] = xm-requ[r];

receive-response: FILLER ⟶ RESPONSE ∪ ERROR-MESSAGE;

receive-response[null] = x-resp['null'],

where "FILLER" is an intrinsic set whose only element is the constant "'null'." The database process successor function is specified as follows:

database-cycle[d] = finalize-transaction[perform-transaction[(d, receive-request)]];

receive-request: ⟶ REQUEST;

receive-request = x-requ['null'];

perform-transaction: DATABASE × REQUEST ⟶ DATABASE × RESPONSE;

finalize-transaction: DATABASE × RESPONSE ⟶ DATABASE;

finalize-transaction[(d, r)] = proj-2-1[(d, send-response[r])];

send-response: RESPONSE ⟶ FILLER;

send-response[r] = x-resp[r].

By renaming (redefining) the exchange functions, we are able to give them mnemonic names, and also to attach explicit types at the most meaningful place.

"send-request" in a terminal and "receive-request" in the database match with each other to transmit the request. Note that the type "xm's" in the terminals compete for the type "x" in the database; if nothing but "x's" were used, two evaluations of "send-request" in different terminals might match with each other! Since the "xm" and "x" are symmetric with respect to synchronization, either may have to wait for the other.

After the request is processed against the database, "finalize-transaction" disposes of the results. It is defined in terms of the intrinsic function "proj-2-1," which projects an ordered pair onto its first component, in this case the updated database. The second component is evaluated only for its side-effect of sending the response back; the "null" value it returns is thrown away.

"receive-response" could have been defined using type "xm", but an "x" is also correct, because precedence constraints enforced by the functional nesting of "send-request" inside "receive-response" ensure that at most one instance of "receive-response" will be in evaluation at any one time, namely that of the process whose request is now being processed. Thus matching on the channel "resp" is always unique.

"FILLER" and "'null'" are used as place-holders whenever syntactic rules dictate that there must be a set or value, but no semantics need be carried. "send-request," for instance, returns the value "'null'" because every function must have a value. And "receive-response" has "FILLER" as its domain simply because it is composed with "send-request," although the reasons for

REQUIREMENTS SPECIFICATION FOR EMBEDDED SYSTEMS

the composition is sequencing rather than transfer of values. "receive-request" does not need a domain (because a function does not require one), but "x-requ" must have an argument—and so "'null'" is used.

3) *Examples of Free-Running Interactions:* A "free-running" process is one whose only interactions occur via "xr", so that it will never wait to synchronize with another process. The prototypical free-running process is a real-time clock, which "ticks" once per process step, and could not fulfill its intended function if it had any synchronizing interactions. Such a process is specified:

(clock-cycle[0], ...);

clock-cycle: TIME ⟶ TIME;

TIME = INTEGER

clock-cycle[t] = proj-2-1[(increment[t], offer-time[t])];

increment: TIME ⟶ TIME;

offer-time: TIME ⟶ FILLER ∪ TIME;

offer-time[t] = xr-time[t].

Any process wishing to read the current time must evaluate

current-time: ⟶ TIME;

current-time = xm-time['null'].

Concurrent "xm-time's" will compete to match with "xr-time," implying for this particular specification that no two readers will ever get the same clock value.

Another common type of free-running process is a digital simulation of a nondigital, unintelligent environment object. Here is the top-level specification of the processes representing the machines in the environment of a process-control system [Zave and Yeh 1981]:

j#1.. 3

<; machine-j-cycle: MACHINE-STATE ⟶ MACHINE-STATE;

machine-j-cycle[m] =
 proj-2-1
 [(simulate-machine[(m, feedback-j-if-any)],
  offer-machine-j-data[sense[m]]
)];

feedback-j-if-any: ⟶ FEEDBACK ∪ FILLER;

feedback-j-if-any = xr-j-back['null'];

offer-machine-j-data: SENSOR-DATA ⟶ FILLER ∪ SENSOR-DATA;

offer-machine-j-data[s] = xr-j-sens[s]

>;

simulate-machine: MACHINE-STATE × (FEEDBACK ∪ FILLER)
⟶ MACHINE-STATE;

sense: MACHINE-STATE ⟶ SENSOR-DATA.

During each process step two things are done in parallel: (1) "simulate-machine" computes the next process state, which is an element of "MACHINE-STATE" encoding the machine's current status, and (2) the current output of sensors attached to the machine ("sense[m]") is offered to the control system via "xr-j-sens." If the control system is ready to accept the data from this machine cycle an exchange will take place; otherwise the data will be gone forever.

"simulate-machine" has two arguments: the current machine state and the value returned by "feedback-j-if-any." This function is defined as "xr-j-back," an exchange function which interacts with several sites in the control system which provide controlling feedback to the j-th machine. If some actuator is being activated at the moment "xr-j-back" is evaluated, an exchange takes place and a value in "FEEDBACK" is returned. Otherwise the argument "'null'" is returned, indicating that no actuators are being used.

Our final example of a free-running process is a producer-consumer buffer. Its process state is the current buffer contents, and its successor function is:

next-buffer: BUFFER ⟶ BUFFER;

next-buffer[b] = give-to-consumer[get-from-producer[b]];

get-from-producer: BUFFER ⟶ BUFFER;

get-from-producer[b] =
/full[b]: b,
'true' : put-on-tail[(b, xr-prod['null'])]
/;

give-to-consumer: BUFFER ⟶ BUFFER;
/empty[b] : b,
'true' : put-on-head[(xr-cons[first[b]], rest[b])]
/.

On each process step "get-from-producer" provides the opportunity to put one new element in the buffer (assuming it is not already full). If some producer has a pending "xm-prod [new-element]", "new-element" will be returned as the value of "xr-prod" and inserted. Otherwise "xr-prod" returns "'null'", which "put-on-tail" will simply ignore.

Likewise, on each process step "give-to-consumer" offers the element at the head of the buffer ("first[b]") to any process evaluating "xm-cons['null']." If such an evaluation is pending an exchange will take place and "xr-cons[first[b]]" will return "'null'", which "put-on-head" will ignore. Otherwise the unconsumed "first[b]" will be returned, and "put-on-head" will reinstate it.

The expected behavior of this process (at least under light loading) will be to cycle very fast, checking for interactions but not having any on most process steps. This shows that exchange functions are in some sense more primitive than synchronization mechanisms which enable a process to wait for any one of several events to occur. The payoff is a much simpler implementation for exchange functions, and the choice is in keeping with the PAISLey philosophy of simplicity and minimal semantics. It is also arguable that the above specification is as perspicuous as any, largely because of the benefits of applicative style.

4) *Implementation:* Exchange functions can be implemented straightforwardly, even on distributed networks (assuming a simple message-passing facility). In almost all cases the pattern of matches on a channel is one-to-one or many-to-one, the latter for resource competition. In this section we present an efficient distributed algorithm for implementing exchange matching in these cases.

Consider first an exchange channel with many "xm"'s and one "x" (or just two "x"'s, in which case one of them takes the role of the "xm" in this description), all residing at different nodes of a network (see Fig. 8). When an "xm" is initiated, a message carrying its argument is sent to the node where the matching "x" resides. These messages are queued up in arrival order. When the "x" is initiated, if the queue is empty, it waits until it is not. When the queue is not empty, it removes the first entry as the "match," takes the value stored there as its own value, sends a termination message containing its argument to the matching "xm," and continues. Computation can continue at the "xm" as soon as the termination message (with its value) is received.

This implementation uses only two messages per match, and automatically prevents lockout with FIFO queuing. For channels with one "xr" and either one "x" or many "xm's", the queue is formed at the site of the "xr", and the only modification necessary is that if the "xr" is initiated when the queue of possible matches is empty, then it does not go into the wait state. For channels with many "xr's" and one "x", matching is done at the site of the "x", but no queue forms. If an "xr" sends an initiating message but the "x" is not pending, a termination message with the original argument is sent back to the "xr" immediately.

In the rare cases where one party to all matches on a channel is *not* predetermined by the static specification structure, matching on a channel can

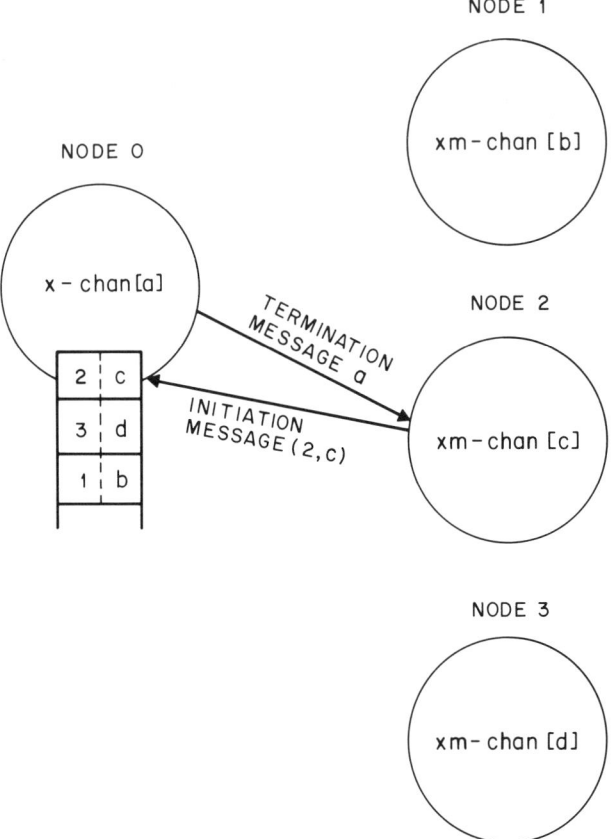

Figure 8. Distributed implementation of exchange matching

be implemented by a "channel controller" situated anywhere in the network. The initiation of any exchange causes a message containing its type and argument to be sent to the controller. The controller queues and matches as appropriate, notifying an exchange function that it has been matched by sending it a termination message containing the value. This is less desirable than the previous strategy only because it requires four messages per match.

5) *Further Properties and Justifications:* Because exchange functions are only "pseudofunctions" and have side effects, expressions containing them cannot be optimized to avoid evaluation of expressions whose *values* are not needed. The most common example of this is a successor function with the form "proj-2-1[(a, b)]", where expression "a" computes the next state and "b" interacts with other processes.

There is also a potential problem with distributing values obtained by interaction, but the formal parameter mechanism does this nicely. Suppose the effect of

/equal[(x-denom['null'], 0]: 'divide-check',
 'true': divide[(numerator, x-denom['null'])]]
/

is wanted, where both usages of the value returned by an exchange are supposed to result from a single evaluation. This can be specified unambiguously by defining "quotient" as

quotient[(n, d)] =
 /equal[(d, 0)]: 'divide-check',
  'true' : divide[(n, d)]
/,

and then using it in the invocation "quotient[(numerator, x-denom['null'])]."

Establishing the internal consistency of a specification with exchange functions requires some attention. The range of a user-chosen function defined as an exchange must agree with the domains of all those with which it can exchange. Furthermore, precedence constraints caused by nested evaluation structures can cause exchange deadlocks. But the channel of an exchange function has been made a constant attribute rather than an argument to it just so that exchange patterns would yield to static analysis, and simple arguments do establish deadlock-freedom in many common cases. For instance, the process hierarchy constructed in Zave and Yeh [1981] expresses the acyclic "dependency" structure of the interactions in the system; the argument that this prevents deadlock is a common one in the operating system literature (e.g., Brinch Hansen [1977]).

There are so many proposals for distributed interaction mechanisms current today that comparison and justification are essential. Most properly, exchange functions are motivated and justified by our goal of fitting processes and asynchronous interactions into an applicative framework, and in this role they are almost unique (see also Milne and Milner [1979]). Their generality is established by Fig. 7(b) and by extensive experience with them, which indicates that the only kind of interaction they cannot specify is *unbounded broadcast*.

Exchange functions can also be justified, however, on the same basis as procedure-based mechanisms, which fall into the two general categories of procedure-call mechanisms [Brinch Hansen 1978], [Hoare 1974], [Ichbiah et al. 1979] and message-passing [Rao 1980]. Exchange functions are more primitive than procedure calls because they specify interaction at only one point in time rather than two (procedure call and return). They are thus more general and easier to implement, while the mutual synchronization of the communication processes provides much of the structure and control usually associated with procedure-call mechanisms.

It is the mutual synchronization that most distinguishes exchange functions from message-passing mechanisms, where (usually) messages are automatically buffered, so that the sender transmits the message and continues, while the message is queued until the receiver is ready for it. The decision against this scheme is based on our concern with performance. Consider a set of terminals sending updates to a central database. With exchange functions a terminal cannot create new work for the system until the system has accepted its previous work. If a terminal could simply send an update message and continue, its speed could increase (unchecked by the ability of the system to handle the work), the queue at the database could grow to unbounded lengths, and no bounds on the performance of the system could ever be established.

At the same time, there is nothing wrong with *bounded* buffering, but this can always be specified in PAISLey. Introducing bounds within an abstract, general-purpose interaction mechanism (such as "message passing up to some bound") would seem a most unfortunate mixture of specification and implementation.

Given that synchronization is going to be two-way, it costs very little in the implementation to preserve the possibility of two-way data transfer, although it is seldom used. It also keeps the number of primitives down by a factor of two, since otherwise each of the three exchange function types would have to come in a "sending data" and a "receiving data" version.

Of all the well-known interaction mechanisms, the most similar to exchange functions is Hoare's input/output primitives [Hoare 1978]. In Hoare's language a pair of statements, "P?input" in process Q and "Q!output" in process P, will come together in the same mutually synchronized manner that two matching exchanges do. "output" is an expression whose value is assigned to the variable "input," assuming appropriate type correspondences. In addition to the relatively unimportant data asymmetry, Hoare's primitives seem to be different from exchange functions in three fundamental ways. (1) There is no way to specify real-time or free-running interactions. (2) There is no straightforward way to specify resource sharing, since all "matches" are one-to-one by process name. In Hoare's language a process representing a shared resource must have a separate command for each process with which it can communicate, and guard that command [Dijkstra 1975] with an input command naming the appropriate process of the many. The guard (and statement) to be executed are chosen nondeterministically from the processes that are ready to communicate. These multiple statements seem distinctly clumsy compared to an "xm"/"x" exchange match. Furthermore, the full knowledge each process must have about the names of the processes with which it communicates makes modularity difficult to achieve. (3) Hoare's primitives belong in a procedural, rather than applicative, framework. The destination of a data transfer, for instance, is specified by an address.

REQUIREMENTS SPECIFICATION FOR EMBEDDED SYSTEMS 163

6.4 Performance Requirements

1) *Definition of Performance Requirements:* So far the only structure that has been needed for complete and formal specification of performance requirements is attachment of timing and reliability attributes to functions in the "functional" requirements specification. A timing attribute refers to the evaluation time of the function. It is a random variable, and any information about its distribution, such as lower or upper bounds, mean, or the distribution itself, may be given.[5]

A reliability attribute can only be attached to a function whose range is divided into two subsets (e.g. "→SUCCESS-RESULT ∪ FAILURE-RESULT"), the first for the values returned by successful evaluations and the second for values returned when the evaluation fails. The attribute itself is a discrete (binary) random variable whose two outcomes denote successful or failed evaluations, and any information about its distribution may be given.

When a primitive function fails it simply returns a value in its failure range. An exchange function fails in the same way, except that even when it fails it must still match another exchange, so that failures do not affect or complicate analysis of exchange patterns. Furthermore, if matching exchange functions *both* have reliability properties, they must succeed or fail together.

Failure of a nonprimitive function simply means that the function delivers a value in the second subset of its range. It is up to the function's definition to ensure that this happens with the specified frequency, since the function is evaluated according to its definition under all circumstances.

Reliability is a difficult and little-understood subject, but this definition of it has several appealing properties. It forces the specified system to have the primary characteristic of a reliable system, namely going into a well-defined and previously anticipated state when something fails. It makes reliability independent of timing and functionality, since a function evaluation must satisfy its timing requirements and deliver a value in its declared range regardless of whether it succeeds or fails. In fact, we have deemed this property so important that we have sacrificed some realism for it: only primitive functions can *really* fail (since nonprimitive ones are always evaluated according to their definitions). Much more knowledge of reliability is needed before we can be sure how successful this approach will be, but its formality and tractability are strong arguments in its favor.

These performance requirements can be simulated by the specification interpreter, and checked (in principle!) for internal consistency, just as the functional ones are. This means, for instance, that if "f[x]" is defined as "g[h[x]]," and there are upper bounds on the evaluation times of all three, then the upper bound on "f" must be strictly greater than (allowing time for

---

5. More generally, the sequence of evaluations of the function over the lifetime of the system could be associated with a stochastic process, so that the time of each evaluation would be a separate random variable, but let us hope such generality will never be needed.

invocation/argument transfer) the sum of the upper bounds on "g" and "h".

2) Examples of "Synchronous Closed-Loop" Performance Requirements: An on-line database system can be called a "synchronous closed-loop" system—"closed-loop" because the entire feedback loop realized by the system is explicitly represented, and "synchronous" because the terminal process (on behalf of the cooperative person behind it) waits for responses, i.e., synchronizes itself with the system. For these systems the basic performance requirements are particularly easy to specify, and all are attached to the terminals. We will refer to the functional terminal specification in Section 6.2, and give performance requirements typical of airline reservation systems [Knight 1972].

Distributions have been left as comments in the PAISLey syntax because we have not yet settled on a formal language for them. Timing requirements normally call for the maximum, minimum, mean, or constant value of the random variable, while reliability requirements normally specify a lower bound on the probability of success.

A response-time limit of 3 s is specified by

$$\text{transact: !} \longrightarrow \text{"maximum = 3 sec."}$$

An average load of 200 transactions/s, assuming 10,000 terminals in the system, is specified by

$$\text{terminal-cycle: !} \longrightarrow \text{"mean = 50 sec,"}$$

which says that on the average a terminal demands a transaction (goes through a cycle) every 50 s. Finally, the requirement that at least 99 percent of all transactions must be processed successfully is expressed as

$$\text{transact: \%} \longrightarrow \text{"prob \{'success'\}} \geq .99\text{"}$$

which, of course, can only be attached to "transact" because its range is divided into success ("RESPONSE") and failure ("ERROR-MESSAGE") subranges.

3) Examples of "Asynchronous Closed-Loop" Performance Requirements: Process-control systems can be called "asynchronous closed-loop" systems — "asynchronous" because the machines, which are the sources and destinations of the feedback loops realized by these systems, are free-running. The systems must keep up with them without their cooperation. Performance requirements for these systems are more of a challenge, but the operational approach enables us to specify them straightforwardly. "Open-loop" specifications, in which not all of the feedback loop (ultimately, the purpose of *any* embedded system is to realize feedback loops) is included explicitly in the model, have performance requirements similar to these. An example of an open-loop specification would be a patient-monitoring system in which treatment of patients was not represented, only display of warning messages.

In Zave and Yeh [1981] a variety of timing requirements for a process-control system are given. These include: (1) the granularity of the discrete simulation of the machines in the environment, (2) a real-time limit on the fully automatic feedback loop realized by the system, (3) a real-time limit on the partially manual feedback loop realized by the system, specified as separate response requirements on the human operator and on the computer system, and (4) a *derived* performance requirement on the system's internal database component which will guarantee that other system components can meet their own performance requirements. Despite the subtleties involved, each one of these requirements is specified simply by attaching a timing constraint to the successor function of a single process!

4) *"Real-World" Properties:* Time and reliability (the fact that sometimes digital components do not do what their definition says they will, for physical reasons forever beyond the reach of digital logic) are nondigital properties that incontrovertibly affect the digital domain. In [Zave 1980b] many other such physical ("real-world") properties are mentioned, weight and distance, for example. Why are these not formalized as performance requirements as well?

The answer is that, to the extent that we know them, the effects of these properties on the computational (digital) domain can be specified in terms of functions, timing, and reliability. Weight constraints, for instance, only affect how many functions can be realized. Even if we did attach weight attributes to components of PAISLey specification, there is nothing that an interpreter could do with them. Therefore an informal comment is just as satisfactory.

Distance is a more interesting example because its effects on the computational domain are more varied. Distance increases the relative time for interprocess interactions, decreases component reliability, and increases the logical complexity of interfaces which must cope with these factors. Yet these three effects are directly expressible in terms of timing, reliability, and functional requirements, respectively.

Factors such as these can nevertheless have a profound effect on requirements. In an airline reservation system, for instance, it may be necessary to divide the response-time or transaction-reliability allowances into portions for the data-communication subsystem and portions for the database subsystem. Although such allocation is technically a design decision, two reasons for doing it during the requirements phase are (1) to enable feasibility analyses of two very different technologies and (2) to contract the work to different organizations.

These allocated requirements can be specified in PAISLey. We have constructed a requirements model in which time limits are given for, and failures can occur in, each of three stages: input transmission, transaction processing, and output transmission. Failure at any stage aborts subsequent stages and propagates an appropriate error message. This is the source of elements in the set "ERROR-MESSAGE" found in the range of "transact" in the terminal specification.

7. EVALUATION AGAINST GOALS FOR REQUIREMENTS SPECIFICATIONS

A thorough evaluation of PAISLey cannot be made until an interpreter has been implemented and specifications of large systems have been written. In the meantime, we present the reasons why we believe our goals for requirements specifications will be met.

It was stated in Section 2.2 that in order to constrain the target system, a requirements specification should be precise, unambiguous, internally consistent, complete, and minimal. The formal nature of a PAISLey specification leaves no doubt as to its precision and lack of ambiguity. If it (1) is syntactically correct, (2) has all its domain declarations in agreement with all its function applications, (3) has all its range declarations in agreement with its function definitions, and (4) can be shown to be free of exchange deadlock, then it is internally consistent. The arguments in Section 5.1 suggest that PAISLey does not obstruct the writing of minimal specifications.

The issue of completeness deserves special attention, because the worst failing a requirements specification language can have is to be unable to express what the requirements analyst wants to say. *This* is the problem that makes analysts revert to English! PAISLey has been used to specify requirements for a wide variety of embedded systems (small examples), and never yet found wanting. In addition to the examples used or referred to here, it was also used to specify (in some 33 pages, see Zave [1978]) a distributed design for an innovative interactive numerical system that was actually implemented directly from the specification [Zave and Rheinboldt 1979; Zave and Cole]. Furthermore, the prompt feedback provided by executable requirements should help to protect against omissions.

Of course, this refers only to properties relevant to the computational domain—it says nothing about constraints on the development process itself, such as deadlines, cost limits, methodological standards, and routine maintenance procedures. PAISLey does not address these, nor does it offer any particular help in posing alternative or prioritized requirements [Yeh 1980]. And the need to supplement formal requirements with diagrams, comments, and other informal avenues of human communication will never disappear.

A requirements specification must be formally manipulable or testable, so that it can be determined whether the final product meets its requirements. Any property of a PAISLey specification relating to the behavior of the system in a given situation is clearly testable, because the behavior of the executable specification can be compared directly to the behavior of the target system. PAISLey specifications should also be suitable for verification, because they are based on a few simple and formal concepts, but this aspect has not yet been explored.

Finally, requirements specifications should be understandable and modifiable. Although these qualities are vague and subjective, there is reason to believe that they can both be achieved by attaining two other qualities which are at least identifiable, if still subjective. These two qualities are (1) providing modeling capabilities which are abstract, intuitive and close to human perceptions of the environment to be modeled and (2) providing means by which complexity can be decomposed. The latter is necessary because a complex specification must be understood (and changed) one small piece at a time. The former is important for understanding because it allows people to think in familiar, problem-oriented terms. It may also be important for modifiability, as explained in Goldman and Wile [1980]. They argue that, since our current best definition of modifiability is that a small change in the environment causes a correspondingly small change in the specification, the property is most possessed by those specifications which are the most direct translations of the natural environment into formalism.

We contend that PAISLey models can be intuitive and close to the natural way people think about embedded systems. The objects in the system's environment can be modeled directly as autonomous parallel processes, using a language with the power to specify simulations of great verisimilitude. The internal process structure of the proposed system model is largely determined by the environment structure and user-oriented system "functions" or capabilities (see Section 8.2).

PAISLey also enables nontrivial decomposition of complexity. The division of a specification into processes is especially useful, for instance, because it decomposes both static and dynamic properties, and because it seems to correlate with divisions meaningful to users. The partitioning even extends to execution of specifications, because any subset of processes can be executed in isolation, simply by leaving all interactions with missing processes as unelaborated primitives in a form such as "receive-message: ⟶ MESSAGE." The interpreter will evaluate this "interaction site" by choosing some message at random. This capability was used in Zave and Yeh [1981] to develop a specification in five versions, each independently executable, and each obtained from the last by adding new processes/functions in an "outside-in" sequence. Decomposition of complexity is discussed further in Zave [1980a].

8. PLANS FOR FUTURE RESEARCH

8.1 Execution of Specifications

We are currently planning the implementation of a system for executing specifications. Specifications will be checked for consistency and compiled into fully parallel runtime process-and-interaction structures. These structures will then be interpreted under interactive control. The most important questions to be answered are: What is it like to test a specification? What kind of control over the course of execution does the analyst need? What display, report, and trace facilities can be used to produce an intelligible outcome?

8.2 Methodology

This work on requirements *specification*, which has been pursued so far with small examples, must be extended in the directions of requirements *analysis*, and "scaling-up" to large systems. In other words, we need to pursue the implications of process-based specifications for a requirements methodology.

The most obvious problem is that process-based descriptions are not intrinsically hierarchical. It is not clear, however, that top-level system requirements are hierarchical either. Preliminary studies indicate that a complex system carries out several parallel functions for its environment, none of which is subservient to any other. ("Top-level" is important here because once the process structure of a PAISLey specification is determined, further decisions are recorded by elaboration of successor functions—which is completely hierarchical.)

This observation has suggested an alternative methodological approach, in which parallel functions are identified and translated into PAISLey processes or hierarchically arranged groups of them (similar to "subsystems" in DDN, see Riddle [1978]). Preliminary work with three process-control examples has even revealed a set of rules which can be used to identify user-oriented functions of these systems; functions defined according to these rules have a one-to-one correspondence with processes in the subsequent PAISLey specification.

Complexity is then decomposed through incremental development: the specification is written and tested one function process at a time. The language semantics already support this mode of use, as explained in Section 7, and our investigations of the interpreter's human interface are also being carried out with the incremental mode in mind.

These ideas are still highly speculative, but they do establish that hierarchical abstraction is not the only approach to a practical requirements methodology. At the highest levels of system description, "flat" structure may not be incompatible with good structure.

8.3 Design

It has been pointed out that PAISLey is capable of specifying the results of design decisions. A logical extension of this is to investigate its properties as a design specification language. The benefits are potentially great, because a uniform language for requirements and design should make possible substantial improvements in the traceability and automatability of design. It might also lead to a better theoretical understanding of design decisions as resource/performance tradeoffs.

ACKNOWLEDGMENTS

Many people have contributed to the work presented here. My thanks especially to D. R. Fitzwater, with whom the foundations for PAISLey were laid, to S. Smoliar, A. Conn, and R. Mittermeir, for stimulating discussions on requirements, to P. Fowler, for the chance to try these ideas on a class at Bell Labs, to G. Cole, for diligent and able assistance, to R. Hamlet, who would read this stuff before anyone else would (or could), to the referees, and to R. Yeh, for support, encouragement, ideas, and good advice.

APPENDIX
A Grammar for PAISLey

[*Appendix deleted*]

CASE STUDIES

Discussion of specification and specification languages would be barren and futile without looking at the applications to substantial and realistic problems. In this third Part we shall look at specifications in action in a selection of important yet diverse case studies.

In the first paper Narain Gehani looks at the controversy surrounding the issue of formal or informal specifications. He looks at one particular working system and considers both approaches to its specification. Despite the fact that there are many problems with informal methods, the conclusions are not one-sided.

In two of the remaining papers specification is employed as an important ingredient in design. In both cases it is used first of all in understanding and then to describe the external behavior of a system without regard to the details of its implementation. John Guttag and Jim Horning look at the design of software in general and Robert Jacob uses specification to help in the design of the man-machine interface.

Three papers are concerned with the specification of software designed for handling text. Bernard Sufrin's paper is concerned with text editors, of the kind used in many computer systems. Prabhaker Mateti addresses the problem of pretty-printing of Pascal programs and Martin Feather looks at text formatters related to the UNIX nroff/troff systems.

The two remaining papers fall into the category of real-time or embedded systems applications. The paper by Carl Sunshine, *et al.* employs the notation of the AFFIRM system to describe communication protocols. In the final paper Pamela Zave and Raymond Yeh illustrate the usability and applicability of their ideas on executable specifications.

NARAIN GEHANI
AT&T Bell Laboratories, Murray Hill, NJ 07974

Specifications: Formal and Informal— A Case Study

1. INTRODUCTION

Informal specifications of systems, while easy to read, tend to be ambiguous, incomplete, imprecise and overspecific. Formal specifications alleviate these problems, and may be used to show the correctness of system implementation and the equivalence of different implementations. They also offer potential for the development of automated aids for the detection of the above problems. [Liskov 1975] is an excellent introduction to formal specifications and their advantages.

The algebraic specification technique of Guttag and Horning [1978a] is favored by many computer scientists. Having seen and used this specification technique on fairly well studied examples such as stacks, queues, lists, symbol tables, etc., I decided to compare the informal specifications of some real system with its algebraic specifications.

For the comparison I selected the EVENT LOG subsystem of the Change Management Automatic Build System for which the informal specifications [Lyons 1977] were available. The EVENT LOG subsystem was selected because it was small, part of a working system with clear informal specifications available, and because members of its design team are accessible. The intent of this paper is not to criticize the informal specifications of the EVENT LOG subsystem, but to compare informal specifications with formal specifications.

The Change Management Automated Build System (CM ABS), a successful software management system, supports the manufacture of software products that generally are

(a) Diverse in their use of language processors, program libraries, and software construction methods,

(b) Too large to be recompiled in their entirety for every release or every version, and

(c) Large enough to constitute a significant engineering records problem.

CM ABS imposes only a minimal set of conventions on software products and is adaptable for use by individual software projects for software construction.

The manufacture of the release of a software product is envisioned as building a series of versions (called builds) of the product. The final version is designated to be the release which is then sent out to the customers. Associated with each release is the EVENT LOG subsystem, a record of the status of the versions of the software product developed in building the release [Lyons and Muenzer 1977; Muenzer 1977].

2. THE ALGEBRAIC SPECIFICATION TECHNIQUE

Algebraic specifications have two parts:

(a) the syntax—the operations of the system are specified indicating the number of arguments, the argument types and the result type

(b) the semantics—algebraic equations (axioms) are given that relate the values created by the operations.

In the basic notation, the operations are functions without side effects; none of the arguments are changed. Guttag [1977] has extended the notation to allow for changes in arguments, that is, to allow procedures.

The algebraic specification technique is illustrated by specifying a rather high-level and abstract version of a relational database [Date 1975]. A relational database consists of a set of relations. Relations are identified by their names. They can be added, deleted and retrieved from a database. Additionally one can check for the membership of a relation in a database. The informal specifications for the operations of a relational database are:

- *new*   returns as its result an empty database.

- $add(d, n, r)$ returns a database which is the result of adding the relation r with the name n to the database d. If a relation with the name n was previously in the database then an error occurs.

- $delete(d, n)$ returns a database d which is the same as d but with the relation named n deleted. If such a relation did not exist then an error occurs.

- $empty(d)$ returns **true** if the database d is empty and **false** otherwise.

- $in(d, n)$ returns **true** if the relation named n is in the database d and **false** otherwise.

- $get(d, n)$ returns the relation with name n if one exists in the database d; otherwise an error is indicated.

In writing the formal specifications an additional operation *insert* is needed. This operation is similar to *add* except that it does not check to see if the relation being added is present or not in the database. It is an internal operation not available to the users of the relational database.

The formal specifications are:

1. **type** *database*

2. **external operations** *new, add, delete, empty, in, get*
3. **internal operation** *insert*

4. **syntax**

5.   *new*: ⟶ *database*
6.   *add*: *database* × *name* × *relation* ⟶ *database* ∪ {ERROR}
7.   *empty*: *database* ⟶ *boolean*
8.   *in*: *database* × *name* ⟶ *boolean*
9.   *delete*: *database* × *name* ⟶ *database* ∪ {ERROR}
10.   *insert*: *database* × *name* × *relation* ⟶ *database*
11.   *get*: *database* × *name* ⟶ *relation* ∪ {ERROR}

12. **semantics**

13.   **var** *d*: *database*; *n, m*: *name*; *r*: *relation*

14. **axioms**

15.   *empty*(*new*) = **true**
16.   *empty*(*insert*(*d, n, r*)) = **false**

17.   *in*(*new, n*) = **false**
18.   *in*(*insert*(*d, m, r*), *n*) = **if** n = m **then true else** *in*(*d, n*)

19.   *delete*(*new, n*) = ERROR
20.   *delete*(*insert*(*d, m, r*), *n*) = **if** *n* = *m* **then** *d*
                          else *insert*(*delete*(*d, n*), *m, r*)

21.   *get*(*new, n*) = ERROR
22.   *get*(*insert*(*d, m, r*), *n*) = **if** *n* = *m* **then** *r* **else** *get*(*d, n*)

23.   *add*(*d, n, r*) = **if** *in*(*d, n*) **then** ERROR **else** *insert*(*d, n, r*)

24. **end** *database*.

In the definition of the *database*, types *name* and *relation* have been used but not defined. Some explanatory notes on the above formal specifications are given below:

    Line 2: specifies the operations available to users of the database.

    Line 3: specifies an operation internal to the database and not available to the user.

Line 5: specifies the syntax of the operation *new*. Operation *new* takes no arguments and returns a value of type *database*.

Line 6: specifies that *add* takes three arguments: a database, a name and a relation. It returns either a database or an error as its result.

Line 13: variable *d* is declared to be type *database*, *n* and *m* to be of type *name*, and *r* of type *relation*.

Line 15: the result of applying the operation *empty* on a database that contains no relations (operation *new* returns such a database) is **true**.

Line 16: *empty* returns **false** if any relation has been inserted into a database.

Line 17: the operation *in* returns **false** when one tries to see if a relation is present in an empty database.

Line 18: operation *in* checks to see if the relation named *n* is in the database by recursively looking at the relations inserted.

Line 19: deleting a relation from an empty database results in an error.

Line 20: a relation named *n* is deleted by recursively looking at all the relations inserted to see if it is present.

Line 23: the operation of adding a relation *r* named *n* to a database *d* results in an error if *n* is already present in *d*; otherwise *add* is equivalent to *insert*.

By convention, any operation that has an ERROR value for an argument returns ERROR as its result. Instead of using one kind of error value, i.e., ERROR, we could have used different error values, i.e., $ERROR_1$, $ERROR_2$, etc. to differentiate error classes.

The use of the axioms in determining the result of applying an operation to the database is now illustrated by means of examples.

2.1 Examples

1. *new* represents the empty database
2. We add a relation *r1* named SUPPLIER to an empty database. We have

    add(*new*, SUPPLIER, *r1*)

    = *insert*(*new*, SUPPLIER, *r1*) — by axiom on line 23,

    i.e., database with one relation named SUPPLIER

SPECIFICATIONS: FORMAL AND INFORMAL 177

3. To the database in (2) we add the relation $r2$ with name PARTS. We get

    $add(insert(new, \text{SUPPLIER}, r1), \text{PARTS}, r2)$

    $= insert(insert(new, \text{SUPPLIER}, r1), \text{PARTS}, r2)$
    — by axiom on line 23

4. We check to see if a relation named SALES is in the above database, i.e.

    $in(insert(insert(new, \text{SUPPLIER}, r1), \text{PARTS}, r2), \text{SALES})$

    $= in(insert(new, \text{SUPPLIER}, r1), \text{SALES})$ — by axiom on line 18

    $= in(new, \text{SALES})$ — by axiom on line 18

    $=$ **false** — by axiom on line 17

    The relation SALES is not in the database.

5. We try to delete the relation named SALES from the database of (3), i.e.,

    $delete(insert(insert(new, \text{SUPPLIER}, r1), \text{PARTS}, r2), \text{SALES})$

    $= insert(delete(insert(new, \text{SUPPLIER}, r1), \text{SALES}), \text{PARTS}, r2)$
    — by axiom on line 20

    $= insert(insert(delete(new, \text{SALES}), \text{SUPPLIER}), \text{PARTS}, r2)$
    — by axiom on line 20

    $= insert(insert(\text{ERROR}, \text{SUPPLIER}, r1), \text{PARTS}, r2)$
    — by axiom on line 19

    $= insert(\text{ERROR}, \text{PARTS}, r2)$ — convention about error arguments

    $= \text{ERROR}$ — convention about error arguments

    Deletion of the relation named SALES leads to an error because it is not in the database.

6. Let us try to retrieve the relation named SUPPLIER, i.e.

    $get(insert(insert(new, \text{SUPPLIER}, r1), \text{PARTS}, r2), \text{SUPPLIER})$

$\quad= get(insert(new, \text{SUPPLIER}, rl), \text{SUPPLIER})$
$\hspace{8em}$ — by axiom on line 22
$\quad= rl$ — by axiom on line 22

It is interesting to note that no axioms were given for the operations *new* and *insert*. As long as the effects of these operations (i.e. "properties") are known in terms of the behavior of the other operations, further specification of behavior of these operations is not required. They may be implemented in any way as long as their effect on the other operations is as specified by the axioms. This should not surprise us too much. Similar examples can be found in other disciplines. For example, when building a bridge we do not care what materials are used as long as they satisfy certain properties. The materials should have a certain elasticity, tensile stress, resistance to corrosion, price, etc. These properties are stated explicitly while in case of the operations *new* and *insert*, the "properties" are implicitly stated by the axioms.

Operations *new* and *insert* are called "constructor" operations. For details of "constructor" operations and how to construct algebraic specifications see Guttag, Horowitz and Musser [1978]; Guttag and Horning [1978a]; Guttag, Horowitz and Musser [1977]. Some limitations of the algebraic specification technique are discussed by Majster [1977], Majster [1979].

3. INFORMAL SPECIFICATIONS OF THE *EVENT LOG* SUBSYSTEM

In this section, the informal specifications of the EVENT LOG subsystem, as given in Lyons [1977], are summarized. Only the essentials are included.

Associated with each release of a product is an eventlog in which status information is entered about all versions (called builds) of a release. The manufacture of a new release of the product is envisioned as building a series of versions starting from the old release. The final version is designated to be the new release.

The eventlog is updated and queried by means of the following operations:

- *create(r)*   creates a null eventlog *r*.
- *newbuild(r)*   updates the eventlog *r* to allow the recording of modifications to build the next version (i.e., build. *Note*: several versions are associated with a release). The new build number is written out on to the standard file. New build numbers range between 1 and 999.
- *append(r, b, e, t)*   text *t* is associated with event *e* of build *b* in the eventlog *r*. Previous text associated with the event *e* is not affected.
- *extract(r, b, le)*   retrieves the text corresponding to the events in

SPECIFICATIONS: FORMAL AND INFORMAL   179

the list *le* associated with build *b* of eventlog *r*. The text is prefixed by the corresponding event. The retrieval order is identical to the order in which these events were entered. If the event list *le* is left out then the event list is assumed to be all the list of the events associated with the build *b*.

- *delete(r, b, e)*   the event *e* of build *b* and the text associated with it are deleted from eventlog *r*.

Destruction of an eventlog is accomplished by destroying its underlying representation which is supposed to be a file.

4. FORMAL SPECIFICATIONS FOR THE *EVENT LOG* SUBSYSTEM

The eventlog as specified by the formal specifications differs from the informally specified eventlog in the following ways.

(a) An operation *destroy* is included to eliminate an eventlog.

(b) An operation *lastbuild#* returns the latest build number (i.e. version number). The operation *newbuild* is now modified so that it does not return a build number. This build number can be determined via the operation *lastbuild#*.

(c) In the simplest form of the algebraic technique, the operations must be functions and not procedures since no side effects are allowed. Consequently all the operations are defined as functions in the formal specifications. In contrast all operations except *extract* are defined as procedures in the informal specifications.

The formal specification of the EVENT LOG subsystem also includes some operations that are not available to the user. These are necessary for the specification of the above system. The operations are:

nbuild   similar to *newbuild* but it does not check to see if the last build number was 999. Only build numbers up to 999 are allowed.

add   similar to *append* except that it does not check to see if the build number being referenced is legal.

extractall   special case of the operation *extract*. It retrieves text associated with all events of a build.

extractlist   also a special case of the operation *extract*. It retrieves text only for the events specified.

1.   **type** *eventlog*

2. **external operations** *create, newbuild, lastbuild#, append, extract,*
$\qquad\qquad\qquad\qquad\qquad\qquad\qquad\qquad\qquad\qquad$ *delete, destroy*
   internal operations *newbuild, add, extractall, extractlist*

3. **syntax**

4. $\qquad$ *create*: $\longrightarrow$ *eventlog*
5. $\qquad$ *newbuild*: *eventlog* $\longrightarrow$ *eventlog* ∪ {ERROR}
6. $\qquad$ *nbuild*: *eventlog* $\longrightarrow$ *eventlog*
7. $\qquad$ *lastbuild#*: *eventlog* $\longrightarrow$ *build#* ∪ {0} ∪ {ERROR}
8. $\qquad$ *add*: *eventlog* × *build#* × *event* × *text* $\longrightarrow$ *eventlog*
9. $\qquad$ *append*: *eventlog* × *build#* × *event* × *text* $\longrightarrow$ *eventlog* ∪ {ERROR}
10. $\qquad$ *extract*: *eventlog* × *build#* × *evenlist* $\longrightarrow$ *text* ∪ {ERROR}
11. $\qquad$ *extractall*: *eventlog* × *build#* $\longrightarrow$ *text* ∪ {ERROR}
12. $\qquad$ *extractlist*: *eventlog* × *build#* × *eventlist* $\longrightarrow$ *text* ∪ {ERROR}
13. $\qquad$ *delete*: *eventlog* × *build#* × *event* $\longrightarrow$ *eventlog* ∪ {ERROR}
14. $\qquad$ *destroy*: *eventlog* $\longrightarrow$ *text*

15. **semantics**

16. $\qquad$ **var** *r*: *eventlog*; *b, b1*: *build#*; *elist*: *eventlist*; *e, e1*: *event*; *t*: *text*

17. **axioms**

18. $\qquad$ *lastbuild#*(*create*) = 0
19. $\qquad$ *lastbuild#*(*nbuild*(*r*)) = 1 + *lastbuild#*(*r*)
20. $\qquad$ *lastbuild#*(*add*(*r, b, e, t*)) = *lastbuild#*(*r*)
21. $\qquad$ *append*(*r, b, e, t*) = **if** *lastbuild#*(*r*) ⩾ *b*
    $\qquad\qquad\qquad\qquad\qquad$ **then** *add*(*r, b, e, t*)
    $\qquad\qquad\qquad\qquad\qquad$ **else** ERROR
22. $\qquad$ *newbuild*(*r*) = **if** *lastbuild#*(*r*) = 999 **then** ERROR **else** *nbuild*(*r*)
23. $\qquad$ *extract*(*r, b, elist*) = **if** *null*(*elist*)
    $\qquad\qquad\qquad\qquad\qquad$ **then** *extractall*(*r, b*)
    $\qquad\qquad\qquad\qquad\qquad$ **else** *extractlist*(*r, b, elist*)
24. $\qquad$ *extractall*(*create, b*) = *empty*
25. $\qquad$ *extractall*(*nbuild*(*r, b*)) = *extractall*(*r, b*)
26. $\qquad$ *extractall*(*add*(*r, b1, e, t*), *b*) = **if** *b* = *b1*
    $\qquad\qquad\qquad\qquad\qquad$ **then** *extractall*(*r, b*)||*attach*(*e, t*)
    $\qquad\qquad\qquad\qquad\qquad$ **else** *extractall*(*r, b*)
27. $\qquad$ *extractlist*(*create, b, elist*) = *empty*
28. $\qquad$ *extractlist*(*newbuild*(*r*), *b, elist*) = *extractlist*(*r, b, elist*)
29. $\qquad$ *extractlist*(*add*(*r, b1, e, t*), *b, elist*) =
    $\qquad\qquad\qquad\qquad\qquad$ **if** *b1* = *b* **and** *in*(*e, elist*)
    $\qquad\qquad\qquad\qquad\qquad$ **then** *extractlist*(*r, b, elist*) || *attach*(*e, t*)
    $\qquad\qquad\qquad\qquad\qquad$ **else** *extractlist*(*r, b, elist*)

SPECIFICATIONS: FORMAL AND INFORMAL

30. $delete(create, b, e) = create$
31. $delete(nbuild(r), b, e) = nbuild(delete(r, b, e))$
32. $delete(add(r, b1, e1), b, e) = $ **if** $b = b1$ **and** $e = e1$
     then $delete(r, b, e)$
     else $add(delete(r, b, e), b1, e1)$
33. $destroy(r) = empty$
34. **end** *eventlog*

In defining the type *eventlog* we have used, but not specified, other types and their operations. They are:

(a) *build#*: subrange of integers from 1 to 999

(b) *text*: sequence of lines;
- *empty* denotes a null sequence of lines
- $||$ used for text concatenation

(c) *line*: character string

(d) *eventlist*: list of events with operations

$in(e, L)$	returns **true** if event e is in eventlist L and **false** otherwise
$null(L)$	returns **true** if eventlist L is null and **false** otherwise

(e) *event*: character string

$attach(e, t)$ prefixes the text t by a line containing the event e for identification.

The formal specifications define two operations, *lastbuild#* and *destroy*, which are not included in the informal specifications. Their inclusion is explained in the comparison. Some notes to help in understanding the formal specification of the EVENT LOG subsystem are given below.

Line 2: Specifies the external operations which are available to eventlog users and internal operations which are hidden from the user. The internal operations are necessary for the specifications.

Lines 4-14: Specify the syntax of all the operations defined in the specifications. For example:

(i) *create*: an operation with no arguments which returns a new eventlog.

(ii) *newbuild*: takes as argument an eventlog and returns either an eventlog or an error.

(iii) *nbuild*: takes as input an eventlog and returns an eventlog

(iv) *extract*: takes as input an eventlog, a build number and an eventlist and returns as result either text or an error.

Line 16: Declares the types of variables used in the axioms defining the semantics of eventlog's operations.

Lines 18-20: Define the behavior of the operation *lastbuild#*. Line 18 specifies that the *lastbuild#* of a new eventlog is 0, line 19 specifies that operation *nbuild* increases the value of *lastbuild#* by 1, and line 20 specifies that operation *add* does not change the *lastbuild#*.

Line 21: Specifies that operation *append* is the same as *add* provided *lastbuild#(r)* $\geqslant b$ where r is the eventlog to which we are adding information about build number b; otherwise we get an error as a result of *append*.

Line 22: Specifies that performing the operation *newbuild* on an eventlog r when the *lastbuild#(r)* = 999 leads to an error; otherwise, *newbuild* is the same as performing *nbuild*.

Line 23: Specifies that the operation *extract* is the same as *extractall* if the event list is null; otherwise it is the same as *extractlist*. Operation *extractall* retrieves all information about a build while *extractlist* only retrieves information about the specified events. So if information about all events of a build is desired, the user does not specify any events when using the operation *extract*.

Line 26: This line is one of the axioms for *extractall*. It says that if the last operation we performed on an eventlog r was to add information t about build number $b1$, then check to see if $b1$ is equal to build number b. If b is equal to $b1$ then perform *extractall* on r and concatenate the information retrieved to t; otherwise just perform extractall on r.

Line 33: The result of destroying an eventlog is a null sequence of lines viz., *empty*. Since a destroyed eventlog is not an object of type *eventlog*, no further operations can be performed on it. This restriction is clear from the syntactic definitions of the operations.

Note that we have again not given any axioms for operations *create*, *nbuild*, and *add*. Instead the other operations are defined in terms of them.

5. COMPARISON OF THE INFORMAL AND FORMAL SPECIFICATIONS

In comparing the formal specifications with the informal specifications (those given in Lyons [1977]), the following points were noted:

(a) **Readability**

The informal specifications are easier to read but formal specifications are clear, and precise. The algebraic specification technique is easy to learn for people with some mathematical background.

(b) **Missing operation**

This observation was the most surprising of all and was possible because formal specifications led me to a better understanding of the EVENT LOG subsystem. In the specifications for *append*, a check has to be made to ensure that the build number being referenced is less than the last build number. It was observed that no operation is provided in the EVENT LOG subsystem to determine the last build number. The last build number is written out to the standard file by the operation *newbuild*. The user has to keep track of the last build number manually. This seemed to be a serious deficiency and was confirmed by Muenzer [1979]. For example, one cannot write a program that retrieves all the text associated with the last build (i.e. version). The inclusion of an operation *lastbuild#* for the EVENT LOG subsystem is now under consideration.

(c) **"Manual" operation**

For some reason, it was decided that destruction of an eventlog will be accomplished manually: one would destroy the eventlog by deleting the file that represented it. We feel that destroying an eventlog should be an operation like *create*, *add*, etc. and have therefore included it in the formal specifications. Having done this, the effect of applying operations on a destroyed eventlog can be defined.

(d) **Clarity, interaction between operations**

The syntactic part of the formal specifications is clearly separated from the semantic part. The operation domains are clearly specified in the formal specifications. Interaction between operations is easily discernible. For example performing a *delete* operation before or after a successful *newbuild* operation has the same result.

(e) **Implementation details**

Specifications should not include implementation details. They should specify what is to be done and not how. The informal specifications contain implementation details e.g "eventlog is represented by a file"; the eventlog will be eliminated by "deleting the file that represents it," lines of text associated with a key are to be stored as one unit, etc. If it is desirable to suggest an implementation then the implementation details should be provided but kept clearly separated from the specifications. The informal specifications do have a section on representation details. However, not all the implementation details are isolated here; some of them are mixed with the specifications of the subsystem.

There are situations where it is essential that a system must be implemented in a certain way. Then specifications detailing the implementation should be provided both for informal specifications and formal specifications [Guttag, Horowitz and Musser 1978]—whichever is being used.

(f) **Errors and boundary conditions**
The informal specifications did not specify what would happen in case operations were applied to an eventlog that had been destroyed, the initial build number, the effect of applying the *newbuild* operation more than 999 times, extracting information about a build number greater than the last build number or a build number that has no information associated with it, what the initialization of the eventlog is supposed to be, etc.

(g) **Imprecision**
The eventfield is defined by the informal specification to be a character string of "moderate" length. What is a moderate length? Such vague specifications will lead to incompatibilities and cannot be used for reference by the user and the implementor.

(h) **Incompleteness**
For the *append* operation "Lines of text are read from the standard file...". It is not specified how this text is terminated.

(i) **Procedures versus functions**
All operations in the formal specifications have been defined as functions. Implementation of these operations as functions will lead to inefficient implementations. As mentioned before, the algebraic specification technique has been extended to allow for defining operations that are procedures.

(j) **Miscellaneous**
The informal specifications are interspersed with environmental details, e.g., version restrictions, the version of the system that maintains it, write permission in the release directory, etc. These are important, but they should be specified separately.

6. CONCLUSIONS

All the points listed in the comparison except for the one about the missing operation were in a sense expected. It took me about a day to understand the EVENT LOG subsystem and its context, and about an hour to write the formal specifications. There was an error in the specifications relating to the definition of the destroy function. This was pointed out by Lyons [1979]. Such an error would probably have not been detected had the specifications been informal. It was fairly easy to modify the axioms to eliminate this error. Although formal specifications may be hard, if not impossible, to write for huge systems such as OS 360, experience in the use of formal specifications and understanding their advantages can lead to the development of better informal specifications.

Formal specifications cannot replace informal specifications—they are complementary. Ideally, system specifications should include both formal and informal specifications. The informal specifications are easier to read and understand while the formal specifications tend to be clearer, precise, unambiguous, etc. Whenever there are any doubts about the informal specifications, the formal specifications should be used to resolve doubts. Additionally, if it is desirable to suggest an implementation, then the implementation details should be specified separately from the specifications—formal or informal.

Liskov and Berzins [1979] point out that formal specifications can also be used in conjunction with automated tools for detection of certain kinds of inconsistency and incompleteness. In addition, formal specifications can sometimes be used to generate implementations automatically although these implementations may not be as efficient as manual ones.

Formal specifications, such as the algebraic specifications, do not allow the specification of the behavioral characteristics of systems such as storage requirements or input and output characteristics. According to Winograd [1979], programming in the future will depend more and more on specifying behavior.

Musa [1979] points out that, in software development, specification defects are the most costly to fix and have the greatest impact on schedules. The larger the system, the larger the proportion of defects due to specifications. Consequently, one must be careful in writing specifications. The use of formal specifications is an effort in this direction.

ACKNOWLEDGEMENT

Thanks are due to T. B. Muenzer for helping me understand the EVENT LOG subsystem, and R. H. Canaday, F. L. Dalrymple, P. V. Guidi, B. W. Kernighan, J. R. Kliegman, T. G. Lyons, D. A. Nowitz and C. S Wetherell for their comments.

JOHN GUTTAG
MIT Laboratory for Computer Science

J. J. HORNING
Xerox Palo Alto Research Center

Formal Specification as a Design Tool

1. INTRODUCTION

There are at least three distinct concerns in the software development process:

1. Developing an intuitive understanding of the problem to be solved. This should involve extensive discussions with members of the anticipated user community, and an examination of any existing software or manual procedures designed to deal with similar problems.

2. Designing a system intended to solve that problem. This may involve multiple iterations, in which partial designs are proposed and carefully analyzed for consistency, completeness, and conformance with intuition.

3. Programming an implementation of the design. This may also involve multiple iterations, in which portions of the program are developed and carefully analyzed for legality, efficiency, and conformance with the design.

In practice, these concerns are never totally separated, nor entirely sequential. Each process is guided by expectations about subsequent processes. Furthermore, the understanding, the design, and (to a lesser extent) the program will generally evolve together, as each analysis provides feedback to previous steps, and as some sort of validation process is undertaken as part of each step.

We have frequently concentrated our attention on the tail end of this process. An obvious symptom of this is the tremendous amount of attention we have lavished on the design of programming languages. A less obvious symptom has been the effort expanded on "program" verification, i.e., on demonstrating the consistency of the result of the second step with the result of the third.

Curiously, many of us working in the areas of programming language design and program verification have, while concentrating our efforts on "programming," also argued that the first two concerns are the key to the construction of excellent software. They are often where the most serious intellectual effort is required. They are therefore also the places where serious mistakes are most likely to be made, and where we believe improved tools and techniques are most likely to lead to substantive improvements.

Our efforts in this area begins with two crucial assumptions:

1. The difficult work associated with phases one and two should be primarily the concern of a relatively small group of well trained and highly capable people. On large software projects those making the critical design decisions should be a small subset of those people involved in building the system. Significant design decisions should not be left to the "programmers." The import of this assumption is that we feel no need to limit ourselves to tools and techniques that can be easily and quickly learned. In particular, we intend to strive for a level of mathematical rigor that may be beyond the abilities of many.

2. Getting the design "right" is much more difficult than implementing the design. This assumption implies that we consider the case of demonstrating the consistency of a design specification and a program to be of secondary importance. The ease with which the design itself can be examined and manipulated is of primary importance. The key verification issue, then, is "What can one prove about a design?"

That we perceive the key issue to be the formulation of questions to be asked and not the exploration of mechanisms for answering questions is probably the distinguishing characteristic of our work. It is not at all clear to us what questions one should or can ask. What is clear to us is that one should ask questions that can be rigorously formulated and objectively answered. This means that one cannot ask whether or not a design is "correct." Correctness is meaningful only with respect to some precise specification of intent, and such a specification is seldom (if ever) available.

The kinds of questions one might ask fall into a spectrum including two extremes: general questions that can be asked about any design specification and problem-specific questions that are applicable only to a particular design. Between these two extremes are questions that are relevant to a class of designs, e.g., designs for data bases. The most general questions deal with the issues of completeness and consistency. We have not yet formulated these two questions precisely, but expect that the completeness question will be closely related to sufficient completeness [Guttag and Horning 1978] and the consistency question to the feasibility of constructing an implementation (model). Posing this latter question will involve a specification of the domain from which the model must be drawn and perhaps the specification of efficiency constraints that must be observed.

Problem-specific questions are, of course, much harder to characterize. Yet they seem to be the more important type of question. Such questions as, "In case of a system crash, is the data base left in a consistent state?" are the heart of a careful review of a design. It is our hope that though these questions will be different for each design, we will be able to discover some general techniques that will prove useful in formulating problem-specific questions. We hope to discover these principles by studying individual designs, formulating questions that we consider appropriate, and finally abstracting from these questions. A necessary prerequisite to this study is a suitable specification language in which to express designs and questions about designs and a set of non-trivial examples.

The rest of this memo describes a preliminary version of a specification language for expressing designs, a non-trivial design expressed in that language, and a discussion of some of the questions we chose to ask (and answer) about the design.

1.1 The specification technique

One can view a system as consisting of a state and a set of mechanisms (which we shall call routines) for changing and extracting information from that state. Actions of the "the external world" will also be modeled as routines, so that the current state of a system is always the result of routines previously performed. Any state can, however, be discussed and even fully understood without reference to these routines. That is to say, one can deal with the information contained in the state without any reference to how that information was created or how it will be used. In our specification technique we do. Our specifications consist of two parts. In the first we specify the possible system states (or a superset of those states), and in the second the routines that deal with those states.

Information (i.e., a state) is static and timeless; that is to say, it involves only constants. This is exactly the kind of thing that algebra traditionally deals with, and the kind of thing that can be handled straightforwardly by the "algebraic axiom" approach to specifications as discussed in Guttag [1977], Liskov and Zilles [1977], and Goguen [1978a], among other places. In this method, one first presents a set of function (operator) names and associated domains and ranges. These can be looked at as defining a set of names that can be used to refer to system states, and a set of questions that can be asked about these states. One next presents a set of equations designed to imply answers to the questions one can pose about states. The information contained in each named state is thus indirectly defined in terms of answers to the questions that may be asked about it.

In most of our previous work, the functions used to name states and to pose questions were identified with the set of mechanisms that would actually be used to interface with the system (or type) being specified. Here, as intimated above, we depart radically from that view. We choose to view the operators defined by the algebraic specification as purely mathematical abstractions. They may appear in specifications of programs or in reasoning about programs, but they are not available to users of programs—be these human users or other programs.

What is available to users is the set of routines. The routines deal with the dynamic behavior of the system being specified. They include mechanisms for establishing initial states, for transforming one state into another, and for extracting information from the current state of the system. The specification of these routines follows and depends upon the specification of the operators. If the routine is a function, it is defined by an equation relating it directly to the operators. If the routine is a statement, i.e., a declaration or a procedure, it is defined using a generalization of Dijkstra's weakest precondition [Dijkstra 1976] in which the assertion language for expressing the predicates to be transformed and the transformation of these predicates includes the operators defined in the first part of the specification.

As an example, we consider type *SimpleDisplay*.[1]

Type *Simple Display*

Operators

Empty: ⟶ *Simple Display*
AddLine: *SimpleDisplay* × *Line* × *Line Number* ⟶ *Simple Display*
ScrollUp: *SimpleDisplay* ⟶ *SimpleDisplay*
Contents: *SimpleDisplay* × *LineNumber* × *CharNumber* ⟶ *Character*
Last: *SimpleDisplay* ⟶ *LineNumber*

Axioms

1) ScrollUp(Empty) = Empty

2) ScrollUp(AddLine(sd, line, ln)) = AddLine(ScrollUp(sd), line, ln−1)

3) Last(Empty) = 0

4) Last(AddLine(sd, line, ln)) = LineNumber.Max(ln, Last(sd))

5) Contents(AddLine(sd, line, ln), ln', cn) = **if** LineNumber.equal(ln, ln')
     then Line.Read(line, cn)
     else Contents(sd, ln', cn)

{*Contents(Empty, ln, cn) intentionally not specified*}[2]

---

1. Introductions to reading and writing this style of algebraic specification are contained in Guttag [1977] and Guttag [1978]. Briefly, an algebraic specification consists of two parts: a syntactic specification and a set of axioms. The syntactic specification provides the syntactic and type checking information: the names, domains and ranges of the operators associated with the type. The axioms are equations that can be used to simplify expressions involving the operators. On occasion, our algebraic specifications will also include a precondition specification. For a discussion of these see Guttag [1980].

2. Formally, this line is merely a comment, i.e., it adds nothing to the proof theory associated with type SimpleDisplay. This implies that our set of axioms is not sufficiently-complete [Guttag and Horning 1978] since such ground terms as Contents(Empty, 2, 2) cannot be further simplified. As part of our methodology we insist that the author of a specification explicitly indicate that such incompletenesses are intentional.

Routines

procedure Clear(**var** *SimpleDisplay*)
    such that wp(Clear(sd), Q) = Q[Empty/sd][3]

procedure Append(**var** *SimpleDisplay, Line*)
    such that wp(Append(sd, lin), Q) =
        [Last(sd) < 24 ⇒ Q[AddLine(sd, lin, Last(sd) + 1)/sd]
        ∧ Last(sd) = 24 ⇒ Q[AddLine(ScrollUp(sd), lin, 24)/sd]]

function GetChar(*SimpleDisplay, LineNumber, CharNumber*)
    such that pre(GetChar, <sd, ln, cn>) = 1 ⩽ ln ⩽ 24[4]
    value GetChar(sd, ln, cn) = Contents(sd, ln, cn)

procedure Replace(**var** *SimpleDisplay, LineNumber, Line*)
    such that wp(Replace(sd, ln, lin), Q) =
        1 ⩽ ln ⩽ 24 ∧ Q[AddLine(sd, lin, ln)/sd]

end Type *SimpleDisplay*

Reasoning about a program that uses routines is a two-step process. First one uses the specification of the routines to construct a predicate in which the routines do not occur. One then simplifies this predicate using the axioms of the operators. Similarly, reading and understanding the specification itself is a two-step process. By separating the specification of the essential properties of the operators from the specification of exceptional conditions and the details of the exact user interface (the routines) the specification is cleanly factored. Consider, for example, trying to understand the vagaries of machine arithmetic. Clearly, one should begin by first understanding the operators of ideal arithmetic. The routines implemented by a particular machine are then understood in terms of their relation to these operators.

2. INTRODUCTION TO THE EXAMPLE

The body of this paper describes a partially completed experiment in the application of our design techniques to a reasonably complex problem. We begin by defining, in a typically imprecise way, the problem to be addressed. We then proceed (part way) through the first two steps outlined at the start of this paper: developing an intuitive understanding of the problem to be solved and designing a solution to that problem. Finally, we review the design. A complete design review would involve:

---

3. Q[x/y] stands for the predicate Q with x substituted for all free occurrences of y.
4. We will, for the most part, associate preconditions and failure specifications [Guttag 1980] with routines rather than with operators.

1. An informal introduction to the system being designed.
2. A presentation of the first stage of the design: the formal specification of the operators.
3. The formulation of questions (or accusations) about this part of the design.
4. An examination of the design to find answers to the questions.
5. A discussion of the suitability of the answers and of the virtues of alternative answers.
6. A presentation of the second stage of the design: the routines.
7. A repetition of steps 3, 4, and 5 for this stage of the design.[5]

One might well question why one should devote significant effort to analyzing the specification of the operators independently of that of the routines. It is, after all, the routines, not the operators, that will actually be used.

If our specification technique is applied as we intend, the specification of the routines will, for the most part, be based on the substitution of expressions built from operators into predicates (cf. the SimpleDisplay example above). If this is the case, proving interesting properties about the operators should enhance greatly our ability to analyze the predicate transformers specifying the routines—simply by dividing the analysis into separate components.

A second reason for devoting considerable effort to the *in vacuo* study of the specification of the operators is that the operators are, in a sense, more fundamental than the routines. It is our intent that the specification of the operators capture the important abstractions that come out of the design experience. We expect that it is this portion of the design that is most likely to prove reusable. It is quite likely, for example, that somewhat different sets of routines may be designed for various users. These different user interfaces would all be related through the common set of operators on which they are based.

2.1 The example problem

We hypothesize the arrival of a new generation of personal computers with powerful display devices attached to them. Once they arrive, we will have to write a large variety of programs to run on them. These will include such things as text editors, calendar programs, circuit design aids, debuggers, etc.

---

5. In this paper we do not deal with steps 6 or 7 of the design review process. We are still in the process of formulating a set of routines that we find acceptable.

FORMAL SPECIFICATIONS AS A DESIGN TOOL

Our problem is to design a standard interface to the display that can be used for all of these programs.

Fortunately, this new display will not be terribly different from the device we are currently using. Therefore, we are able to develop the necessary intuition about the problem area by studying what we consider to be some of the better interfaces to our current display device. In particular, we decide to create abstractions incorporating what we perceive to be the common viewpoints embodied in a text editor, a message system, and a programming language environment. The details of the display interface vary considerably among these three systems. Yet we feel that if we can successfully abstract from these three we can construct a specification that will capture the essence of the knowledge gained through a number of years of experience with the old display device.

2.2 An informal overview of the design

We make no attempt here to describe the design in significant detail. Previous attempts to provide a detailed discussion of the design independently of the formal specification did not prove successful. We therefore leave a careful description of the design to the formal specification, and content ourselves here with presenting a few preliminary comments for the reader. Additional comments accompany the formal specification.

1. A fundamental assumption underlying the viewpoint our design attempts to capture is that the user of the display will wish to have several disjoint blocks of displayable information available at the same time. These blocks are called *pictures*.

2. A *view* is a spatial arrangement of pictures. Any arrangement, including those in which pictures overlap one another, is allowed.

3. A picture may be thought of as consisting of three parts: a *boundary*, a *contents*, and a *spatial (coordinate) transformation* to be applied in viewing the contents. By changing the transformation, one can change the size of the contents, and the portion that falls within the boundary.

4. Pictures have explicit boundaries that correspond to "visible" areas on the display. The boundaries associated with the contents of a picture are implicit, arising from the intrinsic structure of the information to be displayed. That is pictures are clipped and contents are not.

5. Examples of pictures are the entire area of a CRT display, and the interior of a fixed rectangle on the CRT; examples of contents are text documents, figures, and views.

6. Figures 1-4 show examples of major types.

"No real gentleman speaks the
naked truth in the presence
of ladies." -- Mark Twain

Figure 1. Text

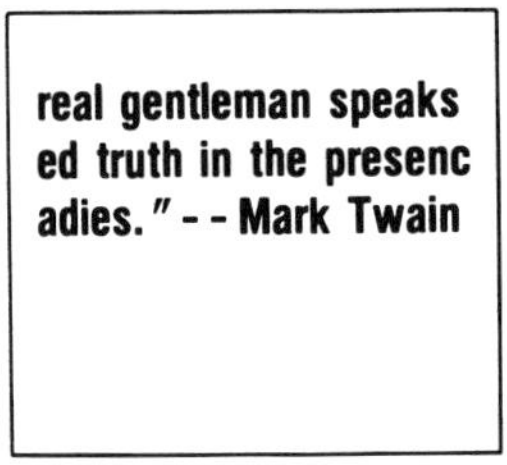

real gentleman speaks
ed truth in the presenc
adies." -- Mark Twain

Figure 2. Picture

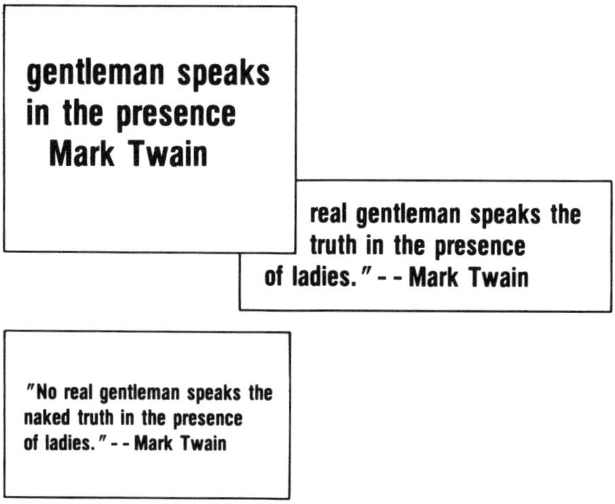

gentleman speaks
in the presence
Mark Twain

real gentleman speaks the
truth in the presence
of ladies." -- Mark Twain

"No real gentleman speaks the
naked truth in the presence
of ladies." -- Mark Twain

Figure 3. View

FORMAL SPECIFICATIONS AS A DESIGN TOOL 195

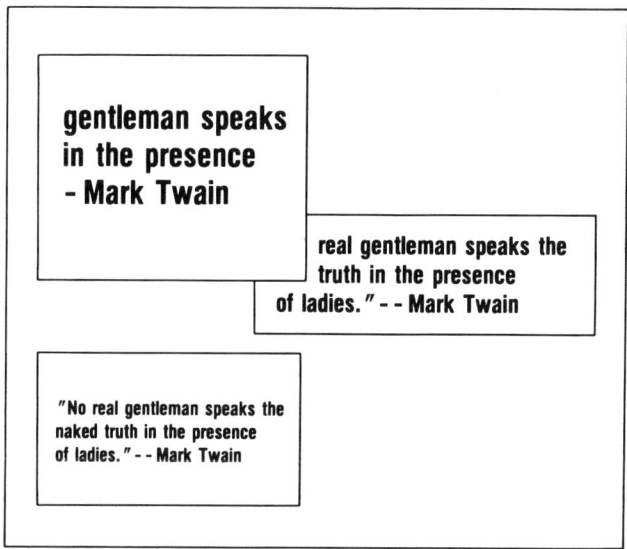

Figure 4. Picture

3. THE FORMAL SPECIFICATION OF THE OPERATORS

3.1 Some remarks on notation

In the process of creating the specification presented in this paper we found ourselves inventing and using a number of notational shorthands. We found these to be a great help. Paradoxically, in presenting this specification to others we found these same notational conventions to be something of a hindrance. We have drawn two inferences from this experience. The first is that if one is going to spend considerable time writing or reading specifications, it is clearly worthwhile to invest some time in becoming comfortable with a compact notation. Since these notations present a considerable hurdle to the uninitiated, we have largely refrained from using them in this paper.

The second, and more interesting, inference is that it seems to be useful to maintain semantically consistent, but notationally distinct versions of the same specification. When we wished an overview of the whole design, we used a notation (similar to the graph of Figure 5) intended to clearly expose some of the relationships among the types, e.g., which types were used in the specification of other types. When we wished an overview of the specification for an individual type, we made extensive use of syntax macros. This made it possible to get an overview of the structure of the specification without getting bogged down in details. When studying individual or small groups of axioms, we found it convenient to expand the macros—thus making the axioms more self-contained. Finally, when we wished to modify the axioms, we found it convenient to use a notation with as little redundancy as possible. No examples of this notation, which is not well-developed, appear in this paper.

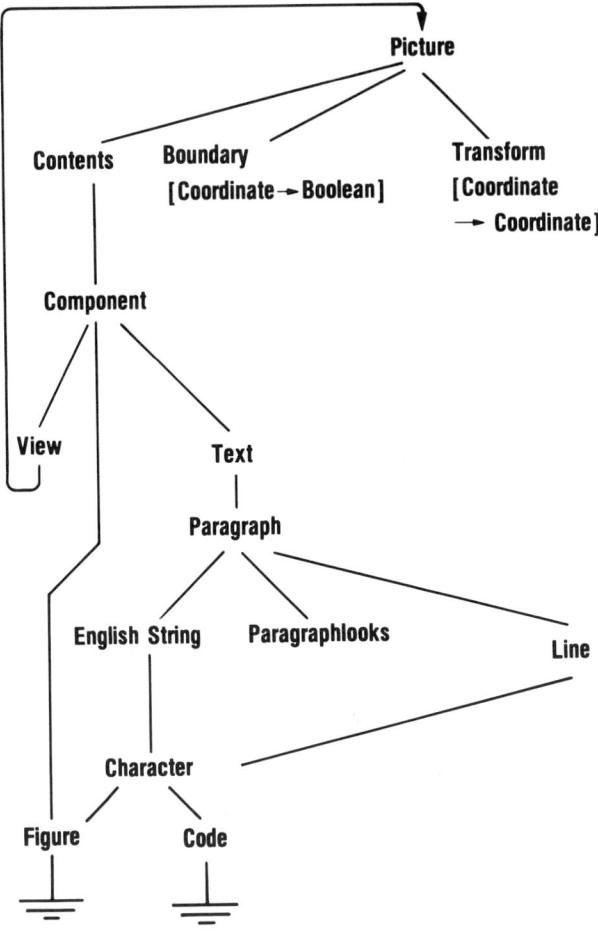

Figure 5. Relations among types

One notational convention we have retained in this paper is the *Let* clause. This is used to define nonrecursive textual macros whose scope is a single type definition. It adds no power to the specification technique, but it can structure and shorten the text of a specification. The primary role of a Let clause, however, is to record the decision that certain subexpressions are to be the same. This is particularly important when understanding or modifying a specification, since it is all too easy to overlook an intended equivalence (or fail to spot pertinent differences) between textually distinct subexpressions.

3.2 The abstractions (types)

We separate the design of the display interface into two groups of abstractions, each of which involves a number of interrelated concepts. The first group is primarily concerned with the structure of areas of the display, and involves the types *Picture, Contents, Component*, and *View*. The second group is primarily concerned with the structure of the data to be displayed, and involves the types *Text* (with subordinate types *Paragraph*,

EnglishString, Line, Character, and *Distance*) and *Figure*. The interface between these two groups is comparatively "narrow." To be acceptable as a component (of a contents), a type must supply an Appearance function, which maps a coordinate into an illumination, and an In predicate on coordinates. *View, Text*, and *Figure* are each acceptable component types. The recursion on *View* and *Picture* permits the structuring of a particular display into any number of levels of views.

Figure 5 portrays the hierarchical structure of the specification. We present it as a road map to be used while reading the specification itself. It is not actually part of the specification, i.e., it plays no role in the formal analysis of the design.

3.3 The generic functions Appearance and In

These functions are "generic," in that the same names are used in different types to identify distinct, but similar, functions. The precise meaning of these functions is contained in the formal specifications of the relevant types. In each type for which they are defined, however, these functions have meanings consistent with the following informal descriptions. To avoid confusion, we precede each use of a generic function name with its type name, except within its type's specification (e.g., *Picture*.Appearance will be shortened to Appearance within the specification of *Picture*.

Appearance plays a central role in this design: It takes a displayable object and a *Coordinate*, and returns the *Illumination* of the object at that point. Most of this design is independent of the nature of types *Coordinate* and *Illumination*. Abstractly, we think of Appearance as mapping from a point in space to a light intensity. Any given implementation will be an approximation to this abstract mapping; for example, it might map discrete two-dimensional Cartesian coordinates into any of

    elements of {Black, White},

    n-bit gray-level intensity values, or

    <hue, saturation, brightness> triples.

In is a binary predicate applicable to many <displayable object, coordinate> pairs. It is true if the coordinate falls "within" the object, false otherwise. Many of our statements about the structure of displays involve this predicate. Although we indicate how its value for composite objects depends on its value for components, we are not concerned here with its computation; indeed, some implementations might never compute it explicitly at all.

3.4 Types *Picture, Contents, Component* and *View*

Each picture has a contents, a boundary predicate (defining the area it occupies), and a transformation function relating the coordinate system of the picture to that of its contents. For a picture, In is determined entirely by its boundary and Appearance by its contents after coordinate transformation.

The contents of a picture is composed of some number (possibly zero) of components, each with a coordinate which is its position within the contents.

Every component is either a text, a figure or a view. *View* is perhaps the most interesting type of component. A view consists of a number (possibly zero) of pictures, each with a coordinate (used to determine its position) and a picture id. The size and shape of each picture are defined by the picture's boundary, not by the view. AddPicture places a new picture at the "front" of a view. Appearance at any given coordinate is determined by the frontmost picture that contains the coordinate. This implies that, at points of overlap, only the frontmost picture's contents will be displayed (a "2½-D" display). FindPictures produces a sequence of picture ids of all the pictures in a view that contain a given coordinate. DeletePicture removes the frontmost picture (if any) bound to the specified picture id.

Type *Picture*

Operators

MakePicture: *Contents* × [*Coordinate* ⟶ *Boolean*] × [*Coordinate* ⟶ *Coordinate*]
⟶ *Picture*

Appearance: *Picture* × *Coordinate* ⟶ *Illumination*
In: *Picture* × *Coordinate* ⟶ *Boolean*

Axioms

1) Appearance(MakePicture(cont, bound, trans), coord)
= *Contents*.Appearance(cont, trans(coord))

2) In(MakePicture(cont, bound, trans), coord) = bound(coord)

end type *Picture*

1. This axiom specifies that the appearance of a picture depends only upon the appearance of its contents and the picture's transformation function. Note that no clipping, based on the boundary, is done here.

2. This axiom states that whether or not a coordinate is in a picture is determined solely by the picture's boundary.

Type *Contents*

Operators

Empty: ⟶ *Contents*
AddComponent: *Contents* × *Component* × *Coordinate* ⟶ *Contents*
Appearance: *Contents* × *Coordinate* ⟶ *Illumination*
In: *Contents* × *Coordinate* ⟶ *Boolean*

Axioms

1) Appearance(AddComponent(cont, comp, coord'), coord) =
           if *Component*.In(comp, Minus(coord, coord'))
           then if In(cont, coord)
               then Combine(*Component*.Appearance(comp,
                       Minus(coord, coord')), Appearance(cont, coord))
               else *Component*.Appearance(comp, Minus(coord, coord'))
           else Appearance(cont, coord)

{*Appearance(Empty, coord) intentionally not specified*}

2) In(Empty, coord) = False

3) In(AddComponent(cont, comp, coord'), coord) =
           Component.In(comp, Minus(coord, coord')) $\lor$ In(cont, coord)

end type *Contents*

1. This axiom specifies that the appearance of a contents at a coordinate is a function, Combine, of the appearance of the top component at that coordinate and the appearance of all the other components at that coordinate (if there are any).

2-3. These axioms specify that whether or not a coordinate is within a contents is based upon whether or not it is contained in one of the contents' components.

Type *Component*

Operators

ViewAsComponent: *View* $\longrightarrow$ *Component*
TextAsComponent: *Text* $\longrightarrow$ *Component*
FigureAsComponent: *Figure* $\longrightarrow$ *Component*
Appearance: *Component* $\times$ *Coordinate* $\longrightarrow$ *Illumination*
In: *Component* $\times$ *Coordinate* $\longrightarrow$ *Boolean*

Axioms

1) Appearance(ViewAsComponent(v), coord) = *View*.Appearance(v, coord)

2) Appearance(TextAsComponent(t), coord) = *Text*.Appearance(t, coord)

3) Appearance(FigureAsComponent(f), coord) = *Figure*Appearance(f, coord)

4) In(ViewAsComponent(v), coord) = *View*.In(v, coord)

5) In(TextAsComponent(t), coord) = *Text*.In(t, coord)

6) In(FigureAsComponent(f), coord) = *Figure*.In(f, coord)

end type *Component*

1-6. These axioms specify that Component is merely a disjoint union type.

Type *View*

Operators

Empty: $\longrightarrow$ *View*
AddPicture: *View* × *Coordinate* × *PictureId* × *Picture* $\longrightarrow$ *View*
Appearance: *View* × *Coordinate* $\longrightarrow$ *Illumination*
In: *View* × *Coordinate* $\longrightarrow$ *Boolean*
FindPictures: *View* × *Coordinate* $\longrightarrow$ *IdList*
DeletePicture: *View* × *PictureId* $\longrightarrow$ *View*

Axioms

1) Appearance(AddPicture(v, coord', id, p), coord) =
                                 if *Picture*.In(p, Minus(coord, coord'))
                                 then *Picture*Appearance(p, Minus(coord, coord'))
                                 else Appearance(v, coord)

{*Appearance(Empty, coord) intentionally not specified*}

2) In(Empty, coord) = False

3) In(AddPicture(v, coord', id, p), coord) =
                                 Picture.In(p, Minus(coord, coord')) $\vee$ In(v, coord)

4) FindPictures(Empty, coord) = *IdList*.Empty

5) FindPictures(AddPicture(v, coord', id, p), coord) =
                                 if *Picture*.In(p, Minus(coord, coord'))
                                 then *IdList*.Insert(id, FindPictures(v, coord))
                                 else FindPictures(v, coord)

6) DeletePicture(Empty, id) = Empty

7) DeletePicture(AddPicture(v, coord, id', p), id) =
                                 if *PictureId*Equal(id, id')
                                 then v
                                 else AddPicture(DeletePicture(v, id), coord, id', p)

end type *View*

1. This axiom specifies that the appearance of a view at a coordinate depends entirely upon the appearance of the topmost picture containing that coordinate. The test in the conditional effects "clipping" for pictures in views.

2-3. These axioms specify that a coordinate is within a view only if it is within one of the pictures placed in the view.

4-5. These axioms specify that the value of FindPictures applied to a view and a coordinate is the sequence of picture ids associated with pictures that contain that coordinate.

6-7. These axioms specify that pictures associated with the same picture id are deleted in a LIFO fashion.

Type IdList

Operators

Empty: $\longrightarrow$ *IdList*
Insert: PictureId × *IdList* $\longrightarrow$ *IdList*
First: *IdList* $\longrightarrow$ *PictureId*
Null: *IdList* $\longrightarrow$ *Boolean*

Axioms

1) First(Insert(p, il)) = **p**

{*First(Empty) intentionally not specified*}

2) Null(Empty) = True

3) Null(Insert(p, il)) = False

end type *IdList*

1-3. These are "standard axioms" for a sequence type.

3.5 Text and its subsidiary types

Text is structured as a sequence of paragraphs; each paragraph consists of paragraph looks and an English string, which is a sequence of characters. *Text*.Appearance is determined by *Paragraph*.Appearance of the first paragraph containing the given coordinate. Each paragraph is offset down by the height of the preceding paragraph. *Paragraph*.Appearance is, in turn, determined by *Line*.Appearance of the first line containing the coordinate, after the paragraph's string has been broken into lines in accordance with the maximum width specified by the paragraph's looks; each line is offset down by the height of the preceding line. *Line*.Appearance is determined by *Character*.Appearance of the first character in the line that contains the coordinate.[6]

When it is displayed, a paragraph is broken into as few lines as possible, consistent with the following intentions:

(a) Lines should not be wider than the paragraph's maximum width.

(b) Each carriage return should terminate a line.

(c) Words should not be broken across lines.

A more precise statement of how a paragraph is to be displayed is contained in the specifications of types *EnglishString* and *Line* appearing in the appendix.

Operators

Empty: ⟶ *Text*
Insert: *Paragraph* × *Text* ⟶ *Text*
Appearance: *Text* × *Coordinate* ⟶ *Illumination*
In: *Text* × *Coordinate* ⟶ *Boolean*

Axioms

Let Down(d) be Minus(coord, Times(d, UnitVectorDown)) in

1) Appearance(Insert(p, t), coord) = **if** *Paragraph*.In(p, coord)
   then *Paragraph*.Appearance(p, coord)
   else Appearance(t, Down(*Paragraph*.Height(p)))

{*Appearance(Empty, coord) intentionally not specified*}

2) In(Empty, coord) = False

3) In(Insert(p, t), coord) = *Paragraph*.In(p, coord) ∨ In(t, Down(*Paragraph*.Height(p)))

end type *Text*

1. This axiom specifies that if a coordinate is in the most recently inserted paragraph, then the appearance of the text at that coordinate is equal to the appearance of the paragraph at that coordinate. It also implies that the inserted paragraph appears above the rest of the text, and that the paragraphs in the rest of the text are offset down by the height of the inserted paragraph.

---

6. Given certain restrictions on the relationship *Character*.Ascent, *Character*.Descent, and *Character*.Width to *Character*.In, one can prove that a coordinate can be in at most one paragraph, one line, and one character.

FORMAL SPECIFICATIONS AS A DESIGN TOOL

2-3. These axioms specify that whether or not a coordinate is in a text depends upon whether or not it is in one of the text's paragraphs. Again we see it implied that the remaining text is displayed below the inserted paragraph.

Type Paragraph

Operators

MakeParagraph: *ParagraphLooks* × *EnglishString* → *Paragraph*
FirstLine: *Paragraph* → *Line*
Balance: *Paragraph* → *Paragraph*
Null: *Paragraph* → *Boolean*
Space: *Paragraph* → *Distance*
Height: *Paragraph* → *Distance*
In: *Paragraph* × *Coordinate* → *Boolean*
Appearance: *Paragraph* × *Coordinate* → *Illumination*

Axioms

Let Down(d) be Minus(coord, Times(d, UnitVectorDown)) in

1) FirstLine(MakeParagraph(look, s)) =
    EnglishString.FirstLine(s, *ParagraphLooks*.Width(look))

2) Balance(MakeParagraph(look, s)) =
    MakeParagraph(look, *EnglishString*.Balance(s, *ParagraphLooks*.Width(look)))

3) Null(MakeParagraph(look, s)) = *String*.Null(s)

4) Space(MakeParagraph(look, s)) = *ParagraphLooks*.Space(look)

5) Height(p) = **if** Null(p)
    then Space(p)
    else *Line*.Height(FirstLine(p)) + Height(Balance(p))

6) In(p, coord) =
    ¬ Null(p)
    ∧ [*Line*.In(FirstLine(p),
        Down(Space(p) + *Line*.Ascent(FirstLine(p))))
        ∨ In(Balance(p), Down(*Line*.Height(FirstLine(p))))]

7) Appearance(p, coord) =
    if *Line*.In(FirstLine(p), Down(Space(p) + *Line*.Ascent(FirstLine(p))))
    then *Line*.Appearance(FirstLine(p), Down(Space(p) + *Line*.Ascent(FirstLine(p))))
    else Appearance(Balance(p), Down(*Line*.Height(FirstLine(p))))

end type *Paragraph*

1. The operator FirstLine maps a paragraph to its first displayable line. The width of that line is based upon the "looks" of the paragraph and conventions for breaking a line of English text. The latter is specified in type *EnglishString*.

2. The operator Balance maps a paragraph to a paragraph whose first displayable line has been removed.

3. This axiom specifies that a paragraph is null if and only if the English string associated with it is null.

4. This axiom specifies that the (leading) space associated with a paragraph is a function of the paragraph's "looks."

5. This axiom specifies that the height of a paragraph is the sum of its (leading) space and the heights of all of its lines. Notice that no mention is made of the space between lines. That is accounted for in the specification of *Line*.Height.

6. This axiom specifies that whether or not a coordinate is within a paragraph depends upon whether it is in one of the paragraph's displayable lines. The complicated second argument to *Line*.In specifies that the origin of a displayable line is offset downwards by the (leading) space of the paragraph and the ascenders of that line. Informally, *Line*.Ascent is the distance the tallest character in the line extends above its base line.

7. This axiom specifies that the appearance of a paragraph at a coordinate is based upon the appearance of the displayable line containing that coordinate. (If a coordinate is not contained in any line, the appearance is not specified.)

The remainder of this specification raises few interesting issues of design or specification methodology, and is therefore relegated to the appendix. The only thing worth noting here is that the specification of type *EnglishString* is unfortunately somewhat complicated. We feel, however, that this reflects the complexity of the conventions used in displaying English text, rather than any property of our specification technique. (Earlier, simpler, specifications were shown to violate those conventions in some cases.)

4. AN ABRIDGED ANALYSIS OF THE OPERATORS

We have spent a great deal of time analyzing this specification and several earlier versions. A complete discussion of this analysis is well beyond the scope of this paper. We therefore limit ourselves here to a presentation of a few representative questions.

The presentation of each question mirrors our analysis. We begin by formulating in English a question about the design. Some of these are questions that we first posed ourselves, but most are reformulations of questions first asked of us by others. As one might suspect, this latter class of questions tended to be the more revealing of peculiarities in our design. Next we present a formal statement designed to get at the issues raised by the informal question. We formulated all of these formal questions ourselves, i.e., we did not ask those who supplied us with informal questions to translate them. Rather, we asked them to examine our translation, and tell us whether or not it was appropriate. Finally, we present the answer to the formal question, an explanation of how we arrived at that answer, and a brief discussion of the question and its answer.

Informal question: Is it the case that pictures are not transparent or even translucent? That is, if two pictures overlap does the bottom one have no effect on what one sees through the top one?

Formal question: Is it true that

$(\forall$ c, c', w, id, vl, v2)[*Picture*.In(w, Minus(c, c')) $\Rightarrow$
 [*View*.Appearance(AddPicture(v1, c', id, w), c) =
  View.Appearance(AddPicture(v2, c', id, w), c)]] ?

Answer: Yes. This theorem follows directly from the first alternative in the second axiom of type View.

Discussion: The formal question posed and answered is somewhat more general than the informal one. It tells us that the appearance of a picture is independent of the context in which the picture is used.

In making the step from the informal to the formal we have often ended up posing a more general question. Sometimes we have done so merely because the more general question was easier to pose or to answer. Often, however, we have done so to reflect the fact that in formalizing the initial question we discovered a number of related questions that struck us as equally interesting.

Informal question: Is it true that the appearance of a contents is determined at each coordinate by the frontmost component containing the coordinate?

Formal question: Is it true that

$(\forall$ cp, c, c', cn1, cn2)[*Component*.In(cp, Minus(c, c')) $\Rightarrow$
  [Appearance(AddComponent(cn1, cp, c'), c) =
   Appearance(AddComponent(cn2, cp, c'), c)]] ?

Answer: Perhaps. The question reduces to whether we can prove

$(\forall$ i1, i2, i3)[Combine(i1, i2) = Combine(i1, i3)].

This question is not answered by our specification.

Discussion: A significant number of the questions we dealt with had "perhaps" as their answer. This meant that the answer depended upon design decisions that had yet to be made, e.g., the properties of Combine. These questions, and their answers, supply us with information that can guide us in continuing the design.

In this case, we decided that the answer to the question should be no. Consequently, Combine(i1, i2) will not be identically i1. Notice, by the way, that this question is quite similar to the first question, and our decision about Combine establishes a critical difference between pictures and components.

Informal question: If I add the same component to the contents of two pictures that appear to be identical, will the resulting pictures also appear to be identical?

Formal question: Is it true that

$(\forall$ cn1, cn2, bd, tr1, tr2)
    $[(\forall$ c)[Appearance(MakePicture(cn1, bd, tr1), c) =
        Appearance(MakePicture(cn2, bd, tr2), c)]
    $\Rightarrow (\forall$ cp, c, c')[Appearance(MakePicture(AddComponent(cn1, cp, c'), bd, tr1), c)
        = Appearance(MakePicture(
            AddComponent(cn2, cp, c'), bd, tr2), c)]] ?

Answer: No. Since the coordinate transformation is associated with the picture, rather than the contents, the new component may undergo quite different transformations in the two pictures.

Discussion: When the informal question was posed about an earlier design, it was obvious to us that the answer was no. We then changed the design with the intent of making the answer yes. It was several weeks later when we formalized the question and attempted a formal proof and discovered that the answer to the informal question was still no.

The informal question that can be answered yes is: If I add the same component to two contents that appear to be identical, will the resulting contents also appear to be identical?

Formally: Is it true that

$(\forall$ cn1, cn2)
    $[(\forall$ c)[Appearance(cn1, c) = Appearance(cn2, c)]
    $\Rightarrow (\forall$ cp, c, c')[Appearance(AddComponent(cn1, cp, c'), c)
        = Appearance(AddComponent(cn2, cp, c'), c)]]?

5. CONCLUSIONS

The most difficult part of this exercise was deciding on the abstractions we wished to have and on the functionalities of the operators associated with these abstractions. This is not surprising. Anyone who has spent time designing software knows that dividing it into appropriate modules is a difficult task. Fortunately, the process of trying to axiomatize the abstractions we had provisionally chosen proved to be a great help. Whenever we discovered that the axioms specifying a type were getting overly complex, we took this to mean that we had not achieved a proper separation of concerns, and consequently revised our choice of abstractions. Since we proceeded in a largely top-down manner, this kept us from spending too much time following unprofitable paths. Writing the axioms also helped to prevent us from making some premature decisions. In our initial specification, for example, we specified type *Coordinate* to be Cartesian coordinate and type *Illumination* to be {Black, White}. In writing the axioms, we noticed that we nowhere depended upon these choices. This prompted us to change our design, leaving them unbound at this stage.

Many readers will doubtless take exception to some of the decisions embodied in our design. (In fact, we hope that our specification is clear enough that they can understand precisely what they don't like about it.) We are not experts on the subject of display interfaces, and our goal was not to design an excellent display interface. It was to develop a tool which, with the help of an expert in the application area, could be used to derive, document, and analyze an excellent design.

We feel that thus far our experiment has been a success. While from time to time we had considerable difficulty in deciding how to design various aspects of the display, we had little trouble expressing our decisions once they were made. Furthermore, we found our formalism useful in clarifying when a decision had to be (or had been) made, what the alternatives were, and what the ramifications of each choice would be. The formal specification also proved to be a useful communication medium. We were able to use it in precise discussions of the design—not only between ourselves, but also with others. We found the latter particularly encouraging. Finally, we were able to modify various portions of the design in a number of significant ways over a considerable period of time.

Our experimentation with this tool is incomplete. We have only just begun to specify the routines for displays. While we do not anticipate any problems, we will doubtless run into unanticipated ones. We also lack significant experience of combining independently constructed designs into the design of a larger system. The ease of difficulty of doing this will have a major effect on the practical utility of these techniques.

ACKNOWLEDGMENTS

We received helpful suggestions from many people in the course of doing this design and writing this paper. Our colleagues at the Xerox Palo Alto Research Center, as well as members of IFIP Working Group 2.3 (Programming Methodology) and the informal ARPA working group on Quality Software for Complex Tasks, were particularly helpful. We owe special thanks to Bill McKeeman and Jeannette Wing for their tenacity in sticking with us over many versions.

The work was supported in part by the National Science Foundation under grant MCS78-01798 and by an Office of Naval Research Contract with DARPA funding #N00014-75-C-0661.

APPENDIX
Collected Formal Specifications

[Appendix deleted]

ROBERT J. K. JACOB
Naval Research Laboratory

Using Formal Specifications in the Design of a Human–Computer Interface

1. INTRODUCTION

Formal specification techniques have been applied to many aspects of software development. Their value is that they permit a designer to describe the external behavior of a system precisely without specifying its internal implementation. However, such techniques have been applied only rarely to the specification of user interfaces, despite the fact that the user interface is increasingly being recognized as a critical element in many software systems. One is handicapped in trying to design a good user interface without a clear and precise technique for specifying such interfaces.

The design of the user interface for a military message system has a special importance because of its role in maintaining the security of classified messages. Enforcement of system security requires that the user understand the security-related consequences of his or her actions, but often such consequences are not intuitively obvious. Recent experimental results indicate that communicating the security implications of an action and obtaining meaningful approval or disapproval from a user can be very difficult [Wilson et al. 1979].

In the Military Message System (MMS) project at the Naval Research Laboratory, formal specification techniques are being used to construct a family of secure message systems [Heitmeyer and Wilson 1980; Heitmeyer 1981]. Compatible specification techniques must therefore be applied to the human–computer interfaces for such systems. Rapid prototypes of military message systems will then be constructed based on these specifications [Heitmeyer, Landwehr and Cornwell 1982], and later, full-scale prototypes will be built.

This paper describes the specification of the user interface module for the family of message systems, surveys specification techniques that can be applied to human–computer interfaces, provides examples of specifications, and presents some conclusions [Jacob].

2. USER INTERFACE SPECIFICATIONS FOR THE MILITARY MESSAGE SYSTEM FAMILY

Each member of the MMS family consists of several components. Two are of interest here: the User Agent and the Data Manager. As shown in Figure 1, the user communicates with the User Agent via a *User Command Language* (UCL). Once it receives a command from the user, the User Agent translates the command into a standard form—a statement in the *Intermediate Command Language* (ICL)—and passes that to the Data Manager. Information returned by the Data Manager in response to user requests is delivered to the User Agent, which is responsible for displaying it to the user. This division permits new systems with different user interfaces to be constructed from an existing system with relative ease. If the user interface is changed, only the User Agent must be modified so that it will translate from the new UCL into the standard ICL; the Data Manager and other system components need not be changed. For example, two members of the MMS family could provide the same basic functions but differ in their user interfaces. They would have two different User Agents but would share the same Data Manager. Separating the user interface in this way makes it possible to experiment with different user interfaces and to evaluate them from their specifications (as Reisner [1981] and Embley [1978] do) as well as from a prototype (as Hanau and Lenorovitz [1980] do).

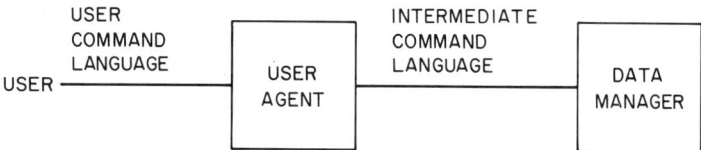

Figure 1. Components of the military message system

This division also makes the specification of the user interface clearer. Previous user interface specifications have suffered because they lacked an acceptable language for describing the "semantics" of the interface, that is, the actions that the system performs in response to the user's commands. Since a complete description of such actions is in fact a specification of the entire system, putting it in the user interface specification clutters that specification with detail that belongs at another level [Dijkstra 1976]. What is needed is a high-level model that describes the operations that the system performs. Then, the user interface specification would describe the user interface in terms of the model, while the internal details of the model would be described in a separate specification.

The design used in the Military Message System project provides one solution to this problem. The ICL is an abstract model of the services performed by a message system and is described in a separate specification [Heitmeyer 1981]. The user interface specification, then, needs only to describe the *syntax* of the UCL using a language specification technique and the *semantics* of the UCL using ICL statements.

3. PROPERTIES OF A SPECIFICATION TECHNIQUE

In selecting a technique for specifying a human–computer interface, one should seek the following properties:

(a) The specification of a user interface should be easy to understand. In particular, it must be easier to understand and take less effort to produce than the software that implements the user interface.

(b) The specification should be precise. It should leave no doubt as to the behavior of the system for each possible input.

(c) It should be easy to check for consistency.

(d) The specification technique should be powerful enough to express nontrivial system behavior with a minimum of complexity.

(e) It should separate what the system does (function) from how it does it (implementation). The technique should make it possible to describe the behavior of a user interface, without constraining the way in which it will be implemented.

(f) It should be possible to construct a prototype of the system directly from the specification of the user interface.

(g) The structure of the specification should be closely related to the user's mental model of the system itself. That is, its principal constructs should represent concepts that will be meaningful to users (such as answering a message or examining a file), rather than internal constructs required by the specification language. Alternatively, the specification should directly yield a reasonable table of contents for a user manual, but not necessarily the material in the manual.

4. SURVEY OF SPECIFICATION TECHNIQUES

Much of the work applicable to techniques for specifying human–computer interfaces has been concerned with static rather than interactive languages. In a static language, an entire text in the input language is conceptually present before any processing begins or any outputs are produced; all of the outputs are then produced together, usually after a fairly long input text, such as a program, has been processed. Processing of an input text is affected little, if at all, by the previous inputs. In an interactive language, the input can be described as a series of brief texts, where the processing of each input generally depends on previous inputs, or, equivalently, as one long text, in which the computer takes actions and produces outputs at various points during the input, resulting in a dialogue. Hence, a specification for such a language must capture not only the system actions and outputs but also their sequence with respect to portions of the input.

Most specifications for both static and interactive languages have been based on one of two formal models: Backus-Naur Form (BNF) [Reisner 1981] and state transition diagrams [Parnas 1969]. Each of these methods provides a syntax for describing legal streams of user inputs. In order to be used to specify interactive languages, the techniques must be modified to describe—in addition to user inputs—the system actions and their sequence with respect to the input.

5. BNF

For BNF, the necessary modification consists of associating an action with each grammar rule. Whenever that rule applies to the input language stream (received thus far), the associated action occurs. (As mentioned, for the MMS family members, these system actions can be described as ICL statements issued by the User Agent to the Data Manager.)

Reisner [1981] provides an example of how BNF can be used to describe a user interface. Unlike several other published specifications, Reisner's specifies a nontrivial, real-world system. It does leave out the semantics of the user interface—the system actions and responses—since Reisner did not need them for her purposes. That is, it provides a standard BNF description of the input language, but no specification of any outputs. Reisner uses formal properties of the BNF specifications of two systems to predict differences in the performance of their users. More complex or less consistent BNF rules lead to predictions of user errors. Several such predictions are then verified experimentally.

Shneiderman [1981] also examines the use of BNF for describing interactive user interfaces and proposes a modified form of BNF in which each nonterminal symbol may be associated with either the computer or the user. With the exception of one unusual nondeterministic case, this type of grammar can be mapped into a state transition diagram similar to Singer's [1979].

A BNF specification can also be used as input to a compiler-compiler such as YACC [Johnson 1980]. Such a program can be given a specification in which an executable action (rather than a routine to generate object code) is associated with each BNF rule; then it can automatically construct a prototype of the specified system. While the input syntax is described in BNF, the actions must generally be given in a conventional programming language.

One general problem that arises with BNF-based techniques is that it is sometimes difficult to determine exactly *when* something will occur, that is, after exactly *what* input tokens have been recognized. This makes it awkward to specify interactive prompting, help messages, and error handling, which must occur at particular points in a dialogue. Often, it requires the introduction of a collection of otherwise irrelevant nonterminal symbols into the specification.

6. STATE TRANSITION DIAGRAMS

To represent interactive languages, state transition diagrams are modified in a way similar to that for BNF based techniques. Each transition is associated with an action; whenever the transition occurs, the system performs the associated action. Since the concept of sequence is explicit in a state diagram (while it is implicit in BNF), the former is more suited to specifying the points in a dialogue at which events occur.

Conway [1963] presents an early use of a notation based on state transition diagrams in which an action is associated with each transition. His goal, however, was to specify and construct a compiler for a static language, so he did not address the problems of interactive user interfaces.

Woods [1970] also describes a notation, "Augmented Transition Networks", based on state transition diagrams for analyzing a static language. His notation includes an extension to conventional state transition diagrams: a (global) data structure. The actions associated with each transition manipulate this structure, and the conditions for making a state transition can include arbitrary Boolean expressions that depend on the data structure.

Conway and Woods both introduce into their state diagrams a feature analogous to BNF nonterminal symbols. With this feature, instead of labeling a state transition with a single input token, the transition may be labeled with the name of a nonterminal symbol. That symbol is, in turn, defined in a separate state transition diagram. The labeled path in the main diagram is then taken if the entire separate diagram can be traversed at the current position in the input stream. This makes it possible to divide complex diagrams into more manageable pieces. It also makes it easier to introduce nondeterminism into the specification.[1] If recursive calls to these separate diagrams are permitted, the notation is equivalent in power to BNF [Hueras 1978]. Adding the actions and conditions (and the ability to create new variables dynamically) either to these state transition diagram notations or to the BNF notations makes the resulting notation equivalent in power to a Turing Machine.

Parnas [1969] proposes the use of state diagrams to describe user interfaces for interactive languages. He differentiates "terminal state" from "complete state" in a way analogous to the separation of syntax from semantics in other specifications. Parnas' paper contains some very simple examples but does not address how the scheme would be extended for more complex real-world systems.

Foley and Wallace [1974] also advocate the use of a state diagram to represent the user interface of an interactive system. While their notation is clear and easy to understand, they, too, do not examine the problem of specifying real-world systems.

The standard for the MUMPS interactive computer language [MUMPS Development Committee 1977] provides an example of a specification of a

---

1. This must be done with care in an interactive system. Even though a deterministic automaton with backtracking can execute a nonrecursive nondeterministic diagram, in an interactive system it is not possible to backtrack over a path that has already generated output to the user.

complex system that uses a notation based on state diagrams. The specification uses nonterminal symbols extensively and gives a precise deterministic procedure for interpreting diagrams containing them (since their use can, in the general case, require a nondeterministic automaton). The specification is noteworthy in that the actions associated with its transitions comprise a complete specification of the semantics of the MUMPS language.

Singer [1979] presents a state diagram-based specification of a nontrivial system. His notation is more precise and more general than most other versions of state diagrams, but it is also more complex and difficult to understand. It uses separate diagrams for nonterminal symbols and a global data structure, which can be set by arbitrary semantic-domain actions. Transitions can only be selected by examining values in this data structure, rather than the input tokens directly. Hence a transition involving receipt of a particular token is described by two transitions in Singer's notation—one to read it into the data structure and one to test the value just stored. While the two notations appear quite different, most aspects of Singer's notation can be mapped into that of the MUMPS specification.

Moran [1981] provides a notation for describing the user's view of a computer system at several levels, from the overall tasks performed to individual key presses. This notation results in an unusually long and detailed specification. At the "Interaction Level," Moran's specification can be mapped onto a state diagram. His notation does not contain a state diagram representation of the Interaction Level of the user interface, but it does record a number of properties such a diagram would have. These properties are sufficient to generate a state diagram specification or (in a specification where only a few properties are specified) a set of diagrams.

7. EXAMPLES OF SPECIFICATIONS

To illustrate the use of some specification techniques, two commands from a hypothetical military message system are specified here. The *Login* command prompts the user to enter his or her name. If it does not recognize that name, it asks the user to reenter it, until he enters a valid name. Then, the system requests a password; if the password entered is incorrect, the user gets one more try to enter a correct one and proceed; otherwise he must begin the whole command again.[2] Next, the system requests a security level for the session, which must be no higher than the user's security clearance. If he enters a level that is too high, he is prompted to reenter it, until he enters an

---

2. In the specifications of this command given below, this counting is performed using an extra state or an extra BNF rule. This approach is clear for the simple command here, but it would obviously be inconvenient if the system allowed the user a maximum of 100 tries to enter his password or if the limit were dependent on some other stored data. In such a case, the action and condition features of either notation, described below, would be used. The state transition or BNF rule corresponding to entry of an incorrect password would have an action that increments a counter variable, and that counter would then be tested in a condition associated with a subsequent state transition or BNF rule.

appropriate level. If he does not enter an appropriate security level, he is given the default level, *Unclassified*.

The *Reply* command permits a user to send a reply to a message he has received. The user can give an optional input indicating to which message he wants to reply; otherwise, the default is *CurrentMsg*. He then enters the text of his reply. Following this, he can enter some optional lists containing additional addressees to which he wants this reply to be sent (in addition to those on the distribution list of the message to which he is replying). Each of these lists consists of the word "To" or "Cc" (depending on how the reply should be addressed to these people) followed by one or more addressees.

In Figure 2, the *Login* command is specified using state transition diagrams; the *Reply* command is specified in Figure 3. The notation follows widely used conventions. Each state is represented by a circle. The start and end states are so named inside the circles. Each transition between two states is shown as a directed arc. It is labeled with the name of an input token, in capital letters, plus, in some cases, a footnote containing Boolean conditions, system responses, and actions. A given state transition will occur if the input token is received and the condition is satisfied; when the transition occurs, the system displays the response and performs the action.

Instead of an input token, a transition may be labeled with the name of another diagram (in lower case). Such a transition will be made if the named diagram is traversed successfully at this point in the input. This notation permits breaking the specification up for clarity; otherwise, the text of the called diagram could simply have been inserted at this point in the calling diagram (provided no recursive calls are made).

In the actions, procedure names in upper case denote ICL statements, but their specific meaning is not material to this discussion. Some simple programming-language-like facilities, such as assignment and comparison, are assumed here, although the corresponding tasks could have been handled by defining some additional ICL statements. A token name preceded by a dollar sign stands for the value most recently read in for that input token. For example, $USER stands for the actual name the user typed.

The special token ANY is defined such that if no other transition can be made, the transition labeled with ANY is made, and the current input token is scanned again when the new state is reached. If the system reaches a state from which no transition can be made, given the current input, then there is an error in the input, and a transition would be made to an error-handling procedure. For clarity, such procedures have not been included in these examples. (Clearly, this cannot arise in a state from which there is a transition with the token ANY.)

The tokens themselves can be defined in a separate specification, which captures lower-level details of the user-computer interaction. For example, the token LOGIN could represent the typed string "Login" a function key, or a hit of a graphic input device on a menu display, without affecting the specification shown here. Similarly, the definition of TEXT would include a

LOGIN

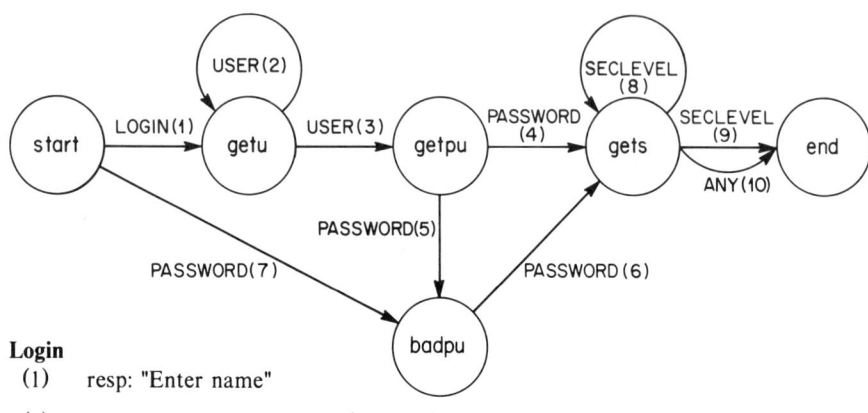

Login
(1) resp: "Enter name"

(2) cond: not EXISTS_USER($USER)
    resp: "Incorrect user name--reenter it"

(3) cond: EXISTS_USER($USER)
    resp: "Enter password"

(4) cond: $PASSWORD = GETPASSWD_USER($USER)
    resp: "Enter security level"

(5) cond: $PASSWORD ≠ GETPSSWD_USER($USER)
    resp: "Incorrect password--reenter it"

(6) cond: $PASSWORD = GETPASSWD_USER($USER)
    resp: "Enter security level"

(7) cond: $PASSWORD ≠ GETPASSWD_USER($USER)
    resp: "Incorrect password--start again"

(8) cond: $SECLEVEL > GETCLEARANCE_USER($USER)
    resp: "Security level too high--reenter it"

(9) cond: $SECLEVEL ≤ GETCLEARANCE_USER($USER)
    act: CREATE_SESSION($USER, $PASSWORD, $SECLEVEL)

(10) resp: "Your security level is Unclassified"
     act: CREATE_SESSION($USER, $PASSWORD, Unclassified)

Figure 2. State diagram specification of the "Login" command.

specification of the delimiter used to indicate the end of an input string.

Figures 4 and 5 show how the specifications can be represented in text form. This is often more convenient for computer input and output than the graphical diagrams. The text representation consists of a list of the transitions that comprise the diagram, each represented by a line of the form

s1: INP resp: "Hello" ⟶ s2

FORMAL SPECIFICATIONS IN THE DESIGN OF AN INTERFACE

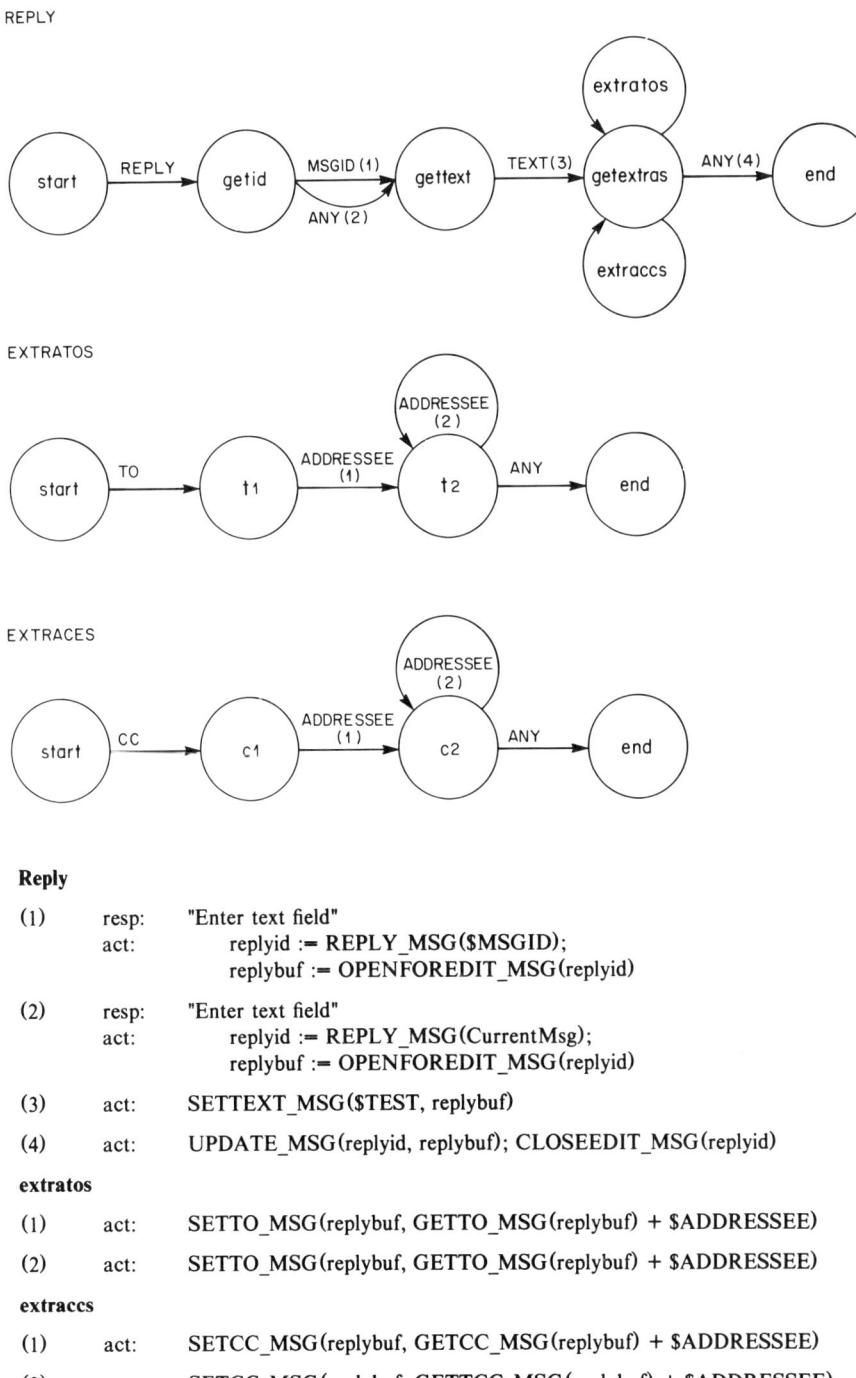

Reply

(1)	resp:	"Enter text field"
	act:	replyid := REPLY_MSG($MSGID);
		replybuf := OPENFOREDIT_MSG(replyid)
(2)	resp:	"Enter text field"
	act:	replyid := REPLY_MSG(CurrentMsg);
		replybuf := OPENFOREDIT_MSG(replyid)
(3)	act:	SETTEXT_MSG($TEST, replybuf)
(4)	act:	UPDATE_MSG(replyid, replybuf); CLOSEEDIT_MSG(replyid)

extratos

(1)	act:	SETTO_MSG(replybuf, GETTO_MSG(replybuf) + $ADDRESSEE)
(2)	act:	SETTO_MSG(replybuf, GETTO_MSG(replybuf) + $ADDRESSEE)

extraccs

(1)	act:	SETCC_MSG(replybuf, GETCC_MSG(replybuf) + $ADDRESSEE)
(2)	act:	SETCC_MSG(replybuf, GETTCC_MSG(replybuf) + $ADDRESSEE)

Figure 3. State diagram specification of the "Reply" command.

denoting a transition from state *s1* to state *s2*, which expects input token INP and displays response "Hello." Conditions or actions are specified in a way similar to the response. Instead of an input token, the name of another diagram could be given (in lower case), meaning that the diagram would be traversed, and, upon exit from it, a transition to state *s2* would be made. Other features of this notation are the same as for the state diagrams above.

Login

start: LOGIN resp: "Enter name" ⟶ getu

getu: USER cond: not EXISTS_USER($USER)
        resp: "Incorrect user name--reenter it" ⟶ getu

getu: USER cond: EXISTS_USER($USER)
        resp: "Enter password" ⟶ getpw

getpw: PASSWORD cond: $PASSWORD = GETPASSWD_USER($USER)
        resp: "Enter security level" ⟶ getsl

getpw: PASSWORD cond: $PASSWORD ≠ GETPASSWD_USER($USER)
        resp: "Incorrect password--reenter it" ⟶ badpw

badpw: PASSWORD cond: $PASSWORD = GETPASSWD_USER($USER)
        resp: "Enter security level" ⟶ getsl

badpw: PASSWORD cond: $PASSWORD≠GETPASSWD_USER($USER)
        resp: "Incorrect password--start again" ⟶ start

getsl: SECLEVEL cond: $SECLEVEL > GETCLEARANCE_USER($USER)
        resp: "Security level too high--reenter it" ⟶ getsl

getsl: SECLEVEL cond: $SECLEVEL ≤ GETCLEARANCE_USER($USER)
        act: CREATE_SESSION($USER, $PASSWORD, $SECLEVEL) ⟶ end

getsl: ANY   resp: "Your security level is Unclassified"
        act: CREATE_SESSION($USER, $PASSWORD, Unclassified) ⟶ end

Figure 4. Text representation of Figure 2.

This notation is directly translatable into that of the graphic state diagrams. In fact, Figures 4 and 5 were the input to a program that produced Figures 2 and 3 automatically.

Reply

start:	REPLY ⟶ getid

getid:	MSGID resp: "Enter text field"
	    act: replyid := REPLY_MSG($MSGID);
	    replybuf := OPENFOREDIT_MSG(replyid) ⟶ gettext

getid:	ANY resp: "Enter text field"
	    act: replyid := REPLY_MSG(CurrentMsg);
	    replybuf := OPENFOREDIT_MSG(replyid) ⟶ gettext

gettext:	TEXT act: SETTEXT_MSG($TEXT, replybuf) ⟶ getextras
getextras:	extratos ⟶ getextras
getextras:	extraccs ⟶ getextras
getextras:	ANY act: UPDATE_MSG(replyid, replybuf); CLOSEEDIT_MSG(replyid) ⟶ end

extratos

start:	TO ⟶ t1
t1:	ADDRESSEE act: SETTO_MSG(replybuf, GETTO_MSG(replybuf) +$ADDRESSEE) ⟶ t2
t2:	ADDRESSEE act: SETTO_MSG(replybuf, GETTOSG(replybuf) +$ADDRESSEE) ⟶ t2
t2:	ANY ⟶ end

extraccs

start:	CC ⟶ c1 ADDRESSEE act: SETCC_MSG(replybuf, GETCC_MSG(replybuf) +$ADDRESSEE) ⟶ c2
c2:	ADDRESSEE act: SETCC_MSG(replybuf, GETCC_MSG(replybuf) +$ADDRESSEE) ⟶ c2
c2:	ANY ⟶ end

Figure 5. Text representation of Figure 3.

Figures 6 and 7 show the same commands in BNF notation. Lower case names denote nonterminal symbols, which are subsequently defined in terms of terminal symbols. Upper case names are terminal symbols, which would be defined in a separate, lower-level specification. Some definition rules are annotated with Boolean conditions, system responses, or actions, all placed in braces. If a rule contains a condition, that condition must be true at the point in the input stream corresponding to its position in the rule for the rule to be matched. When a rule is matched, the system will display the response and perform the action, if any are given.

Login ::=   badpw* goodpw {resp: "Enter security level"} getseclevel

badpw ::=   loguser onetry PASSWORD
               {cond: $PASSWORD ≠ GETPASSWD_USER($USER)
               resp: "Incorrect password--start again"}

goodpw ::=   loguser PASSWORD
               {cond: $PASSWORD = GETPASSWD_USER($USER)}
               loguser onetry PASSWORD
               {cond: $PASSWORD = GETPASSWD_USER($USER)}

loguser ::=   LOGIN {resp: "Enter name"}
               getuser {resp: "Enter password"}

getuser ::=   baduser* USER {cond: EXISTS_USER($USER)}

baduser ::=   USER {cond: not EXISTS_USER($USER)
               resp: "Incorrect user name--reenter it"}

onetry ::=   PASSWORD
               {cond: $PASSWORD ≠ GETPASSWD_USER($USER)
               resp: "Incorrect password--reenter it"}

getseclevel ::= badsl* {resp: "Your security level is Unclassified"
               act: CREATE_SESSION($USER, $PASSWORD, Unclassified)}
               badsl* SECLEVEL
               {cond: $SECLEVEL ≤ GETCLEARANCE_USER($USER)
               act: CREATE_SESSION($USER, $PASSWORD, $SECLEVEL)}

badsl ::=   SECLEVEL
               {cond: $SECLEVEL > GETCLEARANCE_USER($USER)
               resp: "Security level too high--reenter it"}

Figure 6. BNF specifications of the "Login" command

```
Reply ::=          REPLY getid {resp: "Enter text field"
                       act : replybuf:= OPENFOREDIT_MSG(replyid)}
                   TEXT {act: SETTEXT_MSG($TEXT, replybuf)}
                   extras*{act: UPDATE_MSG(replyid, replybuf);
                       CLOSEEDIT_MSG(replyid)}

getid ::=          MSGID {act : replyid := REPLY_MSG($MSGID)}
                   NULL {act: replyid := REPLY_MSG(CurrentMsg)}

extras ::=         extratos | extrraccs

extratos ::=       TO toaddressee toaddressee*

toaddressee ::=    ADDRESSEE {act: SETTO_MSG(replybuf,
                       GETTO_MSG(replybuf) + $ADDRESSEE)}

extraccs ::=       CC ccaddressee ccaddressee*

ccaddressee ::=    ADDRESSEE {act: SETCC_MSG(replybuf,
                       GETCC_MSG(replybuf) + $ADDRESSEE)}
```

Figure 7. BNF specification of the "Reply" command

The special token NULL represents no input. A token or nonterminal name followed by an asterisk stands for "zero or more instances of" that symbol. The other conventions used in the actions are the same as those for the state diagrams above.

The specifications in this notation could have been produced automatically from those above, but the resulting specifications would be difficult to read, as discussed below. Figures 2 and 3 were translated by hand to produce Figures 6 and 7, and several nonterminals thought to be helpful in understanding the specification were introduced in the process.

8. CONCLUSIONS

From examining these and other examples, one can observe that, while the techniques based on BNF and those based on state transition diagrams are formally equivalent, their surface differences have an important effect on the comprehensibility of the specifications. In particular, notations based on state transition diagrams explicitly contain the concept of a state and the transition rules associated with it, while this is implicit in BNF-based notations. Since the concept of state is important in representing sequence in the behavior of an interactive system, state diagrams are preferable to BNF in this regard.

Existing techniques based on state diagrams vary considerably in their syntax and expressive ability, although it is possible to combine the desirable features of several such notations into a new technique. The state diagrams shown above represent such a synthesis.

While the text representations of the state diagrams are somewhat more difficult to read than the graphical ones, they are a more convenient form of computer input. They do contain sufficient information to generate the graphic diagrams automatically (as was done here) and to drive a simulator of the user interface (which has recently been built).

In either state diagram or BNF notation, the judicious use and choice of meaningful nonterminal symbols is important to the overall clarity of the specification, sometimes more so than the choice of notation. The principal difference between the two types of notations in this regard is that a BNF-based specification with very few nonterminals (with respect to the complexity of the system) is generally more difficult to understand than the corresponding state diagram. Thus a direct translation of a typical BNF specification into state diagram notation is likely to contain many very simple diagrams; while a typical state diagram translated into BNF will contain only a few, very complicated rules. BNF, then, requires more nonterminals to make it readable.

A synthesis of the features of several state diagram-based notations was thus selected to specify the user interface for a prototype military message system. The explicit description of states in this notation makes the sequence of actions clearer than in BNF. In addition, some of the states correspond to users' own notions of what a system does ("text entry" state, "logged-out" state). The state diagram examples show how a portion of the User Agent can be specified in this manner. An interpreter has been developed to take such a specification directly and execute the specified user interface, issuing ICL commands to the rest of the message system.

ACKNOWLEDGMENTS

This work has benefited from discussions with my colleagues on the Military Message System project: M. Cornwell, C. Heitmeyer and C. Landwehr, and with L. Chmura.

BERNARD SUFRIN
Oxford University Computing Laboratory

Formal Specification of a Display-Oriented Text Editor

1. INTRODUCTION

In this paper we present the formal specification of a simple, display-oriented text editor which has been in use at the Programming Research Group and elsewhere since late 1979 and which is informally described in Appendix 1. Our original purpose in designing the editor was to offer a comfortable human interface coupled with the possibility of implementation on fairly cheap hardware.

Our goal here is to give a mathematical model which can serve to communicate the essence of our design, to provide a basis for the construction of new implementations, and to act as a touchstone for correctness of those implementations. For this reason we believe that it is unnecessary for the specification to be in a form which is immediately executable; our goals can be met by presenting our design in a manner which facilitates formalization and proof of questions relating to its intended behavior.

Although detailed consideration of algorithms has its place later in the system construction process, at the design stage we are concerned with clearly and unambiguously expressing the relationship between system components. Such an enterprise is entirely different from that of presenting the algorithms which achieve or maintain these relationships. Although it is easy to bend to the temptation to consider a specification simply as a "very high-level program," such an orientation can lead to specifications about which it is considerably harder to prove anything—either formally or informally. We have therefore felt free (but not obliged) to define operations in a way which does not immediately indicate how they might be implemented (for example, see the document-difference functions of Section 2.4).

In short, we do not intend the specification to be read as a direct blueprint for an implementation; it should be read as an indication of *what* the editor is to do not *how* it is to do it.

Design Principles

In general we think that an author using our editor should be able to concentrate on the composition of a document rather than the complexities of the editor interface. This outlook has informed the whole of our design.

The first important design principle is that the editor has *no hidden modes*! Most commands are invoked by a *single keystroke*, and the interpretation of every key on the keyboard is fixed, rather than depending on some non-visible aspect of the history of the edit session so far. The effect of this is that prediction of the effect of a keystroke is simplified; coupled with the fact that the commands are (so to speak) author oriented, this means that many common editing actions can eventually become *reflexes* rather than complicated sequences of keystrokes which must be consciously considered.

The title of the paper alludes to the next design principle: what is visible on the screen is the best approximation to the content of the document that the display device can produce, namely a view of that region of the document which surrounds the place at which commands have their effect. In other words, "you see what you are going to get" rather than having to reconstruct a mental image of the document from the visible remains of the last few commands.

Probably the most important design principle is reflected in the fact that we have not cluttered our design with hosts of features. The payoff for this is that the user manual is just four pages long and most of the editing tasks one ever needs to do can be done once these have been understood. Indeed we have found that given a suitably designed and adequately labeled keyboard a substantial amount of work can be done without ever reading the manual! We are quite happy for implementers to modify our specification to their own taste, but strongly recommend caution. For example, we think that the temptation to encumber an editor with all the power of a general-purpose string-processing *language* should be resisted, although generalizing the notion of a pattern would be quite acceptable. A good guideline for many enhancements is that if they are difficult to add cleanly to the model then they will be difficult to explain to users, and will complicate the editor interface unduly.

Specification Structure

Our specification is in three main sections: first we present the specification of a document editing subsystem; next we specify a document display subsystem; finally we give the desired relationship between these two independently specified components and suggest a modularization for implementations.

We have abstracted away from detailed properties of display devices (such as the repertoire of transformations on the display); editor commands are explained solely as transformations on documents and the role of the display subsystem can be summarized as *keeping in view the region of the document which surrounds the cursor.*

This structure in itself signifies a major design decision. Faced with a sophisticated display device it would be all too tempting to design an editor which utilizes all the facilities provided by that device, and to orient the design either simply or mainly around what will appear on the screen. Unfortunately it is too often the case that computer systems designs are too strongly influenced by the precise characteristics of the hardware on which they will initially be implemented. This adversely affects the designer's ability to come up with a simple and effective human interface—not to mention a comprehensible explanation of his or her design.

Nevertheless, because our initial purpose was the design of a simple editor implementable on cheap hardware, our specification is pitched at a much more concrete level than that chosen by Guttag and Horning [1980]. The abstraction we have chosen as the basis for our model of a display device is a rectangular screen on which characters appear. This abstraction is implementable on a wide variety of display devices, ranging from dumb terminals to bit-map displays.

The basis of our model of a document is also rather unsophisticated: a document is composed of characters, and is viewed as a sequence of lines. This approach precludes generalizations of the editor with the ability to mix text and graphics.

Specification Style

Rather than confronting the reader with a great deal of detail all at once we have chosen to present the specification of the editing subsystem in stages. At each stage we present a mathematical model powerful enough to capture the design decisions we wish to illustrate, then utilize this model to define an editor, giving theorems which indicate its important properties. Our formalism is based on modern set theory, and is summarized in Appendix 3.

For the most part we proceed from model to properties rather than from properties to model. For reasons which are explained in some detail in Sufrin [1981] we believe that this is simply a matter of pedagogy rather than an issue of principle.

A definition in denotational style would involve the invention of an *abstract syntax* of editor commands, the definition of a model for the editor states, and the definition of a *semantic function* to map commands into the state transforming functions which define their effects. The extremely simple structure of the editor "command language" does not warrant the invention of an abstract syntax, however, and we have chosen instead to stay in the world of semantics. At each stage of development of the editor we define a model of the editor state, and describe a set of state-transforming functions each of which corresponds to an editor command.

Since commands are single keystrokes, their "abstract syntax" would simply be a picture of keyboard; the corresponding semantic function would map each key to one of the state transforming functions.

2. EDITING DOCUMENTS

2.1 A Simple Editor Model

We begin by building a small theory powerful enough to define the first editor to be specified, which will have commands permitting insertion, deletion, and motion of just one character at a time. Every command takes effect at, and may change the position of, *the current position* in the document—which henceforth will be called the *cursor*.

The essential observations to be made of the state of the editor are the *content* of the document being edited and the *position* of the cursor. Since we consider the cursor to be *between* characters rather than *at* a character, these two observations can be captured by a pair of sequences of characters—henceforth called a *DOC*. One sequence corresponds to that part of the document which *precedes* the cursor, the other to that which *follows* the cursor. The set of characters which may appear in documents will henceforth be denoted *CH*.

DOC ⎯⎯⎯⎯⎯⎯⎯⎯⎯⎯⎯⎯⎯⎯⎯⎯⎯⎯⎯⎯⎯⎯⎯⎯⎯⎯⎯⎯⎯⎯⎯

$seq[CH] \times seq[CH]$

The following primitive *DOC*-transforming functions will be used to specify the effects of editor commands. Rather than define them by lambda abstraction we present their signatures followed by axioms which specify their properties.

$del: \quad DOC \rightarrowtail DOC$

$move: \quad DOC \rightarrowtail DOC$

$ins: \quad CH \rightarrow DOC \rightarrow DOC$

$content: \quad DOC \rightarrow seq[CH]$

$dom\ move = dom\ del = \{l, r | l \neq \langle\rangle\}$

$(\forall (l, r): DOC;\ ch: CH)$

$move(l * \langle ch \rangle, r) = (l, \langle ch \rangle * r);$

$del(l * \langle ch \rangle, r) = (l, r);$

$ins\ ch\ (l, r) = (l * \langle ch \rangle, r);$

$content(l, r) = (l * r);$

The functions *move* and *del* are partial; their effects are (respectively) to move the cursor backward through the document and to delete the character immediately before the cursor. Both functions are applicable to editor states whose cursor is not positioned at the beginning of the document.

FORMAL SPECIFICATION OF A TEXT EDITOR

Example

$(\langle\text{CURRENT}\rangle, \langle\text{sp POSITION}\rangle)$

move

$(\langle\text{CURREN}\rangle, \langle\text{T sp POSITION}\rangle)$

del

$(\langle\text{CURRE}\rangle, \langle\text{T sp POSITION}\rangle)$

del

$(\langle\text{CURR}\rangle, \langle\text{T sp POSITION}\rangle)$

insert(Y)

$(\langle\text{CURRY}\rangle, \langle\text{T sp POSITION}\rangle)$

These functions are not sufficient to specify even the simplest editor since there is nothing corresponding to rightward motion. Rather than remedy this *ad hoc*, we introduce a *method* for defining direction by defining a pair of directional combinators which we will use throughout the paper. First we add to our theory a function which maps a document to its mirror image.

mirror: $DOC \rightarrow DOC$

mirror(l, r) = (*reverse r, reverse l*)

Example *mirror* applied to:

$(\langle\text{FOO}\rangle, \langle\text{BAZ}\rangle)$

gives:

$(\langle\text{ZAB}\rangle, \langle\text{OOF}\rangle)$

following this by a *move* we get:

$(\langle\text{ZA}\rangle, \langle\text{BOOF}\rangle)$

then by another *mirror* we get:

$(\langle\text{FOOB}\rangle, \langle\text{AZ}\rangle)$

in other words a rightward move!

It is easy to see that rightward delete and rightward insert can be described similarly and for this reason we introduce the following "directional" combinators.

---

right,
left: $(DOC \leftrightarrow DOC) \rightarrow (DOC \leftrightarrow DOC)$

---

right f = *mirror* $\circ$ *f* $\circ$ *mirror*
left f = *f*

The function *right* maps any *DOC*-transforming function to its "rightward" counterpart, while *left* is simply a mnemonic remaining of the identity on *DOC*-transforming functions. We are now in a position to specify a family of simple editors whose commands correspond to the functions:

left move   *left del*   *left*(*ins c*)   (for all c: *CH*)
right move *right del* *right*(*ins c*) (for all c: *CH*)

and which have the following desirable properties:

1. An insertion followed by a deletion has no net effect on the document.

2. A *legal* move in one direction followed by a move in the opposite direction has no net effect.

3. A *legal* deletion in one direction can be achieved by a move in that direction followed by a delete in the opposite direction.

4. *Legal* moves have no net effect on the content of a document.

Proving the theorems which formalize these properties is relatively easy and is left as an exercise for the reader.

FORMAL SPECIFICATION OF A TEXT EDITOR

DOC PROPERTIES

⊢ $(\forall c\colon CH)$
         left del $\circ$ *left(ins c)* = *id (DOC)* ∧
         right del $\circ$ *right(ins c)* = *id (DOC)*

⊢   *left move* $\circ$ *right move* = $id\{l, r \mid r \neq \langle\rangle\}$ ∧
         right move $\circ$ *left move* = $id\{l, r \mid l \neq \langle\rangle\}$

⊢   *left del* $\circ$ *right move* = *right del* ∧
         right del $\circ$ *left move* = *left del*

⊢ $(\forall (l, r)\colon DOC \mid l \neq \langle\rangle)$
         (*content* $\circ$ *left move*) (l, r) = *content*(l, r)

⊢ $(\forall (l, r)\colon DOC \mid r \neq \langle\rangle)$
         (*content* $\circ$ *right move*) (l, r) = *content*(l, r)

Hint: use the following generic properties of sequences.

$$X$$

SEQ PROPERTIES

⊢ $(\forall s, s_1, s_2\colon seq[X];\ x\colon X)$
         reverse(*reverse s*) = *s*
         reverse$(s_1 * s_2)$ = *reverse* s_2 * *reverse* s_1

Quantifying over actions and directions

The two kinds of function defined above are going to be used as the basic building blocks from which we will construct editor specifications. These specifications will comprise definitions of higher order functions whose argument are the document transformations and the directional combinators; we therefore give names to two sets of functions:

ACTION: $\mathbb{P}(DOC \leftrightarrow DOC)$
DIRECTION: $\mathbb{P}((DOC \leftrightarrow DOC) \rightarrow (DOC \leftrightarrow DOC))$

ACTION =   {*del, move*}
DIRECTION =   {*left, right*}

The *ACTION*s are the *DOC*-transforming functions; the *DIRECTIONS*s are the directional combinators.

2.2 A Simple Editor

The *DOC* model and the functions thereon say a great deal of what needs to be said of *any* simple editor. In order to define the human interface to a particular editor with greater precision we need to present a more detailed specification of the available commands; our general approach to such presentations is exemplified below.

The effect of each command will be modeled by a state-to-state function. Editor states—henceforth denoted *ED*—are modeled here by a single *DOC*:

    ED _____
        DOC
    _____

We face a small problem in specifying the effect of commands on editor states: despite the fact that we wish the effect of every command to be completely defined, the functions we can specify using only *ACTION*s and *DIRECTION*s are not all total. For example, ⟨*right move*⟩ is defined only for documents which have text following the cursor but we wish to define the effect of an attempt to move the cursor rightwards beyond the end of the document as "no change to the content of the document nor the position of the cursor."

Once again we avoid solving the problem *ad hoc*; instead we develop a *method* by which we can transform the partial functions of our supporting theories into the total functions by which we specify human interfaces to complex systems. This reflects a separation of concerns which vastly simplifies reasoning in the supporting theories.

The combinator, *try*, which is introduced below, maps a partial function, f, into a total function which agrees with f on its domain (a subset of the *generic* set X) and elsewhere agrees with the identify function on X.

$$X$$

$try: (X \nrightarrow X) \longrightarrow (X \longrightarrow X)$

$try\ f = id\ X \oplus f$

This *generic* form of definition—signified by the X above the double bar—denotes a schema which can be instantiated for any *actual* set. Thus for a set Y

$try[Y]$ denotes a function of type $(Y \nrightarrow Y) \longrightarrow (Y \longrightarrow Y)$.

Example

$try[ED]\ move\ (\langle e\ n \rangle, \langle d \rangle) = (\langle end \rangle, \langle \rangle)$

but:

$try[ED]\ move\ (\langle end \rangle, \langle \rangle) = (\langle end \rangle, \langle \rangle)$

As is customary we will omit the *generic argument* ([ED] above) when invoking generically defined functions such as *try*, since their intended type is usually evident from context.

Keyboard Design

In the simple specification which appears below, we use the "totalizing" function *try* to define two families of functions which are intended to model the effects of commands on the editor. The *FUNCTION* family is indexed by a *DIRECTION* and an *ACTION*, thus permitting motion and deletion in both directions. The *INSERT* family is just indexed by a character; this records our decision to support only the conventional (left-to-right) direction of insertion.

$INSERT: CH \rightarrow ED \rightarrow ED$
$FUNCTION: (DIRECTION \times ACTION) \rightarrow ED \rightarrow ED$

$(\forall a: ACTION; d: DIRECTION; c: CH)$
 $INSERT\ c = ins\ c$
 $FUNCTION(d, a) = try(d\ a)$

We summarize the commands we wish to make available to users of the simple editor by defining *cmd* as a subset of the *ED*-transforming functions.

$cmd: \mathbb{P}(ED \rightarrow ED)$

$cmd = ran\ INSERT \cup ran\ FUNCTION$

One of the tasks of the designer of an *implementation* of this editor would be to provide a mapping from *keys* on the chosen keyboard to each of the *cmds* specified above. Although a detailed discussion of keyboard layout is beyond the scope of this paper, we suggest in Figure 1 a mapping for a keyboard with four function keys; each letter on the keyboard corresponds to a one of a pair of the *cmd* functions—the choice is indicated by whether or not the *shift* button is depressed.

This mapping may be interpreted as the semantic function to which we alluded in our discussion of specification style, and as we add more commands to the repertoire of the editor we will add more keys to the keyboard diagram.

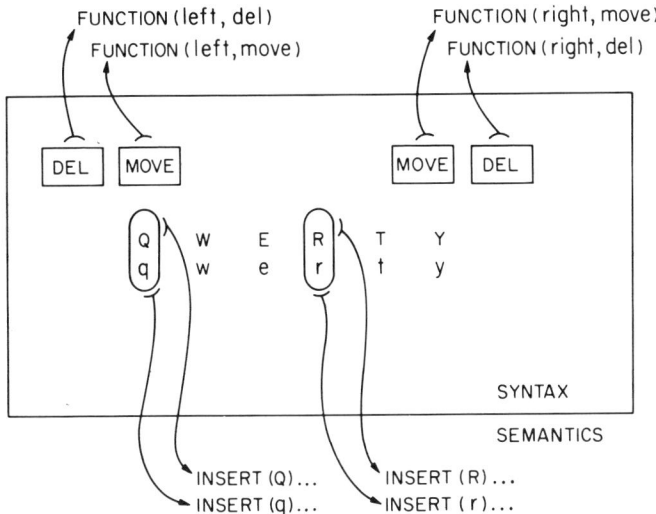

Figure 1. Keyboard design for the simple editor

2.3 Enriching the Simple Model

Defining Significant Places in Documents

We wish to specify commands which act on larger units, namely words, lines, and even the whole document. In order to be able to specify such commands we need to enrich our simple model by formalizing the idea of *word, line* and *document* boundaries.

To exemplify our approach to the definition of unit boundaries we first define the set —*line*— of documents whose cursor is positioned at the beginning of a line by introducing a (constant) character to stand for *newline*.

$$nl: \quad CH$$
$$line: \quad \mathbb{P}(DOC)$$

$$line = \{l, r \mid l = \langle \rangle \vee last\ l = nl\}$$

Example

$$(\langle \text{last nl}\rangle, \langle \text{next}\rangle) \in line$$

but:

$$(\langle \text{last} \rangle, \langle \text{nl next} \rangle) \notin \textit{line}$$

The image through the function *mirror* of this set of documents is written:

mirror⟦*line*⟧

and is equivalent to the set:

$$\{l, r \mid r = \langle \rangle \vee \textit{first}(r) = nl\}.$$

Example

$$(\langle \text{last} \rangle, \langle \text{nl next} \rangle) \in \textit{mirror}⟦\textit{line}⟧$$

So the *mirror* image characterizes the documents whose cursors are positioned at the *end* of a line!

Next we introduce a different constant which stands for *space* and define the set of documents whose cursor is positioned at the beginning of a word.

---

sp: $\quad CH$
$wordb$: $\quad \mathbb{P}(DOC)$

$sp \neq nl$
$wordb = \{l, r \mid \textit{last}(l) \in \{sp, nl\} \vee \textit{first}(r) \notin \{sp, nl\}\}$

Example

$$(\langle \text{purple sp sp} \rangle, \langle \text{prose} \rangle) \in \textit{wordb}$$
$$(\langle \text{final nl} \rangle, \langle \text{draft} \rangle) \in \textit{wordb}$$

but:

$$(\langle \text{painful} \rangle, \langle \text{sp problem} \rangle) \notin \textit{wordb}$$

The *mirror* image of this set of documents is:

mirror⟦*wordb*⟧ =
$\quad \{l, r \mid \textit{last}(l) \notin \{sp, nl\} \vee \textit{first}(r) \in \{sp, nl\}\}$

Example

$$(\langle \text{painful} \rangle, \langle \text{sp problem} \rangle) \in \textit{mirror}⟦\textit{wordb}⟧$$

FORMAL SPECIFICATION OF A TEXT EDITOR

So the *mirror* image of *wordb* describes the set of documents whose cursors are at the end of a word.

For reasons which we shall explain later it is convenient to somewhat widen our definition of word boundaries:

---

word: $\mathbb{P}(DOC)$

---

word = *wordb* ∪ *line*

Lastly we introduce the set of documents whose cursors are at the beginning of the document, and the set whose cursors are positioned at a character boundary (i.e., the *entire* set of documents).

---

document: $\mathbb{P}(DOC)$
character: $\mathbb{P}(DOC)$

---

document = $\{l, r \mid l = \langle \rangle\}$
character = DOC

It will be useful to give names to the function *mirror* and the identity function on documents—$id(DOC)$—which more closely reflect the role they can play in specifying which side of a word, line or document we mean.

---

beginning,
ending: $DOC \rightarrow DOC$

---

beginning = $id(DOC)$
ending = *mirror*

The following sets correspond to documents whose cursors are positioned at significant boundaries:

beginning⟦*character*⟧   *ending*⟦*character*⟧
beginning⟦*word*⟧   *ending*⟦*line*⟧
beginning⟦*line*⟧   *ending*⟦*line*⟧
beginning⟦*document*⟧   *ending*⟦*document*⟧

with the obvious property that

beginning⟦*character*⟧ = *ending*⟦*character*⟧ = *character*

Since we later want to define higher order functions over the sides and the unit boundaries we name these two sets *SIDE* and *UNIT*.

SIDE: $\mathbb{P}(DOC \rightarrow DOC)$
UNIT: $\mathbb{P}(\mathbb{P}(DOC))$

$SIDE = \{beginning, ending\}$
$UNIT = \{character, word, line, document\}$

Motion and Deletion to Significant Places

In order to specify motion or deletion "to the next (previous) ... boundary," we first define functions which map documents into their *distance* (i.e., number of moves) to the nearest "...boundary" in a given direction *if such a place exists*. The conditional nature of these functions is reflected in the partial lambda abstraction by which they are defined. Notice that we have not given an *algorithm* which discovers the distances, simply specified what they are.

---

dist: $DIRECTION \rightarrow \mathbb{P}(DOC) \rightarrow DOC \rightarrowtail \mathbb{N}$

---

dist dir place =
  (λ *doc* | *distances* ≠ { }) *(min distances)*
  where *distances* =
    $\{d:\mathbb{N} \mid d>0 \wedge dir\ move^d\ doc \in place\}$

FORMAL SPECIFICATION OF A TEXT EDITOR

Example

$$\textit{dist right ending}[\![\textit{word}]\!] \, (\langle \text{her} \rangle, \langle \text{sp hand sp is} \rangle) = 5$$

but

$$(\langle \text{her} \rangle, \langle \text{sp hand sp is} \rangle) \notin \textit{dom}(\textit{dist right ending}[\![\textit{line}]\!])$$

Moving or deleting to a given kind of boundary in a given direction is specified simply as an iteration of the action. The effect is undefined for documents in which such a boundary is unreachable, but we will once again invoke the totalizing function *try* when we use these functions to specify commands:

---

to: $((\textit{ACTION} \times \textit{DIRECTION}) \times \mathbb{P}(\textit{DOC})) \rightarrow \textit{DOC} \rightarrowtail \textit{DOC}$

$(\textit{action}, \textit{dir})$ **to** place =
$(\lambda \, \textit{doc} | \textit{doc} \in \textit{dom}(\textit{dist dir place}) \, (\textit{dir action}^n \, \textit{doc})$
where $n = \textit{dist dir place doc}$

Example

$$(\textit{del}, \textit{right}) \, \textbf{to} \, \textit{ending}[\![\textit{word}]\!]$$

maps

$$(\langle \text{her} \rangle, \langle \text{sp hand sp is} \rangle)$$

to

$$(\langle \text{her} \rangle \langle \text{sp is} \rangle)$$

The functions:

$(\textit{move}, \textit{left})$ **to** *character*
$(\textit{move}, \textit{right})$ **to** *character*
$(\textit{del}, \textit{left})$ **to** *character*
$(\textit{del}, \textit{right})$ **to** *character*

obviously correspond to *left*(*move*), *right*(*move*), *left*(*del*), and *right*(*del*) of our original model.

The functions:

(*move, left*)	**to** *beginning* ⟦*word*⟧
(*del, left*)	**to** *beginning* ⟦*word*⟧
(*move, left*)	**to** *beginning* ⟦*line*⟧
(*del, left*)	**to** *beginning* ⟦*line*⟧
(*move, left*)	**to** *beginning* ⟦*document*⟧
(*del, left*)	**to** *beginning* ⟦*document*⟧
(*move, left*)	**to** *ending* ⟦*word*⟧
(*del, left*)	**to** *ending* ⟦*word*⟧
(*move, left*)	**to** *ending* ⟦*line*⟧
(*del, left*)	**to** *ending* ⟦*line*⟧
(*move, left*)	**to** *ending* ⟦*document*⟧
(*del, left*)	**to** *ending* ⟦*document*⟧

together with their rightward-acting counterparts are suitable for modeling commands whose properties are obvious generalizations of the desirable properties of the simple model:

1. Following a successful move from a (character, word, line) boundary to the same kind of boundary by a move in the opposite direction to the same kind of boundary has no net effect.

2. A deletion can be achieved by motion in the appropriate direction followed by deletion in the opposite direction.

3. Motion has no net effect on the content of a document.

These properties are formalized by the following theorem, whose proof is once more left as an exercise for the reader.

PLACE THEOREM _____

$lmove \circ rmove = id\,(place \cap dom\,(rmove)) \land$
$rmove \circ lmove = id\,(place \cap dom\,(lmove))$

$rdel \restriction place = ldel \circ rmove \restriction place \land$
$ldel \restriction place = rdel \circ lmove \restriction place \land$

$content \circ try\,(lmove) = content \land$
$content \circ try\,(rmove) = content$

where $rmove = ((move, right)\text{ to } place)$
and $lmove = ((move, left)\text{ to } place)$
and $ldel = ((del, left)\text{ to } place)$
and $rdel = ((del, right)\text{ to } place)$

Hint: use the following lemmas.

DIRECTION LEMMAS

⊢ *mirror* ∘ *mirror* = *id* (*DOC*)
⊢ *right* ∘ *right* = *id* (*DOC* ↣ *DOC*)
⊢ (∀ *n*: ℕ)
  (*right move*)^n = *right*(*move*^{n}) ∧
  (*right del*) = *right*(*del*^{n})

We have now developed a rather rich set of primitives; the question naturally arises whether we will ever need *all* of them for a particular editor design. We will begin to answer it when we next discuss keyboard design.

2.4 Further Enriching the Simple Model

Since it is all too easy to mistakenly hit a key which deletes a substantial amount of text we will include a *recall* command, which undoes the most recent delete command. We will also include a cut-and-paste facility which permits excision and/or movement of substantial portions of documents.

In order to specify the effect of such commands we enrich our theory further by defining functions which are the *DOC* analogues of sequence concatenation and difference. We also define relations analogous to sequence prefix and suffix.

In fact the theory defined in this section will be utilized in the definition of a surprisingly wide variety of commands; these range from the *recall* command to the pattern-matching and replacement commands.

**:   *DOC* × *DOC* → *DOC*
//:   *DOC* × *DOC* ↣ *DOC*
\\\\:   *DOC* × *DOC* ↣ *DOC*
infixes: *DOC* ↔ *DOC*
outfixes: *DOC* ↔ *DOC*

(*l*, *r*) ** (*l'*, *r'*) = (*l* * *l'*, *r'* * *r*)
(∀ *d*, *d'*: *DOC*)
  (*d* **infixes** *d'*) ⇔ (∃ *d''*: *DOC* | *d''* ** *d* = *d'*)
  (*d* **outfixes** *d'*) ⇔ (∃ *d''*: *DOC* | *d* ** *d''* = *d'*)
(∀ *d*$_1$, *d*$_2$: *DOC* | *d*$_2$ **outfixes** *d*$_1$)
          d$_2$ ** (*d*$_1$ // *d*$_2$) = *d*$_1$
(∀ *d*$_1$, *d*$_2$: *DOC* | *d*$_2$**infixes** *d*$_1$)
          (*d*$_1$ \\\\ *d*$_2$) ** *d*$_2$ = *d*$_1$

Examples

$$(\langle FO\rangle, \langle AZ\rangle) \mathbin{**} (\langle O\ B\rangle, \langle\,\rangle) = (\langle FOOB\rangle, \langle AZ\rangle)$$
$$(\langle FO\rangle, \langle AZ\rangle)\ \textbf{outfixes}\ (\langle FOOB\rangle, \langle AZ\rangle)$$
$$(\langle OB\rangle, \langle\,\rangle)\ \textbf{infixes}\ (\langle FOOB\rangle, \langle AZ\rangle)$$
$$(\langle FOOB\rangle, \langle AZ\rangle)\ //\ (\langle FO\rangle, \langle AZ\rangle) = (\langle OB\rangle, \langle\,\rangle)$$
$$(\langle FOOB\rangle, \langle AZ\rangle)\ \backslash\backslash\ (\langle O\ B\rangle, \langle\,\rangle) = (\langle FO\rangle, \langle AZ\rangle)$$

It is easy to show that every deletion maps a document to one of its outfixes, and that consequently the outer difference between a *DOC*ument and a deletion applied to it is well defined. More formally:

$$\vdash (\forall\, d\colon DOC\,;\ dir\colon DIRECTION\,;\ n\colon \mathbb{N})$$
$$try\,(dir\ del)^n\ d\,\textbf{outfixes}\ d)$$

Methodological Note

The difference functions are specified *implicitly* by (conditional) axioms rather than *explicitly* by lambda abstraction. As we noted in our introduction this form of definition does not immediately suggest an implementation. Indeed there is no *guarantee* of the existence of mathematical functions which satisfy the given axioms. Strictly speaking we should produce evidence of their existence in the form of *constructively defined* functions which we prove to have the required properties. As we also noted in our introduction, however, the property-oriented specification is easier to read, and easier to reason about—and we often relegate the evidence to an appendix or dispense with it altogether.

2.5 The Basic Document Editor

We now define a more powerful editor which supports character word and line motion and deletion, together with a limited form of recovery from erroneous deletions.

We can now observe two attributes of the editor state, namely the text being edited and the last deletion.

ED	
text:	DOC
deleted:	DOC

Editor commands are, as before, modeled by *ED* to *ED* functions—of which there are now three families, namely the *FUNCTION* commands, the *INSERT*ion commands, and the *RECALL* command. Notice that neither insertion nor motion commands affect the last deleted text. This means that a rudimentary form of "cut and paste" can be performed by deleting, moving and recalling. A more general form of cut and paste is specified in Appendix 2.

FUNCTION: *DIRECTION* × *ACTION* × *SIDE* × *UNIT* ⟶ *ED* ⟶ *ED*
INSERT: *CH* ⟶ *ED* ⟶ *ED*
RECALL: *ED* ⟶ *ED*

($\forall$ *d*: *DIRECTION*; *a*: *ACTION*; *s*: *SIDE*; *u*: *UNIT*; *c*: *CH*)
  INSERT c =
    (λ *ED*)
     (μ *ED'*)
      text' = *ins c text*;
      deleted' = *deleted*
  FUNCTION(*d*, *a*, *s*, *u*) =
    (λ *ED*)
     (μ *ED'*)
      text' = *try*((*a*, *d*) **to** *s*⟦*u*⟧) *text*;
      a = *del* ⇒
       deleted' = *text* / / *text'*;
      a = *move* ⇒
       deleted' = *deleted*;
  RECALL =
    (λ *ED*)
     (μ *ED'*)
      text' = *text* ** *deleted*;
      deleted' = *deleted*

Notational Interlude

Here we exemplify the use of the *schema notation* for the first time. The definition of *ED* given above was in a form which permits its utilization as a sort of textual macro when juxtaposed to quantifiers. Thus the expression

    (λ *ED*) ...

denotes exactly the same function as:

    (λ *text*: *DOC*; *deleted*: *DOC*) ...

in which the text of the *ED* schema is substituted for the occurrence of *ED*. The names of the components of *ED* are *bound* within "..." by the quantifier λ.

The expression

$(\mu\ ED')$ ... list of predicates ...

denotes an element of ED for which all of the given predicates hold (μ may be pronounced "make-an"). The names of the components of ED', i.e. *deleted'* and *text'* are *bound* by the μ quantifier, just as the names *deleted* and *text* were bound by the λ quantifier. The "dashing" permits components of the arguments and results of $\lambda-\mu$ functions to be distinguished.

Writing down a μ expression does not in itself guarantee the existence of an element with the required properties; this must (in general) be *proved independently* by showing that the predicates are mutually consistent. In the above case this is trivially evident. When an invariant is added to the schema definition (as, for example, in Section 4) we must also prove consistency of the predicates with the invariant when writing μ expressions.

When S is the name of a schema and *id* is the name of one of its components then the form $S\ .\ id$ is syntactic sugar for the form $(\lambda\ S)(id)$. So, for example, the functions $ED\ .\ text$ and $ED\ .\ deleted$ are the projections from the editor state ED to the values of its components.

For a more comprehensive explanation of the schema notation and its relation to mathematical quantifiers, and an illustration of the expressive power of the μ quantifier see Sufrin [1981].

Properties of the Recall Command

It is evident from the above definition that the $RECALL$ command corrects the effect of a single erroneous deletion on the textual component of the state. More formally:

$\vdash (\forall\ e: ED;\ dir: DIRECTION;\ side: SIDE;\ place: UNIT)$
$\quad ED\ .\ text\ (RECALL\ (deletion\ e)) = ED\ .\ text\ e$
where $deletion = FUNCTION\ (dir, del, side, place)$

Designing the Keyboard

There are actually fewer *useful FUNCTION*s than there might seem to be at first sight. For example, the end of a document can never be found to the left of the cursor, the beginning of a document is never to the right of the cursor and the beginning and ending of a *character* are identical.

The commands *delete left* to *ending* of *line* and *delete right* to *beginning* of *line* are needed so infrequently that they can be omitted from the keyboard and simulated with a couple of other keystrokes when necessary.

Furthermore, practical experience indicates that the availability of both the *beginning(word)* and the *ending(word)* positions complicates the keyboard designer's task. Worse still, it gives a typist several alternative ways of performing word-related tasks, and consequently increases the rate at which *conscious* decisions have to be made, thereby increasing fatigue.

FORMAL SPECIFICATION OF A TEXT EDITOR

In our experience the *ending(word)* positions are the best ones to omit, and we record this and the other decisions outlined above in the following definition of the set of available commands:

$cmd : \mathbb{P}(ED \rightarrow ED)$

$cmd = ran\ INSERT\ \cup\ ran\ FUNCTION\ \cup\ \{RECALL\} - excluded$
where *excluded* =
  $FUNCTION\llbracket DIRECTION \times ACTION \times \{ending\} \times \{word\}\rrbracket\ \cup$
  $FUNCTION\llbracket \{right\} \times ACTION \times \{beginning\} \times \{document\}\rrbracket\ \cup$
  $FUNCTION\llbracket \{left\} \times ACTION \times \{ending\} \times \{document\}\rrbracket\ \cup$
  $\{FUNCTION(left, delete, ending, line)\}\ \cup$
  $\{FUNCTION(right, delete, beginning, line)\}$

This is a somewhat unorthodox approach: describing a *general toolkit* of functions which we then use in order to define a *specific* set of commands by excluding some of those which are potentially specifiable. From a theoretical point of view what we are doing is analogous to giving a *static well-formedness* criterion independently of the denotational semantics of a programming language.

From a practical point of view it is worthwhile observing that it was only the experience of using implementations of *several* of the potentially specifiable sets of commands that led us to make the choice documented above. We find it hard to imagine any theoretical principle which would have enabled us to make that choice in advance of the experience.

2.6 Searching and Systematic Substitution

The commands defined in the previous section form the basic repertoire of the editor. In this section we specify the effects of searching and substitution commands.

We begin to specify these commands by ignoring the problem of how the typist supplies their arguments. The *find* functions specify motion of the cursor in the given direction to the nearest place in the document which matches a given pattern (if such a match occurs). The *replace* functions specify removal of the matching text from a document positioned at an instance of a pattern, and insertion of the replacement in its place. Notice that *replace* remembers the text which was removed.

$$
\begin{aligned}
&\textit{find}: \quad (DOC \times DIRECTION) \longrightarrow ED \rightarrowtail ED \\
&\textit{replace}: \quad (DOC \times DOC) \longrightarrow ED \rightarrowtail ED
\end{aligned}
$$

$\textit{find}\,(\textit{pattern}, \textit{dir}) =$
  $(\lambda\ ED\,|\,\textit{text} \in \textit{dom}\,((\textit{move}, \textit{dir})\ \textbf{to}\ \textit{match}))$
  $(\mu\ ED')\ \textit{text}' = ((\textit{move}, \textit{dir})\ \textbf{to}\ \textit{match})\ \textit{text}\,;$
      $\textit{deleted}' = \textit{deleted}$
    $\textbf{where}\ \textit{match} = \{d : DOC\,|\,\textit{pattern}\ \textbf{infixes}\ d\}$
$\textit{replace}\,(\textit{pattern}, \textit{repl}) =$
  $(\lambda\ ED\,|\,\textit{pattern}\ \textbf{infixes}\ \textit{text})$
  $(\mu\ ED')$
    $\textit{text}' = (\textit{text}\ \backslash\backslash\ \textit{pattern})\ **\ \textit{repl}\,;$
    $\textit{deleted}' = \textit{pattern}$

A formal definition in a more traditional style might well leave to the implementer the task of choosing a method for the typist to supply patterns for the *find* command and replacements for the *replace* command. For a highly interactive program the human interface needs to be specified more precisely, and so we specify below (first informally, and then formally) the details of a suitable method.

Hitherto every character typed has been inserted into the current document. In order to specify patterns and replacements we need to be able to type text which does not have an immediate effect on the document. The *QUOTE* key signals the start of such a text—which can be composed using all of the basic editing commands and without having any effect on the document itself. The *FIND* and *REPLACE* keys signal the completion of pattern (replacement) text, and have an appropriate effect. In the case of the *FIND* key the effect is to move the cursor (if possible) to the next instance of the pattern in the document. The *REPLACE* key changes the text of a document *which is already positioned at an instance of the FIND pattern* by substituting the replacement text for the *FIND* pattern.

Thus to change the next instance of FOO to BAZ, one types:

QUOTE FOO **FIND QUOTE** BAZ **REPLACE**

Both the **FIND** and the **REPLACE** keys remember their last argument, so that (for example) to replace the next instance of FOO one simply types:

FIND REPLACE

whereas to delete the next instance one would have typed:

FIND QUOTE REPLACE

subsequent deletions being performed by:

FIND REPLACE

Later we will show that these definitions do not contradict our strictures about hidden modes; one of the properties of the complete editor is that the quoted text must always be displayed.

We now begin to formalize the informal definition given above. Editor states are denoted by the schema *EDSTATE* whose *main, quoted* and *mode* components reflect the fact that one is either editing the document or composing quoted text. The *pattern* and *replacement* components reflect the fact that the *FIND* and *REPLACE* keys remember their last arguments.

$$
\begin{array}{ll}
\textit{EDSTATE} & \\
\quad main: & ED \\
\quad quoted: & ED \\
\quad pattern: & DOC \\
\quad repl: & DOC \\
\quad mode: & \{MAINTEXT, QUOTEDTEXT\}
\end{array}
$$

The effect of each key depends on whether one is composing the quoted or the main text. For example, a *BASIC* command is simply one of those developed in Section 2.5. It affects either the quoted or the main text, but has no effect on any other component.

$$BASIC: cmd \rightarrow EDSTATE \rightarrow EDSTATE$$

$$
\begin{array}{l}
BASIC\ c = \\
\quad (\lambda\ EDSTATE) \\
\quad (\mu\ EDSTATE') \\
\quad\quad pattern' = pattern\,; \\
\quad\quad repl' = repl\,; \\
\quad\quad mode' = mode\,; \\
\quad\quad mode = MAINTEXT \Rightarrow \\
\quad\quad\quad main' = c\ main\ \wedge \\
\quad\quad\quad quoted' = quoted\,; \\
\quad\quad mode = QUOTEDTEXT \Rightarrow \\
\quad\quad\quad main' = main\ \wedge \\
\quad\quad\quad quoted' = c\ quoted\,;
\end{array}
$$

The *QUOTE* command changes modes, and starts a new quoted text if necessary.

$QUOTE : EDSTATE \rightarrow EDSTATE$

$QUOTE = (\lambda\ EDSTATE)$
$\quad\quad\quad\ (\mu\ EDSTATE')$
$\quad\quad\quad\ pattern' = pattern\ ;$
$\quad\quad\quad\ repl' = repl\ ;$
$\quad\quad\quad\ mode' = mode\ ;$
$\quad\quad\quad\ mode = MAINTEXT \Rightarrow$
$\quad\quad\quad\quad\quad\quad quoted' = emptyED\ \wedge$
$\quad\quad\quad\quad\quad\quad mode' = QUOTEDTEXT\ ;$
$\quad\quad\quad\ mode = QUOTEDTEXT \Rightarrow$
$\quad\quad\quad\quad\quad\quad mode' = MAINTEXT\ \wedge$
$\quad\quad\quad\quad\quad\quad quoted' = quoted$
where $emptyED = \mu\ ED$
$\quad\quad\quad\quad\quad\quad text = (\langle\ \rangle, \langle\ \rangle);$
$\quad\quad\quad\quad\quad\quad deleted = (\langle\ \rangle, \langle\ \rangle)$

Notice that a *QUOTE* in *QUOTEDTEXT* mode is specified as if it just changes to *MAINTEXT* mode. Although their formal definition is beyond the scope of this paper, this is actually a suitable place to incorporate commands which interface the editor to its environment. In our implementations, for example, the command which leaves the editor is typed: *QUOTE q QUOTE*.

FIND and *REPLACE* both recall their last arguments when used in *MAINTEXT* mode. In *QUOTEDTEXT* mode the argument is derived from the quoted text. Notice that the derivation of the pattern used by *FIND* is such as to always leave the cursor positioned at the beginning of the matched text; this permits easy specification of *REPLACE*.

$FIND:$ $\quad DIRECTION \rightarrow EDSTATE \rightarrow EDSTATE$
$REPLACE:$ $EDSTATE \rightarrow EDSTATE$

$FIND\ dir =$
  $(\lambda\ EDSTATE)$
   $(\mu\ EDSTATE')$
   $main' = try\ (find\ (pattern',\ dir))\ main\ ;$
   $repl' = repl\ ;$
   $quoted' = quoted$
   $mode = QUOTEDTEXT \Rightarrow$
       $pattern' = (\langle\ \rangle,\ content\ (ED\ .text\ quoted)) \wedge$
       $mode' = MAINTEXT\ ;$
   $mode = MAINTEXT \Rightarrow$
       $pattern' = pattern \wedge$
       $mode' = mode$

$REPLACE =$
  $(\lambda\ EDSTATE)$
   $(\mu\ EDSTATE')$
   $main' = try\ (replace\ (pattern,\ repl'))\ main\ ;$
   $quoted' = quoted\ ;$
   $pattern' = pattern\ ;$
   $mode = QUOTEDTEXT \Rightarrow$
      $repl' = ED\ .textquoted \wedge$
      $mode' = MAINTEXT;$
   $mode = MAINTEXT \Rightarrow$
      $repl' = repl \wedge$
      $mode' = mode$

Keyboard Design

Once more we conclude our discussion by summarizing the commands which are to be made available, observing that these include all the commands of the basic editor, to which we have added the two *FIND* commands, the *replace* command and the *QUOTE* command:

$key: \mathbb{P}(EDSTATE \rightarrow EDSTATE)$

$key = ran\ BASIC \cup ran\ FIND \cup \{REPLACE, QUOTE\}$

In Figure 2 we suggest a layout for a keyboard with ten function keys. When shifted the function keys marked *char*, *word* and *line* should be mapped to deletion functions, otherwise they should be mapped onto motion functions. Those on the left-hand side of the keyboard should be mapped to leftward functions and those on the right to the rightward functions. The *find* key should be mapped to the rightward variant of *FIND* when unshifted and the leftward variant when shifted.

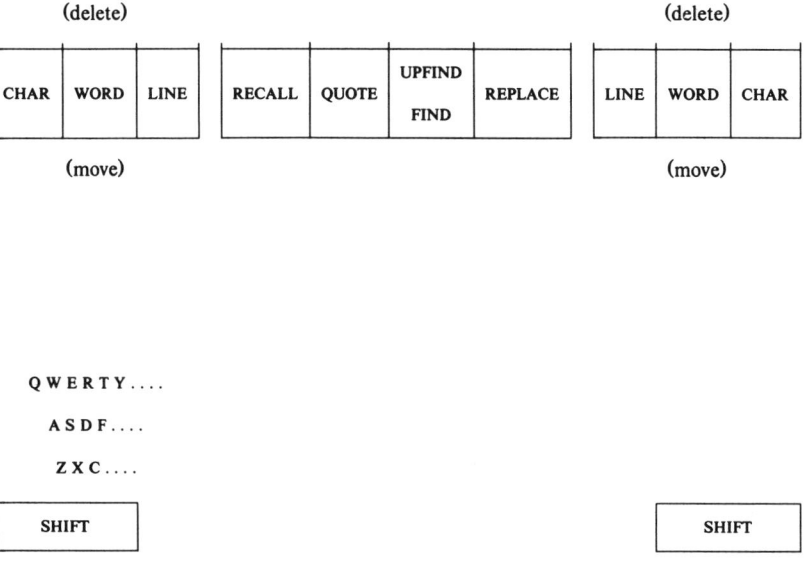

Figure 2. Suggested keyword design (partial); When shifted the function keys marked *CHAR*, *WORD* and *LINE* should map to deletions, otherwise they should map to motions

3. DISPLAYING DOCUMENTS

Editor commands were specified as transformations on the more-or-less one-dimensional *DOC* model. In order to specify the way in which documents are displayed we need a model which reflects the fact that most(!) real displays are two-dimensional and bounded. Indeed this boundedness forces us to have a policy for choosing which part of a document to display. In our view the best policy is to display the part of the document which immediately surrounds the current position and to indicate the current position by means of some distinctive symbol (such symbols are usually called *cursors*). This policy can be likened to looking at the document through a movable *window* which locates itself so as to keep the current position in view. When composing a document the typist always sees on the display an exact picture of the region of the document which has most recently changed, and can quickly discover any mistakes.

Unbounded displays

We begin to formalize the idea of a two-dimensional display by ignoring the fact that real ones are bounded. A *LINE* is a sequence of characters which doesn't contain the newline character.

$$LINE$$
$$seq[CH - \{nl\}]$$

An unbounded display and its current position can be completely characterized by four quantities—the sequence of *LINE*s above the current position, the sequence of *LINE*s below the current position, and the sequences of characters to the left and to the right of the current position, neither of which contain newline characters (for example see Figure 3).

Relating Unbounded Displays To Documents

We formalize the correspondence between an unbounded display and a document by developing a one-to-one relation—*displays*. First we define the function *flatten*—which maps a (nonempty) sequence of lines to a sequence of characters which has newline characters separating the text of the original lines.

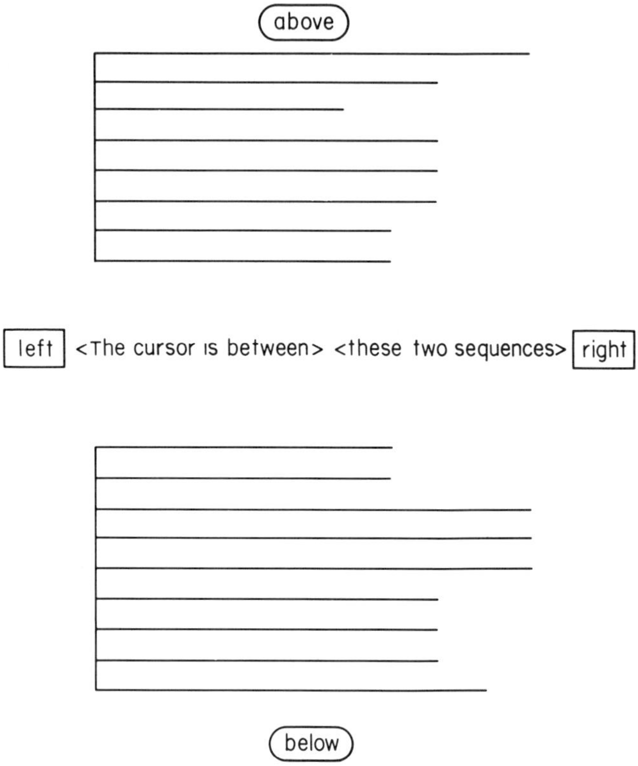

Figure 3.

$$\begin{array}{|l}\hline DISP \\ \quad above: \quad seq[LINE] \\ \quad left: \quad seq[CH - \{nl\}] \\ \quad right: \quad seq[CH - \{nl\}] \\ \quad below: \quad seq[LINE] \\ \hline\end{array}$$

$flatten: \; seql[LINE] \longrightarrow seq[CH]$

$(\forall \; ln: LINE \, ; \, s: seql[LINE\,])$
$\quad flatten(\langle ln \rangle) = ln \; \wedge$
$\quad flatten(\langle ln \rangle * s) = ln * \langle nl \rangle * flatten(s)$

FORMAL SPECIFICATION OF A TEXT EDITOR

Example

$$flatten(\langle\!\langle 1LINE \rangle\!\rangle) = \langle 1LINE \rangle$$
$$flatten(\langle\!\langle LINE1 \rangle\langle LINE2 \rangle\!\rangle) = \langle LINE1 \text{ nl } LINE2 \rangle$$

An unbounded display corresponds (through the *displays* relation) to a *DOC*ument under the following conditions.

1. Flattening the lines *above* and to the *left* of the display cursor gives the sequence of characters to the left of the document cursor, and

2. Flattening the lines to the *right* and *below* the display cursor gives the sequence of characters to the right of the document cursor.

(For example see Figure 4.)

```
< < line 1 >
  < line 2 >
  < line 3 >
  < left > < right >
< < line 5 >
  < line 6 > >
```

Displays

```
(< line 1nl line 2 nl line 3 nl left >,
 < right nl line 5 nl line 6 > )
```

Figure 4.

$displays : DISP \leftrightarrow DOC$

$(\forall disp : DISP; (l, r): DOC)$
 $(disp\ displays\ (l, r)) \Leftrightarrow$
  $l = flatten(above\ disp * \langle left\ disp \rangle) \wedge$
  $r = flatten(\langle right\ disp \rangle * below\ disp)$

It is easy to prove that flatten is a bijection, i.e. that it maps different (nonempty) sequences of lines into different sequences of characters and vice versa. An easily-proven consequence of this is that the *displays* relation is also a bijection, i.e. that every unbounded display corresponds to a unique *DOC*ument, and vice versa. This is hardly surprising; our initial one-dimensional formalization of documents would have been rather implausible but for our intuition that such a one-to-one correspondence existed.

FLATTEN LEMMA

$\vdash (\forall s_1, s_2: seql[\, LINE\,])$
$(flatten\ s_1 = flatten\ s_2 \Leftrightarrow s_1 = s_2)$

DISPLAY THEOREM

$\vdash (\forall d_1, d_2, d: DISP\,;\, doc_1, doc_2, doc: DOC)$
$((d_1\ displays\ doc) \wedge (d_2\ displays\ doc)) \Leftrightarrow d_1 = d_2\ \wedge$
$((d\ displays\ doc_1) \wedge (d\ displays\ doc_2)) \Leftrightarrow doc_1 = doc_2$

The formal proofs are omitted here since they are of no intrinsic interest, although the properties may prove useful when we come to design an implementation.

Screens

We now introduce a little more realism into our discussion of displays by formalizing the idea of a screen. A screen of a given height and width is characterized by its *appearance*—a function which maps every character position on the screen to the character which appears there, and its *cursor*—which must either be on the surface or at the left-hand edge of the screen. (On an ideal screen the cursor would appear just to the right of the character indexed by its column component. Unfortunately on many cheap screens the cursor appears *under* that character.)

height : $\mathbb{N}$
width : $\mathbb{N}$
screensurface : $\mathbb{P}(\mathbb{N} \times \mathbb{N})$
leftedge : $\mathbb{P}(\mathbb{N} \times \mathbb{N})$

screensurface $= 1\,..\,height \times 1\,..\,width$
leftedge $= 1\,..\,height \times \{0\}$

The two *SCREEN* components are linked here by an explicit invariant which in our notation appears beneath their signatures as a list of predicates.

SCREEN ─────────────────────────────

appearance: $(\mathbb{N} \times \mathbb{N}) \rightarrowtail CH$
cursor: $(\mathbb{N} \times \mathbb{N})$

───────

cursor $\in$ *screensurface* $\cup$ *leftedge*
dom *appearance* = *screensurface*

In order to formalize the idea of a screen acting as a window onto an unbounded display it is convenient to introduce three additional attributes of such a display, namely its content viewed as a sequence of lines, its *appearance* (idealized to the extent of being unbounded) and its *current* position.

---

lines: $DISP \rightarrow seq[\,LINE\,]$
appearance: $DISP \rightarrow (\mathbb{N} \times \mathbb{N}) \rightarrowtail CH$
current: $DISP \rightarrow (\mathbb{N} \times \mathbb{N})$

───────

lines = $(\lambda\ DISP)(above * \langle left * right \rangle * below)$
$r \in (1\,..\,\#(lines\ d))\ \wedge$
$c \in (1\,..\,\#(lines\ d\ r)) \Rightarrow$
  appearance $d(r, c)$ = *lines* $d\ r\ c$

current = $(\lambda\ DISP)(1 + \#\ above,\ \#\ left)$

The examination of two boundary conditions gives us some insight into the consistency of our formalizations of documents, displays, appearances and cursors.

The cursor can be to the left of any character in a line or to the right of its last character; there are therefore more cursor positions on a line than there are characters.

A completely empty document corresponds to a display which has a single (empty) line, an empty appearance function, and a cursor at (1, 0).

CURSOR LEMMAS

$\vdash (\forall d : DISP; r, c : \mathbb{N} | (r, c) = cursor\ d)$
$\quad r \in 1\ ..\ \#(lines\ d)\ \wedge$
$\quad c \in 0\ ..\ \#(lines\ d\ r)$

$\vdash (\forall doc : DOC; disp : DISP | content\ doc = \langle\rangle$
$\quad disp\ displays\ doc \Rightarrow$
$\quad\quad cursor\ disp = (1, 0)\ \wedge$
$\quad\quad dom\ (appearance\ disp) = \{\ \}\ \wedge$
$\quad\quad lines\ disp = \langle\!\langle\ \rangle\!\rangle$

Windows

The function *project* is the only additional tool we need to formalize the idea

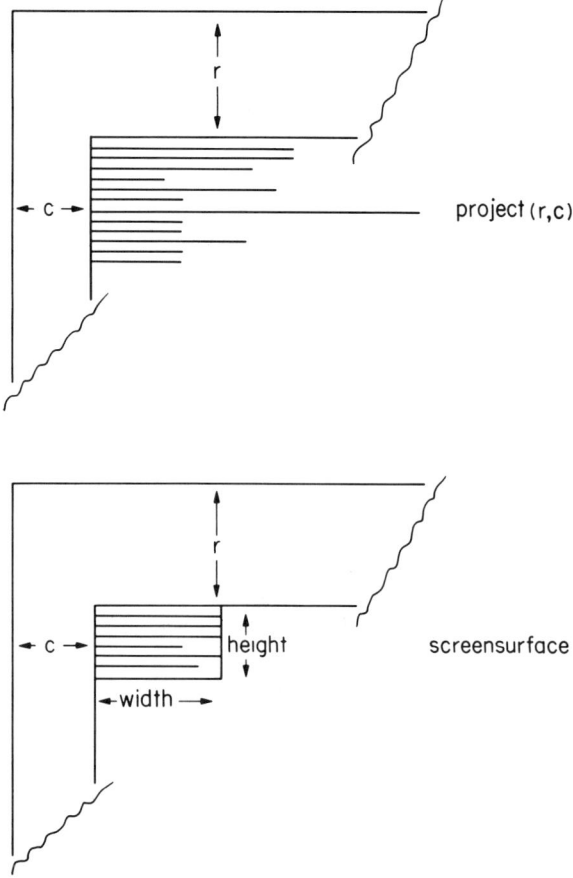

Figure 5.

of a window. Composition with a projection moves the "top left-hand corner" of an appearance function; restricting its domain by *screensurface* puts a rectangular boundary of the right size around it (see Figure 5).

$project: (\mathbb{N} \times \mathbb{N}) \rightarrow (\mathbb{N} \times \mathbb{N}) \rightarrow (\mathbb{N} \times \mathbb{N})$

$project\,(r, c)\,(i, j) = (r + i, c + j)$

The function *window* maps an origin into a function which (if possible) maps a display into a screen with the following attributes:

1. Its appearance is the same as that of the display seen from the origin and restricted by the area of the screen. It has spaces at the positions where no characters appear on the display.

2. Its cursor represents the current position of the display consistently, i.e. projecting it through the origin places the cursor position over the current position.

$window: (\mathbb{N} \times \mathbb{N}) \rightarrow DISP \rightarrowtail SCREEN$

$window\ origin\ d =$
$\quad (\mu\ SCREEN')$
$\qquad appearance' = (spaces \oplus projected) \upharpoonright screensurface;$
$\qquad current\ d = (projectorigin)cursor'$
where
$\qquad projected = (appearance\ d) \circ (project\ origin)$
$\qquad spaces = (\lambda\ i, j: \mathbb{N})(sp)$

Notice that the windowing functions are *partial*. For a given origin it is not always possible to project the current position into a cursor which falls on the surface of the screen. This is reflected formally by the fact that the equations defining the resulting screen are not always compatible with the *SCREEN* invariants.

For a given document, however, there are usually several origins which do permit the current position to be projected correctly (for example see Figure 6). These are given by the function *origins* defined by:

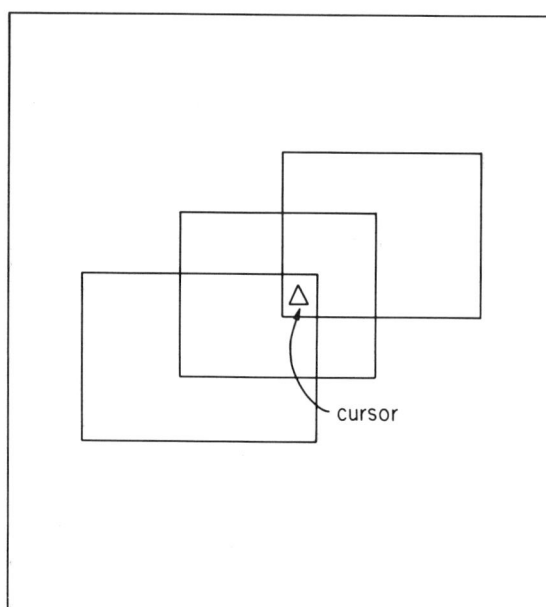

Figure 6.

origins : $DISP \rightarrow \mathbb{P}(\mathbb{N} \times \mathbb{N})$

origins $d = \{r, c \,|\, cursor\ d \in projectedscreen\}$
where *projectedscreen* =
  project (r, c)〖*screensurface* ∪ *leftside*〗

It is easy to show that the function *origins* really does give what is required, and that there is always at least one origin which permits a given display to be windowed. More formally:

ORIGIN LEMMAS

⊢ $(\forall d : DISP\,;\, pos : (\mathbb{N} \times \mathbb{N}) \,|\, pos \in origins\ d)$
  $d \in dom(window\ pos)$
⊢ $(\forall d : DISP\,;\, r, c : \mathbb{N} \,|\, (r, c) = cursor\ d)$
  $(r - 1, c) \in origins\ d$

In fact the only display where there is no choice in the matter (i.e. with *exactly* one origin) is the one which corresponds to the empty document, and

FORMAL SPECIFICATION OF A TEXT EDITOR

it is a good (if somewhat tedious) check on the consistency of this part of the specification to *prove* this.

4. DISPLAYING THE EDITED DOCUMENT

The Complete Editor State

In this section we formalize the hitherto informally stated requirement that the screen should be a window onto the (unbounded display corresponding to the) document being edited. We also suggest a method of displaying quoted text while it is being prepared, namely to embed it in the display of the main document—separating it from the document text by (implementation dependent) sequences which play the role of quotation marks. This reflects our view that it is important to see the main text while composing quoted text but otherwise make a concession to the fact that many cheap displays are too small or too slow to permit efficient maintenance of multiple windows.

A document editing module is mapped into an idealized display by the function *show*, which takes account of whether quoted text is being composed. The role of a display module will be to choose an appropriate window onto this idealized display.

---

quote : seq[*CH*]
unquote : seq[*CH*]
─────────
lastquote = *nl* ;
firstunquote = *nl*

---

show :   *EDSTATE* ⟶ *DISP*
─────────
show = (λ *EDSTATE*) (*ideal*)
where
  mode = *QUOTEDTEXT* ⇒
    ideal **displays** *document* ** *quotes* ** *quotation*
  mode = *MAINTEXT* ⇒
    ideal **displays** *document*
  document = *ED* . *text main*
  quotation = *ED* . *text quoted*
  quotes = (*quote*, *unquote*)

Notice that the quotes are specified in such a way that the quoted text will occupy at least one separate line on the screen.

The complete editor state has a component—*editor*—which models the state of the editing module, and components—*screen*, and *origin*—which model the state of the display module. The single invariant indicates the desired relationship between the two modules.

STATE
editor : *EDSTATE*
screen : *SCREEN*
origin : $(\mathbb{N} \times \mathbb{N})$

screen = *window origin* (*show editor*)

Specifying a Windowing Policy

The task of the editing module has already been specified (at least in the sense that we have given formalizations of the effects of every key as functions on its state). The task of the display module after each keystroke is to derive a *window origin* and *screen content* from the editing module in such a way as to maintain the given invariant. It is evident from the considerations of the previous section that in general there will be some freedom to choose the origin, and that a *policy* will therefore be necessary.

We suggest an *incremental* windowing policy which tries to keep the origin constant for as long as it can. When the current position can no longer be shown on the screen another origin is selected. The advantages of this policy relate both to human factors and to the potential efficiency of implementations:

1. When inserting material the typist does not get distracted by the task of finding the cursor after every keystroke, since it behaves "like pen on paper."

2. Most keystrokes result in relatively small changes to the screen, and these take place at or near the cursor. This facilitates implementation on slow and/or dumb terminals.

Below we formalize our requirements for such a policy function. Given the current origin, and a new unbounded display, the policy function must map them to an offset which permits the current position to be shown on the screen.

Notice that our specification *does not uniquely define the policy function*, it merely gives an overall requirement. At the design state we are not too much concerned with the exact details of the policy; *any* function satisfying the outlined requirements will suffice. This freedom is intended to allow a proof of correctness of a particular display strategy to be made independently of the details of the windowing policy.

$policy: (\mathbb{N} \times \mathbb{N}) \rightarrow (DISP \rightarrow (\mathbb{N} \times \mathbb{N}))$

$(\forall d': DISP; org, org': (\mathbb{N} \times \mathbb{N}) | org' = policy\ org\ d')$
$\quad org \in origins\ d' \Rightarrow org' = org\ \wedge$
$\quad org \notin origins\ d' \Rightarrow org' \in origins\ d'$

We can now summarize the effect of a single keystroke on the state of the display editor.

$effect: key \rightarrow (STATE \rightarrow STATE)$

$effect\ k =$
$\quad (\lambda\ STATE)$
$\quad\quad (\mu\ STATE')$
$\quad\quad\quad editor' = k\ editor$
$\quad\quad\quad origin' = policy\ origin\ idealdisp'$
$\quad\quad\quad screen' = window\ origin'\ idealdisp$
$\quad\quad\textbf{where}\ idealdisp' = showeditor'$

The definition of *effect* concludes our specification. Proof that this function maintains the editor state invariant is extremely simple—once again we leave it as an exercise for the reader.

5. SUMMARY

The specification herein is a revised version of the one from which our first implementation was built [Sufrin 1980]. In that specification we adopted a more orthodox denotational approach, modeled the document as a sequence of lines with a cursor position, and gave completely constructive definitions of all the editor operations. The choice of document model meant that we needed to deal with an enormous number of special cases when specifying operations, the key problem being the description of the wrapping around of operations at the end of lines. Our treatment of windowing was also more complex.

The simplified model of document and cursor position which we use here makes reasoning about properties of the editor commands considerably simpler since there are almost no special cases to consider; even the treatment of directionality is easy. Nevertheless the characterization of movements to word and line boundaries has too much of an algorithmic flavor to it, and the abstraction seems to be stretched to (beyond?) its limit in our treatment of cut-and-paste and automatic indentation [Appendix 2], where one can almost hear the clanking of the machinery!

The unbounded display model plays an important role in the specification insofar as it permits a simple bridge to be built between documents and screens. In a note to be published later we exploit the fact that this model is a natural basis for a formalization of the properties of smart terminals to prove the correctness of an implementation strategy suitable for use with such terminals.

The strategy involves the editing module giving hints to the display module whenever the screen needs to be changed. Such hints indicate, where possible, the *incremental* change to the screen which are necessary to maintain the required relationship between the screen and the document. When the incremental policy breaks down (for example after a *FIND* command moves the cursor off the screen) the hint indicates this, and the display module regenerates the screen completely. The strategy gives good performance even for dumb terminals—the only time when one consciously waits for the screen to reflect a change in the underlying document is when the display module is forced to *tilt* (move the window vertically) more than the height of the screen, or to *pan* (move the window horizontally).

Further Work

The key techniques employed in this paper seem to us to be the abstraction of positional information by using collections of sequences, the use of higher-order functions to model the directionality of operations, and the use of invariants to characterize the required relationships between the states of our abstract modules.

In order to adapt these techniques to the description of more ambitious document-preparation systems we need to remedy some of the above-mentioned deficiencies of the simple document model. One promising approach to this is as follows: the document can be observed *simultaneously* as (pairs of) sequences of characters, of words, of lines, and of paragraphs; these sequences would be *related by appropriate invariants*. The word-related operations (for example) can be defined as $\lambda-\mu$ functions in which we state explicitly only how the word-related aspects of the document change and use the power of the μ quantifier to avoid specifying *explicitly* how the remaining aspects change.

An obvious extension to this approach would be in the treatment of structure-oriented editors, in which the "document" is now a tree, the operations are tree-oriented, and the *displays* relation would correspond to the informal notion that what should be seen is a "pretty-printed" representation of the tree.

6. CONCLUSION

As we stated in our introduction, our goal was to give a mathematical model serving to communicate our ideas about editor design, to permit exploration of the consequences of our design and to provide an unambiguous definition against which the correctness of implementation strategies might be proven.

In other engineering disciplines this sort of thing is a matter of course. Bridge-builders, architects and airplane designers all expect to have to reason more or less formally about their artifacts before building them. They also have well-understood techniques by which to express their final designs unambiguously, and the craftspeople who transform these expressions into reality do so by means which are sound enough to ensure a faithful realization.

Computer scientist have also developed the intellectual tools necessary to permit the description and faithful construction of large classes of program in just as sound a fashion [Jones 1980]. There remain, however, important barriers to acceptance by a majority of practicing programmers of the desirability of reasoning about the design of their programs in advance of their construction, although the utility of doing so has been eloquently expounded by several authors over several years. We hope that this case study is a contribution to breaking down these barriers.

ACKNOWLEDGMENTS

I am deeply indebted to Jean-Raymond Abrial for introducing me to the art of specification, and reawakening my mathematical interest after it had been dormant for many years. Thanks also to Tony Hoare and Ib Sorenson for many fruitful discussions, to John Hughes for discovering a serious flaw in an earlier formalization, and to Geraint Jones and Tim Clement for critically reading parts of the manuscript. It was the challenge of trying to formalize Richard Bornat's lovely but complicated screen-editor—DED—which began this enterprise.

The work is part of a program of research into Software Engineering Methods supported by the United Kingdom Science and Engineering Research Council under grant GRA/A/43124.

APPENDIX 1

Informal Description of the Editor

The description which follows is extracted from a slightly revised version of the documentation of an implementation of the editor which has been in use since late 1979. So that our readers may judge for themselves the extent to which the formalization can capture the behavior of the implementation we have included the descriptions of some of the "custom" features of the implementation, i.e. those not described in the formal specification.

The editor permits the composition, alteration and examination of documents. The typist communicates with the editor through a keyboard which is equipped with a number of special function-keys; the document is shown on a screen on which the typist's current position is highlighted by means of a *cursor*. Once the document becomes too large to be seen on the screen, the editor ensures that the region surrounding the typist's current position is shown on the screen, for it is at or very close to the current position that all the typist's actions have their effect.

Single-Character Insertion, Deletion and Motion

visible-character	The character is inserted in the document at the cursor; the cursor moves to the right; the remainder of the current line is pushed right to make room.
NEWLINE	Inserts a new line in the document at the cursor; any text to the right of the cursor becomes part of the new line.
	In *auto-indent mode (qv)*, spaces are inserted so that the cursor (and any text to its right) appear underneath the first nonblank character of the previous line.
LEFT-DELETE	Rubs out the character to the left of the cursor. When the cursor is at the left-hand end of a line this joins the current line to the previous one.
RIGHT-DELETE	Rubs out the character at the cursor. When the cursor is at the right-hand end of a line this joins the line to the next one.
LEFT-MOVE	Moves the cursor leftwards one character position in the document. If the cursor was at the left-hand end of a line, then it will "wrap around" to the right-hand end of the previous line.
RIGHT-MOVE	Moves the cursor rightwards one character position in the document. If the cursor was at the right-hand end of a line, then it will "wrap around" to the left-hand end of the next line.

Multiple-Character Insertion, Deletion and Motion

A *WORD* begins where a space is followed by a character which is not a space.

LEFT-MOVE(WORD)	Moves the cursor to the beginning of the previous *WORD*, or the start of the current line if that is nearer.
RIGHT-MOVE(WORD)	Moves the cursor to the beginning of the next *WORD*, or the end of the current line if that is nearer.
LEFT-MOVE(LINE)	Moves the cursor to the beginning of the line, or the beginning of the previous line if it is already at the beginning of a line.
RIGHT-MOVE(LINE)	Moves the cursor to the end of the line, or the end of the next line if it is already at the end of a line.
LEFT-DELETE(WORD)	Deletes text between the cursor and the place to which *LEFT-MOVE(WORD)* would move.
RIGHT-DELETE(WORD)	Deletes text between the cursor and the place to which *RIGHT-MOVE(WORD)* would move.
LEFT-DELETE(LINE)	Deletes text between the cursor and the place to which *LEFT-MOVE(LINE)* would move.
RIGHT-DELETE(LINE)	Deletes text between the cursor and the place to which *RIGHT-MOVE(LINE)* would move.
TAB	Inserts enough spaces in the line to put the cursor at the next tab position—these are at eight column intervals.

Miscellaneous Useful Commands

MARK	Place the *mark* at the cursor.
CUT	Cut the text between the cursor and the mark out of the document.
PASTE	Insert the most-recently *CUT* text into the document at the cursor.

RECALL	Inserts the text deleted by the last word-delete, line-delete, or *REPLACE* back into the document.
MARGIN	Sets the right margin at the current column. When the right margin is set at a column other than the leftmost column, then whenever a character is typed to the right of the margin, the "word" of which it is a part will automatically be moved to the beginning of the next line.
NEXTPAGE	Display the next screenful of the document.
PREVPAGE	Display the previous screenful of the document.

Moving to Specified Places in the Document

QUOTE	After pressing this key any of the keys so far described may be used to compose a *quotation*—so called because the keys typed during its composition do not have an immediate effect on the document. When the quotation is completed, by typing one of the keys *FIND, UPFIND, REPLACE, QUOTE*, it has an effect which depends on the key typed. The quoted text is displayed between distinctive marks on the screen as if it had been typed as part of the document, but when completed is removed from the screen.

If the quotation is completed by typing the *FIND* key, then the cursor is placed at the start of the next place in the document which matches it; the *UPFIND* key moves the cursor to the previous place which matches it. If there is no such place in the document then the cursor stays in the same place, and the bell rings. The quoted text is retained so there is no need to retype it in order to find the same text more than once.

If the quotation is completed by typing the *REPLACE* key, and the current *FIND* text matches the document at the cursor then it will be replaced by the quoted text. The quoted text will be retained so that there is no need to retype it in order to *REPLACE* with the same text more than once.

If the quotation is completed by typing the *QUOTE* key, then the line is interpreted as a *special command*, and performed immediately.

Special commands are:

t(op	Move the cursor to the top of the document.
b(ottom	Move the cursor to the end of the document.
q(uit	Leave the editor, putting the altered document back in the file from which it was originally taken.
w(rite	Copy the document to the file but do not leave the editor (it's a good idea to do this from time to time, in case the power supply to your computer fails).
i*NAME*	Add the document stored in the file called *NAME* to the current document below the current line.
o*NAME*	Make a new document from lines between the marked line and the current line and store it in the file called *NAME*.
mk	Exchange the positions of the mark and the cursor.
i(ndent	Set auto-indent mode.
n(oindent	Clear auto-ident mode.
abort	Leave the editor, abandoning any work done in the document since it was last stored in a file.
wd(find	Changes to *word match* mode (*qv*).
lif(find	Changes to *literal match* mode (*qv*).
FIND	Finds the last *FIND* text (downwards).
UPFIND	Finds the last *FIND* text (upwards).
REPLACE	If the text at the cursor matches the last *FIND* text, then it is replaced by the last *REPLACE* text.

Matching Criteria

In *literal match* mode, a *FIND* succeeds where the text at the cursor exactly matches the characters of the *FIND* text. In *word match* mode and when the *FIND* text consists entirely of letters or digits, a *FIND* succeeds only where the text at the cursor matches the *FIND* text and the characters immediately preceding and following the match are neither letters or digits.

APPENDIX 2
Some Additional Features

[*Appendix deleted*]

APPENDIX 3
Summary of Notation

[*Appendix deleted*]

PRABHAKER MATETI*
University of Melbourne

A Specification Schema for Indenting Programs

1. PREFACE

The present paper is one of a triplet on an indenting program for Pascal. We undertook this exercise with three objectives in mind:

1. The literature sadly lacks real-life programs whose correctness is established by proof rather than by testing. On the other hand, those who have practiced proving correctness have been raising the hopes of the readers to such an extent that a single mistake in a published proof gets the widest adverse publicity. We hope that our indenting program and its specifications and proof will serve as examples in this regard.

2. The practicing programmer, we find, often uses the lowest level of formalism whereas a student who has just been through correctness methods employs formidable notation and an excess of formalism. The right level for a given program escapes both. It is not easy to say what is a right level. This can only be communicated through examples.

3. There is a myth that giving precise specifications for "real-life" programs is often not possible. We are quite willing to accept this as a definition of "real-life" programs but not as a corollary. Another myth is to equate precision with formalism. We hope that these papers will serve as examples where sufficient precision is attained with very little formalism.

Only the reader can tell how far we succeed in fulfilling our objectives.

2. INTRODUCTION

That written material expected to be read by humans should be laid out with thought and care is widely appreciated. Yet the layout of many computer programs is poor. To make matters worse, programs written in modern programming languages have many nested levels of control structures and

---

* Present affiliation: Case Western Reserve University.

declarations. While compilers for these languages accept "free-format" input and can distinguish the nesting regardless of how the text input is laid out, most humans are yet to adapt themselves in this fashion.

Laying out the text of a program so that its structure is readily apparent has come to be called "pretty-printing". Many sets of rules for pretty-printing exist (e.g. [Grogono 1979], [Ledgard, Singer and Hueras 1977], [Sale 1978]). These rules range from such typewriting conventions as always following a comma by a blank and flanking an equality sign by blanks to insisting that reserved words such as *goto* appear only at the beginning of a line and never hidden somewhere in the middle of a line. Much of the work in the layout of a program text is routine once a set of systematic pretty-printing rules is chosen. In fact, several programs that pretty-print the given input exist.

In this paper, we limit ourselves to programs written for Pascal, and use the less pretentious word "indenting" in preference to "pretty-printing". We develop the basic mathematical functions required to specify precisely the input-to-output transformation performed by a class of indenting programs. The companion paper [Mateti and Jaffar 1983] proves the correctness of an indenting program meeting the specifications developed here, and [Mateti 1980] discusses global issues about the program.

The indentation scheme embodied in our specifications below has evolved over a period of years accommodating and adapting the many schemes proposed in the literature. The author finds it satisfactory but is aware of others who do not. The goal of this paper is not to promote this scheme but to show that specification for such programs can be developed with sufficient precision employing simple mathematical notions. Section 3 discusses our expectations of indenting programs. Section 4 establishes notation. Section 5 gives the input-to-output transformation performed by these programs using the syntax definition of Pascal. Section 6 specifies the transformation independently of this syntax definition. Section 7 shows that if the input file contains a legal construct of Pascal then the specifications of Sections 5 and 6 are equivalent.

3. WHAT SHOULD INDENTING PROGRAMS DO?

The specifications of a program are simply our requirements and expectations of it but stated precisely without ambiguity. We ignore certain specifications of a program such as that its length be so much, or that it be written in language X without *goto*s. Instead we will concentrate only on the relationship between the input and output of indenting programs. Such specifications are called functional specifications [Liskov and Berzins 1979].

We list some of our expectations of indenting programs below.

1. The most obvious and yet oft-forgotten requirement is that the output of an indenting program should be "lexically equivalent" to the text input given. Should indenting programs accept only syntactically correct text? No. We believe that indenting programs must accept any text input; if the input happens to be a syntactically correct program, we

then expect its output to be properly indented. And if the input is not syntactically correct, the output text should be indented as reasonably as possible. A notion of reasonableness underlies our low level specifications. The main reasons for insisting that indenting programs also accept "incorrect" text are:

(a) Syntactic checking unnecessarily overburdens indenting programs.

(b) Properly indented text helps us quickly identify syntax errors.

(c) There are many variations of the Pascal language in existence.

In fact, only minor modifications should be sufficient to produce an indenting program for other Pascal-like languages.

2. The output from an indenting program should appear "properly indented". This notion is made precise in later sections. (The particular indentation scheme that we suggest may not appear "pretty" to some, but we remind that our interest in the scheme here is only as a concrete running example.) Proper indentation involves essentially three independent activities:

(a) Each line should be started at the appropriate left margin.

(b) Certain constructs of the language should not be hidden in the middle of a line. For instance, it appears important that reserved words such as *while, repeat, procedure* always appear at the beginning of a line and are never embedded in a line. Reading many Pascal programs convinced us that no line of a listing should contain more than one statement. Multiple assignments on one input line should be split up.

(c) Adjusting the inter-word blank spacing so that it is visually appealing. Subjective preferences and special circumstances abound in this matter, and we specify here that this spacing be left unaltered except for splitting.

We believe that each input line should generate an integral number of output lines. Combining two or more input lines and then splitting them up is often unsatisfactory and leads to complicated "control language" to specify (in the program being indented) how the lines are to be split.

3. We also believe that indenting programs which produce output always different from their inputs are undesirable. More specifically, if we feed the indented text back to the indenting program as input, the output must be identical to the input. This characteristic of indenting programs is important from a psychological point of view.

It should be borne in mind that no matter how well we specify the input to output transformation whether an alleged indenting program should indeed be called an indenting program, and for what language, has to be judged by subjective considerations. For instance, our definition of lexical analysis is sure to startle some.

```
function nexttoken : token;
    var
        i, j, d : cx;
        t : token;
    procedure dlmtoken;
        begin
        end;
    procedure stdtoken;
        var
            ctemp : packed array [1..tknlMAX] of char;
            k : cx;
        begin
        end;
    procedure gettoken;
        (* Changes the following global vars :
        .   nextcx    of main prog
        .   tox of main prog
        .   j,t    of nexttoken
        *)
        var
            i : cx;
            d : (1..2);
        begin
        i := nextcx;
        while c[i] in WHITECHARS do i := i + 1;
        j := i;
        while not (c[j] in DELIMITERS) do j := j + 1;
        if i = j then begin
            dlmtoken;
            j := j + d
            end
        else
            stdtoken;
        end (* gettoken *);
begin
tox := nextcx - 1;
while nextcx > lastcx do
        begin
        ...
        end;
    ...
    gettoken;
    ...
    nexttoken := t;
    end;
```

Figure 1. An example of an indented function

Figure 1 gives an example function indented according to our specifications. There are many inputs which produce the indented output. For the sake of concreteness, assume that the input was the text of Figure 1 as shown, but with all leading white space in each line deleted. The reader is encouraged to compute the various functions and predicates that we define below on this input.

4. NOTATION

We denote by \b, \t, \n, \e the characters blank, tab, end-of-line and end-of-file marker, respectively. The first three of these characters are referred to as white characters; we denote by % any one of these. For simplicity in this paper, we replace each tab by a fixed number, say 8, of blanks and assume from now on that tabs do not occur. By *white space* we mean any (possibly mixed) string of white characters. A *line* is a string, not containing end-of-lines or end-of-file markers, followed by the end-of-line character. A *file* is a sequence of lines followed by the pseudo-line containing exactly the single character \e.

We deal with several kinds of sequences. We adopt the convention that any single object is also a sequence of length one consisting of that object. The concatenations of strings, segment sequences and token sequences are denoted by |, ! and o respectively. Note that sequences of lines, or of segments, are also strings. We use regular expression notation when requiring sequences of a certain pattern. Thus, $x**k$ stands for the sequence x repeated k times, and $x*$ stands for $x**k$, for some $k \geq 0$. Unless explicitly stated otherwise, by string we mean a string of characters free of \e. We show strings enclosed in double quotes. A string x is a prefix of z if $z = x|y$ for some y; x is a suffix of z if $z = y|x$, for some y. The words prefix and suffix have analogous meaning when referring to other kinds of sequences. Empty string, token sequence and segment sequences are denoted respectively by "", 0o and 0ss.

The specifications require many predicates and mathematical functions. We use names with upper-case letters in them for these. In the definitions read "::=" as "is defined as".

5. HIGH-LEVEL SPECIFICATIONS

In this section we specify the layout of programs using the Extended BNF grammar [Wirth 1978] of Pascal. As the lexical structure of Pascal is left undefined there we expect the reader to use his own intuitive understanding of how a string is mapped to a token sequence, for the time being. We also ignore, until the next section, the presence of comments, as does the above syntax definition. We also make minor changes to the grammar. For instance, all occurrences of terminal strings are replaced by non-terminals whose names are composed of the letters *nt* followed by the name of the token (in upper case). Thus the nonterminal *nt*REPEAT produces w | *"repeat"*, where w stands for a (possibly empty) white space.

Given a string s with no white space suffix, $s = s_1 | s_2 |...| s_k$, and the corresponding production rule $n = n_1 n_2 ... n_k$, such that $n \longrightarrow^* s$, $n_j \longrightarrow^* s_j$, we assume that the s_j do not have white space suffix. However, the s_j may have a prefix white space. This is significant as the white space prefix of each line is, so to speak, all that matters.

We say that a given string s corresponding to a non-terminal n is "properly laid out" starting at margin m if PLOT$(n, s, m) = true$. The definition of PLOT is given compactly in a syntax-directed way in Figure 2. Each production acts as a template for a conjunction of NEWL and PLOT predicates, which are defined below; substituting actual strings for the non-terminals gives a logical conjunction which can then be evaluated. Each line in the diagram contains one terminal (which we show by the appropriate token) or one non-terminal (and possibly a metabracket) whose indentation from the reference vertical gives the "ruling margin" increment for it. The presence of a NEWL predicate is indicated by a \n character to the left of the reference vertical.

To conserve space, we have omitted from Figure 2 all productions whose specifications are of the form

```
n    =            e.g., block =
| n₁    *                | | [label declaration part]
| n₂    *                | | [constant definition part]
|       *                | | [type definition part]
| ...   *                | | [var declaration part]
|       *                | | procedure and function declaration part
| ...   *                | | compound statement
| nₖ    *
        *
```

where all the n_j are right next to the references vertical and have no \n character appearing to its left.

```
program =
  |program heading
  |    block

program heading =
\n|ntPROGRAM
  |    identifier
  |    ntLPAREN
  |        ident list
  |    ntRPAREN
  |    ntSEMICOLON

label declaration part =
\n|ntLABEL
  |    label
  |    {ntCOMMA
  |    label}
  |    ntSEMICOLON

const definition part =
\n|ntCONST
  |    constant definition
  |    ntSEMICOLON
\n|    {constant definition
  |    ntSEMICOLON}

type definition part =
\n|ntTYPE
  |    type definition
  |    ntSEMICOLON
\n|    {type definition
  |    lntSEMICOLON}

var declaration part =
\n|ntVAR
  |    var declaration
  |    ntSEMICOLON
\n|    {var declaration
  |    ntSEMICOLON}

var declaration =
  |identifier
  |{ntCOMMA
  |identifier}
  |ntCOLON
  |    type

procedure declaration =
  |procedure heading
  |    block

procedure heading =
\n|nt PROCEDURE
  |    identifier
  |    [formal parameter list]
  |    ntSEMICOLON

function declaration =
  |function heading
  |    block

function heading =
\n|ntFUNCTION
  |    identifier
  |    [formal parameter list]
  |    ntCOLON
  |        type identifier
  |    ntSEMICOLON

formal parameter list =
  |ntLPAREN
  |    formal parameter section
  |    {ntSEMICOLON
\n|    formal parameter section}
  |PAREN

formal parameter section =
  |[ntVAR |
  |ntFUNCTION ]
  |ident list
  |ntCOLON
  |type identifier |
  |ntPROCEDURE
  |ident list

actual parameter list =
  |ntLPAREN
  |    expression
  |    {ntCOMMA
  |    expression}
  |ntRPAREN

factor =
  |ntLPAREN
  |    expression
  |ntRPAREN

compound statement =
  |ntBEGIN
  |statement
  |{ntSEMICOLON
\n|statement}
  |ntEND
```

```
statement =                      with statement =
  |(label                        \n|ntWITH
  |ntCOLON                         |variable
  |    unlabelled statement |      |{ntCOMMA
  |unlabelled statement )          |variable}
                                   |ntDO
                                   |    statement
if statement =
\n|ntIF                          goto statement =
  |expression                    \n|ntGOTO
  |ntTHEN                          |label
  |    statement
\n|[ntELSE                       scalar type =
  |    statement]                  |ntLPAREN
                                   |    ident list
case statement =                   |ntRPAREN
\n|ntCASE
  |expression                    record type =
  |ntOF                            |ntRECORD
  |    case                        |    field list
  |    {ntSEMICOLON                |ntEND
\n|    case}
  |ntEND                         record section =
                                   |[ident list
case =                             |ntCOLON
  |[case label list                |    type]
  |ntCOLON
  |    statement]                variant part =
                                 \n|ntCASE
while statement =                  |    (identifier
\n|ntWHILE                         |    ntCOLON
  |expression                      |       type identifier
  |ntDO                            |       ntOF |
  |    statement                   |    type identifier
                                   |    ntOF )
repeat statement =                 |    variant
\n|ntREPEAT                        |    {ntSEMICOLON
  |    statement                 \n|    variant}
  |    {ntSEMICOLON
\n|    statement }               variant =
\n|ntUNTIL                         |case label list
  |expression                      |ntCOLON
                                   |    ntLPAREN
for statement =                    |       field list
\n|ntFOR                           |    ntRPAREN
  |identifier
  |ntASSIGN
  |for list
  |ntDO
  |    statement
```

Figure 2. High level specifications of our indenting scheme

5.1 The predicate properly laid out

For example, we say that a string named *rptst* produced by the non-terminal repeat statement is properly laid out at m if (1) the reserved word *repeat* is the first word on that line starting at a margin of m, (2) the statements of the loop body obey the rules of Figure 2 recursively, (3) the reserved word *until* is the first word on that line starting at margin m and (4) the expression after *until* obeys the rules recursively. More formally, if the instance *rptst* we are considering had two statements, say $st1$ and $st2$, in its body and exp as its expression, and $w1$, $w2$ are white spaces, i.e.

$$rpts = w1 \mid \text{"repeat"} \mid st1 \mid \text{";"} \mid st2 \mid w2 \mid \text{"until"} \mid exp$$

then the logical conjunction given by the diagram is:

PLOT(*repeat statement, rptst, m*) =
    PLOT(*nt*REPEAT, $w1 \mid$ "repeat", m) & NEWL($w1 \mid$ "repeat")
  & PLOT(*statement, st1, m*+UOI)
  & PLOT(*ny*SEMICOLON, ";", m+UOI)
  & PLOT(*statement, st2, m*+UOI) & NEWL($st2$)
  & PLOT(*nt*UNTIL, $w2 \mid$ "until", m) & NEWL($w2 \mid$ "until")
  & PLOT(*expression, exp, m*+UOI)

where UOI stands for the unit of indentation. We now define PLOT and NEWL more precisely.

Definition of PLOT

PLOT is a predicate on triplets consisting of a non-terminal, a string and a margin width.

1. PLOT($n, s \mid c, m$) ::= PLOT(n, s, m), where c is either % or \e. Thus we assume below that s has no trailing white space.

2. PLOT(n, s, m) ::= **false**, if n does not produce s. Thus we further assume below that $n \longrightarrow * s$.

3. PLOT(*empty*, "", m) ::= **true**, for all m.

4. PLOT(t, s, m) ::= ISAT(s, m), where t is a (non-terminal) token.

5. Let $n = n_1 n_2 ... n_k$ be a syntax rule of the language. Let $s, s_1, s_2, ..., s_k$ be corresponding strings generated from the non-terminals n and the n_i. Then

    PLOT(n, s, m) ::=
        PLOT(n_1, s_1, m)
    & PLOT(n_2, m+RMI (n_1, n_2))
    & ...
    & PLOT(n_k, s_k, m+RMI ($n_1 n_2 ... n_{k-1}, n_k$))

& NEWL(s_{i1}) & NEWL(s_{i2}) & ... & NEWL(s_{ip})

where RMI$(n_1 \ldots n_{j-1}, n_j)$ is the ruling margin increment for the n_j as shown in Figure 2 for that production rule and only the nonterminals $n_{i1}, n_{i2} \ldots n_{ip}$ has the \n to the left of the reference vertical.

Thus, the above PLOT(*repeat statement, rpsts, m*) would be *true* for $m = 0$, for example, if *st*1 and *st*2 were empty strings, *w*1 and *w*2 were equal to \n and *exp* did not contain \n.

Definition of ISAT

ISAT*(s, m)* ::= **true** if either $s =$ % * | \n | \b ** m | c | y, for some string y and non-white character c, or s does not contain \n.
 If s does have a \n, then ISAT*(s, m)* will be true if the left-most non-white character of s is exactly m blanks away from the preceding \n.

Definition of NEWL

NEWL*(s)* ::= **true** iff s = % * | \n | x, for some string x.

That is, NEWL*(s)* is true iff s has a \n preceding which there are no non-white characters.

5.2 The indented file

We say that a string s is lexically equivalent to t if both produce the same sequence of tokens. More formally, s and t are lexically equivalent if by replacing the inter-token white space by a single blank, and by deleting any white space prefix/suffix, if any, the resulting strings $s1$ and $t1$ become equal. (See also the next section.)

Given for file FI (the input) an indenting program should produce file FU such that

1. for each i, $1 \leqslant i \leqslant$ number of lines in FI, there exists a u, $1 \leqslant u \leqslant$ number of lines in FU, such that FI[1 .. i] and FU[1 .. u] are lexically equivalent where F[1 .. n] stands for the first n lines of file F,

2. PLOT$(nt, \n|FU, 0) =$ **true**, and

3. no file with fewer lines than are in FU satisfies the above, whenever FI is a sentence corresponding to a non-terminal nt of Pascal grammar.

This is the specification of indenting programs that appeals to us. Part (3) guarantees that input lines are not split up unnecessarily. In part (2), a \n is prefixed to FU so as to treat the end of line character as a "new line" character. Without this \n, a NEWL predicate might be false even though the first token of the very first line is at the correct margin. Note that the behaviour of the indenting program is unspecified when FI does not contain a legal construct of Pascal. Note also that part (1) of the specification implies that FU will have at least as many lines as in FI. It also rules out recombination of input lines and then splitting them up into output lines.

6. LOW-LEVEL SPECIFICATIONS

We now develop a set of specifications that appear independent of Pascal grammar. Whereas the previous section left undefined the behaviour of indenting programs when invalid constructs of Pascal are given as input, this section specifies what transformation is to be done for an arbitrary input string, and hence an arbitrary sequence of tokens. This latter transformation is designed to coincide with that given above for all syntactically valid constructs of Pascal. An outline of a proof of this fact is given in the next section.

6.1 Lexical analysis

Lexical analysis is a process that breaks up strings into sequences of "words", more widely known as tokens. We say a character string w is a *word* if TKN(w) is not undefined, where TKN is a partial function that maps character strings to tokens as elaborated below.

Definition of TKN

For a given string w, TKN(w) is defined as t if there is a pair $<w, t>$ in one of the following sets; otherwise TKN(w) is undefined.

1. Let w be free of delimiters, namely the following characters: blank, tab, end-of-line, end-of-file, parentheses, braces, semicolon, colon, asterisk, quote and period. (Other conventional delimiters do not concern us.)

{   <*"procedure"*,   PROCEDURE>,
        <*"function"*,   FUNCTION>,
        <*"program"*,   PROGRAM>,
        <*"forward"*,   FORWARD>
        <*"repeat"*,   REPEAT>,
        <*"record"*,   RECORD>,
        <*"extern"*,   EXTERN>,
        <*"while"*,   WHILE>,
        <*"until"*,   UNTIL>,
        <*"label"*,   LABEL>,
        <*"const"*,   CONST>,
        <*"begin"*,   BEGIN>,
        <*"with"*,   WITH>,
        <*"type"*,   TYPE>,
        <*"then"*,   THEN>,
        <*"goto"*,   GOTO>,
        <*"else"*,   ELSE>,
        <*"case"*,   CASE>,

           <"var"   , VAR>,
           <"for"   , FOR>,
           <"end"   , END>,
           <"of"   , OF>,
           <"if"   , IF>,
           <"do"   , DO>,
           <other w   , ORDINARY> }

2. Let w contain delimiters.

    {   <";"   , SEMICOLON>,
         <"'"   , QUOTE>,
         <":"   , COLON>,
         <"("   , LPAREN>,
         <")"   , RPAREN>,
         <"{"   , COMBGN>,
         <"}"   , COMEND>,
         <"*"   , ORDINARY>,
         <"."   , ORDINARY>,
         <\e   , ENDFILE>,
         <"(*"   , COMBGN>,
         <"*)"   , COMEND>,
         <"::="   , ASSIGN>}

Note the obvious fact that any string consisting of exactly one non-white character is a token.

The essence of lexical analysis is captured in LEX which produces the token sequence of z in the context of a token sequence T already produced. Recall that 00 denotes the empty token sequence, and o denotes concatenation of token sequences.

Definition of LEX

1. LEX(T, " ") ::= 00.

2. LEX(T, % | y) ::= LEX(T, y).

3. Let z be free of leading white space. The

$$\text{LEX}(T, z) ::= t \circ \text{LEX}(T \circ t, x),$$

where $z = w \mid x$, and w is the longest prefix of z such that TKN(w) is defined. The token t is TKN(w) unless

  (a) TKN(w) $\neq$ COMEND and T = S o COMBGN o ORDINARY*, or

(b) TKN(w) ≠ QUOTE and T = S ∘ QUOTE ∘ ORDINARY*,

for some S free of unmatched QUOTES. In the latter cases, t = ORDINARY.

Definition of TKNSEQ

TKNSEQ(z) ::= LEX(00, z).

Since syntactically correct Pascal programs have one of the delimiters immediately following reserved words, we do not risk non-recognition of such words by ignoring other conventional delimiters (such as operators). Lexical analysis performed by a typical Pascal compiler otherwise matches with LEX except when dealing with comments and strings. In compilers, comments are simply swallowed and the strings are returned as tokens. For our purpose here, however, the layout of comments is important. It would seem logical then to split a comment into three tokens, namely, COMBGN, the comment contained, followed by COMEND. Since comments can span several lines, this decision would complicate the definitions of functions given in subsequent sections. Thus, we define LEX(T, z) based on the longest prefix of z that is a word, and change the token to ORDINARY if T has an unmatched COMBGN or QUOTE.

For example, the string "(*(*)" is broken into words as "(*" | "(*" | ")" giving the token sequence T1 ∘ T3 is a reduced token sequence of T1 ∘ T2 T3 if T2 is the token " *'doesn''t it* " is tokenized as " ' " | "*doesn*" | " ' " | " ' " | "*t*" | "*it*" | " ' ". Note, however, that our line splitting rules do not split a Pascal string that was contained in one source line. Good style for visual appeal demand that reserved words and comments be flanked by white spaces and we do not see the need to rectify these 'anomalies'.

6.2 Reduced token sequences

We introduce the notion of "reduced" token sequences which makes it easy to define the functions that give the left margin width of output lines. Intuitively speaking, a token sequence T1 ∘ T3 is a reduced token sequence of T1 ∘ T2 ∘ T3 if T2 is the token sequence of a syntactically "sensible" Pascal statement. One might insist that T2 correspond to a syntactically correct statement. This, we believe, is overburdening the indenting programs; guaranteeing syntactic correctness is the function of a compiler, not indenting programs. What is syntactically sensible is made clear in the way the mathematical function RED maps a given token sequence to its reduction.

The P, Q, R, S and T below denote token sequences, and s and t denote single tokens. Expressions of the kind "if T = R ∘ DECL ∘ S for some R and S" are abbreviated as "if T = R ∘ DECL ∘ S". The special tokens DECL and PF are devised for the purposes of the RED function below and do not have corresponding words.

Definition of RED (see notes below)

1. RED(T o *t*) ::= RED(RED(T) o *t*) Thus we assume below that the sequence denoted by T is not reducible any further.

2. Let *t* = PROCEDURE, FUNCTION or PROGRAM. Then

    RED(T o *t*) ::= R o DECL o PF,

    where R = S if T = S o DECL, R = T if T does not end with either DECL or LPAREN; ::= T, if T does end with LPAREN.

3. Let *t* = LABEL, CONST, TYPE or VAR. Then

    RED(T o *t*) ::= R o DECL,

    where R = S if T = S o DECL, R = T if T does not end with either DECL or LPAREN; ::= T, if T does end with LPAREN.

4. Let *t* = FORWARD, or EXTERN. Then RED(T o *t*) ::= S, if T = S o PF; ::= T, otherwise.

5. RED(T o BEGIN) ::= S o BEGIN, if T = S o PF, or if T = S o PF o DECL; ::= T o BEGIN, otherwise.

6. Let *t* = RECORD, LPAREN, REPEAT, CASE, DO, THEN or COLON. Then RED(T o *t*) ::= T o *t*.

7. RED(T o OF) ::= S o CASE if T = S o CASE o COLON; :: = T, otherwise.

8. Let the pair <*t*, *s*> be one of <RPAREN, LPAREN>, <UNTIL, REPEAT>. Then RED(T o *t*) ::= R, if T = R o *s* o S where S does not have any tokens *s*; ::= 00, otherwise.

9. RED(T o END) ::= R, if T = R o RECORD o S where S is free of RECORDS; ::=P, if T is free of RECORDS and T = P o *s* o Q where *s* is either a BEGIN, or a CASE and Q does not have any of these tokens; ::= 00, otherwise.

10. RED(T o ELSE) ::= R o ELSE, if T = R o THEN o S where S is free of THENs; ::= ELSE, otherwise.

11. RED(T o SEMICOLON) ::= R o *s*, if T = R o *s* o S where *s* is any token but THEN, ELSE, DO, or COLON and S is a sequence of these tokens only; ::= 00, otherwise.

12. RED(T o *t*) ::= T, for any *t* not covered above.

The many cases in the definition reflect the syntax of the language. It should be clear that many illegal Pascal constructs would result in valid reduced sequences. As mentioned before, syntax validation is not in the domain of indenting programs we are considering.

Cases 2, 3, 4 and 5 would be simpler if Pascal had a different syntax. The special token DECL indicates that declarations (of labels, constants, types, variables and procedure/functions) are due next. If the last token of T is LPAREN, which can arise in a syntactically correct program only inside the parameter list, the tokens VAR, PROCEDURE and FUNCTION have no effect. The declarations end when a BEGIN is encountered; this is shown in case 5. Case 4 arises because FORWARD and EXTERN are not reserved words. They have the special meaning only when they appear immediately following the procedure headline.

Case 7 arises because of variant records with tag fields. In our specification COLON indents and it is, in this case, terminated by the OF.

6.3 Line splitting

Each split-up part of a line is called a *segment*. As we shall see, there is a one-to-one correspondence between input segments and output lines. These two are in fact identical but for the prefix and suffix white spaces.

The function FIRSTSEG maps non-white prefixes of a line to its first segment, using the sets LO and LC. The function SEGSEQ maps arbitrary strings to segment sequences. The set LO contains all (line opening) tokens whose corresponding words should always appear as the first non-white string in an output line. Similarly, the set LC contains all tokens which always close an output line but allow any immediately following comments. Thus the occurrence of a token from LO in the middle of an input line will split it just to the left of the token. The sets LO, LC are chosen to match the specifications of Figure 2.

LO ::= { PROCEDURE, FUNCTION, PROGRAM, LABEL, CONST, TYPE, VAR, WHILE, REPEAT, UNTIL, IF, ELSE, CASE, GOTO }

LC ::= { SEMICOLON }

Intuitively, the segmentation of strings as produced by SEGSEQ can be explained as follows. Place imaginary markers as follows: (1) before the very first and after the very last characters of the string, (2) to the immediate right of every \n, (3) to the immediate left of a token belonging to LO, and (4) to the immediate right of a token belonging to LC but skipping over comments following it. The strings thus enclosed between pairs of consecutive markers are segments. The functions FIRSTSEG and SEGSEQ imitate this process in a non-operational way.

Recall that we denote by 0ss, the empty sequence of segments, and by ! concatenation of segment sequences.

Definition of FIRSTSEG

Let w be a prefix of a line, and let $Q = LEX(T, w)$.

1. Suppose *lc* o COMBGN o ORDINARY* is a suffix of T, where *lc* stands for a token from LC. Then FIRSTSEG(T, w) ::= w, if Q does not contain COMEND; otherwise FIRSTSEG(T, w) ::= x where x is the longest prefix of w such that LEX(T, x) = ORDINARY* o COMEND o (COMBGN o ORDINARY* o COMEND)*.

2. Suppose *lc* o COMBGN o ORDINARY* is not a suffix of T. Then let x be the longest prefix of w such that LEX(T, x) does not contain (i) any token from LO except at its first token, or (ii) the subsequence *lc* o (COMBGN o ORDINARY* o COMEND)* o q, where $q \neq$ COMBGN. Then FIRSTSEG(T, w) = x.

The first segment function FIRSTSEG may be more complex for other indentation schemes. For instance, if we had required that the BEGIN of the code body of a procedure start on a new line, but other BEGINS need not, decomposing an input line into segments can no longer be done on the basis of a set like LO.

Definition of SEGSEQ

Let z be a sequence of lines, and w a prefix of a line.

1. SEGSEQ(" ") ::= 0ss.

2. SEGSEQ(z | w) ::= SEGSEQ(z)! w, if w is all white;
   SEGSEQ(z | w) ::= SEGSEQ(z)! DS(z, w), otherwise.

3. DS(z, w) ::= 0ss, if w is all white. Otherwise,
   DS(z, w) ::= u ! DS(z | u, v) where u = FIRSTSEG(TKNSEQ(z), w), and w = u | v.

As an example, consider the following string, z, where the ends of lines are shown explicitly.

      "**if** *b1* **then** (*loop*) **while** *b2* **do begin**" | \n|

      " " | \n|

      " $x := f(x)$; (*c1*) {*invariant*} $g(x)$" | \n|

      " **end**; (*of while and if *)"

The segments of SEGSEQ(z) are given below.

A SPECIFICATION SCHEMA FOR INDENTING PROGRAMS

"if $b1$ then (*loop*)" !

"while $b2$ do begin " | \n !

"   " | \n !

" $x := f(x)$; (*$c1$*) {invariant}" !

"$g(x)$" | \n !

"end; (*of while and if*)"

6.4 Indentation

Most often the indentation (i.e. the width of the left margin) of a given output line depends on the indentation of the previous line and on the reserved words occurring in it. On rarer occasions, the indentation depends also on the reserved words appearing in that line itself. An example of this is the "until." NMG(T) gives the margin the next line should have if the last token of T corresponds to the last word of the current line; CMG(T) gives the margin the current line should have if the last token of T corresponds to the first word of the current line. The function MG gives the actual margin of each output line.

Definition of NMG

1. NMG(00) ::= 0.
2. NMG(T) ::= NMG(RED(T)). Thus we assume below that the argument of NMG is reduced.
3. Let t = PF, or BEGIN. Then NMG(T o t) ::= NMG(T).
4. Let t = DECL, RECORD, LPAREN, REPEAT, DO, CASE, THEN, ELSE or COLON. Then NMG(T o t) ::= NMG(T)+UOI

Definition of CMG

1. CMG(00) ::= 0
2. Let t = PF, DECL, or ELSE. Then CMG(T o t) ::= NMG(T o t)−UOI.
3. Let t = RECORD, LPAREN, REPEAT, DO, CASE, THEN or COLON. Then CMG(T o t) ::= NMG(T).
4. For all t not covered above, CMG(T o t) ::= NMG(T o t).

It follows from the above, CMG(T) = CMG(RED(T)).

Definition of MG

1. $MG(0ss) ::= 0$.

2. $MG(z ! x) ::= CMG(T \circ t)$, where t is the first token of $LEX(T, x)$, and $T = TKNSEQ(z)$. Note that MG maps segment sequences to margins in contrast to NMG and CMG which map token sequences to margins.

6.5 Final specification

Let $zi\backslash e$ be the input file to indenting program, and let zo be the corresponding output file of an indenting program. Then

$$zo = INDENT(zi) \mid \backslash e$$

is the relation between them, where $INDENT(zi) ::= IND(SEGSEQ(zi))$, and IND is given below.

Definition of IND

IND maps segment sequences to sequences of lines. Let z be a sequence of segments, and x a segment.

1. $IND(0ss) :: = $ " ", the empty string.

2. $IND(z ! x) ::= IND(z) \mid \backslash b ** MG(z ! x) \mid psTRIM(x) \mid \backslash n$, where $psTRIM(x)$ trims x by removing all its prefix and suffix white space.

Note that $psTRIM(ith\ segment\ of\ input\ file) = psTRIM(ith\ output\ line)$.

7. THE EQUIVALENCE OF THE TWO SPECIFICATIONS

The low-level specifications coincide with the high-level specifications in the following sense: Let $zi \mid \backslash e$ be the text input to an indenting program satisfying our low-level specifications. Clearly its output $zo = INDENT(zi) \mid \backslash e$. Then we say the two specifications are *coincident* if $PLOT(nt, \backslash n \mid zo, 0)$ = true whenever $nt \longrightarrow *zi$. Note that if zi were not a valid construct, $PLOT(nt, \backslash n \mid zo, 0)$ would be false for all nt. As Figure 2 completely ignores comments, PLOT does not say how comments should be laid out, and we therefore give INDENT complete freedom in this regard.

A proof that the two specifications are coincident proceeds by induction on the syntactic structure of the input zi. As the base step, we show that if zi can be generated by one application of a production rule then $zo = INDENT(zi)$ would satisfy the high-level specifications. If, for $1 \leqslant j \leqslant k$, $zu_j = INDENT(zi_j)$, and $N = N_1 N_2 ... N_k$ is a production of Pascal grammar such that $N_j \longrightarrow *zi_j$, then the induction hypothesis is that $PLOT(N_j, \backslash n \mid zu_j, 0)$ = true. We need to show that $PLOT(N, \backslash n \mid zo, 0)$ =

true, where $zo = \text{INDENT}(zi)$ and $zi = zi_1 \mid zi_2 \mid ... \mid zi_k$.

Recall that we replaced terminal symbols appearing in the right-hand side of productions by their token names and considered the latter as non-terminals. Thus any zi that can be generated in one application can contain only one token and $\text{INDENT}(zi)$ contains no blank space in front of this token; thus $\text{PLOT}(t, \backslash n \mid \text{INDENT}(zi), 0)$ holds for some appropriate token t.

For the inductive step, note that $zo = \text{INDENT}(zi)$ can be divided such that $zo = zo_1 \mid zo_2 \mid ... \mid zo_k$, no zo_j contains white space suffix, and $N_j \longrightarrow {}^*zo_j$. Further note that the zi_j, zu_j and zo_j are all lexically equivalent. Since $zu_j = \text{INDENT}(zi_j)$, zo_j possibly differs from zu_j only in the width of the margin of each line and by containing an extra $\backslash n$ in the prefix of zo. The rest of the proof of this step follows from these observations and is simple but tedious requiring case analyses for each non-terminal N of the grammar. Here we present two such cases—one for the repeat statement and another for the procedure declaration.

Case N = repeat statement

Clearly $\text{TKNSEQ}(zo_1) = \text{REPEAT}$ and $\text{TKNSEQ}(zo_{k-1}) = \text{UNTIL}$. Also, for $1 < j < k-1$, zo_j must equal $c \mid (zu_j$ with the margin of each line of zu_j increased by UOI blanks.) Here the string c is either empty, or is $\backslash n$ depending on the segment sequence $\text{SEGSEQ}(zi)$. If a segment boundary fell between zi_{j-1} and zi_j, and if zi_{j-1} did not end with a $\backslash n$ then $c = \backslash n$, else $c = $ "". From the definition of SEGSEQ, it follows that a segment boundary falls between z_{j-1} and zi_j either because zi_{j-1} terminated in a $\backslash n$, or in a token from LC followed by (portions of) comments, or because zi_j begins a token from LO. Since LO and LC were chosen so as to make NEWL predicates true, $\text{PLOT}(\textit{repeat statement}, \backslash n \mid zi, 0)$ must be true.

Case N = procedure declaration

We shall make further assumptions below for the sake of simplicity in this illustration. We have that $\text{TKNSEQ}(zo_1) = \text{PROCEDURE}$, $\text{TKNSEQ}(zo_2) = \text{ORDINARY}$ (the corresponding word being the name of the procedure), $\text{TKNSEQ}(zo_3) = \text{SEMICOLON}$, assuming that the procedure heading has no parameters, and $\text{TKNSEQ}(zo_k) = \text{END}$. Further assuming that the procedure has only variable declaration part, we have $\text{TKNSEQ}(zo_4) = \text{VAR}$. Let $zo_5, \ldots, zo_{v-1}$ correspond to this declaration such that $\text{TKNSEQ}(zo_v) = \text{SEMICOLON}$, $\text{TKNSEQ}(zo_{v+1}) = \text{BEGIN}$. Clearly then, $zo_{v+2} \ldots, zo_{k-1}$ correspond to the code body of the procedure. Note that the value of NMG() will be 2*UOI starting from zo_5 until zo_v, both inclusive. After zo_{v+1} it becomes UOI and remains at least UOI until zo_k. As in the previous case, we see that the code body and the variable declaration and hence the procedure thus meet the high-level specifications.

8. CONCLUDING REMARKS

This section contains some remarks based on personal experience with this case study in specifying the behavior of a medium-sized program. I wrote the first version of an indenting program in late 1978 mainly as a reaction to the very long, slow and often clumsy indenting programs that were known to me at that time. A year later, I needed a class-room example of a real life program whose specification and proof are given sufficiently rigorously but with as little formalism as possible.

I began writing these specifications believing that it would take no more than 10 hours. I now estimate that about 150 hours were spent, over 9 months, in choosing the style of presentation, discovering the required functions and specifying the behaviour of the program. (The time spent in writing this paper is not included in the estimate.) In contrast, the original program was designed, written and tested in a total of 30 hours. Two revised versions of the program, eliminating many "minor bugs" in the original, were written during the development of the specifications. A correctness proof of the last version appears in a companion paper [Mateti and Jaffar 1983]. I estimate that the two revisions were done in 20 hours. Thus in my experience, the effort required in specifying a program I thought I understood well was 3 to 4 times more than that required in designing and writing it. I believe that this factor would have been considerably higher if I had less training in this field.

One wonders if the low-level specifications could have been written without a certain program in mind, or if they are needed at all. I did have a certain program in mind, and perhaps some of the inelegance is due to this fact. However, writing down these specifications exhibited the subtle errors and inelegant ways of the program that escaped my attention before. In contrast, the writing of high-level specifications helped only to explain to others how this program indents. It was important to write the low-level specifications because these defined how invalid input would be dealt with. Indeed, half the correctness proof of the indenting program consist of showing that low-level specifications coincide with high-level specifications.

It is not unfair to say that few practising programmers would be comfortable with the level of formalism used here. While there is certainly scope for improving the notations used in the paper, I believe there will be significant loss of precision with any further decrease in the level of formalism and rigor. The complexity of our specifications, however, truly reflects the complexity of any program meeting them.

This experience has been both delightful and frustrating at times. I recommend that everyone who writes programs conduct similar experiments as often as possible. As such experimenters are well aware, specifications can and often do contain bugs just as programs do.

MARTIN S. FEATHER
University of Southern California

Program Specification Applied to a Text Formatter

1. INTRODUCTION

A specification differs from an implementation in that there is no need for it to be efficient in the computational sense; rather, our sole aim in constructing a specification should be to maximize our confidence that the specification in fact denotes the behavior we desire. Within this paper we will be concerned with activities for which no concise specification is available—in such cases we must expend effort to develop a well-organized specification so that despite its size it is nevertheless comprehensible.

Our interest in specification derives from work on program transformation, in particular transformation based upon the methods for manipulating recursion equations, as developed by Burstall and Darlington [1977]. From this work Burstall was motivated to create a simple recursion-equation programming language, NPL [Burstall 1977]. We have used NPL as the language in which to express our specifications, and will consider how its use influenced our construction of specifications. NPL has since been rationalized and extended to become a more powerful language, HOPE [Burstall, MacQueen and Sannella 1980]. The work to be described here was done during the lifetime of NPL; at the end we will comment briefly on how HOPE's additional features might have been of further help.

We consider one particular task, and show how, by using the recursion-equation language and freeing ourselves from all consideration of efficiency during design, we may emerge with a good formal specification. The domain of the task is text formatting; we limit our attention to the simpler end of this domain, and adopt the set of features of an already defined formatter as those we must specify. The formatter we adopt is that described by Kernighan and Plauger [1976, chapter 5]. In this book the authors demonstrate, with the aid of examples, how to organize one's approach to programming to go from an informal task description to a reasonably efficient and well-organized program to perform that task. Hence they provide both an informal description of a text formatter, and a program to do the formatting (written in Ratfor, i.e., preprocessed Fortran). We will construct a formal specification of their formatting task and investigate the benefits we claim for such a formal description.

2. CONSTRUCTING SPECIFICATIONS

We see two main properties that a formal specification should have.

1. It must in fact denote the behavior the writer desires.
2. It must serve as a clear description which can be read and comprehended.

In the case of problems for which no concise specification is apparent it becomes much more difficult to achieve both of these goals. We feel that we have benefited from using NPL in which to express our specifications, insofar as it has encouraged a clear organization of our specifications. The main features of the language that we feel have provided this benefit are as follows.

1. The applicative nature of the language leads to a style of programming which is clearer and less error-prone. Destructive operations, side effects, and iteration are mechanisms appropriate to achieving efficiency but reduce clarity, since their inclusion renders communication between portions of the specification much less transparent. A crucial need in the successful organization of a large specification is to decompose it into separate components, each of which may be understood in isolation, and the communication between which is straightforward enough to permit comprehension of their combination.

2. The language is strongly typed and permits user-defined types. By making liberal use of types defined for the task being specified we get support from the type-checker and provide additional helpful information to the reader.

3. Writing in recursion equations encourages decomposition of the overall large problem into simpler subproblems, which in turn may be decomposed, until finally we emerge with many trivial problems each of which may be easily coded.

In the example to follow we will see the above influences in action. The presence of these features is, of course, no guarantee that we will emerge with a suitable specification. We must adopt a style which makes good use of them. To this end, the freedom to disregard efficiency is of crucial importance. This underlies the crucial difference between our approach and that of structured programming. Whereas the matter is a means for developing a tolerably efficient program, we are concerned (at this stage) solely with developing a specification. Hence, although we may indeed adopt some of the organizational techniques of structured programming, we will typically choose to decompose a problem in a radically different manner, one better suited to satisfying the needs of a specification.

We emphasize that no elements of our approach are new—rather, we are following the techniques already suggested by other researchers. Backus [1978] has argued for the need to escape from conventional imperative programming; Burge [1975] investigates recursive programming. The typed nature of the language ML [Gordon *et al.* 1978] influenced NPL. Noted texts on structured programming include Dahl, Dijkstra and Hoare [1972] and Dijkstra [1976]. Balzer, Goldman and Wile [1976], and Darlington and Burstall [1976] advocate developing programs by first constructing a specification and then transforming to introduce efficiency.

3. THE EXAMPLE TASK

The example task we consider is a (small) text formatter. This we chose as a reasonably well-understood task, one of sufficient complexity that no concise specification is possible (at least, none that we know of), hence suitable as a problem for trying the method of developing a program by formal specification followed by transformation.

3.1 Informal Description of a Text Formatter

We give a (very) brief and informal account of the facilities the text formatter is to provide.

Input to the formatter is a sequence of lines, where lines consist of sequences of characters. Some lines will be text, some will be commands to the formatter. Command lines are identified by the occurrence of a "." in the first column followed by a two letter abbreviation of the name of the command.

In action the formatter may be in a "fill" mode, during which paragraphs are formed by packing as many input words as possible into the output lines, the lines being "right-justified" (to produce an aligned right margin, like this paragraph) by padding out with extra spaces between words if necessary. When not in "fill" mode the input text lines are output without modification. When switching off filling, the words already gathered to go into the next output line are put out without right justification. This action of forcing out a partially collected line is called a break. Some of the commands implicitly cause breaks when they are encountered, even though they may not cause filling to be switched off.

We present the commands and briefly explain their actions:

"Filling" commands

fi   Cause a break and switch on "fill" mode.

nf   Switch off "fill" mode.

br   Cause a break (but does not switch into or out of "fill" mode).

Page commands

bp n   Begin page. *n* is an optional numeric argument, which, if present, is taken as the number of the new page. If not present the default is to increment the current page number by one. Causes a break. If this command would produce an entirely blank page (but for header and footer titles), i.e., occurs at the very top of a page, it merely adjusts the page number without creating the blank page.

pl n Set page length to be *n* lines. Default is *n*=66, does not cause break.

he t Set the header to be printed at top of each page. *t* is a string argument which becomes the new header. The character "#" within the string is replaced by the current page number. Does not cause a break.

fo t Set the footer title to be printed at bottom of each page. Analogous to **he** command.

ls n Set line spacing to *n* (i.e., *n*=2 corresponds to double spacing). Default is *n*=1, does not cause a break.

sp n Causes a break and produces n blank lines. Default is *n*=1. Does not produce blank lines at the very top of a page.

Line commands

ce n Cause a break and center the next *n* text lines (i.e., insert extra spaces if necessary to cause the text lines to be centered within the current margins.) Default is *n*=1. If another **ce** command is encountered while centering text lines, the new command's value of *n* takes precedence.

ul n Does not cause a break. Default is *n*=1. As with **ce** command, encountering another **ul** command will adjust the count of lines to be underlined.

rm n Set right margin to be *n*. Default is *n*=60, does not cause a break.

in n Set left margin (indentation) to be **n**. Default is *n*=0, does not cause a break.

ti n Cause a break and set the left margin for next output line only to be *n*. Default is *n*=0.

Numeric arguments to commands may be preceded by a "+" or −, in which case the value is taken to be the current value of the parameter being set incremented or decremented accordingly. An exception to this is the **ti** command which adjusts relative to the current left margin setting.

In order that the formatter behave reasonably with text containing a minimum of formatting commands, input lines which start with blanks or are entirely blank are treated as follows.

(a) Lines empty but for blanks cause a break and a blank line to be output (even at the top of a new page).

(b) Lines starting with *n* blanks (but followed by other characters) where *n*>0 cause a break and a temporary indent of +*n*.

3.2 The Organization of our Specification

The formatting task may be characterized as follows: from the input representation we extract the lines of text and the associated information which will direct the layout of that text. These lines are processed as directed to produce output lines representing pages containing paragraphs, verbatim text, headers, etc.

Our specification will follow this characterization, i.e., we will have a first stage in which the input is decoded to extract the text lines and associate with each the information to direct the formatting; and a second stage in which these lines + information are processed into paragraphs, pages, etc. from which output lines can be formed.

Thus, already we see a major divergence between our specification and any reasonably efficient program—we have two distinct stages connected by passing of a bulky but conceptually simple data structure, whereas an efficient program would perform the whole operation in a single pass, incrementally maintaining the current information and producing output.

Now we tackle the decomposition of these stages.

Decoding Input to Associate Information with (Text) Lines

This breaks down into two more stages; the first to recognize command lines and decode the type of command and arguments (if any). The output of this is a sequence of elements, each of which is either a (text) line (i.e., sequence of characters) or a command (some types of commands having argument values associated with them). Figure 1 displays the overall organization of our specification, and within it we call this stage of the processing DECODE.

The second stage associates with each text line a data structure to hold the information relevant to formatting that line, e.g., margin values, page size, etc. We call this collection of information an "infomap." Thus output from this, to the second main stage of the whole formatting process is a sequence of elements, each of which is a text-line + infomap. Actually this is a slight oversimplification, insofar as we leave commands of a few types within this sequence rather than trying to force the information implied in the commands into infomaps. The aberrant commands are:

sp (space-down)—left untouched because it is only during page formation that we may determine whether the blank lines this generates would fall at the very top of a page (in which case they are to be discarded), or whether they would fit into the remaining space on the current page (if not they fill it to the bottom, but do *not* overflow onto the next page).

bp (begin page)—left untouched because it is only during page formation that we may determine the page number of the current page, and this command might specify a relative change to the page number rather than absolute.

br (break)—the sole purpose of this command is to delimit collection of words to be accumulated into a single paragraph.

We call this stage DOCOMMANDS within Figure 1. This decomposes further into a separate stage for each command wherever possible. The **fi** and **nf** commands (to switch filling on and off) interact in such a way as to necessitate handling together, as do the **in** and **ti** commands (indent and temporary indent). Apart from these pairs the commands are dealt with in separate passes, the order of which is irrelevant.

lines (each a sequence of characters)

↓ DECODE—*recognizes command lines and decodes them*

(text) lines interspersed with commands

↓ DOCOMMANDS—*associates with each text line on "infomap" to hold formatting information values*

(text) lines + infomaps interspersed with remaining commands

↓ INTERMEDIATE—*local line manipulation (underlining, etc.)*

(text) lines + infomaps interspersed with remaing commands

↓ LINES—*form output lines (involving filling and justifying paragraphs, centering lines between margins, etc.)*

(text) lines + infomaps interspersed with remaining commands

↓ PAGES—*form output pages (generating header and footer titles, padding with blank lines, etc.)*

pages (each a sequence of (text) lines)

↓ OUTPUT—*simplify to a sequence of lines*

lines

Figure 1. Structure of specification

Processing of Text Lines

This breaks down into four distinct stages.

1. *INTERMEDIATE*: Do processing local to individual text lines, i.e., center those lines which need centering by adjusting the margin values within their infomaps, follow each character in text lines whose contents are to be underlined by backspace and underline, and deal appropriately with text lines which start with blanks and/or are entirely blank. Each

of these activities is done in a separate substage— they have been grouped together here because they refer to information and make changes purely within single text lines.

2. *LINES*: Within this stage paragraph formation is performed and overlength lines are dealt with (resulting in a split into two or more lines). The distinction between this and the INTERMEDIATE stage is that this involves actions spread over possibly several text lines. Paragraph formation is the most interesting of the activities done in this stage. We break this down into

   (a) gathering the lines from which words to go into a single paragraph are to be extracted;

   (b) extract the words from these lines (and associate with each word the "infomap" of the line from which it has been extracted);

   (c) squeeze as many of the words as possible into each successive line to form a filled paragraph, and perform justification on each such line. In forming each line we let the infomap of the first word to go onto the line determine the characteristics of the entire line (in particular, its margin sizes).

3. *PAGES*: The text lines to go into pages have been formed in the previous stage, and within this stage these lines are not modified in any way, merely accumulated into pages. Again, a breakdown into subtasks is followed to accumulate page-filling sequences of lines and form actual pages from these.

4. *OUTPUT*: Finally, the sequence of pages is simplified into a sequence of lines for output to some printing device. It is here that we would tailor the output to whatever device was to be the destination (e.g., if the device had no backspace character but could overprint an entire line, we would modify those lines with backspace accordingly.)

We could provide further detail about each stage of processing, but we feel that we have sufficiently demonstrated the overall approach to decomposition of the problem. A portion of the NPL code which forms our specification is provided in the Appendix.

3.3 Implications of Having Constructed a Specification

We consider what benefits there may be from having a formal specification, and reflect on what the exercise has revealed about formatting the specification in general.

1. *Increased Understanding of Task:*

One consequence of our attempt to produce as clear a specification as possible is that it lead us to consider some aspects of formatting that we might otherwise have overlooked.

An example of this arose during specification of paragraphing, when words are extracted from the incoming text lines and put into filled and justified lines. It is clear that the information associated with an input text line should become the information associated with each of the words extracted from that line. However, it is not so trivial to decide how the information associated with several words will be used to determine the information to be associated with the output text line that they are to form. In our specification we chose to let the information associated with the first word to go onto a line determine the information for the entire line.

This is *not* the behavior of Kernighan and Plauger's efficient formatter. Their program, when accumulating the words to go into a filled line, is simultaneously taking notice of the incoming commands to change formatting values (in particular, right margin value). Hence, in the middle of forming a filled line the right margin value might change, and the line formed would reflect the latest value rather than the value prevalent at the start of the line. We speculate that this is an implicit consequence of their aim to design an efficient program rather than the result of a conscious choice between alternatives. Their algorithm may exhibit unusual behavior if during accumulation of words to go into a line the right margin should decrease to less than that needed to accommodate the words accumulated so far—the effect is to cause those words to be put out in a line whose rightmost margin will be neither the old right margin value nor the new smaller value. For example,

Input	Our Specifications' Output	Kernighan & Plauger's Program's Output
.rm 14	AA BB CC DD EE	AA BB CC DD EE
.fi	FF GG HH II JJ	FF GG HH II JJ
AA BB CC DD EE FF	KK LL MM NN OO	KK LL MM
GG HH II JJ KK LL MM	PP QQ	NN OO
.rm 5	RR SS	PP QQ
NN OO PP QQ RR SS		RR SS

Our point is not that our specification exhibits the "right" behavior, but rather that in its construction we were led to consideration of the options available. Regardless of whether we make any further use of our specifications, we would claim that, by being led to such considerations, we benefit in gaining a better understanding of the task in question.

Some further observations that we are led to make are as follows.

Page Formation: There is a close parallel between filling lines with words and filling pages with lines. In each case we must decide what effect commands which adjust line/page parameters should have when they occur in the middle of forming a line/page. (Of course, commands that cause a new line/page to be started have a clear intent— it is only those which adjust parameters without terminating the current line/page whose precise effect is unobvious).

In the same way that we must decide how the information associated with the words to go into a line should determine the information for that line, we also must decide how the information associated with the lines to go into a page should determine the information for that page. To be consistent we choose to let the information of the first line serve as the information for the entire page.

Oddities of Line Filling and Page Formation: Some of the consequences of permitting parameter changes to occur without forcing line/page breaks are rather strange. For example,

Input						Output				
.rm 14						AA	BB	CC	DD	EE
.fi						FF	GG	HH	II	JJ
AA	BB	CC	DD	EE	FF	KK	LL	MM	NN	OO
GG	HH	II	JJ	KK	LL	PP	QQ	RR	SS	TT
.rm 7						UU	VV	WW	XX	YY
MM	NN					ZZ				
.rm 14										
OO	PP	QQ	RR	SS	TT					
UU	VV	WW	XX	YY	ZZ					

We might be surprised to observe no lines with right margin set to 7 in the output. This is a consequence of our decision to let a line's first word's information set the characteristics for the entire line—here the decreased right margin has no effect on the line already in progress, and by the time the next line begins, the margin has been readjusted!

We might also be surprised to learn that the obvious policy of filling up the current line with as many words as possible before starting the next line does not necessarily lead to the paragraph of the shortest overall length! For example,

Input				Our Output				Alternative			
.rm 15				AAA	BBB	CCC	DDD	AAA		BBB	CCC
AAA	BBB	CCC	DDD	EE	FF	GG		DDD	EE	FF	GG	HH
.rm 8				HH	III			III	JJJ		
EE	FF	GG	HH	JJJ							
III	JJJ										

Here by allowing word "DDD" to spill over onto a new (and hence longer) line, more of the following words can be accommodated before the margin shrinkage comes into effect, resulting in a decrease in the paragraph length.

These behaviors suggest that we should consider revising our definition of the formatting process to insist that commands modifying parameters of a line/page always have the effect of terminating the current line/page.

2. Availability of a Clear Specification:

We have more confidence that we understand the behavior implied by our specification than that of Kernighan and Plauger's efficient program. This may be due in part to our having performed the design of our specification, but served only as a reader of their program. However, a good deal of our confidence may be attributed to the deliberately simple structure of our specification, from which we are better able to perceive how the portions interact, and the likelihood of there being anomalous behavior in circumstances that we had not anticipated much reduced.

3. Areas of Dissatisfaction:

We are reasonably happy about the overall quality of our resulting specification; however, we perceive some areas in which we harbor some lingering dissatisfactions.

With respect to clarity, we were forced to make compromises between complicating some portions of the specification in order to simplify others. An example of this is to be found in the method by which information to control line and page formation is gathered and disseminated. Ideally, at any stage which makes use of some of the information it should be evident what information is necessary for the activities of that stage. We have simplified the gathering and passing of information between stages so that each stage receives text lines together with so called "infomaps," containing all the associated information. Hence, it is only through inspection of the activities that we may determine which portions of information are actually required and which are not (e.g., to determine that the pages formation stage makes use of page-length information, but not margin sizes). An alternative would have been to complicate the stage that gathers "infomaps" in order to partition the information so that each stage may be given only the portion of the information necessary for its activities.

Another example is our decision to leave some of the commands (**br, bp,** and **sp**) interspersed with the (text) lines, rather than go to the extra effort of encoding them into infomaps. Again, we see this as a compromise rather than a clear-cut best choice.

4. Availability of a Precise Specification:

Our specification is formal as opposed to informal; hence we may use it in the following ways.

Testing: The NPL interpreter may be used to run the specification on small examples to test its overall behavior. The inefficient nature of the specification prohibits extensive testing; however, its design, in which the overall task is decomposed into smaller and simpler subtasks, permits extensive testing of the components. In practice, our mode of construction and testing of NPL specifications goes as follows: first, we design a specification in the manner outlined for the test formatter; second, we turn this design into an NPL program, which we feed into the type checker, at which point syntactic errors are discovered and removed; third, we are left with a syntactically correct program, which we may try small test cases on, and the components of which we may test extensively. We find that the few errors present in the program are glaringly obvious and relatively simple in nature (both to understand and correct).

Verification: We may attempt to prove properties of our specification. The applicative nature of NPL and the simplicity of our specification make proofs easier. Indeed, Burstall and Darlington acknowledge the influence of Boyer and Moore's successful theorem prover for properties of Lisp programs (see Boyer and Moore [1975] and Boyer and Moore [1979]) on their decision to investigate the transformation of recursion equations. Although we do not have a theorem prover for NPL (or HOPE) programs, the domain of Aubin's prover (Aubin [1976]) is a language recursion equations very similar to NPL, and would seem to be most appropriate.

Transformation: At the start we remarked on how NPL originated from Burstall and Darlington's transformation work. Our intent in producing specifications in NPL is to then transform them into more efficient NPL programs. Darlington [1981] has created a transformation system for NPL. His system is more geared to researching the extent to which transformation techniques may be automated than to performing large transformations which, in the present state of the art, require significant user guidance to be practical. We have engineered a transformation system for NPL which is designed primarily to support the human user in performing large transformations—details of this system may be found in Feather [1982]. With this we were able to transform our text-formatter specification into an NPL program with the structure and behavior of a more conventional algorithm (i.e., a one-pass algorithm in which formatted output is produced as the input is consumed, with the consequent vast improvement in efficiency over our specification, at the expense of clarity). All the steps of this transformation process were machine applied, hence we have confidence that the result of the transformation is in fact equivalent to our specification. Furthermore, the record of human direction to the transformation system is preserved as a manipulable structure in its own right—one which may be read, reapplied, modified, etc.

Maintenance: We would like to see the specification, transformed efficient program, and record of transformation serve together to support maintenance. Rather than attempting to modify the efficient program directly—an error-prone activity at best—we would perform our modifications upon the specification (which, because of its very nature should admit to easier and more error-free maintenance) and reperform the transformation to produce a modified efficient program. Should the nature of the modification be concerned solely with adjusting the efficiency rather than the functional behavior of the program, we would adjust the transformation while leaving the specification the same. These are, at present, wishes only. A good deal of research needs to be done into the maintenance aspect of transformation. See

Darlington and Feather [1980] for a report of preliminary experiment in this direction.

Alternative Evaluation: The NPL interpreter evaluates NPL programs in a straightforward call-by-value fashion. However, the applicative nature of recursion equations makes them neutral to the order of evaluation (except perhaps for loss of termination). [Schwarz 1977] investigates how we may augment an NPL program with control information to direct a more sophisticated interpreter in its selection of evaluation mechanism. By this means we may make some improvement to the efficiency of the interpretation without resorting to transformation; see also [Kowalski 1979] and [Clark and McCabe 1980] for related work on the language Prolog. Darlington has developed some ideas on how to evaluate recursion equations on parallel hardware, and has observed that the specification style of lavish decomposition is suited to taking full advantage of parallel processing power.

4. CONCLUSIONS

4.1 Accomplishments

We have constructed a specification of a simple text formatter, and would like to think that our specification has the virtues of clarity, comprehensibility, and precision. We ascribe the success we might have had to the influences inherent from using an applicative recursion equation language, and to the deliberate decision to disregard all consideration of efficiency. We feel that we have benefited from the experience both by emerging with a formal specification, and by having gained some insights into the actual task of formatting. Further details of our efforts, both specification and transformation, may be found in Feather [1979].

4.2 From NPL to HOPE

As we remarked earlier, the language NPL has since been developed further to become HOPE; the two main extensions, and how they might have been of use to us, are as follows.

Higher Order: NPL is a first-order language, without the power of passing functions as values to functions. We do not think the availability of this feature would have influenced our design of the specification, merely simplified expression of some of the low-level activities.

Modularity: NPL contains a very crude mechanism for information hiding. Within HOPE this mechanism has been significantly extended into a modularization facility. We might make good use of this feature to make explicit the separation of the various stages of our specification. We do not think this would have influenced us to adopting a very different design, rather encouraged us (by the support it provides) to make clearer the communication of information within the established configuration.

4.3 Avenues for Further Research

Restricting our attention to the specification aspect, we see the following possibilities for investigation.

Modularity: We speculate that the apparent compromise between simplicity of some portions of the specification and explicating the necessary and unnecessary communication between portions signifies a weakness in the modularization of our program. We require experience with facilities such as those incorporated into HOPE to determine whether this problem can be partially or wholly overcome by language support.

Explanation: Although we are reasonably happy with our NPL specification, we recognize that it will not suffice as a self-explanatory document; we ascribe its failing in this respect to two factors: first, it is written without redundant information, and makes no attempt to build up from anew to an understanding of the whole; second, the decisions made during construction and the reasons for making those decisions are not evident in the final product of the construction process. There is a need for investigation into providing such support for specifications.

ACKNOWLEDGMENTS

The author would like to thank all his colleagues at the Department of Artificial Intelligence, University of Edinburgh, for their help, in particular R. Burstall and J. Darlington for providing the original inspiration and continuing support and encouragement, and D. MacQueen for revealing discussions about specifications.

APPENDIX

PORTIONS OF NPL SPECIFICATION OF TEXT FORMATTER

[Appendix deleted]

CARL A. SUNSHINE
University of Southern California

DAVID H. THOMPSON
WSAW-TV

RODDY W. ERICKSON and SUSAN L. GERHART
Software Research Associates

DANIEL SCHWABE
Pontificia Universidade Catolica

Specification and Verification of Communication Protocols in AFFIRM Using State Transition Models

1. INTRODUCTION

When we send electronic mail, funds, or programs to another site, we expect many things to happen: the message should be delivered to a particular site and not to others; only one copy of the message should be delivered; the delivery should be timely; the receipt should be acknowledged; etc. In computer-science terms, these properties are often called *safety* (correct delivery), *liveness* (effective work being done), and *performance* (work being done fast enough). The social importance of guaranteeing these properties for electronic media cannot be overvalued: our dependence on such systems increases daily.

Over the past few years, the Internet Concepts Project at ISI has been studying the overall problem of protocol verification, as well as the design of correct protocols. Simultaneously, the ISI Program Verification Project was developing a general-purpose specification and verification system called AFFIRM. This paper reports on joint research between these projects over a year's time. Specific accomplishments include increased understanding of an underlying formalism (state transition models), rendering of such models in the specification language of AFFIRM, experimenting with various ways of expressing the three kinds of properties mentioned above so that they can be proved for state transition specifications, study of several levels of specification (all the way from the user services down to the programming language implementation), an in-depth study of a particular protocol (the alternating bit protocol), and a survey of a number of other protocols. Our overall accomplishment is a general method of specifying and verifying certain aspects of protocols, supported by mechanical assistance. Most of our work has focused on safety properties, rather than liveness and performance properties.

Because we expect at least one of the areas of communication protocols, state transition machines, and abstract data types to be new to most readers, we have included a fairly lengthy introduction to each of these topics in this section. The main part of the paper presents a rather simple example of the integration of these concepts. Thus the emphasis is on *methodology* rather than the results obtained for a particular protocol. Later work [Schwabe 1981a] presents extensive concrete results on protocols of more practical interest.

Our general method of protocol specification and verification is summarized in Section 2. Details of the specification method are illustrated in Section 3. Verification issues are considered in Section 4. The method is applied to the Alternating Bit protocol in Section 5. Section 6 summarizes some of the results obtained with more complex protocols. Extensions and problems are analyzed in Section 7. Our conclusions are presented in Section 8.

1.1 State Transition Models

A variety of methods for modeling the behavior of systems in terms of state transitions has been developed, including finite state automata (FSA) and abstract machines. The key components of these models are as follows.

(1) A set of *commands* (also called *inputs* or *events*).

(2) One or more *state variables*, collectively called the *state*.

(3) A *transition* function (command × state) ⟶ state.

(4) An *initial* state (assigning initial values to all the state variables).

Intuitively, each command can be thought of as a single *state transition function* mapping the current state into a new state. Typically, one distinguished state variable is used to represent the major or control status of the machine, and it features prominently in determining the effects of each command. Generally, commands are considered atomic operations that are processed sequentially; no concurrent commands are allowed. However, the effect of concurrent events may be approximated as discussed in Section 7.2.

A state transition machine operates by starting in its initial state. At unspecified times, the state is transformed by one of the state transition functions (or an input "appears," and is used by the overall transition function to effect a state change). The machine may be designed to operate forever, or may have a specified set of *final* states. When one of these states is reached the machine is considered to have halted.

Within these basic guidelines, there are a number of possible variations. State variables may be defined as value-returning functions. The commands may have parameters. The effects of commands may be made visible to the outside world (i.e., the users of the machine) by defining some of the state variables to be visible, or by producing explicit outputs as additional effects of an operation. *Exceptional* conditions may be specified where a given command has no effect on the state of the system except to produce an error indication or output to the invoking user. If the data types of the state variables are unbounded (e.g., a queue), the model may not have a finite number of states.

State transition models are often written graphically, with circles or boxes representing states and arcs representing transitions. Each arc is labeled with the command causing the transition. Outputs produced are also written on the arcs if needed. Figure 1 gives an example of a state transition model for a very simple message system allowing only a single message in transit from sender to receiver. (This example is explained further in Section 3.)

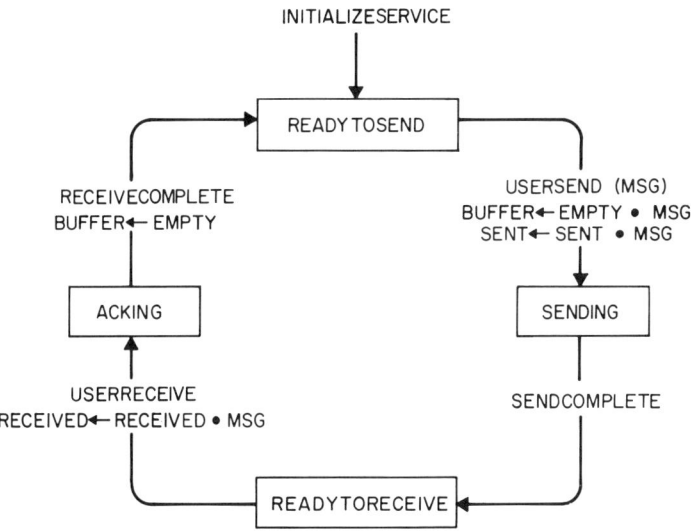

Figure 1. A simple message system

1.2 Specification and Verification in AFFIRM

AFFIRM [Musser 1980; Gerhart *et al.* 1980; Thompson, Gerhart, Erickson, Lee and Bates 1981] is an experimental system for the algebraic specification and verification of user-defined abstract data types. The heart of the system is a natural deduction theorem prover for the interactive proof of data type properties. (These properties are stated in the predicate calculus extended with data types.) Programs, written in a variant of Pascal extended with these abstract data types, may be verified using the inductive assertion method [Floyd 1967]. Additional features include tools for the analysis of algebraic specifications, a library of useful data types, and user interface facilities. Experience includes extensive experimentation with data type specifications, verification of small programs, the specification and partial proof of a large file updating module, and the proof of high-level properties or protocol and security kernels.

The specification and theorem-proving portions of AFFIRM are relevant to the current discussion.

1. *Data Abstraction*

Following Guttag [1975]; Guttag and Horning [1978b]; Guttag, Horowitz and Musser [1978] a data type is specified by first defining three sets of functions.

(a) *Constructors*: These functions create values of the type. Their range is the data type being specified. All values of the type can be described in terms of some functional composition of these functions.

(b) *Extenders (or Modifiers)*: These functions also have the data type being specified as their range, but in contrast to the constructors, they are not needed to express values of the data type. (These functions can be expressed in terms of the constructors.)

(c) *Selectors (or Predicates)*: These functions yield values of types other than the one being specified. The general term is *selector*, but functions yielding values of type *Boolean* are often termed *predicates*.

For example, the constructors of a queue are *NewQueue* (the empty queue) and *Add* (appends an element to a queue). Example extender functions are *Remove* (deletes the first element from a queue) and *Append* (concatenates two queues). Example selector functions are *Front* and *Length*; example predicates are *in* and *nodups* (asks whether there are any duplicate elements).

declare q, q1, q2: QueueOfInteger;
declare i: integer;

interfaces NewQueueOfInteger, q Add i, Remove(q),
          Append(q1, q2): QueueOfInteger;

interfaces Front(q), Length(q): Integer;

interface i in q: Boolean;

The effect of such a specification is to view values of the type in terms of the constructors which build them. Hence, all selectors and extenders are defined in terms of these constructors. For example, the queue of integers

$<1, 2, 3>$

is represented (in infix form) as

((NewQueueOfInteger Add 1) Add 2) Add 3

Thus, the first part of a specification gives the names of all operations, their domains, and their ranges (e.g., the *syntax* of the type).

The second part of a data type specification provides semantics for the operations. Extenders and selectors are defined by equational axioms relating how each function behaves when applied to each of the constructors. (Constructor functions are treated as primitive, unspecified operations.) These axioms look like equations but are treated by AFFIRM as left-to-right rewriting rules. Various methods are used to check the consistency and completeness of the axioms and to check the consistency of the equational theory [Musser 1980, 1977]. For example, some axioms from the type *QueueOfInteger* are

> **axioms**
> Remove(NewQueueOfInteger) == NewQueueOfInteger,
> Remove(q Add i) == **if** q = NewQueueOfInteger
>   **then** q
>   **else** Remove(q) Add i,
>
> Length(NewQueueOfInteger) == 0,
> Length(q Add i) == Length(q) + 1;
>
> Append(q, NewQueueOfInteger) == q,
> Append(q1, q2 Add i) == Append(q1, q2) Add i,

An important use of these data type specifications is to obtain levels of abstraction, in particular to avoid low-level implementation details. For example, in our specification of a queue we do not care whether it is implemented with an array or via pointers and a linked list. Of course, implementation details *do* constrain the abstraction, e.g., by space limitations, but this is a separate problem. A standard method for relating implementations to their abstractions is the *representation* (or *abstraction*) function *rep* mapping from implementation to abstraction [Hoare 1972a; Wulf, London and Shaw 1976b]. For example, we might define a function

> *rep*(a, lb, ub) == **if** lb > ub
>   **then** *NewQueue*
>   **else** *rep*(a, lb, ub-1) Add a[ub]

to map from an array *a* over the sequence of (integer) indexes *lb* to *ub* into queues.

The proof of correctness for an implementation involves showing that all abstract operations of interest have code that computes, via the *rep* function, the proper function. For example, we might have a procedure

> **procedure** *RemoveImplementation*(**var** a: Array; **var** lb, ub: Integer);
>   **pre** wf(a, lb, ub);
>   **post** wf(a, lb, ub) and *rep*(a, lb, ub) = Remove (*rep*(a′, lb′, ub′))
>   ... body of procedure ...

where the primed notation x' denotes the *initial* value of x at the start of the procedure. The expression "wf(a, lb, ub)" is the *implementation* (or *concrete*) invariant *well-formed*, a predicate that shows the variables of the implementation will always map into some abstract object. In the inductive assertion method, the interpretation of the *pre-* and *post*conditions is as follows. If the *pre*condition holds for the variables at entry to the procedure, then the *post*condition will hold for the variables at procedure exit. Note that there is no statement that the procedure terminates.

We will use these concepts in mapping between levels of a specification and from axioms down to programs.

2. Theorem Proving

Typical data type properties might include "*the length of the concatenation of two queues is the sum of their lengths*", stated as

$$\text{Length}(q1 \text{ Append } q2) = \text{Length}(q1) + \text{Length}(q2)$$

and "*the length of any queue is always nonnegative*":

$$\text{Length}(q) \geqslant 0$$

Such properties are proved by induction based on the constructors of the data type, that is, using *structural induction*. For our queue example, the induction schema uses the inference rule

$$\frac{P(\text{NewQueueOfInteger}), \ (\text{all } q, i \ (P(q) \supset P(q \text{ Add } i)))}{(\text{all } q(P(q)))}$$

In other words, we prove the property P for *NewQueueOfInteger* and then, assuming it for some queue q, prove P for q with any element i appended to it (q Add i). These two proofs suffice to prove P for all q. An appropriate induction schema must be included in the specification of each data type.

AFFIRM's style of theorem-proving is interactive. The user develops the proof; the system's role is to follow the user's commands and provide various kinds of necessary information and checking. It does not attempt to search for a proof. AFFIRM simplifies propositions using the data type axioms (as rewrite rules), with built-in simplification procedures for the predicate calculus. The user can ask the system to employ induction, split into subgoals, substitute equalities, and apply lemmas; experimentation with various strategies is often necessary before finding a proof. This experimentation and back-tracking is supported with a model of the proof as a forest of proof trees, and with numerous display and query features.

The overall effect is that the user follows the usual mathematical proof methods, but AFFIRM carries out the mechanics of the proof (down to the axioms or assumptions). Of course, proofs are not iron-clad: there might be a bug (in either our code or the underlying INTERLISP system)[1] or the user might make an invalid assumption. AFFIRM is used to produce *better*, not *guaranteed perfect*, proofs. Such proofs should also be readable (when properly structured in terms of lemmas) and read to be believed.

A more serious problem is that of ascertaining that we have proved (or are trying to prove) what we really want proven. Experience has shown repeatedly that propositions we thought were theorems were *not*; this quickly led us to the conclusion that "the purpose of proving (with AFFIRM) is to turn a *conjecture* into a *theorem*."

1.3 Protocols

In order to apply state transition models and abstract data types to communication protocols, we must first understand specification and verification problems in the protocol domain. The meaning of protocol specification and verification will be described in terms of a model first introduced in Sunshine [1979].

1. *Protocol Specification*

A user's interest in a protocol lies in what kind of *services* it provides. Usually this involves interactions with other entities (such as users or programs) in order to get certain functions performed. For example, one user may wish to interact with another (remote) user by performing various functions such as *SendMessage*. How these functions are actually performed by the protocol is not really of concern; only the end result matters.

Users, then, can regard the protocol as a *black box*, to which one gives a series of commands in order to get certain services performed. The description of this machine is termed the *service specification*. One theorem we may wish to prove about a service specification is that the messages *received* constitute an initial subsequence of the messages *sent* (i.e., messages are not delivered in the wrong order, or garbled, nor are messages spontaneously delivered if they were not sent).

In general, the components used to provide the service can also be regarded as black boxes in their own right. In the case of protocols there is always more than one entity interacting (because we are dealing with distributed systems). In order to provide a given service, it is necessary to have several *stations* (at least one for each physical site) interacting with each other via some *transmission machine* (see Figure 2). The pattern of their interactions constitutes the protocol.

---

1. To our knowledge, AFFIRM has never generated an invalid proof; we consider it unlikely that an error would produce just the right behavior to validate an incorrect theorem, particularly since the user would probably note associated strange behavior. The usual result of a bug is to prevent a valid proof from proceeding. However, soundness cannot be guaranteed.

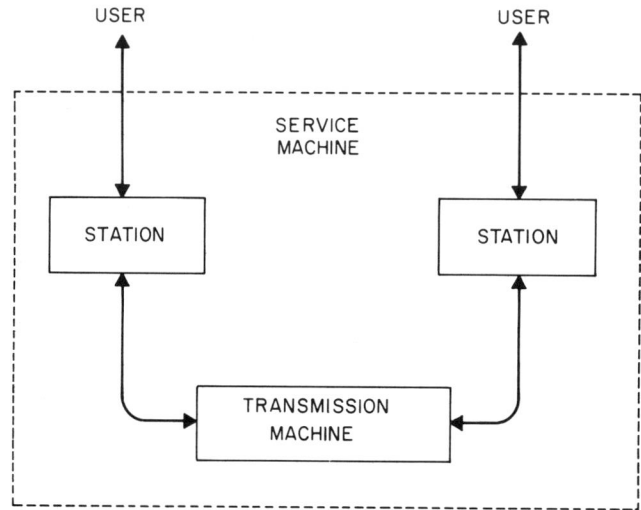

Figure 2. The internal structure of the service machine

This transmission machine is just another level of protocol. Thus we can see a hierarchy of abstract machines developing. In this *uses* hierarchy (following Parnas [Parnas 1978]), each protocol level makes use of the services provided by the lower level. Within each level, there is an *implementation* hierarchy where the service is logically implemented by the abstract protocol specification. The protocol is implemented in turn by an actual program. Thus for each protocol level N, the following information must be provided:

(a) a *service specification*, describing the services provided by the level to the users above, at level $N + 1$;

(b) a *protocol specification*, describing the interaction of the objects in this level in a precise way (assuming services provided by the level below, level $N - 1$); and

(c) a *program* implementing each station in the level (of course, the program may vary from station to station).

This characterization follows closely the model for open system interconnection being proposed by the International Standards Organization [Zimmerman 1980].

2. Protocol Verification

In the context of the model introduced in the previous subsection, we say that *protocol verification* is *a formal demonstration that the logical design of the protocol (the interaction of the stations within one layer) satisfies the service specification of that layer.*

Note that this will depend on the assumed properties (the service specification) of the layer below.

The ultimate task in protocol verification is to demonstrate that an actual program is a valid implementation of the protocol specification. That is, when one has reached a low enough level of abstraction in the specification, it is possible to take an actual program that purportedly implements the protocol, and show it is correct with respect to the specification. This is no different than traditional program verification.

In order to gain greater confidence that specifications are suitable for their intended use, it is useful to prove properties of a single specification. For example, we might want to show that the sequence of messages delivered is equal to the sequence of messages sent. Liveness properties such as eventual termination are also often proved for a single specification. We will discuss these issues at greater length in Section 3.6.

Thus we have three major types of protocol verification problems in each layer of a system:

(a) verification of the *protocol* against its *service*;

(b) verification of an *implementation* against the *protocol*; and

(c) verification of desired properties of the service, protocol, and program *independently*.

1.4 Related Work

To our knowledge, this work is the first combination of state transition machine, protocol, and axiomatic specification notions. However, a large body of work exists in each of these areas individually, and to a lesser extent to each pair.

A variety of methods have been used to specify communication protocols, including Petri nets (and related graph models), formal languages, sequencing expressions, I/O histories, and programming languages. However, the variations on state transition machine methods discussed in Section 1.1 seem to be most popular. Much of this work is either limited in expressive power (e.g., finite state automata) or lacking a solid theory and automated tools for verification. Sunshine [1982] provides a survey and comparison of this work.

In the area of abstract data types, a large body of work also exists [Guttag 1975; Guttag and Horning 1978b; Goguen, Thatcher and Wagner 1978, 1975; Loeckx 1980]. Usually state transition machine (or *abstract machine*) model approaches and axiomatic approaches are viewed as mutually exclusive alternatives [Guttag 1980; Berzins 1979; Liskov and Berzins 1979]. A number of state transition machine models have been proposed [Berzins 1979; Parnas 1972a; Robinson and Roubine 1977; Principato 1978; Razouk and Estrin 1980; Locasso, Scheid, Schorre and Eggert 1980]. Several variations of axiomatic methods have also been developed [Guttag, Horowitz and Musser 1978; Liskov and Zilles 1975; Goguen and Tardo 1979]. The notion of specifying state transition machines axiomatically seems relatively unexplored, although Flon and Misra [1979] hint at it.

We have drawn heavily on the following concepts:

(a) hierarchical layering and cooperating remote stations within a layer from the protocol domain [Sunshine 1979; Zimmerman 1980];

(b) verification of the properties of a specification [Guttag and Horning 1978b; Guttag 1980; Razouk and Estrin 1980; Overman 1977; Brand and Joyner 1978; Hailpern and Owicki 1980; Hailpern 1980; Parnas 1977]; and

(c) verification that a lower level system properly implements a higher level one [Principato 1978; Robinson and Levitt 1977; Guttag, Horowitz and Musser 1976; Good, Cohen and Keeton-Williams 1979]; or that the two systems are "behaviorally equivalent" [Berzins 1979; Subrahmanyan 1979].

Of course, we have had to adapt these concepts to the new environment resulting from the merger of protocol, state transition machine, and axiomatic specification concerns.

2. AN OVERVIEW OF OUR METHOD OF PROTOCOL SPECIFICATION AND VERIFICATION

Our method of specifying and verifying protocols can be summarized as follows.

1. Produce a *service specification*. If a state transition machine description of the service already exists, translate it into an AFFIRM representation. Otherwise, directly state the service specification as a state transition specification in AFFIRM.

2. Validate that the service specification at least partially meets the requirements of the user (either the ultimate user or another layer). Typically this involves proving some *invariant properties* of the specification, e.g., what gets sent by the user at one station gets delivered to the user at the other station in the same order it was sent.

3. Produce the *protocol specification*. Again, if a state transition machine representation exists, simply translate it into an AFFIRM representation.

4. Verify that the protocol specification implements the service specification. This is a two-step process.

    (a) First, define a correspondence (a *rep* function) between the state variables and events of the two specifications.

    (b) Then show that the *axioms* of the service specification, when reformulated using the corresponding data structures of the protocol specification, are *theorems* provable from the axioms of the protocol specification.

    A further validation involves independently stating the service requirements in terms of the state variables of the *protocol* specification, and then proving that the protocol specification satisfies these requirements.

5. Specify an algorithm implementing the protocol specification.
6. Verify that the algorithm implements the protocol.

Sections 3-5 discuss these steps in some detail. Figure 3 displays the relationship of the elements involved in protocol specification and verification.

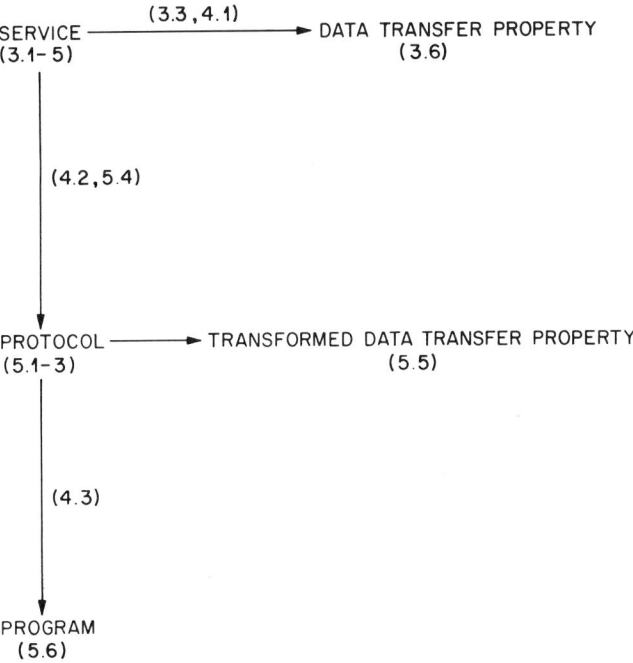

Figure 3. The steps in protocol verification. The references "(3.1)" are to relevant sections of this paper. Vertical lines mean *implemented by*; horizontal lines mean *invariant of*.

3. A SERVICE SPECIFICATION FOR A SIMPLE MESSAGE SYSTEM

Perhaps the simplest data transfer service provides for transmission of one message at a time from a fixed *sender* to a fixed *receiver*. The sender must wait until the previous message is received before sending the next one. There is no possibility of message loss, duplication, or corruption.

The system is shown graphically in Fig. 1. The next section provides an informal English description of the state transition machine. We will show how it can be represented in AFFIRM in the following sections.

3.1 State Variables

There are only a few state variables, each performing a simple function. (Each state variable has an associated data type, as shown.)

State—ControlState: The current status of the service. This state variable simply cycles through the four values of the enumerated type *ControlState*. The four values of the type are *ReadyToSend*, *Sending*, *ReadyToReceive*, and *Acking* (Acknowledging). The state variable *State* is tested by most state transition functions as a general applicability test: the transition function will not change the state unless this variable has the appropriate value.

Sent—QueueOfMessage: The queue of messages that have been sent to the receiver. One of the properties to prove about this service is that the queue of messages sent equals the queue of messages received (except for possibly the very last message of the *Sent* queue, which may not have been received yet).

Received—QueueOfMessage: The queue of messages that have been received by the receiver.

Buffer—QueueOfMessage: The queue of messages that have been sent by the sender but not yet received by the receiver. This state variable represents the *channel* of a real protocol. In the current protocol, this queue is either empty, or has exactly one message in it, the one just sent (but, of course, we have to prove it, not just say it!).

The types of the state variables are assumed to be explicitly defined (e.g. type *ControlState*), or are assumed to have a standard definition (as is the case with type *QueueOfMessage*). Both Sent and Received may be viewed as "ghost" variables used for specification purposes. Their unbounded size causes no problems for AFFIRM due to the axiomatic nature of its specifications.

3.2 State Transitions

A few of the state transition functions would be requested by a user, while others would appear to the user to occur spontaneously. For example, the user would explicitly request the *UserSend* operation, but the *SendComplete* operation, intuitively corresponding to the event "message pops out of the channel at the receiver's end," would appear to be spontaneous to the user. These spontaneous transitions are included to explicitly model the *delay* involved in sending a message. We consider this to be an important aspect of the service.

InitializeService: Initializes the state variables. *Sent, Received*, and *Buffer* are all initialized to the empty queue, and *State* is initialized to *ReadyToSend*.

UserSend(message): Only applicable if *State* is *ReadyToSend*; otherwise, this operation is a no-op. Adds *message* to the *Sent* queue, adds *message* to *Buffer*, and sets *State* to *Sending*.

SendComplete: A spontaneous event (the user cannot directly request it). Applicable only if *State* is *Sending*, i.e., there is an outstanding *Send* operation to be completed. Sets *State* to *ReadyToReceive*.

UserReceive: Applicable only if *State* is *ReadyToReceive*. The message at the front of the *Buffer* queue is added to *Received*, indicating passage of the message to the user. *State* is then updated to *Acking*—an abstraction of the process of sending an acknowledgement to the sender, telling of the receipt of the message.

ReceiveComplete: A spontaneous event, corresponding to the event "sender receives acknowledgment of message receipt." Applicable only if *State* is *Acking*. A message is removed from *Buffer*, and *State* is updated to *ReadyToSend*, indicating the cycle is complete.

3.3 Behavior of the Simple Message System

The state machine starts by performing the *InitializeService* command. The system then repeatedly cycles through the four states *ReadyToSend*, *Sending*, *ReadyToReceive*, and *Acking*. Each of these four states has only two successor states: itself (when a command that is not applicable is issued, in which case there's no change), and the next in the cycle. (Of course, at any time the *InitialService* command can be reissued, in which case the machine is reset to its initial state.)

As the system cycles through the four states, it maintains an invariant: the sequence of messages sent equals the concatenation of the sequence of messages received and the single message currently being sent (if there is one).[2] This and similar properties are called *service requirements*. If the state transition machine is specified correctly, these properties should be straightforward to verify.

3.4 Converting State Transition Specifications to AFFIRM

The AFFIRM representation of a state transition machine is basically just a representation of the *state vector* of the state machine. Each state variable comprising one part of the machine's state vector becomes a selector function. Each state transition function (command) becomes a constructor. There are usually no extender functions in this scheme. The axioms simply state how each state variable is modified by each state transition function.

1. *State Transition Function* → *Constructor*

Each state transition function (command) of the state transition machine becomes a constructor of an AFFIRM type:

    state machine *SimpleMessageSystem*;

    declare s: SimpleMessageSystem;

---

2. Almost. We will discuss the correct formulation of this property later.

declare m: Message;

constructors
    InitializeService, UserSend(s, m), SendComplete(s),
        UserReceive(s), ReceiveComplete(s): SimpleMessageSystem;

Each constructor has as its range the type being defined. And each of the constructors (except the initialization function) is given a parameter of the type being defined. Intuitively, this parameter represents the entire state of the system. Thus state or event histories can be easily represented as compositions of the constructor functions. For example, the sequence of commands

   InitializeService; UserSend(m); SendComplete; UserReceive; ReceiveComplete

would simply be

   ReceiveComplete(UserReceive(SendComplete(UserSend (InitializeService, m))))

This particular sequence of state transitions represents one complete cycle of the machine.

2. *State Variable* → *Selector*

Each state variable of the state transition machine becomes a selector function in the AFFIRM specification. In the AFFIRM specification, each function will take a parameter of the type being defined. Thus each state variable is simply an extraction function of the state vector.

   selector State(s): ControlState;

   selectors Buffer(s), Sent(s), Received(s): QueueOfMessage;

Note that we have chosen to name one of the state variables "State" since it represents the major or control status of the machine (see Section 1.1).

3. *Transition Definition* → *Set of Axioms*

The preceding subsections paved the way by defining the domain and range information of the constructors and selectors. Now we must define their semantics. It will become quite clear why each function carries along the "state" parameter: it provides a natural way of describing a transition. We will demonstrate the method by writing the axioms for the state variable *Sent*. From Section 3.2, we know that the state variable *Sent* is modified by the *InitializeService* operation, possibly modified by the *UserSend* operation, and not modified by the remaining operations *SendComplete*, *UserReceive*, and *ReceiveComplete*.

SPECIFICATION/VERIFICATION OF COMMUNICATION PROTOCOLS

axioms
1. Sent(UserSend(state, message))
   -- **if** State(state) = ReadyToSend
   then Sent(state) Add m
   else Sent(state),
2. Sent(SendComplete(state)) -- Sent(state),
3. Sent(UserReceive(state)) -- Sent(state),
4. Sent(ReceiveComplete(state)) -- Sent(state),
5. Sent(InitializeService) -- NewQueueOfMessage;

Axioms 2, 3, and 4 simply state that the operations have no effect on the state variable. For example, axiom 2 says "the value of the state variable *Sent* after the *SendComplete* event is equal to its value before the event." Similarly, axiom 1 says "if the major state is *ReadyToSend*, then the operation *UserSend* will have an effect on the state variable *Sent*; otherwise it will not." This method of constructing a specification ensures that the specification will be *complete*—the effects of each command on each state variable are detailed.

3.5 The AFFIRM Representation

The following is a stylized representation of AFFIRM input, for the sake of readability. State transition functions that leave a state variable unchanged are not explicitly specified; the convention is "not specified, not modified." The actual AFFIRM input is displayed in Appendix I.

state machine *SimpleMessageSystem*;

declare s: SimpleMessageSystem;
declare m: Message;

constructors
   InitializeService, UserSend(s, m), SendComplete(s),
         UserReceive(s), ReceiveComplete(s);

selectors
   Buffer(s), Sent(s), Received(s): QueueOfMessage;

selector State(s): ControlState;

axioms {*InitializeService*}
   State(InitializeService) -- ReadyToSend,
   Buffer(InitializeService) -- NewQueueOfMessage,
   Sent(InitializeService) -- NewQueueOfMessage,
   Received(InitializeService) -- NewQueueOfMessage;

axioms {*UserSend*}
   State(UserSend(s, m)) -- **if** State(s) = ReadyToSend
                              then Sending
                              else State(s),

```
Buffer(UserSend(s, m)) = = if State(s) = ReadyToSend
                                then Buffer(s) Add m
                                else Buffer(s),
Sent(UserSend(s, m)) = = if State(s) = ReadyToSend
                              then Sent(s) Add m
                              else Sent(s);

axioms {SendComplete}
    State(SendComplete(s)) = = if State(s) = Sending
                                    then ReadyToReceive
                                    else State(s);

axioms {UserReceive}
    State(UserReceive(s)) = = if State(s) = ReadyToReceive
                                   then Acking
                                   else State(s),
    Received(UserReceive(s)) = = if State(s) = ReadyToReceive
                                       then Received(s) Add Front(Buffer(s))
                                       else Received(s);

axioms {ReceiveComplete}
    State(ReceiveComplete(s)) = = if State(s) = Acking
                                       then ReadyToSend
                                       else State(s),
    Buffer(ReceiveComplete(s)) = = if State(s) = Acking
                                         then Remove(Buffer(s))
                                         else Buffer(s);

end {SimpleMessageSystem};
```

3.6 Properties of a Specification

To increase our confidence that the state transition machine we have specified is a reasonable one, we can formulate certain properties we expect to hold during the machine's operation. These service requirements may be proved using structural induction as described in Section 1.2. We present an example of such *service requirements* for the simple data transfer service.

A useful safety property for this service might be

   Sent = Received join *Transit*

stating that the messages received are equal to the messages sent except for any still in transit. We must be a little careful in our definition of *Transit* to take into account the state *Acking* when the message is still in *Buffer*, but has been received.

The exact theorem in AFFIRM would be

   theorem *DataTransferService*, all s (Sent(s) = Received(s) join Transits(s));

   define Transit(s) = = **if** State(s) = Acking

SPECIFICATION/VERIFICATION OF COMMUNICATION PROTOCOLS

> **then** NewQueueOfMessage
> **else** Buffer(s);

This theorem has been proved in AFFIRM.

Another form of the service requirement might be

$$(State(s) = ReadyToSend) \supset (Sent(s) = Received(s))$$

stating that input exactly equals output whenever the system returns to its "idle" state. This turns out to be a special case of the more general theorem above.

Liveness properties for this simple machine are relatively trivial. It is fairly obvious that the allowed progression of states involves a single fixed cycle (ignoring rejected operations having no effects), where a single message is transferred on each cycle. First, formalize the meaning of "ignore rejected operations" as follows:

> **interface** StripNoOps(s): SimpleMessageSystem;
>
> **axioms**
> StripNoOps(InitializeService) = = InitializeService,
> StripNoOps(UserSend(s, m)) = = **if** State(s) = ReadyToSend
>   **then** UserSend(StripNoOps(s), m)
>   **else** StripNoOps(s),
> StripNoOps(SendComplete(s)) = = **if** State(s) = Sending
>   **then** SendComplete(StripNoOps(s))
>   **else** StripNoOps(s),
> StripNoOps(UserReceive(s)) = = **if** State(s) = ReadyToReceive
>   **then** UserReceive(StripNoOps(s))
>   **else** StripNoOps(s),
> StripNoOps(ReceiveComplete(s)) = = **if** State(s) = Acking
>   **then** ReceiveComplete(StripNoOps(s))
>   **else** StripNoOps(s);
>
> **theorem** *StatesMatch*, all s (State(s) = State(StripNoOps(s))
>   and Sent(s) = Sent(StripNoOps(s))
>   and Received(s) = Received(StripNoOps(s))
>   and Buffer(s) = Buffer(StripNoOps(s)));

The definition of *StripNoOps* simply formalizes our intuition about events having no effect because they occur at an inappropriate time. For example, a *SendComplete* event after a *UserReceive* event can have no effect. The theorem *StatesMatch* says that the *effects* of a sequence of events is the same as the effects of a new sequence that has had the no-effect operations filtered out. This theorem was proved in AFFIRM.

In the context of the above definitions, then, the following theorem says that the four operations, in the right order, add a message (and the correct one) to those received, no matter how many additional "rejected" operations may have been interleaved:

theorem *Service Progress*,
   all s1, s2, m (StripNoOps(s2)
                    = ReceiveComplete(UserReceive
                    (SendComplete(UserSend
                    (StripNoOps(s1), m))))
              and State(s1) = ReadyToSend
        imp   State(s2) = ReadyToSend
              and Sent(s2) = Sent(s1) Add m
              and Received(s2) = Received(s1) Add m);

This theorem has also been proved using AFFIRM.

Finally we note that the system will progress around this cycle so long as each operation completes in finite time. This is an assumption at the service level but, of course, must be proved when we see how the protocol implements each operation.

3.7 Alternative Notations

Instead of *implicitly* representing the machine's state vector, we could have represented it *explicitly*, by defining *one* constructor, say *Const*. *Const* takes a number of parameters (one per individual state variable), and creates one state vector out of them:

    constructor *Const*(state, sent, received, buffer): SimpleMessageSystem;

The individual state variables are then defined as *vector-extractors*:

    State(*Const*(state, sent, received, buffer)) = = state;
    Sent(*Const*(state, sent, received, buffer)) = = sent,
    Received(*Const*(state, sent, received, buffer)) = = received,
    Buffer(*Const*(state, sent, received, buffer)) = = buffer;

and the state transition functions, nominally constructors, would become *extenders*:

    UserSend(*Const*(state, sent, received, buffer), message)
        = = **if** state = ReadyToSend
                then *Const*(Sending, sent Add message, received, buffer Add message)
                else {no change} *Const*(state, sent, received, buffer),

    SendComplete(*Const*(state, sent, received, buffer))
        = = **if** state = Sending
                then *Const*(ReadyToReceive, sent, received, buffer)
                else {no change} *Const*(state, sent, received, buffer),

    UserReceive(*Const*(state, sent, received, buffer))
        = = **if** state = ReadyToReceive
                then *Const*(Acking, sent, received Add Front (buffer), buffer)
                else {no change} *Const*(state, sent, received, buffer),

    ReceiveComplete(*Const*(state, sent, received, buffer)) = =

```
        if state = Acking
            then Const(ReadyToSend, sent, received, Remove (buffer))
            else {no change} Const(state, sent, received, buffer),

InitializeService = = Const(ReadyToSend, NewQueueOfMessage,
                      NewQueueOfMessage, NewQueueOfMessage);
```

This notation often results in fewer axioms overall, but each axiom is usually much more complex than those of the notation we described above. This is especially true when one state has a large set of successor states. We have chosen the first notational method for expressing state vectors in AFFIRM because of its convenience. The axioms, with a bit of practice, are generally more understandable because each is relatively simple.

4. VERIFICATION ISSUES

As mentioned in Section 1, ideally we would like to verify three kinds of properties of a specification: *safety* (only correct things happen), *liveness* (eventually something happens), and *performance* (things happen promptly).

Safety properties are typically proved by structural induction (as was described in Section 1.2). Most of our work has focused on this concern.

Liveness properties may be handled by showing the system terminates:

1. some operation is always *enabled*, or the system has reached one of its final states; and

2. each operation decreases some bounded measure function, which at some point (nominally, when it evaluates to zero) *disables* all operations (for example, by setting a special state variable to **false**; presumably all the operations are applicable only if the variable is *true*).

This issue is discussed at length in [Berthomieu 1981]. Temporal logic also provides convenient techniques for stating and proving liveness properties [Hailpern and Owicki 1980; Owicki and Lamport 1980]. We deal only briefly with liveness properties in this paper.

Performance properties have traditionally been dealt with by other methods (e.g., queuing theory); we have not addressed this issue.

4.1 Verifying Properties of a Specification

As noted in Section 1.2, one of the main capabilities of AFFIRM is the ability to verify that a data type has certain desired properties. These properties are specified as theorems and are then proved using the interactive theorem prover of AFFIRM.

Typically these theorems are invariants in the state transition model. That is, they are predicates on the state that are **true** in the initial state, and are preserved across all state transitions. In AFFIRM, these theorems are proved from the axioms of the type being specified (and other predefined types) by structural induction. In the context of the simple message system of the preceding chapter, to prove a theorem $\mathbf{P}(s)$ for all states s, first prove the theorem $\mathbf{P}(\textit{InitializeService})$; then, assuming $\mathbf{P}(s)$ for some state s, prove $\mathbf{P}(\textit{fcn}(s))$ for each constructor *fcn* in the type. This suffices to show $\mathbf{P}(s)$ for all s.

It is also overkill. What is proved is that *any* order of occurrence of the events of the state transition machine is acceptable; the invariant still holds. Carrying out such a proof requires a "ruggedized" machine that has extra tests to make sure that operations invoked at inappropriate times can do no harm: no state change occurs. Real protocols have assumptions about which operations can happen when. It is unlikely, for example, that a time-out can occur if there are no messages that have been sent but not yet acknowledged. Hence proving properties of a program that uses an abstract machine in a certain way may be easier (and allow a simpler machine specification) than proving properties of the machine for arbitrary programs.

4.2 Verifying the Protocol Against the Service Specification

We must show that the detailed system made of stations interacting according to the protocol "does the same thing" as the abstract system specified by the service (see Section 1.3).

This brings us to the problem of what it means for one abstract machine (or set of machines) to *implement* another. There are two aspects of this relationship:

1. a *static* correspondence between each state of the higher level and the state(s) implementing it at the lower level, showing that every higher-level state is in fact implemented; and

2. a *dynamic* correspondence between the transitions of the two levels, showing that the sequences of states reachable in the two levels are the same.

Point 1 is typically handled by giving a representation function *rep* from the state variables of the lower level to the state variables of the higher level. The function is specifically defined in this direction because there may be *several* lower-level states that all represent the same higher-level state (so the function has no inverse). Also, some lower-level states may be *intermediate* states that do not represent any higher-level state. As noted above, it must be shown that there is some lower-level state to represent every higher-level state.

To address point 2, the conventional approach involves specifying a fixed sequence of lower-level operations implementing each higher-level operation. Then it must be proved that if the two systems start in corresponding states, they will end up in corresponding states after corresponding operations.

Let S and s be higher- and lower-level states, respectively. Let *OP* be a higher-level operation and *op* be its lower-level implementation, and let *rep* be a representation function (from s to S). Then this method attempts to show that for each *OP*

$$\forall\ S, s\ (S = \textit{rep}(s) \supset \textit{OP}(S) = \textit{rep}(\textit{op}(s))).$$

The difficulty of this approach in the protocol domain is that a higher-level operation such as sending a message may be accomplished by a *nondeterministic sequence* of lower-level operations, including transmission, loss, time-outs, retransmissions, and receptions. Typically there will be a single low-level operation that starts the accomplishment of the higher-level operation by "posting" some work to be done. This will then be followed by a nondeterministic series of lower-level operations, invisible at the top level, that complete the results of the higher-level operation in the unreliable low-level environment. These latter effects may be viewed as one or more spontaneous transitions of the higher-level machine. Section 5 gives an example of this sort.

In this type of lower-level specification, there are two sorts of operations: one set invoked directly by the users of the system (corresponding to the higher-level operations), and a second set of *internal* operations.

Verification of this type of lower-level specification is similar to the conventional situation discussed above, but must be augmented by a proof that the spontaneous higher-level transitions (and *only* such transitions) are accomplished by the internal operations in a "ruggedized" fashion that includes tests in their definitions to force them to produce no changes if invoked at inappropriate times. The additional theorems to be proved take the following form: from any low-level state corresponding to a higher-level state with spontaneous transitions, the next lower-level state that "maps up" and can be reached by *any* sequence of internal lower-level operations must correspond to the correct higher-level state. We can define this recursively as follows:

$\forall\ S$ such that S has one or more spontaneous transitions
   ($\forall\ s$ such that $S = rep(s)$
      (SpontSucc$(S) = rep($UpSuccessors$(s,S))))$

where *rep* is extended in the natural manner to sets

SpontSucc(S) is the set of states reached from
   S by spontaneous transitions
UpSuccessors$(s,S) =$
   $\{s2$: Successor$(s, s2)$ and MapsUp$(s2)$ and $S \neq rep(s2)\}$
                              $\cup$ UpSuccessors$(s3, S)$
   $\forall\ s3$: Successor$(s, s3)$ and $\sim$MapsUp$(s3)$
Successor$(s1, s2) = \exists\ internalOp$ such that $(s2 = internalOp(s1))$
MapsUp$(s) =$ **true** if s represents some high-level state

This general formulation often simplifies considerably, as shown in the example in Section 5.

4.3 Verifying a Program Against the Protocol Specification

If we followed the pattern of the lower-level (protocol) and higher-level (service) specifications discussed above, each operation of the protocol specification would be implemented by a separate Pascal procedure.

However, an actual implementation of a protocol is somewhat more constrained.

A state transition machine defines a global state and specifies how transitions change the state variables. Since the purpose of protocols is to provide for communication between disjoint processes, an actual implementation will be divided into cooperating stations (as described in Section 1.3); only the state variables describing the communications medium will be shared between stations.

Since losses are a spontaneous behavior of the medium, they are not implemented in either station.

While it was convenient for our specification to allow operations to be invoked in any order, only certain sequences of operations are efficient. (For example, it makes little sense for the sender to retransmit without first checking for acknowledgments.) Hence, the programs typically exhibit only a subset of the allowable behavior (it is hoped that only inefficient event sequences have been omitted).

Of course, many properties of states proved at higher levels may be transferred down to programs. However, the constraints introduced by the program may require *additional* proofs for liveness, e.g., the constraints do not introduce deadlock.

5. DETAILED EXAMPLE: THE ALTERNATING BIT PROTOCOL

We will continue the exposition of our methodology, using the alternating bit protocol as an example. First we will specify a protocol providing the simple data transfer service described earlier. We will then perform the various verification tasks.

5.1 A Brief Description of the Protocol

The alternating bit protocol [Brand and Joyner 1978; Hailpern and Owicki 1980; Bartlett, Scantlebury and Wilkinson 1969; Bochmann and Gecsei 1977; Hajek 1978] is intended to provide a simple but reliable message transfer service over an unreliable transmission medium. It attaches a one-bit sequence number to each message sent, and waits for an acknowledgment of the receipt of the message by the destination. The sequence number is complemented on each new message sent—hence the name of the protocol. If the acknowledgment is not received within a time-out period, the message is retransmitted (with the sequence number unchanged). The protocol guarantees correctly sequenced delivery of messages even if the medium loses messages and acknowledgments, but the medium cannot *reorder* messages.

To accomplish these functions, the sender and receiver stations maintain local sequence number counters. The sender uses its counter to remember the sequence number to attach to the next transmission. The receiver uses its counter to remember the sequence number of the next message it *expects* to receive, thus allowing for the removal of duplicate messages (which will be sent if an acknowledgment is lost).

The alternating bit protocol is a simple instance of a general class of data transfer protocols using *positive acknowledgments* and *retransmission on errors* [Sunshine 1975; Stenning 1976; Kroghdal 1978]. This simple example allows only one unacknowledged message to be transmitted at a time. More complex protocols in this class use larger sequence numbers and allow multiple outstanding messages.

In Section 5.2 we provide an informal definition of a state transition machine for the alternating bit protocol, and in Section 5.3 this specification is translated into an AFFIRM representation. We then discuss the major verification step, showing that the protocol implements its service correctly. We will then discuss an important invariant of the protocol specification (independent of the service). Finally we give algorithms for the sender and receiver stations, and show that these algorithms properly implement the protocol.

5.2 A State Transition Machine for the Alternating Bit Protocol

The protocol machine described in this section closely parallels the service machine described in Section 3, with the addition of details concerning the internal operation of the protocol. The protocol is defined as a single machine rather than as separate sender and receiver components (see Section 7.1). Figure 4 illustrates the main data structures and operations of the protocol.

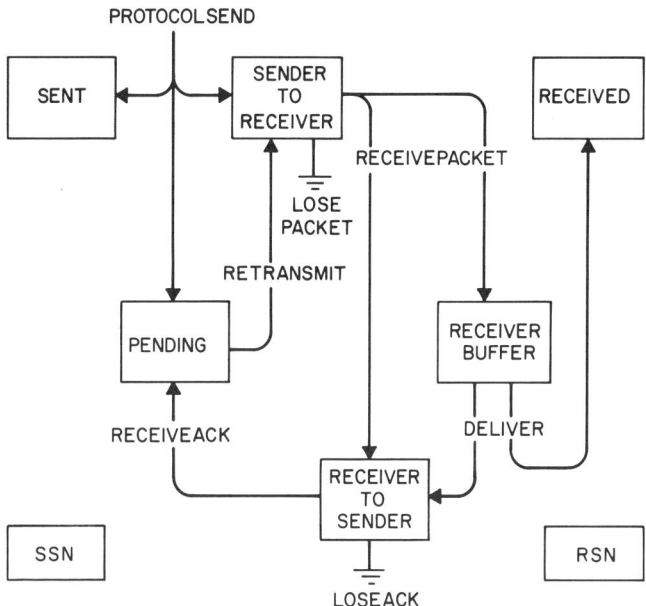

Figure 4. The protocol state transition machine

1. *Data Types Used in the Specification*

The protocol uses a few more data types than the service specification does. Their informal descriptions are gathered here for convenience.

Message: As in the service specification, this type is a minimally defined data type that represents abstract contents.

Bit: An enumerated type with two elements, arbitrarily called *on* and *off*. Functions include a "flip" operation that flips the value (from *on* to *off* or vice versa), represented by the unary *not* operator "~".

Packet: A record (or tuple) with two components: a value of type *Bit* (i.e., a sequence number) and a value of type *Message*.

Medium: Really a *QueueOfPacket* with the addition of operations to "lose" packets. Further enhancements (e.g., to allow the reordering of packets) might be desired in a more realistic medium. The *channels* of the protocol are of this type. The *Transmit* operation takes a value of type *Medium*. Intuitively, it is equivalent to the *Add* operation of the Queue type. Similarly, *Receive* corresponds to the *Queue* operation *Remove*.

QueueOfPacket, *QueueOfMessage*, *SequenceOfMessage*: Standard data types from the AFFIRM Type Library.

2. *State Variables*

SenderToReceiver—Medium: The channel from the sender to the receiver.

ReceiverToSender—Medium: The channel from the receiver to the sender. For convenience, entire packets are returned as acknowledgments, rather than just the sequence numbers.

Pending—QueueOfPacket: The packet currently being transmitted, if any. *Pending* is either empty (i.e., *NewQueueOfPacket*), or contains exactly one packet. A *queue* type was used instead of a simple packet in order to avoid notions of a null packet, and to allow future extensions.

SSN—Bit: The sender's current sequence number (i.e., the next acknowledgment of interest).

RSN—Bit: The receiver's current sequence number (i.e., the number of the next packet expected).

ReceiverBuffer—QueueOfPacket: The packet received but not yet delivered to the user (if any). *ReceiverBuffer* is either empty, or has exactly one element. A *queue* type was used for convenience.

Sent—SequenceOfMessage: A sequence of all the messages sent but not necessarily acknowledged yet. (This variable would not be present in a real implementation; it is for specification purposes.)

Received—SequenceOfMessage: A sequence of all the messages successfully received. (This variable would not be present in a real implementation; it is for specification purposes.)

Of course, not all these data structures are visible or available to both stations (sender and receiver).

3. State Transition Functions

IntializeProtocol: Set the counters and the queues to their initial values.

ProtocolSend(m): Given a message *m*, try to send the message as a packet. If no message is waiting to be acknowledged (*Pending* = *NewQueueOfPacket*) then accept the message *m* (by appending it to *Sent*) and transmit it (by constructing a packet with the current *SSN* and adding the packet to *SenderToReceiver*). Also remember that the packet is waiting to be acknowledged (by putting it in *Pending*).

ReceivePacket: Receive a packet, if one is available. If *SenderToReceiver* is nonempty, remove and examine the first packet. If it is the one expected (its sequence number matches *RSN*), then place it in *ReceiverBuffer* and flip *RSN*. If the packet has *already* been delivered, then send an acknowledgment by copying the packet to *ReceiverToSender*.

Deliver: Deliver a new message (if there is one to be delivered) to the user. If a message is available in *ReceiverBuffer*, append it to the *Received* queue, and acknowledge the message (by copying it to *ReceiverToSender*). Clear *ReceiverBuffer*.

ReceiveAck: Receive an acknowledgment, if any exist to be received. If *ReceiverToSender* is not empty, then remove the first packet. If the packet's sequence number does not match *SSN*, then just ignore the packet. Otherwise, flip *SSN* and empty *Pending* (preparing for another *Send* operation).

Retransmit: Add the message in *Pending*, if any, to *SenderToReceiver*, i.e., resend it.

LosePacket: Lose a packet by removing the front packet from *SenderToReceiver*, if it is not empty.

LoseAck: Lose an acknowledgment by removing the front of *ReceiverToSender*, if it is not empty.

As an example, a typical state of the system might be

ReceiveAck(Deliver(ReceivePacket(ProtocolSend(IntitializeProtocol,m))))

which represents the sequence of operations (reversed from their functional representation)

InitializeProtocol; ProtocolSend(m); ReceivePacket; Deliver; ReceiveAck

5.3 The AFFIRM Representation

As was the case with the service specification, we simply turn state variables into selector functions of a data type; state transition functions (commands) become constructors. The definitions of the state transition functions become axioms. All the functions in the AFFIRM representation carry along an explicit parameter of the type being defined; this is intuitively a characterization of the current state.

What is displayed here is a stylized version of the axioms, omitting all axioms stating that some selector is not modified by some constructor. Appendix II contains the actual AFFIRM input.

state machine *ABProtocol*;

declare s: ABProtocol;
declare m: Message;

constructors
    InitializeProtocol, ProtocolSend(s, m), ReceivePacket(s), Deliver(s), Receive Ack(s), Retransmit(s), LoseAck(s), LosePacket(s);

selectors
    InitialSequenceNumber, RSN(s), SSN(s): Bit;

selectors
    ReceiverToSender(s), SenderToReceiver(s): Medium;

selectors
    Received(s), Sent(s): QueueOfMessage;

selectors
    Pending(s), ReceiverBuffer(s): QueueOfPacket;

axioms {*InitializeProtocol*:}
    Pending(InitializeProtocol) = = NewQueueOfPacket,
    Received(InitializeProtocol) = = NewQueueOfMessage,
    ReceiverBuffer(InitializeProtocol) = = NewQueueOfPacket,
    ReceiverToSender(InitializeProtocol) = = InitializeMedium,
    RSN(InitializeProtocol) = = InitialSequenceNumber,
    SenderToReceiver(InitializeProtocol) = = InitializeMedium,
    Sent(InitializeProtocol) = = NewQueueOfMessage,
    SSN(InitializeProtocol) = = InitialSequenceNumber;

axioms {*ProtocolSend*:}
    Pending(ProtocolSend(s, m)) = = **if** Pending(s) = NewQueueOfPacket
                                  then NewQueueOfPacket Add
                                                MakePacket(m, SSN(s))
                                  else Pending(s),
    SenderToReceiver(ProtocolSend(s, m)) = = **if** Pending(s) = NewQueueOfPacket
                                              then Transmit(SenderToReceiver(s),
                                                    MakePacket(m, SSN(s)))
                                            else SenderToReceiver(s),
    Sent(ProtocolSend(s, m)) = = **if** Pending(s) = NewQueueOfPacket
                                  then Sent(s) Add m
                                  else Sent(s);

axioms {*ReceivePacket*:}
    ReceiverBuffer(ReceivePacket(s)) = = **if** Seq(Front(SenderToReceiver(s))) =
                                              RSN(s) and SenderToReceiver(s)

SPECIFICATION/VERIFICATION OF COMMUNICATION PROTOCOLS 329

$\sim$ = InitializeMedium
then NewQueueOfPacket Add
Front(SenderToReceiver(s))
else Receiver Buffer(s),
ReceiverToSender(ReceivePacket(s)) = = if SenderToReceiver(s) $\sim$ =
InitializeMedium and ReceiverBuffer(s) =
NewQueueOfPacket
and RSN(s) $\sim$ = Seq(Front(SenderToReceiver(s)))
then Transmit(ReceiverToSender(s),
Front(SenderToReceiver(s)))
else ReceiverToSender(s),
RSN(ReceivePacket(s)) = = if Seq(Front(SenderToReceiver(s))) = RSN(s)
and SenderToReceiver(s) $\sim$ = InitializeMedium
then $\sim$RSN(s)
else RSN(s),
SenderToReceiver(ReceivePacket(s)) = = Receive(SenderToReceiver(s));

axioms {*Deliver*:}
Received(Deliver(s)) = = if ReceiverBuffer(s) = NewQueueOfPacket
then Received(s)
else Received(s) Add Text(Front(ReceiverBuffer(s))),
ReceiverBuffer(Deliver(s)) = = NewQueueOfPacket,
ReceiverToSender(Deliver(s)) = = if ReceiverBuffer(s) = NewQueueOfPacket
then ReceiverToSender(s)
else Transmit(ReceiverToSender(s),
Front(ReceiverBuffer(s))));

axioms {*ReceiveAck*:}
Pending(ReceiveAck(s)) = = if Seq(Front(ReceiverToSender(s))) = SSN(s)
and ReceiverToSender(s) $\sim$ = InitializeMedium
then NewQueueOfPacket
else Pending(s),
ReceiverToSender(ReceiveAck(s)) = = Receive(ReceiverToSender(s)),
SSN(ReceiveAck(s)) = = if Seq (Front(ReceiverToSender(s))) = SSN(s)
and ReceiverToSender(s) $\sim$ = InitializeMedium
then $\sim$SSN(s)
else SSN(s);

axiom {*Retransmit*:}
SenderToReceiver(Retransmit(s)) = = if Pending(s) = NewQueueOfPacket
then SenderToReceiver(s)
else Transmit(SenderToReceiver(s),
Front(Pending(s)));

axiom {*LoseAck*:}
ReceiverToSender(LoseAck(s)) = = Receive(ReceiverToSender(s));

axiom {*LosePacket*:}
SenderToReceiver(LosePacket(s)) = = Receive(SenderToReceiver(s));

end {*ABProtocol*};

5.4 Verifying the Protocol Against the Service Specification

This section presents a detailed example of how to verify that a lower-level state transition machine specification implements a higher-level one. In this case the system in question is the alternating bit protocol, and the two levels are the service (higher) and protocol (lower) specifications.

1. *Safety*

The service specification (see Section 3.5) includes *UserSend* and *UserReceive* operations, and an *InitializeService* operation to initialize the system, all meant to be invoked by the users of the service. It also includes spontaneous transitions *SendComplete* and *ReceiveComplete*, modeling the completion of the *UserSend* and *UserReceive* operations within the distributed system providing the service. Hence there are four control states at the service level, as shown in Figure 1, with the two intermediate states explicitly displaying the delay between one user initiating an operation and the other user becoming aware of it. The state variables used at this level include a buffer *Buffer* for messages sent but not yet received (at most one is allowed), and queues *Sent* and *Received* that maintain histories of all messages sent and received (these are only used for specification purposes). There is also a control state variable *State* with four possible values.

The protocol level (see Section 5.3) has operations corresponding to each of the user operations at the service level:

$$\begin{aligned}
InitializeService &\longrightarrow InitializeProtocol \\
UserSend &\longrightarrow ProtocolSend \\
UserReceive &\longrightarrow Deliver.
\end{aligned}$$

There is also a second set of protocol operations that collectively accomplish the spontaneous operations of the service level. These are *ReceivePacket, ReceiveAck, LosePacket, LoseAck,* and *Retransmit*. The service-level state variables *Sent* and *Received* are implemented transparently, while *Buffer* is implemented as the text of the first packet in the queue of packets called *Pending*. The service-level control states (*ReadyToSend, Sending, ReadyToReceive,* and *Acking*) correspond to four defined state classes at the protocol level (*S1, S2, S3,* and *S4*). Figure 5 summarizes these correspondences informally.

Our method of proving that a protocol implements its service specification is to convert each of the service-level *axioms* into a *theorem* at the protocol level, and then to prove these theorems using the protocol specification. This

SPECIFICATION/VERIFICATION OF COMMUNICATION PROTOCOLS

Service	Protocol
InitializeService	*InitializeProtocol*
Sent	*Sent*
Received	*Received*
Buffer	*Text(Front(Pending))*
State	
ReadyToSend	*S1*
Sending	*S2*
ReadyToReceive	*S3*
Acking	*S4*
UserSend	*ProtocolSend*
UserReceive	*Deliver*
SendComplete *ReceiveComplete*	any sequence of the operations {*ReceivePacket, ReceiveAck, Retransmit, LosePacket, LoseAck*}

Figure 5. The correspondence between service and protocol level state variables

follows the method of [Guttag, Horowitz and Musser 1978]. Appendix III.1 shows the formal correspondence between functions at the two levels using a representation function *rep*, and Appendix III.2 defines the protocol-level state classes. The basic method is to replace each occurrence of the service machine state in the axioms of the service specification by the *rep* of its corresponding protocol states, and then to use the other rewrite rules displayed in Appendix III.1 until the expression is reduced to terms involving only protocol-level selectors and constructors.

[*material deleted*]

2. Liveness

In order to deal with liveness concerns, we must show that the implementation for each service-level operation terminates. This is trivial for the user operations, since each is directly implemented by a single protocol operation *assumed* to terminate.

The difficulty comes with the so-called spontaneous operations. We must show that a finite sequence of internal protocol operations serves to accomplish the desired effect. Considering the *SendComplete* operation as an example, an argument of the following sort is necessary.

1. In (protocol) state *S2* (corresponding to service state *Sending*), the *Retransmit* operation is enabled and may place an arbitrary number of packets in the *SenderToReceive* medium.

2. In state *S2*, if one of these packets reaches the receiver, the *ReceivePacket* operation will achieve the desired effects of *SendComplete* (i.e., change the state of *S3*, corresponding to *ReadyToReceive*).

3. If a large enough (but finite) number of packets are transmitted by the sender, one will reach the receiver.

These three points taken together imply that a finite number of protocol internal operations will accomplish the *SendComplete* service operation. Points 1 and 2 follow directly from the axioms for *Retransmit* and *ReceivePacket*. Point 3, however, requires an additional constraint on the simple medium: the number of packets that may be lost is bounded. As yet, there is no convenient method for expressing such eventual delivery constraints in AFFIRM. Our liveness arguments must therefore remain informal. Berthomieu [1981]; Hailpern and Owicki [1980]; Hailpern [1980]; Schwartz and Melliar-Smith [1981] deal with these concerns.

5.5 Protocol Properties and Invariants

As stated in Section 1.3, the essential verification of a protocol involves showing that it meets its service specification. However, it is also possible to prove properties of the protocol specification itself, independently of any service specification. In particular, a state invariant similar to the service requirements discussed in Section 3.6 is worth some discussion. Proving the invariant gives added confidence that the protocol specification is correct.

The system invariant for the alternating bit protocol is the theorem

theorem *MainSystemInvariant*, all s (InS1(s) or InS2(s) or InS3(s) or InS4(s));

This states that the protocol-level system is always in one of the four valid state classes of the protocol. We also note that by the definition of protocol state *S1* (in Appendix III.2),

InS1(s) ⊃ (Sent(s) = Received(s))

which is a protocol-level version of the service requirement.

The system invariant has been proved. The proof makes use of the theorems of Appendix III.6. Those theorems essentially detail how the state changes for each possible event. Most say that no change occurs. As with most abstract data types, much of the difficulty with this proof lies in developing a suitable invariant. We experimented with several versions of the protocol axioms and state class definitions before developing the present form.

5.6 Implementation

Having specified the alternating bit protocol and proven that it has some desired properties, we must provide an implementation which meets these specifications. (See Section 4.3 for a general discussion.) Our implementation (in Appendix IV) has two stations:

1. **Sender** contains procedures *ProtocolSend, SenderTimeout*, and *InitSender*; and

2. **Receiver** contains *ReceivePacket, Deliver*, and *InitReceiver*.

They share the medium variables *SenderToReceiver* and *ReceiverToSender*. Since both stations have local variables, we need two initialization routines. All other procedures correspond to the similarly named events in the protocol specification, except for *SenderTimeout*. It combines the *Retransmit* and *ReceiveAck* events. Like the events of the specification, all procedures have no effect on the system if they are called at an inappropriate time.

Program variables correspond to state variables of the specification. Each procedure has an assertion of the form

VariablesMatch(s, . . vars . .) imp VariablesMatch(event(s), . . new vars . .)

In other words, for the state *s* that corresponds to the *initial* values of the program variables, the state resulting from the listed event will correspond to the variables *after* the routine finishes (see Section 4.4). For example, the assertion *DPost* (Appendix IV.3) says "given any state *s* whose selectors *Sent, ReceiverBuffer*, and *ReceiverToSender* match the corresponding receiver variables, the new state resulting from a *Deliver(s)* event will have selectors that correspond to the values of the variables after *Deliver* is executed." *PSPost* (the assertion for *ProtocolSend*) adds one more stipulation: *ProtocolSend* sets a bit to inform its caller of whether it had any effect.

The partial correctness of all these procedures has been proven using AFFIRM. The proofs were quite straightforward, using only one lemma about the data type definitions and one lemma about the protocol specification:

> **theorem** *SeqMatch*(med, bit) imp ($\sim$Seqmatch(med, $\sim$bit))
> and med $\sim$ = NewQueueOfPacket;

> **theorem** *PendingInvariant*, Remove(Pending(s))
> = NewQueueOfPacket;

Theorem *PendingInvariant* states that *Pending* contains no more than one packet. This was easily proven from the axioms without reference to any other protocol invariants.

Since the implementation is in keeping with the specification, its *safety* follows from the earlier proof (in Section 5.4). *Liveness* has not been formally proven for either level. Any liveness proof must consider that the implementation does not exercise the full range of event sequences possible under the specification. (For example, *Retransmit* is always preceded by *ReceiveAck*.) Informally, it may be seen that only ineffective sequences have been excluded, so progress will not be impeded.

6. FURTHER APPLICATIONS

This section briefly mentions some further work we have accomplished in applying our methodology to several more complex protocols.

6.1 Stenning's Data Transfer Protocol

The protocol described in Stenning [1976] ignores the aspects involved in connection establishment, and instead emphasizes the data transfer aspects. It is designed to operate correctly even though the channel may lose, duplicate, or reorder packets in transit. It is a generalization of the alternating bit protocol as discussed in Section 5.1, since it allows several messages to be in transit at once.

Stenning defined two processes: a *transmitter* and a *receiver*. The transmitter sends messages from a given sequence of messages to the receiver, using a communication line. The receiver in turn accepts messages from the line, stores them in an output sequence, and acknowledges their receipt by sending a message to the transmitter via another communication line. The communication lines are unreliable; hence messages traveling in either direction can be lost, reordered, corrupted, or duplicated. Given such an environment, the protocol is supposed to ensure correct delivery of the messages.

The protocol uses a conventional positive-acknowledgment, retransmission-on-time-out technique, and the receiver and transmitter both maintain windows of messages. The transmitter's window contains messages sent but not yet acknowledged. Similarly, the receiver can buffer-ahead messages received out of order (up to some limit), awaiting receipt of the next expected message.

The AFFIRM specification of the Data Transfer protocol, as well as a proposed safety invariant and documentation of its partial proof, are included in Thompson [1980].

6.2 Transport Service

The transport service represents a protocol layer allowing *many* users to exchange data. Users are identified by *port addresses*. In order to exchange messages, users must first establish a connection between themselves by appropriate requests to the system; once this is done, users may exchange data in both directions independently.

The exchange itself functions as in the data transfer protocol above, but is controlled by the receiving end (in each direction), through the use of explicit *credits*, i.e., permission to send one or more messages. Once users are done communicating, they ask the system to disconnect the established connection.

We have specified a transport service (but not the protocol implementing the service), and proved several properties about the specification. The specification is done in two levels. The lower level describes *one* half-duplex connection that knows about the connection status at both ends. The upper level uses *two* such half-duplex connections, one for each direction, with a shared connection status, thus modeling a full-duplex connection between each pair of users. This division permits the separation of addressing properties from the data transfer properties of the protocol.

Properties proved about this specification show that normal sequences of connection setup and data transfer commands will have their anticipated effects. An interesting detail discovered during these proofs was that the specification precluded a user from establishing a connection with itself.

Complete details of the specification and proven properties may be found in Schwabe [1980].

6.3 Selective Repeat Transport Protocol

In Berthomieu [1980] a transport protocol similar to Stenning's is specified. It involves the transfer of messages between a sender and a receiver over an unreliable medium (it may lose messages, but not reorder them). The sender has a *window* of messages that have been sent but not yet acknowledged. If the acknowledgment does not arrive within a certain (fixed but arbitrary) time, the message is considered to have been lost and is retransmitted. This protocol is proven to be partially correct with respect to the property of "correctly transferring data across the medium."

In Berthomieu [1981], progress properties and their characterization in AFFIRM are examined. In particular, an extension of the "well-founded set" method due to Floyd [1967] is used to show the termination of a data transfer protocol.

6.4 Connection Establishment Protocol

A protocol to provide the kind of connection establishment service described in Section 6.2 has been specified in Goguen [1977]. The protocol modeled in that paper is the *three-way handshake* used in the ARPANET TCP algorithm. Although the protocol has not been verified against a complete service specification, several interesting properties have been proved. The proof attempt also revealed a very unlikely but severe bug in the protocol which was subsequently corrected.

7. PROBLEMS and EXTENSIONS

While we feel that we have had considerable success in handling protocols with AFFIRM, there are several areas where further work is needed. In this section we briefly discuss problems encountered and possible extensions.

7.1 Composition of Specifications

Given that a protocol layer is composed of several interacting stations, it is reasonable to specify the behavior of each station *separately*, i.e., by presenting its *local* view of the rest of the system Schwabe [1981]. In a second step, these several local views could be combined to specify the overall behavior of the layer.

At present, the techniques described in the previous sections do not allow the straightforward composition of such specifications; all specifications thus far have described systems from a *global* reference point.

7.2 Concurrency

A protocol layer supports several users, and hence may receive simultaneous requests for service from them (e.g., one side is sending a long message while the other acknowledges a previous message). A fully adequate specification method should allow for concurrent operations for both service specifications and protocol specifications. Furthermore, since the stations comprising the layer operate independently, the verification method must be able to analyze systems with concurrently executing components.

A basic assumption of most state transition models is that the transitions are atomic, serial operations. This assumption is carried over to the AFFIRM specifications where the axioms define the effects of each atomic operation (constructor function). However, this limitation is not as serious as it might at first appear, because by defining operations with a small enough grain the assumption of atomicity is reasonable. For systems with several independent components, the effect of concurrency can be approximated by considering all possible interleavings of the operations of each component.

The simple message system described in Section 3 illustrates these notions. To model the possible concurrency of sending and receiving operations, it was necessary to break these operations into two finer grained events (e.g., sending becomes UserSend followed by SendComplete). The possibility of a UserReceive operation occurring between the two send events adequately models concurrency in this case. We have used similar decompositions in analyzing the other protocols mentioned in Section 6, and have found this approach to be adequate if somewhat cumbersome.

7.3 Exceptions

The main purpose of a protocol specification is to define *allowed* or *normal* sequences of operations and their effects. Unfortunately, it is a fact of life in the protocol world that users occasionally issue invalid commands, and even protocol stations send inappropriate messages to each other. Thus it is inadequate to merely state that the protocol behavior is undefined for invalid inputs, or that some unspecified party is responsible for guaranteeing that inputs are valid. A richer vocabulary for specifying the handling of such *exceptional conditions* should be supported, including:

1. ignore invalid inputs (i.e., they have no effect);

2. reject them (i.e., they have no effect, but an error indication is returned to the requesting party); and

3. enter an error-recovery portion of the protocol.

Axiomatic specification methods have difficulties with (2) and (3), and the example protocol specifications prepared in AFFIRM to date have been limited to ignoring invalid inputs, or simply not defining the results. Several methods to extend axiomatic techniques to handle exceptions have been proposed [Goguen 1977], but we have not yet determined the best way to proceed in AFFIRM.

7.4 Specification and Verification of Systems with More than Two Interacting Entities

So far, we have considered only protocols that involve essentially two interacting entities over a transmission medium. This covers a large number of protocols being used in practice. Nevertheless, there are protocols involving *more* than two interacting entities (e.g., routing in packet switching networks). It appears that the techniques discussed in this paper can be applied to the specification of these protocols as well [Schwabe 1981a].

As one would expect, there is a combinatorial explosion on the number of possible states of the system. It is at this point that the ability to decompose the overall system description into the description of its components becomes crucial, since it allows the analysis of the behavior of the system through the analysis of the behavior of its components. We are investigating extensions of our techniques to handle such situations.

7.5 Higher-Level Protocols

The main application of formal specification methods to protocols has been at the data transfer level, where the first concerns are overcoming message loss, damage, and reordering. Much less work has been done on formally specifying higher-level protocols that focus more on translation into and out of canonical forms (e.g., a virtual terminal or file). Furthermore, the operations to be specified are more specialized to the area of concern of the protocol (e.g., graphics, terminal handling, speech compression) than to general data transfer. It remains to be seen whether the same methods are applicable at these higher levels, or whether a new set of abstractions (e.g., involving canonical forms) will be more suitable.

8. CONCLUSION

We have chosen to combine the state transition model and abstract data type approaches for several reasons. First of all, we have a strong methodology and a rapidly evolving, powerful supporting tool: AFFIRM. A natural question is whether such a methodology can accommodate a diverse set of formalisms and modeling methods.

This question first arose in conjunction with a toy security kernel [Schwabe 1981a], where we were presented with a state transition specification of an operating system kernel with operations such as *SwapProcesses, RaiseBlockLevel*, etc. It was quite natural to represent the specification as a data type and then do an induction proof of an important invariant about relative block and process levels.

We then applied the same method to protocols and have, on the whole, been quite satisfied. Its limitations are touched upon in Section 7, but within these limits we have conducted a broad exploration of several protocol issues.

All methods have limitations. Some of the limitations of other methods are handled nicely in our approach. For example, we have no problem with unbounded objects which cause difficulties for finite-state modeling approaches. However, we lack the decision ability of algorithms based on finite-state exploration and hence, its ability to simply reveal errors.

Another advantage of our approach is the capability to *executive* specifications: axioms have a natural rewriting rule representation that we exploit. That is, we can take a set of axioms, plug in special values, and see where the rewriting leads. The determinism and executability of axioms is an aid in evaluating the accuracy of specifications, independent of their ability to support proofs. This advantage has been exploited in Schwabe [1981b].

Our method also leads naturally from specification to verification, using the standard data type induction methods. No further mechanisms were needed to adjust AFFIRM to state transition specifications, although a "front-end" to handle our stylized type specifications would be useful and some parts have been implemented.

In conclusion, a basis has been laid for further steps toward practical specification and verification of not just protocols, but also of any system expressible as a state transition machine. Experience indicates that real protocols can be handled [Thompson, Gerhart, Erickson, Lee and Bates 1981]. The major remaining task is to consolidate techniques for proving progress and liveness.

ACKNOWLEDGMENTS

Many colleagues at ISI provided valuable comments on various versions of this paper, including S. Lee, J. Postel, S. Sluizer and D. Wile. The attendees at an informal protocol workshop held at ISI in July 1980 were especially helpful when our ideas were first being applied.

APPENDIX I

Simple Data Transfer Service Specification

[Appendix deleted]

APPENDIX II
Alternating Bit AFFIRM Protocol Representation

[*Appendix deleted*]

APPENDIX III
Service Axioms ⟶ Protocol Theorems

[*Appendix deleted*]

APPENDIX IV
Implementing Procedures and Assertions

[*Appendix deleted*]

PAMELA ZAVE AND RAYMOND T. YEH
Department of Computer Science, University of Maryland

Executable Requirements for Embedded Systems

1. INTRODUCTION

It is becoming increasingly clear that the requirements specification for a system can have a tremendous impact on the quality, usefulness, and longevity of the ultimate product, and on the efficiency and manageability of its development. Meanwhile the special problems of embedded systems, plus their growing prominence, are creating an urgent need for software engineering techniques which are suited to this domain.

This paper addresses requirements for embedded systems. The emphasis is on requirements specification, but the approach recommended will have substantial impact on the activities of requirements analysis, requirements validation, and system design as well.

The approach is based on the idea of constructing an executable model of the proposed system interacting with its environment. This "operational" approach will be explained and motivated, and portions of a specification language embodying it will be introduced.

The heart of the paper is an extended example in which a requirements specification for a process-control system is developed. The example shows a variety of functional and performance requirements presented in unusually precise form, nontrivial decomposition of complexity, and the rudiments of an emerging methodology.

1.1 Goals for Requirements Specification

The requirements specification for a system is already understood to play a central role in the early phases of its development. This document synthesizes a collective understanding of the problem the system is supposed to solve, forms the basis of a contractual agreement with the customer, provides the major channel of communication within the development organization, and serves as the standard against which a design or implementation must be validated.

Copyright © 1981 IEEE. Reprinted, with permission, from 5TH INTERNATIONAL CONFERENCE ON SOFTWARE ENGINEERING, March 9-12, 1981, San Diego, CA, pp. 295-304.

Furthermore, it seems that what we call "maintenance" is actually continuing, evolutionary system development ([Conn 1980]). The system's environment will change, people's ideas about how the system should cope with that environment will change, and the system must change or become obsolete. Each cycle of change is similar to the original development project, and there is no reason to believe that the need for a requirements specification is any less! Needless to say, extending the scope of requirements to the whole life-cycle creates even more demands on their quality. The properties of a good requirements specification include the following:

To define and set the standard for the target system, a requirements specification should be precise, unambiguous, internally consistent, sufficiently complete, minimal (so that the target system is not over-constrained), formally manipulable (if verification will be used to accept/reject an implementation), and testable (if acceptance testing will be used). Most of these properties imply that the specification language will be a formal one. Thus it can be incorporated into a development database, and supported by an integrated set of tools for synthesis and analysis of specifications.

The role of the requirements specification in communication and evolution is equally important, and to play it well a specification must be both understandable and modifiable. Not enough is known about how these goals can be achieved, but we have some suggestions to make in Section 2.

1.2 The Special Nature of Embedded Systems

An "embedded system" is a computer system which is explicitly viewed as being a component of a larger system whose primary purpose is not computation. Process-control systems, switching systems, patient-monitoring systems, flight-guidance systems, defense systems, and even fuel-injection systems are examples of this category. On-line database systems (airline reservation systems, point-of-sale systems) also share some of its properties. The microprocessor revolution is causing an explosion in the extent and variety of embedded systems.

Surely no organization has logged as much experience with embedded systems as the Department of Defense, which spends 56 per cent of its approximately 3 billion dollar annual software budget on them ([Fisher 1978]). Here is a pointed summary of that experience:

> Embedded computer software often exhibits characteristics that are strikingly different from those of other computer applications. The programs are frequently large (50,000 to 100,000 lines of code) and long-lived (10 to 15 years). Personnel turnover is rapid, typically two years. Outputs are not just data, but also control signals. Change is continuous because of evolving system requirements--annual revisions are often of the same magnitude as the original development ([Fisher 1978]).

With respect to software engineering in general, and coping with complexity and change in particular, embedded systems present a special challenge. In addition, there are other characteristic problems:

Embedded systems always have performance requirements, which may be as stringent as absolute real-time constraints and "fail-safe" reliability. Indeed, it may be the urgency of the performance requirements that causes us to emphasize the environment and view these systems as being explicitly "embedded"—since *any* useful program is a part of some operating environment, and could be called "embedded" if we chose to do so [Zave 1980b].

There are often severe restrictions on the weight, volume, power consumption, ruggedness, etc. of the resources from which these systems are implemented, or on their resistance to changes in temperature, pressure, and humidity. This is because the equipment must often be installed in places other than a conventional machine room.

Finally, embedded systems can be extraordinarily hard to test. They interface with their environments through special-purpose devices, in ways that may be distributed. This makes it difficult to write realistic test-driver routines, yet there may be no other choice: it is not feasible to test undebugged guidance software by flying with it, nor to test ballistic-missile-defense software under battle conditions.

2. A PROPOSED APPROACH

2.1 The Operational Approach

Requirements analysis always begins informally, but the operational approach encourages the use of formal models as soon as possible. As long as these models are abstract, they can help rather than hinder the processes of information collection, cost/benefit analysis, clarification, and consensus which are the substance of analysis.

A specification is an executable model of the proposed system interacting with its environment. The environment model consists of those objects with which the computer system will interact. A patient-monitoring system, for example, has such objects as patients, doctors, nurses, sensing devices, and CRT displays in its environment. A point-of-sale system may interact with salespeople at cash registers, warehouse personnel and managers at terminals, and existing or projected electronic funds transfer facilities (via a switching system).

The specification itself is a set of asynchronously interacting processes. Processes within the proposed system represent tasks, data modules, and other virtual structures. Processes in the environment may represent peripheral devices or special interface equipment, or may be digital simulations of nondigital objects such as people.

Computation within processes is specified using an "applicative" (or "functional") language, i.e. one based on side-effect-free evaluation of expressions. Because applicative notation is interpretable, it supports the executability property. It has numerous other theoretical and practical advantages (including a high degree of formal manipulability, see Backus [1978]), the most important being tremendous powers of abstraction—applicative programming is the epitome of the top-down style.

These concepts are embodied in a specification language named PAISLey (Process-oriented, Applicative, Interpretable Specification Language). The complete syntax and semantics of PAISLey, plus many more details and examples, can be found in Zave [1980a].

In the remainder of this section we discuss the major elements of the operational approach, relating them to our general goals for requirements specification, the special problems of embedded systems, and other approaches to requirements.

2.2 Explicit Modeling of the Environment

The purpose of any system (embedded or otherwise) is to support a desired mode of operation in its environment. We believe that the best way to derive the requirements for a system is to model its environment (probably bottom-up, synthesizing many views and diverse pieces of information), and then work "outside-in" to the specification of requirements for an appropriate system. This is followed by top-down design and implementation of a system to meet the requirements.

Even if the analysts can achieve understanding of the requirements in some other way, early concentration on the environment is probably the healthiest approach. It will lead to better communication with users, who are much more interested in their environment than your system. It will also promote open-minded problem solving, unbiased by preconceived notions or similar systems the analysts may have worked on. And it can enhance the modifiability of the specification by making the analysts aware of potential changes—which must, after all, originate with changes in the environment.

Requirements analysis aside, the specification itself also benefits from the presence of the environment model. The reason that the interface between an embedded system and its environment is complex, asynchronous, highly parallel, and distributed is that it consists of interactions among a number of objects which exist in parallel, at different places, and are not synchronized with one another. Organizing these interactions around the objects (processes) which take part in them is an effective way to decompose this sort of complexity. It also makes possible direct documentation of assumptions and expectations on both sides of the boundary. The result is a specification of complex behavior that is far more precise and yet comprehensible than would be possible if either side of the interface were treated as a "black box", which is what happens when the environment is not modeled.

The final advantage of specifying the environment is that most performance requirements belong there. Response time is the time some object in the environment waits for a response, load is a function of the number and speed of the processes which are creating work for the system, etc. Requirements on these performance factors can be expressed formally *and* conveniently by attaching constraints to specifications of objects in the environment.

2.3 Processes

A process is a simple, abstract representation of autonomous (distributed) computation. It is specified by supplying a "state space," or set of all possible states, and a "successor function" on that state space which defines the successor state for each state. It is a model of perpetual, cyclic computation, with the successor function describing the natural cycle of the modeled object.

Processes must interact, a common mechanism for doing so being message-passing. In PAISLey processes interact using the more highly structured mechanism of "exchange functions." Exchange functions also fit more smoothly into the applicative framework, and are explained in Zave [1980a].

There can be no question about the *generality* of processes: they were developed as abstractions of concurrent activities within multiprogramming systems, and are now used routinely for describing parallel computation in all problems domains. The notion of digital simulation of nondigital objects is likewise general. The *appropriateness* of processes for requirements specification stems from the fact that, with embedded systems, asynchronous parallelism—among environment objects, between environment objects and the system, and within the system (if only to meet performance goals)—arises naturally *at the requirements level*.

Processes can be appreciated best by comparing them to the representations of processing found in other requirements languages. Dataflow diagrams show major system functions, and identify the data structures which are their inputs and outputs; they are the basis for SADT [Ross 1977] and PSL/PSA [Teichroew and Hershey 1977]. "Dataflow" is grossly inadequate for embedded systems, in which control is of paramount importance and takes a variety of subtle forms, because it has no explicit notion of control. Stimulus-response paths (the basis of RSL, see Bell, Bixler and Dyer [1977]; Alford [1977]) show the time-sequence of steps needed to produce an output from an input, and are thus much better able to deal with control. They do not, however, represent any state information, and are therefore weak in such areas as shared data structures and internal synchronization. A finite-state machine [Heninger 1979; Davis and Rauscher 1979] has much the power of a single process, and thus permits no explicit parallelism or modeling of the environment.

A set of processes is an abstract model which integrates states, processing, and control in a natural way. The partition into processes also provides intrinsic parallelism and substantial decomposition of complexity.

2.4 Executability

Since PAISLey is a typed language, the domain and range of every function used must be declared. A specification can be executed at *any* stage of development if a means for evaluating as-yet-primitive functions is supplied; two reasonable possibilities are (1) selecting a value at random from the declared range, or (2) displaying the function's arguments at a terminal and asking the analyst to supply a value. Either way the decisions that *have* been made can be tested, with little interference from the decisions that *haven't* been made.

One of the primary means used by programmers to understand the programs they have written is to test them. Requirements analysts should have the same opportunity. We all know that program testing is no panacea, and that requirements testing will suffer from the same problems. Nevertheless, the difficulties inherent in program testing have never caused us to give it up, and requirements testing, once established in common practice, might seem equally indispensable.

There are several other appealing applications for a requirements-language interpreter. It could be used to give demonstrations to customers and users, thereby eliciting meaningful feedback from them early in the requirements phase. It could be used for performance simulation, in cases where the system is suspected of unforeseeable dynamic properties. It could even provide the implementation of a simple system prototype, to be put into trial use among a limited community. Furthermore, the executable model can continue to be useful long after the requirements phase. The environment part of the model can be used as a ready-made test bed during development, and the proposed system model can be used as a concrete standard for acceptance testing.

A final, critically important advantage of executability is the discipline of coherence it imposes on the specification. If an executable requirements specification is shown to be internally consistent, that means it will continue to generate behaviors without ever halting, deadlocking, or going into an undefined state. In other words, it is guaranteed to be a valid specification of *some* system interacting with *some* environment. Clearly this is the utmost that any formally defined notion of internal consistency could do for us, since deciding whether they are the *right* system and environment is a matter of validation by the customer, or verification of consistency with externally defined axioms of correctness.

2.5 Qualms about Operational Requirements

In addition to its obvious advantages, the idea of operational requirements has some apparent disadvantages, which we will now address.

Does an operational requirements specification encroach on design? We believe that the essence of true design is managing scarce resources to meet performance goals, so that a specification does not stray into design unless it introduces resource management strategies. Our language structures are abstract enough to avoid this: (1) applicative notation specifies applications of primitive functions to arguments without constraining in any way the data, control, or processor structures used to do it; (2) the replacement of one process state by its successor is an abstract mechanism which subsumes many techniques for updating persistent data; (3) the fact that processes are virtual rather than physical is easily seen from the evidence of multiprogramming systems, which regularly implement a number of processes by time-multiplexing a single physical processor.

On the other hand, another legitimate view of the requirements/design boundary is that *any* property needed to satisfy the customer is a requirement. It is often the case that the use of specific hardware or software resources is required, because of economic or political pressures on a stand-alone system, or because of the need to interface with an existing system. The operational approach is capable of accommodating these requirements—resources can simply be specified as environment objects. This is a strength of the approach, because any requirements language which is incapable of dealing with design-like properties will be adequate only under the most idealized of circumstances.

PAISLey is certainly too formal and technical to be used directly by untrained personnel, but its rigor can be invaluable to the analyst. There need be no conflict here, however, because the analyst can communicate with users in simplified forms (hopefully generated automatically from the specification database). Processes as semi-autonomous actors seem intuitive to us; perhaps process diagrams similar to those in Section 3 could serve for one type of informal communication.

The greatest barrier of all to understanding large systems is their complexity, but we have not yet discussed the capabilities of executable requirements models for decomposing complexity. This will be done in the course of Sections 3 and 4.

3. EXAMPLE: A PROCESS-CONTROL SYSTEM

In this section a requirements specification for a process-control system is developed. The statement of need says that there are three machines in the factory. Conditions local to individual machines may call for minor adjustments, and must be handled automatically by the system. Conditions arising in the factory as a whole may be quite dangerous, and require more substantial intervention. In addition, the system is to generate reports on such items as production and consumption of raw materials.

This system will turn out to have an interesting variety of activities. Since one of the purposes of the example is to show how operational specifications can decompose complexity, the specification will be developed in five stages. Each version builds incrementally on the previous one, and is an internally consistent, executable model all by itself.

3.1 Version 1: Independent Environment Processes

In Version 1 there are three *machine* processes, each one a digital simulation of one of the three machines. There is also a process representing the printer which produces the reports. The processes do not interact with each other.

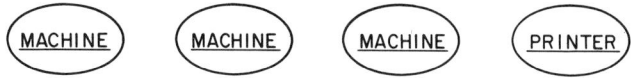

Version 1. Independent Environment Processes

Each step of a machine process represents a simulation step. The successor function of a *machine* process[1] is declared as:

machine-cycle: MACHINE-STATE ⟶ MACHINE-STATE,

where the set "MACHINE-STATE," which is the state space of a *machine* process, contains values which record the state of the machine between steps. "Machine-cycle" must include a computation of the machine's next state, based on its current state.

The machine must also offer sensor data, also based on its current state, to the control system. The two activities can be performed in parallel, so the successor function is defined as:

machine-cycle[m] =
    proj-2-1
        [(simulate-machine[(m, feedback-if-any)],
          offer-machine-data[sense[m]]
)],

where "[ ]" is used to denote function application, "( )" is used for tuple-construction, and the four primitives are declared with domains and ranges:

feedback-if-any: ⟶ FEEDBACK ∪ FILLER

simulate-machine:
    MACHINE-STATE × (FEEDBACK ∪ FILLER) ⟶ MACHINE-STATE

sense: MACHINE-STATE ⟶ SENSOR-DATA

offer-machine-data: SENSOR-DATA ⟶ FILLER ∪ SENSOR-DATA.

Set expressions can be formed using set union ("∪") and cross-product ("×"). The intrinsic set "FILLER" is defined as "{'null'}", and the constant " 'null' " is often used as a place-holder. Because only the value of

---

[1]. Throughout this example we will ignore the detail of identifying individual machines.

"simulate-machine" is needed for the next state, "proj-2-1" is used. This is an intrinsic function which projects an ordered pair onto its first component. The second expression is evaluated only for its side-effect, and the value it returns is thrown away.

"Simulate-machine" simulates change in a machine over a fixed interval of real time. One of its arguments is the current machine state, but the other encodes the possible activation of actuators to control the machine. It must be obtained by an asynchronous interaction with another process, so far denoted only by the primitive function "feedback-if-any." "Offer-machine-data" also denotes an asynchronous interaction, in this case with the purpose of transmitting sensor data to a process in the system to be built.

There is not room here to go into the syntax and semantics of specifying asynchronous interactions via exchange functions. Fortunately, primitive functions are perfect abstractions of them (output data is given as the function's argument, input data is taken from the function's value). Therefore we will only elaborate the specifications down to aptly-named primitive functions (henceforth called interaction "sites"), and explain informally what interactions take place at those sites.

The only other thing the reader needs to know about sites is that there are two kinds: "synchronizing" and "free-running." When the function representing a synchronizing site is evaluated, if the other party to the interaction is not ready, the first party will wait until the second is ready and the interaction can be carried out. A free-running site, on the other hand, will *not* wait—if the other party is not ready, the site function simply returns immediately with a pre-arranged value. Free-running sites never cause synchronization delay, and this is extremely important for modeling real-time systems. In this example, both the sites in a machine process ("feedback-if-any" and "offer-machine-data"), are free-running, enabling the process to be a valid simulation of a real machine, which does not stop to synchronize itself with a computer system, either.

"Feedback-if-any" will return a value in the set "FEEDBACK" whenever some actuator is being activated, and the value " 'null' " otherwise. "Offer-machine-data" will offer its argument to some other process which may want that sensor information, but will not wait for the other process to be ready to read it—it is offered once and then gone forever, like any other real-time data. There is room for a great deal of naturalistic detail in the elaboration of primitive sets such as "SENSOR-DATA," and primitive functions such as "sense."

The printer process needs no state information, and is specified by:

printer-cycle: FILLER ⟶ FILLER
printer-cycle['null'] = print-line[receive-line]

receive-line: ⟶ LINE

print-line: LINE ⟶ FILLER

"Receive-line" is to be an interaction function which *waits* for the next line to be printed, thereby synchronizing itself with whatever process offers the line, unlike the free-running machines. "Print-line" simply represents the physical action of printing, after which the printer process begins its next step, evaluating "receive-line" anew.

The methodology behind Version 1 is straightforward: we have identified from the needs statement the objects in the system's environment. Version 1 could be regarded as an elegant, top-level set of requirements for the system—if the machines keep operating within acceptable bounds of behavior, and the printer keeps printing out reports, who cares how it is done?

Note that we have simplified the environment rather drastically, leaving interactions among machines implicit, and including only the "inner layer" of objects (those that interact *directly* with the system). This will be a common strategy in cases where analysis of the extended environment does not prove necessary.

3.2 Version 2: Machine Monitoring

In Version 2 a process has been added to monitor each machine. The responsibilities of a *"machine-monitor"* process are to read sensor data from its machine, provide minor (localized) feedback to it, and pass selected data on to wherever else it is needed. A process to generate reports has also been added (specification omitted here), communicating on a line-by-line basis with the printer.

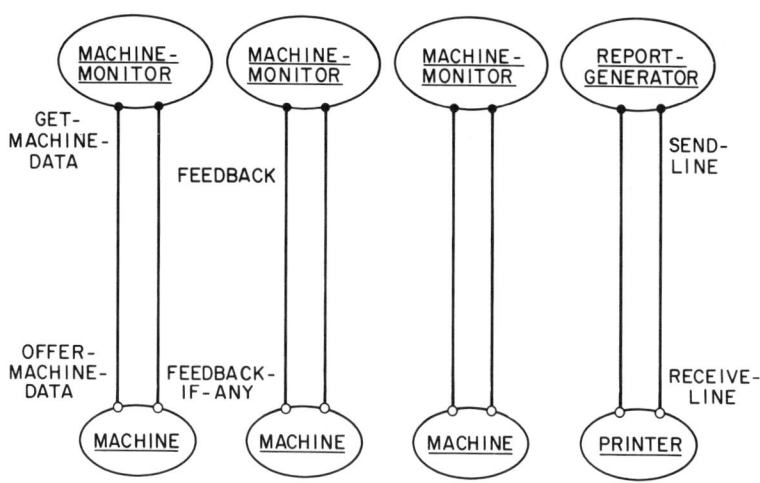

Version 2. Machine Monitoring

The successor function of a *"machine-monitor"* process is

> machine-monitor-cycle: MACHINE-IMAGE ⟶ MACHINE-IMAGE
> machine-monitor-cycle[m] = process-machine-data[(m, get-machine-data)],

where the members of "MACHINE-IMAGE" retain between steps whatever information is needed for history-sensitive decisions, and

get-machine-data: ⟶ SENSOR-DATA

process-machine-data:
MACHINE-IMAGE × SENSOR-DATA ⟶ MACHINE-IMAGE.

"Get-machine-data" interacts with "offer-machine-data" in the corresponding machine. All the hard work is done by:

process-machine-data[(m,d)] =
    proj-3-1
      [(maintain-machine-image[(m, d)],
      feedback-if-needed
            [check-machine-condition[(m, d)]],
      provide-machine-data[(m, d)]
)]

check-machine-condition:
MACHINE-IMAGE × SENSOR-DATA ⟶ FEEDBACK ∪ {'ok'}

feedback-if-needed: FEEDBACK ∪ {'ok'} ⟶ FILLER
feedback-if-needed[f] =
    /equal[f,'ok')]: 'null',
    'true': feedback[f]
    /,

where "maintain-machine-image" provides the next state of the process. Based on the current information, "check-machine-condition" decides whether feedback is needed (producing a value in "FEEDBACK") or not (" 'ok' "). "Feedback-if-needed" is defined using the conditional selection notation "/pl: f1, p2: f2, . . . 'true': fn/", which evaluates to the first "fi" such that the predicate "pi" evaluates to " 'true' ". "Feedback" is the interaction site which interacts with the machine's actuators.

In the diagram of Version 2 sites which can now be elaborated to the point of actually specifying their interaction (i.e., both interacting sites are present in the specification) have been drawn as dots (white for free-running, black for synchronizing), labeled with corresponding function names, and connected to the sites with which they interact.

The process structure of Version 2 was derived from the environment, and of (2) using "sufficient processes" to decompose the system wherever logic, synchronization, or performance suggest. Each machine needs something to accept its sensor data, the acceptor of the sensor data is the natural entity to be providing local feedback, and this function is separate and asynchronous for each machine. In the same way, the existence of the printer outside the system is reflected in the report generator inside the system; separation of the *report-generator* process from other internal system functions will insulate it from the real-time requirements that will be needed elsewhere.

Implicit in these decisions is the need for other processes which will handle global factory monitoring and feedback, support report generation, etc. This fact is documented by the existence of "provide-machine-data", but as long as it is left primitive, *all other decisions as to the nature of these processes can be deferred.*

In establishing the internal consistency of these specifications, the only challenging part is to show the absence of deadlock, in this context a situation where the system cannot proceed because a synchronizing site is waiting for an interaction that will never occur. This would be the case if the other process in the prospective interaction were not, and could not be, in the correct state to interact.

The specification being developed here is free of deadlock. The informal argument that establishes this is a familiar one in the operating system literature (e.g. Brinch Hansen [1977]): one process "depends on" another if the former needs to interact with the latter or else become blocked, and as long as the directed graph of the dependency relation is acyclic, deadlock is impossible.[2] We can see the emerging dependency graph in the processes and communication links of Version 2 (interpreting all links as pointing downward). Later versions of the specification will preserve this acyclic structure.

3.3 Version 3: The Operator

In consulting with factory engineers, the requirements analysts discover that there will always be a human operator on duty. Together the two groups agree that the operator will respond to the factory-wide danger conditions mentioned in the statement of need. The system's responsibility under these circumstances will be to detect the dangerous conditions, sound an alarm for the operator to hear, and provide a quickly accessible source of information about machine status.

These decisions are incorporated into Version 3, which has a process representing the operator. The *operator* process is a newly discovered part of the environment model. The top-level specification of this process is:

```
operator-cycle: FILLER ⟶ FILLER
operator-cycle['null'] =
        /hear-alarm:
                manual-feedback[query-conditions],
        want-report-now: order-report,
        'true': 'null'
        /,
```

---

2. In general, a variety of arguments may be needed to show that a specification is deadlock-free. This argument just happens to be (almost) sufficient for this particular style of specification.

where "hear-alarm" and "want-report-now" are predicates (their range is "{'true', 'false'}").

If the operator hears the alarm, he must first get information ("query-conditions") and then respond appropriately ("manual-feedback"). Otherwise he is free to order the report generator to begin a report. During most process steps the operator will perform neither function, so the dynamic behavior of this process will be to cycle very fast, constantly checking the enabling conditions of its possible activities. The process keeps no state information.

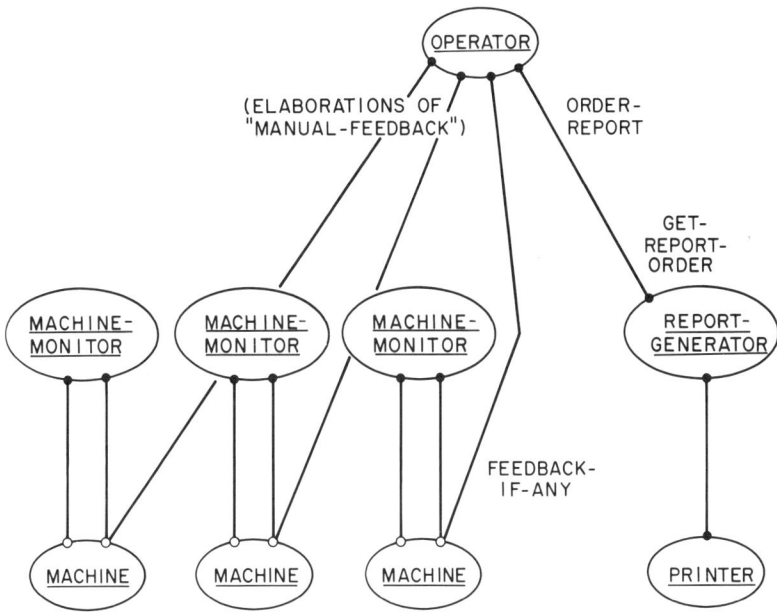

Version 3. The Operator

Quite a number of interactions are implied here. "Hear-alarm" will become a free-running site for interaction with whatever monitors factory conditions. "Query-conditions" will be elaborated into the sites necessary for interacting with an information storage facility. "Manual-feedback" first computes what the operator should do, and then controls the machines via the three sites shown (which would appear as functions in an elaboration of "manual-feedback"). Note that these sites compete with the "feedback" sites in the monitors for interaction with the "feedback-if-any" sites in the machines—the *machine* processes cannot accept feedback from both sources at the same time. "Order-report" interacts with a site in the report generator.

Most of the functions that have been mentioned in this example could be elaborated to any level of detail desired. "Want-report-now" is an exception, because none of the administrative or psychological information that would be needed to decide whether or not the operator wants a report now is available. "Want-report-now" will always be a primitive, nondeterministic function

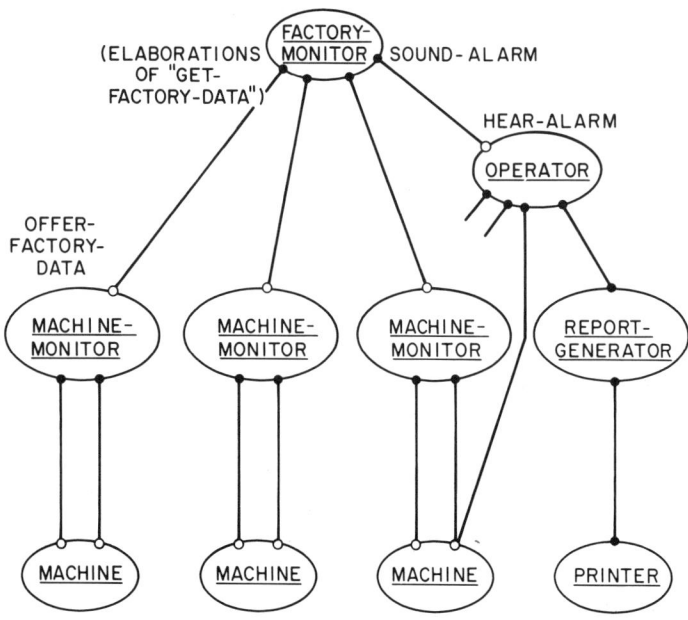

Version 4. Factory Monitoring

representing an interface with the world outside the specification. This is the third interesting interpretation for a primitive function (in addition to a set of deferred decisions, or an asynchronous interaction site).

3.4 Version 4: Factory Monitoring

Version 4 includes a process whose function is to detect factory danger conditions and sound the alarm. Implicit in the decision to have such a process is the necessity to have another process which can act as an information repository (since that function is not yet carried out). Thus we are now in a position to elaborate "provide-machine-data" in the machine monitors, knowing that sensor data has two other destinations. Its definition is:

provide-machine-data[(m, d)] =
 (offer-factory-data[select-for-factory[(m, d)]],
 send-to-database[select-for-database[(m, d)]]
 ),

where the "select-" functions choose appropriate pieces of the data, and "offer-factory-data" and "send-to-database" are interaction sites.

The successor function of the *factory-monitor* process is:

factory-monitor-cycle: FACTORY-IMAGE ⟶ FACTORY-IMAGE
factory-monitor-cycle[f] = process-factory-data[(f, get-factory-data)]

process-factory-data[(f, d)] =
    proj-2-1
    [(maintain-factory-image[(f, d)],
    alarm-if-needed
    [check-factory-condition[(f, d)]]
)]

check-factory-condition: FACTORY-IMAGE × FACTORY-DATA
    ⟶ {'alarm', 'ok'}

alarm-if-needed: {'alarm', 'ok'} ⟶ FILLER
alarm-if-needed[a] =
    /equal[(a,'ok')]: 'null',
    'true': sound-alarm
    /,

where "get-factory-data" will be elaborated into three synchronizing sites to interact with the "offer-factory-data" sites, and "sound-alarm" is the site which interacts with the operator's predicate site "hear-alarm" to cause it to return the value " 'true' ".

The *factory-monitor* process is very similar to a *machine-monitor* process, and the relationship between the factory monitor and each machine monitor is analogous to the relationship between each machine monitor and its machine (note the positions of free-running sites in Version 4). The methodology behind this process is a re-application of working "outside-in" (notice how this is helping to develop the acyclic dependency structure) and of using separate processes for separate functions.

3.5 Version 5: The Database

We have not yet specified what the machine monitors do with the information chosen by "select-for-database", nor where the operator and report generator get their information. Since it is all the *same* information, Version 5 incorporates a *database* process to contain and manage it. The operator and report generator can query this database by evaluating the function:

query-database: QUERY ⟶ RESPONSE
query-database[q] = receive-response[send-query[q]],

where "send-query" and "receive-response" are both synchronizing sites.

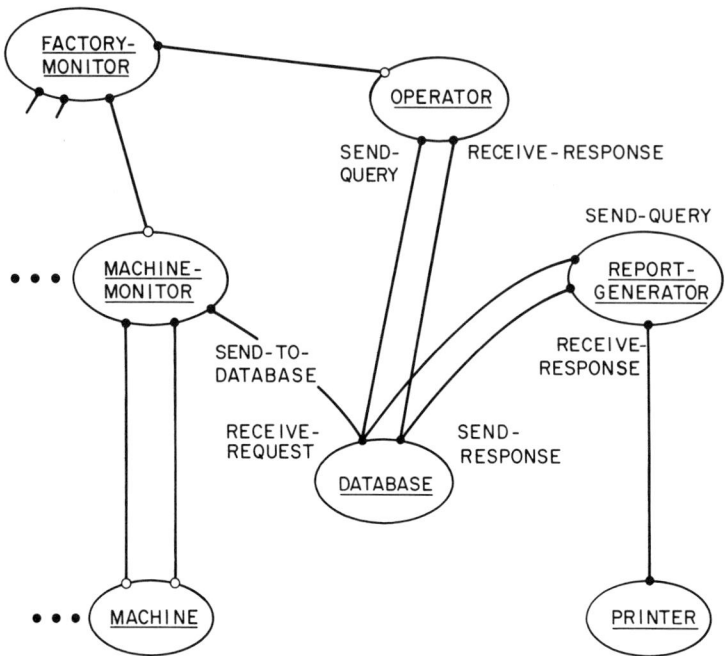

Version 5. The Database

The top-level specification of the *database* process is:

database-cycle: DATABASE ⟶ DATABASE
database-cycle[d] = respond-to-request[(d, receive-request)]

respond-to-request: DATABASE × REQUEST ⟶ DATABASE
respond-to-request[(d, r)] =
  /is-update[r]: update[(d, r)],
   'true': proj-2-1
   [(d,
      send-response[formulate-response[(d, r)]]
)]
  /,

where "receive-request" is the site at which requests for use of the database are received, "is-update" is a predicate dividing members of the set "REQUEST" into queries and updates, "update" and "formulate-response" perform the two major database manipulations, and "send-response" is the site used to return a response to the source of a query.

Version 5 was derived from the need to make explicit some deferred, implicit information paths. At this point "outside-in" development has shifted, from processes that interact directly or indirectly with the environment, to processes that support and interconnect those that do.

This is our final version of the functional specification for this system. If the elaborations that have been mentioned in the course of the example are made, the result will be complete with respect to interprocess interaction, and require only intraprocess elaboration.

3.6 Performance Requirements

Performance constraints are an indispensable part of the requirements for embedded systems. In PAISLey performance requirements are specified by attaching timing and reliability attributes to functions in the "logical" specification. A timing attribute, for instance, refers to the evaluation time of the function: the evaluation time is a random variable, and any information about its distribution can be given.

These performance requirements are also formal and executable (simulatable). [Zave 1980b] explains why timing and reliability seem sufficient for all true performance properties; by presenting the timing requirements for the process-control system, we hope to demonstrate that this simple concept of performance is both powerful and intuitive, because operational specifications provide natural structures to which performance requirements can be attached.

The *machine* processes were designed to carry out a fixed-interval simulation with step time or granularity .1 second. To specify this formally, we state the constraint that the evaluation time of "machine-cycle" is .1 second, using the syntax:

    machine-cycle: "time" ⟶ "is .1 sec" .

There is a real-time response requirement of 3 seconds on the automatic feedback loops provided by the *machine-monitor* processes. Fortunately, each feedback loop is completely contained in one cycle of a machine monitor, leading to the requirement:

    machine-monitor-cycle: "time" ⟶ "maximum is 3 sec" .

There is also a real-time requirement (a limit of 60 seconds) on the manual feedback loop, but it involves action by the environment (the operator) as well as the system. So before the system's requirements can be finalized, some *performance allocation*—of the 60-second leeway—must be done. (Performance allocation is normally a design activity, but this is a typical example of the frequent need to handle "design" at the requirements level.) The operator is allocated 50 seconds to respond to the alarm, and this decision is documented by specifying

    operator-cycle: "time" ⟶ "maximum is 50 sec".

The rest of the manual feedback loop is completely contained within one cycle of the *factory-monitor* process, with the understanding that the data it receives from the machine monitors may already be as much as 3 seconds old. The obvious conclusion is that the factory monitor must complete its cycle within 60 − 50 − 3 = 7 seconds:

factory-monitor-cycle: "time" ⟶ "maximum is 7 sec".

Both the machine monitors and the operator need to access the database during their cycles, and therefore depend on database response to meet their own performance requirements. Although it is not necessary until the design phase, we can derive a performance requirement for the database that will *guarantee* adequate service. Let us say that every process must be guaranteed a database response/access time of 2 seconds, which we judge will enable both machine monitors and the operator to satisfy their other constraints. Since interactions are mutually synchronized, no process can go on to create more work for the database until its previous request has been processed.[3] This means that the maximum number of outstanding requests is five (five processes have access to the database), and a time limit of .4 seconds will guarantee that all are honored within 2 seconds:

database-cycle: "time" ⟶ "maximum is .4 sec".

3.7 Decomposition of Complexity

This example has been a brief one, but it is still possible to draw some conclusions. It is apparently possible to specify a variety of requirements in a uniform notation that is precise, unambiguous, internally consistent, and even executable. It seems likely that we have stayed with requirements and avoided design, because no resources are represented, and all the processes in the specification are either recognizable parts of the environment or are derived quite directly from the required functions.

Our remaining concern is that complexity be managed, but it is in fact decomposed in several ways. The development of the five versions is genuinely incremental, since each can be tested before the next is begun. Within any version, the separation into processes provides a strong partitioning of the specification: states, functions, and interactions can be understood one process at a time.

Perhaps the best way to manage complexity is to create a hierarchy of abstractions. We are well prepared to do this in future elaborations of the specification, because there is nothing left but noninteracting primitive functions to do, and abstraction/elaboration within a purely functional language is straightforward. Processes and their interactions do not lend themselves quite so easily to abstraction hierarchies, but there is encouragement to be found in the hierarchical process structure observable in all the diagrams. All other processes could be viewed as arising from elaborations of primitive functions in the *factory-monitor* process, which is at

---

3. It is always possible to add a buffer process between requesters and the database, but the point is that all structures defined in PAISLey are bounded (and lockout is prevented), so that analyses of this kind can be carried out.

the top of the hierarchy, for instance. More work is needed on abstraction of processes, probably along the lines of "subsystems" in DDN [Riddle et al. 1978].

We can (and will) also claim to have decomposed complexity by providing a process-oriented description of the requirements, and saying only as much about data as was determined by it. Yet data is a vital part of any system, and any specification technique that precludes data-oriented descriptions will be of limited usefulness. The integration of PAISLey and data-oriented specifications is the subject of the next section.

4. RELATION TO DATA-ORIENTED SPECIFICATION TECHNIQUES

The assumption that a requirements model should be an explicit representation of the proposed system interacting with its environment can also lead to a completely different type of specification, based on data objects, database structures, and data-driven computations. The philosophy of data-oriented modeling is explained in Balzer and Goldman [1979] and illustrated in Yeh *et al.* [1979]. Smith and Smith [1979] presents a particular data specification language designed to have all the generality, flexibility, and power needed for complete specification of systems from a data-driven perspective.

It seems clear that a data-oriented technique is a more natural way than using PAISLey to develop requirements for data-processing systems. Our purpose here is to show that the two approaches are compatible (can, in fact, be seen as projections of the same underlying model), so that analysts will be free to use either or both (in parallel), as the application and phase of development suggest.

In both approaches objects in the environment, and objects in the proposed system reflecting objects in the environment (such as machine "images"), are represented by data items. The basic relationships among data items are even the same: database languages classify data items by types, and relate types through "generalization" and "aggregation"; PAISLey also has types (sets), and relates them in the same way through set union and cross-product. Regarding the collection of process states in a PAISLey specification as a database, it differs from a "normal" database only in (1) having a fixed size, and (2) having a simplified structure in which no item is a component of more than one other item. Both properties are appropriate to the nature of embedded systems, but are merely *restrictions* on a more general data model.

In both approaches environment events can change the state of the environment, system events can change the state of the system, and environment and system events can interact. This processing aspect is handled informally in some data-oriented specification techniques, and using formalisms such as predicate calculus in others. In PAISLey processing is specified formally and executably, and in such a way that performance requirements can be stated and guaranteed. PAISLey is well-suited to specifying the overall system structure and control that database languages usually avoid, while database languages are well-suited to specifying the primitive operations on data that PAISLey tends to avoid.

In summary, both process- and data-oriented approaches motivate the same system-plus-environment conceptual model, but they have complementary strengths and weaknesses in the formal specification of it. We believe that well-defined interfaces between the two can be developed.

5. CONCLUSION

The ideas presented here have been applied successfully to a variety of small examples, covering a range of embedded system characteristics. There is a great deal to do, however. Current research plans include: (1) implementing a PAISLey interpreter so as to gain experience with executing specifications, (2) studying the problems of "scaling up" to large systems in general, and abstraction methodology in particular, (3) developing techniques for producing designs from PAISLey specifications, and (4) defining an interface with the data-specification formalism of semantic nets [Yeh and Mittermeir 1980], so that it can be exploited for analyst/user contact.

It must also be remembered that there are aspects of requirements specification for which an operational model is little or no help. These include requirements concerning system development (deadlines, resources, costs, standards) and routine maintenance requirements [Yeh *et al.* 1980]. And the need for pictures, comments, and other informal avenues of human communication will never disappear.

ACKNOWLEDGEMENTS

We are grateful to Bob Fitzwater for his contribution to the theory of operational modeling, and to Alex Conn and Roland Mittermeir for stimulating discussions on requirements problems.

SPECIFICATION SYSTEMS

One of the benefits of any formal language is that it is readily amenable to processing by computer. Formal specifications fall into this category and it is of interest to consider ways in which the computer can be of assistance.

Certainly the syntax of specification can be checked and specifications can be based in system libraries. But other possibilities are more interesting. We have seen that specifications should possess properties such as consistency and completeness; certain approaches to this can be automated. It should be possible to ask questions about specifications and about the consequences of them; in this, theorem proving techniques are a valuable aid. The remaining part of this book is devoted to papers about systems which are used for automating aspects of the specification process.

Some specification systems are concerned only with specification themselves and deductions that can be made from these. The paper by Rod Burstall and Joe Goguen is an important contribution to the literature; it introduces the specification language CLEAR and discusses issues associated with its implementation. The paper by Joe Goguen and Joseph Tardo is concerned with the specification language OBJ which is based on the idea of rewrite rules and is executable. OBJ is seen as an ongoing project; the paper highlights the important early ideas and points the way to later developments.

Other systems may more accurately be called automatic verification systems since the specification content exists almost as a side effect to permit the annotation of programs that have to be verified. The Gypsy system falls into this category and is described and discussed in the paper from the Verification Group at the University of Austin in Texas. The AFFIRM system (paper by Carl Sunshine *et al.*) would also fall into this category.

The final paper by Aviel Klausner and Tom Konchan is concerned with rapid prototyping. To ensure the correctness and accuracy of a specification it can be argued that it is desirable to produce prototype systems. Despite their inevitable inadequacies they do give a rough and ready implementation which can be assessed by a client, modified and finally agreed upon before full-scale development commences.

R. M. BURSTALL
University of Edinburgh

J. A. GOGUEN
UCLA

An Informal Introduction to Specifications Using CLEAR

1. IMPORTANCE OF SPECIFICATIONS

If you want someone to build a house for you, it is wise to employ an architect to make sure that what gets built is what you want. The architect will prepare a detailed specification of the house which you can discuss and amend before anyone starts laying bricks. In the same way before anyone invests time and emotional energy in writing a program it is as well to have a specification to make sure that what is produced is what is required. Of course, this specification is usually an informal affair, a document written in technical English. Individual parts of the program also need to be specified and this is often done even more informally. When the house is to be electrically rewired, or the program is to be altered, the specification is consulted so that the original structure and intentions can be understood. In this maintenance phase, which in the case of programs accounts for much of the cost, a good specification is vital.

Specifications must be understandable, so we need informal specifications. They must be precise, so there is a strong case for formal specifications. We can go the whole way from English, to mathematical discourse, to formal logical language with a machine-checkable syntax.

The notion of program correctness presupposes a precise specification: a program is correct *relative to this specification.* Most work on correctness has had two aims:

(a) to find methods of attaching parts of the specification to the code (invariants, algorithmic or dynamic logic, weakest preconditions, intermittent assertions);

(b) to carry out proofs mechanically, showing that the program agrees with the specification.

We would like to argue here for paying attention to the specification itself, apart from any program. How can we conveniently but precisely say what we want done? In any realistic case saying what we want done will involve the definition of a large number of auxiliary concepts. We may hope that many of these will be well-known, such as "matrix", "graph" or "unification"; others will be peculiar to the project in hand.

So we should turn our attention to specification languages. Even if our correctness proof methods are too weak or laborious to use in practice, precise specifications and careful thought may enable us to write correct programs much of the time.

This paper is an informal account of one such specification language, Clear, touching briefly on the mathematical basis of the language and including some examples of specification.

1.1 State of the Art and Motivation for Clear

The use of particular formalisms and languages for abstract program specifications is a relatively new endeavor. At first our approach was considerably influenced by the success of the algebraic approach to the specification of abstract data types, particularly the work of ADJ. In this tradition, a specification has two parts, one for syntactic declarations, and the other for axioms. The syntactic part is called a *signature* and consists of a set of *sort* names, one for each sort of data involved (such as nat and bool, for natural numbers and truthvalues, respectively), and a set of declarations for *operation* symbols (such as declaring + a binary infix operation on nat, or "not" a unary operation on bool). The axioms in an algebraic specification are *equations*, that is, pairs of terms which are supposed to denote the same value in every valid interpretation. The "initial algebra" school takes such a specification to denote (an isomorphism class of) "prototypical" model(s) [Goguen, Thatcher and Wagner 1978].

The area of software engineering (or program methodology) has a number of "specification languages" of a more or less informal character (see the July 1980 *SIGSOFT Notices* for information on many of these). Prominent among these is the SRI language SPECIAL, part of the HDM methodology [Levitt, Robinson and Silverberg 1979]. While many of these languages have been used for the specification and verification of some fairly complex systems, none has been given a complete formal semantics (this is not, of course, a problem for those who are content to work within the limitations of some already established logical formalism, such as first order predicate logic).

A new generation of specification language is arising, based on experiences with the older work. These languages are more expressive than the formalisms used for abstract data types, and more precise than the languages of the programming methodologies. In general, they make use of strong typing and of parameterization. This paper is concerned with the Clear project, first described in Burstall and Goguen [1977]. Mention should also be made of the interesting and powerful Z language [Abrial, Schuman and Meyer 1979], which is based on axiomatic set theory, and the OBJ system [Goguen and Tardo 1979], which can be seen as implementing an executable subset of Clear. Recent work, based like Clear on initial algebras, has been done by Hupbach, Kaphengst and Reichel [1971]. An extension of these ideas using recursive definitions is proposed in Klaeren [1980]. Bjorner has done a number of specifications based on denotational semantic techniques

[Bjorner 1980] and Guttag and Horning have explored the combination of algebraic specifications with pre- and post-conditions [Guttag and Horning 1980].

General system theory has been another important influence on the development of Clear, in at least two different ways. The first, and rather technical influence, is to provide a mathematical foundation for the basic notion of "putting together", as discussed in Section 1.2.[1] The second and somewhat vaguer influence, was toward generality, in that we did not wish to be restricted to the use of only initial algebra semantics for equational axioms, but wanted to be able to use other kinds of axioms, such as first order sentences, if that seemed more appropriate to the problem at hand; this is discussed briefly in Section 1.4. In addition, we wanted to be able to use specifications for cases where *any* model satisfying the axioms would be acceptable; see Section 1.3.

The intention of Clear has been to provide a precise and flexible tool for the construction of program specifications. However, the primitive operations of Clear are very close to the underlying mathematical theory and they are not as powerful as one might desire for convenience of expression. Perhaps Clear could be thought of as analogous to an assembly language, though one with procedures and user definable types. We hope at some future time to provide higher level languages based on the same semantic ideas, which will be of greater practical value in software engineering.

Another important factor for the practical utilization of abstract specification languages is to build up a library of specifications which can then be used in putting together other larger specifications. Many of these library specifications will, of course, be parameterized. Without such a library, every program specification effort will have to start from scratch, and there will be no significant progress. We believe that program specification should be a communal endeavor.

1.2 Putting Theories Together

Complex problems may have complex specifications. This means that the specifications will be hard to read, write and modify, unless they are somehow broken down into pieces of understandable size. Because specification is a constructive process, this means providing a collection of operations on specifications which permit complex specifications to be put together from simple ones. Perhaps the most important such operation is the application of a parameterized specification to a suitable argument. Other operations will permit specifications to be enriched, or to have some of their parts hidden, or to be additively combined into a whole.

In all of this, we take the point of view that the essential purpose of a specification is to provide a *theory* of what some piece of program is supposed

---

1. This foundation is the categorical notion of colimit, proposed for "putting together" arbitrary systems in Goguen [1971].

to do. Thus, a specification language should consist of *operations upon theories*, and Clear is in fact a language whose expressions denote theories. In particular, Clear takes the view that a parameterized specification is a *procedure* which takes theories as arguments and returns theories as values. An important aspect of this view is that these procedures impose *requirements* on their actual arguments, in the form of certain axioms required to be true before application is meaningful; these requirements are themselves theories.

A complication which must be taken into account in carrying out this program is to insure that shared subtheories are properly treated. For example, we should expect that many particular theories will have the theories Bool of truthvalues and Nat of natural numbers, as subtheories, and we want to be certain that when such particular theories are combined, there remains at the end only one copy each of Bool and Nat. This leads to a concept of environments with sharing.

1.3 Data Constraints

A theory used to specify a not entirely trivial piece of software generally has a number of interesting subtheories. Some of these subtheories specify particular data structures and operations, while others assert some axioms which may be satisfied by any of a variety of structures. For example, Bool specifies the particular (up to isomorphism) structure of truthvalues, while Poset can be satisfied by any partially ordered set. Note that Bool is a subtheory of Poset. We shall call *canonical* those theories which are intended to specify particular structures, and we shall call *loose* those which are used to specify any structure satisfying the axioms. A more complex situation is when we wish to specify some particular structure as canonical only once some other structure, satisfying a loose specification, has been fixed. For example, the parameterized specification List(X) specifies the data structure of lists of X's, once X has been given; but any interpretation of X is permitted, as long as it has at least one sort. We formalize all this with the notion of a *data constraint* which is an assertion that one theory shall be interpreted canonically relative to another (possibly empty) theory. Theories not so constrained are interpreted loosely. Canonical interpretations are defined mathematically by use of initial algebra semantics, using ideas originally due to Kaphengst and Reichel [1971].

1.4 Generality

At this time, it is not entirely clear what underlying logic will be the most appropriate for writing the axioms to be used for program specification. Indeed, it may be that there is no single best choice, but that different logical systems will be more suitable for different applications. Clear has been defined in such a way that any underlying logical system can be used which satisfies certain conditions regarding the relationship between theories and models. We call such suitable logical systems *institutions*; they are discussed further in Section 10. Examples include equational logic, first order logic, temporal logic and (putatively) error and continuous equational logic.

The last three are presumably useful for describing concurrent systems, error (or exception) handling and non-terminating systems (such as operating systems), respectively.

2. THE CLEAR SPECIFICATION LANGUAGE

To specify some concepts in Clear we write them in the form of a theory. This theory will have *sorts, operations* and *equations* (we give examples mostly in equational logic). Further concepts are introduced by enriching this theory; we may add new sorts, operations and equations.

The sorts are different kinds of data, such as numbers, truthvalues or lists of these. They may also be "uninterpreted", as in considering some collection of elements with an ordering. We introduce the former using the word *data*. For example

>   *const* Bool =
>   *theory data sorts* bool
>   *opns* true, false: bool *endth*

This means that the sort bool can only be constructed by the operators true and false (constants count as nullary operations). Furthermore, since there are no equations given, true $\neq$ false. In general when *data* are used, terms using the operators are not equal unless their equality follows from the given equations. The theory of Boolean sequences could be done thus (note that . is an "infix" operation)

>   *const* Bool-sequence =
>   *theory data sorts* bool, sequence
>   *opns* true, false: bool
>   empty: sequence
>   unit: bool $\rightarrow$ sequence
> $-$. $-$: sequence, sequence $\rightarrow$ sequence
>   *eqns* empty.s = s
>   s.empty = s
>   s.(t.u) = (s.t).u
>   *endth*

For example we may deduce from these equations that

>   empty.(unit(true).empty) = unit(true).empty

but

>   unit(true).empty $\neq$ unit(false).empty

since the equality is not deducible. We will write this equality, or indentity, as a Boolean operation "= =". We can then say "not (s = = t)", whereas we do not permit inequations such as s $\neq$ t.

We would like to add extra operations to Bool; this is an *enrichment*, say Booll,

    const Booll =
        Bool *enriched by*
            opns not: bool ⟶ bool
                − and − : bool, bool ⟶ bool
                − or − : bool, bool ⟶ bool
            eqns not(false) = true
                not(true) = false
                b and true = b
                b and false = false
                b or true = true
                b or false = b
        enden

We could more elegantly have written Bool-sequence as an enrichment, thus

    const Bool-sequence =
        Bool *enriched by*
            data sorts sequence
            opns empty: sequence
                unit: bool ⟶ sequence
                − . − : sequence, sequence ⟶ sequence
            eqns empty.s = s
                s.empty = s
                s.(t.u) = (s.t).u
        enden

But what if we want "not", "and", "or", as well as "."? We need to combine theories using "+", thus

    Booll + Bool-sequence

The part which is common to Booll and Bool-sequence, that is Bool, is not duplicated.

Strictly we should put a list of variables before each equation

    forall b: bool. b and true = b

but we will allow ourselves to omit this.

So far we have introduced sorts which are intended to have one particular interpretation (to within isomorphism). But we can also introduce "loosely interpreted" sorts, which are intended to have a variety of interpretations.

For example an automaton is a set of states, with a start state, a transition function and an accept predicate, say,

> Booll *enriched by*
> > *sorts* state
> > *opns* start: state
> > > transition: bool, state ⟶ state
> > > accept: state ⟶ bool
>
> *enden*

We just omit the word *data* before the list of sorts.

The states of the automaton could be realized by many different (nonisomorphic) data types, for example, numbers, pairs of numbers or strings of characters; various interpretations could be given to the operations start, transition and accept. We will see later how state can be "bound" to one of these particular data types. Such loosely interpreted sorts occur in theories used to state the requirement for a theory procedure, say one defining further concepts based on the notion of automaton. This procedure could then be applied to some particular automaton.

Other examples of theories with uninterpreted sorts would be concepts like "partially ordered set" and "monoid".

2.1 Models and Inference

In the Boolean sequences example we wrote down three equations. Obviously we intend all the consequences of these equations to also hold, for example

> empty.unit(true) = unit(true)
> s.((t.u).v) = s.(t.(u.v))

Call a set of sorts and a set of operators with given argument and result sorts a *signature*. Thus the signature of a theory is the theory without the equations. An *algebra* for that signature is a structure which has a set associated with each sort and a function associated with each operator (a function from the sets associated with the argument sorts of the operator to the set associated with its result sort). See Burstall and Goguen [1980] or Goguen, Thatcher and Wagner [1978] for a more technical account of all this.

For example an algebra A for the Bool-sequence signature might have {0, 1} for bool, and the integers ... − 1, 0, 1, 2, ... for sequence. We could let true be 1, false be 0, empty be 0, unit be the identity function and concat be addition.

Now an algebra *satisfies* a theory (is a model of the theory) if it makes each equation in the theory true for any values of the variables. Just pick values for the variables in the sets associated with their sorts, evaluate the left- and right-hand sides of the equation using functions for the operators and check that they are equal. In our example A does indeed satisfy Bool-sequence.

Suppose now that we have some set E of equations. Consider all the algebras which satisfy them. There may well be other equations which are also satisfied by all these algebras; these are called the *logical consequences* of the original set E. We call the union of E with its logical consequences the *closure* of E. Actually in Clear we just write a finite set of equations whose closure is the theory we wish to describe. To find whether an equation is in this closure we need inference rules and a theorem prover.

But something is not right with our algebra A as a model for Bool-sequence! We were trying to describe strings of truth values. There is no harm in using 0 and 1 instead of "TRUE" and "FALSE" since we are only interested in the mathematical properties of truth values and do not care whether they are represented by 0 and 1 or by Charlie Chaplin and Maggie Thatcher so long as negation, conjunction and disjunction do the right thing. But the integers with identity and addition really will not do for sequences. Consider unit(false) and empty; they would both be represented by 0. Also unit(true).unit(false) and unit(false).unit(true) would both stand for 1. There would be no way to denote -1.

We need algebras for which two extra conditions hold:

(1) Two expressions have the same value in the algebra if and only if the equations compel them to do so, that is if and only if they have the same value in every algebra which satisfies the equations.

(2) Every element in the algebra is the value of some expression.

It turns out that although there are many such algebras they are all "isomorphic", i.e. if the conditions hold for both A and B we can make a one to one correspondence between their elements which "respects" the sorts and operations. We can do an operation in A or on the corresponding elements of B and get corresponding results.

The slogans are:

(1) "no confusion"—expressions should not be equal unless they are forced to be so by the equations;

(2) "no junk"—the algebra should not have unnecessary elements.

We call such an algebra *initial*.[2] The initial algebra satisfying Bool is easy: just take the domain to be $\{0, 1\}$, let true denote 1 and false denote 0.

What is an initial algebra for Bool-sequence? We can take bit-strings, with "empty" meaning the empty string and "." meaning concatenation of strings. This satisfies the equations but no two terms evaluate to the same value unless the equations compel them to do so; also each string is denoted by at least one term. Had we taken the integers as the denotation of sort "sequence" neither of these conditions would have held.

Consider now a "loose" theory "Poset" of partially ordered sets

---

2. There is a good (categorical) reason for this name but it does not concern us here.

const Poset =
    Bool *enriched by*
        sorts element
        opns $-\leqslant-$, $==$: element, element $\to$ bool
        eqns $x \leqslant x$ = true
              $x \leqslant y$ and $y \leqslant x => x == y$ = true
              $x \leqslant y$ and $y \leqslant z => x \leqslant z$ = true
enden

(Here "= =" is the operation used for identity, whilst "=" is part of the notation for an equation. When a data sort is introduced it automatically gets an identity operation.)

Now consider a theory of sequences of partially ordered elements,

const Poset-sequence =
    Poset *enriched by*
        data sorts sequence
           opns empty: sequence
                unit: bool $\to$ sequence
                $-\,.\,-$: sequence, sequence $\to$ sequence
        eqns empty.s = s
            s.empty = s
            s.(t.u) = (s.t).u
enden

Which algebras satisfy Poset? Which satisfy Poset-sequence?

For Poset we must interpret the Bool part initially but we may take any set as the interpretation of sort element with any reflexive and transitive relation for $\leqslant$. (Indeed the initial algebra has the empty set as the interpretation of element; so it is dull.) However given an interpretation of element and $\leqslant$ there is only one way we wish to interpret Poset-sequence, as strings of such elements. Thus the enrichment in Poset-sequence denotes an algebra which is initial *relative to* a given Poset algebra A. We call this the *free* Poset-sequence algebra on A. It has the property that the two Poset-sequence terms only have the same value if they do so in all algebras which extend A and satisfy the equations of the enrichment, also that each value is denoted by at least one term.

Thus for an algebra to satisfy Poset-sequence not only must it obey all the equations but it must also interpret the data enrichments freely. This means that a Clear specification represents more than just a signature and some equations; we must also remember which parts are to be interpreted freely. We call the constraint that an enrichment is to be interpreted freely a *data constraint*, and call a theory together with a set of data constraints on parts of it a *data theory*. An algebra satisfies a data theory if it satisfies the theory and also satisfies the data constraints in the sense that the indicated parts have the free interpretation. The technical details, using the notion of theory morphism, are given in Burstall and Goguen [1980].

Since we have a notion of an algebra satisfying a data constraint we can treat constraints just as we do equations. We ask which algebras satisfy a set of equations and data constraints, and then what other equations are satisfied by the same set. These are the logical consequences. Thus we have defined logical consequence for data theories. A data constraint acts like an induction principle, for example it might be an enrichment introducing operations empty, unit and ".", in which case the associated induction principle says "prove it for empty, for unit(x) and assuming it for s and t prove it for s.t". Thus the data constraint has extra equations as its logical consequences, and even extra data constraints (derived induction principles).

The idea of data constraints on a theory is due to Kaphengst and Reichel [1971]. It was developed in its present form by Reichel [1980], and independently by us.[3] Reichel uses the term *canon* for essentially the same concept as our data theory. It seems an important notion and one which elegantly overcomes a number of difficulties encountered in defining the notion of parameterized theory and in permitting "loose" specifications which can be realized in more than one way.

2.2 Derive

We have seen how to enrich a theory by adding new sorts and operators, but we may sometimes wish to hide or to rename certain sorts and operators. Suppose for example that we wish to construct a theory of "characters" with a certain order relation "$\leqslant$", say $A \leqslant \ldots \leqslant Z \leqslant 0 \ldots \leqslant 9$. It may be convenient to use the existing theory of natural numbers with "$\leqslant$", but we do not require the operations of addition and multiplication on characters. We can accomplish this by giving the new sorts and operators (but not necessarily the equations they obey) and also giving a map from new sorts and operators to old ones.

> *const* Characters = *derive sorts* character
> *opns* A, ..., Z, 0, ..., 9: character
> $-\leqslant-$: character, character $\rightarrow$ bool
> *using* Bool
> *from* Natleq
> *by* character *is* nat,
> A *is* 0, ..., Z *is* 25, 0 *is* 26, ..., 9 *is* 35
> $\leqslant$ *is* $\leqslant$
> *endde*

The new sort "character" and the new operations "A", "B" etc. form an enrichment of Bool. The equations they obey are derived from those of

---

3. One of us (RMB) had heard a talk by Reichel in 1977 using his original notion but failed to appreciate the idea and later "re-invented" a slightly extended form of it.

Natleq, a theory of natural numbers with a "less than or equal" ordering, via the map which takes "character" to "nat", A to 0 etc. To find out whether an equation holds in the character theory we use this map to translate it into the number theory and check whether it holds there. Thus "A ⩽ B" holds because "0 ⩽ 1" holds for natural numbers. Note that Bool is a common subtheory of Natleq and the new theory of characters.

Here is another example, Rationals derived from integers. We first enrich the integers to get a theory, R, with a new sort, r, consisting of equivalence classes of pairs of integers. The binary operation "//", written as an infix, takes a pair of integers to their equivalence class. We define operations of addition, subtraction, etc. on these equivalence classes, and also the "injection", i, of the integers into R. Now R has the structure of the rationals but it still bears marks of its construction, the operation //. So we derive Rationals from R, "hiding" the // operation. It is a nuisance to write out a long description of the translation map with "0 is 0", "1 is 1" etc. so we permit operations with the same name in each case to be omitted. This example will involve "errors", the further discussion of which we defer until after giving the Clear text.

  const Rat =
   let R = Integers *enriched by*
       data sorts r
       opns − // − : int, int ⟶ r
       err-opns OVFL: r
       eqns
         (k∗m)//(k∗n) = m//n if k ≠ 0 and n ≠ 0
         (n//0) = OVFL *enden*
    enriched by
      opns i: int ⟶ r
      eqns i(n) = n//1 *enden*
    enriched by
      opns 0, 1: r
        +, −, ∗, /: r, r ⟶ r
      eqns 0 = i(0)
        1 = i(1)
        (m1//n1) + (m2//n2) =
         (m1∗n2 + m2∗n1)//(n1∗n2)
        (m1//n1) − (m2//n2) =
         (m1∗n2 − m2∗n1)//(n1∗n2)
        (m1//n1)∗(m2//n2) = (m1∗m2)∗(n1∗n2)
        (m1//n1)/(m2//n2) = (m1∗n2)//(n1∗m2) *enden*
  in
    derive sorts rat

> *opns* 0, 1: rat
> +, −, *, /: rat, rat ⟶ rat
> rational: int ⟶ rat
> *using* Integers
> *from* R
> *by* rat *is* r, rational *is* i *endde*

The intuitive idea of errors is that the elements of sort s can be of two subsorts: *ok* or *error*. The ok elements are the normal expected ones, and the error elements are the exceptional ones, the error messages. Similarly, there are ok operators and error operators. The ok operators normally produce ok values, but may sometimes produce error values (e.g. 1//0 = OVFL, where "OVFL" is the error message for "overflow"); the error operators always produce error values (e.g. X IS-UNDEFINED-VARIABLE, where "IS-UNDEFINED-VARIABLE" is a post-fix error message producing function). It is required that all operations "preserve errors", in the sense that if any argument is an error, then so must the result be.

The above Clear text first defines, with an unnamed data theory, an error algebra having as its ok values of sort r equivalence classes of pairs of integers (e.g. {1//1, 2//2, 3//3, . . .}, {2//1, 4//2, . . .}) representing the usual rationals, and as its error values of sort r, the single equivalence class {OVFL, 0//0, 1//0, 2//0, . . .}, using the convention that anything equivalent to an error is an error. We next form the theory R, which enriches this structure with some new operations, which are the usual field operations, and defines them, for ok-values, in terms of the previous values given by R. Because these definitions are given by "ok-eqns" (just called *eqns*), nothing is said about what is to happen if an error arises; in this sense the enrichment is "loose". For example, nothing is said about the value of ((1//0)//0) + 2 (except that it is an error element). Finally, we use *derive* to hide the operation // and change the operation "i" to "rational", thus arriving at a specification whose ok part of sort rat is the usual rationals, and whose error part of sort rat is some algebra of error messages.

Clear gives you the choice of specifying what you mean (a) directly by a set of equations (abstract specification), or (b) by deriving it from some pre-existing concepts by first constructing a model from these and then hiding or renaming some of the sorts and operators (constructive specification). The abstract method is more elegant but more prone to mistakes. The ordinary programmer would probably do better with constructive specification most of the time; an exception is when he wants to define an operation as the inverse of another operation.

2.3 Parameterized Theories

We defined above the theory of Boolean sequences. But what if we want sequences of natural numbers? Do we have to start all over again? We need do that in general too, but it can only be done for elements which have a partial order defined on them. These are examples of *parameterized theories*, otherwise known as *theory procedures* since they take a theory as argument and deliver a new theory as result. As we have just seen, the argument must satisfy certain conditions; for example, the procedure which produces the theory of sorting will accept any theory which has a sort with a partial ordering over it. For instance, given the natural numbers with the usual "less than or equal" operation it produces the theory of natural numbers, sequences of natural numbers and the operation for sorting these sequences. We express the constraint that the parameter must have a sort with a partial order by associating Poset, the theory of partial orders, with this parameter, writing:

procedure Sorting(P: Poset) = ...

We call Poset the "requirement" for P ("requirement" replaces our previous term "metasort" in Burstall and Goguen [1977]). The procedure sorting will accept any theory T which is an "example" of Poset, in the sense that we can specify a map from the sorts of Posets to the sorts of T and from operations of Poset to operations of T such that if we translate via this map any equation holding in Poset then the translation holds in T. We write the map in brackets after the argument theory. As for derive, if an operation maps into another with the same name we may omit it. Thus

Sorting(Natleq[element *is* nat, $\leqslant$ *is* leq])

We will work out this example in detail. We start with the notion of sequence. The sequence procedure has a quite trivial requirement, it just needs a sort and no operations. We first define this requirement theory, then sequences.

const Triv = *theory sorts* element *endth*

procedure Sequence(X: Triv) =
   X *enriched by data sorts* sequence
      opns empty: sequence
           unit: element $\longrightarrow$ sequence
           − . − : sequence, sequence $\longrightarrow$ sequence
      eqns empty.s = s
           s.empty = s
           s.(t.u) = (s.t).u
   enden

Note that we refer to "element"; this is more properly "element *of* X" since there might be another parameter "Y: Triv", but we may omit "*of* X" when no confusion is possible.

a theory of sequences of anything. How about a theory of sorting which has an operation which sorts a sequence into ascending order? We would like to

Now for Sorting we use the requirement Poset, then define the procedure Ascending which defines "ascending sequence".

procedure Ascending(SP: Sequence(Poset)) =
SP *enriched by*
    opns $- \leqslant -$: sequence, sequence $\rightarrow$ bool
    eqns empty $\leqslant$ s = true
        unit(x) $\leqslant$ unit(y) = x $\leqslant$ y
        s $\leqslant$ t.u = s $\leqslant$ t and s $\leqslant$ u
        s.t $\leqslant$ u = s $\leqslant$ u and t $\leqslant$ u *enden*
enriched by
    opns ascending: sequence $\rightarrow$ bool
    eqns ascending(empty) = true
        ascending(unit(x)) = true
        ascending(s.t) = ascending(s) and s $\leqslant$ t and ascending(t)
enden

We need to say that the ascending sequence is a permutation of the original one. How can we express this? A convenient way is to introduce the notion of "bag", that is, unordered sequence. A sequence is then a permutation of another if they yield the same bag. Bag and Perms define these concepts. We then use Ascending and Perms to define Sorting.

procedure Bag(X: Triv) =
X *enriched by data sorts* bag
    opns empty: bag
        unit: element $\rightarrow$ bag
        $-$ union $-$: bag, bag $\rightarrow$ bag
    eqns empty union b = b
        b union c = c union b
        b union (c union d) = (b union c) union d
enden

procedure Perms(ST: Sequences(Triv)) =
ST + Bag(ST) *enriched by*
    opns bagof: sequence $\rightarrow$ bag
        is-perm: sequence, sequence $\rightarrow$ bool
    eqns bagof(empty) = empty
        bagof(unit(x)) = unit(x)
        bagof(s.t) = bagof(s) union bagof(t)
        is-perm(s, t) = (bagof(s) = = bagof(t))
enden

> *procedure* Sorting(P: Poset) =
>   Ascending(Sequence(P)) + Perms(Sequence(P)) *enriched by*
>   *opns* sort-up: sequence ⟶ sequence
>   *eqns* is-perm(s, sort-up(s)) = true
>   ascending(sort-up(s)) = true *enden*

A facility which we have not mentioned so far is introducing a local name for a theory using *let* ... = ... *in* .... For example

> *proc* P(X: Poset) =
>   *let* F = Map(X, X) *in*
>   ...X...F...   (expression using F as well as X)

2.4 Shared Subtheories

As we build up our Clear specification we define a number of constant theories (like Bool), and we introduce parameter theories (X in *proc* P(X:T) = ...) and local theories (Y in *let* Y = ... *in* ...). Now these theories are not independent. Bool may be used in defining T, and both X and Bool may be used in defining Y. If Bool is used to define T we may call it an "ancestor" of T. Clear keeps this ancestry relation as part of the environment so that when we combine two theories, Y + Z, the new theory has the *disjoint* union of their sorts and operators, *except* that common ancestor theories are not duplicated. This means that if two people working on different parts of the specification happen to choose the same name for an operator they are still regarded as distinct. Also each application of a procedure gives a fresh copy of the new sorts and operators which it introduces. For example Set(X) + Set(X) will have two sorts called Set and two union operators, but *let* S = Set(X) *in* S + S only has one sort and one operator.

It may be that in our desire to avoid global names and unintentional clashes we have gone a bit too far in making names different, one might like Set(X) to mean the same thing whenever it is written. Our semantics (using the notion of "pushout") is consistent but may cause undue "proliferation" of distinct names, an inconvenience when writing Clear specifications. This needs further exploration.

3. IMPLEMENTATION

Clear is a specification language, not a programming language; its purpose is communication rather than calculation. Nevertheless a computer implementation can help us to answer two questions:

(a) Have we written a valid specification?

(b) What are its consequences?

For the first of these, validation, we must show that: (1) the specification is syntactically correct; (2) it typechecks; (3) each time a Clear procedure is used its arguments fulfill their respective requirements.

Let us examine these in turn.

1. For this we need a syntax checker. A general one written by David MacQueen has been adapted for Clear by Don Sannella.

2. To typecheck the equations we need to determine the local environment of sorts and operators. This means implementing the signature part of the definitions of the Clear operations, "+", enrich and derive, also dealing with procedure application. Shared subtheories must be handled correctly. We then need a typechecker for expressions (again we have one provided by MacQueen but not yet adapted for Clear).

3. To check that arguments of procedures satisfy the requirement theories we need to use the definitions of the Clear operations and of procedure applications, this time to determine what equations are in the environment at a particular point. We then need a theorem prover to show that each equation in the requirement, suitably instantiated, can be derived from the argument theory. For example, if the requirement is for a partially ordered set and we supply the theory of natural numbers with arithmetic "less than or equal", we must show that this operation is reflexive, transitive and symmetric.

Turning to our second question, how do we discover the consequences of the specification? We may follow the Z language and allow the user to insert "theorems" at any point in addition to the specifying equations. To prove such a theorem follows from the specification involves just the same mechanisms as checking that a requirement is fulfilled.

Thus we have to implement the Clear operations on theories and provide a theorem prover. We have not attempted the latter, but Don Sannella and David Rydeheard as part of their Ph.D. work at Edinburgh have done a pilot implementation of the Clear operations, including procedure application, working from an abstract syntax. Their program is coded in the functional language Hope [Burstall, MacQueen and Sannella 1980], and it follows closely the categorical semantics in Burstall and Goguen [1980]. The categorical definitions are implemented by the methods described in Burstall [1980], an approach which we believe to be novel and interesting. However, this implementation "from first principles", although very transparent, is far from efficient in time or space. It has recently been completed, compiled and run on some small examples; further testing is in progress. It has led to discovery of two "bugs" in the semantic definition. Part of the categorical definitions have been recoded more efficiently in POP-2 by Sannella, and he is designing a more practical implementation.

Coding up the mathematical definitions in a strongly typed functional language seems to provide a good basis for understanding and checking out the language definitions. We feel that we were right to do a formal semantics before attempting an implementation.

4. LIMITATIONS AND EXTENSIONS

The Clear language here described suffers from a number of limitations which make it more difficult to write certain specifications. In particular it lacks quantifiers, infinite data objects and higher order operators.

4.1 Quantifiers

We have an implicit universal quantifier around the equations, but no existential quantifier. So we cannot make a straightforward definition like

$$\text{Prime}(n) \text{ iff not } exists \text{ i } exists \text{ j. i} \neq 1 \text{ and j} \neq 1 \text{ and i} * \text{j} = \text{n}$$

We can wriggle round this by using bounded quantifiers "*exists* x $\in$ S" where S is a finite set. Thus since we need only check divisors up to n

$$\text{Prime}(n) = \text{not } exists \text{ i} \in \text{Upto}(n).exists \text{ j} \in \text{Upto}(n).2 \leqslant \text{i}$$
$$\text{and } 2 \leqslant \text{j and i} * \text{j} = \text{n}$$

where Upto(n) is (straightforwardly) defined to be $\{1,...,n\}$. This doesn't look much better, but in fact we can code up such bounded quantifiers in Clear. Consider

$$exists \text{ n} \in \text{S. Nice}(n)$$

We can make an auxiliary definition of an operation

$$\text{Exists-nice: set(nat)} \longrightarrow \text{bool}$$

with

Exists-nice(empty-set) = false
Exists-nice($\{n\}$) = Nice(n)
Exists-nice(S1 union S2) = Exists-nice(S1) or Exists-nice(S2)

We can use this technique to code up the above definition of Prime with two auxiliaries; but it is rather clumsy.

Much better is to extend Clear to permit axioms using quantifiers. Now equational theories have a "best" model, the initial one, but predicate calculus theories do not. The solution is to use equations for introducing new data, with constructor operations, but to permit predicate calculus sentences with *for all* x and *exists* x when we introduce other operators. (We will call them axioms rather than equations.) Of course, we can still use equality in these predicate calculus axioms.

> *const* Natprime =
> *theory data sorts* nat
> *opns* 0: nat

$$\text{succ: nat} \to \text{nat } \textit{endth}$$
$$\textit{enriched by opns } - + -: \text{nat, nat} \to \text{nat}$$
$$\textit{eqns } 0 + n = n$$
$$\text{succ}(m) + n = \text{succ}(m + n)$$
$$\textit{enriched by predicate } - \leqslant -: \text{nat, nat}$$
$$\textit{axioms } m \leqslant n \textit{ iff exists } k. (m + k = n)$$

Now the Clear semantics in Burstall and Goguen [1980] does not permit this. We need to extend the general scheme of semantics to deal with two kinds of theory, equational and predicate. We believe we know how to do this and it is not hard, but the technical details are out of place here.

4.2 Infinite Values

The data sorts are introduced as initial algebras which may be thought of as consisting of equivalence classes of finite terms. Thus it is not possible to have a data type whose elements are infinite sequences. Even though such infinite objects do not occur as stored values in a computer they are very useful in describing computations, for example the infinite set of strings generated by a grammar, or the infinite sequences of values produced by a non-terminating program, say an airline reservation system.

One remedy is to pass from algebras to continuous algebras, for which some initiality results are known. The equations then involve infinite terms and a fixed point or recursive notation would have to be used for these.

Another remedy is to embed set theory, say presented in first order logic, in Clear. Data sorts would have to include (possibly infinite) sets, not just data defined by initial algebras. This would follow the lead of the Z language [Abrial, Schuman and Meyer 1979], which takes set theory as its basis and constructively defines all other data types in terms of sets. This follows the widely accepted approach for the foundations of mathematics. The question would then arise as to whether initial algebra definitions should be abolished or whether it would be convenient to retain them alongside the set constructions. How do you merge the good ideas in Clear with those in Z?

4.3 Scott Domains

In programming language semantics, and more recently in tackling other specification problems, good use has been made of Scott domains. These can be defined as the solution of recursive domain equations. They permit infinite objects and partial functions and functionals to be described. These more sophisticated data types can also be introduced using initiality, but our thoughts in this direction are preliminary. We would like to explore the connection with Milner's work on LCF [Gordon, Milner and Wadsworth 1979].

4.4 Higher Order Logic

Another related but distinct direction of development is higher order logic, dealing with total functions rather than partial functions. An equational system of higher order logic, based on Cartesian closed categories and total functions, is the subject of the forthcoming thesis at UCLA of K. Parsaye-Ghomi.

4.5 Intensional Logics

Another direction of development for Clear is to incorporate intensional logics, algorithmic logic [Salwicki 1970], dynamic logic [Harel 1979]. These enable us to reason about imperative programs with implicit state. Another intensional logic is temporal logic [Pnueli 1979] which has found favor recently as a means of reasoning about parallel programs. The possibility of putting these into the Clear framework is worth investigation; it would provide structure for large theories in intensional logics.

5. GENERALITY AND INSTITUTIONS

We have introduced operations for combining, enriching and deriving theories, together with a parameter mechanism. All this has been done for first order equational theories. But as we have suggested, analogous methods would work for "putting together" more sophisticated kinds of theory. What are the requirements on a notion of "theory" for it to be amenable to our "putting together" techniques? In Burstall and Goguen [1980] we provided a precise mathematical answer to this question. This is the notion of an *institution*.[4] An institution is a kind of logical formalism with its semantics and including a means of changing the vocabulary. For example predicate calculus is an institution and it permits different vocabularies of functions and relation names. We give here a non-technical definition of institution; for a precise one couched in the elegant language of category theory see the paper cited above.

An institution has:

1. A notion of *signature* (some vocabulary of names for sorts, operators, predicates or whatever) together with a notion of *translations* from one signature to another (mapping sorts of the first vocabulary to sorts of the other, operators to operators, etc.).

2. A notion of *combining* two signatures which share some common sub-signature (disjoint union of vocabularies but respecting the shared part).

3. For each signature a set of *models*, together with a rule which given a translation from signature Σ to signature Σ' and a Σ'-model reduces it to a Σ-model.

---

4. In Burstall and Goguen [1980] it is called a "language" (Section 2.9), but we now prefer the term "institution" as less overworked. Think of institutions such as the Bank of England or the Supreme Court.

4. For each signature a set of *sentences*, together with a way of extending a translation from signature Σ to signature Σ' to a translation from Σ-sentences to Σ'-sentences.

5. For each signature a binary relation "satisfies" between models of the signature and sentences of the signature. This relation must obey the "naturalness" condition: For any translation from Σ to Σ', a Σ'-model satisfies the translation of a Σ-sentence if and only if its reduction satisfies the Σ-sentence.

Consider, as an example, equational logic.

(a) A signature is a set of sorts with a set of operators, and translations map sorts to sorts and operators to operators in a compatible way.

(b) Combination of two signatures is just the disjoint union of the respective sort sets and operator sets respecting shared subsets.

(c) The models of a signature Σ are the algebras with sort and operator names in Σ.

(d) The sentences of Σ are the equations with sort and operator names in Σ.

(e) If f is a translation from Σ to Σ', then a Σ'-algebra is a map form operators in Σ' to functions over the carrier of the algebra. If we compose f with this map, we get a Σ-algebra. This is the reduction of Σ'-models to Σ-models.

(f) Given such an f and a Σ-sentence "$t_1 = t_2$" we can get a Σ'-sentence by just replacing the operators in t_1 and t_2 by their translations under f.

(g) The satisfaction relation is rather obvious. We just evaluate the terms in the equation "$t_1 = t_2$" using the operations of the algebra, doing this for all possible values of the variables. If t_1 always has the same value as t_2 then the algebra satisfies the equation. It is easy to see that this satisfaction relation has the naturalness property required.

Thus equational logic is an institution. So are predicate calculus and the various other systems in the previous section. It also turns out that given an institution with suitable initial models the corresponding data theory is itself an institution [Burstall and Goguen 1980].

(a) *Data Enrichment for Institutions: Duplicity*

How do we handle data enrichment in such a general setting? Given a signature the set of its models must have some extra structure, so that we can talk about initial models, and a translation from one theory to another must define the *free* extension of a model of the source theory.

At first sight this imposes considerable limitations on the kind of institution we may deal with, for example, predicate calculus does not enjoy these free extensions (or even initial models). Recently, however, we have seen how to get around this, by a device which we like to call "duplicity". The idea is that although arbitrary translations in the institution may not give rise to free extensions there may be a well-defined subclass of translations between theories which do. For example if we take a predicate calculus theory and just add new sorts, operators and *equations* (no quantified sentences) then we do get a free extension of any model. So the "duplicity" idea is to have an institution together with a "sub-institution" with limited kinds of translation which permit free extensions.[5] In data enrichments we restrict ourselves to these simpler translations. Thus we might use just equations to introduce new data types but allow ourselves quantifiers when we define new operators over them. A finite graph may be defined equationally, but the operator "paths-from _ to _" might be specified using quantifiers.

Such duplicity may seem obvious, but in fact lack of initial algebras has tended to inhibit people from developing richer specification languages in the algebraic style.

6. SYNTACTIC SUGAR

Clear was designed in an attempt to understand what mathematical operations on theories are needed to build up large theories from small pieces. In order to make the underlying operations on theories transparent we kept the syntax as simple as possible making only minor concessions to readability. The user of a specification language would like a little more "syntactic sugar". A pleasanter syntax would make use of the fact that many definitions of theories take standard forms; we could thus avoid the use of words like *theory, enrich* and *derive* as far as possible and thus keep the declarations and equations uncluttered. Proposals in this direction have been made by Don Sannella at Edinburgh, and we are engaged at SRI in the design of a more readable specification language "Ordinary" which has its semantics defined by translation into Clear.

In order to make the example which follows a little more readable we will introduce a little syntactic sugar in this paper. Note that we will use predicate calculus in enrichments which are not data enrichments (the notation is as usual *exists, all, and, or, not iff, if* $\cdots$ *then* and for convenience Q *if* P as a synonym for *if* P *then* Q). This extension was justified informally by "duplicity" in our previous discussion of institutions. The syntactic changes are as follows.

---

5. Technically we have an institution with a category of theories and a subcategory in which each theory morphism gives rise to a free functor between the category of models of its source and those of its target. (We have not yet written this up.)

1. Write *spec* for *const* and for *proc*.
2. Omit = after *const* P and after *proc* P(...).
3. Omit *in* after *let* ... = ...
4. Write *end* for *endth* and for *enden*.
5. Omit X *enriched by* where X is the sum of the formal parameters and locals.
6. Write *axioms* for *eqns* when an enrichment is not a data enrichment.
7. In an equation or axiom omit the *for all* $x_1,...,x_n$, relying on the reader to recognize the variables.
8. Write ... *where* ... = ... for ... *if* ... = ... to introduce local definitions. Thus a = f(a) *where* a = b + 1 means a = f(a) *if* a = b + 1.

With these rules the following transformation takes place

```
proc P(X: T) =              spec P(X: T)
    let Y = ... in              let Y = ...
    let Z = ... in              let Z = ...
    X + Y + Z enriched by       sorts ...
    sorts ...                   opns ...
    opns ...                    axioms ...
    eqns ...                end
enden
```

We also introduce one simple new semantic construct "renaming"; this is very useful although its effects can be obtained using derive. Thus

T *renaming* x1 *is* x, y1 *is* y

means T with sort or operator names x and y replaced by x1 and y1 (its semantics is very similar to that of enrich: composition of a based theory with a name-changing signature morphism).

7. AN EXAMPLE: LIST PROCESSING WITH GARBAGE COLLECTION

We now present a somewhat more substantial example, list processing with garbage collection.

We assume the existence of a theory Set analogous to Bag already given, adding just the equation S union S=S. This must provide the usual operations such as membership. It has requirement Ident, a theory like Triv but with an equality. We also assume a theory Map with requirement Ident, where a map is a finite function, with operations

f[x] — applying the map f to argument x
insert(f, x, y) — takes f and produces a new map with the addition of (x, y)
domain(f) — the domain Set of a map, i.e. all first members of (x, y)-pairs
f restricted-to S — the restriction of map f to the set S of arguments.

We further assume a theory Relation. A relation R over a finite set S is S together with a set of pairs of S elements. We define a sort rel with

domain(R) — the set S
R[x, y] — true iff (x, y) is one of the pairs
empty(S) — the empty relation over S
insert(R, x, y) — takes R and produces a relation with the addition of (x, y)

Note that if S is a set of elements of sort t then the requirement of Relation is a theory of sets of t.[6] We define the state of a list processing machine as a finite function (map) taking a cell to a pair of values, its car and cdr, where a value is either a cell or an atom. This requires a theory Sum, giving the disjoint union of two sorts with injection functions, and a theory Prod, giving the Cartesian product of two sorts with a pairing function.

We can now define the operation of garbage collection which takes a root cell and a state and produces a "cleaned" state by removing all cells not reachable from the root. In order to define this notion of "reachable" we need a theory of "Reachability"; this is quite general and not restricted to list processing.

We can also define list operations. The operation "cons" takes a pair of values and a state and produces a new cell together with a new state in which the new cell has the given values as its car and cdr. To define cons we need a general theory "Choice" to provide an operation "new" which given a set produces some element not in the set. We also define car, cdr, newcar and newcdr; the latter update the car and cdr parts, respectively, of a given cell with a given value.

All this is done for some arbitrary notion of atom. Finally, we take atoms to be character sequences and combine garbage collection with the list operations to produce a theory of list processing.

    spec Sum(X: Triv, Y: Triv)
        data sorts sum
            opns inl: X $\rightarrow$ sum
                inr: Y $\rightarrow$ sum
    end

---

6. If this theory were defined internally in Relation using Set it would give a different copy from any use of Set outside; this is an irritating feature of our semantics which we referred to above as "proliferation".

spec Prod(X: Triv, Y: Triv)
    data sorts prod
        opns < −,− >: X, Y → prod
    end

spec Choice(S: Set(Ident))
    opns new: set → element
    axioms not (new(S) member S)
    end

spec Reachability(R: Relation(Set(Ident)))
    opns −.− : rel, rel → rel
        −power− : rel, nat → rel
        repeat: rel → rel
        reachables: element, rel → set
    axioms
        (R.R1)[x, z] iff exists y (R[x, y] and R1[y, z])
        (R power 0)[x, y] = (x == y) and x member domain(R)
        R power (n + 1) = (R power n).R
        (repeat R)[x, y] iff exists n ((R power n)[x, y])
        y member reachables(x, R) iff (repeat(R))[x, y]
    end

spec State(Atom: Ident)
    let Cell = *derive sorts* cell
        opns −==−: cell, cell → bool
        using Bool *from* Nat *by* cell *is* nat
    endde
    enriched by opns nil: cell *end*
    let Value = Sum(Atom, Cell) *renaming* value *is* sum
    Map(Cell, Prod(Value, Value))
        renaming   state *is* map,
                      cell-set *is* domain-set,
                      empty-state *is* nilmap

spec Garbage-collection(S: State(Ident))
    let R = Reachability(Relation(S[element *is* cell,
                                        set *is* cell-set]))
        renaming cellrel *is* rel
    opns cellsof: value → cell-set
        cellrelof: state → cellrel
        cleaned-state: cell, state → state
    axioms

$$\begin{aligned}
&\text{cellsof}(\text{inl}(a)) = \text{empty-set}\\
&\text{cellsof}(\text{inr}(c)) = \{c\}\\
&\text{cellrelof}(s)[c,c1] = c1 \text{ member cellsof}(v1) \text{ or}\\
&\qquad\qquad\qquad\qquad c1 \text{ member cellsof}(v2)\\
&\qquad\qquad\qquad\qquad\quad \textit{where } <v1, v2> = s[c]\\
&\text{cleaned-state}(\text{rootcell},s) = s \text{ restricted-to}\\
&\qquad\qquad\qquad\qquad \text{reachables}(\text{cellrelof}(s), \text{rootcell})
\end{aligned}$$

end

spec List-operations(S: State(Ident))
    let Ch = Choice(S[element *is* cell, set *is* cell-set])
    opns cons: value, value, state $\rightarrow$ Prod(State[element *is* cell],
                                                     State[element *is* state])
        car, cdr: cell, state $\rightarrow$ value
        newcar, newcdr: value, cell, state $\rightarrow$ state
    axioms
        cons(v1, v2, s) = $<$c, insert(s, c, $<$v1, v2$>$)$>$
                where c = new(domain(s) union {nil})
        car(c, insert(s, c, $<$v1, v2$>$)) = v1
        cdr(c, insert(s, c, $<$v1, v2$>$)) = v2
        newcar(v, c, s) = insert(s, c, $<$v, v2$>$)
                where $<$v1, v2$>$ = s[c]
        newcdr(v, c, s) = insert(s, c, $<$v1, v$>$)
                where $<$v1, v2$>$ = s[c]

end

spec List-processing
    let Atom = Sequence(Character)
    let St = State(Atom[element *is* sequence])
    Garbage-collection(St) + List-operations(St)

8. PROGRAM DEVELOPMENT

We have shown how to write specifications in Clear but so far we have said nothing about program development. First we should emphasize that even without any formal tools for program development the precise specification of the concepts involved is a valuable aid to writing correct programs. But what can we say about systematic development of programs?

One would like the development to be as well-structured as the Clear specification, that is one should be able to develop implementations of the individual pieces of the Clear specification and then combine these implementations (perhaps breaking the modularity structure in places for the sake of efficiency). This suggests some "calculus of program development", but we are still groping for a suitable mathematical formulation, possibly one based on the notion of 2-category [Goguen and Burstall 1980b].

Another approach is to note that Clear has an executable sub-language. First consider data. A data sort whose constructor operations are subject to no equations is immediately implementable, for example stack with empty and push; call this an *anarchic* data definition. Next consider functions defined over such data. We can implement them if each equation has a simple left-hand side of the form $f(x,...,z)$ where $x,...,z$ are variables, or more generously $f(s,...,t)$ where $s,...,t$ are terms using only anarchic constructor operations. (The implementation does not guarantee termination.) Call these definitions *explicit*, as opposed to implicit ones like $f(g(x)) = x$. Anarchic data and explicit function definitions form the executable sublanguage.

Now we can take a Clear specification and rewrite it a piece at a time, *preserving its denotation*, until we arrive at a version in the executable sublanguage. This can be done by introducing *derive* expressions. Note that we do not restrict Clear itself to this sublanguage because non-anarchic data and implicit function definitions may give much simpler specifications, easier to get right.

Thus we could do program development in Clear if we were content with a functional programming language. Using, say, dynamic logic as the institution we might be able to have an imperative target language.

There are still problems, notably connected with many-one representations and quotienting, but we think that this approach may be fruitful.

For other interesting work in this area see Ehrich [1978]; Ehrig, Kreowski, Mahr and Padawitz [1980]; Hupbach [1980].

9. CONCLUSION

Our research on the Clear project has concentrated on a specific issue: modularity in specifications. We have devoted little attention to the other important issues of good notation for the detailed presentation and of a good library of primitive concepts. Rather we have striven to make these issues orthogonal to the modularity issue and we have managed to express this orthogonality in mathematical form. We have also shown how the data/procedure distinction can be handled in a general way using the idea of free constructions and "data theories". Quite apart from the particular language, Clear, which we have defined, we hope that our approach to orthogonality in semantics may be fruitful. We hope that the discussion here may motivate some people to read our semantics paper [Burstall and Goguen 1980].

Open areas for future investigation include:

(a) implementation of Clear;

(b) a more model-theoretic semantics for Clear with procedure denotations being functors instead of theory morphisms (Jim Thatcher has argued forcefully for this);

(c) various mutations, both semantic and syntactic, to make Clear more usable;

(d) a theory of the modular development of programs from Clear specifications.

ACKNOWLEDGMENTS

Our work on Clear stemmed from work of the ADJ group (Goguen, Thatcher, Wagner and Wright), and we have continued to benefit from the insights of the other members of this group. Our students David Rydeheard, Don Sannella and Joe Tardo have done a lot of hard work on implementations; they have provided valuable discussions, as have other colleagues at Edinburgh and Los Angeles. Don Sannella has done a number of Clear examples and has helped with the ones herein. David MacQueen's work on Hope provided a valuable tool. We much appreciate Eleanor Kerse's typing. RMB would like to thank IBM for the Visiting Professorship at the University of Liège, and the Computer Science Department there, especially Professor Danny Ribbens, for their friendly and stimulating reception. The work has been funded by the Science Research Council and the National Science Foundation.

JOSEPH A. GOGUEN
University of California

JOSEPH J. TARDO
Hughes Aircraft Company
and
University of California

AN INTRODUCTION TO OBJ:
A Language for Writing and Testing Formal Algebraic Program Specifications

1. INTRODUCTION

This paper describes a formal language, called OBJ, for writing and testing algebraic program specifications. OBJ is also a programming language, since it allows algebraic specifications to be executed.

OBJ is an on-going experimental project, and there are already several different designs and implementations. The basic idea of a rewrite rule implementation for the initial algebra approach to abstract data types (as in Goguen, Thatcher, Wagner and Wright [1977]) was first presented in Goguen's class at UCLA in the fall of 1974, and Tardo did the first implementation on UCLA's IBM 360/91 in the Winter of 1976. Goguen and Tardo [1977] describe a somewhat later incarnation of this version, called OBJ-0. Subsequently, UCLA acquired a PDP-10, and the OBJ effort was shifted to this facility. There now exists a relatively stable version, also called OBJ-0, to which most of this paper is devoted. In addition, a version called OBJ-T is now partially implemented, and many of its features are discussed here. Finally, we are beginning to plan OBJ-1, and we wish to share our ideas. Hopefully, this will not be too confusing to the reader.

An important practical use of OBJ is in testing and debugging specifications. Experience has shown that specifications can be very helpful in program development in connection with a top-down or stepwise refinement methodology [Dijkstra 1968a; Wirth 1971a] both as an initial design to guide the implementation, and also as a standard against which to measure the correctness of a final implementation. Unfortunately, experience also clearly shows that it is not trivial to produce good specifications, particularly for large systems. Indeed, most published specifications, even of simple data types, are actually wrong in detail, if not in principle; and many specifications of large systems are seriously wrong. Thus, it is important to provide ways both of checking the details of simple specifications, and also of handling the complexity of large specifications.

OBJ provides a number of features which are helpful in creating correct specifications. These include the following: breaking large specifications into an interconnection of smaller, "mind sized" pieces (see Burstall and Goguen [1977]); testing the pieces, and the interconnection, by executing test cases;

very strong typing; flexible user-definable notation; systematic use of error conditions; and a number of internal consistency checks, both syntactic and semantic.

The underlying algebraic semantics of OBJ may be contrasted with the more popular logic-based approach [Floyd 1967; Hoare 1969; Manna 1969], as applied, for example, in Robinson and Levitt [1977], and Nakajima, Honda, and Nakahara [1977].

A number of interesting programs have been written in OBJ. Harm [1977a] specified a simple programming language with expressions, assignments, gotos, and iterations, and then ran a number of programs in it. Harm [1977b] contains an artificial intelligence "robot planner" for problems in rearranging a world of blocks; this was subsequently extended by Wong [1979] to handle conflicting subgoals. Kaufman [1977] specified and tested a simple text editor. Goguen, Tardo, Williamson and Zamfir [1978] specify a keyed file data structure, including sorting and retrieval operations, following the work of [Melkanoff and Zamfir 1978] on algebraic specification of data base structures; Zamfir has also programmed some of the other data base structures from the above paper in OBJ. Goguen has used OBT-T with extensive use of parameterized objects to specify a programming language with block structure and DO-WHILE, in addition to assignments, conditional, and the usual expressions, but at this time has not tested it. The Appendix of this paper specifies the data base system for an airport scheduler.

It is entirely possible that complex programs, such as operating systems and data base query systems, can be algebraically specified and then simulated in OBJ. OBJ would assist in establishing the correctness of these specifications in two ways: by allowing direct testing at the user (or some internal) interface; and by performing consistency checks, in a semi-automatic mode, directly on the form of the specifications.

OBJ is not intended for "performance" requirements, such as execution speed (see Liskov and Berzins [1979]). In this respect, OBJ may be classified with the DDN notation of DREAM [Riddle, Wileden, Sayler, Segal and Stavy 1978], TOPD [Henderson 1975], and SPECIAL [Robinson and Roubine 1977], for example. Other languages, such as SEMANOL [Anderson, Belz, and Blum 1976], may be of use for some performance requirements; certainly there is a general tendency to develop specification languages in this direction by providing appropriate operational semantics. However, none of the above mentioned languages has a precise underlying mathematical semantics, as far as we are aware.

Languages and systems which are closer in spirit to OBJ include NPL, now called HOPE [Burstall 1978], CLEAR [Burstall and Goguen 1977], TEL [Levi and Sirovich 1975], and AFFIRM, formerly DTVS [Musser 1977, 1980]. HOPE is close enough to OBJ that a similar mathematical semantics could be provided for many of its features; the primary differences lie in HOPE's pattern matching type system and its intended primary use as a programming language in connection with program transformation systems. CLEAR has inspired OBJ's modularity, and in particular OBJ-T's IMAGE feature for implementing procedures which produce new modules from old (this feature is similar to what have been called "parameterized types" in the literature). TEL appears not to have an abstract semantics, and neither TEL nor AFFIRM appears to support modularity nor module-valued procedures. AFFIRM has been developed primarily as part of a system to verify abstract data type implementation [Guttag, Horowitz and Musser 1976], and therefore lacks many of the convenience features of a programming or specification language although it appears to be evolving in that direction. An interesting point is that AFFIRM's rewrite rule semantics and inductive verification procedures [Musser 1980] do not appear to be consistent with the ideas of Guttag [1975] and Guttag, Horowitz and Musser [1978], in that any algebra satisfying the equations and sufficient consistency will be acceptable; rather, the initial algebra semantics of Goguen, Thatcher, Wagner and Wright [1977], or equivalently Zilles [1975a], is needed.

It should be noted that of all these languages, only OBJ handles coercions, overloaded operators, or errors in a rigorous and systematic manner. Goguen [1977] argues that it is essential to handle errors in a mathematically precise manner, and Goguen [1978b] generalizes Goguen [1977] to order-sorted algebras; these include coercions, subsorts, union and intersection sorts, overloaded operators, multiple distinguishable sorts of errors (exceptions), and error handling.

Section 2 presents an overview of OBJ, with some examples. Section 3 presents some characteristic features of OBJ-0 in more detail, while Section 4 discusses some implementation issues, particularly for the parser and evaluator. Section 5 discusses the OBJ-T system presently being implemented, and Section 6 discusses the extended example given in the Appendix. The paper concludes in Section 7 with a summary of our experience so far in using OBJ.

For a formal treatment of the algebra underlying OBJ, see Goguen, Thatcher, Wagner and Wright [1977], Goguen, Thatcher and Wagner [1975, 1978], or Goguen [1977, 1978a, 1978b]. Related material appears in Guttag [1975], Guttag, Horowitz and Musser [1978], Zilles [1975a], and Musser [1977, 1980]. Familiarity with the concept of abstract data type is assumed, along with the belief that data types can be effectively modelled by universal (initial) algebras. For readers who are sympathetic with this approach, but are not fluent in algebra, it should suffice to bear in mind that an algebra is essentially a set with some operations defined on it. Many-sorted algebras then have many sets (one for each sort), and some operations among these sets.

We would like to thank: Prof. R. M. Burstall, for his enthusiasm and helpful comments; Drs. Thatcher, Wagner, and Wright, who helped in developing the theoretical foundations; Drs. P. Mosses and J. Schwartz for noticing an error in an early version of Goguen [1977]; D. Harm, M. Zamfir, S. Wong, T. Kaufman, Dr. N. Williamson and several generations of OBJ users at UCLA; Professors M. Melkanoff, D. Martin, A. Avezienis and D. Berry of UCLA for encouragement and comments; F. Nourani, J. Weiner, M. Cutler, K. Parsye-Ghomi, and J. Gallier of the UCLA "SATOC" group for their comments and patience; the referees of this paper for their helpful comments; and for support, financial and otherwise, Naropa Institute, Hughes Aircraft Co., the University of Colorado (Boulder), the University of Edinburgh, the (British) Science Research Council, and the National Science Foundation. J. A. G. also wishes to thank the Venerable Chögyam Trungpa, Rinpoche, and Dr. Charlotte Linde, for personal reasons.

2. THE STRUCTURE OF OBJ

OBJ resembles more traditional languages such as LISP [McCarthy, Abrahams, Edwards, Hart and Levin 1965] and one-line APL [Iverson 1962] in permitting definitions of operations, and then evaluation of expressions. However, OBJ differs from such languages in many important ways, including: operations are defined in modules (or "objects" as we shall say), and have a different character in OBJ in that operator symbols do not denote procedures in the usual sense, because they are defined implicitly by algebraic equations (using the initial algebra model); in particular, there is no assignment function, nor any assignable variables; there are also no side effects, no statements, no goto's, and indeed, none of the serialization constructs associated with the usual programming languages. However, OBJ is very strongly typed, and also supports sub-types, coercions, and the overloading of operators. It should be noted, however, that one can specify in OBJ imperative features such as assignment, and even side effects.

The syntax for objects was inspired by the notation for presenting initial many-sorted algebras, as in Goguen, Thatcher, Wagner and Wright [1977]. It is intended that an object denote a particular many-sorted algebra.

An OBJ object corresponds roughly to a SIMULA class [Dahl and Nygaard 1966], CLU cluster [Liskov 1976], in that it is a means for declaring an abstract data type, assuming the inseparability of data values from their associated operations. However, objects do not necessarily have a distinguished "type of interest," as in Zilles [1975a] or Guttag, Horowitz and Musser [1976]. Furthermore, the use of data type specifications in procedural languages was not an overriding concern in the design of OBJ, so that questions such as the nature of the run time environment need not be addressed, as in CLU and Alphard. Nor is it intended that objects will be separately compiled.

OBJ-0 has three built-in, i.e., already available, objects. These are INT (for integers), BOOL (for Booleans), and ID (for identifiers). The operators provided for INT include increment (denoted INC, with prefix syntax), decrement (denoted DEC, with prefix syntax), greater than (infix >), less than (infix <), plus all the usual constants (0, 1, 10, 108, ...), and the usual operators, infix =, +, *, −, and unary −. Integer arithmetic is implemented with LISP functions. BOOL provides either infix + or | for disjunction, either infix * or & for conjunction, prefix − or ¬ (up-arrow ↑ on the DEC-10), infix ⇒ and ⇔ for implication and if-and-only-if, and T and F for true and false.

ID has a single infix operator =, and its constants are identifiers beginning with a single apostrophe, as 'ATOM.

User defined objects in OBJ begin with the keyword OBJ (or OBJECT) and end with JBO (or TCEJBO).[1] Objects are subdivided into sort, operation and equation sections; the sorts and operations together constitute a signature. Each operator declaration indicates its argument sorts (or arity), its target sort, and its syntactic form. The equations section begins with a declaration of the variables to be used, including their sorts. Figure 1 gives a skeleton of the internal structure of an object.

```
OBJ<name>
SORTS<new sorts>/<old sorts>
OK-OPS...
FIX-OPS...
ERR-OPS...
VARS...
OK-EQNS...
EQNS...
ERR-EQNS...
JBO
```

Figure 1. OBJ-0 skeleton

The name of the object must be a unique single identifier. The SORTS line gives the sort names involved in this object, with a slash separating newly introduced sort names from old ones. More than one new sort can be introduced in an object; there can also be no new sorts.

OBJ distinguishes three types of operators. These are used for ordinary or ok situations, for exceptional or error situations, and for recovery or fix situations. Error operators are used to form error messages. Fix operators are illustrated in Section 3.

Operators are used in expressions, where an expression is either a constant operator, or an operator together with its arguments, which are also expressions. Alternatively, expressions may be viewed as trees, with operator names labelling the leaves and nodes. When we refer to the "the operator" of an expression, we will mean the topmost operator in its tree representation.

Every expression has a sort, the sort of its operator, and is either an ok or an error expression. An expression whose operator is an error operator is always an error expression, as is one whose operator is ok but which contains an error expression argument. An expression whose operator is a fix operator is not necessarily an error expression even if some of its arguments are error expressions.

---

1. This notation is intended as a somewhat humorous negative comment on certain contemporary programming language conventions. Goguen [1977] claims that TCEJBO is Polish for OBJECT.

Operators are declared in a manner which is commonly used in algebra. An example declaration of an operator whose sort is INT, and whose arity is (INT, INT), is

```
G : INT INT -> INT
```

An operator declared with null arity is a constant of the declared sort. For example,

```
CREATE : -> INT
```

The syntax of an operator is determined by its form, which is given to the left of the colon. In the first example above, a prefix syntax is assumed for G, as in the expression

```
G(2,G(4,5))
```

but OBJ also permits users to customize the syntax of their operators, using underbars in the operator form to indicate where the respective arguments go. For example

```
PUSH_ON_ : INT,STACK -> STACK
```

can be used as in the expression

```
PUSH 2 ON CREATE
```

This allows OBJ users to "sugar" their syntax as desired. OBJ also permits coercions, with the form

```
_ : S1 -> S2
```

used to indicate that S1 is to be a sub-sort of S2. What happens during parsing (see later for further details) is that if some operator wants an argument of sort S2, but the sub-expression in that position cannot be parsed as sort S2, then the parser will check to see if the sub-expression can be parsed as being of sort S1. That is, coercion occurs only on backtracking from a failure to parse; however, this does not apply at the top level, where the system interactively asks you what sort you want the expression parsed as, if it is not already indicated in some way.

OBJ also permits distinct operators with the same syntactic form, provided that they have different arities. This situation is often referred to as operator *overloading*. For example, among the built-in operators of OBJ-0 are

```
_+_ : BOOL,BOOL -> BOOL
_+_ : INT,INT -> INT
```

and a number of equality operators, with forms (_=_) or (_==_).

Evidently, this provides tremendous room for ambiguities to arise. However, we define an OBJ expression of sort S to be one which has one and only one parse of sort S; and OBJ will reject any expression not satisfying this condition. Because OBJ is an interactive system, all the user has to do in general is to supply some additional parentheses, and then carry on. For a formal definition of OBJ expression, and more details on parsing coercion and overloading, see Goguen [1978a, 1978b].

This aspect of OBJ has been developed in the belief that it is worth some extra thought at design time, some extra effort at implementation time, and some extra computation at run time, to support a syntax which is as convenient, flexible, and natural as possible. Indeed, the usual limitation to purely prefix operators, without overloading or coercion, seems intolerable in a language which is intended to be used in a practical way for software specification.

It must not be thought that these are purely syntactic issues, with no serious semantic consequences. As Goguen [1978a] shows in some detail, the systematic development and exploitation of the notion of sub-sort leads to a powerful methodology for handling errors and exceptions of all kinds. Also note that the coercion _ : S1 —> S2 means that all items (but not necessarily operations) of sort S1 are also of sort S2, which is clearly a semantic statement. It is, moreover, one which has far-reaching consequences on the notion of algebra which is needed.

Each variable used in the equations must be listed, following the keyword VARS, together with its sort. For example

```
VARS
   I,J : INT ;
   R1,R2 : RECORD
```

Variable names cannot duplicate constant names of the same sort. The expressions used in equations can contain variables as well as constants, and variables are always considered to be ok.

Equations are pairs of expressions of the same sort, separated by an equal sign. For example,

```
(G(0,J)= J)
```

There are two types of equation, following Goguen [1977], which follow the keywords OK-EQNS and ERR-EQNS within an object, and apply respectively to ok and error expressions. In addition, OBJ permits a third type of equation, for which the keyword EQNS is used; these apply to both ok and to error expressions.

Error operators are not permitted in OK-EQNS except in expressions which are the arguments of FIX-OPS operators; similarly ERR-EQNS must have right-hand sides which are error expressions. Each equation is of some particular sort, and its constituent expressions must be unambiguous.

A conditional form is also allowed for equations (as in Thatcher, Wagner, and Wright [1976]). The condition must be an expression of the built-in sort BOOL, and appears following an IF in the form. For example

```
(G(I,J)= J IF (I = 0 ))
```

A conditional equation applies only if its conditional expression evaluates (as described in Section 4) to the Boolean constant T.

A simple specification of the factorial function is shown in Figure 2. This object uses the system-provided objects INT and BOOL, for the integers and Boolean truth values, respectively. OK-OPS has a single unary operator, F, with conventional prefix parenthesized syntax.

```
OBJ FACTORIAL
SORTS / INT BOOL
OK-OPS
     F : INT -> INT
ERR-OPS
     NEG-ARG :  -> INT
VARS
     I : INT
OK-EQNS
     (F(O)= 1)
     (F(I)= I * F (I − 1)IF(I > 0))
ERR-EQNS
     (F(I)= NEG-ARG IF(I < 0))
JBO
```

Figure 2. Factorial

There is a null-ary, or constant, error operator, NEG-ARG, declared in ERR-OPS. When this operator appears in an expression, it indicates that the factorial of a negative number was attempted. The VARS declaration tells us that the symbol I is a variable of sort INT in the equations to follow. There are two OK-EQNS and one ERR-EQNS, including two conditional equations.

An example of OBJ evaluation syntax is

```
RUN F(5) NUR
```

requesting computing of the value of F with the argument 5. OBJ responds

```
AS INT: 120
```

An alternative syntax to RUN encloses the expression in parenthesis, as,

```
(F(5))
```

AN INTRODUCTION TO OBJ

OBJ evaluates (i.e., derives the value of) expressions by using the equations as rewrite rules. Equations are inherently symmetric, whereas rules are asymmetric. OBJ treats equations as rules which are oriented in the left to right order in which they are written.

To apply a rule to an expression, OBJ must first find a unifier; that is, it must find an expression for each variable symbol occurring on the left side of the rule, so that, when these expressions are substituted for their respective variables, the original expression results. If the rule is in conditional form, evaluating the condition after substituting the expressions of the unifier for the variables must yield the BOOL value T. When OBJ finds a rule with which it can unify an expression, it replaces the expression with one it obtains from the right side of the rule by substituting the expressions of the unifier for their respective symbols which occur on the right side or, in the case of conditioned equations, in the condition, must also occur on the left side.

For example, in applying the second of the OK-EQNS in Figure 2 to the expression F(3), the unifier consists of the pair (I, 3), and the result of the rule application is

$$3 * F(3 - 1)$$

In most cases, OBJ applies rules first to the innermost nested sub-expressions until no more rules apply; that is, until those sub-expressions are reduced, or in normal form. To apply rules to an expression, all the arguments of its operator must first be reduced. Rewriting is done bottom-up and left-to-right (on the tree representations of expressions) until the entire expression is reduced. This order resembles the "by value" method with which LISP EXPR's are usually evaluated.

For example, the evaluation of F(3) proceeds as follows, omitting trivial steps.

```
        F(3)
        3 * F(2)
        3 *(2 * F(1))
        3 *(2 *(1 * F(0)))
        3 *(2 *(1 * 1))
        3 *(2 * 1)
        3 * 2
        6
AS INT: 6
```

Evaluation is complicated by the error facility. The algebraic semantics of Goguen [1977] demand that error expressions (which do not necessarily contain error operators prior to evaluation) should not evaluate prematurely to ok values. It has been proved [Goguen 1977] that the above evaluation order correctly implements specifications containing error operators, provided that all ERR-EQNS are tried before any OK-EQNS. If an error equation applies, then OK-EQNS are not used on that sub-expression, nor for rewriting any expressions which contain that sub-expression. This does not affect sub-expressions which comprise the other (parallel) arguments of the immediately enclosing expression's operator.

Here is another evaluation using Figure 2.

```
          F(F(5 - 7))+ F(2)
          F(F(- 2))+ F(2)
          F(NEG-ARG)+ F(2)
          F(NEG-ARG)+(2 * F(1))
          F(NEG-ARG)+(2 *(1 * F(0)))
          F(NEG-ARG)+(2 *(1 * 1))
          F(NEG-ARG)+(2 * 1)
          F(NEG-ARG)+ 2
    AS INT:  >>ERROR>>  F(NEG-ARG)+ 2
```

It may seem surprising at first that one gets a compound expression containing error operators (in this example, an error constant) instead of a simple list of error messages, as in the usual compilers. However, there is a consistent philosophy behind this. The main idea is to "under-evaluate" expressions, so that it is possible to trace back to the source of the error, by comparing the result expression with the expression whose evaluation produced it (see Goguen [1977] for a more detailed expression of this idea).

In visualizing the connection between OBJ's operational semantics and its initial algebra semantics, it might help to consider initial algebra semantics in terms of "word" algebras. With no equations, each word or expression would denote a distinct value in the intended semantic domain. The equations identify those expressions which are to have equivalent meanings in the intended semantic domain; that is, those which are to denote the same value (Goguen, Thatcher, and Wagner [1978] give a formal definition of this equivalence relation). OBJ evaluation computes, for any given expression, a reduced expression representing its equivalence class, and this expression is taken as a representative of the entire class. For example, the reduced value of the expression F(3) above is the expression 6. The definition of the equivalence relation in the case of error algebras is given in Goguen [1977]. For a more formal treatment of OBJ evaluation, see Goguen [1978]; see also Wand [1977a, 1977b] and Musser [1977, 1980] for closely related discussions, and Huet [1977]; O'Donnell [1977]; Lankford [1975]; Rosen [1973] for important background information on sub-tree replacement systems.

3. SELECTED FEATURES OF OBJ-0

This section discusses and/or illustrates some of the more distinctive OBJ features, including user defined syntax, error messages, hidden operators, coercion between sorts, associative and commutative operators, and FIX-OPS.

```
OBJ LIST-OF-INT
SORTS LIST / INT
OK-OPS
     __ __ : LIST LIST -> LIST (ASSOCIATIVE)
     _ : INT -> LIST
JBO
```

Figure 3. LIST object

Consider the definition of LIST in Figure 3. We feel this conveys the list concept with a minimum of fuss and notation. Notice that the operator forms consist only of underbars. The first operator constructs lists by juxtaposition of arguments, and the second regards all integers as (one element) lists. Since juxtaposition is declared ASSOCIATIVE, OBJ automatically provides an equation (in EQNS) for (left) associativity; furthermore, associativity permits the OBJ parser to accept LIST expressions which would otherwise be ambiguous, such as in

RUN 1 2 3 NUR

to which OBJ responds

AS LIST: (1,2,3)

Note that all the integers here have been coerced from sort INT to sort LIST.

Suppose we now enter the object shown in Figure 4 to define HEAD and TAIL operations for lists (the error message is actually not optional, since there is no constant for the empty list), and then enter

RUN HEAD(2,3,4 + HEAD(6)) NUR

Because the expression does not have a unique sort, OBJ initiates a dialogue such as the following

```
Which sort would you like it ?
>HOW?

Can be parsed as one of (INT LIST)
>AS INT
AS INT: 2
      OBJ LIST2
      SORTS / LIST INT
      OK-OPS
         HEAD_ : LIST -> INT
         TAIL_ : LIST -> LIST
      ERR-OPS
         NO-TAIL! : -> LIST
      VARS
         I : INT
         L : LIST
      OK-EQNS
         AS INT (HEAD(I,L)= I)
         (TAIL(I,L)= L)
         AS INT (HEAD(I)= I)
      ERR-EQNS
         (TAIL(I)= NO-TAIL!)
      JBO
```

Figure 4. List head and tail operations

If we try

    AS INT RUN HEAD(2,3,4 + HEAD TAIL 6) NUR

Then we get

AS INT: >>ERROR>>(HEAD(2,3,4 + (HEAD NO-TAIL!)))

as a descriptive error message. On input, parentheses and commas may be used as punctuation; on output, however, only the minimum number of parentheses required to remove ambiguity are provided, with no commas. Also, all parentheses may be suppressed on output, if the user feels this improves readability.

Hidden operators may be controversial but they are supported by OBJ. To declare an operator hidden, put (HIDDEN) after its syntactic definition. Hidden operators cannot be used outside the object in which they were declared, but may be used freely within it. The hiding mechanism can be temporarily disabled for evaluation purposes, permitting specifications with hiddens to be debugged.

Hidden operators are used in the traversing stack example of Figure 5. It has been claimed that this data structure cannot be algebraically specified with a finite number of equations unless hidden operators are used (see Majster [1977]; Thatcher, Wagner and Wright [1978]). Incidentally, equations which begin with a single equal sign are understood to use the same left side as the previous equation. This example also illustrates the OBJ comment convention, delineation by matching pairs of ∗∗∗.

```
OBJ TRAVERSING-STACK
SORTS STACK HSTACK / INT BOOL
OK-OPS
    PUSH : STACK INT -> STACK
    CREATE : -> STACK
    DOWN : STACK -> STACK
    POP : STACK -> STACK
    READ : STACK -> INT
    RETURN : STACK -> STACK
    __ : HSTACK INT -> STACK
    HPUSH : HSTACK INT -> HSTACK
    HT_ : HSTACK -> INT (HIDDEN)
    BOTTOM : -> HSTACK (HIDDEN)
ERR-OPS
    UNDERFLOW : -> STACK
        *** POP EMPTY STACK ***
    NOELEM : -> INT
        *** READ EMPTY STACK ***
    PTR-NOT-UP : -> STACK
        *** READ OTHER THAN TOP
        ELEMENT ***
    PTR-AT-BOTTOM : -> STACK
        *** DOWN WHEN AT BOTTOM ***
VARS
    I J K : INT
    HS : HSTACK
OK-EQNS
    (CREATE = BOTTOM 0)
    (READ(HPUSH(HS,I)J)= I IF J = INC(HT HS))
    (= READ(HS,J)IF NOT(J = INC(HT HS)))
    (PUSH((HS J),K)=(HPUSH(HS,K),INC(J))
        IF J =(HT HS))
    (HT BOTTOM = 0)
    (HT(HPUSH(HS,J))= INC(HT HS))
    (RETURN(HS,J)= HS DEC(J)IF(J > 0))
    (DOWN(HS,J)=(HS,DEC(J))IF J > 0)
    (POP(HPUSH(HS,J),K)= HS DEC(K)IF
        K = INC(HT HS))
ERR-EQNS
```

```
    (READ(BOTTOM,0)= NOELEM)
    (POP(BOTTOM,0)= UNDERFLOW)
    (PUSH(HS I,J)= PTR-NOT-UP IF NOT(I = HT HS))
    (DOWN(HS,0)= PTR-AT-BOTTOM)
    (POP(HS,I)= PTR-NOT-UP IF NOT(I = HT HS))
JBO
```

Figure 5. Traversing stack

The following are a few evaluations of traversing stack expressions:

```
    RUN READ(PUSH(PUSH(PUSH(CREATE,1),2),3)) NUR
AS INT: 3
    RUN READ(DOWN(PUSH(PUSH(PUSH(CREATE,1),2),3))) NUR
AS INT: 2
    RUN READ(POP(RETURN(DOWN(PUSH(PUSH(PUSH(CREATE,
       1),2),3)))))  NUR
AS INT: >>ERROR>> READ(PTR-NOT-UP)
    RUN HPUSH(1,BOTTOM) NUR
?Warning: EXPRESSION CANNOT BE PARSED
    RUN PUSH(DOWN(PUSH(CREATE,1)),2) NUR
AS STACK: >>ERROR>> PTR-NOT-UP
```

Now consider the specification for integer sets in Figure 6 (see Liskov and Zilles [1977]). The first of the OK-OPS, INSERT, is declared to have the PERMUTING attribute. When evaluating an expression whose operator is declared PERMUTING, OBJ remembers the intermediate values resulting from successful rule applications to that expression. This is facilitated by the current evaluation strategy, it is in normal form. Each new expression is compared with the remembered ones; if a previously seen expression reappears, OBJ refuses to apply the rule which produced that expression, but it will try other rules. Evaluation of expressions whose operator is not PERMUTING proceeds as before.

```
CBJ SET
SORTS SET / INT BOOL
OK-OPS
   INSERT : SET INT -> SET (PERMUTING)
   REMOVE : SET INT -> SET
   HAS?   : SET INT -> BOOL
   EMPTY  : -> SET
VARS
   I J : INT
   S   : SET
OK-EQNS
```

```
          (INSERT(INSERT(S,I),J)= INSERT(INSERT
             (S,J),I)IF NOT(I = J))
          (= INSERT(S,I)IF I = J)
          (REMOVE(INSERT(S,I),J)= REMOVE(S,J)IF I = J)
          (= INSERT (REMOVE(S,J),I)IF NOT(I = J))
          (REMOVE(EMPTY,I)= EMPTY)
          (HAS?(INSERT(S,I),J)=(I = J)OR HAS?(S,J))
          (= T IF(I = J))
          (HAS?(EMPTY,I)= F)
     JBO
```

Figure 6. A set object

For the specification of Figure 6, many evaluations in the normal mode would never terminate because of the first equation, which "permutes" the order of the arguments of the operator INSERT. For example, the evaluation sequence

```
         INSERT(INSERT(INSERT(EMPTY,1),2),3)
         INSERT(INSERT(INSERT(EMPTY,2),1),3)
         INSERT(INSERT(INSERT(EMPTY,1),2),3)
```

could occur. The PERMUTING feature causes evaluation to terminate; however, it can be costly.

An alternative to PERMUTING is the "run-with-memory" evaluation mode, in which all intermediate values for all evaluations are remembered, as though all operators were PERMUTING. To command this form of evaluation, use the form

```
         RUM INSERT(INSERT(EMPTY,1),2) MUR
```

instead of the usual syntax.

The error algebra theory of Goguen [1977] requires that all operators preserve errors. But in practice, this can be inconvenient, and OBJ provides a number of built-in operators which can turn error values into ok values. These include an operator ERR for each declared sort which will return T if its argument is an error value and F otherwise; and a built-in equality for each sort, with infix syntax, _==_, which returns T if both its arguments evaluate to the same value, even if that value is an error value, and returns F otherwise, unless one or both of the evaluations fails to terminate. Users can declare their own equality operators by use of the attribute (EQUALITY), and such operators may be either OK-OPS or FIX-OPS. For example

```
         _IS-SAME-AS_? : S1,S1 -> BOOL (EQUALITY)
```

It should be noted that this operator will not in general work correctly if there are PERMUTING operators involved in the arguments. Although an evaluation strategy is known which handles this case, it was not deemed cost-effective for implementation in either OBJ-0 or OBT-T.

OBJ also provides a conditional with syntax IF_THEN_ELSE_FI for each declared sort. The semantic issues associated with conditionals are rather complex and interesting; they are discussed at some length beginning after the next paragraph. This long discussion is justified by the interest and confusion which conditionals have engendered in the literature.

In addition to the built-in operators mentioned above, OBJ permits users to define their own operators having the capability of turning error values to ok values; these operators are called FIX-OPS, and they can be defined and used in OBJ objects much as are OK-OPS and ERR-OPS. FIX-OPS are useful in treating error recovery and exception handling, to complement the capabilities for error (or exception) detection and error message production already provided in the strict error algebra framework. The theory which underlies this facility is rather complex and very general, and there is no room to discuss it here. Let it suffice to say that it involves algebras whose set of sorts is partially ordered, so that it makes sense to speak of sub-sorts and union sorts; error algebras have the property that each sort S is a disjoint union of sub-sorts S-OK and S-ERR; see Goguen [1978b].

We now discuss conditionals. First, it is necessary to distinguish between conditional equations, having the form (_=_ IF _) in OBJ, and equations involving the conditional operator IF_THEN_ELSE_FI, which appears as part of expressions. Ignoring errors for the moment, the former can be defined in terms of the latter, because

$$(E1 = E2 \text{ IF } B)$$

is true if

$$(E1 = \text{IF } B \text{ THEN } E2 \text{ ELSE } E1 \text{ FI})$$

is true, moreover, the conditional expression form can also replace the conditional equation form when both are viewed as rewrite rules, if some way is provided to prevent the conditional expression rule from being repeatedly applied to itself. Some versions of OBJ have incorporated such a mechanism. All that it is necessary to do is to compare the new rewritten expression with the old expression to which the rule was applied, and then refuse to apply a rule for which these expressions are the same. The OBJ "run with memory" mode of evaluation will also accomplish this, but at the greater expense of remembering the whole history of evaluation. Conversely, Goguen [1978a] gives an algorithm for translating an equation with possibly nested conditional operators into a set of conditional equations involving no conditional operators, although further ERR-EQNS should be added to handle the error behaviors.

Thatcher, Wagner and Wright [1978] discuss conditional equations of the form

$$(E1 = E2 \text{ IF } E3 = E4)$$

and show that these have more definitional power than the forms allowed in OBJ. However, this is only because they allow the equality relation in the condition clause to be "absolute," i.e., potentially uncomputable. But it seems to us that anything which would normally be called a "data type" will have a decidable (indeed, an equationally definable) equality relation. And in fact, the example given by Thatcher, Wagner and Wright [1978] is pathological in that it does not have a decidable equality. If all data types are assumed to have equationally definable equalities, then conditional equations add nothing except notational convenience (remember that we are ignoring errors for the moment). Goguen, Thatcher, Wagner and Wright [1977] showed how to give a purely equational definition for the conditional. In OBJ notation, this definition can be expressed as in Figure 7. Thus, for practical data types, and still ignoring errors, there is no reason for any built-in conditional, except convenience; and actually built-in conditionals are somewhat of a nuisance if put into the theoretical development, as in Zilles [1975a].

The situation regarding conditional is more complex if errors are taken into account. For example, consider the expression

$$(\text{COND}(0 = 0, 1, 0 * \text{NFG-ARG}))$$

with COND as in Figure 7, and NEG-ARG an error constant of sort INT. In line with the error algebra approach of Goguen [1977], this expression must evaluate to an error. In fact, OBJ-0 evaluates it to

$$(\text{COND}(T, 1, 0 * \text{NEG-ARG}))$$

```
OBJ COND
SORTS / INT BOOL
OK-OPS
    COND : BOOL INT INT -> INT
VARS
    I J : INT
OK-EQNS
    (COND(T,I,J)= I)
    (COND(F,I,J)= J)
JBO
```

Figure 7. A conditional operator for INT

```
OBJ FACT#2
SORTS / INT BOOL
OK-OPS
    F : INT -> INT
ERR-OPS
    NEG-ARG : -> INT
VARS
    I : INT
OK-EQNS
    (F(I)= COND(I = 0, 1,I * F(I - 1)))
ERR-EQNS
    (F(I)= NEG-ARG IF I < 0)
JBO
```

Figure 8. Factorial using COND

But there certainly are situations in which a conditional with one error argument should evaluate to an ok expression. For example, in evaluating F(0) with the definition of F as factorial in Figure 8, we expect to get the value 1; but if conditional is defined as in Figure 7, in fact we get the above complex conditional expression. Similarly, F(1) will evaluate to

(COND(F, 1, 1 *(COND(T, 1, 0 * NFG-ARG))))

and F(2) to

(COND(F, 1, 2 *(COND(F, 1, 1 *
    (COND(T, 1, 0 * NEG-ARG)))))

using the definitions of Figures 7 and 8. However, if the COND of Figure 7 is replaced by the built-in IF_THEN_ELSE_FI, then things work out as expected (see Figure 9).

```
OBJ FACT#2
SORTS / INT BOOL
OK-OPS
    F2 : INT -> INT
ERR-OPS
    NEG-ARG : -> INT
VARS
    I : INT
OK-EQNS
    (F2(I)= IF I = 0 THEN 1 ELSE I *
        F2(I - 1)FI)
ERR-EQNS
    (F2(I)= NEG-ARG IF I < 0)
JBO
```

Figure 9. Another factorial

AN INTRODUCTION TO OBJ

Figure 10 defines a conditional which can recover from error arguments. For example,

    IF T THEN 1 ELSE NEG-ARG FI

evaluates to the ok value 1, and if this conditional is used with the factorial of Figure 9, then F(3) evaluates to 6, etc. However, it does differ from OBJ-0's built-in conditional in its treatment of errors in the Boolean argument. For example (using the conditional of Figure 10 with the factorial of Figure 9), F(F(−1)) evaluates to

    IF-ERR(NEG-ARG = 0)

whereas using the built-in conditional (with Figure 9) would give

    IF NEG-ARG THEN 1 ELSE F(NEG-ARG - 1)FI

which is more informative about the attempted computation, but it might be argued that it is too detailed. OBJ-T presently implements the conditional of Figure 10, but with form <CONDITION:_> instead of IF-ERR. Incidentally, the factorial of Figure 2 would evaluate F(F(−1)) to F(NEG-ARG), which seems to be the most reasonable answer of all.

```
OBJ COND#2
SORTS / INT BOOL
FIX-OPS
    IF_THEN_ELSE_FI : BOOL INT INT -> INT
ERR-OPS
    IF-ERR_ : BOOL -> INT
VARS
    I J : INT
    B : BOOL
EQNS
    (IF T THEN I ELSE J FI = I)
    (IF F THEN I ELSE J FI = J)
ERR-EQNS
    (IF B THEN I ELSE J FI = IF-ERR B IF ERR B)
JBO
```

Figure 10. A better conditional

Actually, the OBJ-0 built-in conditional cannot be defined in OBJ-0, for two separate reasons, neither of which is very serious. First, notice that we need the three argument error message form IF_THEN_ELSE_FI instead of IF−ERR. We can introduce this into ERR−OPS, but then the parser will find every expression which uses IF_THEN_ELSE_FI to be ambiguous. This difficulty would be solved if we could give the error operator an arity which showed that its use is to be restricted to the case where its Boolean argument is an error; that is, we would like to be able to write

```
FIX-OPS
    IF_THEN_ELSE_FI : BOOL-OK,INT,INT -> INT
ERR-OPS
    IF_THEN_ELSE_FI : BOOL-ERR,INT,INT -> INT
```

regarding BOOL-OK and BOOL-ERR as sub-sorts of BOOL. This makes perfectly good sense in the theory of order sorted algebras, and indeed Goguen [1978b] gives such a definition. However, it does not make sense in the narrower framework of error algebras [Goguen 1977], and it cannot be done in OBJ-0. Our intention is to design OBJ-1 around order sorted algebras, so that such definitions can be given.

The second reason OBJ-0's build-in conditional cannot be defined in OBJ-0 is that the built-in conditional sometimes does not evaluate its arguments. However, this can be easily remedied by providing a LISP-like QUOTE operator which inhibits application of the rewrite rule evaluator to the expression which is its argument. Because the evaluated and unevaluated expressions are in the same equivalence class (of the initial algebra), the implemented version (which sometimes does not evaluate arguments) actually satisfies the order sorted algebraic specification hinted at above. Thus, the conditional non-evaluation can be regarded as an implementation detail. We are considering building QUOTE into OBJ-1 to permit the user to inhibit evaluation in error messages if he wishes to.

Of course, a major practical advantage of a built-in conditional is that it can be coded to execute faster than any user defined conditional ever could.

Finally, let us consider the issue of conditional equations versus conditional expressions in the context of errors. Actually, now that we know what the conditional operator should be in the error context, we can see that conditional equations can be translated into equations with conditional expressions, in the error context, in exactly the same way as in the context of ordinary algebras.

Again, we must assume that each sort has an equality operator if we want to translate the form (E1 = E2 IF E3 = E4); but we need no assumptions for the form (E1 = E2 IF B) which is actually used in OBJ. Also again, for the implementation by rewrite rules to work, we need to somehow inhibit infinite application of the resulting translated rule, and this can be done by the same mechanisms.

As an example, the error equation

```
(F(I) = NEG-ARG IF I < 0)
```

translates into the EQNS equation

```
(F(I) = IF I < 0 THEN NEG-ARG ELSE F(I)FI)
```

4. IMPLEMENTING OBJ

OBJ-0 is implemented in Rutgers/UCI LISP. The major components of this implementation are an interactive command interpreter, a nondeterministic parser, an expression evaluator, an object entry interpreter, a deparser, and some file I/O functions. A consistent intention has been to make the system "friendly" to users by making use of structured displays and the DEC-10 interactive capability, wherever appropriate.

The parser translates arbitrary input expressions (strings of LISP atoms) to internal LISP S-expression representations. It operates top-down and tries all appropriate sort-operator combinations; if an operator pattern fits a string, then the parser attempts to parse the strings between the terminal symbols in that operator's form as expressions of the sorts in the operator's arity. Thus, the parser can handle user defined syntactic forms and detect ambiguous expressions. It also suppresses unnecessary steps in parsing expressions with ASSOCIATIVE operators.

The object entry interpreter is fairly straightforward. When invoked by the keyword OBJ (or OBJECT), it reads input until encountering the first JBO (or TCEJBO), or until end-of-file, and then attempts to interpret this "logical record" as an object. If it cannot interpret some entry, it issues a warning and skips to the next object keyword. Thus, OBJ-0 keywords should be considered reserved. The interpreter formats and prints components of the input object as it digests them, with error messages. If there were any mistakes, the user is asked at the end whether he wants the object installed "as is".

Expression evaluation is initiated when a RUN, AS, RUM, or left parenthesis is encountered. When RUM is used, the "memory" flag is temporarily turned on, alerting the expression evaluator to retain intermediate values. Symbols are read until the matching delimiter is encountered, and then the string, if it parses, is evaluated.

The latest OBJ-0 expression evaluator implements a destructive, noncopying reduction strategy (see O'Donnell [1977] or Rosen [1973]), using the LISP RPLACA function. However, "run-with-memory" makes copies at each step, slowing down evaluation somewhat.

When a sub-expression can no longer be rewritten, it is marked "closed". Marking also indicates whether each sub-expression is an error value; this tells the evaluator if the OK-EQNS apply. This mark is passed up to enclosing expressions during bottom-up evaluation, but it is never passed down. An outermost expression whose operator is a FIX-OPS may inhibit propagation of the error mark, but one whose operator is an ERR-OPS always turns it on.

An expression containing hidden operators is treated as a non-parsable expression during normal evaluation. For symmetry, if an evaluated expression contains hidden operators, a REWRITTEN EXPRESSION CANNOT BE DEPARSED message results.

Files may be read in entirely, or certain objects may be selected from them. For example, one may command

      GET PLANES FROM AIR.OBJ TEG

5. OBJ-T

This section summarizes some features of the OBJ-T system currently being implemented. OBJ-T takes greater advantage of the modularization potential of the object construct than OBJ-0 does. It permits independent objects, which have no knowledge of each other. Objects are maintained internally as nodes on an acyclic directed graph. The syntax which accomplishes this in OBJ-T is based on the form

      OBJ <name> / <name-list>

where <name> is the name of the object being declared, and <name-list> contains the names of already defined objects which are used in the new object. By following back through these lists of antecedent objects, the minimal environment for each object can be determined. The OBJ built-in objects will of course occur at the ends of paths through the acyclic graph of antecedent objects. This syntax is similar in function to the explicit assignment of theories to variable names in CLEAR (with syntax let <name> be <theory> in <theory>), but seems to be better integrated with the particularities of OBJ. This feature of OBJ-T is illustrated in Figures 13 and 14, and is used extensively in the example of the Appendix, as described in Section 6.

OBJ-T makes use of a somewhat more English-like syntax for BOOL than OBJ-0 did; we use the forms _AND_, _OR_, NOT_, _IFF_, and _IMPLIES_, instead of *, +, −, ⇔, and ⇒.

OBJ-T is friendlier than OBJ-0 in allowing the editing and retrying of defective objects. Objects may be output to files, as well as read in; the output file then contains all the antecedent objects required by current ones. Users can evaluate with respect to whatever object they choose, and can also purge objects. Moreover, an object A previously entered may be "prettyprinted", using the syntax

      SHOW A WOHS

We are in the process of implementing a facility for instantiation of parameterized algebraic objects in OBJ-T. It differs from the CLU "typegenerator" approach, and from the variable type system of HOPE, where constructs analogous to objects take arguments which are sorts. As in CLEAR, OBJ-T uses a "morphism" to create a target object from a source object, with the target object having possibly differently named sorts and operators. We call the OBJ-T construction IMAGE, and illustrate its syntax in Figure 11 with a rather simple example. The intended effect here is to supply the sort IDLIST in the target object IDLIST with two list operations having the same syntax and semantics as in the source object LIST.

```
OBJ LIST / TRUTH
SORTS
    S LIST
OK-OPS
    __ : LIST,LIST -> LIST (ASSOCIATIVE)
    _ : S -> LIST
JBO

IMAGE (LIST => IDLIST)/ ID
SORTS (LIST => IDLIST),(S => ID)
EGAMI
```

Figure 11. Instantiation of LIST of ID

In Figure 12, IMAGE creates a sort NAT, which is like INT, with INT's values and operations, except for the negative values. Thus, after this IMAGE is executed, evaluations using NAT will produce error messages instead of negative values. For example

$$RUN - 1 NUR$$

should evaluate to

```
AS NAT: >>ERROR>> NEG-ARG

OBJ PRE-NAT / TRUTH
SORTS
    NAT / BOOL
ERR-OPS
    NEG-ARG : -> NAT
JBO

IMAGE (INT => NAT)/ PRE-NAT
SORTS (INT => NAT)
VARS
    I : NAT
ERR-EQNS
    (I = NEG-ARG IF I < 0)
EGAMI
```

Figure 12. NAT created from INIT

An exact algebraic semantics for IMAGE has not been worked out, but it is similar to theoretical concepts developed in Burstall and Goguen [1977]; Goguen and Burstall [1978]; Thatcher, Wagner and Wright [1978]. The major difference is that CLEAR procedures (which produce new objects when old objects are substituted as actuals) place restrictions on the actuals. These conditions, called meta sorts, are equational theories which the actuals must satisfy. The approach of Thatcher, Wagner and Wright [1978] is similar, but is not part of a specification methodology.

Turning to another topic, it is possible to write sets of equations which evaluate in OBJ as the user intends, but which produce different results under different rule application strategies. We are working on a check, inspired by Knuth and Bendix [1970], for verifying that all rewriting sequences of an expression which terminate in fact yield the same value. In the literature, this is called the Church-Rosser or unique termination property; see Goguen [1978a]; Huet [1977]; O'Donnell [1977] for further discussion.

For example, the object in Figure 13 (pointed out to us by Zilles, private communication) defines a trivial, one element initial algebra rather than the expected one. This may be seen by rewriting the expression

```
(REMOVE (2,INSERT (2,INSERT (2,EMPTY))))
```

as follows

```
REMOVE(2,INSERT(2,INSERT(2,EMPTY)))
REMOVE(2,INSERT(2,EMPTY))
EMPTY
```

and also as

```
REMOVE(2,INSERT(2,INSERT(2,EMPTY)))
INSERT(2,EMPTY)
```

This demonstrates that inserting anything into the empty set always yields the empty set, in contrast to the specification of Figure 6.

```
OBJ TRIVIAL-SET / INT BOOL
SORTS SET / INT BOOL
OK-OPS
    INSERT : SET INT -> SET (PERMUTING)
    REMOVE : SET INT -> SET
    EMPTY : -> SET
VARS
    I J : INT
    S : SET
OK-EQNS
    (INSERT(INSERT(S,I),J)= INSERT(INSERT
        (S,J),I)IF NOT(I = J))
    (= INSERT(S,I)IF I = J)
    (REMOVE(INSERT(S,I),J)= S IF I = J)
    (= INSERT(REMOVE(S,J),I)IF NOT(I = J))
    (REMOVE(EMPTY,I)= EMPTY)
JBO
```

Figure 13. Inconsistent SET specification

Briefly, a pair of rewrite rules is <u>overlapping</u> if a substitution of expressions (possibly containing variables) <u>for variable</u> symbols can be found which unifies the left side of one with a sub-expression of the left side of the other. This process is more complicated than the unification used in OBJ evaluation, since both expressions may now contain variables. Intuitively, overlapping equations can cause different order of evaluation strategies to produce different results. An overlapping pair of rewrite rules generates what is called a <u>critical pair</u>, consisting of the corresponding substitution instances of the two <u>right hand</u> sides. A set of rules is Church-Rosser only if, for each critical pair, both expressions reduce to the same expression. Knuth and Bendix [1970] suggest adding critical pairs as new rules in order to get a "complete set" of rules, guaranteed to reduce any expression (see Lankford [1975]). Musser [1980] suggests a way of using this procedure to test the correctness of inductive assertions.

```
OBJ DEMO
SORTS / INT
OK-OPS
    G : INT -> INT
    H : INT -> INT
    F : INT INT -> INT
VARS
    I : INT
EQNS
    (H(I)= G(I))
    (F(0,H(0))= 0)
JBO
```

Figure 14. An object with overlapping equations

To illustrate these ideas, Figure 14 gives an object whose equations, regarded as rewrite rules, have an overlapping instance. In fact, both left hand sides can match the expression F(0,H(0)). If the first rule is applied (using the unifier (I,0)), the resulting expression is F(0, G(0)). If the second rule is applied, the resulting expression is 0. Because the OBJ evaluator works bottom-up, the first case will be its result; note that F(0, G(0)) is reduced. The critical pair given by this overlapping rule pair is (F(0,G(0)),0), and adding it as a rewrite rule will permit the OBJ evaluator to reduce F(0,G(0)) to 0. Notice that adding this pair as an equation, however, has no effect on the resulting initial algebra.

We have implemented an experimental algorithm to generate critical pairs for OBJ-T, and have learned a good deal from the experience. First, it may be a distinct advantage to have an equationally defined conditional operator in the language, because then one doesn't need to make any special provision for conditional equations, which could become a fairly complex undertaking. Secondly, we have to take account of error values in OBJ. Failure to do so properly can produce a tremendous number of phantom critical pairs between error and ok equations whose left hand sides could never overlap in an actual evaluation. The idea of separating ok and error values as distinct sorts [Goguen 1978b] appears to offer an elegant solution, and requiring that each equation have a declared sort will also help. Thirdly, the way in which the built-in sort BOOL is treated can be very important to the endeavor of finding critical pairs. In OBJ-T, the built-in sort TRUTH contains only the constants T and F; over it is built BOOL, with the usual operations described equationally. These equations themselves can produce a lot of critical pairs. If properly chosen, they can also function as a kind of theorem prover (see Musser [1980]). In OBJ-0, BOOL is built-in without the use of equations.

6. AN EXAMPLE

The appendix contains a relatively non-trivial OBJ-T specification, after Ehrig, Kreowski and Weber [1978], of a data base system for an airport scheduler. As originally given, there were no error messages; we have supplied them to specify integrity constraints. The basic data sorts are flight number, plane number, destination, start time, plane type, and number of seats. Two basic relations are used: FLIGHT-SCHEDULE, relating flight numbers, destinations, and start times; and PLANES, relating plane numbers, types, and seats. These relations are maintained in structures similar to lists. There is also a third relation, between flight numbers and plane numbers, which was given implicitly in Ehrig, Kreowski and Weber [1978]. Finally, there is the AIRPORT-SCHEDULE itself, a tupling of these three relations.

The first five objects define the six primitive relations. In the first two, the form for the constructor operations was chosen to enhance readability of expressions; selectors and predicates for cancelling and verifying are also provided. The airport schedule itself includes the operations intended to be visible at the interface to a clerk, who can schedule, cancel, verify the existence of flights, by flight number, and so forth. The constructor in this object is for the tupling of the three relations involved; three hidden untupling operations are also provided, and are used to retrieve the component relations. The instantaneous value of the schedule is that tuple; since it is undesirable that component relations be updated individually, the user interface does not provide access to them via untupling operations on the state of the system. Note that a considerable portion of this object is devoted to bookkeeping tasks, especially as regards processing of error messages for violation of integrity constraints.

The final object is a test object; it is not a part of the specification, but supplies a particular airport-schedule which is convenient for testing the various operators. Some test runs using this object are included.

Entering this specification took around 4 minutes of KI-10 CPU time, in 50K virtual core, using a compiled version of OBJ-T. The entire test run took about 7-1/2 minutes.

7. CLOSING REMARKS

OBJ has not yet been tried out in a large scale practical application, so that our hopes and intentions in this direction must be regarded as unproved. Yet we hope to convince the reader that this is a real potentiality, in view of the success achieved in micro and mini sized applications (i.e., data structures and small systems). Moreover, we have learned a good deal from our experience so far, and we intend to apply it to the design of future systems. For example, this paper partly documents the evolution from OBJ-0 to OBJ-T. We believe that this very process of learning from one's mistakes is too often glossed over in the literature; indeed, we seek a methodology to make this process more explicit and available. The remainder of this section is devoted to presenting various stages of our experience in the use of algebraic specifications.

The sad fact is that a disturbingly large number of published algebraic specifications, even of simple data types, are wrong. Indeed, the first thing one writes is usually wrong. Moreover, it is probably unrealistic to expect that perfection will ever be reached for reasonable sized problems; rather, one should aim for workability in the actual environment in which a program will be used. Obviously, mechanical aids can be very helpful in achieving such a goal. Our work with OBJ strongly confirms this.

Our experience so far has identified the following as significant sources of errors in algebraic specifications:

(1) typographical errors;

(2) incorrect or imprecise notation;

(3) failure to handle certain special cases, particularly boundary cases;

(4) incorrectly handling certain cases;

(5) writing specifications which give different results if applied in different ways;

(6) writing specifications which fail to terminate when they should; and

(7) failure to treat error conditions precisely or even to treat them at all.

Unfortunately, non-algebraic specifications seem to be no better than algebraic specifications in their propensity toward errors.

Difficulties (1) and (2) can be overcome by providing a formal syntax for specifications, and then mechanically checking all attempted specifications against it. Still, it is surprising how rarely this is actually done, and how common such errors are. Even this paper includes some specifications which we could not check because the relevant features of OBJ have not been implemented as of this writing, such as the IMAGE feature of OBJ-T.

Difficulties (3) and (4) are not entirely precisely defined, but our experience is that they occur significantly often, and can be detected by running appropriate test cases. The capability to do this easily was in fact one of the major motivations for OBJ in the first place.

Difficulty (5) can be approached by the method of Knuth and Bendix, mentioned in Section 5. It is known (for the one sorted case) that this provides a complete solution, if termination can be guaranteed. This is difficulty (6), for which there cannot be any general algorithmic solution. Moreover, we actually sometimes want to specify programs which do not necessarily terminate. Theorem provers are one class of such programs. Technically, this requires an extension to continuous algebras.

Difficulty (7) has been discussed in some detail in Goguen [1977, 1978b]. The fact is, one simply hasn't specified STACK unless one says what happens if there is an attempt to take the TOP of the EMPTY stack. Something like the theory of error algebras seems to be necessary for this purpose.

It goes almost without saying by now that strong typing and the systematic checking of types wherever possible provide a significant aid in writing specifications. Moreover, we believe that a precise but abstract semantics is a big help in designing and using a specification language. Obviously, it is impossible even to consider giving rigorous correctness proofs without a precise semantics for the specification language; yet many specification languages lack considerably in this direction. The advantage of an abstract semantics is that correctness proofs can be expected to be simpler, because of the suppression of detail. Yet many specification languages envisage a basic concrete operational semantics. Thus, the hope for computer aided correctness proofs for implementations is a major practical motivation for algebraic specification languages.

We now summarize, in a provisional way, some lessons which may be helpful in the design of OBJ-1, a next generation algebraic specification language; some of these may also be incorporated in the final version of OBJ-T, and some may turn out to be wrong:

(1) Coercions and distributed fix syntax seem to be well worth the extra time required in parsing, and should be maintained;
(2) The acyclic graph representation of antecedent objects, with the associated slash (/) syntax seems to be viable, but more thought needs to be given to the problems of updating and removing objects;
(3) The use of error algebras is thoroughly justified, but should be extended to permit multiple kinds of user definable exceptions, and the use of the "subsort" notion looks promising in this regard;
(4) It would seem useful to require the user to declare a sort for each equation, and for each evaluation;
(5) The use of FIX-OPS is convenient, and should be extended (each of points (3), (4), (5) are covered by the order sorted algebra approach of Goguen [1978b] as is part of (6) following);
(6) Use of the Knuth-Bendix method should be further explored in connection with order sorted algebras, conditionals, and built in objects;

(7) The parser should be more systematically designed, and should provide optimally helpful error messages (it might well be specified in OBJ!);
(8) The use of meta-sorts and procedures, as in CLEAR, should be explored;
(9) The use of underevaluated error message in complex specifications raises the issue of processing error messages (see the example in the Appendix); in general, this seems to be successful, but some thought should be given to how to make it easier and more natural;
(10) It would be convenient to have built-in tupling and untupling operations (as shown by the example in the Appendix);
(11) The systematic breaking of specifications into modules appears to be highly successful, but the implications for the testing of interconnections of already tested modules need to be further explored;
(12) Some larger specifications need to be tried;
(13) Automatic generation of test cases should be explored; and
(14) The use of backwards spelling for closing delimiters should be replaced by a more conventional notation, such as end.

In summary, we are pleased if all we have done is to open up a number of questions, to give some specifications in which we have a relatively high degree of confidence, and to suggest some further progress in the algebraic approach to the specification of reliable software.

APPENDIX

[Appendix deleted]

ALLEN L. AMBLER
Amdahl Corporation

DONALD I. GOOD, JAMES C. BROWNE, WILHELM F. BURGER,
RICHARD M. COHEN, CHARLES G. HOCH, AND ROBERT E. WELLS
The University of Texas at Austin

GYPSY: A Language for Specification and Implementation of Verifiable Programs

1. INTRODUCTION

The design of Gypsy was driven by the development of a comprehensive methodology for constructing verified programs oriented toward communications processing. This methodology consists of an integrated system of methods for formal program specification and verification either by formal proof or by validation at run time. The methodology also contains two tools for applying these methods: the program design language Gypsy and an interactive system for the design and verification of Gypsy programs. Gypsy provides the means of expressing both programs and their formal specifications and is, therefore, the unifying element of the complete methodology. The language provides a precise means of expressing a program throughout all stages of its design—from initial specification through implementation, verification and subsequent evolution. The integration of programming and specification facilities into a common language is the most significant single characteristic of Gypsy. The merged syntax and semantics allows program proofs to be constructed rigorously in conjunction with program development, thereby bringing maximal benefit to the total programming process.

The incorporation of specifications and programming facilities into a single language provides three complementary approaches to program verification. First, formal proofs that the program will conform to specifications can be constructed before execution occurs. Second, specifications can be validated by actual evaluation at run time. Third, trace facilities provide a convenient mechanism for post-execution analysis if desired. The blending of these techniques (particularly the first two) produces desirable results. Those specifications that are to be validated at run time need not be proven and can be assumed to be valid in formal proofs. This, of course, increases program execution time, but an effective mixture of formal proof and run time validation can significantly reduce the size and complexity of formal proofs without creating intolerably inefficient programs.

A second significant characteristic of Gypsy is the inclusion of language features that allow for both the specification and the coding of concurrent processes. The original target of Gypsy was the expression of verifiable programs for communications processing such as those that might be found at the node of a computer network. This led to the incorporation of verifiable features for expressing concurrency and process synchronization and for expressing real-time dependencies. The result has been a high-level language for the development of general systems programs that can be verified to execute in conformity with precisely stated specifications.

A third significant characteristic is the provision for imperfect execution environments. While formal proofs usually assume a perfect execution environment, execution environments are rarely perfect. In recognition of this fact, the span of both specifications and program code has been extended to include facilities for correct execution in imperfect environments. Specifications and program code concerning data integrity, error monitoring, and error isolation and recovery are expressed directly in the language along with the error-free environment statements.

2. DESIGN OF GYSPY

Gypsy was developed as an integrated programming and specification language to support specification, coding and verification of systems software, with particular emphasis on communications software. Specific goals were:

(1) *Complete Verifiability.* Every feature in the language must be rigorously verifiable, either by proof or run time validation.

(2) *Incremental Development.* The language must support modular, incremental program development and verification. As well as possible, the language must simplify the verification process by encouraging small modules with tightly regulated interactions and by isolating and minimizing the effects of modifications to previously verified code. There must also be a facility for partial expression of program units.

(3) *Systems Programming.* The language must support the development of systems software. There must be facilities for expressing process concurrency and synchronizing process communication. There must also be facilities for expressing real-time dependencies.

(4) *Imperfect Execution Environments.* The language must support execution in imperfect environments. It must be possible to detect, isolate and recover from run time anomalies as well as monitor the program state.

(5) *Specification Capability.* The language must provide an extensive specification capability. For every property that is to be verified, there must be an adequate means of expressing it directly in the language. The integration of formal proof, run time validation and monitoring must be consistent and provide a complete whole.

3. EXERCISING RESTRAINT

While we had great latitude in the design of Gypsy, we were constrained by the necessity of producing a usable system. This not only meant that we had to be able to implement and verify features of Gypsy, but that the amount of effort involved in utilizing the resulting product for the construction of actual application programs had to be kept reasonable. In effect, we faced a classical performance versus cost compromise. For each feature, we had to consider whether the merits of its inclusion outweighed the expense of verifying its properties. In many cases the decision was not easy.

Starting from Pascal [Jensen and Wirth 1974], each existing Pascal construct was carefully analyzed and those which inhibited verification were modified or removed. The hierarchical definition structure was eliminated and protection lists were added to provide a tighter, more flexible environment for incremental program development and verification. Facilities for expressing concurrency, communication, synchronization, timing constraints, external events, error recovery and monitoring were added, paying close attention to the requirements of the verification methodology. Each construct in the program code and the specification statements was designed to support the verification methodology. The program code syntax was modified to integrate the specification statements into a logically consistent and hopefully understandable language.

In the succeeding sections the salient features of Gypsy are discussed briefly and are followed by an example program. The interested reader is referred to the "Report on the Language Gypsy" [Ambler, Good and Burger 1976]. It may be helpful in reading the language features to flip back and forth between the examples as most, if not all, features are utilized there.

4. DESIGNING FOR VERIFICATION

A language which is to facilitate coding and specification must not only include capabilities necessary for expressing the problem domain of interest, but must exclude language constructs whose semantics defeat, or impede, verification. We defer a discussion of Gypsy's specification statements until a later section for pedagogical reasons. Their development was, however, closely interwoven with that of the coding statements.

Verification of program code has only recently become a prominent factor in programming language design. While Pascal was influenced by verification considerations Buxton and Randell [1970], more recently Nucleus [Good and Ragland 1973], Alphard [Wulf, London and Shaw 1976a], and Euclid [Lampson, Horning, London, Mitchell and Popek 1978] have been expressly designed for verification by formal proofs. Gypsy also is specifically designed for verification, but verification by run time validation as well as by formal proof. The first phase in the design of Gypsy was to develop a "conventional" language which was free from concepts known to render formal proof verification difficult. To this end, Pascal [Jensen and Wirth 1974] was selected as a model and Gypsy was patterned after Pascal, but with significant differences.

Routines in Pascal can be nested to arbitrary depths which creates a hierarchy of nested "non-local" variables. Routines in Gypsy may not be nested and variables can only be defined within routines; hence, Gypsy has no non-local variables, i.e., all variables are either local variables or parameters. This simplifies verification as well as incremental program development, which will be discussed in the next section.

Functions in Pascal can take either variable or value parameters and can only return values of a simple type. In Gypsy, functions are allowed only constant and value parameters, but they can return values of most types. The restriction to non-variable parameters, together with the absence of non-local variables, guarantees that functions produce no side-effects. This simplifies verification considerably. It also increases the potential for optimization of expression evaluation.

Pascal allows routines to be included as parameters to other routines; Gypsy does not. This decision and the one not allowing non-local variables are instances where the extra burden on the verification process did not appear worth the extra capability.

Certain of Pascal's data types do not appear at all in Gypsy. These are types "real," "class," "pointer" and "file."

Pascal has "if," "case," "for," "while," "repeat" and "goto" statements for execution control. Gypsy has a similar set of statements, "if," "case," "loop" and "leave," modified for proper placement of assertions and to eliminate the need for extra "begin-end" pairs. The "if" statement is conventional except for a trailing "end." The "case" statement has an additional keyword "is" and an optional "else" clause. The "loop" statement subsumes both the "while" and "repeat" constructs as well as the so-called "loop-and-a-half" construct and infinite loops. Termination and looping are controlled by "leave" statements. Gypsy has no "goto" statement.

5. DESIGNING FOR INCREMENTAL DEVELOPMENT

A language that is to support the development and evolution of verified programs also must consider the practical aspects of verification. In developing a verified program of any significant size, it is necessary that the program be written as a large collection of small, independently verifiable units. Otherwise, a formal proof easily can expand into a mass of detail and become unmanageable. Also for proofs to be maximally effective they should be carried out on a unit-by-unit basis as the program is developed. Further, it is the nature of systems programs that they are continuously undergoing evolution, and reverification is necessary. It is, therefore, essential that the amount of reverification be kept to a minimum. For these reasons, we sought language features which supported unit-by-unit manipulation, increased unit independence and isolated unit interactions.

A Gypsy program consists of a series of "routine," "macro," "constant" and "type" units; which may appear in any order. If a reference cannot be resolved locally within a particular unit, a search of the other external unit names is made. When an unresolved local reference is found to be an external unit name, then the appropriate information is extracted and the analysis continued. Access rights to any unit may be stated in an "access list." These access lists will be checked during the process of resolving references. The combination of units and access lists provides a high degree of code independence, plus a tightly controlled environment.

A "routine" is a "function," a "procedure," a "process," or a "program." A "program" unit defines the initial program execution point. Routine declarations can only appear at the unit level; hence, Gypsy does not permit a nested hierarchy of routine definitions. Besides favoring unit independence, it was felt (1) that a hierarchical structure failed to provide adequate program protection without access lists and (2) that with access lists and without nonlocal variables a hierarchical structure was unnecessary. Routine calls may be recursive.

A macro unit binds a parameterized expression to a name. While macro expansions can be nested, they may not be recursively expanded as there would be no way to terminate a recursive expansion.

A constant unit parallels the constant declarations of Pascal except that a constant may be of any non-buffer type including a structured type. This provides the means for referencing global values without allowing global variables or requiring them to be passed as parameters if they are not to be modified.

A type unit declares a new type either by itemizing its value set or by composing existing types. A type unit which includes an access list is the equivalent of an abstract data structure [Dahl 1972; Liskov and Zilles 1973; Wulf, London and Shaw 1976a; Brinch Hansen 1975; Flon 1974]. The intent of an abstract data type is to be able to construct a new type and to restrict access to the components of that type to operations representative of the type. It is then possible, with a proper implementation, to alter the implementation of the abstract type and the corresponding operations without impacting the program. A comparison of the Gypsy access control to that of Pascal, Concurrent Pascal, Euclid, and CLU can be found in Ambler and Hoch [1976].

6. DESIGNING FOR CONCURRENCY AND REAL-TIME

Programming languages have traditionally avoided concurrency; there have, however, been exceptions. The Burroughs family of extended Algol languages [Lyle 1971] provides processes and process communication, Bliss [Wulf, Russell and Habermann 1971] provides coroutines and processes; Concurrent Pascal [Brinch Hansen 1975] combines processes and monitors, and Algol 68 [van Wijngaarden 1969] provides collateral elaboration of clauses. Several other languages have primitive means of accessing operating system functions which provide concurrency. Operating system research has generated a large number of concurrency and synchronization techniques which we will not attempt to reference. Two systems, RC4000 [Brinch Hansen 1970] and HYDRA [Wulf, Levin and Pierson 1975], were significant factors in our decision on how to specify and implement concurrency.

Gypsy has a routine type called a "process." It differs from a "procedure" only in the types of parameters allowed and in the manner of its invocation. Processes communicate only through message buffers [Brinch Hansen 1973]. This is a natural choice for communications processing applications. A message "buffer" is a finite length queue on which there are only two operations defined, "send" (enqueue) and "receive" (dequeue). The queue is manipulated by a strict FCFS algorithm. Whenever a "send" is made on a full buffer the sending process is suspended until the condition is remedied. Likewise, a "receive" on an empty buffer will cause the process to be suspended. Associated with every buffer is a semaphore which guarantees mutually exclusive access to the buffer.

Concurrent processes are initiated by a "cobegin end" statement and may or may not terminate. Only when all processes called within a "cobegin" statement terminate will the statement following the "cobegin" be executed.

Polling is an important function of real-time systems; hence, it must be possible to poll a buffer without being suspended indefinitely trying to receive from an empty buffer. Gypsy has an "await" statement which allows the simultaneous waiting on the completion of any one of several buffer operations. An "await" is in many respects a guarded command [Dijkstra 1975], except that it has a very restricted set of guards and it has an optional time-out clause. The time-out clause specifies what is to be done if none of the requested operations completes by a certain time.

The concept of (real) time is provided by "clock" variables. A clock variable is a special variable which may not be modified by the program, but which is always changing. There may be any number of clocks in a program, but there is no guarantee that they will be synchronized. As Gypsy programs may be distributed across many machines, synchronization would be virtually impossible.

7. DESIGNING FOR IMPERFECT EXECUTION ENVIRONMENTS

An attribute of real-time software often overlooked in programming languages is the existence of both hardware and software faults. Fault detection, isolation and recovery is an essential function in real-time software and consequently, languages for expressing such software should (1) provide capabilities for fault control programming and (2) provide an interface to the hardware which allows for the detection, isolation and recovery of faults. The work of the Newcastle group [Randell 1975] represents virtually all of the previous efforts on this topic.

A "condition" in Gypsy is an instantaneous event which may occur during the execution of a program. There is a large class of predefined "conditions" which correspond to hardware errors and dynamic language semantics errors, such as "caseerror." Programmers may, in addition, name and signal fault conditions by using a "signal" statement or an "otherwise" clause on a specification (discussed in the next section).

Any statement ending with the word "end," may optionally end with a "condition clause" followed by the word "end." The effect of the condition clause is that whenever a condition occurs, an immediate branch is taken to the condition clause, of the innermost containing statement, which specifies an action for that condition. Searching for the innermost condition clause may involve exiting a routine. After the condition clause is executed, control does not return to where it was before the fault, but instead drops out of the statement whose condition clause was executed. In some sense, a condition clause is a restricted version of a PL/I "on" condition which resembles one of Zahn's event driven case statements [Zahn 1974].

8. DESIGNING FOR SPECIFICATION

Gypsy plays the dual role of programming and specification language. The specification component of the language permits the precise expression of desired functional properties of key parts of the program. These properties are stated in terms of valid states that are to be maintained on the data objects of the program at various points in the program computation. The objective of a verification is to show that the computation always proceeds in conformity with the stated specifications. The conformity of the program with its specification can in most cases be either proved prior to execution or validated during execution. The same specification methods are used in both approaches to verification.

All specifications in Gypsy are stated as Boolean-valued expressions. These specifications are designated to be verified either by proof, by run time validation, or both, or they may simply be assumed. Specifications that are proved or assumed need not be evaluated at run time, and therefore they are permitted to contain special operations and types that could not otherwise be permitted. For example, Boolean expressions may contain the logical quantifiers "for all" and "there exists" and refer to rational numbers and infinite sequences. These special operations and types may not be used in parts of the program that are to be executed, but they are assigned precise definitions for purposes of specification.

The most familiar kinds of specifications used in Gypsy are the "entry," "exit" and "assert" statements for procedures and functions. These follow the same form as that introduced by Igarashi, London and Luckham [1973] for proving Pascal programs. The "exit" specification is interpreted in the weak sense, i.e. it holds if the program terminates.

"Entry," "exit" and "assert" specifications also can be used with processes. However, processes often are intentionally programmed never to terminate, and therefore an "exit" specification may be of no value. Specifications can be stated for non-terminating processes through "block" specifications. A "block" specification holds whenever the process is suspended by a buffer operation. This provides a temporary halting point.

Specifications for routines performing buffer manipulations normally are stated in terms of effects on buffer histories. In the terminology of Clint [1973], these are "mythical variables," but they are provided in a predefined way by the language rather than being installed by the programmer. Associated with every buffer b are several histories that are relevant to specifications and to the proof methodology. For example, "b.infrom" refers to the sequence of objects received "in" from the buffer by the process, and "b.outto" is the sequence of objects sent "out" to the buffer from the process.

Any sequence of "var" declarations in a routine can be followed by a "keep" specification. The "keep" expression must be maintained throughout the immediate scope of the "var" declaration. A procedure or function call releases the "keep," but the called unit must reestablish it before returning. This type of assertion is similar to those used by Stucki [1975] for run time validation.

Any routine that is granted access to the concrete representation of an abstract type may have both unrestricted (entry, exit, block) and restricted (centry, cexit, cblock) external specifications. The external specifications of a routine are visible to the external environment of the routine; internal specifications (assert, keep) are not. Unrestricted external specifications are stated strictly in abstract terms and are visible to any calling routine. Restricted external specifications may be stated in both abstract and concrete terms and typically are used to define the desired relationship between the abstract and concrete. These restricted specifications are visible only to calling routines that also have access to the same set (or possibly a superset) or the abstract types that are accessible to the called routine. Thus, the concrete structure of an abstract type is revealed, through the restricted external specifications, only to other routines that also are granted access to the type. The centry and cexit types were motivated by similar specifications in Alphard.

Two kinds of specifications can be stated for Gypsy type definitions, "require" and "axiom." The require specification follows Alphard and is a precondition on the type parameters that is necessary for the proper creation of an object of that type. The axiom is a relation among the functions that have access to the type.

This set of specification methods provides powerful mechanisms for stating functional properties of programs, and formal proof methods have been defined for proving each of these types of properties. The specifications do not, at this time, directly permit the definition of quantitative aspects of program behavior such as resource utilization.

9. A MESSAGE SWITCHING NETWORK

The following example follows part of the development of a simple message switching network and illustrates many of the important features of Gypsy. Only the specification and implementation of the network will be discussed. Its verification is beyond the current scope. The development of the network will be top-down, but Gypsy admits any kind of program design strategy.

The top-level structure of the network is shown in Figure 1. Network switches messages among a fixed number of users, each of which communicates with the network through a port. We will ignore protocols and assume that each message is a separate, complete communication. Even at

GYPSY: A LANGUAGE FOR VERIFIABLE PROGRAMS

this early stage of development, the network can be written in Gypsy.

```
program Network(var upa: PortArray) = pending;

type PortArray = array(UserId) of Port;

type UserId = integer(1 .. NUsers);
const NUsers: integer = pending;

type Port = record(Get, Put: Line);
type Line = buffer(Csize) of Message;
const Csize:integer = pending;

type Message = pending;
```

This program gives a precise description of the lines of communication between the network and its external environment. Communication is through an "array(UserId) of Port." Each port is a record consisting of two buffers, and each buffer contains a maximum of Csize messages. The type UserId is an integer restricted to the range (1 .. NUsers). The actual number of users, the maximal buffer size, the structure of messages and the implementation of the network are left pending.

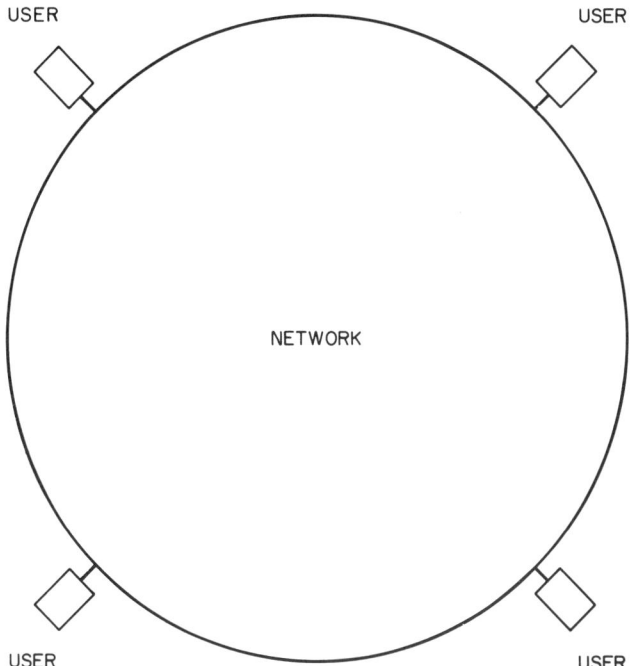

Figure 1. Top level structure of network

In a simple network with no protocols, the fundamental specification that is desired is that messages are delivered properly among all possible pairs of users. This specification for the network can be written as

```
program Network(var upa: PortArray) =
begin
  block all i, j: UserId,
      ProperDelivery(i, j, upa);
  pending;
end;
```

The specification is written as a block, instead of an exit, specification because we intend the message network to be non-terminating. The network being blocked means that all processes in the network are blocked. This could happen for any number of reasons, including deadlock, but in this example, it will mean that there is no further input available from any user.

Before we can proceed with the implementation of the network, it is necessary that we be more specific about the meaning of "ProperDelivery." Loosely speaking, what we mean is that user j receives only those messages that were intended for j. We will make this definition precise with a macro.

```
define ProperDelivery(i, j, pa) =
  mail(pa(j).Put.outto, i, j)
      sub mail(pa(i).Get.infrom, i, j);
```

(The macro definition was chosen to illustrate the use of macros. ProperDelivery also could have been defined using a function.) Pa(j).Put.outto is the sequence of all messages sent out to buffer pa(j).Put by the network, and pa(i).Get.infrom is the sequence of messages received in from buffer upa(i).Get. The function mail(ms, i, j) is the subsequence of messages in message sequence ms that are directed from port i to j.

The completion of the definition of ProperDelivery requires a precise definition of the mail function, and mail in turn will require some additional information about messages.

```
function mail(ms: MessageSequence; i, j: UserId): MessageSequence =
begin
  exit (assume mail(ms, i, j) =
    if ms=MessageSequence( )
    then MessageSequence( )
    else if i = Source(first(ms)) and
        j = Destination(first(ms))
      then MessageSequence(first(ms))
        @ Mail(nonfirst(ms), i, j)
      else Mail(nonfirst(ms), i, j)
    fi   fi);
end;

type MessageSequence = sequence of Message;

type Message <Source, Destination, Text, Compose, Equal> =
begin
  axiom all m: Message,
      Equal(Compose(Source(m), Destination(m), Text(m)), m);
  pending;
end;
```

```
function Source(m: Message): UserId = pending;
function Destination(m: Message): UserId = pending;
function Text(m: Message): CString = pending;
function Compose(s, d: UserId; t: CString): Message = pending;
function Equal(m1, m2: Message): boolean = pending;

type CString = sequence (100) of char;
```

The definition of mail(ms, i, j) is given as an assumed exit specification which gives a complete recursive definition of mail. The definition of mail requires a new type, MessageSequence. The type definition "sequence of Message" defines a potentially infinite sequence of messages. Sequences are given a precise meaning by the semantics of Gypsy, but it is not necessary that they be implemented. Gypsy has a number of these kinds of constructs. They are included for purposes of formal program analysis, and may appear anywhere in a program where execution is not required, such as in specifications that are proved or assumed. In contrast, the type CString is a sequence of ASCII characters of maximal size 100. Normally a Gypsy implementation would contain finite sequences but not infinite ones. Size restrictions can be enforced by run time checks, and both kinds of sequences share a common semantics. MessageSequence( ) denotes the empty sequence of messages. In general, type names can be used to construct objects of that type. The @ operator is the sequence append operator.

The definition of mail makes use of two functions on messages, Source and Destination. The type definition of message permits these functions, as well as Text, Compose and Equal, access to the internal structure of messages, which is temporarily left pending. The axiom states an identity relation that must be maintained among this set of functions. This axiom implies that three kinds of information can be extracted from a message, a source, destination and text part. The source and destination are the means of directing a message from one user to another, and the text is the actual content of the message to be transmitted. The Compose function builds a message from these three parts, and Equal defines a message equality. This is the only information that we will need to know about messages to carry out the full specification, implementation and verification of the network process. Eventually, of course, we must choose a concrete representation of messages and prove that the representation and the implementation of the functions that can access it satisfy the axioms.

Now we can give a completely precise interpretation to ProperDelivery. For every i, j pair, the mail from source i that is sent out to port j must be a subsequence of the mail received in from port i that is designated for destination j. This requires that the messages be the same and that they arrive in the same order that they were sent. The subsequence relation permits the network to drop messages. This is a concession to the reality of potentially unrecoverable transmission failures. This completes the specification of network.

We can proceed with the top-down design at any place in the current Gypsy program where a pending appears. There are many ways this program could be implemented to satisfy the block specification, but we will choose the following:

```
program network (var upa: PortArray) =
begin
  block all i, j: UserId,
        ProperDelivery(i, j, upa);
  var npa: PortArray;
  cobegin
    Node(upa(i), npa(i), i) each i : UserId;
    switch(npa);
  end;
end;

process Node(var up, np: Port; i: UserId) =
begin
  block up.Put.outto sub np.Put.infrom
    and np.Get.outto sub up.Get.infrom;
  pending;
end;

process Switch(var npa: PortArray) =
begin
  block all i, j: UserId,
        ProperDelivery(i, j, npa);
  pending;
end;
```

This implements the program as a star network where each user is attached to exactly one node, and all of the nodes are connected to a single switch as shown in Figure 2. Each node is similar to a full-duplex channel program passing messages unaltered, and in sequence, between the user and the central switch. All of the nodes and the switch are set into concurrent execution by the cobegin in the network program.

A node can be implemented by decomposing it into two one-way channels operating asynchronously.

```
process Node(var up, np: Port; i: UserId) =
begin
  block up.Put.outto sub np.Putinfrom
    and np.Get.outto sub up.Get. infrom;
  cobegin
    Pass(np.Put, up.Put, i, Depart);
    Pass(up.Get, np.Get, i, Arrive);
  end;
end;
```

GYPSY: A LANGUAGE FOR VERIFIABLE PROGRAMS

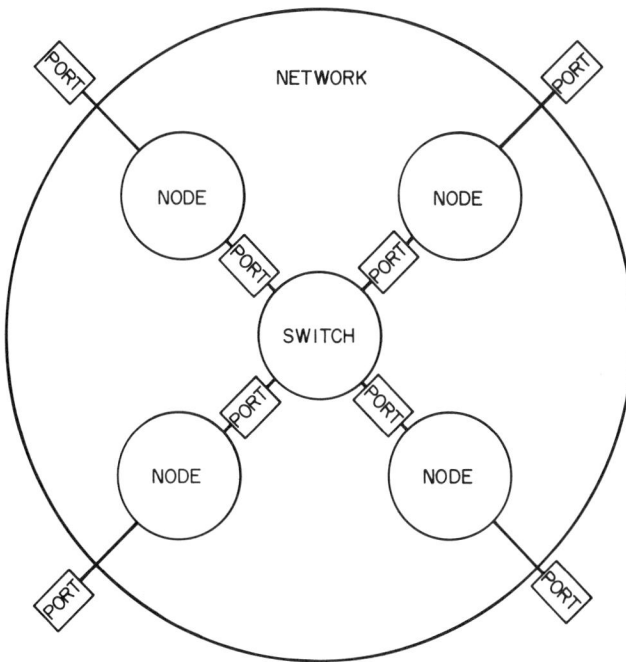

Figure 2. Implementation of network

```
process Pass(var x,y: Line; i: UserId; d: Direction) =
begin
  block y.outto sub x.infrom;
  var m: Message;
  loop
    assert y.outto sub x.infrom
    receive m from x;
    trace i = if d = Depart
       then Destination(m)
       else Source(m) fi;
    send m to y;
  end;
end;
```

type direction = (Arrive, Depart);

Pass is intentionally programmed as a non-termination loop. The loop simply receives messages from line x and passes them to line y performing a trace depending on the value of d. The send and receive statements are potential blockage points, and these are the points where the block specification must hold. A cobegin, as in node or network, also is a potential blockage point.

The Switch process also loops forever waiting on each buffer in its turn for a small time slice. If input is ready it will receive it; otherwise, it will time out and go on to the next buffer.

```
process Switch(var npa: PortArray) =
begin
  block all i, j: UserId,
      ProperDelivery(i, j, npa);
  var m: Message;
  var k: UserId;
  cond DestinationErr;
  keep Destination(m) in (1 .. NUsers)
      otherwise DestinationErr:
  loop
    k := 1;
    loop
      if k > NUsers then leave end;
      assert all i, j: UserId,
          ProperDelivery(i, j, npa);
      await
      on receive m from npa(k).Get:
          send m to npa(destination(m)).Put;
      after TimeSlice: ;
      when
      is DestinationErr: ;
      end;
      k := k + 1;
    end;
  end;
end;

const TimeSlice: integer = pending;
```

Switch repeatedly iterates through the Get buffers of the ports attempting to receive a message. Control leaves the inner loop at the leave statement, and the outer loop runs indefinitely. If a message is not received in TimeSlice amount of time, the await is exited and the next buffer is considered. If a message is received within the allocated amount of time, it is sent to the appropriate destination. The keep specification of Switch is evaluated each time one of its variables is assigned a new value. If the specification ever is violated, a destination error is signaled. The keep prevents an invalid array index in the send statement. If the error occurs, control is transferred to the when clause of the await and the DestinationErr part of the when is performed. In this case, Switch does nothing, thus dropping the message. This conforms with the subsequence relation specified in ProperDelivery.

The process structure of the complete network is shown in Figure 3. All of these processes run concurrently. The intermediate level of a node process was not necessary. The Pass processes could have been invoked explicitly from the cobegin in Network. The extra level of decomposition is helpful conceptually and in breaking the network into small, individually verifiable components.

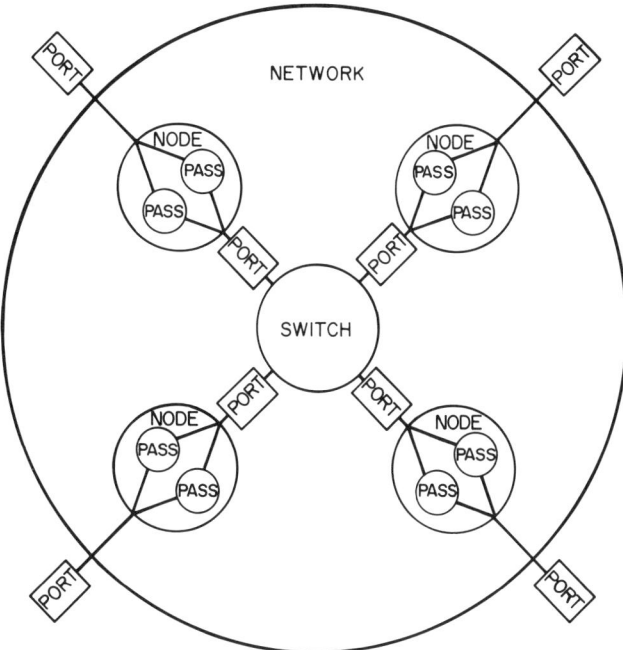

Figure 3. Full network implementation

Now let us return to the implementation of messages. They will be implemented in the obvious way as a record of three fields.

```
type Message <Source, Destination, Text, Compose, Equal> =
begin
   axiom all m: Message,
       Equal(Compose(Source(m), Destination(m), Text(m)), m);
   record(s, d: UserId; t: CString);
end;

function Source(m: Message): UserId =
begin
   cexit Source(m) = m.s;
   result := m.s;
end;
```

```
function Destination(m: Message): UserId =
begin
  cexit Destination(m) = m.d;
  result := m.d;
end;

function Text(m: Message): CString =
begin
  cexit Text(m) = m.t;
  result := m.t;
end;

function Compose(s, d: UserId; t: CString): Message =
begin
  cexit Compose(s, d, t) = Message(s, d, t);
  result := Message(s, d, t);
end;

function Equal(m1, m2: Message): boolean =
begin
  exit Equal(m1, m2) iff Equal(m2, m1);
  cexit Equal(m1, m2) iff
          m1.s = m2.s and m1.d = m2.d and m1.t = m2.t;
  result : =  m1.s = m2.s and m1.d = m2.d
          and m1.t = m2.t;
end;
```

In the functions that are permitted access to internal structure of messages, centry and cexit specifications also are permitted access to the internal structure, but entry and exit specifications are not. Entry and exit specifications are visible externally to all routines that call the functions, but the visibility of centry and cexit specifications is restricted. In this example, the cexits of Source, Destination, Text, Compose and Equal are each visible to the other. This prevents the external specifications from revealing the internal structure of messages to the other routines in the program. In a function the local variable with the reserved name "result" is the value assigned to the function upon exit. It can be used in the same way as any other local variable. In the function Compose, Message(s, d, t) is another example of the type name used to construct an object of that type. Message(s, d, t) creates a message with successive fields equal to s, d and t.

This completes the program and its specifications except for assigning values to the pending constants NUsers, Csize and TimeSlice. The program at this stage of development can be written as

```
program network(var upa: PortArray) =
begin
  block all i, j: UserId,
      ProperDelivery(i, j, upa);
  var npa: PortArray;
  cobegin
```

GYPSY: A LANGUAGE FOR VERIFIABLE PROGRAMS 437

```
        Node(upa(i), npa(i), i) each i : UserId;
        switch(npa);
    end;
end;

type PortArray = array(UserId) of Port;

type UserId = integer(1 .. NUsers);
const NUsers: integer = pending;

type Port = record(Get,Put: Line);
type Line = buffer(Csize) of Message;
const Csize: integer = pending;
define ProperDelivery(i, j, pa) =
    mail (pa(j).put.outto, i, j) sub mail(pa(i).get.infrom, i, j):

function mail(ms: MessageSequence; i, j: UserId): MessageSequence =
begin
    exit (assume mail(ms, i, j) =
        if ms = MessageSequence( )
        then MessageSequence( )
        else if i = Source(first(ms)) and
                j = Destination(first(ms))
            then MessageSequence(first(ms))
                @ Mail(nonfirst(ms), i, j)
            else Mail(nonfirst(ms), i, j)
        fi  fi);
end;

type MessageSequence = sequence of Message;

process Node(var up, np: Port; i: UserId) =
begin
    block up.Put.outto sub np.Put.infrom
        and np.Get.outto sub up.Get.infrom;
    cobegin
        Pass(np.Put, up.Put, i, Depart);
        Pass(up.Get, np.Get, i, Arrive);
    end;
end;

process Pass(var x, y: Line; i: UserId; d: Direction) =
begin
    block y.outto sub x.infrom;
    var m: Message;
    loop
        assert y.outto sub x.infrom;
        receive m from x;
        trace i = if d = Depart
            then Destination(m)
            else Source(m) fi
        send m to y;
    end;
end;
```

```
type direction = (Arrive, Depart);

process Switch(var npa: PortArray) =
begin
  block all i, j: UserId,
      ProperDelivery(i, j, npa);
  var m: Message;
  var k: UserId;
  cond DestinationErr;
  keep Destination(m) in (1 .. NUsers)
      otherwise DestinationErr;
  loop
    k := 1;
    loop
      if k > NUsers then leave end;
      assert all i, j: UserId, ProperDelivery(i, j, npa);
      await
      on receive m from npa(k).Get:
          send m to npa (destination(m)).Put;
      after TimeSlice: ;
      when
      is DestinationErr: ;
      end;
      k := k + 1;
    end;
  end;
end;

const TimeSlice: integer = pending;

type Message <Source, Destination, Text, Compose, Equal> =
begin
  axiom all m: Message,
      Equal(Compose(Source(m), Destination(m), Text(m)), m);
  record(s, d: UserId; t: CString);
end;

type CString = sequence (100) of char;

function Source(m: Message): UserId =
begin
  cexit Source(m) = m.s;
  result := m.s;
end;

function Destination(m: Message): UserId =
begin
  cexit Destination(m) = m.d;
  result := m.d;
end;
```

```
function Text(m: Message): CString =
begin
  cexit Text(m) = m.t;
  result := m.t;
end;

function Compose(s,d: UserId; t: CString): Message =
begin
  cexit Compose(s, d, t) = Message(s, d, t);
  result := Message(s, d, t);
end;

function Equal(m1, m2: Message): boolean =
begin
  exit Equal(m1, m2) iff Equal(m2, m1);
  cexit Equal(m1, m2) iff
      m1.s = m2.s and m1.d = m2.d and m1.t = m2.t;
  result := m1.s = m2.s and m1.d = m2.d
      and m1.t = m2.t;
end;
```

There are many details of Gypsy that this example does not illustrate, but the development of this program and its specifications provides a good overview of the philosophy and capabilities of the language.

10. CONCLUSION

The initial design of Gypsy is complete. The design has been driven by the development of a comprehensive methodology for constructing verified communications processing software, and the trial application of the methodology to realistic problems [Wells 1976]. A report on the full methodology is in preparation. It is expected that the language will continue to develop as methodology is tested and refined in further applications. A full report on the language can be found in Ambler, Good and Burger [1976]. This report gives a formal definition of the syntax, and an informal description of semantics. A formal definition of the semantics is in preparation. An interactive design and verification system for Gypsy programs is under construction. The system consists of a table-driven syntax analyzer, a verification condition generator, and an interactive theorem prover. First implementations of these components are operational for most of Gypsy. These components are being integrated under a program design management component that maintains a data base of Gypsy program units and supports incremental program development and verification. Implementation of Gypsy is planned, but has not yet begun.

Gypsy has a number of important and distinctive aspects. It is a high-level language for general purpose computing that also supports the development of systems programs. It includes facilities for concurrency and timing, execution in imperfect run time environments and an access control mechanism. Gypsy includes extensive facilities for expressing functional specifications of its programs and of the units from which its programs are structured. All constructs in Gypsy are verifiable either by formal proof or run time validation. Run time validation can be used effectively to reduce the size and complexity of the formal proofs. Facilities are provided for decomposing both routines and data into small, logically meaningful units that can be verified independently. This modularity greatly enhances the practical feasibility of formal proofs. We believe that integrating these features smoothly into a common language is a significant step in the design of languages to support the systematic development of highly reliable computer programs.

A. KLAUSNER *and* T. E. KONCHAN
Harvard University

Rapid Prototyping and Requirements Specification Using PDS

1. INTRODUCTION

Rapid prototyping can make the development of software systems cheaper and easier by aiding the requirements definition and design processes, and by aiding the coding of the system's final version. Section 2, Rapid Prototyping, discusses rapid prototyping and its impact on the entire software life cycle.

Ideally, rapid prototyping is supported by an integrated software development environment, consisting of an appropriate programming language and various tools. The Program Development System (PDS), based on EL1 (Extensible Language 1), provides an integrated environment to aid in developing small and large scale software systems. A case study by the authors used this environment to build a prototype of a relational database system. In doing so, the authors made several observations about both rapid prototyping and PDS as an environment for supporting it. PDS and the case study exemplifying its use are described in Section 3.

The incorporation of a requirements specification language in PDS, along with appropriate analysis tools, would make PDS a more complete programming environment and even more supportive of rapid prototyping. This is recommended in Section 4, Requirements Specification in PDS. The requirements specification language proposed, though not rigorously defined, would be a natural and integral extension to PDS.

2. RAPID PROTOTYPING

Rapid prototyping is the process of quickly producing a prototype of a software system according to its requirements. The prototype exhibits the functional behavior of the target system, although it may not meet all its real-time requirements. Use of the prototype provides feedback to the software designers as to the suitability of the system, and gives valuable early experience to future users [Redwine, Seigel and Berglass 1981].

Rapid prototyping results in the early establishment of more complete and correct requirements and design [Gomaa and Scott 1981]. In addition, the target version of the system can be derived directly from the prototype by refinement, rather than being coded from scratch. The overall effect of rapid prototyping is to make the software development life cycle more cost-effective.

2.1 The Impact on Requirements Definition and Design

A common problem with software products is disagreement between what the customer expects and what he gets. The problem can often be traced to a deficiency in the specification of the software requirements. Often the user does not know exactly what he wants, nor what is feasible to implement in software. Also, fully specifying requirements is inherently difficult because of the detailed formal description necessary. Thus, the requirements specification is often inconsistent, incomplete, or ambiguous, necessitating changes in requirements and subsequent redesign and recoding later in development. If these deficiencies could be discovered sooner, time and money would be saved.

Deficiencies in software requirements are not usually perceived until the customer interacts with the systems. Using a prototype the user can interact with the system and can discover requirements deficiencies early, enabling prompt correction and completion of the requirements.

Deficiencies in the software design often are not perceived until the developer can check the feasibility of the design sooner, before effort is expended on developing the target version of the system. Deficiencies in the global aspects of the design are easier to correct on the prototype, before the detailed design of the target version is developed.

The cycle of requirements change, redesign, and recode requires less time when done on a prototype before the target version is coded. Time is also saved when coding and testing the final version because less requirements and design problems are found.

2.2 The Impact on Coding

Rapid prototyping affects the manner in which the target version of a system is created. Instead of coding the target version directly from the design, it can be derived more easily by using the prototype as a model. This derivation can be done mechanically or by hand. If the target version is to be written in a language different from the prototype, then translation and refinement (e.g. replacement of algorithms by more efficient ones) of the prototype code must be performed. If they are written in the same language then refinement of the prototype code is all that is necessary to obtain the target version.

In a case study done by Zelkowitz [1980], the final version of a language interpreter was written in PASCAL by hand translation and refinement of its prototype version, written in SNOBOL4. The result of the translation was nearly error-free version, which was believed to have been developed with less effort than if no prototype had been used. However, Zelkowitz observed that the prototype relied heavily on SNOBOL4 storage management, a feature not supported by PASCAL, and this accounted for most of the translation effort.

Derivation of the target system from its prototype may be easier if both versions are written in the same language, eliminating the need for translation. Furthermore, when an integrated programming environment supports all stages of software development and has tools for transforming and refining code, then the target version can be derived mechanically and systematically from the prototype by a series of stepwise refinements.

2.3 The Impact on the Software Life cycle

Although a prototype adds a small additional cost to the development effort, the improvement in the requirements definition, design, and coding processes result in an overall reduction in cost. Gomaa and Scott [1981] found that the cost of developing and running a prototype of a management information system they built was less than 10% of the total development cost, and the prototype more than paid for itself by revealing requirements and design problems early.

The traditional software life cycle consists of the phases: requirements definition, design, code, test, and maintenance. The coding and testing phases are relatively long partly because they involve correcting problems discovered in the requirements and design, and debugging the code. Figure 2.1 depicts the relative cumulative effort devoted to each life cycle phase. The order of the phases is according to that incurred during the software life cycle. Although the phases often overlap in practice, we simplified the figure by not showing this.

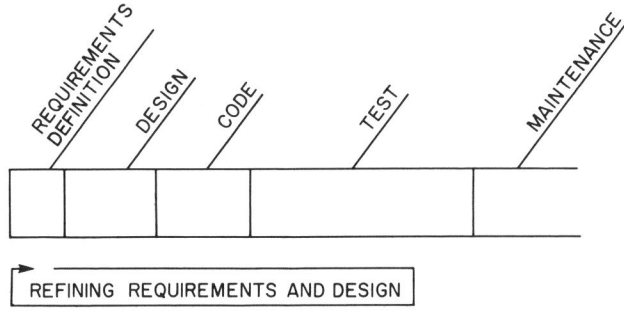

Figure 2.1 The traditional software life cycle

Rapid prototyping differs from traditional software development by the addition of two phases: coding the prototype and testing it (as shown in Figure 2.2). It improves the development process in many ways. Testing time is significantly shortened because many requirements and design problems are discovered and corrected on the prototype. The result is that the test phases combined require less time than the traditional test phase. Time spent coding the target version is shortened because it contains fewer bugs, and can be refined directly from the prototype (the prototype itself is developed quickly because of its small scale). Overall, rapid prototyping has the effect of shortening the software development effort.

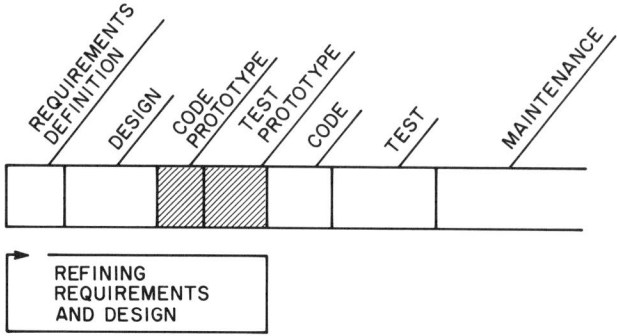

Figure 2.2 The software life cycle with rapid prototyping

3. PDS AND RAPID PROTOTYPING

The Program Development System (PDS) [Hausen and Mullerburg 1981; Cheatham, Townley and Holloway 1979] is an integrated programming environment which supports rapid prototyping. An outstanding feature of PDS is its provision for program refinement by transformation. PDS encourages methodical software development through modular top-down design and stepwise refinement. It manages multiple versions and levels of modules, while hiding file management from the user. PDS is user-friendly, increases programmer productivity, and can be used to enforce programming standards. As a rapid prototyping environment, PDS expedites the process of developing a prototype, thus providing a running system early in the development effort. It also supports the natural evolution of a prototype into an efficient final version.

PDS is based on EL1 (Extensible Language 1) [Cheatham and Townley 1975; Holloway, Townley, Spitzen and Wegbreit 1974], an extensible programming language developed especially for supporting an integrated software development environment [Goodwin 1981]. By extensible we mean it has facilities for extending and modifying the syntax, the set of operators, the data structures, and the control structures available in the language [Cheatham 1971]. The advantage of having an extensible language in PDS is that it can be used as a program design language (PDL) to develop the high level representation of a system and it can also be used to code the executable version of the system.

EL1 is an interpretive language, and has the advantage of being interactive—which facilitates debugging. An outstanding feature of EL1 is that not only can it be interpreted but it can also be efficiently compiled, thus making it feasible for coding a system's target version.

3.1 Overview of the System

PDS is made up of three components: a database of programs, a collection of development tools, and a controlling executive which, among other things, provides an interactive user interface. The data in the database is hierarchically ordered as follows:

1. Module—the largest data item in the database, corresponds to a file.
2. Scope—a group of entities within a module.
3. Entity—the substance of a module, which can be, for example, a procedure or data type definition.
4. Attribute—contains information about a module, scope, or entity. There are many kinds of attributes, for example, **Name**, **Comment**, and **Uses** (a description of relationships between modules). All the information in a module is contained in its attributes.

In PDS, a software system is decomposed into modules, each representing a subsection of the system. When using PDS, one first creates *abstract* modules which contain a high level representation of the system. This representation can be written in any form suitable for the problem being solved, and need not necessarily be written in executable EL1 code. A separate module is used to describe the syntax of this representation. Modules which make up the software system are written with the use of a structure editor which enforces syntactical correctness.

To refine the high level representation into a more concrete form, separate *refinement* modules are used. These modules contain comments, data type definitions, procedures, functions and rewrites. The data types are flexible and their behavior is user definable. Likewise, the procedures and functions can be defined in a flexible manner. The rewrites are operators for transforming abstract problem representations into more concrete representations. Their function is to replace a given pattern of code by different, more detailed, code.

A transformation tool is used to combine abstract and refinement modules, applying the refinements to derive new lower level modules in which abstract constructs have been replaced by more concrete equivalents. There are also analysis tools within PDS for checking the consistency and integrity of abstract, refinement, and concrete modules. For instance, one such tool finds undeclared identifiers.

Refinement modules do not necessarily contain the lowest level version (executable EL1 code) of the software system: rather, they may contain representations which in themselves require further refinement by way of separate refinement modules. Several stages of this process are possible, resulting in a new module containing executable EL1 code. This facilitates top-down development of the system, starting from its initial high level representation, and refining it step-by-step into its final executable form.

PDS allows the user to write alternative refinement modules for any abstract module. This facilitates the testing of alternative design decisions such as which data types and algorithms are best for the particular application. In addition, this allows the same abstract modules to be used for the creation of different target versions for different environments or machines. For example, an abstract module containing a network communications protocol can be refined into various executable versions for the different machines and operating systems in the network. The result can be a family of modules and derivations representing various versions of the system. PDS supports the development by maintaining a database of all the modules and versions in the software system, and their derivation history.

3.2 Rapid Prototyping Using PDS

PDS has several features which make it especially supportive of rapid prototyping. As a programming environment, it expedites the top-down development of an executable prototype by stepwise refinement. The testing and debugging of the prototype, and the subsequent changes to the system requirements and design, are aided by the interactive nature of PDS. PDS supports the development and testing of alternative designs by enabling the use of alternative modules, thus improving design decisions.

In PDS, the target version of a system is written in the same language as the prototype. This enables the direct derivation of the target version from the prototype—eliminating the need for translation. The target version is refined from the prototype, based upon the same abstract modules, only using different refinements reflecting more suitable data types and more efficient algorithms. All versions of the system are maintained in the PDS database.

3.3 An Example of Prototyping in PDS

During the Spring of 1981, the authors used PDS to develop a prototype of a relational database system [Konchan and Klausner 1981]. This effort was part of a course in Programming Methodologies taught by Professor T. E. Cheatham at Harvard University. The goals of the project were:

(a) To learn about the implementation of a new relational database language.

(b) To build a prototype of a complex software system according to an initially incomplete set of requirements.

(c) To experiment with PDS as a rapid prototyping environment.

The project was concerned with extending an existing general purpose programming language with relational database facilities. The language extension was to consist of high level operations which enable a user to manipulate data in a database. The high level operations included operations on various levels of data in the relational database hierarchy, such as operations on databases, operations on relations, and operations on tuples (see Figure 3.1).

REQUIREMENTS SPECIFICATION USING PDS

Operations on Databases	**Operations on Relations**	**Operations on Tuples**
InitializeSystem	CreateRelation	TupleOf
CreateDataBase	CreateTemporaryRelation	Declaration
OpenDataBase	AssociateWithRelation	ForEachTuple
CloseDataBase	OpenRelationToUpdate	Augment
DeleteDataBase	OpenRelationToRetrieve	Modify
PrintDirectories	CloseRelation	Delete
	DeleteRelation	FieldSelection
	PrintRelation	PrintTuple

Figure 3.1 Language primitives

The requirements for the project included a description of the language primitives; for example, two of these were described as follows:

"**ForEachTuple t in r REPEAT body END** -- *a loop in which a variable named* **t** *is bound, in turn, to each tuple of* **r** *and then* **body** *is executed.*

. . .

Augment r with t -- *adds the tuple* **t** *to the relation controlled by* **r**. **r** *must be open in update mode.*"

In addition, some general and vague requirements were included. For example, the user was not to be concerned with storage representation details, but was to be able to specify how the tuples of the relation were to be managed between primary and secondary memory. Another example of a general requirement is that the database system was to be a convenient and consistent extension to the underlying programming language. The requirements did not specify implementation details such as data structures, I/O, and file management.

The first stage in the development was the writing of an abstract module containing the high level representation of the language primitives. This module was divided into three scopes corresponding to the hierarchy of data in the database system (databases, relations, tuples). A separate module contained the necessary syntax.

Figure 3.2 shows an entity (Entity 3.5) containing the abstract version of one of the language primitives, **OpenRelationToUpdate**. This entity consists of two attributes, a **Comment** and a **Binding**. The **Binding** assigns (<-) an explicit procedure (**EXPR**) to the name **OpenRelationToUpdate**. The procedure accepts one parameter, an object block for the use of a relation, but at this level it is not defined in detail. The selection function (.) in the last line of the procedure is used to access, in a yet unspecified manner, information in **RelationControlBlock**.

```
Module <DBS>
   ...
+++++++++++ 3 Scope (OperationsOnRelations) ++++++++++++
   ...
3-5 OpenRelationToUpdate

   Comment
      This procedure accepts a given relation in the
      database and opens it for update. First, check
      whether the database is open, then, according to
      information in the given RelationControlBlock,
      open the necessary file for accessing the
      relation, and update the RelationControlBlock to
      reflect its new status;
   EndComment;

   OpenRelationToUpdate <—
      EXPR(RelationControlBlock: Relation)
         BEGIN
            DataBaseOpen #> ERROR;
               /* If not open, then give an error
                  message and exit block; */
               OpenRelationFile(RelationControlBlock);
               RelationControlBlock.OpenForUpdate <— TRUE;
         END;
   ...
```

Figure 3.2 The abstract version of a language primitive

The second stage of development was the writing of two refinement modules containing two levels of refinement. The first level consisted of data type definitions, file structures, and more detailed descriptions of the language primitive. It was at this level of refinement that many requirements deficiencies were uncovered. The second level of refinement contained implementations of the high level I/O utilities used in the first refinement module.

Figure 3.3 shows a data type definition (Entity 3.4) and one of the rewrites (in Entity 3.9) used to refine the language primitive OpenRelationToUpdate. The data type definition shows a compound record (**STRUCT**) consisting of many fields of different types. The rewrite shown within the entity named **RelationFile** depicts a pattern on the left side of the rewrite operator (<—>), which, when matched, is replaced by the **BEGIN-END** block on the right side.

```
Module <DBSI>
   ...
++++++++++++ 3 Scope(OperationsOnRelations) ++++++++++++
   ...
3-4 Relation <-
   STRUCT(Prt: PORT,
          Length: INT,
          OpenForUpdate: BOOL,
          OpenForRetrieve: BOOL,
          Permanent: BOOL,
          Data: PageList,
          ShadowName: SYMBOL,
          ShadowPrt: PORT,
          ShadowLength: INT,
          DeleteList: DeletedTupleList,
          NextR: Relation,
          RCs: RelationCharacteristics
          TMode: MODE,
          PMode: MODE );
   ...
3-9 RelationFile

   Rewrites
     ...
   OpenRelationFile(RelationControlBlock) <->
      BEGIN
         Valid(RelationControlBlock) #> ERROR;
         RelationControlBlock.Prt <-
            OpenFile(RelationControlBlock.RCs.FileName,
                    "UPDATE", "BINARY");
         RelationControlBlock.Length <-
            FileLength(RelationControlBlock.Prt);
         ResetFile(RelationControlBlock.Prt);
      END;
   ...
```

Figure 3.3   Refinements of a language primitive

The final development stage of the prototype was the application of the transformation tool to form an executable version. Debugging of this version was aided by the interpretive nature of EL1. Changing the refinement modules and reuse of the transformation tool were required to incorporate any corrections. This forced the use of a methodical debugging technique. It is important to note that although we completed the abstract and refinement modules before beginning debugging, we could have begun debugging sooner. In general, debugging can begin whenever any part of the system can be transformed into executable code. During this stage of development, we continued to make changes to the initial system requirements.

The completion of a working prototype was accomplished quickly and successfully. It was used to write meaningful examples of relational database programs which were then executed. Use of the relational database language, and a subsequent analysis of its merits and shortcomings, resulted in a better understanding of the semantic difficulty of merging general purpose programming languages with relational database languages.

The development of an efficient target version of the system has not yet taken place, although it can be developed relatively easily from the prototype.

3.4 Useful Additions to PDS

PDS is in the experimental stage and would benefit from some extensions and additional tools. The incorporation of a requirements specification language and tools to be used in conjunction with it would be especially useful for supporting rapid prototyping. This addition is discussed in more detail in the following chapter.

Some other potentially useful additions to PDS, which won't be discussed in detail, are:

(a) *Restrictions to rewrites.* Such a class of restrictions could prevent the improper use of rewrites and the resultant unmaintainable system, and could help establish a disciplined refinement methodology.

(b) *Quality metrics and tools.* Automated tools for determining the values of metrics such as module coupling and cohesion would be a natural extension to PDS.

4. REQUIREMENTS SPECIFICATION IN PDS

Requirements specification is especially important to rapid prototyping [Peters 1978], but is an inherently difficult task because it involves specifying and defining the problem being solved in a formal and logical manner. To deal with this problem, use can be made of a requirements specification language. The key advantages of a requirements specification language are:

(a) It provides a systematic approach to specifying requirements. This is especially good for large projects, as it results in more comprehensible requirements.

(b) Its formal basis encourages unambiguous and complete descriptions of requirements.

(c) It enables systematic checking of the requirements because of uniformity in the specification.

(d) It enables the use of various automated tools. Compiler technology can be used to check for inconsistency, incompleteness, and ambiguities in the requirements specification. Also, the use of reporting tools is enabled, along with tools which support modifiability—an important feature for a rapid prototyping environment.

It is important that a requirements specification language provide a concise, unambiguous way of defining requirements, but that is not enough; the statement of requirements must also be modifiable, as the majority of maintenance costs are related to changes in system functionality, rather than correction of coding errors.

During the development and use of a system, its requirements change. Thus it behooves us to make requirements modifiable. Modifiability is system wide and spans all phases of software development. Having tools to evaluate the impact of requirements changes, to assist in making requirements changes, etc., is crucial.

A requirements specification language must have a formal basis in order to support sophisticated tools such as analysis tools which perform consistency checks on the inputs and outputs of hierarchically decomposed functional requirements. PDS appears flexible enough, because of its use of modules, a central database, etc., to support any type of requirements specification language. Although many formalized requirements specification languages exist [Zave and Yeh 1981; Davis and Rataj 1978; Smoliar 1981], none of them are general enough to support diverse applications. Thus, they are not appropriate for PDS, which is meant to be a general purpose programming environment.

The purpose of this section is to show how naturally PDS can support requirements specification as a part of an integrated programming environment. Representation of requirements instances and tools to check them (e.g. to ensure consistency with the design) are also presented.

4.1 The Requirements Specification Language

Riddle and Wileden [1978] suggest that languages characterized as *relational* are the most appropriate for specifying requirements because they support problem oriented descriptions of software problems. By relational they mean languages which specify relationships between the functional components of the system, without suggesting or constraining the way in which these functional components will eventually be organized and implemented.

A relational language for requirements specification should be introduced into PDS as a natural complement to its design implementation facilities. Functional requirements instances (single, identifiable functional requirements) would be contained in modules, scopes, and entities, with requirements attributes being used to describe their properties and interrelationships. These requirements attributes would be in addition to the attributes presently in PDS, and would describe the various behavior requirements of the functional instances. Examples of such requirements attributes are:

(a) Name

(b) Type

(c) Inputs

(d) Outputs

(e) Assumptions

(f) Requirement Statement

(g) Constraints

(h) Comment.

As is true in the PDS data hierarchy, the functional requirements instances would be described solely by their attributes. All attributes would be created and maintained by structure editors, and kept in the PDS database.

PDS would support the hierarchical organization of functional requirements instances, which is important for large systems, but would also allow the use of other topologies. Thus, hierarchical functional decomposition (such as described by Rosenbaum and Hackler [1980]), along with other requirements specification methodologies, could be supported.

4.2 The Relationship Between Requirements and Design

The requirements of a system describe its functional behavior, while the design of a system is a high level description of its implementation. This suggests that different language facilities and capabilities are necessary for these two types of descriptions. Because the design is a reflection of the requirements, these languages should be related, and provisions should be made for establishing and verifying the traceability between them.

The functional requirements, structured logically, and the design or system architecture, structured to represent the physical implementation, are seldom structured identically [Rosenbaum and Hackler 1980]. However, there always exists a mapping between them, and to establish this mapping in PDS, a special **Implements** attribute could be added to design modules, scopes, or entities. This attribute would enumerate the requirement modules, scopes, and entities which this design instance implements. Tools described in the following section would access the **Implements** attributes to verify the completeness of the design, to support modifications to the design resulting from requirements changes, etc.

The process of developing and changing requirements and design modules would be supported by maintaining multiple versions of these modules in the PDS database. Thus PDS enhances the modifiability of requirements and design—an important plus in support of a rapid prototyping methodology. PDS would allow more than one design for the same set of requirements—facilitating the examination of alternative designs. Each design module would have its own set of **Implements** attributes, describing the way it relates to the requirements.

4.3 Tools for Use in Conjunction with the Requirements Specification Language

The classes of tools which can be utilized in conjunction with a requirements or design specification language (as suggested by Riddle and Wileden [1978]) are described in the following paragraphs. These classes are meant to represent the entire spectrum of such tools. The classes of tools are first described independent of any particular requirements or design specification language. Then, particular tools are described as examples of those which would be supported by the requirements language presented in Section 4.1.

Bookkeeping Tools. Tools of this class support the creation, alteration, and integrity of a requirements baseline. In order to support such a tool, the individual requirements instances or groups of requirements instances in a requirements specification language which make up a baseline must be accessible and modifiable. In PDS, structure editors would provide this accessibility and modifiability. Furthermore, PDS could support various versions of a baseline—enabling a return to an earlier version should decisions be reversed.

Supervisory Tools. These tools provide assurance that established software development practices and procedures are followed during the specification and design of a system. As these tools are dependent on the particular development procedures in use for a given project, it is difficult to specify a tool that would always be useful, independent of the underlying requirements or design specification language and the given project. An example of such a tool for use with PDS and the requirements specification language described in Section 4.1 is one which would constrain the use of rewrites, thereby placing added control over the refinement methodology.

Managerial Tools. These tools provide information indicating the status of a development effort. From this information progress, problem areas, and critical remaining development tasks can be assessed. In PDS, managerial tools which make use of information in the special **Implements** attributes could provide reports such as requirements-to-design traceability matrices, or the percentage of requirements as yet unimplemented. Report generation tools ideally will provide reports which are comprehensible by personnel who are not necessarily closely associated with PDS or computers.

Decision-making Tools. Tools of this class support the development of more correct requirements and design by providing an analysis capability. The purpose of these tools is to: detect errors in, quantify, predict properties of, bolster confidence in, and guide the specification or design of a system. Some decision-making tools which PDS should support are:

(a) *Requirements self-consistency checkers*. One such tool would check the names and types of data which is passed between functions, revealing any undefined or multiple-defined data.

(b) *Traceability checkers.* These tools ensure compliance of the design to the requirements. An example of a straightforward requirements traceability tool can be found in a paper by Pierce [1978]. This paper describes the data fields which make up a requirements instance and the function of its report generator.

(c) *Evaluators of the impact of requirements changes on design.* An example of such a tool is one which determines how many design modules are affected by the deletion or modification of a requirements instance.

5. CONCLUSION

We find rapid prototyping to be a significant notion and important enough to warrant continued study. It has many effects on software development, all of which culminate in a more cost effective development cycle. Rapid prototyping is supported by PDS, which is an extensive programming environment for supporting small and large scale software systems. One advantage of rapid prototyping is in improving the specification of programs. For this, it is useful to have a special language for specifying requirements. We proposed the addition of requirements specification capabilities to PDS as an integral and natural extension.

Future work should be done on defining and presenting rapid prototyping languages and capabilities, and on incorporating these into existing programming environments. PDS is presently in experimental use, and work is being done to improve its rapid prototyping capabilities. As part of this work, consideration could be given to rigorously defining and implementing the requirements specification language presented here. Such an addition would cause PDS to be a more complete programming environment and more supportive of rapid prototyping.

References

(Papers marked with an * are included in this book.)

Abrial, J. R., S. A. Schuman and B. Meyer 1979. Specification Language Z. Massachusetts Computer Associates Inc., Boston, MA.

Abrial, J.-R. 1980. The Specification Language Z: Basic Library. Specification Group Working Paper, Programming Research Group, Oxford, U.K.

Aczel, P. 1982. A Note on Program Verification. Manuscript.

Alford, M. W. 1977. A Requirements Engineering Methodology for Real-time Processing Requirements. *IEEE Trans. Software Eng.*, vol. SE-3 (January), pp. 60-69.

*Ambler, A. L., D. I. Good, J. C. Browne, W. F. Burger, R. M. Cohen, C. G. Hoch and R. E. Wells 1977. GYPSY: A Language for Specification and Implementation of Verifiable Programs. *Proceedings of an ACM Conference on Language Design for Reliable Software, SIGPLAN Notices* vol. 12 no. 3 (March).

Ambler, A. L., D. I. Good and W. F. Burger 1976. Report on the Language Gypsy. ICSCA-CMP-1, The University of Texas, Austin, TX.

Ambler, A. L., C. G. Hoch 1976. A Study of Protection in Programming Languages. ICSCA-CMP-3, The University of Texas at Austin.

Anderson, E. R., F. C. Belz and E. K. Blum 1976. SEMANOL (73), A Metalanguage for Programming the Semantics of Programming Languages. *Acta Informatica*, vol. 6, pp. 109-131.

Apt, K. R. 1981. Ten Years of Hoare's Logic: A Survey — Part 1. *ACM TOPLAS*, vol. 3, no. 4 (October).

Aubin, R. 1976. Mechanizing Structural Induction. Ph.D. Dissertation, Univ. Edinburgh, Edinburgh.

Backus, J. 1978. Can Programming be Liberated From The Von Neumann style? A Functional Style and Its Algebra of Programs. *CACM*, vol. 21 (August), pp. 613-641.

Balzer, R. M. 1967. Dataless Programming. Full Joint Computer Conference, 1967, pp. 535-545.

Balzer, R. M. 1981. Transformational Implementation: An Example. *IEEE Trans. Software Engineering*, January, 3–14. Also published as USC/Information Sciences Institute RR-79-79, May.

*Balzer, R. and N. Goldman 1979. Principles of Good Software Specification and Their Implications for Specification Language. In *Proc. Specifications of Reliable Software Conf.* (April), Cambridge, MA, pp. 58-67.

Balzer, R., N. Goldman and D. Wile 1976. On the Transformational Implementation Approach to Programming. In *Proc. 2nd Int. Conf. Software Eng.* (October), pp. 337-344.

Balzer, R., N. Goldman and D. Wile 1977. Informality in Program Specification. *Fifth International Joint Conference on Artificial Intelligence* (August) and *IEEE Transactions of Software Engineering* (April), vol. SE-4, no. 2; also USC/Information Science Institute, ISI-RR-77-59 (April 1977).

Barringer, H., J. H. Cheng and C. B. Jones 1983. A Logic Covering Undefinedness in Program Proofs. Submitted to *ACTA Informatica* for publication.

Bartlett, K. A., R. A. Scantlebury and P. T. A. Wilkinson 1969. Note on Reliable Full Duplex Transmission Over Half Duplex Links. *CACM*, vol. 12 (May), pp. 260-261.

Bauer, F. L. 1976. Programming as an Evolutionary Process. *Proceedings of the Second International Conference on Software Engineering*, pp. 223-234.

Bauer, F. L., P. Partsch, P. Pepper and H. Wossner 1977. Techniques for Program Development. In *Infotech State of the Art Report: Software Engineering Techniques* pp. 25-50. Infotech Inform. Ltd.

Belady, L. A. and M. M. Lehman 1979. The Characteristics of Large Systems. In *Research Directions in Software Technology* edited by Peter Wegner, pp. 106-138, MIT Press, Cambridge, MA.

Bell, D. E. and L. J. LaPadula 1973. Secure Computer Systems. Report ESD-TR-73-278, Mitre Corp., Bedford, MA.

Bell, T. E., D. C. Bixler and M. E. Dyer 1977. An Extendable Approach to Computer-Aided Software Requirements Engineering, *IEEE Trans. Software Eng.*, vol. SE-3 (January), pp. 49-60.

Bell, T. E. and T. A. Thayer 1976. Software Requirements: Are They Really a Problem? In *Proc. 2nd Int. Conf. Software Eng.* (October), pp. 61-68, San Francisco, CA.

Berthomieu, B. 1980. Selective Repeat Protocol: Axiomatization and Proofs. USC/Inform. Sci. Inst., Program Verification Project, Affirm Memo. 36, September.

Berthomieu, B. 1981. Algebraic Specification of Communication Protocols. USC/Inform. Sci. Inst., Report RR-81-98, December.

Berzins, V. A. 1979. Abstract Model Specifications for Data Abstractions. MIT, Technical Report MIT/LCS/TR-221, July.

Bierman, A. 1976. Approaches to Automatic Programming. *Advances in Computers*, vol. 15, pp. 1-63.

Birkhoff, G. and J. D. Lipson 1970. Heterogeneous Algebras. *J. of Combinatorial Theory*, vol. 8, pp. 115-133.

Bjorner, D. 1980. Formal Description of Programming Concepts—A Software Engineering Viewpoint. *Proceedings of Mathematical Foundations of Computer Science, Lecture Notes in Computer Science*, vol. 88, pp. 1-21. Springer-Verlag.

Bjorner, D. 1981. The VDM Principles of Software Specification and Program Design. In *Formalization of Programming Concepts, Lecture Notes in Computer Science* 107, pp. 44-74, Springer-Verlag.

Bjorner and Jones 1982. *Formal Specification and Software Development*, Prentice-Hall International.

Bochmann, G. V. and J. Gecsei 1977. A Unified Method for the Specification and Verification of Protocols. In *Proc. IFIP Cong.* (August), pp. 229-234, Toronto, Canada.

Boehm, B. W. 1976. Software Engineering. *IEEE Trans Comput.*, vol. C-25 (December), pp 1226-1241.

Bothe, K. 1981. A Comparative Study of Abstract Data Type Concepts. *Elektronische Informationsverarbeitung und Kybernetik*, EIK 17, vol. 4, no. 6, 237-257.

Boyer, R. S. and J. S. Moore 1975. Proving Theorems About LISP Functions. *JACM* (January), vol. 22, pp. 129-144.

Boyer, R. S. and J. S. Moore 1979. *A Computational Logic*. Academic Press, New York.

Brand, D. and W. H. Joyner, Jr. 1978. Verification of Protocols Using Symbolic Execution. *Comput. Networks*, vol. 2 (September/October).

Brinch Hansen, P. 1970. The Nucleus of a Multiprogramming System. *CACM* vol. 13, no. 4.

Brinch Hansen, P. 1973. *Operating Systems Principles*. Prentice-Hall.

Brinch Hansen, P. 1975. The Purpose of Concurrent Pascal. *Proceedings ICRS*.

Brinch Hansen, P. 1977. *The Architecture of Concurrent Programs*. Prentice-Hall, Englewood Cliffs, N.J.

Brinch Hansen, P. 1978. Distributed Processes: A Concurrent Programming Concept. *CACM*, vol. 21 (November), pp. 934-941.

Bron, C., M. M. Fokkinga and A. C. M. de Haas 1976. A Proposal for Dealing With Abnormal Termination of Programs, T. H. Twente, Memo no. 150.

Burge, W. H. 1975. *Recursive Programming Techniques*. Addison-Wesley, Reading, MA.

Burstall, R. M. 1977. Design Considerations for a Functional Programming Language. The Software Revolution In *Proc. Infotech State of the Art Conf.*, Copenhagen, pp. 45-57.

Burstall, R. M. 1978. Design Considerations for a Functional Programming Language. To appear.

Burstall, R. M. 1980. Electronic Category Theory. *Proceedings of Mathematical Foundations of Computer Science, Lecture Notes in Computer Science*, vol. 88, pp. 22-39. Springer-Verlag.

Burstall, R. M. and J. Darlington 1975. Some Transformations for Developing Recursive Programs. *Proceedings of the International Conference on Reliable Software*, Los Angeles, CA. (April), pp. 465-472.

Burstall, R. M. and J. Darlington 1977. A Transformation System for Developing Recursive Programs. *JACM* (January), vol. 24, pp. 44-67.

Burstall, R. M. and J. A. Goguen 1977. Putting Theories Together to Make Specifications. *Proceedings, Fifth International Joint Conference on Artificial Intelligence* (August), pp. 1045-1058.

Burstall, R. M. and J. A. Goguen 1980. The Semantics of CLEAR, a Specification Language. In *Proceedings of the 1979 Copenhagen Winter School on Abstract Software Specification, Lecture Notes in Computer Science*, vol. 86, pp. 292-332. Springer-Verlag.

Burstall, R. M., D. B. MacQueen and D. T. Sannella 1980. HOPE: An Experimental Applicative Language. In *Proc. 1980 LISP Conf.*, pp. 136-143, Stanford, CA.

Buxton, J. N. and B. Randell (Eds.) 1970. *Software Engineering Techniques*. Report of a conference sponsored by the NATO Science Committee, pp. 27-31 (October), Rome, Italy.

Campbell, R. H. and A. N. Habermann 1974. The Specification of Process Synchronization by Path Expressions. *Lecture Notes on Computer Science*, vol. 16, Springer-Verlag, Heidelberg-Berlin-New York.

Cheatham, T. E. 1971. *The Recent Evolution of Programming Languages*. Technical Report TR-17-71, Center for Research in Computing Technology, Harvard University, Cambridge, MA.

Cheatham, T. E. and J. A. Townley 1975. *A Look at Programming and Programming Systems*. Technical Report TR-18-75, Center for Research in Computing Technology, Harvard University, Cambridge, MA.

Cheatham, T. E., J. A. Townley and G. H. Holloway 1979. *A System for Program Refinement*. Technical Report TR-05-79, Center for Research in Computing Technology, Harvard University, Cambridge, MA.

Chen, P. P. S. 1976. The Entity-Relationship Model: Toward a Unified View of Data. *ACM Transactions on Data Base Systems* (March), vol. 1, no. 1, pp. 9-36.

Clark, K. L. and F. G. McCabe 1980. The Control Facilities of IC-PROLOG. In *Expert Systems in the Microelectronics Age 1980, Proc. AISB Summer School on Expert Syst.*, (July), Edinburgh.

Clint, M. 1973. Program Proving: Co-routines. *Acta Informatica* vol. 2.

Codd, E. F. 1971. Normalized Data Base Structure: A Brief Tutorial. *Proceedings of ACM SIGFIDET Workshop on Data Description, Access and Control*, San Diego, CA.

REFERENCES

Conn, A. P. 1980. Maintenance: A Key Element in Computer Requirements Definition. In *Proc. COMPSAC '80* (October), pp. 401-406, Chicago, IL.

Conway, M. E. 1963. Design of a Separate Transition-Diagram Compiler. *CACM*, vol. 6, no. 7 (July), 396-408.

Cottam, I. D. 1984. The Rigorous Development of a System Version Control Program. *IEEE Trans. on Software Engineering* (March).

Courtois, P. J., F. Heymans and D. L. Parnas 1971. Concurrent Control With 'Readers' and 'Writers.' *CACM*, vol. 14, no. 10 (October), pp. 667-668.

Cristian, F. 1982. Robust Data Types. *Acta Informatica*, to be published.

Cristian, F. 1984. Correct and Robust Programs. *IEEE Trans. on Software Engineering* (March).

Dahl, O.-J., B. Myhrhaug and K. Nygaard 1970. The Simula 67 Common Base Language. Publication No. S-22, Norwegian Computing Center, Oslo, Norway.

Dahl, O.-J. 1972. Notes on Data Structuring. In *Structured Programming*, édited by Dahl, O.-J., E. W. Dijkstra and C. A. R. Hoare, Academic Press.

Dahl, O. J. 1978. Can Program Proving Be Made Practical? Institute of Informatics, University of Oslo, Norway.

Dahl, O.-J., E. W. Dijkstra and C. A. R. Hoare 1972. *Structured Programming*. Academic Press, N.Y.

Dahl, O.-J. and K. Nygaard 1966. SIMULA—An ALGOL Based Simulation Language. *CACM*, vol. 9, pp. 671-678.

Dahl, O. J., K. Nygaard and B. Myhrhuag 1968. The SIMULA 67 Common Base Language. Norwegian Computing Centre, Forskningsveien 1B, Oslo, Norway.

Darlington, J. 1981. Program Transformation and Synthesis: Present Capabilities. Dep. Artificial Intell., Univ. Edinburgh, Technical Report DAI43, 1977; appeared in *Artificial Intell.*, Mar. 1981.

Darlington, J. and R. M. Burstall 1976. A System Which Automatically Improves Programs. *Acta Informatica*, vol. 6, pp. 41-60.

Darlington, J. and M. S. Feather 1980. A Transformational Approach to Program Modification. Technical Report 80/3, Dep. Comput. Contr., Imperial College, London.

Date, C. J. 1975. *An Introduction to Data Base Systems*. Addison-Wesley, Massachusetts.

Davis, A. M. and W. J. Rataj 1978. Requirements Language Processing for the Effective Testing of Real-Time Systems. In *Proceedings of the Software Quality and Assurance Workshop*, pp. 61-66. *ACM SIGMETRICS* (November).

Davis, A. M. and T. G. Rauscher 1979. Formal Techniques and Automatic Processing to Ensure Correctness in Requirements Specifications. In *Proc. Specifications of Reliable Software Conf.* (April), pp. 15-35, Cambridge, MA.

Davis, C. G., and C. R. Vick 1977. The Software Development System. *IEEE Trans. Software Eng.*, vol. SE-3 (January), pp. 69-84.

Dijkstra, E. W. 1968a. A Constructive Approach to the Problem of Program Correctness. *BIT*, vol. 8, pp. 174-186.

Dijkstra, E. W. 1968b. Cooperating Sequential Processes. In *Programming Languages* edited by F. Genuys, Academic Press, New York.

Dijkstra, E. W. 1972. Notes on Structured Programming. In *Structured Programming* edited by O.-J. Dahl, E. W. Dijkstra and C. A. R. Hoare. Academic Press, New York.

Dijkstra, E. W. 1975. Guarded Commands, Nondeterminacy and Formal Derivation of Programs. *CACM*, vol. 18, no. 8 (August), pp. 453-457.

Dijkstra, E. W. 1976. *A Discipline of Programming* (pp. 209-217). Prentice-Hall, Englewood Cliffs, N.J.

Donahue, J. E. 1976. Complementary Definitions of Programming Language Semantics. *Lecture Notes in Computer Science*, vol. 42, Springer-Verlag.

Ehrich, H. D. 1978. Extensions and Implementations of Abstract Data Type Specifications. *Proceedings of Mathematical Foundations of Computer Science, Lecture Notes in Computer Science*, vol. 64, pp. 155-163. Springer-Verlag.

Ehrig, E., J.-H. Kreowski and H. Weber 1978. Algebraic Specification Schemes for Data Base Systems. Hahn-Meitner-Institut, Berlin.

Ehrig, H., J.-H. Kreowski, B. Mahr and P. Padawitz 1980. Compound Algebraic Implementations: An Approach to Stepwise Refinement of Software Systems. *Proceedings of Mathematical Foundations of Computer Science, Lecture Notes in Computer Science*, vol. 88, pp. 231-245. Springer-Verlag.

Embley, D. W. 1978. Empirical and Formal Language Design Applied to a Unified Control Construct for Interactive Computing. *Int. J. Man-Machine Studies*, vol. 10, no. 2 (March) pp. 197-216.

Feather, M. S. 1979. A System for Developing Programs by Transformation. Ph.D. Dissertation, Dep. Artificial Intell., Univ. Edinburgh, Edinburgh.

Feather, M. S. 1982. A System for Assisting Program Transformation. Dep. Artificial Intell., Univ. Edinburgh, Edinburgh, Technical Report DAI124; see also *TOPLAS* (January).

Filman, R. E. and D. P. Friedman. *Languages and Models for Distributed Computing.* To be published.

Fisher, D. A. 1978. DoD's Common Programming Language Effort. *Computer* (March), vol. 11, pp. 24-33.

Fitzwater, D. R. and P. Zave 1977. The Use of Formal Asynchronous Process Specifications in a System Development Process. In *Proc. 6th Texas Conf. Comput. Syst.* (November), pp. 2B-21-2B-30, Austin, TX.

Flon, L. 1974. A Survey of Some Issues Concerning Abstract Data Types, Technical Report, Carnegie-Mellon University, Pittsburg, PA.

REFERENCES

Flon, L. and A. N. Habermann 1976. Towards the Construction of Verifiable Software Systems. *Proceedings Conf. on Data: Abstraction, Definition and Structure, SIGPLAN Notices* vol. 8, no. 2, pp. 141-148.

Flon, L. and J. Misra 1979. A Unified Approach to the Specification and Verification of Abstract Data Types. In *Proc. Specifications of Reliable Software Conf.* (April), IEEE Computer Society, pp. 162-169, Cambridge, MA.

Floyd, R. W. 1964. Treesort 3 Algorithm 245. *CACM*, vol. 7, no. 12 (December), p. 701.

Floyd, R. W. 1967. Assigning Meaning to Programs. *Mathematical Aspects of Computer Science* edited by J. T. Schwartz, Proceedings, *Symposium in Applied Math*, vol. 19, pp. 19-32, American Mathematical Society, Providence, RI.

Foley and V. L. Wallace 1974. The Art of Graphic Man-Machine conversation. *Proceedings of the IEEE 62*, vol. 4 (April), pp. 462-471.

Friedman, D. P. and D. S. Wise 1977. Aspects of Applicative Programming for File Systems. In *Proc. ACM Conf. Language Design for Reliable Software* (March), pp. 41-55, Raleigh, NC.

Friedman, D. P. and D. S. Wise 1978a. Aspects of Applicative Programming for Parallel Processing. *IEEE Trans. Comput.* vol. C-27 (April), pp. 289-296.

Friedman, D. P. and D. S. Wise 1978b. Unbounded Computational Structures. *Software-Practice and Experience* (July-August), vol. 8 pp. 407-416.

Friedman, D. P. and D. S. Wise 1979. An Approach to Fair Applicative Multiprogramming. In *Semantics of Concurrent Computation (Lecture Notes in Comput. Sci.)* edited by G. Kahn, vol. 70, pp. 203-226, Springer-Verlag, Berlin.

Friedman, D. P. and D. S. Wise 1980. An Indeterminate Constructor for Applicative Programming. In *Proc. 7th Annu. ACM Symp. Principles of Programming Languages* (January) pp. 245-250, Las Vegas, Nevada.

Gannon, J. D. 1975. Language Design to Enhance Programming Reliability. Ph.D. Thesis, Technical Report CSRG-47, Department of Computer Science, University of Toronto, Toronto, Canada.

Ganzinger, H. 1983. Parameterized Specifications: Parameter Passing and Implementation with Respect to Observability, *ACM TOPLAS*, vol. 5, no. 3 (July).

Gerhart, S. L., D. R. Musser, D. H. Thompson, D. A. Baker, R. W. Bates, R. W. Erickson, R. L. London, D. G. Taylor and D. S. Wile 1980. An Overview of AFFIRM: A Specification and Verification System. In *Proc. IFIP Congr.* (October), pp. 343-348, Australia.

Goguen, J. A. 1971. Mathematical Representation of Hierarchically Organized Systems. Global Systems Dynamics, S. Karger, pp. 112-128, Basle.

Goguen, J. A. 1977. Abstract Errors for Abstract Data Types. *Proceedings IFIP Working Conference on Formal Description of Programming Concepts*

(August) pp. 21.1-21.32; also in *Formal Description of Programming Concepts* edited by E. Neuhold, pp. 491-526, North Holland, 1978.

Goguen, J. A. 1978a. Some Design Principles and Theory for OBJ-0, a Language for Expressing and Executing Algebraic Specifications of Programs. *Proceedings, International Conference on Mathematical Studies of Information Processing* (August), pp. 429-475, Kyoto, Japan.

Goguen, J. A. 1978b. Order-Sorted Algebras, Subsorts, Coercions, Overloaded Operators, Exceptions, and Recovery. UCLA Semantics and Theory of Computation Report 14 (December), Computer Science Dept., UCLA.

Goguen, J. A. 1979. Some Ideas in Algebraic Semantics. To appear in *Proceedings, Third IBM Symposium on Mathematical Foundations of Computer Science*, Kobe, Japan.

Goguen, J. A. 1980. Thoughts on Program Specification, Design and Verification. *Software Engineering Notes*, vol. 5, no. 3.

Goguen, J. A. and R. M. Burstall 1978. Some Fundamental Properties of Algebraic Theories: A Tool for Semantics of Computation. Submitted to *Theoretical Computer Science*.

Goguen, J. A. and R. M. Burstall 1980a. An Ordinary Design. Technical Report, SRI International. Draft report.

Goguen, J. A. and R. M. Burstall 1980b. CAT, a System for the Structured Elaboration of Correct Programs from Structured Specifications. Technical Report, SRI International, Computer Science Lab. Based on unpublished working draft, UCLA and SRI, 1979.

Goguen, J. A. and J. J. Tardo 1977. OBJ-0 Preliminary Users Manual. UCLA Computer Science Semantics and Theory of Computation Report 10 (July), Computer Science Dept., UCLA, Los Angeles, CA.

*Goguen, J. A. and J. J. Tardo 1979. An Introduction to OBJ: A Language for Writing and Testing Algebraic Program Specifications. In *Proc. Specifications of Reliable Software Conf.* (April), pp. 170-189, IEEE Computer Society, Cambridge, MA., pp. 170-189.

Goguen, J. A., J. J. Tardo, N. Williamson and M. Zamfir 1978. A Practical Method for Testing Algebraic Specifications. To appear, UCLA Computer Science Dept. Quarterly.

Goguen, J. A., J. W. Thatcher and E. G. Wagner 1975. Abstract Data Types as Initial Algebras and the Correctness of Data Representations. *Proc. Conference on Computer Graphics Pattern Recognition and Data Structure*, pp. 89-93.

Goguen, J. A., J. W. Thatcher and E. G. Wagner 1978. An Initial Algebra Approach to the Specification, Correctness, and Implementation of Abstract Data Types. *Current Trends in Programming Methodology* (vol. IV), edited by Raymond T. Yeh, pp. 80-149, Prentice-Hall, Englewood Cliffs, N.J.

Goguen, J. A., J. W. Thatcher, E. G. Wagner and J. B. Wright 1977. Initial Algebra Semantics and Continuous Algebras. *JACM*, vol. 24, pp. 68-95.

Goldman, N. 1978. AP 2 Pocket Guide. Draft Copy (April).

Goldman, N. M. and D. S. Wile 1980. A Relational Database Foundation for Process Specifications. In *Entity-Relationship Approach to Systems Analysis and Design* edited by P. P. Chen, North-Holland, Amsterdam.

Gomaa, H. and D. Scott 1981. Prototyping as a Tool in the Specification of User Requirements. In *Proceedings of the Fifth International Conference on Software Engineering* (March), pp. 333-339, IEEE.

Good, D. I., R. M. Cohen and J. Keeton-Williams 1979. Principles of Proving Concurrent Programs in GYPSY. In *Proc. 6th ACM Symp. Principles of Programming Languages, ACM SIGPLAN*, pp. 42-52.

Good, D. I. and L. C. Ragland 1973. Nucleus—A Language for Provable Programs. In *Program Test Methods* edited by Hetzel, Prentice-Hall.

Goodenough, J. B. 1975. Exception Handling: Issues and a Proposed Notation. *CACM*, vol. 18, no. 12 (December).

Goodwin, J. W. 1981. Why Programming Environments Need Dynamic Data Types. *IEEE Transactions on Software Engineering*, vol. SE-7, pp. 451-457 (September).

Gordon, M. J. C., A. J. R. G. Milner, L. Morris, M. Newey and C. Wadsworth 1978. A Metalanguage for Interactive Proof LCF. In *Proc. 5th ACM POPL Symp.*, pp. 119-130, Tucson, AZ.

Gordon, M. J., A. J. R. Milner and C. P. Wadsworth 1979. Edinburgh LCF. *Lecture Notes in Computer Science*, vol. 78, Springer-Verlag.

Greif, I. 1972. Induction in Proofs About Programs. Master's Thesis, Technical Report MAC TR-93, Laboratory for Computer Science, MIT, Cambridge, MA.

Greif, I. 1975. Semantics of Communicating Parallel Processes. Ph.D. Thesis, Technical Report MAC TR-154, Laboratory for Computer Science, MIT, Cambridge, MA.

Gries, D. 1981. *The Science of Programming*. Springer-Verlag.

Grogono, P. 1979. On Layout Identifiers and Semicolons in Pascal Programs. *SIGPLAN Notices*, vol. 14, no. 4, pp. 35-40.

Guttag, J. V. 1975. The Specification and Application to Programming of Abstract Data Types. Ph. D. Dissertation, Report No. CSRG-59, Computational Sciences Group, Univ. of Toronto.

Guttag, J. 1976. Private communication.

Guttag, J. V. 1977. Abstract Data Types and the Development of Data Structures. *CACM*, vol. 20, no. 6, pp. 396-404.

*Guttag, J. V. 1980. Notes on Type Abstraction. *IEEE Transactions on Software Engineering*, vol. SE-6 (January), pp. 13-23. Also in *Proc. Specifications of Reliable Software Conference*, pp. 36-46, IEEE Cat. No. 79 CH1401-9C.

Guttag, J. V. and J. J. Horning 1978a. The Algebraic Specification of Abstract Data Types. *Acta Informatica*, vol. 10, no. 1, pp. 27-52.

Guttag, J. V. and J. J. Horning 1978b. The Design of Data Type Specifications. In *Current Trends in Programming Methodology*, pp. 60-79, edited by R. T. Yeh, Prentice-Hall, Englewood Cliffs, NJ. (an expanded version of a paper which appeared in *Proc. 2nd Int. Conf. Software Eng.*, Oct. 1976).

*Guttag, J. and J. J. Horning 1980. Formal Specification as a Design Tool. *Proc. 7th ACM Symposium Principles of Programming Language*, pp. 251-261.

Guttag, J. V., E. Horowitz and D. R. Musser 1977. Some Extensions to Algebraic Specifications. *Proc. Language Design for Reliable Software* (March), pp. 63-67.

Guttag, J. V., E. Horowitz and D. R. Musser 1978. Abstract Data Types and Software Validation. *CACM*, vol. 21, no. 12 (December), pp. 1048-1064.

Habermann, A. N. 1975. Path Expressions. Dept. of Computer Science, Carnegie-Mellon University.

Hack, M. H. T. 1972. Analysis of Production Schemata by Petri Nets. Master's Thesis, Technical Report MAC TR-94, Laboratory for Computer Science, MIT, Cambridge, MA.

Hailpern, B. T. 1980. Verifying Concurrent Processes Using Temporal Logic. Ph.D. Dissertation, Comput. Syst. Lab., Stanford Univ., Tech. Rep. 195, August.

Hailpern, B. and S. Owicki 1980. Verifying Network Protocols Using Temporal Logic. In *Proc. 1980 Trends and Applications Symp. Comput. Network Protocols* (May), pp. 18-28, National Bureau of Standards, Gaithersburg, MD.

Hajek, J. 1978. Automatically verified data transfer protocols, in *Proc. Int. Conf. Comput. Commun. Int. Council for Comput. Commun.*, pp. 749-756.

Hammer, M. M., W. G. Howe and I. Wladawsky. An Interactive Business Definition System. *SIGPLAN*, vol. 9.

Hammer, M. and D. McLeod 1978. The Semantic Data Model: A Modelling Mechanism for Data Base Applications. *Proceedings of the ACM SIGMOD International Conference on the Management of Data* (May), Austin, TX.

Hanau, P. R. and D. R. Lenorovitz 1980. Prototyping and Simulation Tools for User/Computer Dialogue Design. *Computer Graphics*, vol. 14, no. 3 (July) pp. 271-278.

Harel, D. 1979. First-order Dynamic Logic. *Lecture Notes in Computer Science*, vol. 68, Springer-Verlag.

Harm, D. 1977a. SCHEMER: An Initial Implementation. UCLA Artificial Intelligence Memo 8 (July), Computer Science Dept., UCLA, Los Angeles, CA.

Harm, D. 1977b. An Abstract Specification of Programming Language. UCLA Semantics and Theory of Computation Report 11 (March), Computer Science Dept., UCLA, Los Angeles, CA.

REFERENCES

Hausen, H. and M. Mullerburg 1981. Conspectus of Software Engineering Environments. In *Fifth International Conference on Software Engineering* (March), pp. 34-43, IEEE.

Heitmeyer, C. L. 1981. An Intermediate Command Language (ICL) or the Family of Military Message Systems. Technical Memorandum 7590-450:CH:ch (November), Naval Research Laboratory, Washington, D.C.

Heitmeyer, C. L., C. E. Landwehr and M. R. Cornwell 1982. The Use of Quick Prototypes in the Military Message System Project *ACM SIGSOFT Software Engineering Notes*, vol. 7, no. 5 (December).

Heitmeyer, C. L. and S. H. Wilson 1980. Military Message Systems: Current Status and Future Directions. *IEEE Transactions on Communications*, vol. COM-28-9, no. 9 (September), pp. 1645-1654.

Henderson, P. 1975. Finite State Modelling in Program Development. *Proceedings, International Conference on Reliable Software* (April), pp. 221-227, Los Angeles, CA.

Heninger, K. L. 1979. Specifying Software Requirements for Complex Systems: New Techniques and Their Application. In *Proc. Specifications of Reliable Software. Conf.* (April), pp. 1-14, Cambridge, MA.

Hewitt, C. and R. Atkinson 1976. Parallelism and Synchronization in Actor Systems. Laboratory for Computer Science, MIT, Cambridge, MA.

Hoare, C. A. R. 1969. An Axiomatic Basis for Computer Programming. *CACM*, vol. 12, pp. 576-583.

Hoare, C. A. R. 1971a. Proof of a Program FIND. *CACM*, vol. 14, no. 1 (January), pp. 39-45.

Hoare, C. A. R. 1971b. Procedure and Parameters—An Axiomatic Approach. In *Symposium on the Semantics of Algorithmic Languages* edited by E. Engeler, Springer-Verlag, Berlin-Heidelberg-New York.

Hoare, C. A. R. 1972a. Proofs of Correctness of Data Representations. *Acta Informatica*, vol. 1, no. 1, pp. 271-281.

Hoare, C. A. R. 1972b. Notes on Data Structuring. In *Structured Programming* edited by O.-J. Dahl, E. W. Dijkstra and C. A. R. Hoare, Academic Press.

Hoare, C. A. R. 1974. Monitors: An Operating System Structuring Concept. *CACM*, vol. 17 (October), pp. 549-557.

Hoare, C. A. R. 1978. Communicating Sequential Processes. *CACM*, vol. 21 (August), pp. 666-677.

Hoare, C. A. R. and N. Wirth 1973. An Axiomatic Definition of the Programming Language Pascal. *Acta Informatica*, vol. 2, no. 4, pp. 335-355.

Holloway, G., J. Townley, J. Spitzen and B. Wegbreit 1974. ECL Programmer's Manual. Technical Report TR-23-74, Center for Research in Computing Technology, Harvard University, Cambridge, MA.

Hommel, G. (Editor) 1980. Vergleich verschiedener Spezifikationsverfahren am Beispiel einer Paketverteilanlage. Kernforschungszentrum Karlsruhe GmbH, PDV-Report, KfK-PDV 186, Part I.

Horning, J. J. and B. Randell 1973. Process Structuring. *Computing Surveys*, vol. 5 (March), pp. 5-30.

Howard, J. H. 1976. Proving Monitors. *CACM*, vol. 1, no. 5 (May).

Hueras, J. F. 1978. A Formalization of Syntax Diagrams as K-Deterministic Language Recognizers. M. S. Thesis, Computer Science Dept., Univ. of California, Irvine, California.

Huet, G. 1977. Confluent Reductions: Abstract Properties and Applications to Term Rewriting Systems. IRIA-Report No. 250, Rocquencourt, France; also in *IEEE Symposium on Foundations of Computer Science* (October), pp. 30-45, Providence, R.I.

Hupbach. U. 1980. Abstract Implementation of Abstract Data Types. *Mathematical Foundations of Computer Science, Lecture Notes in Computer Science*, vol. 88, pp. 291-304, Springer-Verlag.

Hupbach, U., H. Kaphengst and H. Reichel 1980. Initiale Algebraische Spezifikation von Datentypen, Parameterisierten Datentypen und Algorithmen. VEB Robotron, Zentrum fur Forschung und Technik, Dresden, WIB.

Ichbiah, J. D. et al. 1979. Rationale for The Design of The Ada Programming Language. *SIGPLAN Notices*, vol. 14 (June) part B.

Igarashi, S., R. L. London and D. C. Luckham 1973. Automatic program Verification I: A Logical Basis and Its Implementation. Report ISI/RR-73-11, USC, Information Science Institute.

Ingalls, D. H. H. 1978. The Smalltalk-76 Programming System Design and Implementation. In *Proc. 5th Annu. ACM Symp. Principles of Programming Languages* Tucson, AZ, pp. 9-16.

Iverson, K. 1962. *A Programming Language*, Wiley, New York, N.Y.

Iverson, K. E. 1980. Notation as a Tool of Thought. *CACM*, vol. 23 (August), pp. 444-465.

Jacob, R. J. K. Survey and Examples of Specification Techniques for User Interfaces. NRL Report, Naval Research Laboratory, Washington, D.C.

Jensen, K. and N. Wirth 1974. *Pascal User Manual and Report*. Springer-Verlag.

Johnson, S. C. 1980. Language Development Tools on the Unix System. *IEEE Computer*, vol. 13, no. 8 (August).

Jones, C. B. 1979. Constructing a Theory of a Data Structure as an Aid to Program Development. *Acta Informatica*, vol. 11, pp. 119-137.

Jones, C. B. 1980. *Software Development: a Rigorous Approach*. Prentice-Hall, Englewood Cliffs, N.J.

Jones, C. B. 1981. Development Methods for Computer Program Including a Notion of Interference. PRG 25, Oxford University.

Jones, C. B. 1983a. Specification and Design of (Parallel) Programs, *IFIP 1983*, Paris, France.

Jones, C. B. 1983b. Tentative Steps Toward a Development Method for Interfering Programs. *ACM TOPLAS*, vol. 5, no. 4 (October), pp. 596-619.

Kamin, S. 1983. Final Data Types and Their Specification. *ACM TOPLAS*, vol. 5, no. 1 (January), pp. 97-123.

Kaphengst, H. and H. Reichel 1971. Algebraische Algorithmentheorie. VEB Robotron, Zentrum fur Forschung und Technik, Dresden, WIB.

Kaufman, T. M. 1977. TED: A Text Editor Specified in OBJ. M.S. Comprehensive Exam (December), Computer Science Dept., UCLA, Los Angeles, CA.

Kernighan, B. W. and P. J. Plauger 1976. *Software Tools*. Reading, Addison-Wesley, MA.

King, J. C. 1971. Proving Programs to be Correct. *IEEE Trans. on Computers*, vol. C-20, no. 11 (November).

Klaeren, H. A. 1980. A Simple Class of Algorithmic Specifications for Abstract Software Modules. *Proceedings of Mathematical Foundations of Computer Science, Lecture Notes in Computer Science*, vol. 88, pp. 362-374, Springer-Verlag.

Knight, J. R. 1972. A Case Study: Airlines Reservations Systems. *Proc. IEEE,* vol. 60 (November), pp. 1423-1431.

Knuth, D. E. 1974. Structured Programming with Goto Statements. *Computing Surveys*, vol. 6, no. 4 (December).

Knuth, D. and P. Bendix 1970. Simple Word Problems in Universal Algebra. In *Computational Problems in Abstract Algebra* edited by J. Leech, pp. 263-297, Pergamon Press.

Konchan, T. E. and A. Klausner 1981. DBS—A Relational Database System. Technical Report TR-18-81, Center for Research in Computing Technology, Harvard University, Cambridge, MA.

Kowalski, R. 1979. Algorithm = Logic + Control. *CACM* (July), vol. 22, pp. 424-436.

Krogdahl, S. 1978. Verification of a Class of Link-Level Protocols. *BIT*, vol. 18, pp. 436-448.

Lampson, B. W., J. J. Horning, R. L. London, J. G. Mitchell and G. J. Popek 1978. Revised Report on the Programming Language Euclid, Xerox Research Center, to appear. An earlier version appeared in *SIGPLAN Notices*, vol. 12, no. 2 (February 1977).

Langefors, B. Information System Design Computations Using Generalized Matrix Algebra. *BIT*, vol. 5, no. 2.

Lankford, D. S. 1975. Canonical Algebraic Simplification in Computational Logic. Math Dept. Memo ATP-25, University of Texas, Austin, TX.

Lauer, P. E. and R. H. Campbell 1975. A Description of Path Expressions by Petri Nets. *Conference Record of the Second Symposium on Principles of Programming Languages* (January).

Ledgard, H., A. Singer and J. Hueras 1977. A Basis for Executing Pascal Programmers. *SIGPLAN Notices*, vol. 12, no. 7, pp. 101-105.

Lehman, M. M. 1980. Programs, Life Cycles and Laws of Software Evolution. *Proc. IEEE,* vol. 68 (September), pp. 1060-1076.

Levi, G. and F. Sirovich 1975. Proving Program Properties, Symbolic Evaluation, and Logical Procedural Semantics. *4th Symposium, Mathematical Foundations of Computer Science* (September), Springer-Verlag Lecture Notes No. 32, pp. 294-301.

Levitt, K., L. Robinson and B. Silverberg 1979. *The HDM Handbook*, vols. I, II, III. Technical Report, Computer Science Lab., SRI International.

Liskov, B. H. 1975. Specification Techniques for Data Abstractions. *IEEE Conference on Reliable Software Engineering*, vol. 1, no. 1 (March).

Liskov, B. H. 1976. An Introduction to CLU. In *New Directions in Algorithmic Languages* edited by S. Schuman, pp. 139-156, IRIA, Paris, France.

*Liskov, B. H. and V. Berzins 1979. An Appraisal of Program Specifications. In *Research Directions in Software Technology* edited by Peter Wegner, The MIT Press, Massachusetts, pp. 276-301.

Liskov, B., A. Snyder, R. Atkinson and C. Schaffert 1977. Abstraction Mechanisms in CLU. *CACM* vol. 20, no. 8 (August), pp. 564-576.

Liskov, B. and S. Zilles 1973. An Approach to Abstraction. Computation Structures Group Memo 88, MIT.

Liskov, B. H. and S. Zilles 1974. Programming With Abstract Data Types. *Proceedings of the ACM SIGPLAN Conference on Very High Level Languages, SIGPLAN Notices*, vol. 9, no. 4 (April), pp. 50-59.

Liskov, B. H. and S. N. Zilles 1975. Specification Techniques for Data Abstractions. *IEEE Trans. Software Eng.*, vol. SE-1 (January), pp. 7-19.

Liskov, B. H. and S. Zilles 1977. An Introduction to Formal Specifications of Data Abstractions. In *Current Trends in Programming Methodology*, (vol. I) edited by R. Yeh, pp. 1-32, Prentice-Hall, Englewood Cliffs, N.J.

Locasso, R., J. Scheid, D. V. Schorre and P. Eggert 1980. The **Ina Jo** Specification Language Reference Manual. Syst. Develop. Corp., Technical Report TM-(L)-6021/001/00, June.

Loeckx, J. 1980. Algorithmic Specifications of Abstract Data Types. Technical Report, Univ. Saarlandes, Saarbrücken.

London, R. L., J. V. Guttag, J. J. Horning, B. W. Lampson, J. G. Mitchell and G. J. Popek 1978. Proof Rules for the Programming Language Euclid. *Acta Informatica*, vol. 10, pp. 1-26.

Lyle, D. M. 1971. A Hierarchy of High Order Languages for Systems Programming. *Proceedings of SIGPLAN Symposium on Languages for Systems Implementation*.

Lyons, T. G. 1977. Change Management Automated Build System EVENT LOG Sub-System Design Specification. Bell Labs (November).

REFERENCES

Lyons, T. G. 1979. Private Communication (August 30).

Lyons, T. G. and T. B. Muenzer 1977. Proposal for the Field Trial of the Change Management Automated Build System (CM ABS) by the Division of Revenues Processing (DRP) Project. Bell Labs (November).

Majster, M. E. 1977. Limits of the Algebraic Specification of Data Types. *SIGPLAN Notices*, vol. 12, pp. 37-41.

Majster, M. E. 1979. Treatment of Partial Operations in the Algebraic Specification Technique. *Proc. of Specifications of Reliable Software* (April).

Manna, Z. 1969. The Correctness of Programs. *J. of Computer and System Sciences*, vol. 3, no. 2 (May), pp. 119-127.

Manna, Z. 1974. *Mathematical Theory of Computation*, McGraw-Hill, New York, N.Y.

Mao, W. T. and R. T. Yeh 1980. Communication Port: A Language Concept for Concurrent Programming. *IEEE Trans. Software Eng.*, vol. SE-6 (March), pp. 194-204.

Mateti, P. 1980. Documentation of Program *indent*: A Model for the Complete Documentation of Computer Programs. Unpublished class notes, Department of Computer Science, University of Melbourne, Parkville 3052, Australia.

Mateti, P. and J. Jaffar 1983. A Correctness Proof of an Indenting Program. *Software—Practice and Experience*, vol. 13, no. 3.

McCarthy, J. 1963. A Basis for a Mathematical Theory of Computation. In *Computer Programming and Formal Systems* edited by Braffort and Hirschberg, North Holland Publishing Co., Amsterdam-London.

McCarthy, J., D. W. Abrahams, D. J. Edwards, T. P. Hart and M. I. Levin 1965. *LISP 1.5 Programmer's Manual*, MIT Press, Cambridge, MA.

Melkanoff, M. A. and M. Zamfir 1978. The Axiomatization of Data Base Conceptual Models by Abstract Data Types. Computer Science Dept. Report UCLA-ENG-7785, UCLA, Los Angeles, CA.

Millen, J. K. 1979. Operating System Security Verification. MITRE Corp., TR M79-223, September.

Milne, G. and R. Milner 1979. Concurrent Processes and Their Syntax. *JACM*, vol. 26 (April), pp. 302-321.

Mittermeir, R. T. 1980. Semantic Nets for Modeling the Requirements of Evolvable Systems-An Example. Inst. Digitale Anlagen, Tech. Univ. Wien, Vienna, Austria, (May).

Moniconi, M. and R. L. Schwartz 1981. Automatic Construction of Verification Condition Generators from Hoare Logics. In *Proceedings, 8th International Colloquium on Automata, Languages and Programming*. Springer-Verlag, Lecture Notes in Computer Science.

Moran, T. P. 1981. The Command Language Grammar: A Representation for the User Interface of Interactive Computer Systems. *Int. J. Man-Machine Studies*, vol. 15, no. 1 (July), pp. 3-50.

Morris, J. H. 1973. Types are not Sets. *ACM Symposium on the Principles of Programming Languages* (October), pp. 120-124.

Muenzer, T. B. 1977. Change Management Automated Build System. Bell Labs (March).

Muenzer, T. B. 1979. Private Communication (June).

MUMPS Development Committee 1977. MUMPS Language Standard. American National Standards Institute, N.Y.

Musa, J. 1979. Program Specifications: A Mini-Tutorial. Bell Labs (June).

Musser, D. R. 1977. A Data Type Verification System Based on Rewrite Rules. *Proceedings, Sixth Texas Conference on Computing Systems*, (November), Section 1A, pp. 22-31, Austin, TX.

Musser, D. R. 1980. Abstract Data Types in the AFFIRM System. *IEEE Transactions on Software Engineering*, vol. SE-6 (January), pp. 24-32.

Nakajima, R., M. Honda and H. Nakahara 1977. Describing and Verifying Programs with Abstract Data Types. *Proceedings, IFIP Working Conference on Formal Description of Programming Concepts*, pp. 22.1-22.29, MIT; also in *Formal Description of Programming Concepts* edited by E. Neuhold, pp. 527-556, North-Holland.

Naur, P. 1966. Proof of Algorithms by General Snapshots. *Bit*, vol. 6, no. 4, pp. 310-316.

Neumann, P. G., R. S. Boyer, R. S. Feiertag, K. N. Levitt and R. S. Robinson 1977. A Provably Secure Operating System: The System, Its Applications and Proofs. Final Report, Stanford Research Institute (February), pp. 11, Menlo Park, CA.

O'Donnell, M. J. 1977. *Computing in Systems Described by Equations*. Lecture Notes in Computer Science 58, Springer-Verlag.

Overman, W. T. 1977. Formal Verification of GMBs. Dep. Comput. Sci., Univ. California, Los Angeles, Internal Memo. 176, July.

Owicki, S. S. 1975. Axiomatic Proof Techniques for Parallel Programs. Ph.D. Thesis, Report TR-75-251, Cornell University, Ithaca, N.Y.

Owicki, S. and L. Lamport 1980. Proving Liveness Properties of Concurrent Programs. Stanford Univ., Technical Report S&L 1 (Op. 57), October.

Parnas, D. L. 1969. On the Use of Transition Diagrams in the Design of a User Interface for an Interactive Computer System. *Proc. 24th National ACM Conference*, pp. 379-385.

Parnas, D. L. 1971a. Information Distribution Aspects of Design Methodology. Technical Report, Depart. of Comput. Science, Carnegie-Mellon University. Presented at the IFIP Congress, 1971, Ljubljana, Yugoslavia and included in the proceedings.

Parnas, D. L. 1971b. Sample Specification for the Man Machine Interface. Presented at the NATO Advanced Study Institute on Graphics and the Man Machine Interface (April), Erlangen, West Germany (to be included in the proceedings of that institute).

REFERENCES

*Parnas, D. L. 1972a. A Technique for the Specification of Software Modules with Examples. *CACM*, vol. 15, no. 5 (May), pp. 330-336.

Parnas, D. L. 1972b. On the Criteria to be Used in Decomposing Systems into Modules. *CACM*, vol. 15, no. 2 (December), pp. 1053-1058.

Parnas, D. L. 1977. The Use of Precise Specifications in the Development of Software. *Proc. IFIP Congress* 1977, North-Holland Publishing Company.

Parnas, D. 1978. Designing Software for East of Extension and Contraction. In *Proc. 3rd Int. Conf. Software Eng.* (May), IEEE-ACM, pp. 264-277.

Parnas, D. L. and G. Handzel 1975. More on Specification Techniques for Software Modules. Technical Report, Technische Hochschule Darmstadt, Darmstadt, West Germany (February).

Parnas, D. L., G. Handzel and H. Wuerges 1976. Design and Specification of the Minimal Subset of an Operating System Family. Presented at *2nd International Conference on Software Engineering* (October); also published in special issue of *IEEE Transactions on Software Engineering* (December).

Parnas, D. L. and W. R. Price 1973. The Design of the Virtual Memory Aspects of a Virtual Machine. *Proceedings of the ACM SIGARC-SIGOPS Workshop on Virtual Computer Systems* (March).

Parnas, D. L. and W. R. Price 1974. Using Memory Access Control as the Only Protection Mechanism. *Proc. of International Workshop on Protection in Operating System* (August), pp. 13-14, IRIA.

Parnas, D. L., J. E. Shore and D. Weiss 1976. Abstract Types Defined as Classes of Variables. *Proc. Conference on Data: Abstraction, Definition and Structure*, pp. 22-24, Salt Lake City, Utah (March).

Parnas, D. L. and H. Wuerges 1976. Response to Undesired Events in Software Systems. *Proc. of the 2nd International Conference on Software Engineering* (October), pp. 13-15, San Francisco, CA.

Peters, L. 1978. Relating Software Requirements and Design. In *Proceedings of the Software Quality and Assurance Workshop*, pp. 67-71. *ACM SIGMETRICS* (November).

Petri, C. A. 1962. Kommunikation mit Automaten (Communication with Automata). Ph.D. Thesis, Technische Hochschule, Darmstadt, West Germany.

Pierce, R. A. 1978. A Requirements Tracing Tool. In *Proceedings of the Software Quality and Assurance Workshop*, pp. 53-60. *ACM SIGMETRICS* (November).

Pirotte, A. 1977. The Entity-Property-Association Model: An Information-Oriented Data Base System. Technical Report, M.B.L.E. Research Laboratory, Brussels, Belgium.

Pnueli, A. 1979. The Temporal Semantics of Concurrent Programs. *Proceedings of Conference on Semantics of Concurrent Computation, Lecture Notes in Computer Science*, vol. 70, pp. 1-20, Springer-Verlag.

Price, W. R. 1973. Implications of a Virtual Memory Mechanism for Implementing Protection in a Family of Operating Systems. Technical Report (Ph.D. Thesis), Carnegie-Mellon University (June), AD766292.

Principato, R. N., Jr. 1978. A Formalization of the State Machine Specification Technique. MIT, Technical Report MIT.LCS/TR-202, May.

Prywes, N. S. 1977. Automatic Generation of Computer Programs. In *Advances in Computers*, vol. 16, Academic Press.

Quillian, M. R. 1968. Semantic Memory. In *Semantic Information Processing*, pp. 227-268, M.I.T. Press, Cambridge, MA.

Ragland, L. C. 1973. A Verified Program Verifier. Ph.D. Thesis, Technical Report TR-18, University of Texas at Austin, TX.

Randell, B. 1975. System Structure for Software Fault Tolerance. *Proceedings ICRS*.

Rao, R. 1980. Design and Evaluation of Distributed Communication Primitives. Comput. Sci. Rep. 80-04-01 (April), University of Washington, Seattle.

Razouk, R. R. and G. Estrin 1980. Validation of the X.21 Interface Specification Using SARA. In *Proc. 1980 Trends and Applications Symp. Comput. Network Protocols* (May), pp. 155-167, National Bureau of Standards, Gaithersburg, MD.

Redwine, S. T., Jr., E. D. Seigel and G. R. Berglass 1981. Candidate R&D Thrusts for the Software Technology Initiative. DoD Report (May), Department of Defense, USA.

Reichel, H. 1980. Initially-Restricting Algebraic Theories. *Proceedings of Mathematical Foundations of Computer Science, Lecture Notes in Computer Science*, vol. 88, pp. 504-514, Springer-Verlag.

Reisner, P. 1981. Formal Grammar and Human Factors Design of an Interactive Graphics System. *IEEE Trans. Software Eng.*, vol. SE-7, no. 2 (March), pp. 229-240.

Reynolds, J. C. 1983. *The Craft of Programming*. Prentice-Hall International.

Riddle, W. E. et al. 1978. Behavior Modeling During Software Design. *IEEE Trans. Software Eng.*, vol. SE-4 (July), pp. 283-292.

Riddle, W. E. and J. D. Wileden 1978. Languages for Representing Software Specifications and Designs. *ACM SIGSOFT, Software Engineering Notes*, vol. 3, no. 4 (October), pp. 7-11.

Robinson, L. and R. C. Holt. Formal Specifications for Solutions to Synchronization Problems. Computer Science Group, Stanford Research Institute, Menlo Park, CA.

Robinson, L. and K. N. Levitt 1977. Proof Techniques for Hierarchically Structured Programs. *CACM*, vol. 20 (April), pp. 271-283.

Robinson, L. and O. Roubine 1977. SPECIAL, A Specification and Assertion Language. SRI International Report CSL-46 (January), Menlo Park, CA.

Rosen, B. 1973. Tree Manipulating Systems and Church-Rosser Theorems. *JACM*, vol. 20, pp. 160-187.

Rosenbaum, J. D. and W. R. Hackler 1980. Requirements Specifications for Embedded Astronautic Systems. In *Space—Enhancing Technological Leadership, 1980 Annual Meeting* (October), pp. 1-21. American Astronautical Society.

Ross, D. T. 1977. Structured Analysis (SA): A Language for Communicating Ideas. *IEEE Trans. Software Eng.*, vol. SE-3 (January), pp. 16-34.

Ross, D. T. and K. R. Schoman 1977. Structured Analysis for Requirements Definition. *IEEE Trans. Software Eng.*, vol. SE-3 (January), pp. 6-15.

Roubine, O. and L. Robinson 1977. Special Reference Manual (Second Edition). Technical Report CSG-45, Stanford Research Institute, Menlo Park, CA.

Roussopoulos, N. 1979. CSDL: A Conceptual Schema Definition Language for the Design of Database Applications. *IEEE Trans. Software Eng.*, vol. SE-5 (September), pp. 481-496.

Sale, A. 1978. Stylistics in Languages with Compound Statements. *The Australian Computer Journal*, vol. 10, no. 2, pp. 58-59.

Salwicki, A. 1970. Formalized Algorithmic Languages. *Bull. Acad. Pol. Sci. Ser. Math*, vol. 18, pp. 227-232.

Sannella, D. and M. Wirsing 1983. A Kernel Language for Algebraic Specification and Implementation. To appear in *Proc. Intl. Conference on Foundations of Computing Theory* (August), Bergholm, Sweden.

Schaffert, J. C. Specifying Meaning in Object-Oriented Languages. Master's Thesis, Dept. of Electrical Engineering and Computer Science, MIT, Cambridge, MA.

Schoett, O. 1982. A Theory of Program Modules, Their Specification and Implementation. Private communication.

Schwabe, D. 1980. Transport Protocol Specification in AFFIRM. USC/Inform. Sci. Inst., Program Verification Project, Affirm Memo. 19, March.

Schwabe, D. 1981a. Formal Techniques for Specification and Verification of Protocols. Ph.D. Dissertation, Univ. California, Los Angeles, April.

Schwabe, D. 1981b. Formal Specification and Verification of a Connection Establishment Protocol. In *Proc. 7th Data Commun. Symp.*, Mexico City, ACM/IEEE, Oct., pp. 11-26.

Schwarz, J., 1977. Using Annotations to Make Recursion Equations Behave. Dep. Artificial Intell., Technical Report DAI43, Univ. Edinburgh, Edinburgh.

Schwartz, R. L. and P. M. Melliar-Smith 1981. Temporal Logic Specification of Distributed Systems. In *Proc. 2nd Int. Conf. Distributed Comput. Syst.* (April), pp. 446-454, Paris, France.

Scott, D. 1970. Outline of a Mathematical Theory of Computation. *Proceedings of the Fourth Annual Princeton Conference on Information Science and Systems*, pp. 169-176.

Shaw, M., W. A. Wulf and R. L. London 1977. Abstraction and Verification in ALPHARD: Defining and Specifying Iteration and Generators. *CACM*, vol. 20, no. 8 (August), pp. 553-564.

Shneiderman, B. 1981. Multi-Party Grammars and Related Features for Defining Interactive Systems. *IEEE Trans. Systems, Man, and Cybernetics*, vol. SMC-12, no. 2 (March), pp. 148-154.

Singer, A. 1979. Formal Methods and Human Factors in the Design of Interactive Languages. Ph.D. Dissertation, Computer and Information Science Dept., Univ. of Massachusetts, Amherst, MA.

Smith, J. M. and D. C. P. Smith 1977a. Database Abstractions: Aggregation. *CACM* (June), vol. 20, no. 6, pp. 405-413.

Smith, J. M. and D. C. P. Smith 1977b. Database Abstractions: Aggregation and Generalization. *ACM Transactions on Database Systems* (June), vol. 2, no. 2, pp. 105-133.

Smith, J. M. and D. C. P. Smith 1979. A Database Approach to Software Specification. In *Proc. Software Develop. Tools Workshop* (May), Pingree Park, CO, edited by W. E. Riddle and R. E. Fairley, pp. 176-200, Springer-Verlag, N.Y.

Smoliar, S. W. 1979. Using Applicative Technique to Design Distributed Systems. In *Proc. Specifications of Reliable Software Conf.*, pp. 150-161, Cambridge, MA.

Smoliar, S. W. 1981. Operational Requirements Accommodation in Distributed System Design. *IEEE Transactions on Software Engineering*, vol. SE-7 (November), pp. 531-537.

Smoliar, S. W. Applicative and Functional Programming. In *Software Engineering Handbook* edited by C. V. Ramamoorthy and C. R. Vick, Prentice-Hall Englewood Cliffs, N.J.

Spitzen, J. and B. Wegbreit 1975. The Verification and Synthesis of Data Structures. *Acta Informatica*, vol. 4, pp. 127-144.

Stenning, N. V. 1976. A Data Transfer Protocol. *Comput. Networks.* vol. 1, pp. 99-110.

Stucki, L. G. 1975. Testing Impact on the Future of Software Engineering. *Proceedings of Fourth Texas Conference on Computing Systems*, University of Texas.

Subrahmanyan, P. A. 1979. On Proving the Correctness of Data Type Implementations. Dep. Comput. Sci., Univ. Utah, Technical Report, September.

Sufrin, B. 1980. Specification of a Display Editor. Specification Group Working Paper, Programming Research Group, Oxford, U.K.

Sufrin, B. 1981. Reading Formal Specifications. Technical Monograph PRG-24, Programming Research Group, Oxford, U.K.

Sufrin, B. Formal Specification: Notation and Examples. *Proc. INRIA Winder School on Tools and Notions for Program Construction*, Cambridge University Press, London, U.K. To appear.

Sunshine, C. A. 1975. Interprocess Communication Protocols for Computer Networks. Ph.D. Dissertation, Stanford University, Palo Alto, CA.

Sunshine, C. A. 1979. Formal Methods for Protocol Specification and Verification. *Computer*, vol. 12 (September), pp. 20-27.

Sunshine, C. A. 1982. Formal Modeling of Communication Protocols. In *Computer Networks and Simulation* edited by S. Shoemaker. North-Holland (also USC/ISI Technical Report RR-81-89, March 1981).

Teichroew, D. and M. J. Bastarche 1975. PSL User's Manual. ISDOS Working Paper No. 98, University of Michigan.

Teichroew, D. and E. A. Hershey, III 1977. PSL/PSA: A Computer Aided Technique for Structured Documentation and Analysis of Information Processing Systems. *IEEE Trans. Software Eng.*, vol. SE-3 (January), pp. 41-48.

Thatcher, J. W., E. G. Wagner and J. B. Wright 1976. Specification of Abstract Data Types Using Conditional Axioms. IBM Research Report RC-6214 (September), Yorktown Heights, N.Y.

Thatcher, J. W., E. G. Wagner and J. B. Wright 1978. Data Type Specification: Parameterization and the Power of Specification Techniques. *Proceedings, SIGACT 10th Annual Symposium on Theory of Computing* (May), pp. 119-132, San Diego, CA.

Thompson, D. H. 1980. A Behavioral Axiomatization of the Stenning Data Transfer Protocol. USC/Inform. Sci. Inst., Program Verification Project, Affirm Memo. 16, June.

Thompson, D. H., S. L. Gerhart, R. W. Erickson, S. Lee and R. L. Bates 1981. Eds., *The AFFIRM Reference Library*, 5 vols. (*Reference Manual, User's Guide, Type Library, Annotated Transcripts* and *Collected Papers*). USC Inform. Sci. Inst.

U.S. Air Force 1965. Air Force Weapons Effectiveness Testing (AFWET) Instrumentation System. Air Proving Ground Center, Eglin Air Force Base, FL, R&D Exhibit PGVE 64-40.

van Wijngaarden, A. 1969. Report on the Algorithmic Language ALGOL 68. *Numerische Mathematik*, vol.14.

Wand, M. 1977a. Algebraic Theories and Tree Rewriting Systems. Technical Report 66 (July), Computer Science Dept., Indiana University, Bloomington, IN.

Wand, M. 1977b. Compiling Lambda Expressions Using Continuations and Factorizations. Technical Report 55 (July), Computer Science Dept., Indiana University, Bloomington, IN.

Wegbreit, B. 1976. Verifying Program Performance. *JACM*, vol. 23, no. 4 (October), pp. 691-699.

Wells, R. 1976. The Specification and Implementation of a Verifiable Communications System. Masters Thesis, The University of Texas at Austin.

Wilson, S. H., J. W. Kallander, N. M. Thomas III, L. C. Klitzkie and J. R. Bunch Jr. 1979. MME Quick Look Report. Memorandum Report 3992, Naval Research Laboratory, Washington, D. C.

Winograd, T. 1979. Beyond Programming Languages. *CACM*, vol. 22, no. 7 (July).

Wirth, N. 1971a. Program Development by Stepwise Refinement. *CACM* vol. 14, no. 4 (April), pp. 221-227.

Wirth, N. 1971b. The Programming Language Pascal. *Acta Informatica*, vol. 1, no. 1, pp. 35-63.

Wirth, N. 1978. Syntax of Pascal in Extended BNF. *Pascal News*, vol. 12, pp. 52-53.

Wirth, N. and H. Weber 1966. Euler: A Generalization of ALGOL and its Formal Definition. *CACM*, vol. 9, no. 1 (January), pp. 13-23.

Wong, S. 1979. Subgoal Interaction in a SCHEMER Planning System. M.S. Thesis, Computer Science Dept., UCLA, Los Angeles, CA.

Woods, W. A. 1970. Transition Network Grammars for Natural Language Analysis. *CACM*, vol. 13, no. 10 (October), pp. 591-606.

Wulf, W. A., R. Levin and C. Pierson 1975. Overview of the Hydra Operating System Development. Proceedings of Fifth Symposium on Operating Systems Principles.

Wulf, W. A., R. L. London and M. Shaw 1976a. Abstraction and Verification in Alphard: Introduction to Language and Methodology. Research Report ISI/RR-76-46, ARPA.

Wulf, W. A., R. L. London and M. Shaw 1976b. An Introduction to the Construction and Verification of ALPHARD Programs. *IEEE Transactions on Software Engineering* vol. SE-2, no. 4 (December), pp. 253-265.

Wulf, W. A., D. B. Russell and A. N. Habermann 1971. BLISS: A Language for Systems Programming. *CACM* vol. 14, no. 12.

Yeh, R. T. 1980. Software Requirements: A Report on the State of the Art. Univ. Maryland, College Park, Comput. Sci. Technical Report TR-949 (October), University of Maryland, College Park; to appear as "Software Requirements: New Directions and Perspectives" in *Software Engineering Handbook* edited by C. V. Ramamoorthy and C. R. Vick, Prentice-Hall, Englewood Cliffs, N.J.

Yeh, R. T. and R. T. Mittermeir 1980. Conceptual Modeling as a Basis for Deriving Software Requirements. *Proc. Intl. Computer Symp.*, (December), Taipei, Taiwan.

Yeh, R. T. et al. 1979. Software Requirement Engineering—A Perspective. Computer Science Report SDBEG-7 (March) University of Texas, Austin, TX.

Yeh, R. T., N. Roussopoulos and P. Chang 1979. Systematic Derivation of Software Requirements Through Structured Analysis. Comput. Sci. Technical Report SDBEG-15, University of Texas, Austin, TX.

Zahn, C. T. 1974. A Control Statement for Natural Top-Down Structured Programming. Symposium on Programming Languages.

Zave, P. 1978. The Formal Specification of an Adaptive, Parallel Finite-Element System. Technical Report TR-715 (December), University of Maryland, College Park, MD.

*Zave, P. 1980a. An Operational Approach to Requirements Specification for Embedded Systems. Technical Report TR-976 (December), University of Maryland, College Park, MD. (Also in *IEEE Transactions on Software Engineering*, **SE-8** (3), 250-269, 1982.)

Zave, P. 1980b. Real-World Properties in the Requirements for Embedded Systems. In *Proc. 19th Annu. Washington D.C. ACM Tech. Symp.*. pp. 21-26, Gaithersburg, MD.

Zave, P. Extending Applicative Specification Techniques to Embedded Systems. To Be Published.

Zave, P. and G. E. Cole, Jr. A Quantitative Evaluation of the Feasibility of, and Suitable Hardware Architectures for, an Adaptive, Parallel Finite-Element System. To be published.

Zave, P. and W. C. Rheinboldt 1979. Design of an Adaptive, Parallel Finite-Element System. *ACM Trans. Math. Software*, vol. 5 (March), pp. 1-17.

*Zave, P. and R. T. Yeh 1981. Executable Requirements for Embedded Systems. In *Proc. 5th Int. Conf. Software Eng.* (March), pp. 295-304, San Diego, CA.

Zelkowitz, M. V. 1980. A Case Study in Rapid Prototyping. *Software — Practice and Experience*, vol. 10, no. 12 (December), pp. 1037-1042.

Zilles, S. 1974. Algebraic Specification of Data Types. *Progress Report XI*, Laboratory for Computer Science, MIT, Cambridge, MA, pp. 52-58; also Computation Structures Group Memo 119, Laboratory for Computer Science, MIT, Cambridge, MA.

Zilles, S. N. 1975a. An Introduction to Data Algebras. IBM Research, San Jose, CA.

Zilles, S. N. 1975b. Abstract Specifications for Data Types. IBM Research Laboratory, San Jose, CA.

Zimmermann, H. 1980. OSI Reference Model—The ISO Model of Architecture for Open Systems Interconnection. *IEEE Trans. Commun.*, vol. COM-28 (April), pp. 425-432.